D1563373

Performance and Gender in Ancient Greece

Performance and Gender in Ancient Greece

NONDRAMATIC POETRY IN ITS SETTING

Eva Stehle

PRINCETON UNIVERSITY PRESS

PRINCETON, NEW JERSEY

Published by Princeton University Press, 41 William Street,
Princeton, New Jersey 08540
In the United Kingdom: Princeton University Press, Chichester, West Sussex

Library of Congress Cataloging-in-Publication Data

Stehle, Eva, 1944–
    Performance and gender in ancient Greece : nondramatic poetry
in its setting / Eva Stehle.
        p.   cm.
    Includes bibliographical references and index.
    ISBN 0-691-03617-9 (cloth : alk. paper)
    1. Greek poetry—History and criticism.   2. Women in the performing arts—
Greece—History.   3. Oral interpretation of poetry—History.   4. Women and
literature—Greece—History.   5. Bards and bardism—Greece—History.
6. Greece—Social life and customs.   7. Oral tradition—Greece—History.
8. Sappho—Friends and associates.   9. Sex role—Greece—History.   I. Title.
PA3067.S74   1996
881'.0109—dc20   96-3522

This book has been composed in Bembo

For Norman

Contents

Preface

LIKE GOOD TIMES in the old song, this book has been long, long on the way. It had its genesis in the weekly seminar of the Pembroke Center for Teaching and Research on Women at Brown University in the fall of 1986. In that stimulating atmosphere it was possible to think about Sappho and Jacques Derrida together. Although in the book as it has evolved Derrida is never mentioned, questions about what speech as a sign of presence meant for Greek performance culture and for Sappho determined the form of my initial inquiry. As it ultimately evolved, the focus of the work is on gendered speech in performance and on subversive rhetorical strategies opened up by the system of writing. One goal served by framing the question this way is to understand Sappho's "difference" as a poet and a woman poet. From this point of view, the first five chapters are preliminary, providing a context for Sappho. The other inspiration for my work is love for live performance, for the energy that passes between actors and audience in dance, theater, improvisation, even a good lecture. Although the physical excitement of the performances that characterized Greek culture of the archaic and early classical period can be recaptured only by our imaginings, I have tried to analyze how the dynamic of performance might have interacted with poetic texts in the eyes and minds of the viewers. From this perspective the first five chapters are not preliminary but central, and Sappho's poetry reveals something of its "difference" by contrast. I hope that the whole adds to readers' appreciation of the complexity of gender ideology and of the relations of speech and writing in ancient Greece. I avoid the question of performance and self-presentation in drama because that is a large topic in its own right and a somewhat different one.

Translations are my own unless I indicate otherwise in a note. I can claim neither grace nor vigor for them, but they follow the Greek closely, even to strained word-order on occasion, in an attempt to reproduce the effect of hearing the original. As for transliteration, I only hope that I have been consistent in my inconsistencies. I use the Latinized form of a personal or place-name if it is a familiar one, stricter transliteration if it is not so well known. When I do use the latter, I also commit the impropriety of attaching English adjectival endings to the Greek, e.g., Keos and Kean. A list of transliterated terms that I use repeatedly can be found at the end of this book. A final note on terminology: when I use the term *women,* I mean to refer to women collectively, married or unmarried. These two states are distinguished in Greek, and where relevant I also distinguish.

The abbreviations indicating editions used and any others found in text, notes, or Bibliography are listed following this Preface.

Dates are BCE unless I specify CE. The book ranges over the period roughly from 700 to 300 BCE; it assumes that the function and modes of performance remained largely the same over that period, although developments are discussed in Chapter 1, and the Conclusion sketches the arc of each genre's evolution. For the dates when the various mentioned authors lived, see the chronological chart in the Appendix.

In the Greek that is quoted, I use iota subscript or adscript depending on the practice of the edition from which I take the text. A dot under a Greek letter (usually found in texts from papyrus or inscriptions) indicates that the letter is not certain. Square brackets in a translation mean that the Greek text is damaged and a word or more is missing. When a word is enclosed in square brackets, it has been restored in Greek. In translating very broken texts, I occasionally use ellipses rather than brackets because this makes the text easier to read.

There are a few works cited in the Bibliography to which I do not refer in the notes. These either appeared too late for me to use, or came to my notice too late, or are tangential to my specific discussions but have a general relevance to the subject. In the hope that nonclassicists will find the book of interest, I have translated all the Greek and have provided the chronological list of authors and the lists of transliterated terms and abbreviations mentioned above.

I have sometimes daydreamed of reaching the moment when I could say thank you to those who have helped me and have composed purple patches of fervid gratitude in my head. But, as Aristotle says, writing is more spare than speech, so I will just say that I truly appreciate all the help and support. First thanks go to my colleague at Wheaton College in Massachusetts, Dorothea Wender, who encouraged, exhorted, and read several chapters. Elizabeth Weed, Associate Director of the Pembroke Center, who invited me to join the seminar and from whom I have learned a great deal, also has my special gratitude. For conversations that expanded my ideas, I owe much to Marilyn Skinner. Ian Rutherford and Joseph Russo read the whole typescript and gave me good advice, saving me from numerous mistakes and omissions. I thank also the Press's anonymous referees, my editors Lauren Osborne and Brigitta Van Rheinberg, and my copy editor Marta Steele for her patience and her eagle eye. Egbert Bakker, Deborah Boedeker, David Konstan, Sara Lindheim, William Mullen, Adele Scafuro, and my University of Maryland colleagues Lillian Doherty and James Lesher read part or all of the work. They have all talked over questions with me and been vital to me in stimulating further thought. My mother, Evelyn Stehle, read an early version and encouraged me to make it understandable to a wide audience, as I hope I have done. She and my father, Philip Stehle, were understanding and encouraging when the project seemed interminable. Seth Schein, Charles Segal, and John Winkler offered support at an early stage when it was very good to know that someone thought the project looked promising, and so did Matthew Santirocco at a later point. Amy Day, Stephen Lambert, Margaret Miller, Emmet Robbins, and Andrew Szegedy-Maszak answered burning questions, and Jennifer Roberts advised me and spurred me on, as did Joseph and Leslie Preston Day. The codirectors of the Center for Hellenic Studies in Washington, DC, Deborah Boedeker and Kurt Raaflaub, and the Librarian, Ellen Roth, have all been very generous; I am glad to be able to express my gratitude. Maryland colleagues John Duffy, Judith Hallett, Katie King, Hugh Lee, Gregory Staley, and Marjorie Venit offered practical support as well as the cheerful atmosphere that makes work fun. Ms. Rosalie Wolff of the Solow Art and Architecture Foundation graciously gave me permission to use and obtained for me the photograph on the jacket cover.

I owe thanks to various institutions as well. The Arts and Humanities Research Board of the University of Maryland gave me a grant for a semester's leave in the fall of 1988, when I really began work; I am grateful to them and to Robert Rowland for encouraging me to apply and supporting my work. The Madeleine Clark Wallace Library at Wheaton College has welcomed me back each summer. I wish especially to thank Marsha Grimes for spectacular interlibrary loan services. The Brown University Classics department has been hospitable. The University of Toronto Classics department invited me to join their activities and use their library when I spent a sabbatical in Toronto; my thanks to faculty and graduate students for such a friendly welcome.

There are two people who were so generous with their interest that they always buoyed me up and were very dear to me, whom I can no longer thank in person. The first is Jack Winkler. All who knew him must miss him still. The second is my aunt Dorothy Stehle, who read part of the typescript and had all sorts of suggestions, whose enthusiasm was catching, and whose good opinion I treasured.

Finally, there is one more whom I must thank, without whose gentle steadiness I would not be finished even now. The book is dedicated to him.

Stowe, Vermont
July 1995

Abbreviations

EDITIONS

AHS	Allen, Halliday, and Sikes 1980.
C	Calame 1983.
CA	Powell 1970.
CEG	Hansen 1983.
DK	Diels and Kranz 1966–68.
Dr.	Drachmann 1966–69.
FGH	Jacoby 1954–69.
G	Gentili 1958.
IG	*Inscriptiones Graecae.*
LP	Lobel and Page 1955.
LSJ	Liddell, Scott, and Jones 1940.
MW	Merkelbach and West 1967.
PMG	Page 1962a.
PMGF	Davies 1991.
PW	Wissowa 1893–.
SIG³	Dittenberger 1915.
SLG	Page 1974.
SM	Snell and Maehler 1970 *or* 1987–89.
TrGF	Radt 1977.
V	Voigt 1971.
W	West 1989 *or* 1992b. *W*², second edition specifically.

JOURNALS

AJP	*American Journal of Philology.*
BICS	*Bulletin of the Institute of Classical Studies of the University of London.*
CP	*Classical Philology.*
CQ	*Classical Quarterly.*
CW	*Classical World.*
GRBS	*Greek, Roman, and Byzantine Studies.*
HSCP	*Harvard Studies in Classical Philology.*
JHS	*Journal of Hellenic Studies.*
P. Oxy.	*The Oxyrhynchus Papyri,* a series published under different editors.
QUCC	*Quaderni Urbinati di Cultura Classica.*

SEG	*Supplementum Epigraphicum Graecum*
TAPA	*Transactions of the American Philological Association.*
ZPE	*Zeitschrift für Papyrologie und Epigraphik.*

ANCIENT AUTHORS AND WORKS

Hdt.	Herodotus.
Incert. auct.	Uncertain author.

Ach.	Aristophanes, *Acharnians.*
Anth. Pal.	*Palatine Anthology,* a collection of epigrams by various authors.
Ath. Pol.	Aristotle, *Constitution of Athens.*
Bibl.	Apollodoros, *Bibliotheke,* or Photios, *Bibliotheke.*
Hipp.	Euripides, *Hippolytos.*
Lys.	Aristophanes, *Lysistrata.*
pap. Colon.	Cologne papyrus.
pap. Oxy.	Oxyrhynchus papyrus.
Rep.	Plato, *Republic.*
Symp.	Plato, *Symposium.*
WD	Hesiod, *Works and Days.*

MISCELLANEOUS

ad loc.	referring to a commentary: at the lines indicated.
app. crit.	notes printed with a text that record possible restorations, scholia, and other pertinent details.
BCE	before the common era (equivalent to *BC*).
CE	common era (equivalent to *AD*).
ch.	chapter.
col.	column.
f	following (indicates the paragraph, not "following," in references to Plato or Athenaios).
fig.	figure.
fr.	fragment.
n.s.	new series.
passim	(not an abbreviation) throughout.
pl.	plate.
rev.	revised.
s.v.	under the word (referring to a dictionary entry).
schol.	scholion (pl. scholia), ancient marginal comment in a manuscript.
ser.	series.

test.   testimonium (pl. testimonia), i.e., ancient evidence on an
             author's life and works. Note: in Ch. 6, "Test."
             (capitalized) refers to the testimonia on Sappho in
             Campbell 1982.
tr.   translator *or* translated by.

Performance and Gender in Ancient Greece

Introduction

What is love? 'Tis not hereafter,
Present mirth hath present laughter.
—song from Shakespeare,
    Twelfth Night

I

LIKE LOVE, Greek poetry was not for hereafter but shared in the present mirth and laughter of festival, ceremony, and party. Before the Hellenistic age (and often later), poetry was composed for performance. Men and women, young and adult, had their turns at singing, dancing, parading, or reciting before their neighbors. How can we restore the physicality of body and voice, the energy of interaction between performers and audience, to the nondramatic poetic texts that have survived from ancient Greece?

We could begin with descriptions of performance. These are remarkably few because, paradoxically, performance was so common. No one needed to be told what a choral dance looked like. But there are some passages and passing remarks that offer a hold to the imagination. They will allow us to start from performance as an event peopled by members of a community, and sometimes strangers, then ask what the poetic texts *add* to the occasion—the opposite of the usual procedure, if indeed performance is taken into account at all in the study of nondramatic poetry. I will use the excerpts that follow to throw performers and their audiences into high relief.

Athenaios preserves from Philochoros a brief vignette of the City Dionysia at Athens, when tragedies, comedies, and dithyrambic poems were performed:

> At the competitions of the Dionysia the Athenians would first eat and drink, then go to the show and watch, wearing wreaths, and all during the whole contest wine was poured out for them and sweets were carried around, and as the choruses were coming in, they poured out wine for them to drink; and as they were leaving after performing in the competition they poured (for them) again.[1]

[1] Athenaios 11, 464f citing Philochoros *FGH* 328 F171.

We gain a sudden glimpse of a reveling crowd, of noise and sticky hands and camaraderie.[2] In the midst of it all are the choruses, the troupes of singer-dancers who performed the round-dance known as the dithyramb or joined the actors in tragedy and comedy. Members of each tribe no doubt cheered when one of their dithyrambic choruses appeared, for each of the ten tribes entered two choruses of fifty dancers each, one of men and one of boys, in the annual contest.[3]

Demosthenes adds to our impression of the dithyrambic contest when he recounts his tribulations in serving as *chorēgos,* or "sponsor," for his tribe in his oration against his nemesis Meidias (21 *Meidias*). Elaborate in dance and song, performance required months of rehearsal and afforded Demosthenes' enemy any number of chances to derail the Pandionis tribe's showing.[4] Demosthenes complains that Meidias broke into the goldsmith's shop and destroyed some of the gold crowns Demosthenes was having made for the chorus members (21.16). He corrupted the trainer, and if the pipes-player (21.17)

> hadn't himself thought it necessary to hammer together and train the chorus, we would not have been able to compete, O men of Athens, but the chorus would have come in untrained and we would have suffered a most shameful thing.

Furthermore, Meidias somehow was responsible for his tribe's not getting the prize even though they were winning (21.18). To top it all off, Meidias struck Demosthenes in public while he was involved in the ceremonies (21.1, 6–7, and 74). Demosthenes' taut competitiveness complements the communal jollity depicted by Philochoros.

Women performed as well. In Aristophanes' comedy *Acharnians* the protagonist, Dikaiopolis, celebrates the rural Dionysia with his family. His daughter is to carry a ritual basket in the procession. As he organizes the participants, he gives her some advice (253–58):

> Make sure, daughter, that, pretty as you are, you carry the basket prettily, looking sour pickles. For he will be blessed who marries you and begets pole-cats no less good than you at farting at daybreak. Start off, and guard yourself well in the crowd so that no one sneakily nibbles at your gold.

The slave Xanthias is to walk behind her holding erect the phallus on a pole, while Dikaiopolis follows singing a phallus-song. The daughter does not join his ribald song, but young women did sometimes sing in processions. The location of the performance is again in the midst of a

---

[2] Cf. Cole 1993: 27–29 on the Dionysiac aspects of the City Dionysia, with a procession of phalluses and dancing in the agora.

[3] Cf. Pickard-Cambridge 1962: 32–38; 1968: 74–79.

[4] Cf. Antiphon 6 *On the Choreut* 11–13 on organizing a boys' chorus.

crowd.[5] Though part of a comedy, this scene must evoke the day of the rural Dionysia, for it is meant to arouse nostalgia in members of the theater audience cut off by war from their country homes.

Very different is another kind of performance. In his dialogue *Ion,* Plato puts into the mouth of the rhapsode Ion an account of his performance of Homeric epic.[6] Ion throws himself bodily into his recitation as he stands on a platform above the crowd. Yet Ion—the character created by Plato— also assesses crowd reaction in a detached way as he recites, since his living depends on his success in moving the audience emotionally (535cd):

ION   (Yes, I am inspired,) for when I recite something pitiable my eyes fill with tears, and when (I recite) something frightful or awe-inspiring my hair stands on end for fear and my heart jumps.

SOC.   What then, Ion? Shall we say that this man is in his right mind, who, dressed in multicolored garment and gold wreaths, cries in the midst of sacrifice and festival?

Socrates asks Ion whether he knows that he produces the same effect in the audience, and Ion answers (535e):

ION   Indeed I know it well; for I look down each time from up on the platform at people crying and looking awestruck and acting astounded at my words. For it is necessary for me to pay close attention to them, since whenever I set them to crying I myself will laugh when I take the prize-money, but whenever (I cause) laughter I will cry myself, losing the prize.

Ion uses his body differently from the dithyrambic dancers, histrionically rather than rhythmically (though both are richly dressed), and creates a hypercharged emotional atmosphere that contrasts with the crowd's welcoming revelry in the first two instances.

The account that Plutarch gives of Solon's performance of his elegy *Salamis* is probably (though not necessarily) fantasy.[7] In *Salamis* Solon urged the Athenians to take up their abandoned war to annex the wealthy island Salamis. According to Plutarch Solon started a rumor that he was mad, then rushed out of his house wearing a herald's cap, mounted the herald's stone in the agora (marketplace), and recited his poem. Plutarch gives the opening lines (1 *W*):

I myself, a herald, come from desirable Salamis, setting my arrangement of words as a song instead of a speech.

[5] The crowd is only imagined by Dikaiopolis, who alone can celebrate since he has a private treaty with Sparta, with whom Athens was at war.

[6] On the *Ion* as a description of performance, see Herington 1985: 10–13.

[7] Plutarch *Solon* 8.1–3, quoted in West 1992b *ad* Solon 1.

The poem contravened an Athenian law against speaking about the war with Salamis, says Plutarch, but by this means Solon made his harangue without being held accountable for it. The spectacle of an apparently raving Solon would draw everyone at a run to witness it—and hear his words.

Finally, in Aristophanes' *Wasps,* Bdelykleon tries to teach his father Philokleon the proper etiquette for singing at a symposium, an all-male gathering of friends to eat and then drink. After advice on how to recline, how to compliment the host, how to make conversation, Bdelykleon turns to the proper mode of singing together (1222–39):

BD.   (after listing the guests): Finding yourself in company with these, watch that you take up the songs well.
PH.   Are you kidding? Like no hillman I will!
BD.   I'll find out. Now suppose that I am Kleon; I first start singing the Harmodios song then you will take it up. "No man ever born to Athens was—"
PH.   "—ever such a miscreant or thief!"
BD.   Is that what you'll do? You'll throw away your life, knocked out by the shouting. For he'll say that he will destroy you and ruin you and drive you out of this land.
PH.   And if he threatens, then by Zeus I'll sing another song: "O human, you who are grasping at great power, you will yet overturn the city. She hangs in the balance."
BD.   Well, then, when Theoros, reclining at your feet, takes Kleon's right hand and sings, "Taking to heart the saying of Admetos, O comrade, hold dear those who are good," what *skolion* (little song) will you sing to him?

We can imagine vigorous stage business during this scene. Physical proximity colored and personalized the meaning of songs, and interaction involved bodies—from hand-holding to fistfights—as well as words. Women sang among their female friends in groups like those that gathered at the symposium, as Sappho did and perhaps Korinna, although we have no descriptions of the scene. Vase paintings show women performing for other women in interiors.[8]

In these scenes we see how significant for communication the physical and visual dimension of performance was, as well as observing the pressure of the audience and the intensity of its reactions. When we look at performance through this lens focused on the performers, we can see something else as well, a feature that will provide a way to analyze performance in its totality: in each of these passages (except the first), performers are planning or discussing the use of bodies (combined with words) to

[8] See West 1992a: pl. 7, 22, and cf. 33 (outdoor scene).

make an impression on the audience. Demosthenes arranged for his tribe to be visually splendid and cried foul when they were not judged the best. Dikaiopolis' daughter is showing herself off as ready to be married, for Dikaiopolis' mind leaps from her carriage in the procession to her marriage. Ion calculatedly mimes emotions in order to elicit crowd empathy. Solon stages a theatrical coup in order to ambush the audience with political exhortation. And Philokleon and his son disagree about what attitude he should project toward his drinking companions, while the opening of Kleon's Harmodios song ("No man ever was . . .") could be meant, with the right gestures, to describe himself (as Philokleon certainly takes it).[9] I actually did not pick the passages with this in mind, but what they show is that performance in pre-Hellenistic Greece was in the first instance the self-presentation of performers as social actors to their audiences. Their performances are not simply vocalizations of poetry, but acts of staging themselves. Now, it is a truism that oral performance is inescapably the self-presentation of a performer. Meaning comes to the audience not simply as a fabric of words but shaped by the voice and body of the interpreting performer. But performers may or may not use performance to present their extraperformance selves. It is my contention that nondramatic performance in its lived form in archaic and classical Greece, with physical, visual, aural, as well as verbal dimensions, can best be recreated by envisioning it as a medium in which, among other things, individuals enacted their own identities (actual or idealized) for the audience.

To say this is to say that performance was part of the "theatrical" public life of a culture governed by honor and shame.[10] Those who wished to participate in public business acted out a dramatized identity in a variety of ways in agora, public meeting, court and council, on military service, and in the symposium. Herodotus' stories of notable individuals, Plato's dialogues, Plutarch's *Lives*, among other sources, attest to the quality of bluff and posturing (to use John Winkler's words), the staginess (to use Adele Scafuro's term) that animated social life.[11] Robert Connor has pointed out the importance of dramatic self-presentation in public to those who would

---

[9] As Reitzenstein 1970: 26 points out. For more on this scene, see Ch. 5 and cf. MacDowell 1971 *ad loc.*

[10] Mediterranean anthropology highlights competitive posturing in contemporary societies dominated by constant public assessment of honor and shame: Campbell 1964 and Herzfeld 1985 both emphasize interfamilial competition in the Greek villages they investigate; Pitt-Rivers 1977 treats the Mediterranean basin as a cultural and historical unity with respect to the centrality of shame and honor. Seremetakis 1991 studies women's response in lament.

[11] Winkler 1990a: 4 and passim. He uses the fundamental work of Gouldner 1965, who applies the term *zero-sum game* to the competition for honor so prominent throughout the ancient Greek world. Scafuro forthcoming, Ch. 1.

8 · Introduction

be prominent.[12] To show how poetic performance participates in the same system is the burden of this book.[13]

In sum, if we wish to recapture a sense of Greek nondramatic poetry as it entered the lives of its original audience, we must think of it not as reified texts or even simply as occasional poetry, but as blueprints or librettos for performers' self-presentation. In this book I try to resurrect performers whose appearance and identity interacted with their words to produce the "message" for the audience. In other words, rather than treat the performer as a medium for the poetry, I propose to treat the poetry as a medium for the performer. Attending to performers means attending to audience and context also. The scenes described above attest to the variety of situations in which performers sang or recited. I investigate these further in the next section.

Two questions may be troubling the reader by now: given that in general we have only the texts of performed poetry, why and how do I take this approach? As to *why*, I have two answers. First, it highlights the character of Greek oral culture. Communication was to a significant extent oral in archaic and classical Greece, as scholars have realized for some time, and there are disputes over how much of a role writing played even in preservation and transmission of poetry.[14] But the critical issue for understanding Greek culture in this period is not orality but performance. By focusing on orality as a global condition, scholars of Greek poetry have tended to define the relevant issues and problems as those of style, occasion, and transmission.[15] The physical actuality of performance then drops out of sight, and the specific effects of oral communication are lost to view. So by insisting on putting the performer at the center, we gain an imaginative shift. Second, as I hope this book demonstrates, reconstituting performance enriches rather than narrows the meaning of texts. I do not set myself against effects detected by close

[12] Connor 1987. His major example is Peisistratos' staged return to Athens in a chariot driven by a tall woman dressed up as Athena (Hdt. 1.60). Of the citizens' response, he notes (46): "[They are] participants in a theatricality whose rules and roles they understand and enjoy. These are alert, even sophisticated, actors in a ritual drama affirming the establishment of a new civic order, and a renewed rapport among people, leader and protecting divinity." Rehm 1992: 3–11 emphasizes the range and importance of performance at Athens.

[13] Cf. Griffith 1990: 191 apropos of the agonistic style in poetic texts: "Poems were usually designed to *defeat other poems* [his italics]" and "[T]he case of the Greeks is special, I think, in the prevalence of overtly agonistic mannerisms, and in the extent to which awareness of (an) immediately present judge(s), and the challenge of a viable but contradictory alternative to the poet's present statement, may influence the choice of subject, treatment, and self-presentation."

[14] Havelock 1963 first made the case for the primacy of oral communication until the late fifth century. Thomas 1992, esp. 101–27, gives an overview of current scholarship.

[15] Cf. the major work of Gentili 1988: 3–49, who emphasizes occasion; Nagy 1990a and 1990b, who focuses on transmission; Rösler 1980, who looks at occasion and style.

reading, on the grounds that the audience would not have noticed them, but show that in various ways utterances would interact with other aspects of a performance.

To begin the answer to the question *how*, let me mention some of the work that has influenced mine, including recent work on performance in anthropology. I try to unite focus on the speaker with attention to the function and effect of speaking within particular contexts, drawing in part on Ruth Finnegan and the "ethnography of speaking." In her 1977 book, *Oral Poetry*, Finnegan surveys practices of oral communication from all over the world and emphasizes the importance of realization in performance to an audience, a feature that has been relatively neglected in the study of oral poetry.[16] Ethnography of speaking treats performance as heightened communication taking place within culturally recognized patterns of situation and style.[17] Speaking is a form of power, the access to which and modes of which can be studied.[18] These approaches, combined with the theatrical self-presentation that I have referred to, lead me to the idea that performance is self-presentation within enabling and legitimating contexts.[19]

Given this model to orient research, it is still essential to study specific cultural constructions of performance: the mode of self-presentation and the function of performance in various enabling contexts. Here several studies of performance in ancient Greece are very helpful. Richard Martin, in *The Language of Heroes,* begins from speech-act theory to give an account of *mythos* as authoritative self-presentation and performance of identity in a competitive situation.[20] *Mythoi* are authoritative speeches falling into the categories of command, boast-and-insult, and narrative of remembered events (for the purpose of persuasion).[21] He calls attention to the description of Thoas (*Iliad* 15.282–84):

[16] Finnegan 1977: 118–26 and passim.

[17] Bauman and Sherzer 1989: ix–xxvii give an overview of the field, which they date from Hymes 1962; another founding text is Bauman 1978. Foley 1992: 282–85 gives a synopsis. The performances studied are often much more informal than the ones I treat. Cf. also Stewart 1989, an ethnographical study of speaking relevant to my Ch. 5.

[18] On this dimension of performance, see Bloch 1975: 1–28.

[19] Foley 1992, taking a different tack, proposes to combine ethnography of speaking with oral formulaic theory, arguing that formulas provide heightened meaning by evoking the whole tradition. See also Herzfeld 1985 on the "poetics" of male self-presentation in everyday life in a Cretan village, esp. 10–19 giving a theoretical background for his study of self-presentation as social drama.

[20] Martin 1989: 14–15, 22–23, and ch. 1 passim. He contrasts *mythos* with *epos*, the other common word for speech in Homeric epic. For heroic performers of *mythoi*, see esp. 82–83 on the contrast between Odysseus and Nestor as speakers and ch. 3, "Heroes as Performers." Martin extends the work of Muellner 1976, who studies the Homeric verb *euchomai* and finds that its basic meaning is "say in a marked way." It too directs attention to the speaker.

[21] Martin 1989: 47, discussed 47–88.

Αἰτωλῶν ὄχ' ἄριστος, ἐπιστάμενος μὲν ἄκοντι,
ἐσθλὸς δ' ἐν σταδίῃ· ἀγορῇ δέ ἑ παῦροι Ἀχαιῶν
νίκων, ὁππότε κοῦροι ἐρίσσειαν περὶ μύθων.

Best by far of the Aetolians, skilled with a spear and good at close fighting, and
few Achaeans could have the better of him in the assembly when the young men
contested in speaking (= *mythos*).

As the *Iliad* depicts it, the Greek cultural construction of a speaker is a man
who has or claims authority and presses his character on others as he seeks
to increase his honor.

In his final chapter Martin argues that Homer himself is a speaker of
mythoi and that his poem is a competitive self-presentation meant to drive
other performers' versions out of contention.[22] Epic belongs to the category of narrative of remembered events, the most powerful kind of *mythos*
in the poem, and the poet aligns himself with Achilles, the most powerful
human speaker of *mythoi*.[23] I assume that the kind of speaker presupposed
by *mythos*—one who seeks to impress his or her authority and identity on
others—is a basic constituent of Greek social life in post-Homeric days as
well and that other important kinds of poetry also fall into the categories
that epic labels *mythos,* that is, narrative of stories for persuasive purposes,
boast, and lament (named a *mythos* when performed by women in the
Iliad).[24]

To these prayer must be added, which the *Iliad* portrays as private communication and does not name *mythos*.[25] For public, performed prayer as a
form of self-presentation, we can turn to Lutz Käppel, who studies the
paian as a genre embodying communication from a petitioner to a god as
bringer of well-being, either to request aid or in thanks for aid given.[26] He
shows that it thematizes the identity of the speaker: the "I" presents itself as
needing and as being worthy of help.[27] The genre of praise similarly the-

---

[22] Ibid.: 231–39. Martin also draws on anthropological accounts of "epic" performers in
various traditions: see his Ch. 1. Nagy 1990b: 221–24 points out that Pindar asserts a parallel
between *logioi* (masters of speech) and *aoidoi* (singers of epic).

[23] Cf. Wyatt 1987–88, who uses narratological technique to analyze the scene between
Thetis and Achilles in *Iliad* 1.348–427 for its effect in performance. The scene repeats the
quarrel from Achilles' point of view, adopted by the performer, to a sympathetic audience,
Thetis, whose role is given to the actual audience.

[24] Martin 1989: 86–88.

[25] Ibid.: 38.

[26] Käppel 1992: 63–64.

[27] Käppel 1992: 71–72. He refers to the creation of a dialogue with the god addressed, but
as D'Alessio 1994: 64 points out, the real recipient is the human audience, to make it content
with its lot.

matizes the speaker's identity, as we know from Pindar.[28] Lament, praise, and prayer are not agonistic forms, but they share the characteristic identified by both Martin and Käppel of claiming authority and status in the act of speaking.

But a practical problem remains: how is it possible to study self-presentation? It is true that often some indication of the circumstances of performance can be deduced from the poetry, and sometimes information about the circumstances is recorded. But there is one aspect of the identity and appearance of performers of nondramatic poetry that is systematically recoverable: their gender. Gender is the only area in which it is possible, normally, to link texts with the physical presence of the performer, for the gender of speakers can be determined by textual markers. Furthermore, since gender is an inevitable part of self-presentation in the flesh and cultural assumptions about gender attach themselves to speakers prior to any speech and inform its reception, oral texts must be read as gendered speech.[29]

Plato attests that a system existed for signaling participants' gender (and class) in musical performance and dance. Adapting choral performance to his ideal state in the *Laws*, he says it causes harm if the ensemble of words, tune, and dance are not scrutinized for inconsistencies perpetrated by human composers, who are less skillful than the Muses. For (669c)

> the Muses would never make so gross an error as to compose words suitable for men, and then give the melody a colouring proper to women, to put together melody and postures of free men, and then fit to them rhythms proper to slaves and servile persons.[30]

It is significant that Plato thinks about the total effect of performance in terms of gendered self-presentation. Musical idiom is not recoverable, of course, but the point for us is that gender identity was such an important aspect of performers' communication that melody and rhythm were perceived as expressing gender.

For men gender was a powerful code through which self-display and competition with others was channeled. Maud Gleason illustrates in her study of physiognomical literature her dictum that "masculinity in the ancient world was an achieved state, radically underdetermined by ana-

---

[28] Hubbard 1985: 3, speaking of Pindar's epinician odes, refers to the poems' "persistent auto-referentiality." Cf. Goldhill 1991: 166 on the construction of an authoritative speaking position in the act of praising.

[29] Butler 1990 gives a sophisticated description of gender as constructed through "performance" in daily life. Cowan 1990: 59 makes the same point and adds (91) that by means of dance ideology is reinforced and attached to sensuous experience.

[30] Translation from Barker 1984: 154.

tomical sex."[31] Men enacted their manhood through body language—the firm walk and glance, controlled body, athletic dancing. Women's self-presentation affected their reputations as well, although aggressive assertion of gender identity would be self-defeating for them.

If speakers also identify themselves verbally as gendered or use sexual language about themselves or even about others, they produce a composite self-presentation created from the interaction between their body language and their words. The two codes, physical and verbal, may simply be mutually reinforcing, but, as we shall see, they can also create more complex identities.

Now let us return to the scenarios given earlier and consider how gender identity is implicated. Dikaiopolis' daughter gives the simplest performance, for she does not speak but only shows herself to the audience. She walks to the tune of her father's phallus-song, so her visual self-presentation is framed by male sexuality. Yet note that even her message is composite: although she is "pretty," she must not smile lest she seem too inviting. In this context the finery she wore must have suggested her family's ability to give her a good dowry. (One can garner some idea of basket-bearers' adornment at a more pretentious level of society from the sixth-century *korē* figures, statues of aristocratic young women, dedicated on the Athenian Acropolis.[32] They wear earrings and necklaces, sometimes a tiara, and embroidered gowns.) By balancing his compliment to her with insult and warning, Dikaiopolis represents for his daughter the position she must occupy: valuable and desirable, yet object and animal for male spectators, yet self-conscious enough to withhold herself from them. In her case it is her father's verbal definition of her that interacts with "her" (actually a male actor's) appearance and movements to characterize her for the audience in the theater.

We should note parenthetically at this point that physical self-presentation may involve enacting social status as well as gender. By putting themselves before an audience, well-dressed, especially in ritual contexts, performers offer themselves as worthy to be the center of attention. At the same time performers whose high status was established would reinforce other messages encoded in performance. Social status intersects gender in self-presentation (though in ways very difficult to trace, since we know so little about the individual identity of performers).[33] That both are involved in the role of basket-bearer can be illustrated by the episode of the

[31] Gleason 1990: 391.

[32] See Richter 1968: 6–12 on costumes and jewelry; plates.

[33] Cf. Winkler 1990a: 45–70, who shows that surveillance (the other side of self-presentation) of sexual practices is political and directed at an elite who participate in government.

tyrannicides, Harmodios and Aristogeiton, related by Thucydides (6.54–58): Harmodios was the beloved of Aristogeiton and rejected the bid of Hipparchos, brother of the Athenian tyrant Hippias, to become a rival lover. In revenge Hipparchos pronounced Harmodios' sister unworthy to serve as basket-bearer in the procession at the Panathenaia. It was this insult to the family's social standing, as well as the sister's virginity, that impelled the two young men to assassinate Hipparchos.[34] The issue of status in performance will only occasionally be noted in the present work, but I want to point out that it too is operative.

We can now return to considering visual self-presentation as gendered in our initial examples. Choral performance included the spectacle of bodies in "dance"; dance ranged from moving in procession to military exhibitions like the dance in armor. Men's dithyrambic dancing must have been impressively athletic and coordinated, since dancers were excused from military service in order to rehearse. The Athenian citizens making up the chorus of Aristophanes' *Wasps* (1060–61) boast that they were once "strong in choral-dancing and strong in battle." Body language in the symposium was different, including a diffused eroticism to which Philokleon is too peppery to submit. He reappears on stage, after going off to a "real" symposium following his lesson, with the flute-girl he abducted from the party (1341–47). Gender is always automatically implicated, for all these bodily self-presentations will be evaluated in terms of the gender roles prescribed by the dominant ideology, an assessment that the use of gender as a code for male competition can only intensify.

To visual self-presentation is added the song or spoken poem. The words then intertwine with visual messages. The dithyramb might combine vigorous dancing with sensuous, captivating language. Pindar composed a dithyramb for Athens (fr. 76 *SM*), probably for one of the competing choruses at the city Dionysia, in which the performers called the city *iostephanoi* (violet-crowned) and *liparai* (shining)—terms often applied to women, especially goddesses.[35] Implicit in the performers' presentation is perhaps the old religious pattern of young men in the service of a goddess, so the audience could feel collectively flattered and exalted.[36] In fact Aristophanes' chorus in the *Acharnians* (636–40) criticizes the Athenians for allowing embassies to flatter them by using these two words lifted from

---

[34] Aristotle *Ath. Pol.* 18.2 has a slightly different version that also includes the insult to the sister. Harmodios and Aristogeiton were later celebrated in song as liberators. The "Harmodios song" that figures in the scene from the *Wasps* quoted above was one of several.

[35] "Violet-crowned": *Homeric Hymn* 6.18 and Solon 19.4 *W* (Aphrodite), Theognis 250 (Muses). "Shining": *Iliad* 14.186 (Hera's feet), Hesiod *Theogony* 901 (Themis), Bacchylides 7.1 (daughter of Time and Night) and 5.169 (wife).

[36] On the pattern see Burkert 1985: 212.

the dithyramb; but it applies the first to the audience members themselves, not the city, suggesting that they have let themselves be put in the position of women!

Solon's physical appearance as "mad"—out of control, bereft of identity— is qualified by the gender ideology of his message. What that is can be brought out by contrast with a scene from Plutarch's *Pericles*. When the Spartans under King Archidamos invaded Attica in 431, Pericles refused to lead an army out to meet them. "Many of his friends urged him on by entreaty," says Plutarch (33.7), "and many of his enemies by threatening and denouncing him, and choruses sang songs and mockeries to shame him, insulting his generalship as unmasculine.[37] "Masculinity," as re- marked above, is code for aggressive defense of honor, explicit here and implicit in Solon's urging the Athenians to fight. Verbally, therefore, So- lon counteracts the initial impression he gives.

Philokleon disrupts male bonding in the symposium with his insults; for better symposium technique let us take a poem sung in Athenian sym- posia in the fifth century BCE, Timokreon's anti-Themistoklean sympo- sium song (727 *PMG*). The performer asserts himself at once by means of a priamel (1–5):

> Now if *you* praise Pausanias or again you praise Xanthippos or you Leotychides, I on the other hand praise Aristeides, the one best man to come from holy Athens, for Leto developed an antipathy to Themistokles, that liar, perverter of justice, traitor.

The poem continues its denunciation of Themistokles, culminating in an assault on Themistokles' manhood in a passage of sexual double entendre that portrays him as a pathic prostitute (10–12):[38]

> And full of silver he laughably kept an inn at the Isthmos, supplying meats that were cold. The others ate and hoped that no joint (of sacrificial meat) of Themistokles would (a)rise.

Self-assertion gives way to common laughter at the expense of an emblem of the enemy. Whereas Solon's words overrode his initial bodily message, this singer complements the physical dynamic, affirming his (and the others') masculinity in latently erotic intimacy with other men by creating a "female" and mercenary figure of contrast.

Poetry was an embedded part of the semiotics of these scenes as wholes. It was performers' speech: what they said expanded their dramatized iden- tities, while the meaning of the text was influenced by their appearance and

---

[37] The choruses meant are comic choruses, for Plutarch goes on to quote some verses from the comic poet Hermippos.

[38] For this reading of the last three lines, see Stehle 1994: 516–20.

social status. And gender was a crucial element of the total effect, inhering in both visual presentation and speech. Issues of gender both require and permit analysis of texts as embodied communication with an audience, and, as it turns out, gender as a code is used for ideological ends and manipulated between visual and linguistic levels in very interesting ways.

I want to end this section with a final observation. My approach, especially since I see speech as gendered by the body of the speaker, takes it for granted that the performers were conceived by the audience to be speaking "spontaneously," by which I mean that the words they spoke were assumed to be their own.[39] In very few cases were the utterances actually original with the performers, but what mattered was not whether the performers had put together the text but the fact that they *affirmed* it by speaking the words in public.[40] The act of speaking meant that they committed themselves and linked their prestige to the sentiments they expressed. The modern convention is the same as far as politics goes. Everybody knows, for instance, that George Bush's speech-writer Peggy Noonan wrote the line "Read my lips, no new taxes!" What mattered was that Bush spoke it at the 1988 Republican Convention and thereby committed himself to its message. It was the job of poets, as it would be of logographers (speechwriters) beginning in the fifth century, to create speaking positions for the performers.

That grammatical first person markers in performed poetry refer to the performer is generally accepted, with two exceptions of tangential interest to this book: rhapsodic recital of the *Iliad* and *Odyssey,* and performance of Pindar's epinician poetry (poetry celebrating athletic victories), if one believes, as I do, that it was normally choral.[41] I will say a little more about each type. As for performers of epic, no one (so far as I know) now thinks that recording the two monumental poems put an end to the activities of bards who recomposed in performance.[42] These performers continued to shape their stories according to their talents. The guild of Homeridai may have had a fixed text of the *Iliad* as early as the eighth century that they

---

[39] Barrett 1964 *ad* Euripides *Hipp.* 1423–30, comments apropos of "song-making care" of maidens for Hippolytos that it is "as if the girls composed their own songs: perhaps they did, but it is a common fiction of lyric poetry that it is extemporized by the singer."

[40] The view that choral poetry is the performers' speech may explain why the record of victories at the City Dionysia, *IG* ii² 2318, gives only the winning tribe and *chorēgos,* not the poet, for the dithyrambic contests. Cf. Pickard-Cambridge 1968: 72 and the text of the inscription on 104–6.

[41] On the controversy over whether Pindar's epinicians received solo or choral performance, see Heath and Lefkowitz 1991; Carey 1991 with bibliography. The majority of commentators from antiquity on have assumed choral performance. Morgan 1993 is closer to my view but does not distinguish the spoken from the written medium.

[42] Janko 1982: 191. For the difference between earlier singers and later rhapsodes and more detailed discussion, see Ch. 4 below.

alone performed, but the audience would have no particular reason to be aware of the poem's existing in disembodied form.[43] Once Athens owned a text of Homer and demanded that rhapsodes recite it from memory at the Panathenaia, then the Athenians, at least, would think of the performers as subservient.[44] Yet a rhapsode like Ion performed in competition with other rhapsodes, and competition throws the limelight onto the individual competing. Plato's *Ion* can in fact be read as a dispute about whether or not Ion is a speaker in his own right, with Socrates proposing the simile of the iron ring (rhapsode) attracted to a magnet (Homer) as an alternative to Ion's insistence that he knows everything because he knows Homer. The debate culminates in Ion's asserting that he would make an excellent general (540d-541c) because he knows from Homer what sort of speech is appropriate to a general. Here is a glimpse of the strain that speaking another's words put on the amour propre of a rhapsode. In this book I am not concerned with Ion's situation, however, although I have put him on his platform for the purposes of the Introduction, but with bards who had a choice of poems to perform or some ability to shape poems for particular audiences. They must have been a vanishing breed in the fifth century BCE, but in the sixth fresh versions of hexameter poems were still being created.[45]

The other exception, epinician poetry, is a different case. Choral performers normally presented the poems they had learned as their own speech, for no *canonized* text stood behind a choral performance.[46] The idea that epinician, atypically, presents the poet speaking through the medium of the chorus is scholarly interpretation based on reading texts.[47] In fact, the first person of Pindar's odes is impossible to identify uniquely, and many Pindarists have now adopted the idea that it is a "first person indefinite" that includes the chorus.[48] In the case of *spoken* language, however, listeners attach "I" automatically to the speaker they see speaking,

[43] Janko 1982: 228–31 places the fixing of the text of the *Iliad* in the eighth century. On the Homeridai see Burkert 1987b: 48–50, Nagy 1990b: 22–23. Burkert suggests that the Homeridai advertised themselves as offering "Homer," who thus became the supreme author of epic. Judging from their name, they claimed their "father's" song as an inheritance.

[44] Ps-Plato *Hipparchos* 228b attributes the rule to Hipparchos. The Panathenaia is the only attested occasion for fixed recitation. On visual evidence for epic competition at the Panathenaia before the date of the rule (probably soon after 514) and signs of the new rule, see Shapiro 1993: 98–104. Cf. Burkert 1987b: 47–50 on the changeover from telling stories to reciting "Homer."

[45] Janko 1982: 198.

[46] The feminine pronouns in texts for women to perform as well as statements about identity show that the performers are the speakers.

[47] Lefkowitz 1991 defends this view and distinguishes epinician from other choral poetry, in which she identifies the first person as the chorus's.

[48] Young 1968: 12 and 58. Young's view is accepted by, e.g., Kurke 1991: 188. Cf. Mullen 1982: 21–41, esp. 34. I disagree with his view that Pindar sometimes refers to himself apart

not to a third party. Nothing therefore stands in the way of assuming that an audience took the chorus members to be speaking in their own person, as usual; in fact, Eveline Krummen, who has made the most extensive study of the performance of two epinician odes (*Isthmian* 4 and *Pythian* 5) within the framework of public celebration, identifies the speakers as the chorus in those cases.[49] In the one victory ode that I analyze, therefore, *Olympian* 6, I presuppose choral speakers speaking about themselves.[50]

II

These acts of speaking must be situated in their performance contexts.[51] As remarked above, it is necessary to take into account the context of performance, for the kind of gendered self-presentation called for varies with the function of the performance in public life. We can use the passages given above to make some distinctions between types of performance. There are several criteria we might use, but they yield the same categories. First to strike the eye are the spatial relations between performer(s) and audience. Ion is separated from his audience and elevated; he stands on a platform above the crowd the better to project his voice.[52] Dikaiopolis' daughter and the dithyrambic dancers move through the middle of the throng of neighbors or townspeople. Philokleon will recline with a small group in a closed room. If prior social relations between performer(s) and audience are the key, the result is the same: Ion is a foreigner, while dancers in the dithyramb were members of their tribe who had to be Athenian citizens in good standing and Dikaiopolis' daughter participates as a member of her deme; in contrast with both, guests in a symposium or women's circle had to be invited (or at least welcome).[53] Then too, Ion was a professional; public choral performance was part of education for both sexes and for young men a demonstration of military fitness; but singing in a closed group was an amateur (and aristocratic) accomplishment. By all three criteria it appears that some performances are collective (choral) and cen-

---

from the chorus; see Ch. 3 below for an alternative view of *Olympian* 6.87–91, a passage always read as the poet's self-reference. Similar to Mullen is Most 1985: 199–200 on *Nemean* 7.

[49] Krummen 1990: 55, 138–40.

[50] I will deal with the question of the first person in Pindar at greater length elsewhere.

[51] Martin 1989: 5 stresses the two sides of performance: "Along with a new appreciation for the precious individuality of each verbal performance, a second variable has gained attention in this research [on discourse strategies]—the audience. . . . Oral communication must know and face its audience."

[52] Platforms are also pictured in vase-paintings showing rhapsodic and kitharodic competition at the Panathenaia. See Shapiro 1993: 100, fig. 25; Herington 1985: 17 and n.32.

[53] Ion was from Ephesos (530a). On the requirement of citizenship for dithyrambic performance, see MacDowell 1990 *ad* Demosthenes 21 *Meidias* 56–61.

tered in the community, while foreign/professional performers are set apart and small groups may segregate themselves and perform for each other.

Collective performances engage performers and audience as members of a community, while the implications extend beyond performance into the life of the community. By "community" I mean a collection of families organized under a system of governance, laying claim to a demarcated territory, worshiping common cults, and recognizing one another as fellow members. The dithyrambic singer-dancers articulate Athens into its ten tribes (which are an artificial creation undermining local separatism) and display their physical coordination.[54] Dikaiopolis' daughter manifests the attraction of marriage within the community. Both occasions include sharing food and drink. In fact Dikaiopolis' rural Dionysia and the dithyramb contest at the City Dionysia mark the endpoints of a span of community performances. At one extreme Dikaiopolis' celebration is the minimum sacrificial procession, the fact that it is confined to one family underlining the loss of community for rural Attica because of the Peloponnesian War. At the other extreme dithyrambic performance has become competitive and has been drawn into the political infighting of eminent men, the *chorēgoi*. It is performed in the theater, which increases the distance from the audience. As we see in Chapter 1, it is no longer fully analyzable as community poetry.

The other two types are optional from the point of view of the community. Both define themselves against the community, the symposium guests in forming a closed group and the bard in representing his knowledge as going beyond the community's. Solon's alleged performance was anomalous. Like a bard he pretended to come from elsewhere and mounted the herald's stone for elevation, yet his recitation had immediate implications for the audience. I analyze it in Chapter 1 as an abuse of community poetry.

The three categories also correlate with three major genres of poetry: hexameter narrative (bardic poetry), choral poetry, and monodic lyric (together with elegy and iambos). That is no surprise; the genres developed from performance. What is interesting is how well the genres reflect their conditions of performance. Hexameter narrative contains accounts of travels and events that encompass the whole cosmos; it was performed by one who could come in from outside and who separated himself by station, clothes, and professionalism from his audience. Choral poetry usually expresses the viewpoint of a particular community, and it was sung and danced in the middle by performers from the community.[55]

---

[54] Zimmermann 1992: 35–38.
[55] Cf. Plutarch's remark (*On the Malice of Herodotus* 872de, quoted *ad* Simonides 16 *W²*)

Poetry for small groups speaks of "personal" emotions and wishes and political views to an audience with whom the singer has a personal relationship.[56] All these kinds of performance are "public" in that they bring together members of different families, but the audience has a different character in each.

These three categories of performance are not simply opportunities for performers' self-presentation. They have important functions as occasions of public discourse and contain value-laden formulations of cultural belief. A performer's self-presentation must be in and through the discourse that is meant to influence the audience's conception of life, state, or world. As a result, we cannot generalize about self-presentation until we know the function of each type of performance. Then we will be able to see how a performer presents himself or herself in terms of the effect that the performance seeks to produce.

At this point I want to introduce the term *psychological efficacy*. I borrow the idea of the efficacy of performance from performance theorist Richard Schechner. Considering the continuum of ritual and theater, he says: "The basic opposition is between efficacy and entertainment, not between ritual and theatre. Whether one calls a specific performance ritual or theatre depends on the degree to which the performance tends toward efficacy or entertainment. No performance is pure efficacy or pure entertainment."[57] An efficacious performance is one that accomplishes something through performance itself. He draws an example from Highlands New Guinea: one village may give pig meat away to another through a dramatic performance in which the men of the two villages, who have recently been enemies, engage in mock warfare. After the ceremony the two villages observe friendly relations for a time.[58]

The performances I am concerned with do not automatically accomplish anything outside themselves, but they urge certain views on the audience and try to affect the audience's state of mind. This is what I will call their psychological efficacy. The term *psychological efficacy* suggests that a performance aims to persuade an audience to do something or feel in a certain way that has practical consequences.[59]

---

that Simonides did not offer his praise of Corinth (which Plutarch quotes) "while training a chorus in Corinth or making a song for the city" but put it into an elegy.

[56] Most 1982: 90 and 94 gives an excellent account of the typical differences between monodic and choral lyric that identifies the latter as poetry for a community.

[57] Schechner 1976: 207.

[58] Ibid.: 200–205; cf. 207 for a chart showing the differences between efficacy and entertainment.

[59] For a case of performance gone awry and not efficacious, consider the story that Phrynichos was fined for his tragedy on the fall of Miletos because he reminded Athenians of their failure to rescue the city (Hdt. 6.21).

The book takes up each of the three types of performance in turn. For each it investigates the psychological efficacy of performance as a preliminary to discussing performers' self-presentation. I will briefly indicate the results here. The psychological efficacy of community poetry is to renew the community and provide a unifying discourse. Such performance was predominantly choral but not necessarily so (nor does all choral performance fall into the category of community performance). As we shall see, community performance included prayer, praise, commemoration, or description of the world that naturalized a political system. The texts are often rich in deictics, i.e., first- and second-person pronouns and references to the here and now of performance.[60] The performers, women as well as men, spoke *for* the community in representing its traditions, and also *to* it in moving it to a new stage of communal life.[61] Its centripetal force could serve to counteract or to disguise the agonistic aspects of public interaction.[62] The message of community performance by those of high status is that the community's integrity depends on maintaining the power structure, while among those who qualify competition to showcase members of their families may be intense.

Community poetry has not been studied as a type with a typical pattern of interaction with the audience.[63] However, two major recent attempts to reconstruct choral performance of Pindaric odes can be correlated with the analysis presented here, books by William Mullen and Eveline Krummen.[64] Mullen proposes to recover a sense of Pindar's poetry as danced and as a preliminary offers an excellent account of the qualities expressed through dance in Greek culture.[65] Krummen's book, *Pyrsos Hymnon*, is exemplary in recreating a context for the original performance of Pindar *Isthmian* 4 and *Pythian* 5. She situates the poems convincingly as part of larger festivals important to maintaining the polis (city/city-state).[66] She

[60] Danielewicz 1990 stresses the importance of understanding deictic elements, including pronouns, as referring to the situation of performance and gives examples of the "chorocentric" (12) reference system that is found in choral poetry.

[61] Redfield 1990a: 324 observes that theater is unique among the various kinds of performance in the city (debate, ritual, games, and theater) in speaking both to and for the audience. Drama grew out of choral poetry and preserves this characteristic.

[62] For agonistic and integrative tendencies, compare the contrasting descriptions of fifth- and fourth-century Athens by Halperin 1990a and Patterson 1986. Henderson 1991b and Schmitt-Pantel 1990 both distinguish an inclusive and an exclusive view of the community, the former based on family membership, the latter on citizenship.

[63] Lefkowitz 1991: 11–25 points out several characteristics of community poetry in distinguishing it from epinician poetry.

[64] Mullen 1982; Krummen 1990.

[65] Mullen 1982: 56–70, and see 84–86 for discussion of *Olympian* 14 that is similar to Krummen's approach.

[66] Krummen 1990: 33–151. There are smaller studies that also stress embedded communication. Minchin 1990–91 uses the linguistic concept of pragmatics to study a speech in the

and Lutz Käppel both adapt reception theory to oral communication, look-ing for the "Sitz im Leben" (living context) of performance, which brings them close to the methods of ethnography of speaking.[67] Like these studies, Chapter 1 examines the psychological efficacy of community poetry, look-ing both at texts and at other kinds of evidence for performance. On this basis performers' self-presentation as gendered can be studied. Chapters 2 and 3 take up performance by women and by men, respectively.

Authority to speak within the community was granted by the commu-nity. Both bards and symposium performers resisted communal demands on discourse and claimed an (ostensibly) more individualistic style of speaking. Bards and symposium performers could improvise or choose their texts on the spot, as choral and other community performers could not. Both also had to establish and maintain personal legitimacy as speakers, the bard by his own success in projecting authority, the sympo-sium participant by preserving his standing with the group.[68] In the case of the bard, performance shifted toward the pole of entertainment, while in the symposium the need for efficacy of performance was more immediate, for the group was held together by its own discourse.[69] Only men per-formed in these two settings. Bardic performance is studied in Chapter 4, and in Chapter 5 I examine the gendered identity constructed in sympo-sium poetry.

Chapter 6 takes up Sappho's poetry. I consider the evidence for Sap-pho's audience and the character of her circle, an examination that will lead me to distinguish her poetry for a group audience from her erotic poetry. By attempting to analyze the latter as sung for a collective audience, I show that Sappho's method of self-presentation is unique and that it used rhetor-ical effects such as are found in inscriptions, effects inspired by writing. This poetry invites the recipient to construct a private fantasy world in which an internally created speaker, not necessarily identical with the singer, addresses her alone.

My set of three categories (plus Sappho's erotic poetry) does not cover all types or circumstances of performance. Civic banquets or aristocrats' entertainments with professional singers are a likely setting for perfor-mance, but we are not informed about what was sung on such occasions.

Iliad in its context. Morris 1986 and Slater 1984 examine Homer's epic and Pindar *Nemean* 1 respectively as communication to an audience and identify their function and ideology, al-though without focusing attention on the speakers.

[67] Krummen 1990: 1–30, esp. 5–8; Käppel 1992: 3–31, esp. 17–21 on "Sitz im Leben."

[68] On competition between bardic and choral poetry, see Burkert 1987b: 51–53; Ley 1993: 123–24. Nagy 1990b: 362n.124 takes issue with Burkert's suggestion that there were *profes-sional* choral performers in the archaic period; there is no evidence for them.

[69] Redfield 1975: 30 distinguishes song-for-something and song-for-itself, the latter of which is the bard's song.

Semipublic wedding songs and laments do not come in for consideration, except briefly in Chapters 2 and 6. Nor do official institutions like the Molpoi (see below), for in neither case do we have their poetry. I have little to say about the poetry of the pre-Socratic philosophers, as interesting as it is, because the setting for its performance is unknown. Stesichoros and Simonides are slighted for the same reason.[70] With one exception I avoid epinician poetry, for it is a special development from community poetry and requires separate study.[71]

I also do not consider reperformance, whose importance John Herington so rightly stresses.[72] Some reperformance, such as of ritual poetry like Alkman's *partheneia,* probably occurred under circumstances similar to the original ones. Other instances were no doubt memorial; performance of an epinician ode, for instance, might have been repeated on the anniversary of the original victory. Poetry of all types could be adapted to the symposium. Later performance of "traditional" songs lifted them from their embedded place in community ceremony and used them for a self-conscious evocation of ethnicity. Thus the variety and flexibility of songs especially, their entertainment aspect, is slighted in my account. I work with poetry about whose original context and performers we know or can deduce something because in these cases I can connect performers' self-presentation with the psychological efficacy of the poetry.

III

Since this book puts performers at center stage, we must have some idea what sort of figures to imagine in that position. Of the various types of performance that I have limned, the one least sharp in the imaginations of modern scholars is choral performance. The problem is in large part that we know so little about who performed. We too need to know whose words they are in order to have them come to life (and in the case of Pindar, we attribute them to the poet in order to give them a "speaker"). Anonymous, the chorus appears to us to be an indistinct collective of interchangeable dancer-singers on the analogy of a folk-dance troupe or modern chorus line performing the can-can. It appears to offer "vocal writing," as Jesper Svenbro calls the performance of tragedy when he describes actors as intermediaries between an author who writes and a passive audience that silently receive his words.[73] I would like to claim a

[70] On Stesichoros see West 1971, who thinks that his poems are solo kitharodic works, and Burnett 1988, who treats them as choral. For Simonides see Ch. 4.

[71] Kurke 1991, esp. Part II, shows why epinician poetry is special: it addresses both the victor's community and an interstate network of aristocratic families.

[72] Herington 1985: 48–50.

[73] Svenbro 1993: 169–71; cf. 180–83. I find his phrase unfortunate since it implies that the audience thought of the play primarily as text. But it does make the point that the actual identities of the performers are submerged in drama.

populist stance in studying choral performance; however, the evidence to be gleaned from passing remarks in ancient authors shows that performers might well be the elite of their communities, as befits a traditional form of public, political speaking. I will mention some examples in the hope of making choral poetry less indistinct.

At Athens, according to Pseudo-Xenophon, the people (i.e., the democracy) have robbed those practicing gymnastic and *mousikē* (music, poetry, and dance), that is, the elite, of all influence; instead the people want to be paid to sing and dance.[74] As a similar complaint in Aristophanes' *Frogs* 727–33 shows, choral dancing is particularly meant. What the author had in mind, I believe, is that democracy drove out the old system of self-presentation through choral performance by making speaking in assembly and courts a much more direct path to influence.[75] Yet the notable did perform at Athens, as the following instances show. The young Sophocles led a victory *paian* and dance after the battle of Salamis.[76] As a boy Euripides was wine-pourer for a group known as the Orchestai (Dancers) who danced around the temple of Delian Apollo; these were "among the foremost Athenians" (*tōn prōtōn Athēnaiōn*).[77] Boiotos, son of the wealthy Mantias, performed in a chorus at the Dionysia.[78] Mantitheos, the speaker of the court speech to which we owe the item, reminds the audience of it, giving the impression that it was natural to know who the dancers were. The two leading youths (who were dressed as women) in the Oschophoria procession were chosen from among those eminent in birth and wealth.[79] Among women Harmodios' sister has already been mentioned. Plutarch relates a popular account of Solon's stratagem for taking Salamis that involved laying a trap with "the foremost women" dancing on the shore at a festival to Demeter as the lure.[80]

At Sparta the kings took part in the choral dance for the Hyakinthia, for the fourth-century king Agesilaos, after a major military victory, returned

---

[74] Ps-Xenophon *Constitution of Athens* 1.13. On the problems of translation, see Frisch 1942 *ad loc.*

[75] Ober 1989: 76 points out that the Athenians moved from a democracy of consensus to one of debate. But speeches to the assembly and law-courts, as he analyzes them, took over some of the functions of choral performance. Each speaker seeks to make a favorable presentation of himself by inflecting an integrative ideological discourse. These performances contributed to the stability of the democracy (308): "Public rhetoric not only *revealed* social tension, it was a primary vehicle for *resolving* tension. The evolving vocabulary of symbols of social mediation expressed in the topoi and other rhetorical tactics of legal orations was, therefore, a key ingredient in the maintenance of social peace at Athens" [his italics].

[76] *Life of Sophocles* 3, *TrGF* p. 31; Käppel 1992: 304, Test. 26.

[77] Athenaios 10, 424ef, citing Theophrastos 119 Wimmer.

[78] Demosthenes 39 *Boiotos* 16. On the identity of Boiotos, see Davies 1971: 364–68.

[79] Harpokration s.v. *oschophoroi,* quoting Istros *FGH* 334 F 8. Cf. Hesychios s.v. *ōschophoria* [sic].

[80] Plutarch *Solon* 8.4–6. Plutarch does not actually say that the women were dancing, but his account implies it.

home for the Hyakinthia and "participated in the *paian* to the god in the position in which he was placed by the chorus-organizer."[81] In a choral poem by Alkman, the name Agido figures, a name that looks as though it should be connected with the Agiadai, one of the two kingly houses at Sparta. Other names linked to the kings appear in Alkman's choral poetry, suggesting that the performers were highly placed.[82] Stories of young women abducted for the sake of ransom point in the same direction. For instance, when a chorus of Spartan young women was dancing at the Temple of Artemis at Karyai, Aristomenes of Messenia carried off "those preeminent in money and the worth of their fathers." He released them in return for much money (having defended their virginity from his own soldiers).[83]

At Miletos the Aisymnetes (chief official) of the Molpoi (Singers-and-Dancers), a group that performed a periodic public ritual of procession, song, and dance, was also eponymous official of the city.[84] A similar group held an esteemed rank at Ephesos, as attested in the second century BCE.[85] At Epidauros, as an inscription tells us, a new ceremony was instituted probably shortly before 300 BCE in which the "best men" marched in procession and sang a *paian* in order to give expression to the idea that aristocracy is best able to preserve the city. I discuss this event in Chapter 3. At Cyrene the chorus performing Pindar's *Pythian* 5 hail the aristocratic Aigeid clan as "my fathers" (75–76).[86] They are not necessarily all part of it, for the clan ancestry could be generalized to the whole city, but the way in which this genealogy is thematized suggests that the speakers may have had a special affinity for aristocracy. On Samos men dressed in snowy chitons with gold clasps in the shape of cicadas in their hair marched in procession in honor of Hera; song is not mentioned, but perhaps only because it did not suit the author's topic of luxury.[87] The gold decorations indicate their wealth. At Thebes the procession for the Daphnephoria was led by a family with horse-racing victories in the year that Pindar composed his *partheneion* II for it; the chorus that followed

[81] Xenophon *Agesilaos* 2.17. Cf. Plutarch *Sayings of the Spartans* 208de for an incident in which the boy Agesilaos is assigned to an inconspicuous position in the chorus and says, "Fine, I will show that it isn't the positions that display the men but the men who display the positions as honored." On this story and its variants, see Nagy 1990b: 348–49.

[82] Page 1959: 19–20; Calame 1977, II. 140–41. Cf. Ch. 1 n.99.

[83] Pausanias 4.16.9–10.

[84] *SIG*³ #57; partly given in Käppel 1992: 335–36, Test. 111. The inscription is a copy of one from 450/449 BCE that sets out cult regulations dating from a revision in 479/478: *SIG*³ note 1 *ad loc*. See Käppel 1992: 59–61 with bibliography. Robertson 1987: 357n.1 gives bibliography on political affiliations of the Molpoi.

[85] See *SIG*³ #57, p. 70n.5.

[86] Krummen 1990: 136–40 shows that the statement must be referred to the chorus since it is intimately tied up with both the festival of the Karneia and the history of the city.

[87] Athenaios 12, 525ef citing Asios fr. 13 Bernabé. On the cicadas see O'Sullivan 1981.

must have been of status to do honor to the family whose praises they sang. On this song see Chapter 2. Finally, Sappho was involved with choral performance for weddings and ritual occasions; she came from a prominent family and seems to have associated with other wealthy or aristocratic women.[88] The conclusion that I draw is that choral performance was one of the ways in which prestigious families traditionally staged their centrality in the community and their right to speak for it, to identify its interest with their own.

Choral performance must have been ubiquitous in religious ceremony, as witness the chorus mentioned in passing in an inscription: a mid-fifth-century treaty among Argos and Knossos and Tylisos on Crete specifies that at a certain regular sacrifice participated in by all three, the Knossians should give guest-gifts to the sacrificers and the Argives to the chorus.[89] The dances and songs performed at such events were surely traditional. Most Greek communities were small, villages or minor city-states.[90] Nicholas Jones emphasizes the particularism that characterized Greek political organization. Attica, though united around Athens, is a vivid example: each of the 139 demes (villages) in Attica maintained a series of cults and festivals separate from the city.[91] In these small communities probably everyone knew the songs and perhaps all participated as performers. But it is the more ambitious groups that commissioned new poems for new or refurbished festivals or special occasions, and the poems we have come largely from this set.[92] We should think of them as performed by the prominent.

---

[88] Aloni 1983: 23.

[89] *SIG*³ #56.38; Meiggs and Lewis 1988: #42B (with better punctuation), dated to ca. 450 BCE. Demosthenes 21 *Meidias* 51–53 speaks of forming choruses in the ancestral fashion and quotes several oracles that prescribe sacrifice and choruses.

[90] Starr 1986: 37 emphasizes that the majority of city-states were tiny. He quotes Ehrenberg 1968: 7: the polis was "a human community, often very small indeed, always held together by narrow space, by religion, by pride, by life." Cf. also Starr 46–50 on size and local attachment.

[91] Jones 1987: 61–65 gives a general discussion of the activities overseen by the demes, including religious ritual. See also Whitehead 1986: 176–222.

[92] For occasions of performance see Käppel 1992: 43–65 for *paianes* and 322–41 for testimonia on performance at festivals and in cult settings; Burnett 1985: 158n.4; the appendices in Herington 1985. Webster 1970 collects archaeological and literary evidence for choruses. Barker 1984 is an invaluable collection of literary testimony to musical performance.

CHAPTER ONE

Community Poetry

I

IN THE INTRODUCTION I defined community performance as collective and centered on the community, with implications that extend beyond the performance into the life of the community. Community poetry is poetry composed for the setting and function of community performance. The purpose of this chapter is to investigate the psychological efficacy of community poetry. What does it accomplish and how? The staging of the performer will not, except incidentally, be taken up in this chapter but will be the subject of the next two chapters.

Theognis gives a sketch of a city celebrating its continued well-being as part of a prayer to Apollo to save the city from the Persians, presumably in 480 BCE. In its generality we can see the typical elements of a communal response to evidence of the gods' favor (773–79):

> Φοῖβε ἄναξ, αὐτὸς μὲν ἐπύργωσας πόλιν ἄκρην,
>
> Ἀλκαθόωι Πέλοπος παιδὶ χαριζόμενος·
>
> 775 αὐτὸς δὲ στρατὸν ὑβριστὴν Μήδων ἀπέρυκε
>
> τῆσδε πόλευς, ἵνα σοι λαοὶ ἐν εὐφροσύνηι
>
> ἦρος ἐπερχομένου κλειτὰς πέμπωσ' ἑκατόμβας
>
> τερπόμενοι κιθάρηι καὶ ἐρατῆι θαλίηι
>
> παιάνων τε χοροῖς ἰαχῆισί τε σὸν περὶ βωμόν.

Lord Phoibos, you yourself once fortified the high city, doing a favor for Alkathoos, son of Pelops; now likewise keep the insolent army of the Medes away from this city, so that to you the people may convey memorable hecatombs in joy when spring comes, delighting in the lyre and heartwarming feast and choruses of *paianes* (ritual songs) and shouts around your altar.

The city expresses itself in music, dance, and public meal.[1] The chorus sings *paianes* to Apollo around his altar as part of a celebration involving the whole community, for it is through the chorus that the community addresses the god with thanks and hope for the future. Arthur Fairbanks suggests that the *paian* is a responsive song, with the crowd shouting the

---

[1] Cf. *Iliad* 1.469–74 for a feast combined with choruses of *paianes;* Fairbanks 1900: 25–26 considers this a typical combination in cult practice.

typical refrain *iē paian* along with the chorus.[2] Thus the shouts that accompany the *paian* in this passage would be the audience's response to the singers, making it literally a communal production. This vignette places the chorus in an emotional, spatial, and social context.[3]

To guide further our investigation of community poetry, in its choral form, and confirm that the performers act as representatives of the whole, let us look next at Plato's *Laws*, book 2. Plato offers the nearest thing to an analysis of the role of the chorus in a Greek city-state, for in his last work he turns from reliance on dialectic back to traditional means of educating and shaping individuals as ideal citizens.[4] His discussion allows us to see what he thinks the power and effects of choral performance are.[5]

Plato first identifies choral activity with education because it imposes discipline and harmony on children who are still too young to reason, while implanting the idea that the virtuous life is the sweetest one (653a–654b, 659d–660a; cf. 664bc). From this perspective choral song and dance are a kind of imprinting; their effects are independent of an audience. In other words, choral performance *creates* public speakers: the sentiments provided by the lawgiver via poets should become as "natural" as harmonious movements. Plato aims at producing individuals who affirm the prescribed speech as their own personal belief. His long-term project of combining Socratic individualism with a unified belief system settles in the end on the traditional system of choral performance.

But Plato also thinks of performance as making an impression on an audience (664cd):

> To begin with, then, it will be correct for the chorus of the Muses, which is composed of children, to enter first upon these themes, and to sing them with all its energy before the whole city; and secondly the chorus of those up to thirty years old will call Apollo Paian to witness that what is said is true, and will pray him to come to the young people with grace and persuasion. Thirdly, those between the ages of thirty and sixty must also sing.[6]

Leading up to this point has been discussion of the idea that the just man is happiest. The lawgiver will persuade or compel poets to say this and to provide the rhythms and melodic forms that go with that idea (661c). Then the lawgiver must devise a way to persuade the whole community to

---

[2] Ibid.: 48–49.

[3] Segal 1985: 165–68 emphasizes the importance of choral poetry in the civic life of communities in both its moral and its sensuous aspects.

[4] Cf. Meier 1989 on the educational role of festivals, particularly tragedy. Note esp. 576–77 on the importance of *experiencing* communality in a state without police or established authority.

[5] Cf. Morrow 1960: 302–71; Anderson 1966: 64–110 on Plato's view of music and its place in education; Mullen 1982: 53–56 on music and dance in the *Laws*.

[6] Translation from Barker 1984: 148–49.

agree to this belief without lapse in all its songs, stories, and discourse (664a).[7]

The choruses represent the lawgiver's strategy for impressing on all the idea that just behavior is equated with happiness. To generalize, once the system is in operation, the chorus functions both to reflect the ideology already affirmed by the community and to model that ideology for the audience.[8] Thus the second chorus in the lines quoted above is to pray to Apollo Paian to help it persuade the young men, its counterparts in the audience.[9] The prayer to Paian is simultaneously a directive to the audience: if it does not resist the god of healing, it will yield to the assertions of the chorus.

But the chorus does more than convey the assertion: it makes the assertion "true." As the chorus performs the rhythms and melodies (*harmoniai*) of good men, the dancers give pleasure, so that justice and pleasure are *seen and heard* to be united. We could say that in Plato's ideal state community values are refracted through the chorus in such a way as to become visible and sensuous. Plato calls choral performance *mimēmata tropōn* (655d, "imitations of character"); the qualities that the chorus imitates are made attractive by the rhythm and melodic form of song and dance.

Reflection and modeling, reproduction of hegemonic discourse and intensification of it by personal affirmation and sensuous involvement of bodies—these two aspects describe choral performance in its communication with its audience. The performers present themselves as exemplary members of the community, for they concretize collective attitudes as personal convictions and exhibit the shared beliefs in idealized form.[10] The notion of community performance as providing reflection and model means that community performers speak both for and to the audience and community at large: *for* the community as reflectors of its beliefs and *to* it as models for renewed affirmation of those beliefs.

The idea of reflection and model can also be correlated with the function of community performance to mark a turning point or critical moment in

[7] The third or "Dionysiac" chorus, as the wisest citizens (665d), must sing also. They will not want to (665e) but will sing after wine in a group of moderate size (666bc). They will select and sing the best songs, serving thus as leaders of younger men (670c–671a). I take this to mean that they will sing in the symposium. Belfiore 1986 interprets Plato's somewhat opaque description to mean that they will perform choral poetry.

[8] Cf. *Laws* 799ab, where it is said that every festival will include songs and choruses.

[9] England 1976 *ad* 664c takes the last quoted line to mean that the chorus is persuading others.

[10] Lefkowitz 1991: 23 summarizes the difference between the speaker's self-description in Pindar's epinician poetry and that found in other choral poetry by remarking that the latter fulfils a communal function. The chorus achieves a corporate character through self-description, which may include stress on patriotism (15). She thus sketches out the category of communal poetry.

the life of the community. Performance, as we shall see, marked a specific moment as special, even transformative, and brought out its significance for the audience: a stage in the yearly round or progression of generations, a change of political system or shift in interstate relations, a critical moment in the relationship with the gods, negotiation of relations among individuals.[11] Reflection, then, is oriented toward the past and modeling toward the future. Plato's chorus does not mark and enact moments of transformation for the community, for his ideal community has none. Plato's desire is to eliminate shifts in thinking, so performance should be constant and unchanging in its basic message, though new songs must be introduced constantly in order to maintain pleasure (665c).[12] The model in this case is only an intensification and justification of the reflection, for Plato plans a closed system for the circulation of discourse. Real community poetry is not so involuted, though for it too the recommended future is based on the shared past. I will use the idea of speaking for and to the community, reflection and model, as a framework with which to approach communal poetry.

There are other indications that choral performance served as the primary way for a community to represent itself; cities, for instance, sent choruses to represent them at interstate festivals such as the one on Delos. Philodamos of Skarpheia's *paian* for Dionysus, performed at Delphi, describes communities, including that on Olympus, welcoming the god in turn with choruses.[13] Community poetry is not necessarily choral, but it seems usually to have been so; the corporate body of a chorus suggests a community more easily than does an individual.

With Plato's description as a guide, let us turn now to actual examples of communal poetry to see how they operate as performance. There are very few surviving poems from the archaic period that qualify as communal, but enough to discern a pattern. Plato also shows (what plenty of other evidence, including texts themselves, confirms) that the system of choral performance did not disappear even with the increase in writing and books.[14] Early Hellenistic poems can also illustrate the function of communal poetry, and I will use two in the course of this and the following chapters.

[11] On festivals promoting communal solidarity, see Plato *Laws* 738de. Burkert 1985: 254–55 stresses that ritual creates solidarity. He also remarks (259) on the opportunity ritual offers individuals for expressing their personalities. One example is Xenophon, who set up a shrine to Artemis and served as her priest and the host at the annual festival.

[12] Elsewhere Plato says that the songs must never be changed; Morrow 1960: 355–57 thinks that Plato means the type of song.

[13] *CA* pp. 165–71. The poem is preserved on an inscription, which also records the honors that the Delphians gave Philodamos in return. For its connection with the temple of Apollo, see Stewart 1982.

[14] Mullen 1982: 3 points out that *choreia* (the combination of dance and song) was no

1. Alkman's *Louvre partheneion* (1 *PMGF* = 3 *C*).

The poet Alkman, who flourished in the seventh century BCE, was engaged, apparently by the Spartan government, as composer and chorus-trainer.[15] He became famous for his *partheneia,* songs for a chorus of *parthenoi* (young unmarried women). A large fragment of a song called the *Louvre partheneion* has been recovered on papyrus. The poem itself may have indicated that it was sung by a chorus of eleven *parthenoi;* it does tell us that they were engaged in making an offering to Orthria and wished to please Aotis (who is presumably the same goddess).[16] The chorus praises two women, Hagesichora and Agido, the former of whom seems to be the chorus-leader, as her name indicates, and mentions that they are engaged in some ritual action separate from the chorus.[17] Fragmentary and referring elliptically to its own ritual setting, the poem is difficult to understand.

The first legible part of the papyrus contains the end of a mythic narrative. The name Polydeukes is visible (1), followed by a list of the sons and relations of Hippokoon. One narrative concerning the sons of Hippokoon is part of Spartan legendary history: Hippokoon usurped the throne from Tyndareus, and Heracles fought Hippokoon's sons to recover it for him.[18] The story as known does not include the Dioskouroi (Kastor and Polydeukes = Castor and Pollux), so either Alkman gave a more elaborate version of the known story or he told another unknown one. The gnome (maxim) that closes this narrative (16–21, quoted below) suggests that the story had to do with inappropriate marriages, so it probably dealt with a dispute between the Dioskouroi and the Hippokoontidai over brides.[19]

---

longer a major medium for creative energies by Plato's time. But composition and performance continued. Bremer 1981: 197–203 gives evidence for performance from inscriptions, mainly Hellenistic and later.

[15] For the testimonia on Alkman, see Calame 1983; Campbell 1988.

[16] There is no agreement on the identity of the goddess. See Ch. 2 for possibilities. The restoration indicating that eleven *parthenoi* form the chorus is that of Puelma 1977: 46–48, based on an obscure remark by the scholiast. Others, including *PMGF,* accept a supplement that indicates ten chorus-members but destroys the progression.

[17] The relative status and relationship of Agido and Hagesichora is difficult to determine from the text. I hold with those who see Agido as an officiant more involved in the ritual than with the chorus. Puelma 1977: 13–19 finds in the language used of Agido evidence of her priestly function. So also Eisenberger 1991: 277.

[18] E.g., Diodoros 4.33. 5–6.

[19] Euphorion (*CA* p. 35, #29) mentions a story in which the Hippokoontidai were rival suitors of the Dioskouroi for the daughters of Leukippos. Page 1951: 30–33 and Davison 1968: 148–51 adduce it. Davison speculates that the prominence of Heracles in the later versions is the result of Spartan propaganda subsequent to Alkman's lifetime, legitimizing Heraclid claim to rule in Sparta. Another possibly relevant story is that one of the Hippokoontidai threatened violence toward Helen, sister of the Dioskouroi (Plutarch *Theseus* 31). Robbins 1994: 12–13 has a sensible discussion.

After the gnome a stanza, most of which has been lost, seems to have told another myth, also perhaps connected with marriage.[20] The next stanza opens with a gnome concluding the second myth and makes a transition to the "personal" section in which the chorus sings of the beauty of Hagesichora and Agido, its own deficiency without its leader, and the ceremony.

The first step in examining the interaction of the chorus with the audience is to see what we can infer about the composition of the audience. The assumption is often made that because the *parthenoi* seem to be expressing personal feelings they are performing only for themselves. John Herington says about it, "Something amazing happens: the chorus begins to sing to itself, and about itself."[21] Claude Calame views this poem as composed for an initiation group and takes the *parthenoi* to be expressing their erotic desire for the chorus-leader.[22] But it would be remarkable, and unparalleled, for a chorus, possessed of an elaborate text and having rehearsed, to perform its song and dance for no one but itself.[23] On the other hand, if there was an audience, the chorus's words were directed to the listeners, not to itself. In other words this choral poem is not a private conversation that we overhear but public communication, and the question that faces us is who the audience was. Diane Rayor argues that the poem was directed at the community at large.[24] I believe that her view is in accord with the evidence, and I will follow her lead.

To recover a sense of audience, let us first consider the six lines of gnomic advice (1.16–21 *PMGF*):

μή τις ἀνθ]ρώπων ἐς ὠρανὸν ποτήσθω
μηδὲ πη]ρήτω γαμῆν τὰν Ἀφροδίταν
ϝ]άν[α]σσαν ἤ τιν'
] ἢ παίδα Πόρκω

---

[20] Calame 1983: 320 suggests the story of Otos and Ephialtes, who were punished for trying to rape Artemis. Note again the theme of violence connected with a goddess.

[21] Herington 1985: 21.

[22] On the issue of initiation, see Ch. 2. Gentili 1988: 75–76, relying on Griffiths 1972, thinks the poem was an epithalamium celebrating a "wedding" between Agido and Hagesichora within a closed group. Griffiths thinks the poem to be a wedding poem, but emends too freely.

[23] Calame 1977: I 251–304 adduces references in which choruses of *parthenoi* are said to have performed at one or another temple near the borders of Spartan territory; these he sees as evidence for initiatory withdrawal to the margins, but the occasions were festivals, presumably thronged with celebrants. Cf. Nilsson 1957: 196–99 on the Karyatides, *parthenoi* of Karyai whose local dance for Artemis Karyatis became famous, and the festival for her. There were ritual groups of young women, e.g., the Leukippides, mentioned below, but they had sacerdotal roles and their attested activities were public.

[24] Rayor 1987.

Χά]ριτες δὲ Διὸς δ[ό]μον
]σιν ἐρογλεφάροι·

Let [no one] of humans fly to heaven [or] attempt to marry Aphrodite ruler of
[   ] or any [   ] or a child of Porkos, [   ] but the Graces with love-
inspiring eyes [   ] the house of Zeus.

The people to whom this advice is especially directed are young men of an
age to marry and their families. It is likely that the chorus addresses this
remark to the audience because the viewers included young men. The
illustration of the gnome by an account of a military conflict supports the
idea that men were present. Young women might address men, for Plutarch (*Lykourgos* 14.4–6, quoted below) says that *parthenoi* performed in
public at Sparta and even directed praise or mockery at young men. What
is more immediately relevant, in a following passage (15.1) Plutarch remarks that the Spartans meant to promote marriage by having the *parthenoi* appear so freely in public. If this performance was public, it served
one of the attested purposes of maiden-choruses: to show off marriageable
women of the community to advantage to potential suitors.[25] Compare
these lines from Aphrodite's lying description of herself as a mortal
maiden, part of a chorus for Artemis, in the *Homeric Hymn to Aphrodite*
(119–20):[26]

πολλαὶ δὲ νύμφαι καὶ παρθένοι ἀλφεσίβοιαι
παίζομεν, ἀμφὶ δ᾽ ὅμιλος ἀπείριτος ἐστεφάνωτο·

Many of us nymphs and much-courted maidens were dancing, and an immense
throng encircled us around.

The praise by the chorus of its chorus leader Hagesichora fits this function
perfectly. As Rayor points out, the notion of offering the chorus-leader—
and the chorus—as potential brides provides the link between the mythic
section and the "personal" section.[27] The myth warns against unsuitable
brides, while the chorus presents suitable ones. The final reason for believing that this song was performed in public is that it seems to have com-

---

[25] Rayor, ibid., makes this point and draws the consequences for the understanding of the
poem.

[26] Compare *Iliad* 18.590–604: a chorus of young men and much-courted *parthenoi* dances
while a crowd watches with delight. According to Euripides' *Helen* 1312–14, Persephone
was snatched from a chorus. Plutarch *Theseus* 31.2 depicts Theseus snatching Helen from a
chorus dancing for Artemis Orthia.

[27] Rayor 1987 and Robbins 1994: 10–16 both note the parallelism between the number of
Hippokoontidai and the number of the chorus (although Rayor puts it at ten and Robbins at
eleven). The alignment supports the idea that the chorus members are potential brides. For a
different but related idea, see Calame 1977: II 58.

bined an agricultural ceremony marking the opening of the harvest season with the presentation of the young women.[28]

Assuming, then, a communitywide audience, how does the chorus interact with it? The mythic section, in its preserved portion, is not presented as straight narrative. The chorus gives its own assessment of the Hippokoontidai (2, 12):

οὐκ ἐγώ]ν Λύκαισον καμοῦσιν ἀλέγω

I do [not] count Lykaithos among the dead[29]

and

] παρήσομες

. . . we will [not?] pass over . . .

The *parthenoi* seem to treat the myth as a matter for personal evaluation. But the chorus's assessments would hardly have been idiosyncratic. Some of the Hippokoontidai seem to have been heroes at Sparta, and the chorus is no doubt reproducing the common view of them (hence the honorific roll call in the poem of the names of the defeated), while making that view its own opinion.[30] In expressing as its own the shared assessment of the heroes, the chorus is doing two things: asserting the relevance of the myth to contemporary society and speaking *for* the audience. The first of these I will come back to; for the moment I want to elaborate the second. When the chorus sings, "I do not count . . . ," each choral performer speaks of herself, personally. But her "I" stands equally for what each of the listeners also thinks, at least by convention. By reproducing consensus as her own opinion, the performer stands in for the audience and the whole society. The general applicability of the "I" does not detach it from the individual but makes her an exemplary member of the community. A *parthenos* could perform in public precisely because she could serve as a reflector of social consensus. Her authority was not great enough to give her as an individual the right to participate in public discourse, but in public performance she borrowed authority from the society, as represented by the audience, in order to speak for it, to reflect it back to itself.

The gnome that ends the first narrative, quoted above, is stated so as to conform with the role of the *parthenoi* as reflectors. Rather than use a second-person imperative, which would distinguish an implicit "I" or "we" as advisor(s) and a "you" as recipients of advice, the *parthenoi* adopt a third-person imperative: "Let [no one] of humans fly to heaven." The

---

[28] See Ch. 2 for evidence and argument.

[29] For the supplement and this translation of ἀλέγω see Calame 1983 *ad loc.*

[30] On the Hippokoontidai see Page 1951: 26–29; van Groningen 1935–36: 243–44.

construction generalizes it from a command to a piece of shared cultural wisdom; that is, the gnome could be spoken by anyone and does not single out an addressee. The *parthenoi* are not staged as authoritative vis-à-vis the audience, whereas a direct command would have suggested that they were.

In this connection the passage of Plutarch alluded to above is relevant. It describes the freedom that *parthenoi* had at Sparta. They exercised by engaging in the same activities that the young men did. Plutarch continues (*Lykourgos* 14.4–6):

> Removing daintiness and overprotection and all femaleness, he made the girls no less accustomed than the boys to march in short tunics and to dance in certain festivals and sing when the young men were present and watching. Sometimes (the *parthenoi*) attacked those going astray to their benefit, speaking mockery at each; and again, performing encomia composed in song for the worthy ones, they used to provoke much ambition and rivalry in the youths. For the one exalted for manliness and become illustrious among the *parthenoi* would depart magnified by the praises; but the biting rebukes of jokes and mockery were no less sharp than warnings given in earnest since indeed they (were offered) in the sight of the kings and the assembled elders, together with the other citizens.

The *parthenoi* mocked the young men who did not measure up in public and praised in song those who did. Again, it cannot have been the private opinions of the *parthenoi* that were aired in public to such effect. The *parthenoi* must have voiced general opinions (or some official assessment). The unusual freedom of Spartan girls was not independence but a license to participate in a system of maintaining social pressure on the members of the society.[31]

The particular effect of having *parthenoi* sing praise or mockery of young men was to eroticize the assessment. The power of equating social approval with sexual attraction is obvious. Another small fragment of a *partheneion* (10(b) *PMGF* = 82 C), known only because it is quoted in a scrap of commentary on Alkman's poem, may be doing what Plutarch indicates, though the young men are described as chorus-leaders. The speakers command Hagesidamos, "god-beloved chorus leader, famous son of Damotimos," to "lead the Dumainai." The speakers probably are the Dumainai, which seems to have been a well-established chorus (however transient its members).[32] A little later in the poem, according to the commentary, the chorus describes a group of young men as (15–18)

---

[31] David 1989: 5, 13–14 analyzes the psychology of mockery to ensure gender conformity at Sparta.

[32] Calame 1977: I 274–76.

. γερώχως κῆρατῶς χο[ρα]γώς· αυτα γὰρ ἁμῶν ἥλι[κ]ες νεανίαι
φίλοι τ᾽ ἀγ[έ]νει[οι κ]ἀνύπανοι

noble (?) and desirable chorus-leaders; for they themselves are young men of the
same age with us and dear, unbearded, unmustached.[33]

The adjective ἀγέρωχος (if that was the original word) is employed in epic
to denote admirable figures. Here it is combined with the adjective ἐρατός
(desirable) to produce just the eroticized approval that the Plutarch passage
would suggest.[34] The words ἐρατός and φίλος (dear) are not an expression of the private feelings of the *parthenoi* (except insofar as the *parthenoi*
find desirable those whom they are culturally directed to admire), for the
praise is collective and pre-scripted. The *parthenoi* are lending their persons
for the eroticization of public approval; they speak for audience and
community.

But so far we have considered only the first twenty-one lines of the
Louvre partheneion. After the much-damaged and largely unreadable stanza
with the second myth comes the "personal" part of the poem. Here the
first-person statements are no longer generic in the sense that they could
equally well be spoken by a member of the audience. The first person in
lines 39ff. is specific to the young women, who are now speaking *to* the
audience. For instance:

39   ἐγὼν δ᾽ ἀείδω
        Ἀγιδῶς τὸ φῶς·

And I sing of the light of Agido.

56   διαφάδαν τί τοι λέγω;

Why do I tell you openly?

85   [ἐ]γὼν μὲν αὐτὰ
        παρσένος μάταν ἀπὸ θράνω λέλακα

I myself, a maiden, squawk in vain from the roofbeam

The switch is necessary because the chorus is now seeking to persuade the
audience of the extraordinary beauty of the chorus-leader and Agido. The
performers are no longer repeating what the audience already believes but

[33] The missing first letter of .γερώχως was not α in the papyrus (*PMGF* ad loc.), but
ἀγερώχως is likely to have been the original word. In the translation I also accept αὐτοί,
suggested by Page 1962a *ad loc.*, for αυτα in the papyrus. See also Calame 1983 *ad loc.*
[34] On ἐρατός denoting youth in a choral context, see Calame 1983 *ad loc.*

presenting an opinion that they hope the audience will adopt. They address the audience to provoke its assent (50):

ἦ οὐχ ὁρῆις;

Don't you see?

and "Why do I tell you openly?" (56, quoted above). Their first person belongs to themselves in their character as *parthenoi,* but they use it as an instigation to the audience to react with favorable assessment.

To put it in the terms suggested by Plato, their first-person utterance is no longer a reflection; it is now a model for the audience. By establishing their role as reflectors first, in the mythic section, the performers create the basis for their new role. This switch does not mean that the singers are now expressing their private feelings. Just as they do in the case of the young men, they are offering eroticized approval to Hagesichora. In this case eroticism is the point, not (or not only) a vehicle for approval of other conduct. For the chorus-leader must be a marriageable young woman, whose value is being publicly demonstrated.[35] As pointed out earlier, she is being presented as eligible in contrast to the ineligible women of the myth and the gnome.

If their speech is to be effective, the *parthenoi* in their role as model for the audience must not abjure the role of reflector. Their expressions of desire must preserve the conventional forms so as to be accessible to everyone. By using recurrent imagery of racehorses (47–51, 58–59), the chorus casts Hagesichora and (briefly) Agido according to a standard masculine metaphor of appreciation derived from the world of male activity.[36] (It is possible that the imagery of racing horses was provoked by an actual race that one or both women were to run. But lines 58–59 specify that the one second to Agido *in looks* will run as a Kolaxian horse with an Ibenian.[37] Unless women's ranking in looks is being compared with their ranking in running, the race must be metaphorical.[38]) The adjective *klenna* (44, "illustrious") inserts Hagesichora, the chorus-leader, into the public world of

[35] Public erotic praise would only be directed at a woman at that point in her life. If Agido was an officiant, she would receive praise in that capacity, but praise of her is more formal. Cf. Puelma 1977: 13–15: φῶς (light) is not an image of beauty but of salvation.

[36] Cf. Stigers [Stehle] 1979: 469–70.

[37] The qualities of these two horses are not known in detail; both are good types. As a result the point of the comparison is not clear.

[38] Van Groningen 1935–36: 250 takes the line to mean that the second in beauty after Agido will race as her equal, but he does think that the race is metaphorical (255). Races for *parthenoi* are attested at Sparta: Pausanias 3.13.7 refers to a group called Dionysiades (daughters of Dionysus). Some of these, together with the Leukippides, sacrifice; eleven others run a race.

mythic and historical commemoration.[39] These turns of speech show that the chorus's praise is framed as though from the audience's (that is, the male) point of view.

The chorus also says that the chorus-leader's beauty silences it (43–46):

ἐμὲ δ' οὔτ' ἐπαινῆν
οὔτε μωμήσθαι νιν ἁ κλεννὰ χοραγὸς
οὐδ' ἁμῶς ἐῆι· δοκεῖ γὰρ ἤμεν αὔτα
ἐκπρεπής

But the illustrious chorus-leader even so does not permit me either to praise her (Agido) or to find fault; for she herself appears outstanding.[40]

The *parthenoi* direct the audience away from listening to them and toward looking at the object of their praise. Again, in line 56 the question quoted above—"Why do I tell you openly?"—is followed by the exclamation, "Here is Hagesichora herself!" The singers suggest that though they may praise, the audience's gaze on the chorus-leader will be more persuasive than their words. The communal gaze, in overtaking and superseding the chorus's directives, returns the chorus to the role of reflectors.

Several times in the second part of the poem the chorus uses the second-person plural form ἇμιν (to/for/with us) or the related adjective. It is usually seen as a simple variant of the first person singular that it uses elsewhere.[41] But B. A. van Groningen suggests that the plural is used when the audience is included in the statement.[42] The four instances come at points when the chorus seems to be referring to the ceremony itself. Two of the four contrast singular and plural, making explicit the more inclusive reference for the plural. The chorus says (39–43), "I sing of the light of Agido; I see her like the sun, which Agido calls to be present as witness for us."[43] Agido's act is part of her ceremonial role, performed for the whole community, so the chorus-members distinguish themselves as singers from the larger group of beneficiaries of the ritual. Later in the poem (88–89, quoted in Chapter 2) they say that Aotis is the healer of toil "for us." Since in the following lines they say, "but young women enter

---

[39] Cf. the same word used of young men praised by the *parthenoi* in the quotation from Plutarch above.

[40] The referents of the pronouns in this whole section (43–59) are notoriously difficult to decide. See the chart in Calame 1977: II facing 176 for various scholars' solutions; and add Puelma 1977: 23, who thinks that Agido is the chorus-leader. Calame's view (1977: II 46–48), the commonest one, is that Hagesichora is the chorus-leader and is so outstanding that she inhibits the chorus from praising Agido.

[41] So, e.g., Bowra 1961: 46.

[42] Van Groningen 1935–36: 246–47.

[43] Cf. Puelma 1977: 16–19 on μαρτύρεται φαίνην. Cf. also nn. 17 and 35 above.

delightful peace by Hagesichora's agency," they again contrast themselves with "us," who must be the audience as a whole. The other two uses should follow suit. The instance in line 81 clearly does: Hagesichora "praises our sacrificial offerings (?)," and they must be the offerings of the corporate body, not just of the chorus-members.[44] The last case is more complex. In the difficult lines 60–63, discussed at length in Chapter 2, the chorus says (in part), "The Peleades fight with us as we carry a plow to the Dawn-goddess." The pronoun *us* has a feminine plural participle with it, so it refers to the chorus-members; yet, as van Groningen suggests, the plural simultaneously generalizes the action to include the audience in the struggle and the ritual. The chorus therefore continues to speak *for* the community in referring to the actions and effects of the ritual in progress while it speaks *to* the community about women's attractiveness. The distinction so carefully maintained (while in the first part the singular and plural alternate because the *parthenoi* are speaking only for the community) points to conscious staging of the two functions of the *parthenoi*.

The two modes, therefore, of interaction between performers and audience can be detected in this *partheneion*. The chorus speaks both for and to the audience; they serve as both reflection of and model for the communal opinion. In the poem these two modes are aligned respectively with mythic narrative and ceremony on the one hand and with praise of the new generation on the other. The separation allows us to perceive the temporal dimension of the functions of reflection and modeling as well. The chorus both reanimates the past, speaking for the audience, and uses it as a springboard to the next stage in the community's history, speaking to it. So here the *parthenoi* evoke a negative example of young men's erotic behavior in the past and advise the present young men to choose socially approved brides in order to foster stability. This is, I suggest, the full paradigm of communal poetry, interaction between communal past and modeled future. It negotiates a stage in the life of a community by drawing on the symbolic resources of the community. Because the authority for the negotiation belongs to the community and is articulated in its name by the performers, all groups that are part of the community, including *parthenoi* and children, can perform. We can see in this poem the kind of pattern that Plato was drawing on in the *Laws*.

So far we have examined the relationship between the text as performed and the audience. I touched only once on the question of what effect particular performers had on the meanings of a text when I suggested that putting praise and blame of the young Spartan men into the mouths of *parthenoi* eroticized the judgments. The question is still to ask about this *partheneion*: what effect did performance by *parthenoi* have on the reception

---

[44] Schol. A *ad* 61 (p. 31 *PMGF*) glosses the word θωστήρια as "festival" but "sacrificial offerings" is more likely: see Puelma 1977: 19n.47.

of the song? We can see that only women, precisely because of the social construction of women as sexually passive, can offer sexual praise of other women without arousing fears of just the violence that the myth illustrates.[45] The *parthenoi* as performers cancel the threat of social confusion— of rape/seduction, jealousy, and strife—that would follow from men's praising young women in public. The threat of erotic violence is displaced to the myth and to absent male speakers, but its shadow is part of the process of persuasion that is enacted in performance. The inverse question, how the song stages the *parthenoi,* will be addressed in Chapter 2.

2. Swallow-song (Athenaios 8, 360cd; *PMG* 848).

A Rhodian begging song of a type known as a "swallow-song" has survived. It appears to be a traditional folk song and was sung at a festival in the Rhodian month of Boedromion (probably in the spring). It was recorded by a certain Theognis in his treatise *On the Rhodian Festivals,* from which Athenaios copied it.[46] The singers, who were children, presumably went from house to house, singing and begging, for the ceremony is called *agermos* (collection).[47] One of them must have been dressed as a swallow. The singers announce that the swallow has come, then they ask for food in her name (6–7):

παλάθαν σὺ προκύκλει / ἐκ πίονος οἴκου

You, roll out a fruitcake from the well-stocked house.

They then switch to first-person plurals to threaten their audience with the consequences of not contributing (12–19):

πότερ' ἀπίωμες ἢ λαβώμεθα;
εἰ μέν τι δώσεις· εἰ δὲ μή, οὐκ ἐάσομες·
ἢ τὰν θύραν φέρομες ἢ τὸ ὑπέρθυρον
15 ἢ τὰν γυναῖκα τὰν ἔσω καθημέναν·
μικρὰ μέν ἐστι, ῥαιδίως νιν οἴσομες.
ἂν δὴ †φέρῃις τι, μέγα δή τι† φέροις·
ἄνοιγ' ἄνοιγε τὰν θύραν χελιδόνι·
οὐ γὰρ γέροντές ἐσμεν, ἀλλὰ παιδία.

Shall we go away or shall we grab? If you give something (then good); but if you don't, we won't leave you alone; we are likely to carry off either the door or the

[45] Some scholars take these sentiments to be personal and think that the *parthenoi* express homoerotic feelings for their leaders. See Ch. 2.

[46] It could be harvesttime; the place of the month in the Rhodian calendar is unclear. See Smyth 1900 *ad loc.* Nothing else is known about Theognis.

[47] See Smyth 1900 *ad loc.* Flückiger-Guggenheim 1984: 27–31 and Burkert 1985: 101–2

lintel or the wife who is sitting within; she is small, easily will we carry her off. If
you bring something, please bring something really big (?); open, open the door
to the swallow; for we are not old men, but children.

In this poem performance for and to the audience is combined, but the
audience takes two different forms, the actual audience at each house (the
members of the household) and the community as a whole. In their imperious request for a contribution the children speak *to* the audience at the
house door. But the parallel with Halloween is not complete; the children are collecting not for themselves but for the community, probably
for a communal dinner. So much is suggested by the *aition* (origin story)
that Athenaios gives: "Kleoboulos of Lindos (one of the seven wise men)
first introduced this (sort of) collecting when the need for a collection of
goods/money arose in Lindos." The children are therefore also speaking
for the community and can ask in these forthright tones because they
have authority derived from the community during the time of the festival. The first person belongs to the children specifically, for their song is
directed to the individual audiences, while the address for the collective
audience remains unspoken but understood in the very possibility of the
transaction.[48]

Moreover, performance for the community is indirectly expressed in
the threat that the children make. They threaten to invade the house and
carry off the women, in other words, to behave like enemies. The threat is
no doubt lighthearted and prankish; I am not suggesting real coercion. But
it refers to real and frightful violence that threatens the children as much as
their audience: it reminds members of the community that without collective action there is no safety. A refusal to participate in the community
leaves the household isolated in the face of hostile forces. The children's
demand is therefore a demand in a larger symbolic sense that the community adhere to its collective identity.

Surely this is a heavy message for a children's song to bear. But like the
parthenoi singing Alkman's song, children can be its messengers because
they also cancel its threat. In the mouths of the children, a threat of inva-
sion is playful posturing. Note that the children use the diminutive παιδία
(little children) to describe themselves. Children and *parthenoi,* who are

---

discuss ancient and modern collecting songs; Petropoulos 1994: 5–12, ancient and modern
swallow-songs.

[48] Cf. the Athenian custom of carrying the *eiresiōnē,* an olive branch hung with fruit and
figures made of pastry, at the Pyanopsia: Deubner 1962: 191, 199. Boys carried them around
to the houses, singing a song of which Plutarch (*Theseus* 22.7) records three lines: the *eiresiōnē*
should bring figs, bread, honey, olive oil, and wine, "so that one may get drunk and sleep."
The subject of the last clause is feminine, so if it is not the *eiresiōnē* itself, it must be the wife in
the house.

powerless, are good bearers of disguised warnings because they cannot act on them in their own persons.

The children's message has a happier aspect, too, another reason why they are appropriate singers of this song. The opening lines of the poem say:

ἦλθ' ἦλθε χελιδὼν

καλὰς ὥρας ἄγουσα,

καλοὺς ἐνιαυτούς

The swallow has come, has come, who brings the beautiful seasons, the beautiful cycles of years.

The command at the end of the poem to open the door to the swallow (quoted above) can refer not just to the house-door but to the householders themselves: open yourself to the coming of spring (or harvest); by giving food you presage the new season with its promise of a renewal of the supply; by welcoming the children you welcome rejuvenation.[49] The children contrast themselves at the end with old men; they *are* the renewal that the season promises. Thus the children stage themselves as the regenerating and flourishing aspect of the community. They also, by virtue of arriving as a collective at the individual house, show themselves to be committed to the collectivity that is the community.

In a Hellenistic imitation, the "Crow-song" (Athenaios 8, 359ef; *CA* p. 233), the theme of a new generation is actually expressed (8–14): "O boy, open the door, (for) Wealth knocked, and may the *parthenos* bring figs to the crow. Gods, may the girl be in all ways irreproachable and find a rich husband with a good name and place a son in the hands of her old father and a daughter on the knees of her mother, a shoot to nourish as a wife for her brothers." A swallow-song sung by Samian children collecting at a festival of Apollo describes the house that the collectors approach as wealthy and happy and predicts a wife for the son.[50]

The paradigm of renewal based on past patterns is here the yearly cycle rather than a myth played off against a current situation. Still, the song performs the same function as the *partheneion* in marking a stage in the life of the community, and, like it but in more direct language, negotiates renewed commitment based on the community's ability to renew itself with food and children. Alkman's *partheneion* also marks a stage in the year in its aspect of agricultural ritual.[51]

[49] Cf. *WD* 568–69 and West 1978 *ad loc.* on the coming of the swallow in spring.

[50] *Herodotean Life of Homer* 467–80 Allen. It is found also in the Suda *in Homero* 180–95 Allen with numerous minor variations of wording. The song was called *Eiresiōnē*. Cf. Nilsson 1957: 116–18.

[51] See Ch. 2.

3. Hermokles' (?) song for the Athenians (Athenaios 6, 253d-f; *CA*
pp. 173–75).

This song was composed at a later period than the others, somewhere
around 300 BCE.[52] The poem, possibly by Hermokles, is an "ithyphallic
song" (on which see below). It is said to be one of the songs with which the
Athenians welcomed Demetrios Poliorketes back to Athens from Leukas
in the period after he had liberated Athens from the Macedonians under
Demetrios of Phaleron.[53] It is preserved in Athenaios, who got it from
Douris of Samos.[54] I quote lines 1–8, 15–34 (the opening of the poem
is lost):

. . . .

1   ὡς οἱ μέγιστοι τῶν θεῶν καὶ φίλτατοι
         τῇ πόλει πάρεισιν·
      ἐνταῦθα γὰρ Δήμητρα καὶ Δημήτριον
         ἅμα παρῆχ' ὁ καιρός.
5   χἠ μὲν τὰ σεμνὰ τῆς Κόρης μυστήρια
         ἔρχεθ' ἵνα ποιήσῃ,
      ὁ δ' ἱλαρός, ὥσπερ τὸν θεὸν δεῖ, καὶ καλὸς
         καὶ γελῶν πάρεστι. . . .
15   ἄλλοι μὲν ἢ μακρὰν γὰρ ἀπέχουσιν θεοί,
         ἢ οὐκ ἔχουσιν ὦτα,
      ἢ οὐκ εἶσιν, ἢ οὐ προσέχουσιν ἡμῖν οὐδὲ ἕν,
         σὲ δὲ παρόνθ' ὁρῶμεν,
      οὐ ξύλινον οὐδὲ λίθινον, ἀλλ' ἀληθινόν.
20   εὐχόμεσθα δή σοι·
      πρῶτον μὲν εἰρήνην ποίησον, φίλτατε,
         κύριος γὰρ εἶ σύ,
      τὴν δ' οὐχὶ Θηβῶν, ἀλλ' ὅλης τῆς Ἑλλάδος
         Σφίγγα περικρατοῦσαν,

[52] Burstein 1985: 9n.4 gives the date 291 for Demetrios' return from Leukas.

[53] On the historical situation see Plutarch *Demetrios*. Plutarch says (12.1) that after the
liberation the Athenians decided that Demetrios should be received with the welcome
granted Demeter and Dionysus whenever he came to the city. He also speaks of the extravagant honors the Athenians paid Demetrios on several occasions, e.g., 10.2–4, 12.1, 23.2–3,
26, 40.4. On these honors see also Pritchett 1979: 193–94, with bibliography.

[54] *FGH* 76 F13. Marcovich 1988 gives a text with bibliography and some commentary;
his primary interest is in the religious ideas, which he traces mainly to Epicurus.

25 (Αἰτωλὸς ὅστις ἐπὶ πέτρας καθήμενος,
        ὥσπερ ἡ παλαιά,
    τὰ σώμαθ᾽ ἡμῶν πάντ᾽ ἀναρπάσας φέρει,
        κοὐκ ἔχω μάχεσθαι·
    Αἰτωλικὸν γὰρ ἁρπάσαι τὰ τῶν πέλας,
30   νῦν δὲ καὶ τὰ πόρρω·)
    μάλιστα μὲν δὴ κόλασον αὐτός· εἰ δὲ μή,
        Οἰδίπουν τιν᾽ εὑρέ,
    τὴν Σφίγγα ταύτην ὅστις ἢ κατακρημνιεῖ
        ἢ σπίνον ποιήσει.

Thus (?) the greatest of the gods and dearest to the city are present. For the occasion has brought both Demeter and Demetrios here together. She comes to conduct the solemn mysteries of the Maiden, but he is here, cheerful, as a god ought to be, and handsome and laughing. . . . For the other gods are either far distant or do not have ears or do not exist or do not pay attention to us in anything, but you we see present, neither wood nor stone, but real. We truly beseech you, first of all bring peace, dearest one, for you have the power, and personally punish the sphinx who lords it over not Thebes but all of Greece (an Aetolian one that, sitting on a rock just like the (sphinx) of old, snatches all our bodies and carries them off, and I am not able to fight; for it is Aetolian character to snatch what belongs to the neighbors and now the possessions of those far off). Or else, find an Oedipus who will throw this sphinx headlong off the rock or turn it into a finch.

Athenaios quotes a description of the performance setting, clearly of this song, from Demochares:

When Demetrios returned from Leukas and Corcyra to Athens not only did the Athenians receive him by burning incense and crowning him and pouring libations, but also processional choruses and phallus-bearers met him with dance and song, and being placed among the crowds they sang as they danced, repeating the refrain that he was the only real god.[55]

This song, unlike the first two, is not for a recurring occasion but to mark a critical moment for the Athenians, when they had become "free" but hardly secure in the constant warfare of aggrandizement. Authoriza-

[55] 6, 253bc = *FGH* 75 F2. Demochares' description of the Athenians' flatteries is close enough to the song from Douris to make it certain that this is the song he has in mind. Both speak of Demetrios as ἀληθινός (real), while the other gods are absent, as beautiful and surrounded by friends, and as the son of Poseidon and Aphrodite. Demochares was the nephew of Demosthenes, so he is a contemporary source.

tion for this kind of extraordinary speech on its behalf can only come from the whole community (or a large powerful sector); if the chorus spoke this way without being accepted as representative, the community might wish to disown it. The community did in fact authorize this (or similar) speech on behalf of the whole. According to Athenaios (15, 697a), it held a contest to choose a poem to be sung in welcome of Antigonos and Demetrios. It is in this passage that the name Hermokles is found, as the winner.[56] Even if this surviving song is a different one from his, we should note the use of a procedure to elicit consensus for the words to be sung by the community's representatives—an essential step in such an untraditional situation.[57]

Despite the public imprimatur, the poem must work hard to naturalize its theme that Demetrios is a god. There are in fact two distinct audiences for the poem, Demetrios and the Athenians. Each requires a different message. Addressed to Demetrios, the praise should be extravagant enough to persuade him of the Athenians' gratitude. Addressed to the Athenians, however, it should reassure them that they have not moved to too new a stage and lost their identity. As it is, the conversationalists depicted by Athenaios are disgusted that the Athenians, men of Marathon, would sing such a thing. To observe how the composer meets the demands of the situation, it is necessary to analyze the chorus' speech as reflection and model for the community.

The poem opens with a portrait of Demetrios in the third person, addressed therefore *to* the Athenians, then switches in line 13 to the second person (not quoted above). The rest of the poem addresses Demetrios *for* the Athenians. The first-person plural in line 18, "we see you present," embraces all the onlookers. The prayer in line 20 is on behalf of the whole city. And when in line 27 the chorus refers to the sphinx snatching "all our bodies," the "all" refers to the Athenians at large. The chorus stands, as it were, between the Athenians and Demetrios, negotiating his acceptance. In the first twelve lines, addressed to the Athenians, the poem does not introduce the model for the future (the usual function of speaking *to* the audience) but inserts Demetrios into established ritual, as though the city were merely embellishing its practice.

The poem links Demetrios with Demeter by juxtaposing their similar names (3). The "laughing" Demetrios is also the god Dionysus, for the

---

[56] There is a textual problem at this point. Athenaios names Philochoros (*FGH* 328 F165) as his source for the statement that the Athenians sang the *paianes* composed by Hermippos of Kyzikos for Antigonos and Demetrios. A reference to the contest and Hermokles as winner follows in a genitive absolute construction. This makes no sense, and the alteration of "Hermippos" to "Hermokles" is generally accepted (e.g., by *CA* ad loc.; Burstein 1985: 9n.3; Käppel 1992: 298, Test. 7).

[57] In 6, 253b Athenaios refers to the Athenians singing "*paianes* and processional songs" to Demetrios, so various songs were composed for him, and Hermokles' song may have been a different one from the song Douris preserves.

poem was an "ithyphallic song": it was performed by men accompanied by a large phallus, reminiscent of the processions bearing phalluses at the City Dionysia and other Dionysiac festivals.[58] In mentioning the mysteries, the poem reminds the audience of the mystic aspects of both gods: both blurred the boundaries between human and divine, for each appeared, according to a well-known story, in human guise as a preliminary to establishing rites, and each offered humans a partial escape from the condition of mortality.[59] The phallus points, on the other hand, to theater. Both Demeter and Dionysus were patrons of theater or ritual drama in Attica. Dionysus oversaw tragedy and comedy, and at Eleusis the sacred story was acted out for initiates. Depending on inclination, then, the resistant onlooker could read the reception of Demetrios as a mystic experience or as theater. The poem addresses *to* the audience a reminder that in receiving Demetrios the city is not departing from its traditions. Not that the Athenians as a whole were not enthusiastic, but the opening justifies the welcome they gave him.[60]

Finally, Dionysus was sometimes known as Lysios (the releaser).[61] By a ready train of thought, one might recollect that a typical narrative of Dionysiac myth is the punishment of those who fail to receive the god when he comes to celebrate his rites. The stories of Lykourgos in the *Iliad,* of the sailors who kidnap the god in *Homeric Hymn* 7, of the Proitides in the Argolid, and, above all, of Pentheus at Thebes were well known.[62] The last is the subject of the *Bacchae* of Euripides, a popular playwright at this period. By identifying Demetrios visually with Dionysus, the performers could therefore also suggest the consequences of not greeting him wholeheartedly.

Speaking for the audience from line 13 on, the chorus asserts a different view of the situation: all the other gods are indifferent, and only Demetrios is present for Athens, "neither wood nor stone but real" (a jingle in Greek). This is its new model, embrace of a "god" who will more effectively watch over Athens, a model that it puts into practice right away by praying to Demetrios for two things, peace and suppression of the Aetolian League (the "sphinx"). It is as though the chorus had won the Athenian

---

[58] Pickard-Cambridge 1968: 62. He gives the text of inscriptions indicating that colonies of Athens were expected to send a phallus to the Dionysia. Marcovich 1988: 12 thinks that Demetrios, not Dionysus, is meant in lines 7–8 but does not consider the possibility that Demetrios is equated with Dionysus.

[59] God in human form: *Homeric Hymn to Demeter* 98–267, Euripides' *Bacchae.* Both gods had mysteries: Demeter's at Eleusis promised a more blessed afterlife, while Dionysiac mysteries were established by this time. On both see Burkert 1987a.

[60] According to Athenaios 6, 253f, the Athenians sang this song not only in public but even in their homes, so taken with it were they.

[61] See Farnell 1977: V 120 and 288; cf., e.g., the Sikyonian ritual mentioned below.

[62] *Iliad* 6.130–40; on the Proitides see Bacchylides 11.40–112 *SM.*

audience over by subordinating Demetrios to its traditions in the opening
lines, then used the audience's assent as its basis for presenting the model to
Demetrios. The chorus keeps the idea of theater alive to the end of the
poem, nevertheless, by asking Demetrios to punish the sphinx himself or
find an Oedipus who will destroy her (23–34). Demetrios should play the
role of Oedipus or else the role of Theseus, who welcomed Oedipus at
Colonus and received Oedipus' promise to protect Athens from his grave,
according to Sophocles' other Oedipus play, *Oedipus at Colonus*. This will
be the practical test of the new order.

The section containing the model is more than flattery of Demetrios;
Athens made public acknowledgment of its own weakness. The one first-
person singular usage in the poem, in line 28, is a strategic one. Each singer
says of himself (in relation to the Aetolian League), "I am not able to
fight," making the admission personal. But the chorus and phallus-bearers
are not uniquely responsible for military action, so the first person is not
specific to them. It applies to each of the adult men at Athens and by
extension to everyone; thus the statement acquires the power of collective
personal confession of their dependency by the Athenians. The implied
peril that shadows this poem, the alternative to accepting the model, is
defeat for Athens. The performers this time do not cancel that threat by
their inability to carry it out (as *parthenoi* and children do in the previous
two poems) but rather underline it by their inability to prevent it. The
performers, in sum, enact a message that Athens has a choice of welcome
of a savior or futile struggle against superior and supernatural forces.

Given the context, the phallus invited the audience to attach multiple
meanings to it. It could visually reclaim the masculinity that the performers compromised (in Greek cultural terms) in denying their ability to
fight. It could be read as an expression of Demetrios' revitalizing effect on
the city (as equated with its male citizens). It could be seen, in the company
of Demeter and by a kind of additive logic, as a symbol of the citizen body
collectively. It could also be taken by Demetrios and his friends as the
Athenians' detachment of their "manhood" from their own bodies and
presentation of it to him. We will return in Chapter 3 to the sexual imagery
of phallus and sphinx.

4. Pindar, *paian* 9 for the Thebans (52k *SM*).

Among the fragments of Pindar's *paianes* are some whose performance
context can be discerned.[63] *Paian* 9 is particularly interesting for our purposes. It was written for the Thebans after an eclipse, to pray that the omen

---

[63] For the *paian* as a genre of cult poetry, see Käppel 1992: 54–62. Important also is his
discussion (189–200) of unliterary *paianes;* they linked the act of sacrifice and the gods. Race

be favorable to Thebes, as the poem itself indicates.[64] A further reference within the poem demonstrates that it was performed at the Ismenion, the Theban temple to Apollo.[65] The identity of the performers is unknown beyond that they were masculine (as the participle in line 39 indicates). I assume that it is a choral piece, but nothing in my interpretation depends on it; a solo singer would produce the same effects, though perhaps less impressively.[66]

In this *paian* too, like the song for Demetrios, a community reacts to a general threat by asking for divine aid for itself. What the Thebans fear is that the eclipse may signal a new stage throughout Greece that is worse than the old. The *paian* accordingly requests that divinity turn the universal omen to the good for Thebes. The psychological efficacy aimed at by the poem must be to make the audience feel sanguine about the future, but since it is a matter of changing a mood, with no external correlate (a new season, new politics), the poem must generate the model it proposes (an effective response to the eclipse) rhetorically. As a result, the model is "discovered" in the course of the poem.

We can follow the movement of the poem only tentatively since there are gaps in the text. Two triads are partly preserved. The first survives through the first line of the epode, with one short gap. The first three lines of the second strophe are lost; thereafter the second triad is essentially complete (except for line 40) through the penultimate line of the antistrophe. The epode has disappeared, as have any successive triads that the poem may have had. The poem begins by asking (1–10):

> ἀκτὶς ἀελίου, τί πολύσκοπε μήσεαι,
> ὦ μᾶτερ ὀμμάτων, ἄστρον ὑπέρτατον
> ἐν ἀμέρᾳ κλεπτόμενον; ⟨τί δ'⟩ ἔθηκας ἀμάχανον
> ἰσχύν ⟨τ'⟩ ἀνδράσι καὶ σοφίας ὁδόν,
> 5 ἐπίσκοτον ἀτραπὸν ἐσσυμένα;
> ἐλαύνεις τι νεώτερον ἢ πάρος;

1992: 28–31 analyzes the difference between cultic and rhapsodic hymns: cult hymns have a more personal tone and I-you relationship with the god. Bremer 1981: 193–97 describes the typical structure of "hymns" in the sense of sung prayers.

[64] The eclipse was probably that of 463, according to Schroeder 1900: 429–30. Rutherford forthcoming *ad loc.* thinks that 478 cannot be ruled out.

[65] See below. The Ismenion is one of four places that Fairbanks 1900: 34 identifies as having especially well attested performances of *paianes*. The others are Delphi, Delos, and Sparta.

[66] Demosthenes 21 *Meidias* 52–53 gives the text of four oracles, two from Delphi and two from Dodona, prescribing sacrifice for various reasons, including epidemic. Two of the oracles call for setting up choruses, providing wine, and wearing crowns as well, and a third implies it. MacDowell 1990 *ad loc.* comments, apropos of the response to epidemic, on the

ἀλλά σε πρὸς Διός, ἱπποσόα θοάς,

ἱκετεύω, ἀπήμονα

εἰς ὄλβον τινὰ τράποιο Θήβαις,

10 ὦ πότνια, πάγκοινον τέρας

Ray of the sun, much-seeing, what will you devise, O mother of eyes, preeminent star concealed in the daytime? Why have you made both strength and the
road of wisdom unavailing for men, rushing along a darkened path? Do you
pursue something more novel than before? I supplicate you, driver of swift
horses, in the name of Zeus: please transform the universal portent into a grief-
less blessing for Thebes, O lady.

The performers, sounding helpless, ask whether the sun is bringing on
something new. Almost immediately they replace question with prayer,
but the prayer does not produce any immediate surge of confidence. The
following two and a half lines, the first lines of the antistrophe, are missing, but the rest of the antistrophe contains a list of possible disastrous
meanings for the portent, cast as a question (13–21):

]ῶνος [   ], πολέμοιο δὲ σᾶμα φέρεις τινός,

ἢ καρποῦ φθίσιν, ἢ νιφετοῦ σθένος

15 ὑπέρφατον, ἢ στάσιν οὐλομέναν

ἢ πόντου κενεώσιας ἂμ πέδον,

ἢ παγετὸν χθονός, ἢ νότιον θέρος

ὕδατι ζακότῳ ῥέον,

ἢ γαῖαν κατακλύσαισα θήσεις

20 ἀνδρῶν νέον ἐξ ἀρχᾶς γένος;

ὀλοφύ⟨ρομαι οὐ⟩δέν, ὅ τι πάντων μέτα πείσομαι

[   ] Do you bring the sign of some war, or shriveling of the harvest, or
strength of snow beyond description, or destructive civil strife, or emptying of
the sea over the plain or freezing of the ground or a wet summer awash in roiling
water, or will you flood the earth and set up a new race of men from the beginning? I lament nothing that I will suffer together with all.

As the list rises to a cataclysmic climax, realistic troubles are left behind.
The strophe mimes a state of panic—but in order to effect a catharsis. In
reaction the performers begin to reassert control at the beginning of the

---

"routine advice for times of god-sent affliction." Cf. a similar oracle prescribing choruses in
Demosthenes 43 *Makartatos* 66, in response to a "sign" in the sky, and Rutherford 1990: 173–
76 on a fragmentary *paian* by Simonides that may have been for a sacred embassy in response
to lightning over Mt. Parnes during one of the seasons of the year when lookout was held.
These parallels suggest that *paian* 9 is likely to have been choral as well.

epode: "I lament nothing that I will suffer together with all." It is particularly unfortunate that the rest of the epode is lost so that we cannot tell how this odd opening would have developed.

In the second triad, when the text takes up again with the fourth line of the strophe, the chorus has settled on the divinity to be invoked and the grounds of its appeal (33–49):

[σάματι][67]
ἐκράνθην ὑπὸ δαιμονίῳ τινί
35   λέχει πέλας ἀμβροσίῳ Μελίας
ἀγαυὸν καλάμῳ συνάγεν θρόον
μήδεσί τε φρενὸς ὑμ[ε]τέραν χάριν.
λιτανεύω, ἑκαβόλε,
Μοισαίαις ἀν[α]τιθεὶς τέχνα[ι]σι
40   χρηστήριον . [   ]πωλογτ[   ]ι
ἐν ᾧ Τήνερον εὐρυβίαν θεμίτ[ων
ἐξαίρετον προφάταν ἔτεκ[εν λέχει
κόρα μιγεῖσ' Ὠκεανοῦ Μελία σέο, Πύθι[ε.
τῷ] Κάδμου στρατὸν ἂν Ζεάθου πό[λιν,
45   ἀκερσεκόμα πάτερ, ἀνορέας
ἐπέτρεψας ἔκατι σαόφρονος.
καὶ γὰρ ὁ πόντιος Ὀρσ[ιτ]ρίαινά νιν
περίαλλα βροτῶν τίεν,
Εὐρίπου τε συνέτεινε χῶρον

I was ordained in response to a certain unearthly [sign?] to join together near the ambrosial couch of Melia a noble cry by means of a reed and by the skill of my intellect, a delight to you.[68] I pray, far-shooter, dedicating (as subject) to the Muses' arts the oracular place[69] [   ] in which the daughter of Okeanos, Melia, bore Teneros of broad strength, outstanding prophet of righteous things [   ], mingling with your bed, Pythian one. [To him] you entrusted the people of Kadmos in the city of Zethos, unshorn father, on account of his sound-minded courage. And furthermore, marine Poseidon honored him outstandingly among mortals and the land of Euripos he strove. . . .

[67] I depart here from the Snell-Maehler text, which prints δείματι *exempli gratia*, and adopt σάματι, suggested by Rutherford forthcoming.
[68] Or "for your sake." But this translation loses the force of χάριν.
[69] Since one cannot dedicate an oracular seat in the sense of offering such a thing to a god, either ἀνατιθείς or χρηστήριον must be taken in a metaphorical sense. I have chosen to take the participle metaphorically because schol. *Pythian* 11.5 (II 255 Dr.) states that Teneros had an oracular seat in the Ismenion. For the metaphor cf. Pindar *Pyth.* 8.29–31.

Clearly a change of emotional tone has taken place between the two triads.[70] The second prayer (38) is not an admission of helplessness like the
opening one but an assertion of confidence. Whereas the road of wisdom
was unavailing in the first strophe, now the choreuts claim to exercise their
"skill of intellect" in producing delight for Apollo. Each performer
avows, "I was ordained."[71] The noun δείματι (fear) printed by the Snell-
Maehler edition is surely wrong as a supplement at the end of line 33: first,
the fear to which the poem responds is not vague, whereas the missing
noun is modified by the indefinite adjective τινί (34), and second, fear has
been superseded in this triad by the vigor of the performers' self-assertion.
Ian Rutherford's suggestion σάματι (sign) is much better, though equally
speculative. A supernatural sign would of course give added authority to
this portent-deflecting ritual production.

The chorus's confidence is based on its solution to the problem posed by
the eclipse: an appeal to Apollo as the lover of Melia and father of Teneros.
Speaking *to* the audience in lines 34–37, the chorus announces the ceremonial act that is in fact underway. Then, speaking for all, it calls on Apollo
("I pray," line 38) and reminds him of his liaison with Melia, his son
Teneros, and the honors that he once granted his son. During the performance of this song, the chorus was apparently stationed near Melia's
birthing-couch in the Ismenion (35).[72] By renewing Apollo's tie with
Thebes through these figures imbricated in his cult, the chorus expects to
win his protection. It is significant, I think, that Pindar chooses a story
with *only* local resonance. As L. R. Farnell remarks, Teneros was scarcely
known outside Boeotia.[73] Mention of this hero occurs three times in fragments of Pindar's religious songs for the Thebans and never in the epini-

[70] Rutherford, forthcoming, raises the question of the unity of the poem, since it addresses
first the sun then Apollo. It is as though, he says, an apotropaic *paian* had been joined to a cult
paian. This is an excellent description of the emotional dynamics of the poem: the situation
has been normalized by the shift. Rutherford suggests that the identification of Apollo with
the sun, attested already in the fifth century, eased the transition.

[71] The word is difficult. Farnell 1961 *ad loc.* assumes that the first person refers to Pindar
and interprets the line to mean that Pindar composed the ode under divine inspiration. The
scholiast glosses with ἐπετελέσθην. Slater 1969b s.v. offers the translation "I have been
granted fulfilment." *LSJ* interprets as "I was perfected." Fraenkel 1950 *ad* 369 discusses the
meaning "ordain" for κραίνειν, although he says that Pindar does not use the word this way.
In translating "I was ordained," I take it to mean that the speaker was chosen in a solemn way.
So also Rutherford forthcoming.

[72] Farnell 1961 *ad loc.* points out that line 35 implies a consecrated κλίνη (couch) in the
Ismenion. He also suggests (p. 225 *ad Pythian* 11) that a *hieros gamos,* a ritual marriage between
Apollo and Melia, was celebrated periodically: see Pindar *Pyth.* 11.1–6, where Ino, Semele,
and Alkmene are called on to come to Melia at the Ismenion. Pindar's *Hymn* 1 mentions her
also.

[73] Farnell 1961 *ad loc.*

cian odes.[74] Teneros linked Apollo uniquely with Thebes, excluding any need to share Apollo's fatherly attentions with other claims.

One can dimly guess at another reason for calling on Teneros. Teneros was a prophet, as the chorus mentions (42).[75] If lines 39–40 are correctly interpreted as "dedicating (as subject) to the Muses' arts the oracular place," and if "sign" or something similar is the correct restoration in line 33, then the background may be that one of Teneros' oracles was found to predict the eclipse and offer advice on countermeasures. The assertion of line 34, "I was ordained," may then refer to a directive in the oracle also, and the metaphor of "dedicating" used for taking the oracle as subject of song could point to the idea that the ceremony was to be repeated yearly. If so, then the *paian* achieves psychological efficacy by reproducing the sequence of consternation and revelation played out in finding the oracle.

What is also notable about lines 34–37 at the beginning of the second triad is that the performers draw such overt attention to themselves as agents of Thebes' safety. The first-person ἐκράνθην (I was ordained) is not generalizable. It looks as though at the moment when the chorus begins speaking *to* the audience to reveal the model for a benign new stage for Thebes, the choreuts present themselves. The model, in other words, is not just a ceremony of calling on Apollo but a singling out of the performers as the ones whose prayers will be efficacious. One wonders whether the Theban aristocracy seized on the eclipse as an occasion to stage themselves as saviors of the city (for the fact that Pindar wrote the poem implies that an elaborate ceremony was mounted). The poem then represents its performers' high status as divinely sanctioned wisdom.[76] The threat posed by the eclipse is vivid enough, and the more one wants the ceremony to counter it, the more one is impelled to put faith in the performers.

5. Tyrtaios' *Eunomia* (1–4 *W*).

A different kind of poem from the ones I have been considering is Tyrtaios' *Eunomia* (Good Government). Tyrtaios was a Spartan poet of the seventh century BCE who composed primarily military exhortations. It was not a choral poem, as its elegiac meter indicates. Unfortunately, we

[74] Teneros is found together with Melia in *paian* 7, lines 13 and 4, respectively. Strabo quotes some words from a hymn describing Teneros (51d *SM*). The religious songs have an unqualified local focus that the epinicians do not.

[75] Cf. n.69 above. Strabo 9.2.33–34, cited *ad* fr. 51 *SM*, calls him "interpreter of the oracle" at another Apollo sanctuary at Mt. Ptoon.

[76] Cf. the discussion of Isyllos' *paian* in Ch. 3; Isyllos tells us that the "best" of the city were chosen to perform in the ceremony.

have only two fragments from it and know nothing about the conditions under which it was performed, so we cannot examine it as a performer's speech as we have the others.[77] The *Eunomia* is Tyrtaios' most ambitious poem, so the occasion of its performance was probably a ceremony of reaffirmation of the political order.[78] Tyrtaios' place in early Spartan history is a vexed question, but the poem may have been performed on various occasions long after Tyrtaios' death.[79] It contains the same indicators of local poetry as we have found in the other poems we have examined.

As in Alkman's *partheneion*, the address for the audience and the address to it are separate, the first establishing the performer's communal voice as the basis for the second. The first fragment (2 *W*) tells of the Dorian immigration to the Peloponnesus. Four lines are complete (12–15):

αὐτὸς γὰρ Κρονίων καλλιστεφάνου πόσις Ἥρης
Ζεὺς Ἡρακλείδαις ἄστυ δέδωκε τόδε,
οἷσιν ἅμα προλιπόντες Ἐρινεὸν ἠνεμόεντα
15   εὐρεῖαν Πέλοπος νῆσον ἀφικόμεθα

For the son of Kronos himself, husband of lovely-crowned Hera, Zeus, has given this city to the sons of Heracles, together with whom leaving windy Erineos we came to the broad island of Pelops.

These lines show that the performer was speaking in a definite setting: note the deictic τόδε (this) referring to Sparta. The first-person plural ἀφικόμεθα (we came to) is tellingly used: by saying "we" when describing the actions of the long-gone ancestors who first migrated to the Peloponnesus, the speaker makes one cohesive group of all Dorian Spartans, living and dead. A subjunctive verb, πειθώμεθα (let us obey), hangs in isolation in line 10, just before the lines quoted, and suggests that the speaker is either recommending that the audience submit to higher authority or reporting a speech by an ancestor that advised submission to a higher authority.[80] Embedded in a narrative the advice would come to the actual listeners more indirectly, but they would hardly miss its applicability to

[77] Bowra 1961: 240 comments that Sappho and Archilochos expressed their feelings, whereas Tyrtaios or Solon was "the voice of a class or a people or a public conscience." The difference in locale and function of performance, not just in personality, accounts for the different content.

[78] Bowie 1986: 30–31 includes it in a type he identifies of long elegiac poems given public recitation. Herington 1985: 32–33 observes that Tyrtaios' poems were "instruments of civil and military policy" and that the *Eunomia* was addressed to the community as a whole. Rösler 1990a: 234–35 thinks that it was sung in the *syssitia* (Spartan messes; see Ch. 5).

[79] On the political situation, see Prato 1968: 27–47 and references below, n.81.

[80] Rösler 1990a: 234–35 notes the conflation of past and present. Cf. Mimnermos 9.2 *W*. As Bowie 1986: 30 points out, these lines could come from a speech by a Spartan leader embedded in the narrative.

themselves so long as they accepted continuity of identity with their mythical ancestors.

With the basis of communal solidarity established, the performer then enumerates the principles of the political order as a narrative about Apollo's advice to the Spartans (4 *W*).[81] There is no way to know how much text has been lost between fragments 2 and 4, but if the order of the fragments is right, then the inclusive first person preceded the recital of the provisions of the oracle.

I pointed out in the discussion of Alkman's *partheneion* that even when the *parthenoi* do speak as a model to the audience, they avoid commands and assertions that would present them as more authoritative than the audience. The authority for local performance is drawn from the community and must not presume to independence from its source. So here also the performer does not present the restatement of the political order as a series of injunctions.[82] The principles are quoted in indirect discourse as the command of Apollo (4.1–4 *W*):

> Φοίβου ἀκούσαντες Πυθωνόθεν οἴκαδ' ἔνεικαν
> μαντείας τε θεοῦ καὶ τελέεντ' ἔπεα·
> ἄρχειν μὲν βουλῆς θεοτιμήτους βασιλῆας,
> οἷσι μέλει Σπάρτης ἱμερόεσσα πόλις

Having heard Apollo, they brought home from Pytho (= Delphi) the oracles of the god and his efficacious words; the god-honored kings, to whom the lovely city of Sparta is a care, should preside over the council.

The list of narrated commands continues. In this case, when he ceases simply to draw on community authority but adds to it instead (especially if this reaffirmation of the existing political order is in the face of potential resistance), the performer substitutes an external, divine authority for his own utterance. Apollo's commands in turn are set within the framework of a narrative about the return of the messengers from Delphi. That is to say, the performer further disguises Apollo's indirect commands as a continuation of the integrative history that the poem has apparently been narrating from the first fragment on. Only the last line of the text (as found in Diodoros alone) reveals that the narrative was meant as injunction. Abandoning the narrative frame, the line addresses the audience as though the previous lines had been dictating behavior to it; note the use of γάρ (for) explaining the preceding (10):

---

[81] The question of Tyrtaios' relationship to the Spartan document known as the Great Rhetra and allegedly brought from Delphi is much disputed. The Rhetra was the basis for a revision of the constitution. See Wade-Gery 1943; Podlecki 1984a: 100–105.

[82] On Tyrtaios' use of verb forms to shape his appeal to the audience, see Jaeger 1966. He

Φοῖβος γὰϱ πεϱὶ τῶν ὧδ' ἀνέφηνε πόλει.

For Phoibos declared thus to the city concerning these things.[83]

The *Eunomia* is so careful to embed its prescriptions because the performer is using shared traditions to impose acceptance of a political order. As to the threat of trouble if the audience does not conform, the performer may also have described the grief that reaffirmation of the political order will overcome. Tyrtaios was good at depictions of misery, for in another poem (10 *W*) he vividly expatiates on the consequences of failing to fight to the death. Here more than in the first four poems, the implicitly coercive force of the ideology of communal unity is apparent.[84] Correspondingly, the performer does not assert himself (in the few extant lines) but stages himself as a narrator and thereby assimilates the current Spartan institutions to the heroic age.

Tyrtaios' other extant poems, those urging the Spartans to fight, seem to fall between the categories of public and symposium poetry; they may have been recited at public dinners in military camp.[85] Though they are largely without references to the past and seem like pure exhortation, they too rest on consensus, for they assume the whole Spartan ethos of virtue as military.[86] They are also careful not to present the performer as imperious toward the audience. In 10 *W* after a hortatory subjunctive, "let us fight" (13), the speaker admonishes the young in imperatives (15–20), but at the end of the poem the moral is drawn in the form of a third-person imperative. In 11 *W* second-person imperatives are used in the first three lines

---

comments (115) that infinitives are a favorite form in laws. His observations on the impersonal "I" in 12 *W* (119) and the speaker's inclusion of himself in the citizen body addressed (116) are relevant to the delineation of community poetry.

[83] There is a question about whether this line was in the original poem; Andrewes 1938: 98–99 would reject it. Prato 1968 *ad loc.* rejects the version found in Diodoros (7.12.6) altogether, explaining it as a late variant meant to support agitation for a democratic reform. Thus the poem may have been altered to reflect changing politics, but it presents itself as reflecting continuity with the past.

[84] Jaeger 1966: 120–21 argues that ξυνὸν ἐσθλόν (common good) in Tyrtaios 12.15 *W* is a new political idea. The difference from the individualism in battle depicted by Homer may be not only chronological but also a difference in performance context.

[85] Lykourgos *Against Leokrates* 107: there was a law stating that when they were under arms all should be called to the king's tent to hear Tyrtaios' poems. Cf. Bowie 1990: 224–28; Herington 1985: 33. At Athenaios 14, 630f it is said that soldiers on campaign kept their movement rhythmical by singing Tyrtaios' poetry. These must be the anapestic marching songs attributed to Tyrtaios: so Bowie 1990: 225.

[86] See Shey 1976 for good analysis of the persuasive force of 12 *W*, which does use myth, but for negative exemplars. Fuqua 1981 studies the implicit promise of heroization to all warriors who die in battle.

("be of good courage," "do not fear"), but a third-person form appears in line 4 when it comes to standing in battle ("let each man hold his shield").[87]

These five poems show some of the occasions that could be marked by poetic performance, but there were other important moments for which we do not have any examples of poetry. Among occasions calling for choruses were victory celebrations. Though no substantial examples of poems survive, testimony shows that the pattern of communal poetry that has been traced in the preceding poems was found in these also. For example, Sosibios' description of choral performance at a festival commemorating Spartan victory at Thyrea is reported by Athenaios (15, 678bc):

> The leaders of the choruses that perform at this festival wear them (i.e., Thyreatic wreaths) as a memorial of the victory in Thyrea. There are ⟨three⟩ choruses, one in front of boys, ⟨one on the right of old men⟩, and one on the left of men, dancing nude and singing the songs of Thaletas and Alkman and the *paianes* of Dionysodotos the Lakonian.[88]

The victory was about 546 BCE.[89] Alkman's and Thaletas' songs were still part of the repertoire at that time, a hundred years after Alkman's lifetime. Boys and old men, not of an age to participate in battle, had their place in the ceremony and transformed celebration of victory into an expression of solidarity between generations in a cohesive history like the one Tyrtaios presents. The old songs combined with the parading of the boys make a powerful statement about Spartan viability.

Sosibios' notice has been correlated with one in Plutarch which describes three choruses singing in turn at a Spartan celebration.[90] A chorus of old men sings first, "We once were vigorous youths." A chorus of men in their prime answers, "And we are now, in truth; if you wish, look!" Then a chorus of boys announces, "And we indeed will be stronger by far." Reflection and model are linked by a third term, so that past, present, and future are represented. Although nothing specific connects Plutarch's quotations with celebration of the victory at Thyrea, both organize celebration in the same way: the boys' chorus is in the center in Sosibios'

---

[87] One exhortation to battle by the Ephesian poet Kallinos survives (1 *W*). Its first four lines are accusatory second-person plural questions addressed to the youths. But it switches to third-person imperatives for its advice to fight. The lines perhaps reflect formalized intergenerational conflict, like the three Spartan choruses quoted below. Tedeschi 1978 deduces a symposium setting from the language of the poem.

[88] The translation is from the text of Campbell 1988 *ad* Thaletas 11 (p. 328), which accepts the supplements from Kaibel 1887–90 and Jacoby's striking out of a reference to the Gymnopaideia. For the latter, cf. Sosibios *FGH* 595 F5 and the commentary *ad loc.*

[89] Hdt. 1.82.

[90] *Lykourgos* 21.3; 870 *PMG*. Podlecki 1984b rather speculatively connects the poet and pipes-player Sakadas with this celebration (181).

description and forms the climax of the three boasts in Plutarch. This arrangement of choruses is thought to be the model for Plato's three choruses in *Laws* 664b–665b.[91] Similarly, the boy Sophocles led a chorus singing a victory *paian* after the battle of Salamis.[92]

An inscription records the enhanced celebration of a festival for Dionysus at Eretria in the late fourth century BCE: "Since at the procession of Dionysus the garrison departed and the city was freed [and after] the hymns also adopted democracy, so that there might be a memorial of this day, it seemed good to the council and the people that all the Eretrians and the inhabitants should wear wreaths of ivy in the procession of Dionysus . . . and the choruses should begin [."[93] The inscription breaks off, so the instructions about the choruses are lost. Choruses participate along with "all the Eretrians" in marking a turning point in Eretrian history. The latter will have been the audience for the choral performances, which must have praised both Dionysus and democracy. Celebrating the democracy also exerts pressure toward maintaining it, of course, and dramatizing its inception at the moment when the city was freed from occupation by foreign forces equates it with local autonomy. The memorial is a model for the future as well.

Literature supplies evidence that a chorus was an appropriate way to celebrate victory or resolution of a threat to the community. The watchman in Aeschylus' *Agamemnon,* rejoicing in victory after he spots the signal beacon, calls it the harbinger of the forming of many choruses in Argos (23–24). The chorus in Sophocles' *Antigone* says in response to Theban victory that it wishes to approach all the sanctuaries of the gods in all-night choruses with Dionysus as leader of the dance (152–53). In Euripides' *Heracles* 673–700, the chorus sings a victory *paian*. At the end of Aristophanes' *Lysistrata,* the participants celebrate peace with dancing.

Eveline Krummen's analysis of Pindar *Isthmian* 4 for a Theban victor can be restated within this framework.[94] She argues cogently that the victory ode was performed during a yearly festival for Heracles and his sons held just outside the city. The ceremonies included a sacrificial meal, a *pannychis* (all-night celebration) during which bonfires blazed in honor of the dead warrior sons, and athletic games. The cult may have been connected with the mustering of the new warriors who joined the ranks of the hoplite army each year. Reflection and model in the ode likewise consist of honor to dead warriors and celebration of a fresh rise to triumph. Four of

---

[91] England 1976 *ad loc.*

[92] *Life of Sophocles* 3, *TrGF* p. 31.

[93] Sokolowski 1962: #46. The reading "and after the hymns" is suggested by Sokolowski (98–99), who thinks it refers to a formal announcement. For the date see p. 98.

[94] Krummen 1990: 33–94.

Melissos' relatives who died in war are recalled, but (36–37) "now again after wintery dark of months the colorful earth, as it were, bursts into bloom with red roses by will of the gods." The imagery of renewal refers to Melissos' victory, which again raised his house to honor. Through this image, which resonates with the festival as a whole, the meaning of the cult is transferred to Melissos' family also.[95] The performers are citizens (79) who honor the victor Melissos as representatives of the collective citizenry.[96]

To summarize the results so far, the five poems that I have adduced as examples of community poetry are quite different: choral or solo, for a regular ritual or special occasion, sung every year or newlymade for one year's ritual, addressed to divinities or to the audience at the ceremony, and associated with different times and places. Only one is traditional and anonymous; all the others were acquired by the community from (or at least attributed to) a known poet. The latter are no less authentic communal poetry, for poets knew how their poems were to fit into the proceedings. This local poetry was not a phenomenon of the archaic period only but continued to be created and reperformed as long as it filled a need. Many festivals were founded or developed in the seventh and sixth centuries, and thereafter the creation of new cults, with concomitant need for song and dance, went on into the Hellenistic period.[97] What is underrepresented in the surviving corpus is the vast amount of poetry that must have existed for regularly repeated festivals. Much of it may never have been written down at all.

The two aspects, reflection and model, may be very differently weighted in different situations. I do not want to argue that all local poetry has exactly the same features. The pattern of reflection and model is an abstract one; it describes a function that must be fulfilled constantly and on different levels. In some places (e.g., Sparta) mythic history as a backdrop to action was probably more important than in others. Furthermore, in some places more of the citizens' activities were mediated through public performance. There is less evidence, for instance, of public performance of

[95] Ibid.: 54–59, 88–94, and passim emphasizes the thorough imbrication of poem and cult: Melissos' relatives = Heracles' sons, Melissos = Heracles, the ritual banquet = Heracles' feasting on Olympus.

[96] Ibid.: 55.

[97] See Burnett 1988: 141–43 on the need of Greek settlers in the West to invent ritual and poetry that created a communal identity. Speaking of reworking old myths, she says (141): "These verities would be at their most plangent when cast into the choral form and sung by many voices from the citizenry, and their consolation would be at its most effective, since a myth danced out in public could be ingested at once by an entire community. Instructed by such means in the sacredness of customs peculiar to itself, the city gained direct experience of its separate unity, even as its festival was infused with the common Hellenic mythology."

parthenoi at Athens than at Sparta, although it may have taken place at the deme level instead of the level of the city.[98]

Community poetry negotiates a stage in community life between performer and audience. One of the functions of such poetry is to move a community to the next stage emotionally, based on its established mores. The two aspects of the process, reflection and model, together describe the ideological work that local poetry does. The alternative terminology I use, that performers speak both for and to the audience, defines the ideological work from the point of view of performer-audience relations and emphasizes that performers are the community's means of communication with itself; they are put in the position of making public affirmation of the communal view in their own persons, while at the same time they present their persons as exemplary. Performance is in this way potentially political in a narrower sense. The *parthenoi* who sang Alkman's *partheneia* may have been women from good families who were, among other things, calling attention to their status.[99] The performers of Pindar's *paian* 9 seem to be celebrating their own wisdom. The role played by gender in the composite will be examined in Chapters 2 and 3. There I will continue the analysis of the *Louvre partheneion* and Hermokles' song and will bring in other examples of community poetry.

To round out the discussion, we should turn to a few other descriptions of festivals and performance of community poetry that are recorded in cases where no texts survive. They will add to our sense of the variety of ways in which community poetry was used and fill out our picture of festival settings for performance—while our conception of performance as offering reflection and model lends a sense of the dynamics of performance to the preserved descriptions. There are notices of dozens of occasions when choruses performed at religious or civic ceremonies, but usually no further description, or nothing useful for us, is offered. Occasionally we get more information or a glimpse of a scene.[100]

Community, especially choral, poetry was part of major state festivals.

[98] Cf. Jones 1987: 62: the list of deme business "leaves little doubt but that it was in the deme that citizens found the focus of their public communal activity." Religious activities took up much of the attention (64–65).

[99] An apparent reference to Timasimbrota, probably the daughter of the Spartan king Eurykrates, appears in a line of Alkman quoted in a lacunose papyrus commentary (5 fr. 2 col. ii 14 *PMGF* = 80 *C*, with the commentator's explanation in 14–17). If she was a participant in choral performance, it would prove the exalted status of the young women who presented themselves to the Spartan community. Cf. the Introduction.

[100] Barrett 1954 reconstructs the history of the temple at Asine, where Bacchylides' *paian*, fr. 4 *SM* was performed. The *paian* gives a vivid image of festivity: song and dance and good cheer bloom (56–57), songs and sacrifice, athletics, pipes, and revelry are offspring of peace (61–68), and "streets are full of lovely symposia and songs by (or: about) the young blaze out" (79–80).

Performance at the center of attention of the whole celebrating population could crystallize the meaning of the festivity, as was evident in the description of the Spartan commemoration of victory quoted above. Athenaios preserves a description of another one of Sparta's big public festivals, the Hyakinthia (4, 139d-f, from the *Lakonika* of Polykrates).[101] The Hyakinthia was a ceremony of mourning and renewal. Mourning took place on the first day; the second celebrated the return of joy.[102] On this middle day of the three-day festival, amid the various spectacles and general celebration, "ample choruses of young men enter (the theater) and sing some of the local songs, and dancers among them perform the old-fashioned movement to pipes and song." (Note the self-consciousness about local songs and old-fashioned movements; we will come back to this phenomenon.) Children performed also, according to the passage, while *parthenoi* paraded in carriages. They sacrificed generously, and the citizens held dinners for acquaintances and slaves. At some point a choral performance in which the kings took part presented the eminent men to the assembled.[103] As in the passage from Theognis with which the chapter began, community poetry is here seen to be part of a larger ceremony of communal participation and renewal.[104] Louise Bruit comments that the second day "provides the city with the opportunity of self-celebration through the spectacle furnished by its young men and women."[105]

At Athens, Euripides' *Heracleidae* 777–83 describes song and choral dance of youths and maidens at a *pannychis* on the Acropolis. Ludwig Deubner assigns the passage to the Panathenaia, for which a *pannychis* is attested.[106] Another Athenian ceremony, the Oschophoria, included a procession from Athens to Phaleron led by two noble youths dressed as women and carrying vine branches with grapes attached, followed by a chorus of youths singing "Oschophoria songs." This ceremony was in the charge of the Salaminioi, a subgroup of Athenian families who apparently came from Salamis.[107] The adherence of the Salaminioi to Athens seems to be dramatized and grafted onto icons of fertility, while the whole ceremony was associated with Theseus through its *aition*. Perhaps the political and agricultural themes were linked in the songs; in any event the singing

---

[101] *FGH* 588. Nothing else is known of Polykrates, including his date.

[102] On this festival see Nilsson 1957: 129–40; Bruit 1990: 163–67.

[103] Xenophon *Agesilaos* 2.17. Cf. the Introduction.

[104] Calame 1977: I 305–23, esp. 317–18, thinks that the ritual marked the end of the initiatory period. On the basis of Euripides *Helen* 1365, he attributes nocturnal choruses for young women to the festival.

[105] Bruit 1990: 165.

[106] Deubner 1962: 24. His discussion (22–35) makes vivid the involvement of the whole city in the Panathenaia.

[107] On the Oschophoria, see Ch. 3.

was part of a complex representation of the compatibility between local and Athenian, agricultural and urban allegiance.

The Athenian festival that developed the most complex series of performances is of course the City Dionysia, discussed in the Introduction, at which tragedy, comedy, and dithyrambic choruses performed in competitions. Dithyrambic choruses in this case moved beyond the purposes and limits of community poetry, as we shall see in the next section. However, Simon Goldhill's study of the ceremonies surrounding the plays shows how deeply these performances too were bound up with the city's self-display: male orphans marched in armor on their coming of age; men who had given the city signal service were rewarded with crowns; the tribute was displayed; and the ten generals offered libations.[108] The city's self-display is obviously also the stage for individuals' performance of their identity. In her investigation of the typical features of Dionysiac festivals, Susan Cole comments that balancing the honors for individuals was the custom of *aischrologia* (mocking, obscene jesting) during the phallus-bearing procession, which allowed those of lesser status to jeer at those of greater; *aischrologia* served both as an antidote to competition and as an outlet for aggression.[109]

Noteworthy is the absence of performance by women; at the Dionysia only men performed. As the city grew into an imperial center, it became less a community in which all groups participated in the same public space. Women had their own festivals and were not absent from the great state holidays, but they had no significant share of public speaking in performance in the city itself.

II

Community poetry was not a simple unself-conscious or bounded category. We have seen that highly artistic poems could be commissioned for special occasions. Traditional poetry could itself become evidence for the communal past and could be manipulated for political ends; the limits of the category are blurred; and poetry could fall into or out of the category as its function and style of performance changed. All of these can be illustrated either by texts or by descriptions of performance. They show that community poetry is always in tension with other kinds of performance and always subject to redefinition or fossilization.

The endpoints of the process of self-definition through song can be illustrated from Sikyon. Herodotus says that the sixth-century tyrant Kleisthenes of Sikyon transferred choruses from Adrastos to Dionysus

[108] Goldhill 1990: 100–114.
[109] Cole 1993: 33–34.

because Adrastos was an Argive hero, and Sikyon was hostile to Argos; A. J. Podlecki points out that these choruses must have been filling a civic function in fostering a sense of political identity, and Kleisthenes wanted to alter the kind of identification the Sikyonians claimed.[110] Almost a millennium later, Pausanias visited Sikyon. He reports that the people of Sikyon carry statues once a year at night to the temple of Dionysus, accompanying them with torches and local songs (2.7.5–6). The origin of these statues (and songs?) they attribute to figures in Sikyon's mythical history as symbols of the immemorial sameness of Sikyonian identity. Change and continuity both help to create the meaning of performance in context.

Two fragments will show us the limits of communal poetry, the conditions under which it may cease to be communal.

6. Solon, *Salamis* (1–3 *W*).

Solon's poem exhorts the Athenians to resume the fight for the island of Salamis. Plutarch gives an account of the occasion for performance, cited in the Introduction: out of weariness with the war against Megara for control of Salamis, the Athenians had passed a law forbidding anyone to argue for renewing the fight, on pain of death.[111] Seeing that people were ready to fight again, Solon started a rumor that he had gone mad, then rushed into the agora wearing a herald's cap, mounted the herald's stone, and recited the elegy *Salamis*. This story is probably apocryphal; its genesis may lie in the peculiarity of the poem itself, as we shall see. The actual context of performance, if not the agora, is unknown. The poem could be for the symposium; in that case it is probably commemorative, that is, sung after the fact to evoke the decision to return to the fight. Conceivably it was sung among a group of influential men in a symposium in an effort to muster their support for the war.[112] But a public setting is possible, perhaps at a festival. By discussing it as if it is community poetry, I can demonstrate its difference, a difference that may mean that it was in fact performed elsewhere but may show how Solon used his extraordinary influence.

A total of eight lines from the poem are preserved in quotations. The poem is anomalous in that it does not begin with a reflection of consensus and move the audience to a new stage grounded in that consensus. In its

---

[110] Hdt. 5.67.5; Podlecki 1980: 395.

[111] Plutarch *Solon* 8.1–3. Other references listed in West 1992b *ad loc.*

[112] Bowie 1986: 18–21 discusses the problem of the setting for Solon's poetry and argues for the symposium, whence the message would percolate horizontally and vertically through Athenian society. Tedeschi 1982: 42–45 thinks that it was performed anomalously in the agora, drawing on bardic inspiration and claim of personal observation.

opening lines (1 *W*), quoted by Plutarch, the performer announces his assumed identity: "I myself, a herald, come from desirable Salamis, setting my arrangement of words in a song instead of a speech."[113] By proclaiming himself a herald, he abjures his actual identity and adopts a position and viewpoint closer to a bard's.[114]

Diogenes Laertios quotes two passages from later in the poem (2 and 3 *W*), saying that he is quoting them in order:

> εἴην δὴ τότ' ἐγὼ Φολεγάνδριος ἢ Σικινήτης
> ἀντί γ' Ἀθηναίου πατρίδ' ἀμειψάμενος·
> αἶψα γὰρ ἂν φάτις ἥδε μετ' ἀνθρώποισι γένοιτο·
> "Ἀττικὸς οὗτος ἀνήρ, τῶν Σαλαμιναφετέων."

then

> ἴομεν ἐς Σαλαμῖνα μαχησόμενοι περὶ νήσου
> ἱμερτῆς χαλεπόν τ' αἶσχος ἀπωσόμενοι.

In that case would that I were Pholegandrian or Sikinetan, giving up in exchange the fatherland of an Athenian; for quickly would this remark arise among people: this man is Attic, one of the Salamis-relinquishers.

then

Let us go to Salamis to fight for the desirable island and thrust off harsh shame.

Far from seeking to represent the Athenians, the performer expresses shame and the wish to belong elsewhere. He picks perilous ground from which to present a model for communal behavior, yet the lines quoted next open with a first person plural that unites speaker and audience: "let us go. . . ." The poem here makes a pitch for consensus based on the model of resuming battle, so that the poem can *end* by reflecting its audience. Solon is reported to have carried his point; the Athenians took up the fight again and won Salamis.

Plutarch's story (unless it has a core of truth) seems to have developed as a way to account for the poem's remarkable staging of its performer. The story solves a problem posed by the poem, namely that it is without a basis in communal authority. It offers a reason, the law against speaking about Salamis, for Solon's devious way of bringing up the question of Salamis; then it accounts for Solon's success by taking the herald of the opening as a

[113] West 1992b *ad loc.* thinks that ᾠδήν in the text is a gloss on κόσμον ἐπέων.
[114] Bowie 1986: 19 compares Archilochos 1 *W* and Theognis 257 as examples of metaphorical identities taken on by singers, but they are not close parallels. As he points out, the stance of the returning traveler is found in Theognis 783–88.

sign of a larger theatrical coup. The story says in effect that Solon arranged that his words should be taken as meaningless and have the character of an announcement so that he could speak them to the citizens before they could respond to the real violation of the social code. Plutarch also remarks that many members of the community felt the way Solon did, so that he in fact had a hidden consensus. Plutarch's story of the performance is a measure of how transgressive it was to speak to and about the community without the community's assent.

This poem presents its performer as an individual distinct from the community. If the community joins the individual in the decision expressed in the line "let us go . . . ," then the poem arrives at the place that local poetry begins from. The failure that this poem risks (or represents itself as risking) is that the performer will not bring the community over and that his inclusive ending will not be identified by his audience as including it. The very fact that Solon's proposal was cast as poetry suggests that he was drawing on the consensual basis of local poetry as part of his effort to reach people before they rejected the course he was proposing. If it was performed in public, the poem is in a sense an abuse of the function of local poetry. On the other hand, if it was sung as a symposium poem after the fact, then it would stage the performer as one whose individual prestige outweighs the pressure of conventional public opinion. It becomes a delineation of Solon's unique power to direct Athens, of which we will see another example in Chapter 5. We learn from poem and story that the alternative to the kind of performer-audience relations constructed by local poetry is performance by an individual on his own authority.

7. Archilochos 98–99 *W.*

Another example of solo poetry that may escape the limits of local poetry is Archilochos 98–99 *W,* a description of a seventh-century battle, preserved on an inscription probably set up in a hero-shrine to Archilochos and supplemented by a papyrus fragment.[115] So little of it is preserved that to analyze its character seems frivolous; nevertheless I proffer a very tentative discussion. From the inscribed commentary, which quotes from the poems as evidence for its assertions, we learn that several poems were connected with Thasos, but it cannot be determined that this one was. Even from the broken text, we can see that it was a lively account, made vivid in part by the use of the first person plural. The following lines, heavily supplemented, are the most intelligible section (7–21):

[115] See Peek 1985; West 1985a.

παῖς] Ἀθηναίη Διός·

ἀμφ[ὶ] δ' ὑψ[ηλὰς ἐπάλξεις ἤρ]κεσαν πρὸ π[α]τρίη[ς

χρημ[κ]εῖτο πύργος ἀμφα[ή]ς,

10 θαυ[μ]α[   ] ἐκ λίθων ἐδε[ίμαμ]ε[ν

ἄν]δ[ρ]ε[ς] αὐτοὶ Λεσβίω[   ]ει[

τῶ]ν δ' ἀ[μ]φ[ιθ]έντες χερσὶν ο[   ]δια

ἰμεγωι. [   ]ων ἐσο[   ]σει Ζεὺς Ὀλυμπίω[ν]ο. ι[

αἰχμ]ῆ[ι]σιν θοῆισι πημονὴν ἐπήγομ[εν

15 ει . εθ[   ]ότ' ἀμφὶ πύργον ἔστασαν πονε[όμενοι

κλίμακας, μ]έγαν δ' ἔθεντο θυμὸν ἀμφε[

βαρὺ δ' ὑπεβρ]όμε[ι σίδ]ηρον εἱμένη καλ[

μηχανὴ   ἀ]μειπτή· πολλὰ δ' ἐρρύ[η βέλεα

] φαρέτραι δ' οὐκέτ' ἔκρυ[πτον φόνον

20]σαν ἰῶν· οἱ δ' ἐπε[

στρέψα]ντες ἶνας καὶ ταγ[ύσσαντες βιούς

. . . Athena, child of Zeus; and around the high [battlements] they fended off on behalf of the fatherland [a grievous thing ?] . . . there was set a tower visible all around, a wonder [to all, which ?] . . . [we built] from stones . . . men themselves (of ?) Lesbos . . . setting around (their) hands their [shields ?] . . . Zeus, of the Olympians [the strength ?] . . . with swift [spears] we brought grief [on them ?] . . . laboring they set up [ladders ?] around the tower and they set (their) hearts high . . . an iron-clad [siege-machine ? was rumbling heavily] . . . in return . . . and many [weapons] poured and quivers no longer hid [death ?] . . . of arrows; but they . . . [twisting] strings and stretching [bows[116]

If fragments 96 and 97a belong to the same poem or set of poems, it also included (teasing?) blame for the general Glaukos and the second-person accusation, "you were afraid" (97a.4), both plausibly part of a narrative. Assuming that the fragments capture the tone of the whole poem, dramatic narrative predominated. Where and for whom the poem was performed, we do not know. Perhaps it was within military circles. But possibly Archilochos and/or others recited it at a festival or public gathering.[117] If he did participate in the battle as a mercenary, Archilochos' ac-

[116] The text is the slightly improved one of West 1985a: 11. In the translation I have included some of his *exempli gratia* supplements, marked with a question-mark. Of the poem he says (13): "Archilochus appears to be with the defenders (10, 14), but in 8 he uses the third person, not the first, to say that 'they defended their fatherland.' This suggests that the city is not his own, that he is there as a member of an allied force or as a mercenary. The pervading tone is exhilarated, giving us the impression that the defence was ultimately successful." I have made use of the translation in West 1993.

[117] Notopoulos 1966 argues that Archilochos must have had training as a bard.

count would have no community dimension, although it might contain praise of Glaukos and suggest a model of good soldiering.[118] Its narrative interest is strong and may well have been the point of the poem.

One can see that in a different way from Solon's this poem too lends itself to presentation of an individual separate from the community. The performer of Archilochos 98–99 *W* presents himself as a soldier and includes the audience (insofar as they identify with his first person plural) as fellow-soldiers. For some of the audience, at least, the poem solicits a fictional sense of solidarity with the speaker. That in itself is unremarkable; Tyrtaios' *Eunomia* does the same. But if a modeling function, bringing the past to bear on the present, is absent, then this partly fictional connection between performer and audience is the only one. It is an easy move to treat the whole poem as a fictional narrative, detached from its context and performed by anyone with a flair for self-dramatization to any audience that quickens to tales of fighting. The poem approaches epic in its straightforward narrative. Indeed it was perhaps this kind of poem as well as mythic narratives that the rhapsodes who performed Archilochos recited.[119]

The poems of Solon and Archilochos threaten in different ways to depart from the system of communication that works through communal poetry. If the performer speaks only *to* the audience or only *for* it, the sense of transaction is lost, of performance as marking and negotiating a transition. The poem becomes personal—didactic or fictional (in the sense of narrative that is entertaining for its own sake).[120]

Poetry can also be drawn into the system of communal performance although it was not composed for that purpose or can become fossilized and lose its function as transaction. The first happened to Solon's poetry, one example of which, as we have seen, was marginally communal in its implied interaction with the audience. Much of his extant poetry seems to have been composed for a symposium setting but was later reperformed as community poetry. A passage in Plato's *Timaeus* (21b) mentions boys reciting poetry, including Solon's, at the Apatouria for prizes set by their fathers. The Apatouria was the festival at which young men were received into the phratry. The point of the performances is easy to see: boys recited

[118] Glaukos appears in other poems of Archilochos, and his gravestone was found on Thasos. He would be known to the original audience.

[119] Plato *Ion* 531a lists Archilochos among the poets whose work rhapsodes performed. For notices of mythic narrative by Archilochos, see 286–89 *W* and Bowie 1986: 34, esp. n.110; Notopoulos 1966.

[120] Any kind of poetry could be enjoyed for its own sake in the symposium, a setting in which a composition could easily shift from functional communication to aesthetic object. Athenaios 6, 250b indicates, for instance, that the *paianes* of Phrynichos, Stesichoros, and Pindar were sung after dinner in the time of Dionysios the Younger of Syracuse.

poetry that shaped their consciousness of political and ethnic identity at a festival confirming legitimacy, the basis of citizenship. In this case reflection and model work through the idealization of the figure of Solon.[121] The boys identify with Solon, for his political poetry has an individual first person, and by producing an imitation of him they affirm his status as the paradigmatic statesman and also present themselves as committed to democratic principles. This ceremony, in which the future is projected as loyalty to the past and the performer takes on the identity of the virtuous man, has more in common with Plato's scheme in the *Laws* than the poetry examined hitherto.

Polybios supplies an example of poetry shifting from interactive to emblematic. He comments that among the Arcadians boys were required to learn the local poetry (4.20.8–9):

> This is well-known and familiar to all, that, among the Arcadians almost alone, the boys first of all from infancy are made accustomed to sing by law (or, in measure) the songs and *paianes* with which each (community) in traditional fashion hymns the local heroes and gods; after this, learning the compositions of Philoxenos and Timotheos they dance with great rivalry each year to professional pipes-players in the theater, the boys in juvenile contests, the young men in those called the men's (contests).

Polybios was an Arcadian; he was writing in the second century BCE, but he attributes the emphasis on song and dance to "the men of old" (4.21.1). Furthermore, he continues, "they made customary common gatherings and many sacrifices for men and women alike, and also choruses of *parthenoi* and of children" (4.21.3). Polybios thinks that the purpose was to "soften" and civilize the Arcadians, but more mundane considerations may have moved the Arcadians also. One of them was probably the fostering of Arcadian ethnic identity after the restoration of independence in 370.[122] The traditional songs are part of an educational program whose upper reaches are the showpieces of Philoxenos and Timotheos; they seem to be transformed into a token of ethnic identity whose appeal was perhaps mainly sentimental, but which still served as a means for young men to represent themselves as "Arcadian." Similar is the singing of "local songs" and dancing of "old-fashioned movement" at the Hyakinthia according to the description quoted above.

Precedence for a shift in the meaning of performance can be found at the Athenian dithyrambic contests, where the sort of composition favored by Philoxenos and Timotheos developed. Not much is known about the form of the dithyramb prior to the end of the sixth century when the

[121] The speaker explains that Solon's poetry was "new" at the time, although in fact it was not. On idealization of lawgivers, cf. Szegedy-Maszak 1978.

[122] Cf. Nilsson 1972: 18–22 on the policy of centralizing Arcadian cults at Megalopolis.

contests began.[123] Presumably it was, like the *paian,* a form in which a community could address a god, although it may always have been more flamboyant than the *paian.* The contest at the City Dionysia included twenty fifty-person choruses, one of men and one of boys from each tribe.[124] A smaller contest with ten choruses (one of men and one of boys from pairs of tribes) took place at the Thargelia, a festival in honor of Apollo, and there were others.[125] The contest dithyrambs required new texts for each production; in this they were probably different from most choral performance more closely linked to ritual. An ambitious *chorēgos* might seek out a famous poet.[126] The choruses were released from military service to train.[127] This spectacular display of "rhythm and *harmoniae,*" in Plato's words, was the city showing itself off to itself on a grand scale. Each chorus was the expression of its tribe's identity, while the contest had an integrative function for the city as a whole: the tribes were artificial creations, and each tribe included demes from various parts of Attica, so regional attachments were undercut by tribal affiliation.[128] On the other hand, the chorus (so far as the evidence shows) did not speak about the tribe that it represented—yet no one chorus represented Athens in a collective way.[129] Instead, the competitive framework changed the purpose of performance to display of virtuosity. As is well attested, by the mid-fifth century dithyrambic producers had begun to emphasize music and special effects at the expense of poetry.[130] Exploration of language was the province of drama, so dithyramb seems to have seized on musical and visual dazzle as its forte.[131]

[123] See Pickard-Cambridge 1962: 1–59, esp. 9–15; Zimmermann 1992: 19–31 on early dithyramb. Arion of Lesbos is said by Hdt. 1.23 to have been the first to compose them, at Corinth in the late seventh century; he may have been providing choruses for festivals established by the tyrant Periander.

[124] On the contest see Pickard-Cambridge 1962: 32–38 and 1968: 74–79. Cf. the Introduction for Demosthenes' tale of difficult sponsorship.

[125] Zimmermann 1992: 37–38n.15 lists the festivals for which dithyrambs are attested, with sources; others are the lesser Panathenaia, Hephaistia, Prometheia, and (in the third century BCE) Lenaia.

[126] For known poets who provided texts in the early period, see Herington 1985: 94, who points out that more of them are foreign than Athenian. On Simonides' victories see Molyneux 1992: 102–4, 318–25.

[127] Demosthenes 21 *Meidias* 15 and 193.

[128] Cf. Connor 1987: 41–42; Zimmermann 1992: 32–38, who stresses its antiaristocratic character.

[129] Zimmermann 1992: 39 remarks on the treatment of local myth implied by the name *Bouzyges* given to a dithyramb by Lasos of Hermione in the generation before Pindar. In 61–63, summarizing the typical elements of Pindar's dithyrambs, he includes praise of the city and narration of a myth relevant to the city; cf., e.g., 41–43 on 70a *SM* for Argos.

[130] On the later development of the dithyramb, see Pickard-Cambridge 1962: 38–58; Zimmermann 1992: 117–26.

[131] Competition between *chorēgoi* was fierce, as Demosthenes 21 *Meidias* attests. Cf. also Xenophon *Memorabilia* 3.4.3–5; Lysias 21.1–4.

Pindar and Bacchylides, who composed in the first half of the fifth century for one or both of the contests (the Dionysia and Thargelia), did use arresting poetic themes. Bacchylides cast one dithyramb (18 *SM*) as an interchange between King Aigeus and the people of Athens about the approach of an unknown hero whom the audience would recognize as Theseus.[132] Pindar composed praises of Athens so glorious that the Athenians are said to have voted him special honors.[133] But these apparently offered no long-term guide to development of a poetry suited to the occasion. Another dithyramb by Bacchylides for performance at Athens survives in part (19 *SM*), telling the story of Io, leading up to the birth of Dionysus. Some lines from it are indicative of the changed atmosphere (8–11):

> ὕφαινέ νυν ἐν
> ταῖς πολυηράτοις τι καινὸν
> 10   ὀλβίαις Ἀθάναις,
> εὐαίνετε Κηΐα μέριμνα.

Weave then something new in beauteous happy Athens, you praiseworthy Kean object of our regard.

The chorus asks for something new, addressing the *poet*. The song, it seems, should surprise the audience, not engage with it or address a figure, divine or human, on its behalf. The next three lines continue with praise of the poet. Bacchylides is no doubt tooting his horn, but the chorus also advertises that it has a new song from a poet favored by the Muses. The need for "something new" no doubt drove performance toward the resplendent.[134] In this situation the song expands mythic representations to occupy the whole text and moves in the direction of entertainment.

This closes the sketch of types and occasions for communal poetry. It remains to draw some consequences from the character of this poetry.

---

[132] The roles of Aigeus and the people of Athens are sometimes assigned to different singers. The fact that the King's stanzas have no second-person forms and only one verb that could be heard as first-person (but also as third-person, 30) suggests that the poem was not dialogue and that the whole chorus sang the poem. Only the subject connects this poem with Athens. Jebb 1967: 234–35 suggests that it would have been appropriate to the Thargelia, whose rites were said to have been founded by Theseus. Merkelbach 1973 has proposed performance at an ephebic ceremony; Ieranò 1987 develops the idea, pointing out if young men danced it, displaying their strength, the assertion in 13–14 that Athens has strong youths to protect it would gain resonance. There is no evidence for ephebic ritual in the fifth century, but performance at the Thargelia would produce the same effect.

[133] Fragments 74a–77 *SM* come from dithyrambs for Athens, on which cf. Van der Weiden 1991: 182–215. For the honors given Pindar, see Isokrates *Antidosis* 166 (10,000 drachmas); Pausanias 1.8.4 (statue). Cf. the Introduction for his praises of Athens.

[134] Jebb 1967: 234 sees Bacchylides already as a forerunner of the "new dithyramb" of the later fifth century.

Most of the poetry that has been adduced is choral. From prescriptions found in oracles and notices of victory celebrations one gets the strong impression that it was almost always choral. Performers could represent the community more effectively if they were a corporate body.[135] Multiple voices all speaking the same words would provide an image of communal harmony, and individual style would be to some extent submerged in the coordinated movements of dance or procession. In a battered fragment from what was probably a *paian* by Simonides for the Athenians from the early fifth century, the chorus says as much (519 fr. 35.8–10 *PMG*):[136]

καὶ σέ, ἄναξ ἑκαβ[
]. ετα ἱέμενοι ἐνοπὰν ἀγανοῖσιν [
10   ] εὔφαμον ἀπὸ φρενὸς ὁμορρόθο[υ

Also you, Lord Apollo [   ] (we) sending forth an auspicious cry with gentle [   ] from a mind that moves in unison.

"A mind that moves in unison" applies the image of coordination in dance to the thoughts of the dancers, expressing what choral dancing ideally implied: unity of thought.

If performers speak for the community, the community must be conceivable as a harmonious, hierarchical whole. Performance actually creates (or recreates) the image of unity that it seems to evoke, often by referring to the community's cults, possession of land, or genealogy and kinship.[137] Narratives that can put the past into a form usable as a model for the present include especially stories of victory, the favor of a god, marriage, or birth. Thus in Tyrtaios the story about winning Sparta with the gods' favor is the unifying background to the reassertion of the political order. In *paian* 9 Melia is the unifying figure who demonstrates Apollo's concern for Thebes. The boys who danced in the victory celebration recorded by Sosibios should become victorious warriors in their turn.

Each group within the community has its place, ratified by the narratives. Each set of performers dramatizes the perspective of its gender and

[135] Davies 1988b emphasizes that the ancients do not (except for Plato once) make the distinction between choral and solo poetry. But while arguing that poets cannot be classified as composers of only one or the other type, he allows that there are choral and solo poems (61). That conclusion leaves ancient writers' failure to use these categories unexplained. It must be that in principle any lyric song could be performed either way depending on what the occasion called for. Plato makes the distinction (*Laws* 764de) when he is discussing performance. Thus we cannot tell by inspection whether a poem is solo or choral but only try to determine the setting for its performance. Cf. Ley 1993.

[136] On this fragment see Rutherford 1990: 171–76.

[137] Cf. Raymond Williams' point that hegemony must always be renewed, quoted by Cowan 1990: 14.

age group on the collective ideology of the community. The act of speaking for and to the community is also a speaking about itself. A connection between the identity of the performers discussed in this chapter and the model for the future they propose is discernable. On the children of the Swallow-song rests the duty of the "renewal" promised by the song. The men who welcome Demetrios speak as soldiers and citizens whose decision it is to fight or not to fight. Alkman's *parthenoi* suggest marriage, which is their goal. The men who perform *paian* 9 present themselves as the community's best representatives to address Apollo. Each set of performers positions itself in the community in the course of projecting unity through the communal past. Francis Vian similarly comments about the Panathenaia that it reflected an image of the community as articulated by its constituent groups.[138]

I must stress that this unity exists only at the level of ideology. Communal performance is not prepolitical. One of the effects of projecting a unifying view of the community is that the power structure is made to appear natural. Whatever the tensions and factions characterizing daily life in the community, they are not directly articulated in ceremonial performances attendant on religious and civic celebration.[139] Thaletas could cure civic strife with music, not only because of the emotional power of music but because the words conveyed by the performer via music imposed structure on the audience.[140] In Chapter 2 we see how women present themselves as figures who hold the community together, and in Chapter 3 we see how male performers arrogate unifying imagery to themselves.

[138] Vian 1952: 255–58.
[139] Calame 1977: I 385 summarizes the place of choruses in Spartan life as both political and religious and representative of the hegemonic social body.
[140] Plutarch *Lykourgos* 4.2–3.

Women in Performance in the Community

I

CHAPTER 1 looked at community performance as marking a transitional moment in the common life of a group; it analyzed texts in terms of their address to the audience, evocation of local myth and religion, and vision of the immediate future. As I argued in the Introduction, performance combines psychological efficacy for the audience with staging of the performers, and the time has come to turn our attention to the performers themselves.

The phrase "staging the performer" can mean various things. Performers present themselves both visually and as speakers. These two dimensions of their communication about themselves necessarily interact, whether they reinforce one another or play off one another in creating a composite statement of identity. We must therefore keep in mind the visual, physical part of performance when we analyze texts for their gendering of the speakers, even though we can only guess at the effect of bodies moving rhythmically, of distinctive dress or nudity, of movement within significant spaces. Sexuality is always present when bodies are on display. We need only recall the spectators' shouts of amazement at Antheia and Habrokomes as they lead their respective age-mates in procession at the beginning of the *Ephesiaka* (1.2) by Xenophon of Ephesos or the effect on the crowd of the procession at Delphi in Heliodoros' *Aithiopika* (3.2–3) to conjure up the excitement generated by visually pleasing performers.

An audience will interpret the statements that performers make within the framework created by the performers' physical appearance, movements, location, so their speech will automatically be perceived as gendered. But the speech of performers also adds to the gender identity that they fabricate in performance, extending or modifying the meaning of visual clues. Thus performers may go beyond representation of their "real" identity to idealized versions of themselves. Boys who recited Solon's poetry at the Apatouria were adopting a "voice" that their physical development belied and thereby anticipating their future role as (male) citizens.[1] Performers' social status and reputation must also have influenced the total effect, but that part of the mix is more difficult to trace than

---

[1] Plato *Timaeus* 21b.

the interaction of body and words. Thersites speaking does not have the same effect as Achilles; Achilles is beautiful and noble, while Thersites is ugly and has no honor (*Iliad* 2.211–23).

It is obvious, then, that performers can stage their gender identity through performance: they present themselves visually while speaking about their sense of themselves. In effect they publicly demonstrate their internalization of their gender roles, while reinforcing the construction of those roles for the audience. Plato's account of the effectiveness of choral performance as education explains perfectly how it functions as a system for the reproduction of gender ideology.[2]

In this chapter I take up performance by women. I study women's performance before men's not only as an indication of my own interest but also because texts for women's performance articulate their gender identity much more explicitly than do texts for men's performance. Female performers, at least *parthenoi* for whom alone we have actual texts of any length, declare themselves to be female and express the implications thereof. Male identity is both so much a norm and so extensively manipulated that paradoxically we can best approach it in light of women's performance. To put it another way, women claimed the gender roles that the society assigned them and only those roles; any idealized identity they might adopt remained tied to the kind of character expected of them in fact. Men's metaphorical gendering was much more wide-ranging.

Women performed within the community in many places.[3] Choruses of women performing in public at Sparta, Arcadia, and Athens were mentioned in the last chapter; and female performers are attested from Thebes, Delos, Delphi, Elis, Aigina, Lesbos, Rhegion, Argos, Ephesos, and elsewhere.[4] In *Laws* 12 (947d) Plato specifies that at state funerals girls (*korai*) and women past childbearing age should march in the procession. Perhaps these are the two groups who regularly performed in public.[5]

But between their gender and their public speaking *about themselves* a contradiction hovers: according to the construction of gender in Greece men, not women, had the right to define women's identity, but when women spoke in public about themselves they appeared to be articulating

[2] See the Introduction and cf. Butler 1990.

[3] In the Hellenistic period women traveled in order to perform and even competed in poetic contests: see Pomeroy 1977: 54–55.

[4] Calame 1977: I passim is a wonderful collection of evidence for performance by *parthenoi*, although his study of choruses of *parthenoi* treats them all as participating in initiatory rituals, not public address. Prudhommeau 1965: pls. 6–8 shows choruses of women on Greek vases. Webster 1970: 6 gives early (eighth century) archaeological evidence for women's dances; it adds attestation from Mycenae, Tiryns, Tegea, and Corinth to the places I have listed.

[5] Cf. Sappho 44.25–31 *V* where the same two groups are mentioned.

their own identity.[6] One could respond that most public performance by women was based on traditional texts or texts composed by men; that fact is very important, for it clearly represents one of the forms of social control exercised. Yet it does not entirely answer the question, in part because women in performance would still be perceived as speaking about themselves. The answer is inadequate in a more important way, too, because the conflict is reproduced in performance itself. If women are to exhibit formally their internalization of the commandments of gender ideology, they must have a public "voice," the authority to make themselves heard in public. But if they do internalize the prescriptions of the social system, then they must renounce a public voice.[7] What is needed is that they should publicly demonstrate their lack of voice. The question posed by the very project of studying women's gendered self-presentation in performance, then, is how texts for women's performance negotiate this contradiction in order to domesticate women's speaking about their gender identity.

The two statuses *gynaikes* (married women) and *parthenoi* (unmarried women) were kept apart. The surviving poetry is largely for performance by *parthenoi,* so the analysis will perforce concentrate on them initially. They are the ones who had to show that they understood the proper exercise of their sexuality—an issue of burning interest to the community.[8] Since almost no poetry performed by *gynaikes* survives, we cannot directly compare the self-presentation of the two groups, but clearly performance will have had a different function in the case of married women. I will consider some references to performance by *gynaikes* later which will tell us something about the stories that they told or to which they alluded in performance.

The most important fragment of a choral piece for *parthenoi* is Alkman's *Louvre partheneion* (1 *PMGF* = 3 *C*), of which the first part has already been scrutinized in Chapter 1.[9] Here I examine the latter part of the poem, in which the *parthenoi* speak of themselves. It will be the paradigm example for this chapter also, since it so clearly reveals contradiction and, when viewed as a whole, the complexity of the social transactions negotiated through the performance of *parthenoi*. Since we are now examining the

[6] The contradiction of women speaking in public has been studied in the case of tragedy. See especially Goff 1990 and Zeitlin 1990 (esp. 85: a woman speaking on the stage transgresses the social rules if she speaks on her own behalf).

[7] MacMullen 1980: 216 remarks that although women held public offices in the Roman Empire they seldom filled roles requiring them to speak in public.

[8] On song as education in sexuality for *parthenoi,* see Hallett 1979.

[9] For the circumstances of performance, see Ch. 1 and Most 1982: 91–92. Most thinks that only Agido is being presented as ready for marriage, but with that difference our views are compatible.

singer–dancers' self-presentation, the nature of the audience is of paramount importance. In Chapter 1 I argued for public performance, not performance within a self-contained initiatory group, and will assume here that the *parthenoi* speak to the Spartan community at large.

As I pointed out in Chapter 1, the *parthenoi* maintain a communal perspective by suggesting that the audience's gaze at the women praised is more persuasive than their own words; thus they hint from the beginning at the inadequacy and superfluity of their speech. In none of the other communal poems examined in Chapter 1 do the performers renounce their words. Furthermore, it may not be pure accident that the two verbs preserved from the mythical section express a negative relationship to the figures spoken of: οὐκ] . . . ἀλέγω (2, "I do [not] count") and παρήσομες (12, "we will pass over"). If it is not chance, then the *parthenoi* systematically avoid assertions that are both positive grammatically and affirmative in meaning about the status of the mythic figures (see pp. 30, 33). Some commentators restore a negative in front of παρήσομες. That would produce a negative grammatical structure, litotes, but an affirmative stance toward the heroes. Throughout the early part of the poem, then, the *parthenoi* use modes of expression whose negativity or abdication undermines the authority of their voices even as they offer reflection and model to the audience.

In the latter part of the *partheneion,* the inadequacy of the performers becomes an explicit theme. The *parthenoi* depreciate both their voices and their sexual attractiveness. I will look at their treatment of their voices first. Because I will be discussing the poem in detail, it is easiest to quote the whole latter section now (57–101):

>   Ἀγησιχόρα μὲν αὖτα·
>   ἁ δὲ δευτέρα πεδ' Ἀγιδὼ τὸ ϝεῖδος
>   ἵππος Ἰβηνῶι Κολαξαῖος δραμήται·
> 60   ταὶ Πεληάδες γὰρ ἇμιν
>   ὀρθρίαι φᾶρος φεροίσαις
>   νύκτα δι' ἀμβροσίαν ἅτε σήριον
>   ἄστρον ἀυηρομέναι μάχονται·
>
>   οὔτε γάρ τι πορφύρας
> 65   τόσσος κόρος ὥστ' ἀμύναι,
>   οὔτε ποικίλος δράκων
>   παγχρύσιος, οὐδὲ μίτρα
>   Λυδία, νεανίδων
>   ἰανογ[λ]εφάρων ἄγαλμα,

70 οὐδὲ ταὶ Ναννῶς κόμαι,
    ἀλλ' οὐ[δ'] Ἀρέτα σιειδής,
    οὐδὲ Σύλακίς τε καὶ Κλεησισήρα,
    οὐδ' ἐς Αἰνησιμβρ[ό]τας ἐνθοῖσα φασεῖς·
    Ἀσταφίς [τ]έ μοι γένοιτο
75 καὶ ποτιγλέποι Φίλυλλα
    Δαμαρ[έ]τα τ' ἐρατά τε ϝιανθεμίς·
    ἀλλ' Ἁγησιχόρα με τηρεῖ.¹⁰
    ──────
    οὐ γὰρ ἁ κ[α]λλίσφυρος
    Ἁγησιχ[ό]ρ[α] πάρ' αὐτεῖ,
80 Ἀγιδοῖ [ ]αρμένει
    θωστήρ[ιά τ'] ἄμ' ἐπαινεῖ.
    ἀλλὰ τᾶν [   ]σιοὶ
    δέξασθε· [σι]ῶν γὰρ ἄνα
    καὶ τέλος· [χο]ροστάτις,
85 ϝείποιμί κ', [ἐ]γὼν μὲν αὐτὰ
    παρσένος μάταν ἀπὸ θράνω λέλακα
    γλαύξ· ἐγὼ[ν] δὲ τᾶι μὲν Ἀώτι μάλιστα
    ϝανδάνην ἐρῶ· πόνων γὰρ
    ἄμιν ἰάτωρ ἔγεντο·
90 ἐξ Ἁγησιχόρ[ας] δὲ νεάνιδες
    ἰρ]ήνας ἐρατ[ᾶ]ς ἐπέβαν·
    ──────
    τῶ]ι τε γὰρ σηραφόρωι
      ]τῶς εδ[
    τ[ῶι] κυβερνάται δὲ χρὴ
95 κ[ἠ]ν νᾶϊ μάλιστ' ἀκούην·
    ἁ δὲ τᾶν Σηρην[ί]δων
    ἀοιδοτέρα μ[ὲν οὐχί,
    σιαὶ γάρ, ἀντ[ὶ δ' ἔνδεκα
    παίδων δεκ[ὰς ὡς ἀείδ]ει·¹¹

¹⁰ I depart here from the text of *PMGF.* Hooker 1979: 220 opts for τηρεῖ and Campbell 1992 prints it. On the alternative, see below.
¹¹ I substitute ὡς from Puelma 1977: 46 for ἅδ' printed by *PMGF.* Accepting from schol. A *ad* 98, p. 31 *PMGF,* that "ten" and "eleven" are juxtaposed, Puelma thinks that 98–99 say that she sings like ten over against a chorus of eleven. Robbins 1994: 10 adopts this view. Davies's text makes 98–99 a parenthetical reference to the chorus; likewise Calame 1977: II 130–32 and 142–43n.9. The lines and scholia are too damaged to supplement with any confidence.

100   φθέγγεται δ' [ἄρ'] ὥ[τ' ἐπὶ] Ξάνθω ῥοαῖσι
κύκνος· ἁ δ' ἐπιμέρωι ξανθᾶι κομίσκαι

Here is Hagesichora herself.[12] The second in beauty after Agido will run with her as a Kolaxian horse with an Ibenian one,[13] for the Peleades, rising like Sirius through the ambrosial night as we carry a plow (or robe) to Orthria (Dawn-goddess), fight with us. For a surfeit of purple cloth is not enough to provide defence[14] nor is an intricate golden serpent-bracelet nor a Lydian headdress, ornament of violet-eyed young women, nor the hair of Nanno, and further neither godlike Areta (is able) nor Thylakis and Kleesithera, nor will you go to Ainesimbrota's and say, "Might Astaphis be mine and might Philylla and Damareta and lovely Wianthemis look toward me," but Hagesichora guards me.[15] For the lovely-ankled Hagesichora is not nearby [but] she stands [beside] Agido and praises our sacrificial offerings. But receive their [prayers?], gods; for the accomplishment and end belong to the [gods]. Chorus-leader, I would say (if I may): I myself, a *parthenos,* screech in vain from the roofbeam, an owl; yet I long especially to please Aotis (= Orthria). For she is the healer of toil for us; but young women enter into delightful peace by Hagesichora's agency. For just as to the trace-horse [   ] and it is necessary to listen especially to the steersman also in a ship. But she (Hagesichora) than the Sirens is [not] more songful, for they are goddesses, but [she sings like ?] ten over against [eleven?] children; and she gives voice [just as at ?] the streams of Xanthos the swan (does); but she with (?) lovely light brown ringlets . . . "

The climax of the poem from the point of view of the ritual is the request to the gods in lines 82–83. At that point, at which the *parthenoi* take on the burden of communal representation most decisively, they most fully possess authority transferred from the community. Directly after the line in which they address the gods (for δέξασθε must have the gods as its recipient), the *parthenoi* disavow the power they had momentarily wielded. They turn to address the chorus-leader Hagesichora instead, with a deferential request to speak. In explanation of their request, the *parthenoi* assert their own inadequacy: "I myself, a *parthenos,* screech in vain from the roofbeam, an owl." The owl's screeching is ugly, so the chorus-members

[12] The translation offered is my interpretation of lines that can be taken in a number of different ways. There are numerous problems in these lines whose solution does not affect my argument and which I pass over in silence.

[13] The interpretation of these lines is disputed. I follow West 1965a: 197 in thinking that neither woman is directly compared with the other. Cf. Ch. 1 n.40.

[14] Earlier scholars supplied ἔστιν ἁμιν and took this sentence to say, "I do not have such an abundance of purple, etc., as to ward off" the Pleiades. So, e.g., van Groningen 1935–36: 254 (although he makes it a question). But Puelma 1977: 37–38n.68 makes τόσσος predicative and assumes τοῖος ὥστ' ἀμῦναι with the following items. Although less easy, this view makes more sense of Nanno's hair.

[15] The alternative reading here is "wears me down." See below.

cast aspersion on the delight they can give as performers.[16] But the word
μάταν (86, "in vain") implies that more than aesthetics is involved: they
wish to speak, but their utterance is ritually futile. Worse, an owl's hoot
was ill-omened.[17] The performers say that because they are *parthenoi* their
act of speaking will destroy the meaning of what they want to say. Furthermore, Hagesichora is elsewhere, not nearby to grant permission.[18]
The status of their speech becomes dubious. Here is an interim solution to
the contradiction of women's speaking in public: the performers themselves can disavow their own voices.

On the other hand, complete deficiency on the part of the *parthenoi*
would threaten the ceremony. They immediately reestablish an attitude of
reverence to preserve the connection with the deity in whose honor they
sing. But now the link is based on their desire. The Greek word ἐρῶ (88)
denotes longing or yearning. As Plato defined it much later, it is desire for
what one cannot have.[19] Without importing that crystallization into this
text, we can use it to measure the significance of the way the *parthenoi*
position themselves. Their appeal to the goddess is based on their perception of the distance between themselves and what is pleasing; they substitute longing for success as their offering to her in place of brilliance.

The chorus explains the consequences of having a desire that falls short
of fulfillment in the following lines. The goddess Aotis is healer of toils for
the community, but the chorus-members must arrive at a happy state
through Hagesichora's agency: they must rely on her to include them in
the new state of peace that the goddess brings to the group and obey her as
those on shipboard obey the steersman (90–95). In this final statement of
their position, the chorus-members have produced a more stable solution
to the contradiction. They interpret their performance as an act of obedience to the chorus leader, through whom their words must be channeled
to acquire meaning. From this ground they turn again to praise Hagesichora (96–101).

The chorus's final praise of Hagesichora is based on difference: she is
wonderful because she is so much better than they. Thus they can praise
without authority. And because they have established themselves as the
negative term of the comparison, whatever beauty and delight they in fact
create goes to exalt Hagesichora. In this scheme the *parthenoi* stand in for
men in praising Hagesichora, while she stands in for men in commanding
the obedience of the *parthenoi* when she is implicitly compared to a steersman. The imagery makes the gender switch evident in her case so that

[16] On the ugliness of the owl's cry, see Calame 1983: 343 s.v. γλαύξ. The verb λέλακα
(I screech) in the perfect is typically used of animals.
[17] Van Groningen 1935–36: 257.
[18] Some editors put a question mark at the end of 79: "Is Hagesichora not nearby?"
[19] *Symp*. 200e.

when the *parthenoi* refer their speaking to her they can acknowledge the real source of authority.

In attributing their legitimation to Hagesichora, the *parthenoi* only displace the problem of women's public speaking. Hagesichora apparently does not participate in performance of this poem, but she must have sung (100). Consequently, at the end of this poem, a parallel process of (partially) deauthorizing Hagesichora works to destabilize the displacement. Lines 96–101 are very lacunose, but their strategy is detectable. The first sentence seems to be about to compare Hagesichora's singing favorably with the song of the Sirens, the bird-women who inhabit a rock by a distant sea.[20] Yet the sentence almost certainly ended in a negative; Hagesichora cannot sing like them. Instead she can sing as well as ten children (?) or a swan. Hagesichora is implicitly denied adult human social status and her voice lauded as beautiful by means of a simile that confines it to aesthetic power. The cry of the owl is both ugly and ill-omened; Hagesichora's swan is contrasted on the scale of beauty and does not have negative ritual connotations, but she is left without claim to the significant speech characteristic of men.[21] She is demoted from her momentary authority just as the *parthenoi* had retreated from authority after their address to the gods.

Still, the complete solution contained in the poem to the problem of women performing is not yet exposed. Since this is a poem about the sexual attractiveness of young women, the contradiction I spoke of takes in not just women's public speaking but women as subjects of their bodies. Greek culture generally insisted on a construction of the socially acceptable female body as sexually passive. One consequence is that women could praise other women sexually without compromising men's appropriation of those women; for that reason the performance of *parthenoi* is necessary to present women to the community. But how can *parthenoi* speak of other women without adopting a notion of their own value that might lead to assertion of control over their bodies? The poem solves this aspect of the contradiction by alienating the *parthenoi* from their bodies through self-depreciation: like their voices, the bodies of the *parthenoi* are staged as deficient. The contrast of owl and swan that characterizes the two in terms of voice has implications for their visual attractiveness as

---

[20] On Sirens see below. Alkman places "Siren" in apposition to the Muse in a choral context in 30 *PMGF*, where he also uses the verb κέκλαγ' (screams), often used of birds and seldom of articulate speech (so *LSJ* s.v.).

[21] Cf. Alkman 39 *PMGF* = 91 *C* and Calame 1983 *ad loc*. The lines may say, "Alkman discovered these words and song by heeding the talkative voice of partridges." If, as Calame suggests, this fragment comes from a *partheneion*, then the singers both identify their own song with that of a bird and attribute the translation into human terms, the interpretive activity, to Alkman. But see Gallavotti 1972 for a different reading.

well. It is in fact part of a system of comparisons in sensuous terms between Hagesichora and the *parthenoi* who praise her.

But before this effect can be demonstrated, it is necessary to take a position on the meaning of the intensely debated lines 60–63 and on the train of thought leading up to and away from them. We will have to detour through an investigation of the festival before returning to the *parthenoi*. I begin from the premise that the language is straightforward, while the difficulty lies in the denseness of the thought patterns absorbed in it.

The clause of 60–63 says, " . . . for the Peleades, rising like Sirius through the ambrosial night as we carry a plow to Orthria, fight with us." Who are the Peleades and in what sense do they "fight" with us? The word means "dove." Three views on the identity of the Peleades have supporters: the term refers to a rival chorus, or to Hagesichora and Agido, or to the star cluster, the Pleiades.[22] Since the name Peleades appears in the description of a ritual for a goddess of the dawn and they are said to be "rising," it is most natural to take them as the star cluster.[23] So we have the line, "the star cluster 'fights' with us." Most interpretations of the verb *fights* attempt to drain it of at least some of its hostility.[24] But the Pleiades are in fact potentially inimical. Anne Burnett has pointed out that the Pleiades are a sign of the change of season.[25] At their heliacal rising in mid-

[22] The first has little support now. Page 1951: 52–57 chooses it, followed by, e.g., Bowra 1961: 56–57, 60; Eisenberger 1991: 283 (seeing it as a riddle). Rosenmeyer 1966 defends the idea that the *partheneion* was sung by competing half-choruses. Schol. A *ad* 60ff., p. 31 *PMGF,* identifies Agido and Hagesichora with doves (i.e., the Peleades) and is followed by, e.g., Caudatella 1972: 28; Calame 1977: II 72; Puelma 1977: 33–35; *PMGF* p. 30; Robbins 1994: 9. Diels 1896: 360 thinks that the grammar is against it. Schol. B fr. 6 col. ii 16–22, p. 33 *PMGF* appears to also; Barrett 1961: 686 remarks that the fragment is "very little help" but points out that the scholiasts knew of more than one interpretation of the passage. For the view that the Pleiades are meant, see the next note. Bowra's agonizing (1961: 54–60) is a good exposé of the problems. For more complete bibliography, see Calame 1977: II 72–73n.52; Gerber 1987; *PMGF* ad loc.

[23] Davison 1968: 159–61 takes the Peleades as the constellation. The comparison with Sirius is often felt to be a problem for this view since the Pleiades are dim. The meaning of μάχονται is another: how do stars fight with a chorus? Davison solves both problems by pointing out that the Pleiades must be baleful. I think that this is right; see below. Burnett 1964: 31–32 also understands the Peleades as the stars but takes the comparison to be in the idea of rising and the "fight" to be the young women's race to complete their ritual before sunrise. Diels 1896: 359–60 and West 1965a: 197 interpret "Peleades" as the star-cluster standing for a chorus.

[24] E.g., Puelma 1977: 36n.66, who says that despite paucity of evidence from the archaic period one must take it in a weakened sense: the two leaders "contend" with the chorus. Davison 1968: 159 points out that the word refers to physical struggle. Calame 1983 *ad* 60–63 and Caudatella 1972: 29 keep the meaning "fight" and argue for taking the dative to mean "on our behalf." *PMGF* notes: "μάχονται quid significet incertum."

[25] Burnett 1964: 32; likewise Diels 1896: 359–60. Burnett cites the passage from Hesiod given just below but gives a positive tone to the idea of summer.

May, they usher in summer heat and the beginning of harvest.[26] If we look at Hesiod, *Works and Days* 571–81, we see that heat is the enemy and Dawn the helper; the work of harvesting is the toil at which Dawn assists:

> ἀλλ' ὁπότ' ἂν φερέοικος ἀπὸ χθονὸς ἂμ φυτὰ βαίνῃ
> Πληιάδας φεύγων, τότε δὴ σκάφος οὐκέτι οἰνέων,
> ἀλλ' ἅρπας τε χαρασσέμεναι καὶ δμῶας ἐγείρειν.
> φεύγειν δὲ σκιεροὺς θώκους καὶ ἐπ' ἠῶ κοῖτον
> 575 ὥρῃ ἐν ἀμήτου, ὅτε τ' ἠέλιος χρόα κάρφει·
> τημοῦτος σπεύδειν καὶ οἴκαδε καρπὸν ἀγινεῖν
> ὄρθρου ἀνιστάμενος, ἵνα τοι βίος ἄρκιος εἴη.
> ἠὼς γάρ τ' ἔργοιο τρίτην ἀπομείρεται αἶσαν·
> ἠώς τοι προφέρει μὲν ὁδοῦ, προφέρει δὲ καὶ ἔργου,
> 580 ἠώς, ἥ τε φανεῖσα πολέας ἐπέβησε κελεύθου
> ἀνθρώπους, πολλοῖσι δ' ἐπὶ ζυγὰ βουσὶ τίθησιν.

But whenever the snail climbs up plant-stalks away from the earth fleeing the Pleiades, then indeed there is no longer digging of the vines, but (one should) sharpen the sickles and rouse the slaves. Flee shady seats and sleeping in until dawn in the harvest season when the sun parches the skin; at this time put your energy into it and bring home the grain, rising at morning twilight in order that you have sufficient sustenance. For dawn gives out a third share of the work; dawn puts you ahead on the road, puts you ahead in work also, dawn, who when she appears sets many people on their path and places yokes on many oxen.

The tone of Hesiod's paragraph is very different from Alkman's, but the nexus of thought may be the same without any direct influence either way.[27] In Hesiod the Pleiades stand in for heat that makes the ground burn and dries out the skin and enervates the laborer.[28] Dawn is personified because its relief is so crucial to getting the work done (and it brings dew to keep the grain from burning).[29] Summer follows in Hesiod's text, with

[26] Rising just before sunrise is the heliacal rising. See West 1978 *ad* 383–84 for calculation that the date was May 11. Cf. also West's chart on 253 for the farmer's year divided by the position of the Pleiades, Sirius, Orion, Arcturus, and the solstices.

[27] Caudatella 1972: 36 cites *WD* 614–17, where the setting of the Pleiades is the sign that it is time to plow. He suggests that the plow in the song is not an offering but a badge of identity for the chorus, whose name is punningly equated with the star-cluster. Thus the Peleades are Agido and Hagesichora, the chorus, and the stars.

[28] Schol. *ad loc.* makes the connection between the Pleiades and heat: see Brumfield 1981: 31. Cf. Nilsson 1957: 7–8 on a sacrifice to Zeus "Ikmaios" on Keos for help in averting summer heat, attested by Apollonios of Rhodes, *Argonautica* 2.518–29. As Nilsson observes, the name Ikmaios shows that Zeus is here the dew- and rain-god.

[29] Petropoulos 1994: 19–25 describes the "grueling" task of harvest in modern Greece:

Sirius as its symbol (587), as the next stage in the progression of the year. In Alkman the Pleiades, "like Sirius" (the star most associated with heat), beset or fight with the community, while in lines 88–89 the goddess of the dawn heals the labors of the community.[30] Note that ἇμιν (to/for/with us), referring to the community as a whole, occurs in both passages.[31] The verb μάχονται (fight) is metaphorical in this interpretation, as in other explanations of the sentence, but it does retain its full meaning of hostile attack. It also gains relevance to the central ceremony, the community's counterattack through its ritual for the Dawn goddess. If Alkman's song is for a preharvest ceremony to a goddess whose composite identity includes association with the dawn, then nothing is strange about setting her in opposition to the threatening heat of summer.[32] Goddesses who have been suggested include Artemis, Helen, Eileithyia, Aphrodite, and the Leukippid Phoibe, all of whom could be connected with the dawn.[33] What is more, the plow, if that is what the chorus was carrying to dedicate to the goddess, may have been in token of work now complete. Farmers plowed not just to raise furrows for seed but also (like the digging that Hesiod mentions) to keep the ground open in vineyards and orchards so that it could absorb moisture. Such plowing comes to an end in the summer.[34]

If heat and harvest are the subject of lines 60–63, what do they have to do with the lines before and after? In that question lies the central bewilderment of this poem. The logical structure of the sequence is as follows: two beautiful women are present, *for* the Peleades fight with us, *for* surfeit of purple and so on are not enough to provide a defense, and godlike Areta and others (cannot), but Hagesichora protects me.[35] Women's splendor is

"The harvest begins at dawn, when the stalks are still damp with dew and more easily cut. An early start will ensure a few hours of relatively comfortable work; after 10 o'clock the heat scorches" (21).

[30] The Pleiades are not "like" Sirius in brightness, but in their agricultural implications. Those who see in the comparison to Sirius a compliment to the beauty of Hagesichora and Agido ignore the negative associations of the star.

[31] On ἇμιν, see Ch. 1, pp. 37–38. A feminine participle agrees with the pronoun in 60, but I argue in Ch. 1 that it unites the community with the chorus in the ritual.

[32] See Nilsson 1957: 113–15 on preharvest festivals in May. Davison 1968: 159–60 suggests the Athenian Thargelia as an analogy.

[33] Calame 1977: II 122 argues for Helen and gives a list (121n.146) of earlier suggestions, mainly various forms of Artemis. Page 1951: 71–82 and Davison 1968: 154–57 and 165–69 think that ancient commentators were probably right that it was Orthia. Burnett 1964: 32–33 proposes Eileithyia. Gentili 1988: 75 suggests Aphrodite (= morning star). Phoibe is put forward by Garvie 1965 and adopted by Robbins 1994: 14.

[34] Brumfield 1981: 30–32. An Athenian festival offers a parallel, the Skira, which was an early-summer women's festival that included a procession to Skiron and a ritual plowing. See Deubner 1962: 40–50, esp. 47–48.

[35] The other interpretation of this verb is τείρει (exhausts, wears out). τείρει is found in the papyrus of both the poem and a commentary (schol. B fr. 7 col. i(b), p. 34 *PMGF*). The

somehow crucial to fighting the threat of the Peleades.[36] The most eco-
nomical explanation is that a beautiful woman was pleasing to the goddess
of the dawn.[37] Other festivals are known in which it is specified that the
most good-looking man or woman should have a special role.[38] Perhaps
here a specially chosen woman was to lead the chorus and participate in the
act of making the offering; she is called Hagesichora on this occasion, or
always.[39] If the goddess was any of those mentioned just above in connection with the dawn, her interest in marriageable young women would be
natural, for all are also connected with marriage or childbirth. The ceremony would have a composite character as preparation for harvest and
showing off of young women ready to marry.[40] The plow, then, may
have a second meaning as well as its agricultural symbolism. Plowing is
common imagery for sexual intercourse, perhaps particularly for intercourse within marriage.[41] If so, then fostering of harvest and mar-

difference depends on distinctions in spelling that were not made in the original script, as
Davison 1968: 189–90 points out. Those who read "exhausts" take it in an erotic sense, citing
Hesiod fr. 298 *MW* and Telestes 805 *PMG*. But in those lines the subject is δεινὸς ἔρως and
ὀξὺς ἔρως respectively. The verb describes what a *harsh* desire does to someone; it does not in
itself have any erotic overtones. Nor can the statement "Hagesichora wears me down" be
taken as the equivalent of "love wears me down." Page 1959: 19 cites σοῦ τρυχόμεθα at *Peace*
989, but it is not parallel since the genitive does not represent the agent. As Bowra 1961: 61
says, τείρει does not naturally refer to love; he suggests "Hagesichora wears me out (with
praising her)."

[36] See Page 1951: 52n.1 on the meaning of ἀμύνειν.

[37] Diels 1896: 369 points out that the goddess's anger must be softened by beauty. Similarly Puelma 1977: 52. Athenaios 13, 566a quotes Herakleides Lembos as saying that at
Sparta the most beautiful man and most beautiful woman are marveled at; perhaps the remark points to a ritual judgment.

[38] Nilsson 1957: 57 and 94 understands the "beauty contests" attested on Lesbos (Alkaios
130B.17–20 *V*) and elsewhere as a ritual choice of the most beautiful to approach the divinity.
The priest of Apollo at Thebes had to be of good appearance according to Pausanias 9.10.4.
Pausanias 9.22.1 says that at Tanagra the most handsome youth carries a ram for Hermes.
Athenaios 13, 609e–610a, citing Theophrastos and others, mentions contests also at Tenedos,
Basilis, and Elis. The last is for men, with prizes, and the winner, decked with ribbons, leads
a procession to the temple of Athena; see also Athenaios 565f and Crowther 1985: 285–86.
Graf 1985: 275 gives an overview of evidence for "beauty-contests" for women in connection
with the contest at Basilis. Cf. also Graf 60–61: some kind of contest for girls is attested by
inscription in connection with the cult of Leto on Chios. Cf. Hdt. 4.180.3 on a Libyan
custom, Redfield 1990b: esp. 125 for a ritual *aition* that involves a specially beautiful man and
woman. Aristophanes *Lys.* 1314–15 describes Helen as the "pure, beautiful chorus-leader" of
Spartan maiden-choruses, a hint that Spartan chorus-leaders were chosen for their beauty.

[39] I agree with Nagy 1990b: 345–49 that Hagesichora (Chorus-leader) is probably the
name granted to the young woman chosen each year to play the role.

[40] Calame 1986: 161 points out the connection between agriculture and marriage in a
different Spartan ritual directed to Hera.

[41] As Burnett 1964: 34n.22 points out.

riage/production of children in the face of heat were intertwined motifs at the heart of the ceremony.

The train of thought is then: here is Hagesichora in her beauty (and Agido is outstanding too), for the Peleades are hostile, for I cannot combat them by showing my splendor, but Hagesichora will win the goddess's help. The audience must accept Hagesichora's beauty in order for the ritual to be efficacious. Note that on this interpretation the poem-as-model would expand to preparation for harvest, which would engage the whole community, as well as preparation for marriage. The role of the chorus has more to do with the latter, but the two ideas are amalgamated.

The chorus in fact distinguishes two aspects of the ritual in lines 88–91. The goddess is a healer of toils, but young women enter into delightful peace by agency of Hagesichora.[42] Earlier it was suggested that Hagesichora was the intermediary through whom the chorus participated in the ritual and its rewards. Now one could surmise that "peace" refers to the marriage aspect of the festival and healing of toil to the agricultural one. The two aspects are deeply linked, of course, by the agricultural view of women so endemic to Greek cultural imagery.[43] Two passages from the *Works and Days* illuminate the threat that heat poses to *parthenoi* and the use of the term *peace* to describe their successful escape from its force.

The first passage follows shortly after the lines quoted above and describes high summer. When the cicada sings (585–88):

585   τῆμος πιόταταί τ' αἶγες καὶ οἶνος ἄριστος,

μαχλόταται δὲ γυναῖκες, ἀφαυρότατοι δέ τοι ἄνδρες

εἰσίν, ἐπεὶ κεφαλὴν καὶ γούνατα Σείριος ἄζει,

αὐαλέος δέ τε χρὼς ὑπὸ καύματος·

Then goats are fattest and wine best, women most lusty and men most limp, since Sirius desiccates the head and knees and the skin is parched with heat.

The threat that the "Peleades, rising like Sirius through the ambrosial night" bring to the *parthenoi* is one of sexual disorder. Hesiod's view of the problem is the opposite of what Alkman's text and the image of the Pleiades (who flee Orion) overtly suggest. For Alkman the expressed problem is male violence and persuading men to pick the right women; but the problem of overlusty women arises very obliquely in Alkman's poem in that the *parthenoi* are staged as renouncing the possibility for themselves. To see how they are doing so, we can compare Hesiod's un-

---

[42] I take the aorists in 89 and 91 as gnomic.

[43] duBois 1988: 39–85. Puelma 1977: 22n.50 compares *Orphic Hymn* 2.2ff. for πόνος and 36.4ff. for εἰρήνη, both in connection with childbirth. Calame 1977: II 116–20 connects them with the process of initiation.

packing of the word *peace* in the second of the two passages from the *Works and Days* (225–35):

225 οἳ δὲ δίκας ξείνοισι καὶ ἐνδήμοισι διδοῦσιν
ἰθείας καὶ μή τι παρεκβαίνουσι δικαίου,
τοῖσι τέθηλε πόλις, λαοὶ δ᾽ ἀνθέουσιν ἐν αὐτῇ·
Εἰρήνη δ᾽ ἀνὰ γῆν κουροτρόφος, οὐδέ ποτ᾽ αὐτοῖς
ἀργαλέον πόλεμον τεκμαίρεται εὐρύοπα Ζεύς·
230 οὐδέ ποτ᾽ ἰθυδίκῃσι μετ᾽ ἀνδράσι Λιμὸς ὀπηδεῖ
οὐδ᾽ Ἄτη, θαλίῃς δὲ μεμηλότα ἔργα νέμονται.
τοῖσι φέρει μὲν γαῖα πολὺν βίον, οὔρεσι δὲ δρῦς
ἄκρη μέν τε φέρει βαλάνους, μέσση δὲ μελίσσας·
εἰροπόκοι δ᾽ οἴες μαλλοῖς καταβεβρίθασιν·
235 τίκτουσιν δὲ γυναῖκες ἐοικότα τέκνα γονεῦσιν·

As to those who give straight judgments to strangers and fellow-townsmen and never deviate from the just, their city flourishes and the people in it blossom; Peace is a child-nurturer across the land, nor does wide-seeing Zeus assign painful war to them; nor does Hunger ever attend straight-judging men nor Ruin, and they enjoy the well-tended substance of lush growth. For the earth bears much sustenance for them and the hardwood in the mountains bears chestnuts on high, bees in the middle; the fleecy sheep are heavy with wool; and women give birth to children who resemble their fathers.

Peace, though subordinated to Hesiod's defense of δίκη (justice), is emotionally linked to reproductive abundance, agricultural and human, within a social order in which women confine sexual activity to relations with their husbands.[44] If "peace" in connection with young women means the same thing in Alkman as in Hesiod, then the parallel between the two results in Alkman's poem is obvious: just as the harvest will be successful with the help of the goddess, so the *parthenoi* will find orderly sexual fulfillment in marriage and reproduction with the help of Hagesichora. They will escape the violence of wanton sexuality induced by heat.[45] But we should note that in addition to heralding the summer heat, the Pleiades also evoke the opposite danger, namely that the *parthenoi* will refuse reproductive sexuality altogether.[46] As the Pleiades flee from Orion, so the Spartan virgin might reject all men. The desire for virginity equally in-

[44] See the parallels in Greek literature cited by West 1978 *ad loc.*, especially Herodotus 3.65.7: "may women and flocks give birth."

[45] On the connection between heat and female sexuality widely attested in Greek writing, see Carson 1990: 139–41.

[46] Cf. King 1993 on mythic expression of fear that the virgin's body will remain closed up and fail to bleed, that is, fail to become sexual.

volves a young woman's claiming control of her body and sexuality and so must equally, from the hegemonic viewpoint, be suppressed.

Now we can proceed to examine the poem's modes of alienating the *parthenoi* from their bodies. The *parthenoi* speak disparagingly of themselves. They also leave unexpressed the threat that they themselves pose—refusal of (exclusively) marital sexuality—while embracing the obedience that will avert it. These are linked phenomena; between them they work to hinder the possibility that the *parthenoi* will articulate either their desire or a subjectivity based on consciousness of beauty. Yet they are presenting themselves in public; are we meant to take their words about their deficient attractiveness at face value? The text and the occasion both suggest that we should not. The stanza 64ff. should be looked at again.

The *parthenoi* say that a surfeit of purple, a gold bracelet, and Lydian headdress cannot ward off the threat posed by the Pleiades (64–69). They may be wearing these things (although not necessarily; the statement may be a general observation), but the wealth of adornment does not make up for their deficiency in beauty. With Nanno's hair they switch to declaring themselves inadequate. The first items show that they are not proud on the basis of their families' wealth (while perhaps pointing out that wealth), but the list as a whole must have called attention to the disparity between their self-description and their actual appearance. It may stage them as attractive but unaware of it. This effect operates between the visual and verbal levels, creating figures whose perception is not directed to their own bodies. We must guess at it, but it only confirms an analogous effect within the language itself. The chorus-members insist on the inadequacy of their own beauty in a stanza swamped with negatives, yet the language is erotic. "Godlike" Areta cannot please the goddess. The projected subject ("nor will you go," 73) will *not* ask that "lovely" Wianthemis and Astaphis and Philylla and Damareta look toward her.[47] These may be fictitious names with respect to any given performance, but they are nonmythic, so they refer to *parthenoi* like those singing.[48] In the very act of denying that the addressee would want these young women to intercede with the goddess, the chorus supplies lover's phrases as a protreptic to the audience, and the negatives call attention to their own desirability. Nor are the terms λέλακα

[47] The participle in line 73, ἐνθοῖσα (going), is feminine singular. Calame 1977: I 26 takes it that the chorus members are speaking to each other, rejecting one another in favor of Hagesichora, whom they all desire. I assume with Burnett (1964: 34n. 17) that they are speaking to the audience, perhaps especially to the woman or women who chose Hagesichora (while the feminine participle avoids the representation of Spartan men as praising or seeking out *parthenoi*). Against the notion that the chorus members are rejecting alternatives to a liaison with Hagesichora is the conjunction *and* connecting the list of young women in 74–76.

[48] It is a generally accepted hypothesis that the names given are those of the chorus members. But if this poem was performed yearly, the names would not be those of the actual dancers.

(I screech) and γλαύξ (owl) a straightforward description of themselves or their singing. Throughout the latter part of the poem, the *parthenoi* present themselves through negatives designed to produce a double message for the audience, that they are desirable and that they are without knowledge of it.

Their self-presentation culminates in their statement that they must obey as those in a ship obey the steersman. Here is the key to the preceding: the *parthenoi* present themselves as trained to be compliant, to have no sense of authorization or power.[49] By virtue of this lack, they will enter into peace, that is, be fruitful within the structures of the social system. The stable solution that Alkman has found to the contradiction consists of absorbing it into the text itself and having the *parthenoi* stage it verbally as a disjunct between their bodies and their self-awareness. Their eroticism must not be suppressed any more than it is acknowledged, for they must accept husbands, but its expression must be at a nonverbal level.[50] The Spartans seem to have highlighted young women's beauty, as witness the worship of Helen. If an especially beautiful woman was chosen for the role of Hagesichora, then the value of women's beauty had ritual confirmation, but all others beside the one chosen could thereby be made to speak of themselves as "inadequate."[51]

The negative statements of the singers about themselves have of course been noticed, but usually to dismiss them. Claude Calame explains the chorus's "dissonance" as a sign that their initiation is not yet complete, and Glenn Most sees it as a mild form of apotropaic banter.[52] "Light-hearted joking" is another description.[53] However, the *parthenoi* probably did not present the lines as a joke, given the immediate context of appeal to the gods; it was left to the audience to find humor (or satisfaction) in their self-depreciation. Within a ritual and on the subject of women's sexuality, humor must be seen as a functional part of the composite presentation.

If the *parthenoi* are showing themselves and not just Hagesichora off to

[49] The Hippokoontid myth at the beginning of the poem may itself be about control of women.

[50] Cowan 1990: 198–205 analyzes the contradictory expectations the community has of women who present themselves in dance, who are judged by their attractiveness but always in danger of appearing immodest.

[51] If Hagesichora was chosen for her role by women, then she gained no public basis for high self-valuation vis-à-vis men, just as she was praised by *parthenoi* who acknowledged that they did not count. We do not know how she was positioned by the ceremony as a whole.

[52] Calame 1983: 343 s.v. λέλακα (cf. 1977: II 77–79). Most 1982: 92.

[53] Cf. Van Groningen 1935–36: 257; Segal 1985: 176. Gentili 1988: 74–75 explains that they resign themselves to losing the contest for the love of Hagesichora or Agido (since the poem celebrates a "wedding" between these two). Puelma 1977: 37 describes the lines as irony.

the audience, then the difference between them and Hagesichora is perhaps relatively minor. She is the one singled out by the ceremony as beautiful and as chorus-leader and adjutant in the ritual, but she may not be much older or more authoritative. In Euripides' *Electra* (175–80), Electra remarks that it does not please her to go to the festival of Hera and "direct choruses." She means, apparently, that because of her status she will be chosen as chorus-leader or expected to organize the dances.[54] Hagesichora's position is not necessarily much more official and long-term than that. However, the division between her and the chorus is useful for adjusting the poem to the prohibitions surrounding the construction of women's sexuality. Perhaps after all this emphasis on the poem's production of negative imagery, it should be said that the overall impression it gives is lively, colorful, and engaging. It naturalizes its effects very successfully.

In Chapter 1 I studied this poem as reflection and model for the community and concluded that the *parthenoi* urge young men to marry within the community while presenting Hagesichora and themselves as eligible. The results of that earlier discussion can be integrated with this one: the *parthenoi* explicitly warn against trying to win brides from elsewhere (figured as Aphrodite or a nymph) and implicitly demonstrate that they themselves will make good brides, neither fleeing nor causing trouble. The psychological efficacy they seek, therefore, lies in exerting centripetal sexual force. From this perspective women hold the community together; they draw men's emotional and sexual energy to themselves rather than allowing it to dissipate. We know that the Spartans relied on a closely knit, homogeneous social organization in order to maintain themselves in control of a subservient population. Alkman's poem predates the thoroughly militaristic system attested later, and it illustrates the role of public performance in maintaining both a cohesive ideology and an inward-focused social and sexual dynamic in Greek communities. A social hierarchy is probably also reinforced in performance, but that aspect is less perspicuous.

This interpretation of the poem is at odds with Claude Calame's view of it as part of initiatory ritual and a ritualized expression by *parthenoi* of desire for their chorus leader.[55] There is no direct evidence for a system of initia-

---

[54] See Denniston 1939 *ad* 178, who argues that the verb ἵστημι cannot of itself mean "participate in" a chorus but must mean "institute" or "direct" a chorus, although Electra envisions dancing as well. Calame 1977: I 96–99 connects the verb with the activity of the chorus-leader.

[55] Calame 1977: I passim. Diels 1896: 352–58 already outlines this interpretation, including a comparison with Sappho (on which see Ch. 6). Young women had choral groups and ritual groups; but there is no indication that these performed in private. With the exception of the interpretation of choral performance as closed, Calame's study is extremely valuable for every aspect of Alkman's poetry.

tions in the strict sense for young women at Sparta.[56] Alkman's poem, in fact, is thought to be one of the main supports for the hypothesis, based on a reading of it as the chorus's address to itself. Yet the *parthenoi* do not direct erotic language toward Hagesichora or Agido; the only suggestive language in the poem is in the lines in which the *parthenoi* assert that they themselves are not able to ward off danger. What they offer is praise, a well-attested function of choral poetry.

A similar process of deauthorization occurs in the only other *partheneion* (3 *PMGF* = 26 *C*) by Alkman of which more than scrappy fragments survive. In this poem both eroticism directed at a particular woman and reference to the public setting are found; it allows us to confirm that the *parthenoi* express in their own persons longing and admiration on behalf of the people as a whole. Much less of this poem is left than of the *Louvre partheneion*. Not enough survives to say how the chorus articulated the functions of reflection and modeling overall. The myth, assuming that the poem contained one, must have been located in the largely missing portion between the two preserved sections.[57] The papyrus does, however, preserve the opening lines, so we can get an impression both of the setting and of the method by which the *parthenoi* introduce themselves (1–10):

> Ὀλ]υμπιάδες περί με φρένας
>]ς ἀοιδας
>]ω δ' ἀκούσαι
>]ας ὀπός

[56] Calame 1977: I 372–74 argues from a phrase of Pindar's, Λάκαινα μὲν παρθένων ἀγέλα (112 *SM*, "a Spartan band of *parthenoi*," cited by Athenaios in a discussion of dance), that initiatory groups of young women organized in choruses were found at Sparta, parallel to the boys' ἀγέλαι. But Pindar need not refer to a specific institution in his use of ἀγέλα. Cf. fr. 122.17–20 *SM*:

> ὦ Κύπρου δέσποινα, τεὸν δεῦτ' ἐς ἄλσος
> φορβάδων κορᾶν ἀγέλαν ἑκατόγγυι-
> ον Ξενοφῶν τελέαις
> 20 ἐπάγαγ' εὐχωλαῖς ἰανθείς.

O mistress of Cyprus, here to your grove Xenophon led a hundred-limbed band of girls who graze, (Xenophon) cheered by the accomplishment of his prayers.

The reference is to Xenophon's gift of fifty sacred prostitutes to join those serving Aphrodite in her temple at Corinth.

[57] So Calame 1983: 395. At least one column of thirty lines intervened between the two legible portions.

5   ] .. ϱα καλὸν ὑμνιοισᾶν μέλος

    ] . οι

   ὕπνον ἀ]πὸ γλεφάϱων σκεδ[α]σεῖ γλυκύν

    ]ς δέ μ' ἄγει πεδ' ἀγῶγ' ἴμεν

   ἆχι μά]λιστα κόμ[αν ξ]ανθὰν τινάξω·

10   ] . σχ[ἁπ]αλοὶ πόδες[58]

The Olympian goddesses [fill?] me about my mind [with desire ?] for song, and
I [am eager ?] to hear the [ ] voice [ ] of (women) singing a beautiful
song [ ] will scatter sweet [sleep] from my eyelids and [ ] leads me to
go to the assembly [where] I will especially (?) shake my light brown hair.
[   ] tender feet

First we should look at the evidence for public performance. Line 8 refers
to an ἀγών, a public gathering ("assembly" rather than "contest").[59] The
speaker describes herself as waking and going to the ἀγών, which must be
the location where she is already singing. It has been suggested that a solo
singer sang the introduction to the song because it seems odd for performers to speak as though they had not yet begun to sing.[60] But the
"performative future" is well-attested, and Pindar uses the same device, as
Claude Calame points out.[61] This setting is again referred to in lines 73–
74, where the chorus puns on the name of Astymeloisa (Care of the city),
the woman who is singled out for attention:

   Ἀ]στυμέλοισα κατὰ στρατόν

    ] μέλημα δάμωι

Astymeloisa among the people [ ] darling of the community

These lines are apparently part of a description of what Astymeloisa is
doing at the moment of the song, so they should identify her location as
well.[62] By analogy with the *Louvre partheneion*, Astymeloisa may be the
chorus-leader, although nothing in the fragment indicates it.[63] This song,

[58] For the supplements suggested by Page and Barrett for the opening lines, see *PMGF ad
loc.* Calame 1983 *ad loc.* has a more complete apparatus.

[59] So Calame 1983 *ad loc.*

[60] Page 1959: 16–17; he rightly denies that it is Alkman speaking through the chorus but
does not think that the chorus would sing about itself in this way.

[61] Calame 1983 *ad loc.* with bibliography on previous views. Similarly *PMGF ad loc.* For
the performative future, see Slater 1969a.

[62] Even if they are more general, they depict Astymeloisa as the object of public attention.

[63] Calame 1977: II 92 makes this supposition.

then, appears to parallel the *Louvre partheneion* in that both praise the beauty of a woman who is engaged in ritual to a public audience.[64]

We can now examine the self-presentation of the *parthenoi*. In the extant portion the *parthenoi* give less attention to themselves than in the first poem, but they are the subject of the opening lines. There the chorus-members apparently wish to hear the voice of women singing a lovely tune, either themselves or, less likely, I think, the Muses (since humans do not listen to the Muses except to reproduce their song). In either case the chorus-members displace themselves as the subject of their activity; they want to hear a song rather than sing it. By this means they take on a generalized first person, speaking for rather than to the audience in their opening lines, reflecting the excitement of the day, but not as though they were its source. The speaker does not become the subject of a verb until the very last word of the stanza, τινάξω (I will shake). The following line has "tender feet" visible in the nominative, which means that the chorus-members immediately lose their position as subject. As in the first *partheneion,* the *parthenoi* are dissociated from subjectivity over their bodies and voices.

When the papyrus becomes legible again, the chorus is praising Astymeloisa in highly sensuous language (61–82):

       λυσιμελεῖ τε πόσωι, τακερώτερα
       δ' ὕπνω καὶ σανάτω ποτιδέρεκεται·
       οὐδέ τι μαψιδίως γλυκ . . ήνα·

       Ἀ[σ]τυμέλοισα δέ μ' οὐδὲν ἀμείβεται
65   ἀλλὰ τὸ]ν πυλεῶν' ἔχοισα
       [ὥ] τις αἰγλά[ε]ντος ἀστήρ
       ὠρανῶ διαιπετής
       ἢ χρύσιον ἔρνος ἢ ἁπαλὸ[ν ψίλ]ον
             ]ν
70   ]. διέβα ταναοῖς πο[σί·]
       -κ]ομος νοτία Κινύρα χ[άρ]ις
       ἐπὶ π]αρσενικᾶν χαίταισιν ἴσδει·

       Ἀ]στυμέλοισα κατὰ στρατόν
       ] μέλημα δάμωι
75   ]μαν ἑλοῖσα
          ]λέγω·

---

[64] The πυλεών (wreath) in 65 is usually taken to be an offering that Astymeloisa is about to dedicate to a divinity, since Athenaios 15, 678a says that Spartans call thus a wreath that they

]ϵναβαλ' α[ὶ] γὰρ ἄργυριν
]ία
]α ἴδοιμ' αἴ πως μϵ . . ον φίλοι
80   ᾶσ]σον [ὶο]ῖς' ἀπαλᾶς χηρὸς λάβοι,
αἶψά κ' [ἐγὼν ἰ]κέτις κήνας γενοίμαν·
νῦν δ' [

. . . with limb-loosening desire, and more meltingly than sleep and death she
gazes toward (me), nor is she sweet in a lightheaded way. But Astymeloisa
answers me nothing, [but] holding the wreath [like] a falling[65] star of the glittering heavens or a golden sapling or a soft [feather   ] she crossed on long feet.
The moist hair[-enhancing?] gift of Kinyras (i.e., perfume) sits on the hair of the
maiden (?).[66] [   ] Astymeloisa among the people [   ] darling of the community [4 lines fragmentary] I might see if somehow [   ] (she) [approaching]
take (my) soft hand, immediately I would become her suppliant (?).[67] As it
is . . .

The praise is punctuated by the chorus's two admissions of failure to win a
response from Astymeloisa. In line 64, at the beginning of a stanza, the
chorus says, "Astymeloisa answers me nothing." Astymeloisa *looks* at the
chorus (if one supplies "me" as the object of "gazes toward" in line 62) but
does not return speech for the chorus's speech. The chorus describes its
own words as ineffectual; therefore, while the words may charge the air
with eroticism, they do not construct an acknowledged subject position
for their speakers. The chorus's speech creates no obligation for Astymeloisa to answer, hence a fortiori has no authority in the world of
public discourse.

    Later, in line 81, each chorus-member singly says that if Astymeloisa
were to take notice of her, "I would become her suppliant."[68] The con-

---

offer to Hera. Calame 1977: II 107–9 argues that it might have been worn by Astymeloisa
herself, thereby divesting the poem of a public ritual context.
   [65] The meaning of this adjective is not known. I give the usual translation, but see *PMGF*
ad loc.
   [66] The text says: ἐπὶ π]αρσϵνικᾶν χαίταισιν ἴσδϵι. παρσϵνικᾶν is plural, so the chorus
should then be describing itself. But the abrupt and unsignaled switch of attention from
Astymeloisa to the chorus is very strange. Campbell 1988 emends to παρσϵνικᾶς (following
Page's suggestion in *PMG* ad loc.); Calame 1977: II 103 assumes that the text as it stands refers
to Astymeloisa.
   [67] The text in the two preceding lines is very difficult to reconstruct. Barrett 1961: 685
labels the relationship of the clauses in lines 77–81 obscure. Calame 1983 *ad loc.* suggests ϝίδοι
μ' in 79 to go with αἰ γὰρ in 77 (if only she might look at me).
   [68] Calame 1983 *ad loc.* does not accept the restoration ἰκέτις (suppliant) on the grounds
that it is not an erotic word. Davies 1986a defends it as a metaphor for desire and points out

struction is apparently a future-less-vivid condition, which means that no immediate possibility of Astymeloisa's approach is envisioned (as the following words seem to acknowledge). The suppliant position itself puts the one who supplicates into a dependent state, but the chorus does not achieve even that kind of contact with and claim on Astymeloisa. In these lines the singer-dancers' power of erotic attraction rather than their language seems to be at issue: they represent themselves as lacking the charisma to affect Astymeloisa as she affects them. Just as in the first poem, they depreciate both their speaking and their attractiveness, and their praise is based on their sense of difference from the one they praise. Their desire both provides a model to the audience for its perception of Astymeloisa and simultaneously marks their own lack.

Astymeloisa herself is described in lines 61–72 in terms that dissolve her into a revery of sensuality. Is melting into sleep her effect on others or her own state? She is a figure for yielding to loss of consciousness. In the following lines images pile up, incompatible in their aura, shifting from bright to soft, celestial to humble.[69] Then she is fragmented as her feet and hair, or rather the exotic perfume on her hair, are noticed in turn. The excess of language creates a diffused picture, offering Astymeloisa no coherent reflection on which she might base a sense of herself as a subject.

In the first *partheneion,* as I argued, the chorus portrays itself as inadequate in beauty to please the goddess, although it longs to; that is, desire replaces beauty as the grounds of the chorus's approach to the goddess. In this poem there is apparently no external judge. The chorus and Astymeloisa form a system of mirrors through which both are staged for the audience. Each looks at the other for the audience, neither possessing the gaze of mastery. Astymeloisa's looking, as described by the chorus (61–62), is, on one hand, an expression of loveliness that causes others to desire her, and, on the other, a disguised solicitation to the audience to look at the chorus. Both are to be looked at; each stands in for the audience vis-à-vis the other. At the same time, Astymeloisa neither speaks nor approaches, while the chorus's speech is unavailing. For the audience both are constituted as passive. Astymeloisa is yielding and immobilized as an object of desire, while the chorus members desire to put themselves into a position of dependency. Because all are female, what is predicated of each can be generalized by the audience to all: each is desirable and desires to be desired

---

that grasping the hand is an element of supplication. Eroticism suffuses the earlier lines, and the image must continue it, but its most striking aspect is the powerlessness of the suppliant.

[69] Cf. Barrett 1961: 684, who comments on the lack of any common element among the images. Bruschi 1994 takes the lines as an explanation of the preceding images, but his argument is strained. As he points out (41–43), basis for the supplement ψίλον (feather) is very weak. Calame 1983 *ad loc.* thinks that the chorus introduces its own desire in 76 with a line similar to Alkman 1.56: "Why do I tell you?"

by another who will define her. Into this empty space created by the distance between Astymeloisa and the chorus, the audience can insert itself imaginatively in the figure of a husband. Thus, again, young women can present themselves to the community as speakers and promote themselves and others as sexually desirable while demonstrating their lack of a sense of subjectivity or personal authority.

This analysis must remain tentative because so much of the poem is missing. It is also true that Astymeloisa (or the young woman who played her role) had presence and actions independent of the chorus's description of her. However, while the chorus is singing, at least, its words intervene between the audience and Astymeloisa, guiding what the audience sees—a ravishingly beautiful Astymeloisa, an interplay of looks—and so defining Astymeloisa.

In both of Alkman's *partheneia,* the chorus is staged in such a way that the chorus-members can fulfil their role of offering reflection and model to the community while presenting themselves as proper *parthenoi,* that is, as lacking authority and subjectivity. The deauthorizing of the performers is so overt precisely because their function is praise of women's sexual attractiveness—for the contradiction of women's participation in the community appears most intense when women become public speakers about women's sexual identity. It follows from this view of their function that neither of the poems is an expression of young women's real physical/emotional attachment to their leader, which Alkman knew or intuited. On the other hand, since women were called on to praise other women in public, the idea of desire between women was not repressed. On the level of ideology, at least, the very system of male possessiveness meant that space was left open for erotic attachments between women.

In the other extant, though fragmentary, poem to be performed by *parthenoi,* the contradiction of women's speaking appears in a different form, for the performance had a different function in its ritual context. The poem is a processional song composed by Pindar for a performance during the Daphnephoria at Thebes in the fifth century (*partheneion* II = fr. 94b *SM*). The Daphnephoria is described by Proklos, who tells us that the procession was in honor of Apollo and went in turn to two of his temples, the Ismenion and the Galaxion: a boy with both parents living led the procession, followed by a near relative holding aloft a garlanded branch called *kōpō,* then by the *daphnēphoros* (laurel-bearer).[70] He was followed by a chorus of *parthenoi* who held out sprays (of laurel) as a sign of supplica-

---

[70] Proklos in Photios, *Bibl.* 321b23, quoted in *SM* ad loc., and cf. Pausanias 9.10.4. See for discussion Nilsson 1957: 164–65; Schachter 1981: 83–85; Ferrari 1991: 396, who thinks that Pausanias 9.10.4 is not relevant to this festival. Proklos' description does not quite match up with Pindar's text. Pindar does not mention two young men, as required if the leading boy and the *daphnēphoros* are distinct people.

tion to the god and sang hymns called *daphnēphorika*. As Proklos puts it, "The priests hymned (Apollo) through a chorus of *parthenoi*."[71] It is incidental, but interesting, that Proklos (who is viewing the event through texts) or his source sees the chorus as a medium for the officials of the cult: he assumes that the *parthenoi* do not speak in their own right.

In the first stanza the chorus indicates that it has a dual task: the young women will sing both of Apollo and of the family of Aioladas, whose members are serving as leaders of the procession. The performance requires a different "voice" for each task; to see why, let us consider the ceremony further. The two shrines of Apollo to which the procession went promoted fertility and reproduction. The temple of Apollo Ismenios, the Ismenion (site of the performance of Pindar's *paian* 9 also), seems to have contained the couch of Melia, who gave birth to Teneros and perhaps celebrated a "sacred marriage."[72] An *aition* for the cult of Apollo Galaxios, moreover, credits Apollo with causing the herds to give milk.[73] The leader of the procession had to be a boy both of whose parents were alive. And the *kōpō* may have been dressed to look like a female figure.[74] This aspect of the ceremony explains the participation of the *parthenoi*, for they will soon be involved in reproduction themselves. Their performance therefore has the same function as performance of Alkman's *partheneia* by Spartan *parthenoi*: they should appear in public in an appropriate context to indicate their approaching readiness for marriage.

Joined to this celebration of women's role is a ceremony of honor dedicated to the family whose members lead the procession.[75] The family must have been chosen each time from among the prominent families of the city, and the praise is no doubt offered in return for benefactions the city has enjoyed. In this aspect the ceremony is political in a narrower sense. The first aspect of the ritual calls for the *parthenoi* to show themselves off as young women devoid of any sense of power. But the second aspect, homage to the leading family, requires that they have enough authority to speak public praise. The song consequently spends much effort in adjusting the performers' self-presentation to meet these two conflicting demands.

The singers begin, after what was probably an invocation, by describing Apollo's arrival and their response (3–17):

[71] 321a34, quoted in *SM* ad loc.
[72] See Ch. 1, p. 50; Farnell 1961 *ad paian* 9.35 and *Pythian* 11.1–6.
[73] Farnell 1961: 426; Schachter 1981: 48–49. Cf. the fragment of a *daphnēphorikon* 104b *SM;* Farnell 1977: IV 123 and 361.
[74] This is Schachter's (1981: 84) interpretation.
[75] Lehnus 1984: 77 stresses that the festival was for a particular family as well as the city, a fact that makes the song resemble an epinician ode.

ἥϰε]ι γὰρ ὁ [Λοξ]ίας
π]ρ[ό]φρω[ν] ἀθανάταν χάριν
5   Θήβαις ἐπιμ⟨ε⟩ίξων.

ἀλλὰ ζωσαμένα τε πέπλον ὠκέως
χερσίν τ’ ἐν μαλαϰαῖσιν ὄρπαϰ’ ἀγλαόν
δάφνας ὀχέοισα πάν-
δοξον Αἰολάδα σταθμόν
10   υἱοῦ τε Παγώνδα

ὑμνήσω στεφάνοισι θάλ-
λοισα παρθένιον ϰάρα,
σειρῆνα δὲ ϰόμπον
αὐλίσϰων ὑπὸ λωτίνων
15   μιμήσομ’ ἀοιδαῖς

ϰεῖνον, ὃς Ζεφύρου τε σιγάζει πνοὰς
αἰψηράς.

For Loxias (= Apollo) [has come], well-disposed, mingling immortal grace
with Thebes. But belting my garment quickly and holding a bright branch of
laurel in my soft hands, I shall sing of the all-glorious establishment of Aioladas
and of his son Pagondas, verdant with wreaths on my maiden head, and I will
imitate the Siren in her vaunt with songs to lotus pipes, (the vaunt) that silences
the sudden blasts of the west wind.

Apollo "mingles" grace with Thebes in quasi-sexual language appropriate
to the theme of fertility. When the *parthenoi* continue by mentioning their
dress and their "soft hands," they are drawing attention to their appearance, and in their hurry they seem to be responsive to his arrival. But this
beginning of their erotic self-presentation (the fertility theme) is interrupted when they announce that they will sing of the family of Aioladas.
The ἀλλά (but) of line 6 turns out to introduce the other theme of the
ceremony. Then they return to self-description; note that θάλλοισα (verdant) and παρθένιον (maiden) are juxtaposed, for the two words delineate
the young women, though the first strictly defines the effect of their
wreaths. Overall, their description of themselves in ritual garb supports
their right to sing of the Aioladadai, while their duty to praise subordinates
their self-presentation to its requirements.

At this point the *parthenoi* offer their first definition of the status of their
voices: they will imitate the Siren in her "vaunt," a cry that silences the
winds. Alkman had equated Siren with Muse, so the song may be refer-

ring to the genre of *partheneion* as Alkman elaborated it.[76] But performers of Pindar's epinician poetry never derive inspiration from the Sirens. The voices of the *parthenoi* are marked as different from men's by association with the Sirens, and we must determine the nature of the difference.[77]

We have two different testimonies to the effects of Siren song. In the *Odyssey* the Sirens seduce sailors by singing of heroic deeds such as they offer to recount for Odysseus (12.184–91):

> Come here, much-praised Odysseus, great glory of the Achaeans, and halt your ship so that you can listen to our voice. For no one ever passed by this place in his black ship before listening to the honey-sweet voice from our mouths, but rather he goes his way delighted and knowing more. For we know indeed all that the Argives and the Trojans labored at by will of the gods in broad Troy; and we know all that happens on the much-nourishing earth.

In the Hesiodic *Catalogue of Women,* the Sirens are magicians who lull the winds.[78] The Sirens whom the *parthenoi* imitate are the latter sort, and the audience is like a wind or storm that they "silence" as the Siren does. However, the song that soothes the winds according to the *parthenoi* is a κόμπον (vaunt), which makes it similar to what the Odyssean Sirens sing. The Odyssean idea of Sirens who sing of deeds is grafted lightly onto the Hesiodic Sirens.

The image of Sirens as the prototypes of the *parthenoi* is useful in that it allows Pindar to position the young women's voices appropriately. On one hand, by hinting at the Odyssean Sirens, it suggests a source for praise of the Aioladadai that heroizes them and implies that their praises are sung, their deeds memorialized, near the end of the earth. On the other hand, although flattering to the object of their song, comparison with the Sirens does not grant status to the *parthenoi* as speakers. The *parthenoi* do not claim access to the Muses, who are the culturally validated link with the divine world. The Sirens are located in the wilds, far from civilization or Olympus. And the Hesiodic Sirens, unlike the Odyssean Sirens or the Muses, are not depicted as either knowledgeable or seductive. What is

[76] Cf. 30 *PMGF* and Alkman 1.96 above. Lehnus 1984: 80 compares the two. Various opening lines (e.g., 14, 27 *PMGF,* both choral) are quoted from Alkman in which the speaker does call on the Muses.

[77] Molyneux 1992: 69 and 78n.21 lists various meanings of "Siren" used as a term of comparison; much later it is usually complimentary, but in Euripides' *Helen* 167–69 it is associated with lamentation and in *Andromache* 936 with a deceitful woman. Aischines 3.228 is also negative.

[78] Cf. frs. 27–28 *MW* on the island of the Sirens and their control of the winds. The same power is implied by the *Odyssey,* for Odysseus says that the wind dropped when they neared the Sirens' island (12.168–69). Pindar's text continues with three and one-half more lines of description of storm, but the text is corrupt. On it see Ferrari 1991: 390–93.

more, the *parthenoi* do not draw direct inspiration from the Sirens; rather, they "imitate" them without actual contact with them as a source of knowledge.

Yet this solution to the problem of the singers' authority is inadequate because it is unstable. The message of validated praise by the unvalidated voices of the *parthenoi* will collapse in on itself if not shored up. On the one hand, intrusive memory of the Odyssean Sirens may attribute seductive power to the voices of the *parthenoi*. Marginal figures, eternal virgins, autonomous, enticing speakers, the Sirens are not really auspicious models (from the point of view of hegemonic culture) for human *parthenoi*. The threat that erotic young women will escape from the system of exchange among men is submerged but not absent. On the other hand, the auditor who is oblivious to the threat of female knowledge and seductive speech will also not appreciate the emotive power attributed to praise of the Aioladadai.

Luigi Lehnus has pointed out the associations of the phrase "lotus pipes," which contains a similar ambivalence.[79] Pipes, which are made of reeds (including lotus), are prominent in worship of Apollo and notably in a Delphic version of a Daphnephoria; while reeds give the Kephisos River in Boeotia its character. Thus they are doubly appropriate to a Boeotian Daphnephoria. At the same time, the Sirens are sometimes depicted as offering mythic lotus, a plant that causes the one who eats it to forget all else except the pleasure it brings. Lehnus observes that lotus pipes link the festival with a Siren image for the young women's singing, but he does not comment on the danger implied by lotus or the Sirens. One image tries to hold in suspension two incompatible meanings of the voices of the *parthenoi*, but the two set up interference.

Therefore Pindar continues (or takes up again) the process of defining the speech of the *parthenoi*. After a frustrating lacuna we find (31–41):

πολ]λὰ μὲν [τ]ὰ πάροιθ[
   δαιδάλλοισ' ἔπεσιν, τὰ δ' α[
Ζεὺς οἶδ', ἐμὲ δὲ πρέπει
   παρθενήϊα μὲν φρονεῖν
35 γλώσσᾳ τε λέγεσθαι·
   ἀνδρὸς δ' οὔτε γυναικός, ὧν θάλεσσιν ἔγ-
   κειμαι, χρή μ[ε] λαθεῖν ἀοιδὰν πρόσφορον.
πιστὰ δ' Ἀγασικλέει
   μάρτυς ἤλυθον ἐς χορόν

---

[79] Lehnus 1984: 82.

40   ἐσλοῖς τε γονεῦσιν

    ἀμφὶ προξενίαισι·

Many things from the past [   ] embellishing in words, but [   ] things Zeus knows, but for me it is appropriate to think things suitable for a maiden and to say them in speech. I must not forget the song fitting for either the man or the woman to whose children I am devoted. As a faithful witness for Agasikles and for his good parents, I have come to the chorus on account of their ties of friendship with men from other states.

If δαιδάλλοισ' (embellishing) is correctly interpreted as a feminine participle, it is most likely part of a further self-description by the *parthenoi*. Bruno Snell suggests the following restoration of lines 31–32 by way of example:[80]

πολ]λὰ μὲν [τ]ὰ πάροιθ' [ἀείδοιμ' ἂν καλοῖς

    δαιδάλλοισ' ἔπεσιν, τὰ δ' ἀ[τρεκῆ μόνος

Ζεὺς οἶδ', . . .

I might sing many things of the past, embellishing them with beautiful words. But Zeus alone knows unerring things.

At all events a double contrast between Zeus and the *parthenoi* appears to be set up, first between their verbal adornment and his knowledge, then between his knowledge and what is appropriate for *parthenoi* to think and say.[81] The first contrast is an ordinary enough sentiment for archaic and early classical Greece, although it confirms that these *parthenoi* as singers do not have access to the Muses. But a second is added, which now distinguishes, not between what Zeus and the *parthenoi* know, but between the full story as Zeus might give it and the social and intellectual constraints that inhibit the young women's speech. The *parthenoi*, it implies, will speak less fulsomely, less assertively in recounting the praises of the Aioladadai than men would. Thus Pindar turns the constraints on the singers' speech to account in proposing that the praise is even greater than the chorus can enunciate.

At the same time the second contrast makes the *parthenoi* present themselves as aware of and obedient to the social demand for modesty on their part. They have been tamed since their initial description of themselves: to be *parthenoi* now means not having Sirenlike power to fascinate but to be limited even in one's thoughts. Note the two uses of an adjective derived from *parthenos*, παρθένιον (12) just before the Siren is introduced and

[80] Cited in the apparatus of *SM*. Ferrari 1991: 393 takes δαιδάλλοισ' as third-person plural, suggesting, e.g., ἀοιδοί as subject. That is possible and makes the *parthenoi* contrast their song with other heroic narrative.

[81] Dionysios of Halikarnassos *Demosthenes* 39 comments on the difference in style between the *partheneia* and other compositions by Pindar.

παρθενήϊα (34), defining how the singers must think and speak. In these two occurrences the whole shift in their self-presentation is summed up. Following their statement of their role, they admonish themselves not to forget their words of praise. The danger that is actually articulated is not that they will be too potent or seductive as speakers but that they will fail to speak at all. Therefore the *parthenoi* present themselves as earnest to live up to others' expectations. The praise has been implicitly detached from their authority, almost as if it came from Zeus even though they do not speak for Zeus. By this maneuver the *parthenoi* have been redefined while the validity of the praise and the effect of singing it remain what they were.

The *parthenoi* thus arrive at a summary statement of their position: they are "faithful witnesses" (38–39). The phrase connotes both the truth of their words and their obedience to the social imperative. Here the praise of the Aioladadai actually begins.[82] The young women are "witnesses" to diplomacy and horse-racing triumphs, ordinary aristocratic boasts. However, after another lacuna the end (apparently) of the section in praise of the Aioladadai is partly preserved and says something about "hateful strife" (63). The *parthenoi* may have alluded to political disruptions; their statements may have been less uncontroversial than they appear at the beginning of the section and their speech more assertive. Such would account for the long preparation for the praise section.

Thereupon (66) the singers turn to address the leaders of the procession, singling out two women by name, Damaina and Andaisistrota (her mother ?), and calling on Damaina's father to lead them.[83] With this shift the song probably returns to its first task, celebration of the rites of Apollo in his aspect of fosterer of reproduction. Damaina may be the chorus leader, since she follows directly after her father. Andaisistrota has rehearsed or dressed her skillfully (ἐπάσκησε μήδεσ[ι, 71–72). In praising other women, the chorus also returns to a more traditional role. But just as the papyrus gives out, the young women apparently take up once more the issue of their speaking: in 76–77 the words μὴ νῦν νέκτα[ρ   ]νας ἐμᾶς / διψῶντ' (don't now [   ] nectar of my [   ] thirsting) are visible. The nectar may be a metaphor for song, but the point is lost.[84] Still, the new metaphor is appropriate to the theme of fertility and flowing milk, so the *parthenoi* may position themselves anew as proleptic providers of nourishing liquids.

This song does not stage its performers either as evoking female eroti-

---

[82] Lehnus 1984: 80 sees this line as the suture between a song of para-epinician praise and a *partheneion*.

[83] Lehnus 1984: 83–85 discusses the relationship among the people mentioned on the basis of a new reading of line 66 that supplies the word *father*. His reading and his genealogical scheme are accepted by *SM* ad loc.

[84] See Lehnus 1984: 79 on this passage and the idea, which he discusses indecisively, that the first person refers to Pindar himself.

cism or as depreciating their voices to the extent that Alkman's two *partheneia* do. The chorus does do both, but its function in the ceremony is a double one, so it cannot devote its whole attention to presenting itself and the women it praises. Moreover, the chorus's role is described by Proklos as "supplication," so it had a further task on behalf of the community. Visually, supplication in the context of fertility has something of the same quality as the assertion by the Spartan *parthenoi* that they must obey Hagesichora and through her agency enter into peace; in both, the *parthenoi* humbly, as it were, seek reproductive abundance. The community's use of the chorus as representative is very clear, precisely because this performance fulfills so many functions, but the combination makes staging the *parthenoi* as speakers a complicated matter.

The poems we have examined were written by men for women's performance. Male composition of the words is a form of control over women's speech, for (as is clear from the feminine pronouns) the words in performance were meant to be taken as those of the performers themselves. Would women composing for women's public performance encode a different perspective? The only fragments we possess that might tell us are those of Sappho and Korinna. Small snatches of Sappho's wedding hymns are known, but the extant lines are too few to help with this question. I will examine them in Chapter 6. Korinna was a poet from Tanagra in Boeotia. Several long fragments of her poetry have turned up on papyri, but they present manifold problems. Nothing about the circumstances of performance is known except what can be speculatively deduced from one fragment. The question is made more complicated by the fact that Korinna's date is disputed.[85] If she is Hellenistic, as M. L. West maintains, then her monodic poetry was not necessarily performed (although it might have been); it could have been presented in book form. However, if she wrote choral songs for *parthenoi,* those at least must have been sung in public.[86]

Nevertheless, in a chapter about women's performance, we cannot pass up that fragment, and we can learn something about possibilities from it. The text of most of the fragment follows (655.1–16 *PMG*):

ἐπί με Τερψιχόρα [
καλὰ ϝεροῖ᾽ ἀισομ[έναν
Ταναγρίδεσσι λε[υκοπέπλυς
μέγα δ᾽ ἐμῆς γέγ[αθε πόλις

[85] Korinna has traditionally been dated to the fifth century on the basis of anecdotes connecting her with Pindar. West 1970b proposes a Hellenistic date. Davies 1988a argues that Korinna's date is indeterminable; West 1990 responds.

[86] A fragment entitled *Orestes* (690 *PMG*), probably by Korinna, contains a reference

5   λιγουροκω[τί]λυ[ς ἐνοπῆς.[87]
     ὅττι γὰρ μεγαλ . [
     ψευδ[   ]σ . [   ]αδομε[
         ]ω γῆαν εὐρού[χορον
     λόγια δ' ἐπ πατέρω[ν
10   κοσμείσασα ϝιδιο[
     παρθ[έ]νυσι κατα[
     πο]λλὰ μὲν Καφ[ισὸν ἰών-
     γ' ἀρχ]αγὸν κόσμ[εισα λόγυ]ς,
     πολλὰ δ' Ὠρί[ωνα] μέγαν
15   κὴ πεντεί[κοντ'] οὐψιβίας
     πῆδα[ς οὓς νού]μφησι μιγ[ί]ς

Terpsichora [summons?] me as I undertake to sing beautiful tales to the white-garbed women of Tanagra, and the city rejoices greatly in my clear-chirping voice.[88] For whatever greatly (?) [without?] falsehood [   ] the land of broad [dancing-places], and adorning stories from the time of the fathers [   ] for *parthenoi* [I initiate a ritual action ?]. Often/much [I] adorn[ed] the founder Kephisos [in words] and often/much great Orion and the fifty powerful sons whom he [begat], mating with nymphs. . . .

The poem refers to song-producing. If Korinna is taken as the speaker, then what does it say about her audience?[89] She seems to name two different audiences when she speaks of singing ϝεροῖα (tales) for the women of Tanagra (marital status unspecified) and of pleasing the city. The following sentence seems to explain her activity (γάρ) and perhaps distinguishes between two types of song: "whatever greatly . . . " of lines 6–8 (perhaps the same as the tales of line 2), and "stories from the time of the fathers" (9).[90] The second category of song she connects with *parthenoi*. If we line up the two sets of distinctions, then we arrive at the conclusion that Korinna both sings tales to the Tanagran women and delights the city by

---

to "season" and "in the flowers of spring" and the words "chorus throughout the seven-gated . . . " in its opening lines. These may indicate performance at Thebes, perhaps at a spring festival (so Page 1953: 28; West 1970b: 280).

[87] The restoration of these four lines is certain since they are quoted by Hephaistion *Encheiridion* 16.3.

[88] Campbell 1992 prints χαλῖ (summons) in the lacuna of line 1.

[89] West 1970b: 283–84 and 1990: 553 proposes that it was composed as a written introduction to a collection of her poems, not as a piece to be sung; this is one of his grounds for dating Korinna down.

[90] It depends on whether one takes the δ' of line 9 to signal an alternative or represent a continuative. If the latter, Korinna would be continuing to describe the type of poetry already mentioned.

composing choral poetry on traditional themes for performance by *par-thenoi*. Her "voice" in line 5 will be metaphorical; it is the voices of the *parthenoi* that the city actually hears.[91] By this reconstruction Korinna's activity was similar to Sappho's; both composed poetry for public perfor-mance by *parthenoi* (wedding poetry in Sappho's case) and poems for a circle of friends. One fragment of Korinna's (a hexameter) includes an address to Korinna, with "Korinna" in the vocative—reminiscent of poems in which Sappho recounts a conversation. The poem under consid-eration, then, like some of Sappho's (e.g., 71 *V*, discussed in Chapter 6), could be a programmatic statement performed to her group of friends.

On the other hand, lines 6–11 may not distinguish two types of poetry, and in any event the term ϝεροῖα and the words "[without?] falsehood" and "land of broad [dancing-places]" in lines 6–8, which would describe the first kind of poetry, do not seem appropriate to characterize poetry among friends. Another solution may be to assume that the "Tanagran women" are *parthenoi* and that the whole passage describes Korinna's ac-tivity as chorus-trainer.[92] This poem would then either be meant for read-ing as an introduction to a collection of her choral poetry or else have been sung to an unknown audience.

A third solution is to take the poem as choral. The Muse invoked, Ter-psichore (Delighting in the chorus), is an appropriate one, although the meter is apparently stichic instead of strophic.[93] The future in line 2 would be a performative future, designating what the performers are actually doing. The participle κοσμείσασα (adorning) would mean "honoring in performance" rather than "composing."[94] The phrase κοσμείσασα . . . παρθένυσι (10–11, "adorning . . . for *parthenoi*") is perhaps a problem because the participle is singular and the noun plural, so the *parthenoi* could not be referring to themselves. On the other hand, the dative παρθένυσι could be a dative of interest with the verb κατά[ρχομη (I initiate a ritual action), if that is the correct supplement, and could indicate that the singers begin an action in the interest of other *parthenoi* by singing.[95] Singing for

[91] I ignore the permutation that would have Korinna sing solo to the city, for it is unlikely, and if she did I do not know what the occasion would be.

[92] West 1970b: 280 considers ϝεροῖα to be choral songs for *parthenoi*. Snyder 1989: 50 also equates "Tanagran women" and *parthenoi*.

[93] West 1990: 554, although the ends of only 1–5, 14–16 are preserved, so six-line strophes (as in 654 col. i *PMG*) would be undetectable if not marked in the left margin. Stichic composition (by the line rather than in stanzas) does not rule out choral performance; there is a Spartan marching song in stichic paroemiacs, 856 *PMG*. Cf. the *paian* in the same meter, 858 *PMG*. Rutherford 1990: 200n.111 mentions these. The *paian* and processional of Lime-nios (*CA* pp. 149–59; cf. Käppel 1992: 389–91 #46) to which West 1970b: 281 compares the meter was performed by a chorus. It is lines 36–49 in *CA*, presumably the processional part (West 1992a: 299), that is comparable.

[94] For a close parallel see Euripides *Erechtheus* fr. 65.80 Austin.

[95] κατά[ρχομη was supplied in line 11 by Lobel (*PMG* ad loc.) and approved by Page and by Campbell 1992, who prints it. For *parthenoi* singing on behalf of others, cf. Theocritus

Tanagran women would then either specify the current performance as one among women or represent the *parthenoi* as addressing women in order to avoid the notion of their engaging in authoritative speech to men.[96] The one past tense (13) is restored; the poem may not have referred to past performance at all. If it did, the chorus would have to be an ongoing one, like the Deliades or the Spartan Dumainai.[97]

If this is a choral poem, it is different from the others we have looked at in that it does not limit or depreciate women's ability to speak effectively. It would limit their implied audience instead, but once they say that they speak to women, the speakers can boast of the delight they give.[98] Instead, the solution to the problem of women's public voices is on a different plane. For, however we take the poem, we are left with one bit of information. Korinna characterizes songs for *parthenoi* as "stories from the time of the fathers." The speaker emphasizes the patriarchal content. Kephisos (the river-god), Orion with his sons—the speech and sexual activities of men—are accepted by the speaker as defining the community and her place in it. The broken lines that follow the quoted section contain the words κόραν, καλὰ ϝιδεῖν, τίϰτ[, and τέϰετο ("girl," "beautiful to see," "was giving birth (?)," and "begot"). It may be the birth of one of Orion's sons that is described, underlining the point about male sexual possession of women.[99] Another surviving poem, 654 col. iii *PMG* (on the fates of the daughters of Asopos), also deals with gods' rape of young women. And striking among the attested subjects of Korinna's lost poetry are stories about sets of daughters. In addition to the daughters of Asopos, she told the stories of the daughters of Orion, who sacrificed themselves to save the city (656 *PMG*); the daughters of Euonymos, a son of the Kephisos River (660); and the daughters of Minyas, who resisted Dionysus (665).[100] If these were choral pieces, then these paradigmatic or cautionary tales about

---

18.22–24, where a chorus of twelve young women says, "we are all age-mates . . . four times sixty girls, the female youth of the city."

[96] Rayor 1993: 224 identifies the two audiences of Tanagran women and city. For *parthenoi* addressing women in public performance, cf. the feminine participle in Alkman 1.73 *PMGF*.

[97] On the Deliades, see below, n.124. On the Dumainai, who appear more than once in Alkman's fragments, see Calame 1983: 388–89.

[98] If Korinna is Hellenistic, the conventions for women's public speech may have changed by her time. On the other hand, if this is a choral poem, then one of the major reasons for dating Korinna to the Hellenistic period, namely that this poem looks like an introduction to a collection, vanishes.

[99] If so, then lines 12ff. are not a catalogue of subjects for different songs (as West 1990: 554 thinks) but the introduction to the subject of this song; some of the nymphs were surely daughters of the river Kephisos.

[100] The subject matter is entirely local Boeotian myth, appropriate for community poetry. Page 1953 surveys her known titles. He finds Korinna unique in her parochialism among early Greek poets: "Not even Sappho is so strictly confined to the interests of a province" (45). He points out (28) that her *Orestes*, the least obviously local poem, may have been performed at the Ismenion at Thebes, comparing Pindar *Pythian* 11. See n.86 above.

groups of women must have seemed directly applicable to the *parthenoi* who performed them. Korinna's may be another, more traditional, way of inhibiting a sense of authority in *parthenoi*: the young women celebrate patriarchy and male power, specifically sexual power, over women.[101]

Korinna has been treated critically as variously "patriarchal" and "feeble as a poet."[102] The category of community poetry helps to bring her work into focus. If she was composing for communal choral performance, she must have had to meet public expectations, both in matters of gender and of local focus. One can, indeed, note shifts and exaggerations in her versions of myths that intimate the possibility of another perspective; perhaps her two audiences, Tanagran men and Tanagran women, were meant to hear slightly different messages.[103] But there, with a woman's voice devoid of context and a glimpse of further texts for choral performance, we must leave the matter.

Actual *partheneia* are preserved only from Sparta and Thebes (and possibly Tanagra). Alkman and Pindar were both male poets very conscious of the power of language. Texts for performance by *parthenoi* cannot normally have deauthorized their voices in such a sophisticated way. However, *parthenoi* could also be positioned within the community by the content of their song, as the examination of Korinna 655 *PMG* suggests. Other evidence can be adduced to show that male control of women's bodies was a common theme for the songs of *parthenoi*. In a sense this is hardly surprising, since they sing of mythical childbearing in order to unite their social function with the tales that define the community. But sometimes more than celebration of reproduction is at stake. A notice about a recurring performance will serve as example.

In a well-known passage (5.16.2–8), Pausanias describes the activities of the board of Sixteen Women at Elis. He gives two stories about the origin of this board, one mythical and one historical (whether accurate or not). Both are significant for the role the women play in community self-definition. The mythical story is that Hippodameia, daughter of the king, gathered the women and with them established the quadrennial Heraian games, doing honor to Hera in return for her marriage to Pelops. (The games are races for three age-classes of girls, run in the stadium at Olympia, with the winner receiving an olive crown and a portion of the sacrifice

---

[101] On the other hand, 654 col. i *PMG,* a poem about a singing contest, honors Rhea for rescuing her son Zeus and hiding him in a mountain cave.

[102] Rayor 1993 disputes these views. Cf. Snyder 1989: 46–50 on Korinna's skill in narrative.

[103] Rayor 1993 argues that Korinna is a "woman-identified" poet and points out traces of her alteration of traditional myth. It is also possible to see in the Asopos-poem a mocking exaggeration of the theme of rape that calls attention to male violence and presumptions about possession of female bodies. See Maclean 1987 for women's using such techniques to change the valence of traditional narratives.

to Hera.) The historical story is that after the death of Damophon, a sixth-century tyrant of Pisa, women were chosen from the cities of Elis to make peace with Pisa. In his time, adds Pausanias, the Elians are divided into eight tribes, and two women are chosen from each tribe.[104] In addition to overseeing the Heraia, the women organized two choruses, one in honor of Hippodameia, the other dedicated to Physkoa. Physkoa (still according to Pausanias) was a local woman to whom Dionysus made love. Their son was Narkaios, who became a great warrior and together with his mother established worship of Dionysus. Pausanias implies that other honors were given to Physkoa as well. Pausanias does not say who performed the choruses, but we can guess from the women's involvement with girls and *parthenoi,* as well as the connection with Hippodameia and the theme of marriage attached to her, that the dancers were *parthenoi,* that the performances were public, and that the stories of Hippodameia and Physkoa figured in the poetry performed.[105] This institution was probably similar, as Claude Calame argues, to the Spartan performances for which Alkman wrote.[106]

If we first consider the information Pausanias gives on the mythic background, we can see how the content of this ceremony solved the problem of women speaking in public. Both women were taken perforce by men: Pelops won Hippodameia by outracing her father and carrying her off in his chariot, while Dionysus raped/seduced Physkoa. Both women made public gestures of thanks for their encounters with men: Hippodameia founded the Heraian games and Physkoa the local worship of Dionysus. The message that women embrace the definition given them by men is clear enough. But another aspect of the pairing is just as interesting. Hippodameia was married by a human hero, Physkoa raped by a god. In combination these stories *both* prescribe marriage as the state to which a *parthenos* must aspire *and* certify the availability of her body to the male figure who takes possession.[107] In retelling them, *parthenoi* stage themselves as acceding to alienation from their bodies in that, though they would be punished for the transgression, they express no outrage at or right to resist a male figure's violation of them.

With the Elian practice we can compare an epinician ode in which Bacchylides describes *parthenoi* singing in honor of Aigina, eponym of the

---

[104] The board of Sixteen Women seems to have had political functions, as well as directing girls' "education." They are also said to have woven a robe for Hera every four years.

[105] On the marriage theme and a hypothetical women's reading of Hippodameia on the east pediment of the Temple of Zeus at Olympia, see Stehle and Day, 1996.

[106] Calame 1977: I 210–14.

[107] But the latter story may also have functioned to legitimate bearing children outside marriage. Cf. stories of rape followed by punishment of the woman raped but ultimate vindication, as in the Kallisto story. On this pattern, the "girl's tragedy" in Euripides, see Scafuro 1990.

island Aigina, who bore Aiakos to Zeus, and of Endais, wife of Aiakos, who bore Peleus and Telamon (13.91–99 *SM*):

> ταὶ δὲ στεφανωσάμε[ναι φοιν]ιϰέων
> ἀνθέων δόναϰός τ' ἐ[πιχω-
> ρίαν ἄθυρσιν
> παρθένοι μέλπουσι τ[   ]ς, ὦ
> 95 δέσποινα παγξε[ίνου χθονός,
> Ἐν]δαΐδα τε ῥοδό[παχυν,
> ἃ το[   ]ων ἔτι[ϰτε Πηλέα
> καὶ Τελαμ[ῶ]γα [ϰρα]τ[α]ι[ὸν
> Αἰαϰῶι μιχθεῖσ' ἐν εὐ[ναῖ·

Garlanded with [crimson] flowers and reeds the maidens dance and sing [your fame?] as a local festivity, O mistress of the hospitable [land], and rosy[-armed] Endais, who bore [Peleus] and [strong] Telamon, mingling with Aiakos in bed.

As at Elis, a divine rape and a human marriage are celebrated. Aigina bore Aiakos to Zeus on the island that bears her name. She is identified with the land and has no story apart from the sexual encounter and birth-giving. Aigina's irregular liaison with Zeus (and lack of any later marriage) is balanced by Endais' marriage to a human hero. Bacchylides' ode was performed presumably by a male chorus, but it may well reflect actual celebrations of Aigina by choruses of *parthenoi*, who thus exalt men's colonizing of their bodies, as at Elis.

However, Bacchylides is also imagining an ideal scene, and certainly the preceding lines (83–90) describing a ϰόρα (girl) dancing like a fawn with her companions owe much to fancy. As a vision this vignette takes us into a different realm: the meanings assigned to a chorus of *parthenoi* as a fantasy image. I do not want to pursue this direction more than a short way, far enough to suggest a more elusive aspect of performance by *parthenoi*. More than any other group, choruses of *parthenoi* figure in imagined scenes of communities or enclosed places. Such images must have interacted with real performances in that they establish another set of desires for *parthenoi* to meet. Here too contradictory impulses arise.

The *parthenoi* in Bacchylides' ode praise Aigina and Endais (and Eriboia a bit later, 102) in celebration of heroic lovemaking and the birth of heroes. They implicitly promise a continued genesis of stalwart men. Contrast this image with Pindar's description in *Pythian* 10.31–44 of life among the Hyperboreans, which includes feasting, music, dancing of *parthenoi*, and absence of sickness, old age, struggles, and wars.[108] Pindar makes a joke of

---

[108] Calame 1977: I 172–74 thinks that choruses among the blessed reflect the theme of marriage.

male sexuality, which he attributes to the donkeys, in this sensuous setting.[109] *Parthenoi* here seem to symbolize the absence of strife or *eros* (longing for what one cannot have) and therefore of politics.[110] They bespeak
utter harmony among the elements of the scene, a kind of suspended sensuousness that never issues in the isolating act of lovemaking.[111] Female
choruses also predominate among depictions of choruses on Greek vases,
perhaps because of the fantasies they evoke.[112]

   If we take these images seriously as forms of cultural significance attached to choruses of *parthenoi,* we can see other possible dimensions of
actual performance. The audience's demand on *parthenoi* representing the
community may be deeper than a simple wish to include them as a re-
source for the community but exclude them as subjects who have control
over their bodies. It can descend into levels of fantasy in which *parthenoi*
reflect an unaging, united community, with food and music replacing
sexuality and reproduction, on the one hand, and provoke patriarchal desire to beget "heroic" children on the other. The conflict that *parthenoi*
sustain in the realm of fantasy can be pictured as a desire for the idyllic
community of the Hyperboreans and simultaneously for the heroic society represented in myth by Aiakos. This conflict is not another version of
the one I have been outlining between body and self-consciousness but
presumes that one: the *parthenos* is treated here as a body on which contradictory cultural impulses are inscribed. In other words the alienation of the
female from her body produced by her acculturation also makes her body
available as a sign for types of ideal male unions: collective horizontal
friendship or individual vertical kinship.

II

What then of *gynaikes* (married women)? Can we learn anything from
notices and descriptions about their performance and whether they too
represented themselves as constructed in contradiction? There is no way to
tell whether voices of *gynaikes* were undermined in the same way as those
of *parthenoi* without having actual poems to consider. It is possible that

[109] The *hybris* of the donkeys may refer to their braying also; cf. Kirkwood 1982 *ad loc.*
[110] A collective of women providing an image of peaceful relations is found elsewhere,
e.g., the women of Aristophanes' *Lysistrata;* and cf. Antigone's claim, in Sophocles' play,
that it is her role to συμφιλεῖν (523, "return affection"). Or a woman can be shared: the
Athenians and Spartans divide up *Diallage* (Reconciliation) at the end of the *Lysistrata,* as
David Konstan points out to me.
[111] Contrast the chorus of nymphs dancing in a beautiful "natural" spot who represent a
danger to men. Theocritus *Idyll* 13 on the fate of Hylas depicts a man's succumbing to female
sexuality as loss of consciousness. A fragment of a dithyramb (*CA* pp. 192–93) places choruses of *parthenoi* in a flowery, enveloping landscape. Culture must control the sexuality
revealed by women's dancing in such settings.
[112] Calame 1977: I 62.

parthenoi in performance are deauthorized in part because they are not *gynaikes,* that they lack the marital status to function as speakers. The loss of texts can be to some extent circumvented and tentative answers to these questions given by considering the *aitia* and circumstances of married women's performance offered by our sources.

One of the most remarkable narratives connected with women's performance comes from Olympia in Elis, relayed by Pausanias (6.20.4–5). This is the tale of Sosipolis (whose name means "savior of the city").[113] When the Arcadians had invaded Elis, so the report goes, and the armies were drawn up ready for battle,

> [a] woman who had a baby at her breast came to the Elian generals and said that she had given birth to the child and that as a result of dreams she was giving it to the Elians as one who would fight on their side. Those in charge—for they thought her to speak trustworthy things—set the child naked in front of the army. Then the Arcadians attacked and the child at that moment became a snake. The Arcadians, flabbergasted at the spectacle and turning in flight, were pursued by the Elians, who won an illustrious victory and give the god the name Sosipolis.

A sanctuary was built on the spot where the snake went into the ground.[114]

This is the *aition* for an old cult that was still active in Pausanias' time.[115] Significant, from our perspective, is the fact that the woman who had brought the child was identified as Eileithyia (goddess of childbirth) and that the sanctuary was dedicated to Olympian Eileithyia. Sosipolis had an inner chamber of her temple, where he received honors, and a priestess, an old woman chosen yearly who alone might go into the chamber (6.20.2–3). When the priestess enters to perform rites, "*parthenoi* and married women, remaining in the chamber of Eileithyia, sing a song." Given the cult of Eileithyia and the *aition,* the song must have focused on the theme of birth. What the *aition* suggests is that women's role in giving birth was linked to the safety of the community and gods' protection of the land.

In fact, the story is almost too transparent a parable about relinquishing children to defence of the territory. In this narrative authority is attributed to the (mythical) female as a way of valorizing both giving birth and giving up the child. Moreover, no father is hinted at in Pausanias' narrative, nor any source for the dreams. Assuming that Pausanias did not merely omit the father, the woman must have been depicted as acting on her own

---

[113] For Sosipolis at Olympia, see Farnell 1977: II 611–12.

[114] Sosipolis' shrine was near the Temple of Hera in the oldest section of the sanctuary at Olympia. See Herrmann 1972: 31 and 70.

[115] At another point in his account of Elis, Pausanias mentions a painting of Sosipolis done according to a dream vision (6.25.4): the god is a boy wrapped in a robe spangled with stars and holding the horn of Amaltheia in one hand.

in order to establish that she voluntarily yielded the child. We cannot tell from Pausanias' account whether the women's song had a communal audience, so that it could count as public poetry in the sense in which I have been using the term. In any case the *aition* interprets the cult of Sosipolis as another version of the alienation of women from themselves that was found in the *partheneia*.[116]

With this story other briefer pieces of evidence can be compared. *Gynaikes* are said to have mourned Achilles at Kroton and Aias at Lokris.[117] This custom, odd at first glance, must have to do with giving up sons to an early but glorious military death (whatever other significance was also involved).[118] If women staged themselves in these ritual dramas as mourning for mythical children, both theatricalizing and depersonalizing grief, they represented loss as a norm for themselves. During the Agrionia festival at Chaironeia in Boeotia, women went hunting for Dionysus but said he had fled to the Muses; the story is reminiscent of the tale of Dionysus and his nurses in *Iliad* 6.130–40 and presupposes a young Dionysus who is lost.[119] For the women, such display must have interacted psychologically with the laments for death of kin that were their province and must have given the latter an added patina of inevitability.[120]

If modern Greek parallels are indicative, lament was a genre in which women did speak powerfully to the community, assigning blame and demanding recompense for the deaths of relatives, especially children.[121] Ritualized lament may then have been, among other things, a way to

[116] It was a theme in Attic tragedy too. A fragment of Euripides' *Erechtheus* (fr. 50 Austin) contains a long speech by Erechtheus' wife Praxithea relinquishing her children to sacrifice on behalf of the city.

[117] Burnett 1988: 143, citing Lykophron *Alexandra* 856–58 and 1131ff. She lists other mourning rituals as well, not all celebrated just by women.

[118] Women were the chief mourners in a family. Alexiou 1974: 10 points out that women have traditionally had the duty to mourn.

[119] Agrionia: Plutarch *Sympotic Questions* 717a, discussed briefly by Nilsson 1957: 274. Plutarch (*Greek Questions* 299f) tells of a grimmer version of the Agrionia at Orchomenos: the daughters of Minyas killed the son of one of them; since then certain women are pursued by the priest of Dionysus at the yearly ritual, and he has the right to kill a woman if he catches her. Plutarch adds that in his time the priest Zoilos did kill a woman.

[120] Loraux 1990: 57–100 analyzes the pathos and anger of the grieving mother in the Greek imagination, projected in myth. Myth depletes the mother's power by making her responsible for her grief and destroyed by it, like Niobe or the nightingale.

[121] For a remarkable account of modern Greek women's mourning in the Mani, see Seremetakis 1991, esp. 99–125. Mourning is "antiphonal," with a group responding to the lead mourner (called the *korifea*, "chorus-leader"), who improvises eight-syllable verses, and one woman taking up from another. The women improvise poetry that is sometimes of great power; see, e.g., 121–22. Good laments are remembered in an oral tradition. On 102 and 124–25 she makes a brief comparison with ancient Greece. Ancient Greek women's laments may have been an equally powerful form of expression, and, like women of the Mani, ancient women may have incited men to revenge by their laments, as Alexiou 1974: 21–22 suggests.

model generic lament devoid of angry demands for recompense.[122] *Gynaikes,* whose bodies were already sexual, could present themselves in performance as cut off from their product, children.

On Delos and doubtless elsewhere, childbirth inspired songs. Delian women danced and sang in honor of Apollo, probably celebrating his birth.[123] A chorus of quasi-professional status existed on Delos, the Deliades; they sang of Apollo, Leto, and Artemis, and also of the men and women of old; perhaps these last were cult-founding stories.[124] Herodotus also mentions (4.35) the "song of Olen" that Delian women sang as they made a collection for Opis and Arge, *parthenoi* who were connected with the birth of Apollo. Olen came from Lycia and, Herodotus says, composed the other ancient Delian hymns as well.[125] It sounds as though Herodotus is attesting to a traditional song to go with an old agricultural custom; Opis and Arge may have been non-Greek agricultural goddesses later equated with Artemis.[126] Yet it gives one pause to learn that Opis and Arge were buried in a tomb behind the Temple of Artemis.[127] Herodotus says nothing about mourning, but the birth of Apollo was somehow linked with the death of *parthenoi.*[128]

Gynaikes also act out alienation of body from subjectivity in one type of

---

Martin 1989: 86–88 identifies lament as the one genre of *mythos* (authoritative speech) performed by women in epic.

[122] For legislation that effectively curbed ancient women's public lament, see Alexiou 1974: 14–18. Holst-Warhaft 1992: 114–19 extends Alexiou's discussion of the danger that women may spur revenge by lamenting.

[123] Euripides *Heracles* 687–90.

[124] *Homeric Hymn to Apollo* 158–61. On the Deliades see Calame 1977: I 194–204. They are referred to as *parthenoi* in the hymn, but Thucydides (3.104.5) calls them *gynaikes*. Homolle 1890: 500–502 collects information from several Hellenistic inscriptions on the activities of "the chorus" and the props for their use: torches or lamps, "vine-branches," etc. This was a chorus of married women (χορὸς γυναικῶν: 501n.4). Homolle identifies it with the Deliades. The chorus participated in numerous festivals and was apparently a standing institution, for the (female) pipes-player who accompanied them was paid by the year (501). Cf. Bruneau 1970: 35–38.

[125] On Olen's hymns, see also Pausanias 8.21.3, 5.7.8.

[126] Sale 1961: 79–80.

[127] Sale 1961 has an excellent discussion of the difference between this pair of maidens and another pair, Hyperoche and Laodike, who also had a grave in the sanctuary of Artemis, according to Herodotus in this same passage, in which he distinguishes their rites. The latter were connected with Eileithyia, Sale believes, and therefore with human fertility.

[128] Some will see an initiatory motif in this, but that idea attaches more readily to the other pair of maidens, who receive gifts of hair from young women about to marry and from young men (Hdt. 4.34). Holst-Warhaft 1992: 101 points out that at Athens the major women's festivals, the Demeter festivals, Anthesteria, and Adonia, have mourning as a component.

ritual, Dionysiac celebrations.[129] One poem invoking Dionysus and performed by *gynaikes* is recorded, the brief hymn that the women of Elis
sang when they called on Dionysus, according to Plutarch (871 *PMG*):

> ἐλθεῖν ἥρω Διόνυσε
> Ἀλείων ἐς ναὸν
> ἁγνὸν σὺν Χαρίτεσσιν
> ἐς ναὸν
> 5 τῶι βοέωι ποδὶ δύων,
> ἄξιε ταῦρε,
> ἄξιε ταῦρε.

Come, hero Dionysus, to the holy shrine of the Elians with the Graces, to the
shrine, entering on your bovine foot, worthy bull, worthy bull.

This may or may not be the whole song that they sang, perhaps at the
festival of the Thyia, in a ritual of calling on the god.[130] If ἡμῖν (to us) was
the original reading in line 1 in place of the anomalous ἥρως (hero) used of
a god, then the first person would be a communal one.[131] Pausanias provides another item about the Thyia: on the evening of the festival the
priests lock away three empty jars, and on the next day they are discovered
to be full of wine. Martin Nilsson therefore suggests that the women may
have performed during the evening or night, and the wine in the jars was
evidence of the god's response. If this is right, then the transaction, renewing Dionysus' commitment to the territory, operates through an exchange
of wine for women who will yield themselves to the force of his coming.
Dionysus is to appear in bull form, but together with the Graces, so the
women's very dancing testifies to his presence.[132] Reflection and model
are condensed into a demonstration of energy that attracts the god and
renews his favor.

Another category of performance by *gynaikes* is mocking festivals, in

[129] See Henrichs 1978 for the activities of women attached to the cult of Dionysus in the
Hellenistic period.

[130] See Nilsson 1957: 291–93 on the Thyia and the connection of the poem with it. Plutarch elsewhere (*Virtues of Women* 251e) refers to "the women sanctified in relation to Dionysus whom they call Sixteen," on the basis of which Nilsson identifies the performers with
the board of Sixteen Women. Plutarch nowhere says that these women were the ones to
dance, so this is dubious. Cf. Pausanias 6.26.1.

[131] As suggested by Brown 1982.

[132] The *Bacchae* of Euripides is the great literary depiction of Dionysus' possession of
women. Teiresias and Kadmos are not inspired by the god, and Pentheus is dressed in
women's garments at the point when Dionysus takes over his mind. In Bacchylides 11.112
SM the Proitides establish a chorus of *gynaikes* after they have been cured of madness.

which women mocked each other or women and men mocked. I will look at one example of each. The ceremony for Damia and Auxesia held at Epidauros and on the island of Aigina is described by Herodotus (5.83.3). In addition to sacrifices, choruses of women mocked "no man, but local women," according to the historian.[133] Herodotus also says that the Aiginetans assigned ten *chorēgoi* to each goddess. These could be chorus-leaders, which would imply that there were twenty choruses, but Herodotus is probably using the word *chorēgos* to mean "sponsor," the one who pays for clothing and rehearsing of the chorus.[134] In the latter case, the *chorēgoi* would also arrange for and therefore control the texts for the choruses, for performance cannot have been a spontaneous shouting match. Perhaps, as in Attic comedy, they jeered at prominent figures, which would explain why Herodotus is at pains to rule out female mockery of men. Between male control of their words and women as their victims, female performers are forced to enact women's subjection to male definition. The tone might have been festive and joshing, the insults generic, or serious shaming of women who were unpopular may have been included. Without knowing more about the level of jibes, we cannot analyze the effect precisely, but it is likely enough that women's performance was used against deviations from the roles assigned to women.[135] Here, as in the case of Eileithyia and Sosipolis, women are empowered to speak in public of their own negative relationship to social power.

Another mocking festival is Argive, the Hybristika; it involves women and men mocking each other. In a way this arrangement makes women public speakers like men, for the two groups ranged against one another share the same public space. The asymmetry is in fact simply displaced, if the *aition* is a guide to the nature of the mocking. According to the *aition* the Argive army was defeated, and the Spartans marched on the city of Argos. Telesilla armed the women, inspiring them to defend the walls; the women were victorious.[136] Thereafter a festival was instituted in which

---

[133] Fluck 1931: 21–22 connects this with the well-attested *aischrologia* (obscenity-speaking) of Demeter festivals. Men are usually barred from such rituals; see the collected testimonia in Fluck.

[134] This is how Fluck 1931: 21 takes it.

[135] I am not arguing against the standard view that these rituals are meant to stimulate fertility, but pointing out that when they are conducted in public they are easily transformed into exercises in shaming. On the fertility-promoting character of *aischrologia,* see Nilsson 1957: 322; Fluck 1931: 25–26.

[136] Plutarch *Virtues of Women* 245d-f gives the story and describes the festival. Henderson 1987 *ad Lys.* 254–386 connects this scene in the play, in which half-choruses of men and women mock each other, with insult festivals. Cf. Nilsson 1957: 369–74 on cults with androgynous figures or cross-dressing. He connects the Hybristika with wedding rituals (371–73).

women and men exchange clothes and mock each other.[137] The mocking festival then seems to center on the question whether the men are adequate warriors. Shaming is directed toward men in this case; if women claim to be better men than the men, while the men are cast as women, they both merely illustrate the insult to the category "male" that failure represents. The shameful category of women is to be occupied by whoever is less valorous. Again, women's public performance is predicated on their agreeing that the female body is the unworthy one. But did women always insult men on the grounds that they were worthless like women, or did they slip in the direction of the opinion that men are worthless? The effort to use the female as the category that can be defined *ad libitum* may backfire if it opens the category "men" up to redefinition.

So far as the evidence goes, it indicates that women performing communal poetry combined the function of providing reflection and model with a staging of their own subordinate status in the community. Yet they did perform. Their self-presentation could not be wholly discredited without jeopardizing the communal function they filled, and they themselves could undermine their words by irony or mocking exaggeration. Dancing is a sensuous activity. Performers cannot in the nature of the event be inhibited from projecting their subjectivity through inflection and body language. The demand that women affirm in their own persons the dominant culture's self-contradictory meaning of the sign "female" gave women a psychological power that they could always try to reclaim.

One might compare the ending of Euripides' *Hippolytus* (1428–29), where Artemis promises Hippolytus that *parthenoi* will sing of Phaedra's love for him. Barbara Goff's analysis of the significance of their song is applicable in a remarkable way to the ambiguity of women's performance as we have traced its effects in *partheneia*.[138] She says about them: "Although the rite and song contain the brides within a traditional role, they also give them voice and therefore a certain power. They are women singing about a woman silenced, but by this song the brides ensure that Phaidra will be heard. As girls on the brink of marriage, the brides are about to become counters in the patriarchal exchange of women; but the signs that are women are uniquely equipped also to make signs themselves, to use language, as the brides do when they sing of Hippolytos and Phaidra."

---

[137] Other festivals with mockery pitting women against men were found at Anaphe (Apollodoros 1.9.26) and Pellene (Pausanias 7.27.10). The first is for Apollo, the second for Demeter.

[138] Goff 1990. The following quotation is from 116–17. Her whole final discussion, 113–29, is relevant.

III

There was, however, opportunity for a very different kind of public "performance" by women through which they could speak to the community without being deauthorized, although it did not allow them to speak for the community. They could set up inscriptions. Objects offered to the gods and grave-markers begin in the eighth century to be engraved with metrical inscriptions, usually hexameters or elegiac couplets, explaining their significance. In fact, most poetic inscriptions of the archaic period are either records of dedicators on votive offerings or epitaphs on grave monuments. Both are meant to address the community for the purpose, like Pindar's *partheneion* II, of promoting attention to particular members of it.

Here I will give some examples of inscriptions with women as subjects. They are taken from *Carmina Epigraphica Graeca* (abbreviated *CEG*).[139] The rhetoric of inscriptions more generally will be examined in Chapter 6, but the point to be made at the moment is women's access to this form of public representation of themselves.

1. *CEG* 138, ca. 550–525?, Troizen.

Δαμοτίμοι τόδε σᾶμα φίλα ϝεργάσατο μάτερ
    Ἀμφιδάμα, οὐ γὰρ παῖδες ἐνὶ μεγάροις ἐγένοντο.
καὶ τρίπος hὸν Θέβασ{σ}ι θέον ἔνικεγ [   ]
    [   ]μα[ ] ἐστ' ἀπαθές, ἐπέθεκε δὲ παιδί.

For Damotimos his loving mother had this marker made, Amphidama, for no children were born in his house. And the tripod that he won at Thebes in running [   ] is uninjured, and she set it over her child.

The inscription is on an octagonal column; the victory tripod once sat atop it. Paul Friedländer comments on its use of epic language, which accords with the mother's evident concern to provide for her son's continuing *kleos* (fame).[140] Amphidama names herself (and not the father) and describes her actions. This is public poetry in the sense that the monument was set up in public where all might recognize its message. But although speaking to the community, it does not speak for it in any way. What validates this claim without a performance context? Her actions explain the existence of the monument, so in a sense Amphidama is the authority for the "speech" of the marker. The community knows who she is, at least in the short term, so can place the monument. Yet the "performer" of this

---

[139] Hansen 1983. For a selection of metrical inscriptions with translation, see Friedländer and Hoffleit 1948.

[140] Friedländer and Hoffleit 1948: 34.

"speech" is not Amphidama, who appears in the third person, but the marker itself, or no one. Amphidama and Damotimos are both replaced by writing. Because it "speaks" in their absence and provides a self-sufficient authority, writing is a system that women can use to represent themselves in speech.

2. *CEG* 38, ca. 530?, Attica.

> [Τ]ερπὸ Μελίσες σῆμα τόδ᾽ ἔχ[ευεν?   θαν]όσες.

Terpo heaped up (?) this grave-marker of Melise, who [died   ].

The women named here are brought into no relationship with men at all. They may have had no permanent connections that would have given them position, but through writing a woman can name herself and another woman as individuals who have claims on others' memory of them.

A different kind of independent naming of a woman is found on votive offerings:

3. *CEG* 273, ca. 470–450?, from the Athenian acropolis. Cf. *CEG* 342.

> [Μ]ικύθη μ᾽ ἀνέ[θηκεν Ἀθ]ηναίηι τό[δ᾽ ἄγαλμα]
> [εὐξ]αμένη δ[εκάτην καὶ] ὑπὲρ πα[ίδων κ]αὶ ἑαυτῆ[ς].

Mikythe dedicated me, this [delight], to Athena, having [vowed] a [tenth] for the sake of her children and herself.

Votive offerings frequently refer to the object in the first person, as this one does: the object "speaks" its own identity. This habit is confirmation that the message is seen to be self-contained, the authority for the statement inhering in the combination of inscription and object. Here the object "speaks" to name Mikythe also in a public record of her activity.

Through the use of writing, women could also participate in the interstate presentations of civic identity, of which the choral performances on Delos discussed in Chapter 3 are an example. It is at Delos, in fact, that a dedication by a woman from Naxos was found.

4. *CEG* 403, ca. 650, Naxos. Cf. *CEG* 413 and 414, 317.

> Νικάνδρη μ᾽ ἀνέθεκεν ἑκηβόλοι ἰοχεαίρηι,
> Ϙόρη Δεινοδίκηο τõ Ναhσίο, ἔhσοχος ἀλήον,
> Δεινομένεος δὲ κασιγνέτη, Φhράhσο δ᾽ ἄλοχος γ⟨ῦν⟩.

Nikandre dedicated me to the far-shooting arrow-pourer (Artemis), (Nikandre) the daughter of Deinodikes the Naxian, eminent beyond other women, the sister of Deinomenes, and wife now of Phraxos.

This inscription is on a votive offering, a marble statue of a female figure. Nikandre is fortified by the names of three male relatives who identify her status, but her name and action occupy the first line and she receives the epithet reminiscent of epic. There is another votive offering with inscription that may have been meant for display on Delos also; the sculptor, who added his name, identifies himself as Parian, which could mean that the monument was to be displayed elsewhere than on Paros:[141]

5. *CEG* 413, ca. 525–500? Paros.

᾽Άρτεμι, σοὶ τόδ᾽ ἄγαλμα Τελεστοδί[κη μ᾽ ἀνέθηκεν]

᾽Ασφαλίο μήτηρ, Θερσέλεω θυγάτηρ.

τõ Παρίο ποίημα Κριτωνίδεω εὔχομ[αι ἔναι].

Artemis, to you Telestodike [dedicated me] this delight, the mother of Asphalios, the daughter of Therseleos. I claim [to be] the work of the Parian Kritonides.

What is striking about this inscription is that Telestodike identifies herself as a mother but not as a wife. As she presents herself, she is a link in a vertical kinship line passing down generations. Perhaps there was a special reason why she does not name her husband, or perhaps she is simply indicating how she views her place in the social system. In speaking of Telestodike as the agent, I am not forgetting that she probably could not have acted without the cooperation of men in paying the sculptor and arranging for the offering to be set up on Delos. She may well not even have composed the verses. The background is unrecoverable, but the fact remains that the inscription presents her as actor and chooses a subset of all possible men to attach to her as indicators of identity.

6. *CEG* 169, ca. 525–500? Erythra.

[   ]ι τόδε σ[ῆ]μα μήτηρ ἐπέθηκε θανόντι

Φανοκρίτη παιδὶ χαριζομένη.

For [   ] who died his mother set up this grave-marker, Phanokrite, making a gesture of affection to her child.

This inscription does not scan correctly. The hexameter has a wrong quantity and the first half of the pentameter is three syllables short. Ulrich von Wilamowitz-Moellendorff commented about it, "What is more obvious than that before the eyes of a woman too little educated was an example such as Καλλιμάχῳ τόδε σῆμα πατὴρ ἐπέθηκε θανόντι Κάλλων τηλυγέτῳ παιδὶ χαριζόμενος (To Kallimachos who died his father Kallon set up this marker, making a gesture of affection to his beloved child)?"[142] Peter Hansen assents to his opinion. Because it is metrically faulty, we are invited to think that this particular inscription was composed by a woman. Rather than comment on the assumptions behind that remark, I prefer to

---

[141] This is the suggestion of ibid., 1948: 106.
[142] Quoted in *CEG ad loc.*

ask *why* it is metrically faulty. It does not scan because its author has wrested the language adapted to expressing men's relationships to her use as a woman.[143] In the first line she has substituted μήτηρ for πατήρ, "mother" for "father," and changed a short syllable to long. In the second line she did not include an ornamental epithet with her name or the word *child,* so the line is short. Perhaps she had no model of a line with a name of the same metrical shape as her name, or perhaps the meanings of the available adjectives did not appeal to her. The metrical faultiness exposes the subversion necessary for a woman to use the conventional language but also illustrates women's manipulation of language in contrast to the linguistic manipulation of women in performance.

I have treated the evidence from different times and places as though it all contributed to one homogeneous picture. I do not mean to suggest homogeneity in local performance except at an abstract level. In spite of the terrible state of the evidence, it is possible to make some suggestions about differences in the way women were included in the community through performance in different places. One is tempted to find in Elis an unusually prominent role played by women. This impression could also be an effect of Pausanias' having better sources for women's activities in Elis than elsewhere, for most of the information comes from him. At Thebes too, women's participation in public ceremony is better attested than it is at most places. At Sparta *parthenoi,* at least, were apparently more visible in public than elsewhere and participated in the system of maintaining pressure on young men to become admirable warriors, but in return were staged as alienated from themselves perhaps more overtly than elsewhere. On Lesbos a high degree of segregation by sex seems to have been the rule. Groups like Sappho's give little indication of participating in common festivals other than weddings. Alkaios (130B *V*) contrasts the political gathering of the assembly with a women's gathering in a temple precinct. At Athens very little evidence about women's performance survives in spite of the relative richness of the sources for that city.[144] The democracy had the effect of suppressing women's public appearances because democratic ideology was inimical to women's self-presentation as

---

[143] Svenbro 1993: 48–55 discusses another inscription that does not scan. The problem is again a woman's name, although in this case it does not appear that trying to change the gender of a known pattern was at the root of the problem. Svenbro has a different explanation.

[144] Euripides *Heracleidae* 777–83 mentions *parthenoi* dancing on the Acropolis at an all-night festival, probably the Panathenaia. In Euripides' *Erechtheus* (Fr. 65.80 Austin) Athena prescribes choral dances of *parthenoi* in honor of the daughters of Erechtheus; this must reflect actual practice. Plutarch *Theseus* 18 refers to a procession of girls to the temple of Apollo Delphinios but does not mention song. The Thorikos calendar has references to "singing (?) women"; see Whitehead 1986: 194–95n.102. The list of women's ways of participating in ritual in the city at *Lys.* 638–47 does not mention choral performance.

representatives of the community.[145] Women's speech in single-sex groups
is a different matter. At the Athenian Thesmophoria and at the Haloa,
women celebrating by themselves are reported to have indulged in obscene joking, and fantasy suggested to men that at the Haloa women medi-
tated on indulgence in adultery.[146] At Sparta a banquet for women is mentioned that featured cakes shaped like breasts and performance by a chorus
of *parthenoi*. Plutarch says that Spartan *gynaikes* had eros for *parthenoi*.[147]

[145] Cf. Halperin 1990a on the operation of Athenian ideology in making the male body the
ground of equality.

[146] Schol. Lucian *Dialogues of Courtesans* 7.4; pp. 279–81 Rabe; Fluck 1931: 13–15. See
Winkler 1990a: 188–209 on women's perspective as expressed in rituals celebrated by women
apart from men, and 194–95 for translation of the scholion.

[147] Athenaios 14, 646a citing Sosibios *FGH* 595 F6: the *parthenoi* sing an encomium of "the
parthenos" (whose identity, goddess or human, is not clear); Plutarch *Lykourgos* 18.9. Calame
1977: I 433–36 overstates the evidence for female homosexuality at Sparta.

CHAPTER THREE

Male Performers in the Community

I

WE NOW TURN to men in community performance. Here one might expect
to find that men would either announce their gender identity as a positive
counterpart of women's self-identification or would say nothing about
their sexual identity because to be male was the norm. These modes are
indeed common, but male use of gender goes beyond them: while men as
speakers could rely on an unspoken or merely asserted gender identity,
they could also adopt a metaphorical identity. I will begin with simple
assertions. In Chapter 2 we examined the statement from Alkman's *Louvre
partheneion,* "I myself, a *parthenos,* screech in vain from the roofbeam, an
owl." A self-identifying statement by male performers will expose a basic
difference in the way male and female performers assert their gender identity as a basis for their public voices.

Plutarch quotes lines, probably old, spoken by three Spartan choruses
composed respectively of older men, younger men, and boys. The lines
were quoted in English in Chapter 1; I quote them here with the Greek
(870 *PMG*):

ἁμές ποκ' ἦμες ἄλκιμοι νεανίαι.
ἁμὲς δέ γ' εἰμές· αἰ δὲ λῆις, αὐγάσδεο.
ἁμὲς δέ γ' ἐσσόμεσθα πολλῶι κάρρονες.

We once were vigorous young men.
And we now are, in truth; if you will, look!
And we indeed will be stronger by far.

The members of the middle chorus assert their identity as "vigorous
young men," then point to their bodies. They do not need to speak further
because the audience can look. Their bodies give the performers adequate
grounds for speech and boasting self-presentation, for they validate the
men's claim to represent Spartan strength. If these lines were connected
with the celebration to commemorate the victory at Thyrea, then the men
were nude and were presenting themselves as worthy to revive the memory of past success.[1] In this case the men do speak, as well as display

---

[1] See Ch. 1, p. 55.

themselves, in order to articulate self-conscious pride in their bodies, for the context is military, and aggressive self-confidence is an important ingredient of military success. Orestes in Euripides' *Electra* (388–90) says that *physis* (nature) and *eupsychia* (high spirit) make a man steadfast in battle.[2] These dancers are no doubt presenting their *eupsychia*. The whole of Plutarch's *Lykourgos* 21 is a eulogy of the Spartan linking of "music" (including song and dance) with valor.

In the contrast between this line and Alkman's *Louvre partheneion*, we see encapsulated the difference between male and female performance at Sparta. The *parthenoi* speak of their speaking as ineffectual and their bodies as inadequate to attract. By means of the contradiction between their statements and the ritually efficacious, attractive performance, they create a negative position from which to speak without authority. The male performers treat their speaking not as ineffectual but as unnecessary because their bodies are adequate to ground their self-presentation. Furthermore, the *parthenoi* of Alkman's two *partheneia* direct the audience's gaze at Hagesichora and Agido (in the first case) and at Astymeloisa (in the second case), away from themselves. If the audience did in fact gaze at them, as they must have, they did so despite the words of the *parthenoi*. The young men ask the audience to gaze at them, while their boast inhibits the audience from objectifying them. The erotic charge of this performance, based on the young men's exuberant self-consciousness, is of a different sort from the effect produced by the *parthenoi*. Lucian (*On the Dance* 12) adds confirmation that the dance movements of the young men and women expressed the difference when he describes the Spartan dance called the *hormos* (necklace):

> The necklace is a dance of ephebes and *parthenoi* together performing in a single line and truly resembling a necklace. The ephebe leads, dancing steps of young men's type such as later he will use in war, and the *parthenos* follows, showing how to dance decorously a woman's part, so that the necklace is woven of chastity (σωφροσύνη) and masculinity (ἀνδρεία).[3]

Thus the eroticized public praise and blame of young men by Spartan *parthenoi* (discussed in Chapter 1) fit into a system of display linking sexual attractiveness with military fitness. The two are combined in Tyrtaios' lines on the beauty of a young warrior dead on the battlefield (10.27–30 *W*):

---

[2] Similarly Heracles prays at Pindar *Isthmian* 6.45–49 that Telamon's son should have a body as "unbreakable" as Heracles' lion pelt and a spirit to accord with it.

[3] Cf. *Iliad* 18.590–98 for a dance of men with daggers and marriageable *parthenoi* with wreaths; Webster 1970: 46–48.

νέοισι δὲ πάντ’ ἐπέοικεν,
ὄφρ’ ἐρατῆς ἥβης ἀγλαὸν ἄνθος ἔχηι,
ἀνδράσι μὲν θηητὸς ἰδεῖν, ἐρατὸς δὲ γυναιξὶ
30   ζωὸς ἐών, καλὸς δ’ ἐν προμάχοισι πεσών.

But it is completely fitting for young men (to lie dead on the field), so long as one is in the glorious flower of lovely youth, a wonder for men to see, lovely to women while he is alive, beautiful if he falls among the front ranks of fighters.

As Jean-Pierre Vernant has commented, young men were prepared for war as young women were for marriage.[4] We can see, in the case of Sparta, what different ways of constructing self-consciousness that preparation involved.[5]

There are parallels elsewhere for Spartan men's visual staging of themselves as the embodiment of Spartan power.[6] It is recorded of Sophocles that, nude, anointed with oil, and playing the lyre, he led those performing the *paian* in celebration of the Athenian victory over the Persians at Salamis.[7] Various athletic dances, including the *pyrrhichē*, or dance in armor, displayed strength.[8] Plato in the *Laws* (796b) speaks of armed dances at Athens for Athena, at Sparta for the Dioskouroi, and on Crete for Zeus. At the Athenian Panathenaia youths danced the *pyrrhichē* naked and brandishing a shield.[9] This must be the Athenian dance that Plato has in mind; in fact, it is probably the model for the dance he prescribes at *Laws* 815a.[10] In that passage Plato says that the young men are to mime avoidance of blows and missiles by dodging, pulling back, leaping on high and into a crouch and to take on aggressive postures as well; if this depicts the dance at the Panathenaia, it must have been spirited.[11] Athenaios (14, 630d) says

[4] Vernant 1988: 34.

[5] Sometimes men sang and women danced, e.g., Ps-Hesiod *Shield* 278–80 (although probably the men are to be pictured dancing as well and the women singing); Callimachus *Hymn* 4.304–6. This accords with the distinction drawn here: the men speak and the women show themselves off.

[6] Martin 1989: 132 cites Fingerle 1939: 148 for the idea that Hector's lines at *Iliad* 7.235–41 are an old song for a sword-dance and concurs that Hector is conflating battle with display performance here.

[7] *Life of Sophocles* 3, TrGF p. 31.

[8] Cf. Schol. Pindar *Pythian* 2.127 (II 52–53 *Dr.*) on the *kastoreion*, a Spartan dance in armor, and the *pyrrhichē*. It also says that Thaletas was the first to compose *hyporchēmata* (dance songs) to accompany the *pyrrhichē*. Nagy 1979: 330–32 connects the *pyrrhichē* with fire and warrior "force."

[9] Lysias 21.1–4. On this passage see Kyle 1992: 94–95.

[10] Wheeler 1982: 231, who also compares Euripides *Andromache* 1129–36, where Neoptolemos avoiding Delphian weapons is said to be doing the *pyrrhichē*.

[11] Poursat 1968 collects vase-paintings that show armed dancers. Sometimes a procession is shown because the pipes-player marches ahead of the dancers; sometimes the pipes-player

that the *pyrrhichē* is a fast and warlike dance. In Xenophon's *Anabasis* (6.1.11) some Arcadians are described as putting on a show by marching in armor to pipes and singing a *paian* and dancing "just as (they do) in their processions to the gods."[12] Armed dances are also attested from the west.[13] To return to Sparta, a Dorian marching song speaks of actions that must have been performed as the singers sang the words (856 *PMG*):

> ἄγετ' ὦ Σπάρτας εὐάνδρου
> κοῦροι πατέρων πολιητᾶν,
> λαιᾶι μὲν ἴτυν προβάλεσθε,
> δόρυ δ' εὐτόλμως πάλλοντες,
> 5   μὴ φειδόμενοι τᾶς ζωᾶς
> οὐ γὰρ πάτριον τᾶι Σπάρται.

Come on, youths of well-manned Sparta from citizen fathers, thrust your shield forward with the left hand while shaking the spear boldly, not sparing (your) life, for it is not the tradition at Sparta.

In performance of military dances, men make the point that they are worthy to represent the community in war, so their visual demonstration of strength and aggressiveness creates a feeling of renewal for the audience.[14]

Very relevant to the militaristic construction of the masculine body in performance is Maud Gleason's conclusion in her study of physiognomists' advice for evaluating the character of men:

The physiognomists, astrologers, and popular moralists of antiquity thought in terms of degrees of gender conformity and gender deviance. They shared a notion of gender identity built upon polarized distinctions (smooth/hirsute, pantherine/leonine) that purported to characterize the gulf between men and women, but actually served to divide the male sex into legitimate and illegiti-

---

faces them, indicating a dance in place (552–65). The dancers hold their shields forward and sometimes horizontally, their right arms pulled back with spears in hand; their step is high and quick. See his illustration #16 for probable Panathenaic dancers. Borthwick 1970 points out that on the vases and in literary evidence the dancer turns his head to the side, perhaps in mimesis of Athena fighting the Gorgon (319–22), perhaps to represent avoidance of blows (329–30).

[12] Other more specialized dances are also described in this passage (6.1.5–13), which records a set of impromptu after-dinner entertainments. They include the *pyrrhichē* danced by a dancing-girl with a light shield.

[13] Burnett 1988: 143nn.123 and 127 gives examples.

[14] See Pritchett 1979: 202–9 on military festivals, some with dancing and races in armor. Cf. also Morrow 1960: 335–37; Brelich 1969: 113–207 on initiation as strenuous military training. Strabo 10.4.16 gives an account of training, including war dances. Crowther 1985 discusses contests in male beauty and physical fitness.

mate members, some of whom were unmistakable androgynes, while others were subtly deceitful impostors.[15]

Gleason is writing about the second century CE, but the system of classifying men that she describes was clearly much older.[16] She cites features of it from Aristotle, and the scene between Better Argument and Worse Argument in Aristophanes' *Clouds* is based on it.[17] According to this system a firm carriage, fearless look, and deep steady voice indicated a man, while deviations from the ideal revealed a tendency toward the feminine or even a predilection for the "feminine" sexual position.[18] As she points out, masculinity "constituted a system of signs. It was a language that anatomical males were taught to speak with their bodies."[19] In other words, it was largely visual. Men performing their military capacity in dance were declaring themselves the manliest of men.[20]

In the *Clouds* the issue is educating boys rather than manliness *per se,* but the argument is over whether education should produce an admired sort of man or a physically weak but verbally slick type who can indulge himself and escape (or shrug off) the consequences. Better Argument connects boys' admirable physique with performance of traditional songs and dances and ignorance of rhetoric (964–68):

> Then (it was necessary) for the neighborhood boys to walk in good order in the roads to the kithara-master's, lightly clothed, in a throng, even if it was snowing like coarse-ground barley. Then, moreover, he taught them to learn a song by heart, not holding their thighs together, either "Dread Pallas, city-sacker" or "A far-carrying cry," singing the tune that their fathers handed down.[21]

This is the system that produced the men of Marathon (986), that makes one burst into anger at a jeer (992), and that produces a well-developed body (1012–14): "a shining chest, bright skin, large shoulders, a small tongue, large buttocks, and a small organ." Those educated by Worse

---

[15] Gleason 1990: 412.

[16] Cf. Dover 1978: 68–73 on ideal male beauty as deduced from sixth- and fifth-century vase-painting; Winkler 1990a: 45–70 on classical Athens.

[17] On Aristotle, Gleason 1990: 396n.30; 412–13.

[18] Cf. Dover 1978: 73–76 and the treatment of Agathon in Aristophanes *Women at the Thesmophoria* 101–208. Plato in *Laws* 665e remarks on the leanness required for choral dancing in competition.

[19] Gleason 1990: 402.

[20] Cf. Dover 1978: 144: "In the Athens of Aristophanes the supreme effeminacy was cowardice on the battlefield; Eupolis' comedy *Astrateutoi* ('men who have not been on military service') had the alternative title *Androgunoi* ('women-men')."

[21] The point of the boys' not holding their thighs together is not clear. Dover 1968 *ad loc.*

Argument have the opposite appearance, "pale skin, small shoulders, slender chest, large tongue . . . " and so on (1017–19). These boys will be stuffed with *katapygosynē* (1023, "assholery").[22] They cannot perform the *pyrrhichē* creditably (988–89):

> You (with your coddling) make me gag whenever they have to dance at the Panathenaia and one of them shows disdain for Athena by holding his shield in front of his haunch.

The point seems to be that the boy is letting his shield sag too low rather than holding it up and deploying it as he should.[23] The contrast between "masculinity" written on the body displayed in performance and command of rhetoric suitable for the assembly and the courts is Aristophanes' version of the contrast between real and fake men (or women-men) that Gleason studies.

What Aristophanes and Gleason suggest is that not only do male performers "perform" their gender by calling attention to their bodies, but even when military discipline is not the point they should always present a sufficiently "masculine" appearance to validate their performance.[24] If they were not convincing, the audience would not accept them as its representatives and the performance would not reach the level of psychological efficacy. On the other hand, speaking about masculinity would be either redundant or else useless and an invitation to laughter. Thus male gender identity would often have been signaled in performance at the visual level, unmodified by performers' speech about themselves.[25] "Masculine" mu-

---

considers that it refers to boys' not manipulating their genitals somehow with their thighs. But cf. Archilochos 114 *W*:

1   οὐ φιλέω μέλαν στρατηγὸν οὐδὲ διαπεπλιγμένον . . .
3   ἀλλά μοι σμικρός τις εἴη καὶ περὶ κνήμας ἰδεῖν
    ῥοικός, ἀσφαλέως βεβηκὼς ποσσί, καρδίης πλέως.

> I do not feel friendly toward a tall general (who stands) with legs crossed . . . rather give me a short man and bow-legged to look at who stands firmly planted on his feet, full of heart.

Aristophanes may also refer to a "masculine" stance.

[22] On *katapygosynē* and related words, see Dover 1978: 113 and 142–43.

[23] This is the explanation of Dover 1968 *ad loc.* Cf. Henderson 1991a: 129 and n.115 for a possible obscene meaning.

[24] With the proviso that styles changed somewhat (Dover 1978: 79–81). The attitudes noted by Gleason 1990 seem to have lasted (as attitudes, at least) through most of antiquity. Cowan 1990: 189 describes men's dancing in a modern Greek town as an expression of power and prestige among men; though it displays the body, it is not "sexual" in the narrow sense.

[25] Cf. David 1989: 6–13 on the Spartans forcing the helots to perform obscene and grotesque songs and dances, including probably (11) an obscene dance in female disguise and wearing "ugly feminine masks" (Hesychios s.v. *brudalicha*). The social relevance of self-presentation in performance could not be clearer.

sical modes and arrangements of hair and beard would help to underscore gender also.[26]

This masculinity of bodily display is an aggressive stance. The boy raised by Better Argument will flare up at an insulting joke. A pugnacious attitude is an appropriate posture for demonstration of the city's power, no doubt. The problem for community performance is that masculinity is asserted against other men, as Gleason shows, so male performers need some method of mitigating the challenge to the audience that their self-display inevitably creates. In the Spartan song with which I began the chapter, competition is between generations, which means that each chorus's "we" can include the others of its age group. Men's performance sometimes involved making the body humorous or adding a deflating disguise. Choruses of "padded dancers" are attested on vases, men with padding on buttocks and stomach so that they look the opposite of athletic.[27] The satyr costume seen on vases and taken over by the chorus of satyr plays includes an erect phallus—a mark of undignified sexuality. Choruses of men in animal disguise are found on vases and in Aristophanes' comedies: cocks and other birds, wasps, horses and riders, dolphins and riders, frogs.[28] Most of these have emphatically sexual metaphorical meanings.[29] Pindar fr. 107a *SM,* from a *hyporchēma* (dance song), has the singers compare themselves to animals (1–5):

Πελασγὸν ἵππον ἢ κύνα
Ἀμυκλαίαν ἀγωνίῳ
ἐλελιζόμενος ποδὶ μιμέο καμπύλον μέλος διώκων,
οἷ᾽ ἀνὰ Δώτιον ἀνθεμόεν πεδί-
ον πέταται θάνατον κεροέσσᾳ
5   εὑρέμεν ματεῖσ᾽ ἐλάφῳ·

Imitate a Pelasgian horse or an Amyklaian dog, as you whirl on rivalrous foot pursuing the curving dance, such as flies along the flowery Dotion plain seeking to discover death for the horned deer!

Their dance may have mimed these animals. Male sexuality is displayed, but in joking terms, inviting an exuberance that remains good-humored.

---

[26] On "masculine" musical modes, see Plato *Laws* 802e. Note too the prominent beards that adult men on Greek vases usually sport.

[27] See Winkler 1990c on the social meanings of taut and slack male bodies as represented in tragedy and comedy.

[28] See Sifakis 1971: 73–102 for animal costumes.

[29] For wasplike men who give pain to enemies, see Aristophanes *Wealth* 561. Phallus-headed birds are often depicted on vases, e.g., Keuls 1985: figs. 63 and 64. Theognis 1249–52 and 1267–70 refer to a boy as a horse who needs a rider. For the image in erotic contexts, cf. Vetta 1980 *ad loc.* Cf. also Burnett 1988: 143–44.

Through these screens the body is partially disjoined from the ego. Here too belongs the huge phallus, suggesting a collective masculine sexuality, that is at home in Dionysiac revels like the procession at the City Dionysia at Athens.[30]

From this perspective we can better understand Hermokles' "ithyphallic song" for Demetrios, discussed in Chapter 1, and see how cleverly it negotiates a difficult position for the performers. Here the performers speak of themselves as inadequate men when they say, "I am not able to fight." Yet in the phallus they carried they had a prop that recuperated their gender identity—one whose Dionysiac exaggeration could deflect any appearance of being aggressive toward Demetrios. That the Dionysiac phallus belonged in a setting of release from competitive posturing made it perfect for negotiating the presentation of masculine identity in this situation.

At the same time the Aetolian League, the enemy who robs the men performing the "ithyphallic song" of potency, is figured as female and monstrous, a Sphinx. The final lines of the poem ask Demetrios to find an Oedipus who will throw headlong off the rock or turn into a finch τὴν Σφίγγα ταύτην (32–34; "this Sphinx"—the feminine gender is prominent). By labelling the enemy of the community "feminine," the community as a whole can think of itself as masculine. For the Athenians, therefore, the phallus is the community's collective masculinity and the supernatural female its opponent. Together they neutralize the admission of weakness—detach sexual impotence from the impotence of their weapons—and ensure that no destabilization of the masculine identity of the chorus and by extension of the community occurs.

II

The result of the discussion so far, that physical demonstration of achieved masculinity was a necessary basis for men's effective performance, is important in the investigation that follows, of men's verbal self-presentation in performance. To embark on it, we must return to Plutarch's lines quoted at the beginning of the chapter. The other two choruses in that series enhance the physical appearance of the men's bodies through speech. The

[30] Athenaios 14, 622b–d = 851 PMG (partial text), quotes from Semos of Delos (FGH 396 F23) a compressed and obscure description of performances by *ithyphalloi* (those with upright phallus) and *phallophoroi* (phallus-bearers). The former ask the crowd to make way for the "erect, bursting" god, which implies that they should precede an oversized phallus. The latter also perform in the theater; they come out singing a song that promises a new song, then run forward and jeer, while the "phallus-bearer" walking straight. . . . The last sentence is lacking a verb and has other problems. Cf. Cole 1993 on these, esp. 32 on an inscription honoring the ritual attendant of the phallus-bearer for a spectacular dance that ended with hoisting the phallus.

older men recall their past strength. The chorus of boys, however, idealizes itself by asserting that its strength will be much greater than that of the current men. These boys do not yet have the physical stature to represent the community as a military power, but they arrogate to themselves the authority to do so by claiming an identity that extends even beyond the plausible. The boys' dance must have been vigorous enough to make that declaration other than laughable, but the point of interest for us is that they could gain stature through a fiction that also added to the persuasive power of the performance. The boys' idealized identity comes last in the sequence and clinches the psychological efficacy of the performance by predicting that in the future the community will be even more successful than in the past.

What this minimally verbal performance (as Plutarch records it) shows us is that male performers can highlight their bodies as the ground of their worthiness to speak, but they can also create an idealized, extended gender identity that garners assent from the audience because it abets the psychological efficacy of the performance.[31] In this case the idealized identity is simply greater strength than that of normal men, but the same principle allows men to create more complex identities. Of the few extant texts that were performed by men, some stage their performers as taking on this sort of gendered identity, although the fictions are more surprising.

My first example of a text with a significant idealized identity for its performers is Pindar's *paian* 2 for the people of Abdera, of which substantial portions have been recovered on papyrus. The preserved fragments do not indicate the sex of the performers, but the fact that it is a *paian* as well as the political and military focus of the poem make it certain that they are male. The occasion may have been a regular cult observation or, more likely I think, a special ceremony brought on by stress.[32]

There were three triads. In the first, of which the second half of the strophe and the antistrophe are missing, the chorus opens with an appeal to Abderos, eponymous hero of the city, then describes itself in the epode.[33] The second triad, of which some lines are incomplete, begins on the

[31] Cf. Cowan 1990: 16–17 on modern Greek men's creation of an identity through dance. She points out that it is easier for men to "invent" themselves this way than it is for women. I mean verbal idealization, but dance interacted with it.

[32] Dougherty 1994: 205 adopts the former view, passing over the signs of strife and the reference to the "last battle." Whatever the occasion, her analysis complements mine by stressing colonial themes as integrative discourse.

[33] Radt 1958: 28, who is predisposed to attach the first person to Pindar himself, takes the "I" in this poem as the chorus's throughout and quotes von Arnim 1909 with approval: a shift in the first person from Pindar to the chorus is not in theory impossible, but "in a poem like this, where the chorus represents the entire citizenry of a city (cf. 24f. ναίω Θραϊκίαν γαῖαν, 28f. νεόπολίς εἰμι κτλ., 39), it seems out of the question. 'The civic chorus of Abdera, that at a public city festival calls on the tutelary goddess (sic!) of the city for assistance, could not be used by Pindar as a mere mouthpiece like a chorus of paid professional singers' (Arnim 9)."

subject of war in the present. In the antistrophe (48–58) the poem made some reference to civil strife (in a damaged part of the papyrus).[34] Connected with the same theme is the puzzling statement ἤδη φθόνος οἴχεται / τῶν πάλαι προθανόντων (55–56, "now envy has departed of those who died much earlier"). Is the envy of or felt by "those who died much earlier"?[35] Envy connected with ancestors may be an oblique reference to ethnic or class strife; in any event, the fact that it is brought up means that its effects have not entirely dissipated. The epode moves back into history with a review of Abdera's struggle to maintain itself in the face of dispossessed, hostile neighbors. The third triad returns to the present with a prophecy by Hekate, arguably about a battle yet to come.[36] The antistrophe is missing. In the epode the chorus describes song on Delos and the *parthenoi* of Delphi singing and dancing in a chorus. A final address to Abderos and prayer for help in the "last battle" followed by a *paian* refrain close the poem.[37] Both internal and external threats face Abdera, it seems, and the function of the *paian* must be to unify the community for the coming "last battle" mentioned at the end.

The opening lines indicate the place of performance (1–5):

> Ναΐδ]ος Θρονίας Ἄβδηρε χαλκοθώραξ
> Ποσ]ειδᾶνός τε παῖ,
> σέθ]εν Ἰάονι τόνδε λαῷ
> παι]ᾶνα [δι]ώξω
> 5 Δηρηνὸν Ἀπόλλωνα πάρ τ' Ἀφρο[δίταν

Bronze-armored Abderos, child of the [Naiad] Thronia and of Poseidon, (beginning) from [you] I will pursue this *paian* for the Ionian people [going?] to (the shrine of) Apollo Derenos and Aphrodite. . . .

The first lines reveal that the *paian* was performed near or in procession to the shrines of Derenos Apollo and Aphrodite in Abdera; "Derenos" is a

---

[34] So the scholia to 46 and 48, quoted by *SM* ad loc., indicate. D'Alessio 1992 discusses them in light of inscriptional evidence and concludes that Tean colonists at Abdera are creating unrest.

[35] The genitive is either objective or subjective. If it is subjective, it must refer to ancestors who fomented dissention. If objective, it must refer to present citizens' recent resentment, now allegedly come to an end, that some group claimed special privilege on the basis of ancestry. In the latter case the genitive names the grounds for envy. Cf. Radt 1958 *ad loc.* for discussion.

[36] I follow Radt 1958 *ad loc.* on the puzzling lines 73–79. Führer 1967: 62–65 and Rutherford, forthcoming, take the prophecy in 73–75 to refer to the battle at Mt. Melamphyllon, mentioned in 68–70. This is possible, although the *paian*-refrain separates it from the prophecy, but does not eliminate the "final battle" (105–6) which must still be ahead.

[37] Rutherford, forthcoming, points out that each triad ends with a reference to victory in battle followed by a *paian*-refrain. The first two may be victory cries, but the third I would take as an appeal, whose positive outcome the pattern predicts.

local epithet of Apollo.[38] The phrase "Ionian people" probably designates the Abderites themselves.[39] This is clearly communal poetry. When we trace out the alternation between speaking for the audience and speaking to it, however, the effects of internal troubles appear in the programmatic effort to disguise speaking to the audience as speaking for it.[40] Understanding this manipulation will help explain the gender imagery also. The first triad opens the poem by speaking for the audience in the prayer and contains the chorus's self-identification (quoted below), which embraces the audience as well. In the second strophe the chorus continues to speak for the audience in its μάρναμαι . . . δᾴοις (39–40, "I do battle with enemies") but follows up with advice, perhaps in favor of using the cavalry, the aristocratic fighting force—a point on which there may have been no consensus.[41] The antistrophe mingles description of the past (speaking for the audience, reflecting the community back to itself) with gnomes that interpret it (speaking to the audience). For instance, the line proclaiming that envy of ancestors has departed leads into a statement that a man ought to convey to his parents their share of praise (57–58), a partisan remark if the importance of ancestors was a point at issue.[42] Reviewing Abdera's history may itself be meant as a vindication of certain ancestors. Furthermore, persistence in the face of defeat is such a strong theme that the *paian* seems to be trying to whip up enthusiasm for an unpopular military venture. In the final triad the chorus openly speaks to the audience in reminding it of the prophecy of Hekate (73–75), which must be recent, then (after the missing antistrophe) speaks for it in the final prayer.[43] The new stage sought by the performance is consensus and confidence, based on Abdera's history (and the oracle of Hekate, for even if it applied to a previous battle, it will appear to apply to any upcoming one as well) as the citizens approach the "last battle" (105–6).

Now we can examine the self-presentation of the performers. Surpris-

[38] Schol. Lykophron *Alexandra* 440, quoted in *SM*. Radt 1958 *ad loc.* shows that Apollo, probably Apollo Derenos, was the chief deity of Abdera. He assumes performance at the shrine; Rutherford, forthcoming, argues for a procession from a hero-shrine of Abderos in the city itself to the sanctuaries of Apollo Derenos and Aphrodite outside the city. Dougherty 1994 does likewise.

[39] So scholia and Radt 1958: 28–29.

[40] Perhaps the poem is rather mediating between positions and skirting contentious issues; it is hard to tell without independent knowledge of the political situation. Hampe 1941 takes the poem as a warning to the Abderites to substitute staunchness for jealousy.

[41] The scholia, quoted by *SM* ad loc., interpret these lines either to mean that Abdera should develop the same type of force as the enemy or that the city should rely on cavalry against all types of force. The lines mention horses, but the advice, whatever it was, must have been expressed with circumspection.

[42] Cf. the gnomes in 50–52 and 66–67.

[43] As Radt 1958: 69–70 points out, Hekate's oracle must be current in order for the audience to recognize it (for it is not identified until after it is quoted).

ingly in this ode on military struggles, the chorus's initial self-presentation in the first epode makes no profession of strength and spirit. Rather, (24–34):

]α τινα [τάνδε] ναίω
25   Θ[ρ]αϊκίαν γ[αῖ]αν ἀμπελό[εσ]σάν τε καὶ
εὔκαρπον· μή μοι μέγας ἔρπων
κάμοι ἐξοπίσω χρόνος ἔμπεδος.
νεόπολίς εἰμι· ματρὸς
δὲ ματέρ' ἐμᾶς ἔτεκον ἔμπαν
30   πολεμίῳ πυρὶ πλαγεῖ-
σαν. εἰ δέ τις ἀρκέων φίλοις
ἐχθροῖσι τραχὺς ὑπαντιάζει,
μόχθος ἡσυχίαν φέρει
καιρῷ καταβαίνων.

. . . I dwell in [this] Thracian land, viney and fertile; may great lasting time as it advances not grow weary in the future, I pray. I am a new city; even so, I gave birth to my mother's mother, (who was) struck by hostile fire. If one goes up against enemies brutally in defense of friends, labor brings rest if it enters the contest at the critical moment.

The chorus identifies itself with the city as birth-giving mother. This remarkable image, apparently referring to the refounding of Teos, permits the chorus to idealize itself as a complete embodiment of the city.[44] Note first that it does not "effeminize" the singers. Rather, it *adds* the ability to give birth to the "masculine" identity that must be signaled by the chorus's appearance. The sufficiency of visible masculine identity allows radically different spoken identities to be compounded with it.

The image of the chorus as city needs to be unpacked. Given that Abdera was experiencing tension and that the *paian* seems to take a position, the choreuts faced the danger that they would not be accepted as speakers for the city and that the performance would not achieve psychological efficacy. They assert in the most radical way they can that they are speaking for the city by speaking as the city. Their "I" is not exclusive; the audience is meant to join in the same identity—and thereby take the chorus as its representative. At the same time it is important that the chorus-members designate themselves female (since the word *city* is female in

[44] Radt 1958 *ad loc.* follows Huxley 1984, who argues that Teos was refounded by the Abderites after capture by the Persians. Radt's discussion shows that Athens cannot be meant. If Teos is the mother's mother, then the chorus is both the city and offspring of the city simultaneously. Dougherty 1994: 210–11, noting the riddle-like quality, points out that riddles are typical of colonial founding stories.

Greek): female figures are unaggressive, and, further, because female identity for them is necessarily symbolic, their boast cannot cause resentment as it would if they were asserting their literal primacy in the state. When they add an image of giving birth, they solidify their symbolic role and add to the audience's sense of the city as self-renewing. If they successfully speak for the city and create in the audience a heightened conviction of being members of a community, then they also forward themselves and their political program. Paradoxically, then, it is by creating for themselves and their audience a unifying, generative female image that the performers hope to induce a sanguine attitude toward a war, whether they are proposing it or see it as inevitable.

After the second triad, with its submerged harangue, and the prophecy of Hekate in the third strophe, the chorus turns in the third and final epode to an analogy between its song for Abderos and songs sung by a chorus of *parthenoi*, with a closing prayer for Abderos' help (96–106):

]ε καλέοντι μολπαί
Δᾶλο]ν ἀν' εὔοδμον ἀμφί τε Παρ[νασ]σίαις
πέτραις ὑψηλαῖς θαμὰ Δ[ελφ]ῶν
λιπαρ]άμπυ[κε]ς ἱστάμεναι χορόν
100   ταχύ]ποδα π[αρ]θένοι χαλ-
    κέᾳ] κελαδ[έον]τι γλυκὺν αὐδᾷ
τρόπ]ον· ἐμο[ὶ δ' ἐπ]έ[ω]ν ἐσ[
    ε]ὐκλέα [   ]ν χά[ρ]ιν,
'Αβδ]ηρε, καὶ στ[ρατὸν] ἱπποχάρμαν
105   σᾷ] βίᾳ πολέ[μ]ῳ τελευ-
    ταί]ῳ προβι[β]άζοις.

. . . songs call [Apollo] throughout scented [Delos], and often around the lofty rocks of Parnassus *parthenoi* of Delphi with [shining] headbands, as they start up the [nimble]-footed dance, sing a sweet [tune] with bronze voice. And to me [of words   ] the well-famed [   ] grace, Abderos, and may you send the mounted army forth by [your] strength to the last battle.

A chorus of *parthenoi* can be, as we saw in Chapter 2, an image of the ideally harmonious community. So again at the end of the *paian* the chorus seeks an integrative metaphorical identity. In this context the image also depicts a vulnerable group safe in the god's protection.[45] This final image

---

[45] Similarly, the chorus of old men in Euripides' *Heracles* juxtaposes itself, in singing *paianes* for Heracles, with the Deliades (687–95). Rather than add female identity to a full male one, this chorus implicitly equates itself with a female chorus by insisting on the old age of its members. (I thank Ian Rutherford for pointing out the relevance of this passage.) In tragedy the chorus may represent (as in the *Heracles*; cf. 107–13, 268–69, 436–41) not the

is part of an appeal to Abderos, eponymous hero of Abdera, that asks him to lead the army forward into the decisive battle. The message for him is that his city relies on his protection as the *parthenoi* do on Apollo; actually, ἐμοὶ δ' both connects and contrasts: "we are like *parthenoi*," but "*parthenoi* dance, while we fight." The verbal/visual juxtaposition of female and male early in the *paian* appears here in the words themselves. In a leap worthy of the finale the chorus moves from dancing *parthenoi* to battle, its composite character modeling for the audience the sequence they must follow too.

Whether the chorus members were actually people whom the audience would accept as able to unite the city and rouse it for war or were members of a faction attempting to unite the populace around themselves by offering a powerful rhetorical statement of their position through this performance we cannot tell. The poem seems to give answers, but we do not know where in the range of possible answers they fell, so the specific politics of the performance must remain opaque.

What *paian* 2 shows us is that the two fantasy images that we identified in Chapter 2 as men's projection onto female performers, the mother who gives birth to heroes and *parthenoi* dancing in collective harmony and suspended sexual invitation, could be taken over by male performers in order to gain the same response for themselves. The image of the mother is especially useful for creating a symbolic figure who personifies a community. Not only as birth-giver but as center of a household, she constitutes her "children" as kin.[46] Asserted masculine identity, given its competitive character, could hardly be used to lend the chorus an integrative appeal, but the overlay of feminine identity, like the costumes mentioned earlier, compounds visual male display with modifying identities.

Another poem that posits female identity for male performers is the *paian* of Isyllos of Epidauros (*CA* pp. 133–36). It is preserved in an inscription that Isyllos set up at Epidauros toward the end of the fourth century BCE.[47] Isyllos recorded several poems: an introductory one, then one describing his proposal for a new ceremony to be instituted at Epidauros, followed by two more brief poems and his *paian*. He does not say that the *paian* was performed as part of the ceremony, but the same two gods are involved in both cases, Apollo Maleatis and Asklepios, and the presence of

---

community in its wholeness but the community as exposed and inadequate. The chorus of Aeschylus' *Agamemnon* is another example.

[46] Goldhill 1990: 112 comments on the way the city appropriates the vocabulary of the family. For a different use of the female, i.e., as the outsider, in symbolic description of territory within narrative, see Calame 1986.

[47] *IG* iv 1 ed. min. 1929, #128; Käppel 1992: 380–83, #40, with bibliography.

the poem on the stele indicates that it belongs in the same setting.[48] The act of founding the ritual and the last line of the second poem (quoted below) suggest that Epidauros was experiencing difficulty, although the nature of it is not indicated. A final poem validates Isyllos' religious insight by describing a vision of Asklepios that he had as a child, when the god announced safety for Sparta. Given that the second poem tells us what social rank the participants in the ceremony are to come from, we have an almost unique opportunity to examine a *paian* as an indirect expression of political ideology.

In the first, preliminary poem, Isyllos announces that the *dēmos* (citizen body) is most secure when it promotes men who ensure aristocracy and explains that he had vowed, should the law that he proposed be passed, to inscribe it. The second poem describes the proposal. I quote all of it (10–26; the poems are numbered continuously, so line 10 is the first of the poem):

```
10   τόνδ᾽ ἱαρὸν θείαι μοίραι νόμον ηὗρεν ῎Ισυλλος
     ἄφθιτον ἀέναον γέρας ἀθανάτοισι θεοῖσιν,
     καί νιν ἅπας δᾶμος θεθμὸν θέτο πατρίδος ἀμᾶς,
     χεῖρας ἀνασχόντες μακάρεσσιν ἐς οὐρανὸν εὐρύ[ν·
     οἳ κεν ἀριστεύωσι πόληος τᾶσδ᾽ Ἐπιδαύρου
15   λέξασθαί τ᾽ ἄνδρας καὶ ἐπαγγεῖλαι κατὰ φυλὰς
     οἷς πολιοῦχος ὑπὸ στέρνοις ἀρετά τε καὶ αἰδώς,
     τοῖσιν ἐπαγγέλλεν καὶ πομπεύεν σφε κομῶντας
     Φοίβωι ἄνακτι υἱῶι τ᾽ Ἀσκλαπιῶι ἰατῆρι
     εἵμασιν ἐν λευκοῖσι δάφνας στεφάνοις ποτ᾽ Ἀπόλλω,
20   ποὶ δ᾽ Ἀσκλαπιὸν ἔρνεσι ἐλαίας ἡμεροφύλλου
     ἁγνῶς πομπεύειν, καὶ ἐπεύχεσθαι πολιάταις
     πᾶσιν ἀεὶ διδόμεν τέκνοις τ᾽ ἐρατὰν ὑγίειαν,
     εὐνομίαν τε καὶ εἰράναν καὶ πλοῦτον ἀμεμφῆ,
     τὰν καλοκαγαθίαν τ᾽ Ἐπιδαυροῖ ἀεὶ ῥέπεν ἀνδρῶν,
25   ὥραις ἐξ ὡρᾶν νόμον ἀεὶ τόνδε σέβοντας·
     οὕτω τοί κ᾽ ἁμῶν περιφείδοιτ᾽ εὐρύοπα Ζεύς.
```

Isyllos discovered this sacred law by divine ordination, an undying everliving honor for the immortal gods, and the whole citizen body made it an institution of our fatherland, holding up their hands toward the wide sky to the gods: (the people) should choose those men who are noblest of this city Epidauros and

---

[48] So Wilamowitz-Moellendorff 1886: 14. The *paian* was not part of the proposal to the assembly, so is not included in the poem describing that decision.

array them by tribes, (men) in whose breasts is city-sustaining courage and sense of reverence, array them and they should go in procession with their hair long to Lord Phoibos and to his son the doctor Asklepios, (proceed) in white cloaks with wreaths of laurel to Apollo and proceed in purity with branches of cultivated olive to Asklepios and pray (to them) always to give to all citizens and to their children lovely health and good government and peace and blameless wealth and that nobility of men always prevail at Epidauros, as they always respect this law from season to season. Thus indeed might far-seeing Zeus spare us.

Note first that Isyllos puts himself in the third person and refers to "our fatherland"; the inscription is composed as though any Epidaurian were the "speaker" of its contents. This rhetorical procedure duplicates the procedure described, in which Isyllos persuades the *dēmos* to adopt his proposal. The description also assimilates the voting to prayer, since the participants raise their hands "to the gods." The rhetoric of the inscription itself reveals that Isyllos is intent on binding the *dēmos* psychologically to the political implications of the ceremony by interweaving politics with religion.[49] The religious ceremony in fact solidifies the political agenda because once performed the ceremony can (ideally) never thereafter be omitted without angering the gods. If there was internal dissension at Epidauros, then this ceremony is meant to help cure (or suppress) it.

The background of communal performance is revealed in the proceedings described here. The *dēmos* agrees to let chosen men represent it. These men are to be staged visually as the community's embassy to the gods: the style of their hair and color of their cloaks are specified. Their hair was to be worn long, a fact that had political significance, for it reflected the old Dorian style.[50] At the same time, it draws on one of the signs of masculinity in the system of gender symbolism.[51] The aristocracy is therefore to be assimilated to traditional Dorian militarism.

In the prayer, which is itself a performance, they speak on behalf of (for) the community. The last two lines of the prayer (24–25), however, are set off grammatically from the preceding list and ask that the political order instantiated in the ceremony itself continue, along with the ceremony that renders it visible. Unlike the other things in the list, this blessing is up to the Epidaurians themselves (to the extent that they retain local autonomy), so the prayer covertly shifts to an address *to* the people of the city. Thus the new stage that this ceremony initiates includes a provision that all future new stages repeat this one.

[49] Note also the insistence on the gods' participation in line 10 (and also 9, not quoted).

[50] As Wilamowitz-Moellendorff 1886: 39 points out. He emphasizes the backward-looking nature of this ceremony in the age of the Macedonian conquerors.

[51] Cf. Gleason 1990: 400–402 on the importance of an abundance of hair.

The process of choosing performers has been ratified by the *dēmos*. But if the ceremony is to *enact* a coming together of the community in conjunction with the address to the gods, the performers will need to present a metaphoric identity that disguises their political adherence under integrative symbolism. Isyllos' *paian* provides the rhetoric that gives them an idealized Epidaurian character.

On the inscription two short texts stand between the one quoted above and the *paian*, one of which tells us that Malos first established the altar of Apollo Maleatis (at Epidauros) and honored the precinct with sacrifices. Now to the *paian*: I quote two sections. The *paian* opens with lines addressed to the audience (37–40):

> ἰὲ Παιᾶνα θεὸν ἀείσατε λαοί,
>
> ζαθέας ἐνναέτα[ι] τᾶσδ' Ἐπιδαύρου.
>
> ὧδε γὰρ φάτις ἐνέπουσ' ἤλυθ' ἐς ἀκοὰς
>
> 40   προγόνων ἀμετέρων, ὦ Φοῖβ' Ἀπόλλων.

Sing, people, the god as Ie Paian, you inhabitants of this divine Epidauros. For a story telling the following came to the ears of our ancestors, O Phoibos Apollo.

Lines 41–47 recount the genealogy of Malos and of Phlegyas, who "inhabited his fatherland Epidauros." It culminates in Aigla, nicknamed Koronis, whose beauty is mentioned.[52] The following lines contain the story of the birth of Asklepios and the closure (48–61):

> κατιδὼν δ' ὁ χρυσότοξος Φοῖβος ἐμ Μά-
>
> λου δόμοις παρθενίαν ὥραν ἔλυσε,
>
> 50   λεχέων δ' ἱμεροέντων ἐπέβας, Λα-
>
> τῶιε κόρε χρυσοκόμα.
>
> σέβομαί σε· ἐν δὲ θυώδει τεμένει τέκε-
>
> το ἶνιν Αἴγλα, γονίμαν δ' ἔλυσεν ὠδῖ-
>
> να Διὸς παῖς μετὰ Μοιρᾶν Λάχεσίς τε μαῖ' ἀγανά·
>
> 55   ἐπίκλησιν δέ νιν Αἴγλας ματρὸς Ἀσκλα-
>
> πιὸν ὠνόμαξε Ἀπόλλων, τὸν νόσων παύ-
>
> [σ]τορα, δωτῆρ' ὑγιείας, μέγα δώρημα βροτοῖς.
>
> ἰὲ Παιάν, ἰὲ Παιάν, χαῖρεν Ἀσκλα-
>
> πιέ, τὰν σὰν Ἐπίδαυρον ματρόπολιν αὔ-

[52] Wilhelm 1949: 25–28 argues that Aigla is Koronis' nickname rather than the reverse, as the poem seems to say. Käppel 1992: 201 takes Koronis as the nickname. The name Aigla avoids invoking the story of her infidelity. On it, see below.

60   ξων, ἐναργῆ δ' ὑγίειαν ἐπιπέμποις

       φρεσὶ καὶ σώμασιν ἁμοῖς· ἰὲ Παιάν, ἰὲ Παιάν.

Espying (her), golden-bowed Phoibos loosed her maiden season in the house of Malos, and you mounted the delightful bed, golden-haired son of Leto. I reverence you—and in the fragrant precinct Aigla gave birth to a son, and the son of Zeus relieved (her) fruitful labor pains, together with the Fates, and (so did) Lachesis the noble midwife; naming him after his mother Aigla, Apollo called him Asklepios, the stayer of diseases, giver of health, a great gift to humans. Ie paian, ie paian, rejoice, Asklepios, increasing your mother-city Epidauros, and may you send manifest health to our minds and bodies, ie paian, ie paian.

The opening lines command the people to honor the god as healer (Paian) on the grounds that "our ancestors" had the story of Apollo's local manifestation. The audience knows this story too, so it is linked to forebears who are revealed in the next lines to be Malos and Phlegyas, probably the mythic ancestors of the Epidaurian aristocracy.[53] In return for honoring the noble families, the audience is implicitly invited to share in their traditions and identify with the originators of the political structure.[54] The poem is communal, then, in its embrace of the community as united by a shared aristocratic past.

The *paian* tells the story of the birth of Asklepios, whose mother Aigla is the daughter of Phlegyas. Aigla gives birth in the sanctuary itself (presumably, however illogical, the famous sanctuary of Asklepios at Epidauros). The figure of Aigla therefore serves as a unifying image for the community by joining humans and gods, city and sanctuary. Lines 48–53 describing Apollo's attraction to Aigla and its consequences (quoted above) repay close attention. The performers have been narrating in the third person. When they come to Apollo's rape of Aigla, they switch suddenly, in mid-sentence, into the second person ἐπέβας (you mounted) and add a three-word vocative address: Λατῶιε κόρε χρυσοκόμα (golden-haired son of Leto). The scene of intercourse is replaced by the chorus's demand for Apollo's attention, *as though they had replaced Aigla*.[55] Apollo's climactic moment in lovemaking is marked by the chorus's responsive ecstasy: σέβομαί σε (I reverence you), the only first-person singular in the poem.

---

[53] Phlegyas is from Thessaly. According to Pausanias (2.26.4) Phlegyas came to the Peloponnesus with his daughter, who bore Asklepios secretly in Epidauros. On the adoption of Phlegyas into Epidaurian genealogy, see Wilamowitz-Moellendorff 1886: 84–90, esp. 89–90.

[54] A community's adoption of the ancestors of the noble families as communal forebears is common. Cf., e.g., the designation of Thebans as Kadmeioi.

[55] Nagy 1990b: 346–47 speaks of performance as a mimesis of the original cult story. This example would evoke ritual mimesis, with the singers standing in for the woman who would play the role of Aigla.

After this dramatic point, the chorus returns to third-person narrative. By implication, then, the chorus inserts itself into the place of Aigla. When the performers thus reenact briefly the story of Aigla, they renew symbolically in their own persons Apollo's rape and Asklepios' appearance in the world. The message is clear: the community is embodied in the aristocratic men whom Apollo loves and who give birth to continued health for the community.

At the same time as the performers put themselves in Aigla's place, they also assert masculine preeminence. The *paian* at every moment transfers attention from Aigla to Apollo. As she gives birth, Apollo relieves her birth pains. Apollo names the child. This attitude correlates with the longing of the poem for a male lineage; it begins its genealogy with "father Zeus" giving the Muse Erato to Malos as a wife (41–42, not quoted). At the end the poem gives away the meaning of Aigla. Earlier it had referred to Epidauros as the πατρίς (43, fatherland). In line 59 the performers ask Asklepios to foster τὰν σὰν Ἐπίδαυρον ματρόπολιν (your mother-city Epidauros). The meaning that ματρόπολιν must take on here, "city of your mother," is unparalleled; usually the word refers to the city either as "mother" of its inhabitants or as the "mother" of a colony.[56] But Aigla is so completely identified with Epidauros that Asklepios has a mother-city instead of a mother—and the performers embody her/it. Thus the performers stage themselves as the most adequate incarnation of Epidauros and enact renewed intercourse between the city and the gods. *Paian* 2 for Abdera may also have attempted a similar presentation of one group as a privileged embodiment of the city.

Note, however, that the story of the death of Aigla/Koronis by a blast of lightning is ignored by the poem. In that version Koronis does not give birth; the baby is torn from her womb by Apollo. In Pindar's *Pythian* 3, dedicated to an ailing Hieron, which also tells the story of the begetting of Asklepios, her demise is emphasized because it suits Pindar's theme. Here, however, Aigla must give birth to preserve the connection with the sanctuary. Furthermore, and equally important, her honor as a member of the Epidaurian founding genealogy must be preserved in order for the citizens to claim through her a connection with Asklepios and Apollo.

If from this poem we look back at *paian* 9, discussed in Chapter 1, which also refers to birth in a sanctuary, we can see some of the same effects operating. In that case the chorus says that it is supplicating Apollo from the place where Melia bore Teneros to him; it aligns itself with her spatially rather than rhetorically.[57] In *paian* 9, too, an opposing system of

---

[56] Wilamowitz-Moellendorff 1886: 17. Cf. Radt 1958: 37–38 for more extensive discussion of the term.

[57] For Melia's couch and celebration of her, see Ch. 1, p. 50.

gender imagery preserves the chorus from unvarnished identification with a female figure. There the sun (normally masculine in Greek) is addressed in the opening lines as "ray of the sun" ("ray" is feminine) and "mother of eyes." In the second triad Apollo is "father" (45). Therefore, a movement from "mother" to "father" vivifies the movement from panic to intellectual control and effective speech that I traced out in the earlier discussion. Since the performers of Isyllos' *paian* go in procession to the sanctuary where Asklepios was born, both it and *paian* 9 combine visual association with birth-giving and verbal progression from female to male. In *paian* 9 the visual identification with the female is stronger, while in Isyllos' *paian* the verbal one prevails.

Identification with a mother is not the only strategy open to a chorus that presents itself as a complete representation of a community. The chorus portrays itself as a child of the mother in Pindar's problematic *paian* 6, where it also associates itself with a chorus of *parthenoi*. This *paian* was performed at Delphi at the Theoxenia, a festival at which gods and ambassadors from other states were feasted in honor of the Delphians' quondam intervention with Apollo to end a famine in Greece.[58] The first difficulty in this fragmentary poem, for us, is in knowing who the performers are. According to the heading supplied by Alexandrian scholars, it was composed for the Delphians, which would mean that the chorus was addressing its own community (as well as delegations from elsewhere). The end of the *paian* gives extensive praise to Aigina, so some think that the Aiginetans must have sent a chorus to the Theoxenia to perform it.[59] But the Aiginetan hero Aiakos was involved in stopping a drought, and Stefan Radt suggests that the two stories have been combined, so that Aiakos' role motivates the praise of Aigina.[60] A. Hoekstra proposes that a Delphian chorus is standing in for an Aiginetan one.[61]

[58] Lines 60–61 indicate the occasion. On the ritual of Theoxenia, see schol. Pindar *Olympian* 3 hypothesis (I 105 *Dr.*); Nilsson 1957: 160–62 (for Apollo), 419–21 (for the Dioskouroi); Krummen 1990: 121–22, 223–26.

[59] So Rutherford, forthcoming. This view can explain the opening as well, but it has problems and means throwing out our one explicit piece of evidence about the performers. I offer another explanation for the opening and praise of Aigina that I think more satisfactory.

[60] Radt 1958 *ad loc.* The Greek leaders who asked Aiakos to intercede did so on the advice of Delphi, according to Pausanias 2.29.7–8, who also says that the embassy was depicted at the entrance to the shrine of Aiakos on Aigina. Cf. Isokrates 9.14–15, who does not mention Delphi; Apollodoros *Bibl.* 3.12.6 and Diodoros 4.61.1, who imply Delphi's involvement. At the Theoxenia it would be appropriate to honor other gods like Zeus; cf. Käppel 1992: 210 on Philodamos' *paian* to Dionysus for the Theoxenia. Rutherford, forthcoming, objects that in this *paian* the Delphians themselves prayed (64); for my view, see below.

[61] Hoekstra 1962. Fogelmark 1972: 117–32 criticizes his theory that the Aiginetans had a privileged part in the Theoxenia on the grounds that it has no basis in evidence. He looks for evidence that other foreign choruses performed and adduces a papyrus scrap (*p. Oxy.* 25, 2430 fr. 35.12), a heading from a poem for a state that is not Aigina to perform at Delphi.

Another view has also been mooted: because of the opening lines, some think that the Delphians could not mount a chorus and that Pindar came to their aid, writing a *paian* for them or even bringing a chorus.[62] Pindar is then the speaker and the chorus has become his mouthpiece. The opening lines, on this view, explain why Pindar is there. I accept the statement of the heading that the *paian* was performed by a Delphian chorus and will begin by explaining why I find implausible the view that the ode is Pindar's personal voice. Here are the opening lines of the *paian* (1–18):

πρὸς Ὀλυμπίου Διός σε, χρυσέα
    κλυτόμαντι Πυθοῖ,
λίσσομαι Χαρίτεσ-
    σίν τε καὶ σὺν Ἀφροδίτᾳ,
5 ἐν ζαθέῳ με δέξαι χρόνῳ
    ἀοίδιμον Πιερίδων προφάταν·
ὕδατι γὰρ ἐπὶ χαλκοπύλῳ
    ψόφον ἀϊὼν Κασταλίας
ὀρφανὸν ἀνδρῶν χορεύσιος ἦλθον
10 ἔταις ἀμαχανίαν ἀ[λ]έξων
    τεοῖσιν ἐμαῖς τε τιμ[α]ῖς·
ἦτορι δὲ φίλῳ παῖς ἅτε ματέρι κεδνᾷ
    πειθόμενος κατέβαν στεφάνων
    καὶ θαλιᾶν τροφὸν ἄλσος Ἀ-
15 πόλλωνος, τόθι Λατοΐδαν
    θαμινὰ Δελφῶν κόραι
χθονὸς ὀμφαλὸν παρὰ σκιάεντα μελπ[ό]μεναι
    ποδὶ κροτέο[ντι γᾶν θο]ῷ

By Olympian Zeus I beg you, golden Pytho famed for prophecy, together with the Graces and Aphrodite, receive me in this most holy time, a songful interpreter of the Muses. For hearing the splash bereft of a chorus of men at the bronze-gated water of Kastalia, I came fending off helplessness from your citi-

---

Delphic Paian I (*CA* pp. 141–48) was performed by Athenians, but he admits that it is much later (138 BCE) and not certainly for the Theoxenia. On it see Käppel 1992: 387–89 #45 (text and bibliography).

[62] Radt 1958: 105–8 takes Pindar as the speaker, in accordance with this view of the circumstances, although he insists on relevance to the festival as a criterion for interpretation of the rest of the *paian*. Hamilton 1974: 113–15 and Fogelmark 1972: 118–21 assign the first person in the *paianes* generally to the poet, ignoring their ritual and ceremonial function. Hoekstra 1962: 9–13 argues cogently that the first person belongs to the chorus. See Radt for earlier bibliography.

zens and my privileges;[63] obeying my heart as a child its honored mother, I came down to the grove of Apollo, nurse of crowns and festivity, where the daughters of the Delphians often, celebrating the son of Leto in song and dance around the shady navel of the earth, beat [the ground] with [quick] foot. . . .

The text speaks as though the performance were spontaneous, and it is this that seems to invite a biographical reading. If one takes lines 7 to 11 quasi-literally, then the first-person speaker has rushed to Delphi because the chorus that was supposed to perform by the Kastalian spring was not going to be able to. The speaker thus saves the citizens of Delphi from embarrassment and preserves his own honors. Once Pindar is accepted as this speaker, two other details seem to be in accord. First, any claim to receive inspiration from the Muses in Pindar's poetry tends to be treated as a personal statement of Pindar's, so Πιερίδων προφάταν (6, "interpreter of the Muses") appears to refer to him. Second, the poem's distinction between "your citizenry" and "my honors" seems to support the idea that Pindar is speaking to the Delphians.[64]

Yet this view implies certain things about the festival of the Theoxenia that I find unpersuasive, apart from my conviction that the first person in performance belongs to the performers. It suggests that the festival was primarily an entertainment mounted by the Delphians for visitors. Their lack of a chorus was lack of a show number; it left an empty slot on the program. Under these circumstances a presentation by a foreigner about himself could substitute for the Delphians' own self-presentation. But if, as I think was the case, it was both religiously and politically important for the Delphians to present themselves as stewards of the god's sanctuary, then they could hardly tolerate having their address to god and audience usurped by another (and one who pointed out their failure!). The reasons given by Stefan Radt for understanding the first person of *paian* 2 as the chorus's are equally valid here.[65] Nor do the considerations listed in the preceding paragraph compel one to take the first person as Pindar's. The Muses inspire not just poets but singers as well.[66] After Elroy Bundy we have learned not to read the epinician odes literally, and the same

[63] Radt 1958 *ad loc.* construes ἐμαῖς τιμαῖς as parallel to ἔταις τεοῖσιν, so that the speaker is warding off ἀμαχανία from both. Hoekstra 1962: 11–13 argues for taking ἐμαῖς τιμαῖς as a dative of purpose.

[64] Then it must be explained how Pindar's honors were jeopardized by the Delphians' lack of a chorus. Radt 1958 *ad loc.* suggests that it must have been Pindar's *prohedria* (right to a front seat), for if there were no performance Pindar would be unable to sit at it.

[65] Cf. note 33 above.

[66] See, for example, Alkman 3 *PMGF*, Euripides *Trojan Women* 511–14, Aristophanes *Ach.* 665 and *Lys.* 1297. Detienne 1967: 10–11 defines the common noun μοῦσα as "la parole chantée, la parole rythmée." The Muses themselves are singers: Hesiod *Theogony* 1–115 passim; *Homeric Hymn to Apollo* 189–91.

sensitivity to Pindar's metaphorical language and to the program to which poetic statements must conform should be applied to his religious poetry.[67]

Why then does the song open in this unusual way? If we consider the *paian* in terms of the staging of the performers and of its efficacious themes, the themes connecting the song with the festival, we arrive at a more cogent view of the first lines. The Theoxenia was a festival of thanks for deliverance from a widespread disaster of a sort that could always recur. Its function was also to persuade the gods to avert another episode of famine; thus it fits Lutz Käppel's description of the *paian* as communication from a petitioner to a god as bringer of well-being.[68] The poem therefore allows the chorus to present its performance as active intervention in a world that is never stable. The reference to Kastalia "bereft of a chorus of men" raises the threat that a lapse of attention might bring renewed disaster—a threat that is canceled by the performance itself. As we saw in Chapter 1, community poetry often alludes obliquely to the calamitous alternative to the audience's accepting the model it proposes. So here the chorus's coming is dramatized as a salvific act, while Pytho is asked to accept it as efficacious (line 5).

What is striking about the opening lines is the double description that the chorus-members give of themselves. In lines 7–11 they say that they came to fend off helplessness from the citizenry of Delphi and preserve their own honors when they perceived that Kastalia was bereft. Here they identify themselves as male, for what the spring lacks is the dancing of *men*. The participle ἀλέξων (10, "fending off") implies active, male protection of the community, exercised here through dancing for the god. The poem glances at the physical strength that male dancing could express. The dancers also ward off helplessness from their own privileges (τιμαί) by dancing. Participation in the chorus may be one of the privileges; in other words, the chorus is ensuring the continuance of its privileges by performing them. The word *privileges* again points to the masculine, public world of competition for honor. The fiction of spontaneity abets the choreuts' self-description as watchful and energetic, for they themselves perceive Delphi's need at this holy period and act to meet it.[69]

Yet in the next lines (12 to 18, where the fragment breaks off), the chorus members begin over again, as it were, this time explaining that

[67] Bundy 1962.

[68] See the Introduction, pp. 10–11.

[69] If an Aiginetan chorus were to claim that it was warding off helplessness from Delphi's citizens it would be both insulting the Delphians and making an absurd statement. Only the Delphians could say this.

they came out of obedience to their hearts, like a child minding its mother. Now images of nurture prevail: the grove of Apollo is "nurse of festivity" and Apollo is called by his matronymic Latoidas. Here the daughters of the Delphians often dance around the omphalos, the navel, of the earth. As the chorus shifts from one identity to the other, Delphi's condition shifts also from lack to fecundity.[70]

At the beginning the chorus establishes two different characters for itself, aligned with male and female gender imagery. Its male identity is associated with the theme of warding off helplessness and preserving honor, its female-oriented identity (child and *parthenos*) with generativity. The two themes structure the *paian*. The chorus-members may have signaled the shift in their self-identification through their dancing.[71] Whether they did or not, their words indicate that dancing is an expression of character for both groups: the men dance out of protectiveness, and the *parthenoi* in the second portrayal dance (it would seem) out of joy. Simply by dancing, the chorus identifies itself with both groups.

To a Delphian audience the speakers might appear in the opening lines to be overstressing their own personal activity and honors in a way not conducive to winning the audience's participation. But another audience was present at the performance, for other states sent delegations to the Theoxenia. The foreign audience explains the forcefulness of the Delphian chorus's self-portrayal, for from an external point of view the Delphian performers represent all the Delphians and assert their collective privileged relationship with Delphi. As outsiders would see it, the privileges the chorus protects by dancing are precisely those of the inhabitants. From an external perspective, "your citizens and my privileges" says the same thing twice over: the inhabitants belong to the sanctuary, which they address, and receive from it their privileges as a result. In other words, the chorus's opening self-presentation is composed to address outsiders to Delphi. Other states' choruses also performed at the Theoxenia, so the Delphian chorus speaks in competition with external points of view, and the performers must present themselves within the framework created by that fact.

The antistrophe and beginning of the epode are lost. In the epode the chorus is still speaking about its own performance (50–61):

[70] This note is sounded already in lines 3–6, since the chorus asks Pytho to receive it "with the Graces and Aphrodite."

[71] The meter shifts slightly, for the single-shorts that elsewhere are interspersed with the double-shorts in this Aeolic rhythm are absent between line 12 and the last word of line 16. It is perhaps worth noting that it is at the same point in the third strophe that Zeus' rape of the *parthenos* Aigina appears (134, not a new sentence). There is a shift in topic at the same point in the second strophe also (although not in the antistrophes).

50   καὶ πόθεν ἀθαν[άτων ἔϱις ἄ]ϱξατο.

      ταῦτα θεοῖσι [μ]έν

      πιθεῖν σοφοὺ[ς] δυνατόν,

      βϱοτοῖσιν δ' ἀμάχανο[ν εὑ]ϱέμεν·

      ἀλλὰ παϱθένοι γάϱ, ἴσθ' ὅτ[ι], Μο[ῖ]σαι,

55   πάντα, κε[λαι]νεφεῖ σὺν

      πατϱὶ Μναμοσ[ύν]ᾳ τε

      τοῦτον ἔσχετ[ε τεθ]μόν,

      κλῦτε νῦν· ἔϱα[ται] δέ μο[ι]

      γλῶσσα μέλιτος ἄωτον γλυκὺν [

60   ἀγῶνα Λοξία{ι} καταβάντ' εὐϱὺν

      ἐν θεῶν ξενίᾳ.

. . . and whence the [strife?] of the immortals arose. These things it is possible for the gods to persuade wise men, but impossible for mortals to discover. But, since as *parthenoi* you hold this [ordinance?], Muses, (namely) that you know all, together with your black-cloud father (= Zeus) and Memory, listen now! My tongue longs [to pour?] the consummate sweetness of honey as I enter the broad assembly of Apollo at the Theoxenia.

The chorus is still warding off helplessness by its performance, now by calling on the Muses for hidden knowledge. The word ἀμάχανον (impossible) picks up the word ἀμαχανία (helplessness) of the first strophe. The needed information may concern what caused the famine but (since the famine seems not to be introduced until the beginning of the second triad) may be more general advice on maintaining good relations with the gods. We now see the connection between the chorus's self-designation as the "interpreter of the Muses" in line 6 and its claim to "ward off helplessness" in line 10: the speakers will bring the gods' precepts to earth. Then in a sudden shift of focus, the chorus-members hope the Muses will enable them to pour out their message like honey. We are back to the second identity with images of abundance and pleasure. The chorus's two identities are now more internalized, characterizing the song rather than the dance.

The next two triads take up and expand the themes of the chorus's two identities, which turn out to correlate in a grand way with the two themes of the Theoxenia itself, Apollo's power to ward off evil and the abundance that the gods can grant. In both of these triads, Delphi's relationship with the rest of Greece is also the subject: Apollo wards off aggression toward Delphi, and Delphi "feeds" Greece with song. Aigina is the state chosen to demonstrate both propositions, for Aiginetan myth provides both the example of Neoptolemos, whose violence toward Delphi was punished by Apollo, and of Aiakos, who cooperated with Delphi in ending a famine apparently identified with the one celebrated at the Theoxenia.[72] The chorus, therefore, takes the occasion of the Theoxenia, when Delphi is offering hospitality to gods and delegations from other states, to express the political meaning of Delphian myth and ritual.

In the second triad, warding off helplessness is the subject, enlarged from the chorus's activity to that of the Delphian ἔθνος (people) and Apollo. In the opening of the strophe, the Delphians approach the gods, now as in the past, on behalf of all Greece (62–65):

> θύεται γὰρ ἀγλαᾶς ὑπὲρ Πανελ-
> λάδος, ἄν τε Δελφῶν
> ἔθ[ν]ος εὔξατο λι-
> 65   μοῦ θ[

For sacrifice is being made on behalf of glorious Greece as a whole, (sacrifice) which the Delphian people vowed [to make in thanks for ending?] famine. . . .[73]

The juxtaposition of "Greece as a whole" with the "Delphian people" sets out the relationship symbolized by performers and audience, each representative of a larger group. As the Delphian performers bring the revelations of the Muses, so the Delphians as a whole intercede with the gods from their special location. Delphi is still the locus of speech that communicates with the gods, but now it is the whole community of Delphi that speaks.

The fragmentary lines that follow this passage must have contained a description of Apollo's aid in ending the famine. The words χρησ[τ]η[ρι (oracle) and Πυ]θωνόθ[εν (from Pytho) are visible at the beginning of successive lines (71, 72).[74] Then the chorus suddenly takes up another instance of Apollo's protection: he fended off the destruction of Troy for as long as possible by killing Achilles (73–104). Once Troy had fallen,

---

[72] Although I think with Radt 1958 (n.60 above) that Aiakos' reputation for ending a famine motivated use of the Aiakidai in the *paian*, I see their function as a larger one. For celebration of Aiakos on Aigina in Pindar's fragmentary *paian* 15, see Rutherford 1992: 62–67.

[73] The relationship of the Delphians' vow/prayer to Aiakos' must be that the Delphians vowed the festival if Aiakos should succeed. Thus Aiakos' part was drawn under Delphi's aegis. If Aiakos' story were not subordinated to the Delphian one, it would be competing (no matter who the speaker is) and therefore unwelcome at this festival.

[74] This may refer to Delphi's recommendation that the Greek leaders ask Aiakos to pray to Zeus, for Κρόν[ιε and πρύτα[νι appear in 68 and 69.

condemned by the fates, he pursued Neoptolemos, Achilles' son, sacker of the city, violator of altars (105–17), and killed him at Delphi (117–20):

> ἀμφιπόλοις δὲ
> κ]υριᾶν περὶ τιμᾶν
> δηρι]αζόμενον κτάνεν
> 120 ⟨ἐν⟩ τεμέ]νεϊ φίλῳ γᾶς παρ' ὀμφαλὸν εὐρύν.

As he was quarreling with the attendants about legitimate privileges, (Apollo) slew him in his familiar [precinct] beside the broad navel of the earth.[75]

We have returned to Delphi. It cannot be a coincidence that the end of the triad also returns to warding off helplessness from privileges. What the chorus did for itself in the opening, the god now does for his attendants. The chorus, it transpires, mirrors the god as well as the Delphian people, and the god protects the Delphians in particular as well as humankind in general. The chorus's initial self-description is transforming itself into a forceful statement that disputing Delphi's privileges will bring destruction on the one who interferes. Quarrelsome Neoptolemos had invaded Delphi as far as the navel of the earth where, according to the opening lines, the Delphian *parthenoi* dance. His violation seems the more flagrant if that initial picture is recalled.[76]

But mention of the omphalos (navel) also prepares for the third triad, in which the chorus's other identity, child and dancer where the *parthenoi* dance, with its associated theme of abundance and pleasure, grows in scope. The choreuts again open the triad with description of their own (and Delphi's) speaking; they will grant speech to the island of Aigina. Their initial address to Aigina is a little startling in its imagery but fits the developing idea (123–31):

> ὀνομακλύτα γ' ἔνεσσι Δωριεῖ
> μ[ε]δέοισα [πό]ντῳ
> 125 νᾶσος, [ὦ] Διὸς Ἑλ-
> λανίου φαεννὸν ἄστρον.
> οὔνεκεν οὔ σε παιηόνων
> ἄδορπον εὐνάξομεν, ἀλλ' ἀοιδᾶν
> ῥόθια δεκομένα κατερεῖς,

---

[75] Or one could read μ]υριᾶν in 118, as referring to countless sacrificial victims. So Radt 1958 *ad loc.*

[76] Neoptolemos had a precinct at Delphi, according to Pindar *Nemean* 7.44–47. Nagy 1979: 123–38 connects the themes of feast, quarrel, and heroization in Neoptolemos' story. Pindar used only the quarrel theme here.

130   πόθεν ἔλαβες ναυπρύτανιν
       δαίμονα καὶ τὰν θεμίξενον ἀρετ[άν.

Island of famous name you lie, ruling over the Dorian sea, [O] bright star of
Zeus Hellanios. Wherefore we will not put you to sleep without dinner of
paianes, but receiving a surf of song you will say whence you got (your) ship-
ruling luck and your goodness, righteous to strangers.

Zeus Hellanios is the god to whom Aiakos, hero of Aigina, prayed to end a
famine, so Delphi is praising Aigina as a participant in the act of securing
abundance to humans. The accolade also compensates for using Neoptolemos as a negative example; Aigina provides the positive example
also, which, because it follows the negative one, overrides it.[77] "We will
not put you to sleep without dinner of *paianes*" can be taken to mean "we
will not dismiss you (after the account of Neoptolemos) without praise."
At the same time the imagery asserts that Delphi feeds Aigina, which the
chorus then enacts metaphorically by speaking for Aigina. Now mother
rather than child, the chorus-members portray themselves (and Delphi) as
the flowing source of songs that nurture by retelling Aigina's founding
legend and Zeus' act of fecundation. As the chorus in the rest of the strophe
(132–43) tells of Zeus' lovemaking with Aigina and the begetting of
Aiakos under a golden cloud, it expands the theme of security and abundance. Zeus pledged prosperity to Aigina. And the tale must have included Zeus' creation of the Myrmidons, whose name is just visible in line
143, to be companions of Aigina's son Aiakos.

In the antistrophe Aiakos probably came in for praise. The epode may
have generalized about the Aiakidai (who include Achilles and Neoptolemos), for Αἰακ]ιδᾶν is restored at the beginning of line 177 and the words
ἀπείρονας ἀρετάς (countless kinds of manly virtue) appear in line 176.
Thus the theme of warding off helplessness may have made one more
appearance. But then in a final prayer the chorus says (177–83):

                φ[ιλεῖ]τε
            ] πόλιν πατρίαν· φι-
            λεῖτε] δ' εὔφ[ρον]α λαόν
180   τόνδε [καὶ] στεφάνοισί νιν
        πανθαλέος ὑγιε[ίας] σκιάζετε· Μοισᾶν

    [77] I do not believe the scholiasts' explanation of *Nemean* 7.102–6, that Pindar is apologiz-
ing for having slandered Neoptolemos. But their view gives us a measure of how important
mythic figures were to communities' self-definition. The *paian* must make up for its treatment of Neoptolemos.

ἐπαβολ[έ]ο̣υτ̣[α] πολλάκι, Παιάν, δέ-
ξ'] ἐννόμων ἐ[νοπ]ᾶν.[78]

[hold dear   ] (their?) ancestral city, and hold dear (?) this festive assembly and shade it with wreaths of blooming health. And, Paian, receive often the one who comprehends the ritually correct [songs] of the Muses.

In wreaths and festivity the theme of abundance has the final word (although the specification that Apollo should receive the one who comprehends "ritually correct" songs reminds the audience that the Delphians have a privileged position in knowing how to approach the god). The poem moves from the threatened disaster of the opening to the imagery of joyous celebration at the end. The chorus's identity grows more idealized and all-embracing until it becomes a model for Delphi at the center of the Greek world, its double gendering making it representative of Delphi's autonomy.

The Theoxenia as a festival combining food and song allows the chorus-members to treat their own speech and by extension speech of Delphians, including Apollo, as efficacious: as nurturant, for the Delphians' prayer ends the famine and the chorus pours out honey and feeds Aigina with song of praise at the end; and as juridical, for the chorus's song "wards off helplessness" at the beginning and reveals information from the gods, while Apollo's oath to prevent Neoptolemos from reaching home or old age (112–17) is fulfilled at Delphi. Delphian song and Delphian feast combine to illustrate the power to feed others, and the cautionary words by analogy imply that Delphi has the potential to withhold food. Neoptolemos was quarreling about his share of the sacrifice when Apollo struck him down.[79]

Male assumption of a female role or identity has a background in traditional ritual performance. It does not conform to a single pattern; ritual transvestism and attachment to a goddess, for instance, create the effect in quite different ways. An example of each will show that these practices are a possible source for the idea that men can present themselves as integrative or representative figures through adding female identity to their own (visual) male identity.

Transvestism is found in different kinds of rituals. The Hybristika at Argos, with its exchange of clothing between men and women, was mentioned in Chapter 2. Vase paintings show men dancing in women's

[78] I give the text of D'Alessio and Ferrari 1988: 180. My translation also follows theirs.

[79] Nagy 1979: 125–26 adduces testimony that the priests at Delphi grabbed off the sacrificial meat or that the meat was apportioned according to what each could grab. This ritual or popular conception of struggle for food at Delphi may also underlie the chorus's presentation of a Delphi that can give or withhold.

clothing, perhaps for the humor of it.[80] Closer to the poetry discussed above is the Oschophoria, an Attic festival. As remarked in Chapter 1, it included a procession from a temple of Dionysus in Athens down to the coast at Phaleron, led by two young men, called Oschophoroi, dressed in women's clothing and carrying vine branches on which grape clusters hung.[81] A chorus of young men accompanied them, singing Oschophoria Songs. Women called Dinner carriers participated in the procession. Sacrifice and dances, presumably at Phaleron, were included; the women must have prepared food. A race for young men was held, either at Phaleron or on the way to Phaleron, and the victor danced a *kōmos* (revel) with the chorus.[82] According to Athenaios (14, 631b) young men danced the dance called *oschophorikos* naked; the dance suggested sports and physical exercises. The visual presentation of the young men was therefore a composite of Dionysiac cross-dressing and athleticism. We do not know how they described themselves verbally or what the effect of the ensemble was.[83]

The pattern of male nurture, replacing the mother, is found in a cult hymn, the apparently traditional *Hymn of the Kouretes* (CA pp. 160–62) known from a second-century CE inscription discovered at Palaikastro in Crete, although it is not adopted by the performers in an explicit way.[84] This is psychologically efficacious poetry of a simple kind; much of the poem is taken up by a repeated refrain calling on the god to come. I quote the refrain and the first two stanzas (1–20):

ἰώ, μέγιστε Κοῦρε,
χαῖρέ μοι, Κρόνειε,
παγκρατὲς γάνος, βέβακες
δαιμόνων ἀγώμενος·

[80] Apart from the Anakreontic vases that show scenes connected with the symposium (on which see Ch. 5), a few early vases seem to show men's choral dance in female dress: Webster 1970: 14 and fig. 3.

[81] For the festival see Deubner 1962: 142–47; Jeanmaire 1939: 344–63. Athenaios 11, 495f, quoting Aristodemos (*FGH* 383 F9), and Proklos (Photios *Bibl.* 322a) are the main sources. Deubner 143 thinks that the "women's" clothing is just the old Ionic chiton, which continued in use as festival dress. If so, it appeared to be female dress to later eyes.

[82] Kadletz 1980 argues for a race to Phaleron followed by the chorus. Rutherford and Irvine 1988 discuss the evidence and a fragment of a papyrus commentary on an Oschophoria song by Pindar that appears to be a victory song for the winner of the race. The song must have been generic, suitable for whoever won, since the winner celebrated immediately after the race. Either there were Oschophoria songs for both the procession and the *kōmos* or the sources have the sequence garbled.

[83] The *aition* in Plutarch *Theseus* 23.2–3 is that when Theseus led the band of victims to Crete to be given to the Minotaur he dressed two young men as women. When they returned, having escaped their fate, these two led the procession, holding vine branches, as did the two Oschophoroi thereafter. This *aition* has been laid over an old Dionysiac festival.

[84] See West 1965b; Jeanmaire 1939: 427–44 on this hymn.

5   Δίκταν εἰς ἐνιαυτὸν
        ἔρπε καὶ γέγαθι μολπᾷ,
        τάν τοι κρέκομεν πακτίσι
        μείξαντες ἄμ᾽ αὐλοῖσιν,
        καὶ στάντες ἀείδομεν τεὸν
10   ἀμφὶ βωμὸν οὐερκῆ.
        ἰώ, μέγιστε Κοῦρε,
        χαῖρέ μοι, Κρόνειε,
        παγκρατὲς γάνος, βέβακες
        δαιμόνων ἀγώμενος·
15   Δίκταν εἰς ἐνιαυτὸν
        ἔρπε καὶ γέγαθι μολπᾷ,
        ἔνθα γὰρ σέ, παῖδ᾽ ἄμβροτον,
        ἀσπιδ[ηφόροι τροφῆες]
        παρ᾽ Ῥέας λαβόντες πόδα
20   κ[ρούοντες ἀντάχον.]

Io, greatest youth, greetings, son of Kronos, all-conquering brightness, you are present, leading the divinities; at the year's turn come to Dikte and delight in the song, that we pluck for you on lyres, mixing it together with pipes, and sing standing about your well-fenced altar. Io, greatest youth, greetings, son of Kronos, all-conquering brightness, you are present, leading the divinities; at the year's turn come to Dikte and delight in the song, for here, immortal child, (your) shield[-bearing nurses ?], receiving you from Rhea, [cried in response, beating ?] their feet.

The "shield[-bearing nurses]" (if the supplement *exempli gratia* is correct) take over from Rhea.[85] Even if the supplement is not close, these figures conflate the imagery of nurture and defense by their action, more explicitly than do Pindar's *paianes,* for they receive the baby. The imagery in the poem probably reproduces the imagery of the cult itself, with the performers leaping when the poem calls on the god to leap (47–50, 57–60, not quoted). By implication the speakers also take on the role of guardians of the baby. This hymn allows us to imagine that Pindar was drawing on a traditional image-pattern in his *paianes.*

The poems examined so far, few as they are, suggest that male performers in politically attuned civic performance may add female identity to their self-presentation in situations when the community is under stress or is presenting a united front to outsiders. Under these circumstances the

---

[85] The restoration is purely *exempli gratia,* and other restorations are possible (see *CA* ad loc., West 1965b: 152).

performers have a special interest in reflecting the community back to the audience as an integrated whole. Female identity does double duty in that through it the performers seem to sum up the community more comprehensively (that is, represent both men and women) and it also symbolizes ideal unity. It may have resonance with local cults as well, like the two just described, themselves a focus of unifying practice.

III

I now want to consider three poems in which the chorus-members do not claim female identity but place themselves in the realm of the female, creating an idealized identity through their proximity to female figures. The third example bears some resemblance to the Palaikastro Hymn. The first two poems, both *paianes,* were probably performed on Delos. Various cities each sent a chorus to Delos to represent it at a festival, most likely the annual Delia/Apollonia.[86] Performance in this context is an extension of community poetry: the performers represent the community and speak for it, but they are no longer speaking to it or modeling a new stage. The reflective role has taken over. Each city must have been keen to give as favorable an impression of itself as possible, for this was one forum for interstate vying for prestige.[87]

Plutarch gives evidence of the importance that fifth-century Athens attached to a good showing on Delos as well as a lively vignette of a moment of performance in his *Nikias* (3.5–6). Nikias sponsored a chorus and led the delegation that included it to the island. But instead of landing directly on Delos, where crowds would meet the ship and demand to hear the chorus sing on the spot, he put in at nearby Rhenaia. He had a bridge of boats strung between the two islands; then at daybreak he led the chorus in procession over the bridge, the chorus grandly costumed and singing. The story suggests, incidentally, that the choruses sent to Delos must have had more than one song in their repertoire. Nikias no doubt won plaudits in Athens for presenting the city so splendidly to the crowd of visitors from all over the Aegean.

Since on Delos cities are representing themselves to others, perfor-

[86] For fragments of Simonides' *paianes* to be performed on Delos and at Delphi, see Rutherford 1990. Pronomos, a famous pipes-player, composed a *paian* for Chalkis to take to Delos (Pausanias 9.12.6). Of Pindar's *paianes* for which the venue of performance is known, three and a possible fourth are for Delos (4, 5, 7b, and perhaps 12). To Eumelos, an early poet, is attributed a *prosodion* or processional song for the people of Ithome for their first delegation to Delos (696 *PMG*); on Eumelos see Janko 1982: 231–33. Xenophon *Memorabilia* 3.3.12 mentions the Athenians sending choruses to Delos.

[87] It is conceivable that the choral performances were competitive, but there is no good evidence for it. Nothing is said, for instance, about whether Nikias won with his spectacular choral production, mentioned below. Käppel 1992: 56–59 discusses the issue and points out that singing *paianes* in contests would harm their communicative function.

mance in this setting poses an interesting question about how men might present themselves as speakers. If *paian* 6 is a guide, we could imagine that they might claim both male and female identity, but perhaps the inevitably, if not officially, competitive aspect of performance affected their self-presentation, making identification of themselves as female a more dubious technique. On the other hand, the founding legend of the cult of Apollo, Artemis, and Leto on Delos was a birth story, and the cult was a rich complex of elements referring to marriage and childbirth.[88] In order to make contact with the Delian ambiance, a chorus might want to address these themes. If it is correct that the two following poems, both for performance by the people of Keos, were sung and danced on Delos, then we can see in them two particular solutions to the question of male performers' style of self-presentation in an external setting.

Pindar's *paian* 4 is the first one.[89] In it the mother in her household is the central image for the attitude of the Keans toward their island and especially the city Karthaia.[90] The chorus presents itself as ready to pass up power in favor of the harmony found in the community-as-household. We can follow the train of thought despite the lacunae. In the half-preserved lines at the beginning of the fragment, a sentence seems to say, "I will [not] exchange Karthaia, [   ] short-backed breast of earth, for Babylon . . . " (13–15). The following lines from the first epode pursue the same idea (21–30):

> ἤτοι καὶ ἐγὼ σ[κόπ]ελον ναίων δια-
> γινώσκομαι μὲν ἀρεταῖς ἀέθλων
> Ἑλλανίσιν, γινώσκ[ο]μα[ι] δὲ καὶ
> μοῖσαν παρέχων ἅλις·
> 25 [ε]ἴ καί τι Διω[νύσ]ου ἄρο[υρ]α φέρει
> βιόδωρον ἀμαχανίας ἄκος,
> ἄνιππός εἰμι καὶ βουνομίας ἀδαέστερος·
> ἀλλ’ ὅ γε Μέλαμπος οὐκ ἤθελεν
> λιπὼν πατρίδα μο[να]ρχε[ῖν] Ἄργει
> 30 θέμενος οἰ[ω]νοπόλον γέρας.

---

[88] See Ch. 4 for the birth-story celebrated on Delos.

[89] The evidence that this poem was performed on Delos is tenuous: the name Delos appears in line 12. Käppel 1992: 141–48 discusses the alternatives of performance on Keos and performance on Delos and decides in favor of the latter on the basis of the name Artemis in 1, for she seems to have received *paianes* along with Apollo only on Delos; likewise the elaborate self-presentation of the chorus speaks for an external audience. It follows that this poem is not connected with Pindar *Isthmian* 1.

[90] Käppel 1992: Ch. 3 has an excellent discussion of this poem. It is possible that the chorus was from Karthaia and not from Keos as a whole. On the relatively abundant testimony for choral activity at Karthaia, see Rutherford, forthcoming.

And I also, though I dwell on a rock, am well-known among the Greeks for prowess in contests, and well-known too for furnishing the Muse in abundance; if my fields also bear Dionysus' life-giving cure for helplessness, I am without horses and untutored in cattle-raising; but certainly Melampos[91] did not readily leave his fatherland to wield sole power in Argos, laying aside the honor of divining from the birds.

The Keans state their virtues, then acknowledge the limitations of the island. The next line, with its example of Melampos, introduces a somewhat compressed train of thought: "but certainly Melampos was hesitant, (because it required) leaving his home, to take up sole power at Argos . . . (so far less would I want to leave my home)." Melampos came from Pylos but received a third of the kingship of Argos because he cured the daughters of Proitos of their madness; thus he had great recompense for giving up his homeland.[92] However, by using the imperfect οὐκ ἤθελεν (kept finding himself unwilling to) the chorus means to suggest that initially even he resisted.[93] The novel detail that he had to give up his divining if he accepted the kingship introduces the chorus's view that such heroes have a choice between power and right relations with the gods.[94]

Melampos is a foil for Euxantios, the Kean hero who is introduced in the second strophe after a gnome about cherishing near relations.[95] Poor though Keos is, unlike Melampos' native territory, Euxantios prefers his homeland and the gods' good will (35–53):

35   λόγο[ν ἄν]ακτος Εὐξαν[τίου
      {σ} ἐπαίνεσα [Κρητ]ῶν μαιομένων ὃς ἀνα[ίνετο
      αὐταρχεῖν, πολίων δ' ἑκατὸν πεδέχει[ν
      μέρος ἕβδομον Πασιφ[ά]ας ⟨σὺν⟩ υἱ-
      οῖ]σι· τέρας δ' ἐὸν εἰ-

[91] The usual form of the name is Melampous.

[92] Melampos demanded part of the kingdom as payment. Farnell 1961 *ad loc.* remarks, "He is the last person in Greek mythology suitable to choose as the type of one who refused to leave his home to take up a better position." The point is that the person least imaginable as a paradigm of attachment to home had some doubts about leaving it.

[93] The phrase οὐκ ἤθελεν has caused problems. It can be translated "was not willing" (i.e., refused), but Käppel 1992: 129–35 points out that in that case it flies in the face of all other versions. He suggests that the negative should be taken only with μοναρχεῖν: Melampos did not want absolute rule. But λιπὼν πατρίδα cannot be incidental in this context. For the verb expressing reluctance to do what one does do, cf. Archilochos 5 *W*: he left his shield behind οὐκ ἐθέλων. Slater 1969b s.v. takes it this way. D'Alessio 1994: 64 also does not accept Käppel's solution.

[94] So Käppel 1992: 136–37, although he contrasts accepting a third of the kingdom with demanding the whole territory of Argos.

[95] Like the Boeotian Teneros, Euxantios is a local figure, though he was known at Miletos. See *PW* ad loc., and on Teneros Ch. 1, pp. 50–51.

40   πέν σφι· "τρέω τοι πόλεμον
     Διὸς Ἐννοσίδαν τε βαρ[ύ]κτυπον.

     χθόνα τοί ποτε καὶ στρατὸν ἀθρόον
     πέμψαν κεραυνῷ τριόδοντί τε
     ἐς τὸν βαθὺν Τάρταρον ἐμὰν μα-
45   τέρα λιπόντες καὶ ὅλον οἶκον εὐερκέα·
     ἔπειτα πλούτου πειρῶν μακάρων τ' ἐπιχώριον
     τεθμὸν π[ά]μπαν ἐρῆμον ἀπωσάμενος
     μέγαν ἄλλοθι κλᾶρον ἔχω; λίαν
     μοι [δέο]ς ἔμπεδον εἴ-
50   η κεν. ἔα, φρήν, κυπάρισ-
     σον, ἔα δὲ νομὸν Περιδάϊον.
     ἐμοὶ δ' ὀλίγον δέδοται θά[μνου
     οὐ πενθέων δ' ἔλαχον, ⟨οὐ⟩ στασίων . . ."

I praise the speech of the [lord] Euxantios, who refused to be a ruler, though the [Cretans] were eager for it, and to hold a seventh share of the hundred cities with the sons of Pasiphae; he told them his guiding sign: "I fear, I tell you, war from Zeus and deep-striking Poseidon. Once indeed they sent the land and the crowded people to deep Tartaros with thunder and trident, leaving my mother and her whole well-walled house. Then making a try for wealth and casting off to complete desolation my native ordinance from the gods, should I have a great holding elsewhere? My [fear] would be too fixed. Let go the cypress, heart, let go the grazing land around Ida (?). Little [place for] vegetation (?) is given to me, but I drew no share of sorrows, no share of faction. . . ."

(The disaster to which the poem refers is Zeus' blasting the Telchines, the previous inhabitants of the island.[96]) Unlike Melampos, Euxantios actually refused to accept the kingship pressed on him. To demonstrate the loyalty that Keos enjoys, the chorus tells of the offer to Euxantios, then takes on Euxantios' voice to respond as he contrasts rule in Crete with remaining in his mother's house.[97] If he were to go to Crete, he would be an absolute ruler (αὐταρχεῖν, 37) and would gain wealth. But Euxantios fears "war" from Zeus and Poseidon should he take up the offer. *War* is not the most obvious word to use in describing the gods' disfavor, but it

[96] For this destruction see Callimachus *Aitia* III fr. 75.64–69 Pfeiffer. The reference to Euxantios' mother's house is explained by Bacchylides 1.112–29, for a Kean victor: after the destruction of the other inhabitants, King Minos stopped at Keos and slept with Dexithea, with whom he left half his retinue. Euxantios was born of that union. Huxley 1965 discusses the mythical history of Keos.

[97] Rutherford, forthcoming, comments that the combination of short introductory formula and long speech is rare and produces the effect of making the chorus impersonate Euxantios.

carries the chorus's theme that the price of power in general is strife and probably active hostility on the part of the gods.

In contrast, the figure of the mother defines the community of Keos as kin and home and suggests stability. The words ἐμὰν ματέρα (my mother) come at the same position in the second triad as does Karthaia, the name of Keos' principal city, in the first triad, where Karthaia is (apparently) preferred to Babylon. And Euxantios summarizes the object of his loyalty as ἐπιχώριον τεθμόν (46–47), a difficult phrase to translate but meaning his whole local set of established ways and relations with the gods.[98] The word *local* resonates with *mother* and *house*.[99]

The poem responds to an unspoken charge that Keos is too small and poor to brag about. The chorus meets the charge by stressing devotion to home all through the extant section (32–34, as well as the lines quoted above). As the fragment breaks off, the chorus, still speaking as Euxantios, is pointing out the positive results of the gods' dispensation to his mother: "Little [place for] vegetation (?) is given to me, but I drew no share of sorrows, no share of faction. . . ." (52–53). Euxantios' lack of grief seems to pick up a theme from the beginning of the poem, where the words ἡ]συχίαν Κέῳ (7, "peace and quiet for Keos") are visible.[100] Through the figure of his mother and Euxantios' choice to remain home, the defects of Keos are transformed into virtues more precious than wealth and power. The burden of the chorus's prayer to Apollo and Artemis (1) must have been for continued enjoyment of their calm. In *paian* 9 the image of the city giving birth is combined with military themes; the mother figure serves to give a collective and constructive slant to armed activity. In this case the mother is a focus for renunciation of military ambitions and substitution of other values.

The chorus's dancing as harmonious movement and analog for the social harmony Euxantios enjoyed confirms that the benefits of living on Keos have continued. By taking on Euxantios' voice after praising his words, the choreuts both identify themselves with the mythic past and confirm his choice as theirs: speaking his words, they refer to "my mother." At the same time the poem presents the Kean performers as a parallel to the people of Delos.[101] The character of Keos, like Delos, is

---

[98] The meaning of τεθμόν is difficult to specify precisely. Farnell 1961 *ad loc.* suggests "worship." Slater 1969b s.v. has "ordinance." Käppel 1992: 122n.122 chooses "ordinance" and makes ἐρῆμον refer to the idea of place implied in ἐπιχώριον.

[99] Käppel 1992: 128–29 points out that the scholia to the lost lines 58–61 indicate that the subject was those children of Euxantios who made Keos their home; they may have been the bridge over which the chorus returned to its own sentiments.

[100] Cf. Käppel 1992: 99n.42 on the meaning of ἡσυχία in Pindar. He translates it as "friedliche Ruhe im Staat."

[101] Käppel 1992: 104 points out that ἤτοι καὶ ἐγώ (and I also) in 21 implies that the previous lines have characterized islands in general. The Delians could easily hear in this line a comparison with themselves.

defined by a mother. Both are small rocky islands (cf. 21), but under the protection of the gods. The Keans can therefore draw on the reverence granted to Delos to explain their own special status in the world and at the same time bring pleasure to the Delians.

Very different in style is Bacchylides' so-called dithyramb (in fact probably a *paian*) for the Keans on Delos (17 *SM*).[102] Bacchylides' poem takes up a narrative immediately and pursues it to its conclusion without bringing the performers into relationship with any addressee until the end of the poem.[103] All staging of the performers is therefore indirect; we can only suggest the interaction of the performers with their story. But we must remember that it was a performance, not the narrative in the abstract, that the Keans offered. As pure narrative it is not entirely coherent, in any event; the demands of its context and the Keans' self-presentation have overridden narrative logic.[104]

The narrative opens with the ship, commanded by Minos, that is carrying Theseus and his fourteen companions (seven male and seven female) to Crete. Minos touches one of the young women in lust. In the first direct speech of the poem, Theseus reproves him and compares their genealogies. Minos in anger at Theseus' boldness asks for and gets a sign from his father Zeus. Then, throwing a ring into the sea, he challenges Theseus to prove that his father is Poseidon by retrieving the ring. Theseus dives in and is borne by dolphins to his father's house, where he sees Nereids (sea nymphs) dancing and Poseidon's wife Amphitrite. She gives him a purple cloak (?) and a wreath of roses that Aphrodite had given her at her marriage. Theseus reappears beside the ship and comes out of the water dry.

It has been remarked that the first half of the poem focuses on masculine figures and the second half on feminine ones.[105] In the first half Aphrodite provokes a man's illegitimate desire; in the second half she gives wedding gifts to a woman. In the first half the chorus takes on Theseus' voice and in

[102] Jebb 1967: 223 and Käppel 1992: 183–89 identify this poem as a *paian*. So also Snell-Maehler 1970: xlviii–xlix. Zimmermann 1992: 91 takes it as a dithyramb, arguing that dithyrambs are attested for Delos by a notice of a dithyramb by Simonides (539 *PMG*) "from the Delian ones." But performance of dithyrambs by foreign choruses is unattested in the fifth century; cf. Pickard-Cambridge 1962: 3. Schmidt 1990 also discusses its genre.

[103] Of the "dithyrambs" whose opening lines are extant, 15 is the only other one to open with narrative; its performance context is unknown. Ode 18 begins immediately with its dramatic presentation. Odes 16, 19, 20 refer to the here and now of performance. On 17 see Käppel 1992: 156–89; Burnett 1985: 15–37; Zimmermann 1992: 77–94.

[104] Burnett 1985: 22–23 points out problems in the narrative. Her solution, in the realm of religious recreation of mythic time, and Käppel's (1992: 178–85), in the context of ceremonial *aition* and historical situation, are very different. Zimmermann 1992: 85–91 believes that the poem was to be danced by young men and women and interprets it as description and enactment of initiation.

[105] Stern 1967: 45–46; Segal 1979, for whom the poem depicts Theseus' initiation into mature sexuality via plunge, encounter with the female, and receiving the robe (31–34). Cf. Burnett 1985: 28–29.

the second half dances as it describes the Nereids dancing. It is this shift that I want to explore.

Theseus' speech is a long one (lines 20–46) and ends with a command and threat, expressed with restraint (39–46):

τῷ σε, πολέμαρχε Κνωσίων,
40   κέλομαι πολύστονον
ἐρύκεν ὕβριν· οὐ γὰρ ἂν θέλοι-
      μ' ἄμβροτον ἐραννὸν Ἀο[ῦς
ἰδεῖν φάος, ἐπεί τιν' ἠϊθέ[ων
σὺ δαμάσειας ἀέκον-
45   τα· πρόσθε χειρῶν βίαν
δε[ί]ξομεν· τὰ δ' ἐπιόντα δα[ίμω]ν κρινεῖ.

Wherefore, commander of the Knossians, I order you to restrain your grievous aggression, for I would not want to see the immortal lovely light of Dawn once you subdued any of the youths against his or her will; we will sooner show the strength of our hands, and a divinity will judge the outcome.

The first person is emphatic in these lines, so that for the audience, watching men perform, it would be easy to allow the chorus and Theseus to merge in their minds. Minos is given two shorter speeches (52–66 and 74–80), but in neither of them is the first person at all prominent: an unemphatic pronoun in the accusative and two adjectives (53, 64, 74).

In the "megaron of the gods" (100–101) that Theseus enters after his dive, the alignment shifts. The chorus now seems to make the Nereids visible as it dances. No explicit interlocking of the two occurs, although the chorus may have mimed the scene by a change in its style of dancing (101–11):

τόθι κλυτὰς ἰδών
ἔδεισε⟨ν⟩ Νηρῆος ὀλ-
βίου κόρας· ἀπὸ γὰρ ἀγλα-
ῶν λάμπε γυίων σέλας
105   ὧτε πυρός, ἀμφὶ χαίταις
δὲ χρυσεόπλοκοι
δίνηντο ταινίαι· χορῷ δ' ἔτερ-
πον κέαρ ὑγροῖσι ποσσίν.
εἶδέν τε πατρὸς ἄλοχον φίλαν
110   σεμνὰν βοῶπιν ἐρατοῖ-
σιν Ἀμφιτρίταν δόμοις·

There, seeing the renowned daughters of blessed Nereus, he was afraid, for brightness shone from their beautiful limbs as of fire, and ribbons braided with gold whirled around their hair; they were delighting their hearts in the dance with limber feet. And he saw his father's cherished wife, august large-eyed Amphitrite, in the lovely house.

Theseus, so bold in confronting Minos, is now fearful. The Nereids dominate the picture with their dance. They are less tame than *parthenoi;* choruses of nymphs dancing in the wild can be dangerous to the young man they fancy. The chorus, by the emphasis in its song, is on the side of the Nereids. When Amphitrite gives Theseus gifts, a purple robe and a crown of roses given to her by Aphrodite for her own wedding (112–16), her "motherly" role is tinged with the erotic. Theseus himself earlier mentions to Minos the golden veil that the Nereids gave his mother (36–38).

As Theseus returned to the ship (123–32),

> ... λάμ-
> πε δ' ἀμφὶ γυίοις θεῶν δῶρ', ἀγλαό-
> 125 θρονοί τε κοῦραι σὺν εὐ-
> θυμίαι νεοκτίτωι
> ὠλόλυξαν, ἔ-
> κλαγεν δὲ πόντος· ἤίθεοι δ' ἐγγύθεν
> νέοι παιάνιξαν ἐραταῖ ὀπί.
> 130 Δάλιε, χοροῖσι Κηΐων
> φρένα ἰανθείς
> ὄπαζε θεόπομπον ἐσθλῶν τύχαν.

The gifts of the gods shone about his limbs, and the splendid-throned maidens gave a ritual shout (*ololygē*) with new-founded enthusiasm and the sea rang, while nearby the young unmarried men shouted a *paian* with lovely voice.[106] Delian one, cheered at heart by the choruses of the Keans, grant god-sent fortune of good things.

Theseus now resembles the Nereids: λάμπε δ' ἀμφὶ γυίοις θεῶν δῶρ' (123–24, "the gifts of the gods shone about his limbs") echoes ἀπὸ γὰρ ἀγλαῶν λάμπε γυίων σέλας (103–4, "brightness shone from their beautiful limbs") of the Nereids. Since ὀλολύζω (shout *ololugē*) is onomatopoeic for the cry that women make, while the youths' *paian* reflects what the chorus is singing, the chorus seems to reproduce both reactions. The youths' *paian* cry at the end blends into the chorus's own parting prayer to Apollo,

[106] I follow Gerber 1982 in taking the κοῦραι of 125 to be the *parthenoi* and not the Nereids.

so that for a moment past and present fuse.[107] The chorus, like its mythic counterparts in the tale, is male and female. All of this is atmospherics, but the song eroticizes its singers and ambiguates their masculinity.[108]

The poem does not have the usual indications of communal poetry, such as the use of first-person statements and references to the context of performance or address to the gods, at least until the last three lines. The chorus-members do not present themselves verbally as representative of the Keans; rather their staging of themselves is dramatic and sensuous. Perhaps the text illustrates the Keans' renunciation of an attempt to compete against boasts of power and wealth, the same attitude we saw expounded in *paian* 4. But Pindar's poem tries to forestall others' taking a contemptuous attitude toward Keos, while Bacchylides' poem tries to seduce its audience. Pindar's text allows its chorus to assert (23–24), "I am well-known for furnishing the Muse in abundance." Bacchylides, who was from Keos himself, tries to demonstrate the truth of that boast in sensuous terms. Mother figure and chorus of female dancers here have nothing to do with the community. Freed of pressure to embody the community and likewise of any need to persuade the community that the speakers do represent it (such as would constrain poetry performed within the community), the chorus uses these figures to create the image of a beautiful ephebe and the vaguer suggestion of enticing androgyny. It is hard to imagine that it was performed by other than young men.

Richard Jebb and others connect the story of Theseus in this poem thematically with the crane dance, danced around a horn altar on Delos and said to have been initiated by Theseus.[109] The crane dance was a dance for young men and women together.[110] Lutz Käppel suggests that the crane dance (for which he thinks this poem to be a libretto) was performed at the Delia.[111] Since the crane dance was danced by men and women, I would

---

[107] Käppel 1992: 177–78 with references to earlier discussions of the effect. On the importance of these lines for the performance context of the poem, see Käppel 178–83.

[108] The tension between the military ideal of masculinity and a more lithe and charming, androgynous image of male beauty, documented by Dover 1978: 73–79 and Gleason 1990: 405–6, comes down here on the side of the latter. Dover 73–75 points out the connection of the androgynous ideal with musical performance. See Scodel 1984 on the gifts making Theseus an erotic figure: he wins Ariadne, who enables him to defeat Minos.

[109] Jebb 1967: 224–25 based on Plutarch *Theseus* 21, who associates the dance with Theseus' dedication of a statue of Aphrodite. Calame 1977: I 108–15 has discussion and bibliography.

[110] The back of the Françoise Vase shows pairs of young men and women dancing in celebration of Theseus' victory over the Minotaur. Coldstream 1968 interprets the dance on several early vases as the crane dance. In Callimachus *Hymn* 4.304–13 to Delos, men sing and women dance, as Theseus and his companions once did. Mineur 1984: 243 has further bibliography on the question.

[111] Käppel 1992: 179–81; cf. 142. He does not set out all the steps in the argument; they are as follows:

guess rather that the Delians themselves performed it, not the visitors. This ode then evokes it as a tribute to Delos. Käppel also proposes a date for the performance around 478–474 on the grounds that the theme of the poem is awareness of moral restraints and that Minos and Theseus, the first unobservant of moral limits, the second attentive to them, reflect the Persians and the Athenians in the recent clash of the Persian Wars.[112] If so, the gendering of the dancers does have an indirect political point in asking Athens to protect and respect the "female" islands of the Aegean sea.

These two poems illustrate further the adaptability a male chorus gained by co-opting female identity or characterizing itself through female figures. The effects are indirect in these poems, for the female characters are figures in the narrative, but interaction there must have been between those who sang and danced and their song. Pindar's *paian* uses the same techniques of gendered self-identification as does poetry to be performed within the community, but Bacchylides' song turns them on their head. I have already referred to performance meant to represent the community to outsiders as an extension of community performance. Bacchylides' *paian* marks the limit of the category, as poems of Archilochos and Solon were shown to in Chapter 1.[113] Like the dithyramb at Athens, it has shifted toward the pole of entertainment. Only the three-line ending anchors it to community and context.

It should be noted here that most of the examples of male choruses claiming female identity come from Pindar. Pindar's religious poetry is almost the only surviving community poetry for men, so inevitably his texts are the example. But it may be that he was especially fond of the technique. It is not prevalent in the epinician odes, which incorporate a

1. Thucydides 3.104.6 says that, after the demise of the old games on Delos (and before the Athenians reinstated a quadrennial festival with games in 426), the islanders and the Athenians continued to send choruses and sacrificial victims to Delos. This must have been a yearly occurrence, since it is distinguished from the quadrennial festival.
2. Nilsson 1957: 145–46 argues that the yearly festival must be the Delia, for only outsiders would give such a name to a Delian festival (all festivals being "Delian" for the Delians) and that Apollonia is the local name of the same festival. (Others make these separate festivals.)
3. If there was only one festival, the yearly *theoria* (delegation) from Athens to Delos mentioned by Plato *Phaedo* 58ab must have coincided with the yearly sending of choruses to the Delia. Plato explains that the *theoria* originated in Theseus' vow to honor Apollo in this way if he were saved from the Minotaur. So the Delia were connected with Theseus.
4. Since Theseus instituted the crane dance on Delos, the crane dance must be connected with the Delia.

[112] Käppel 1992: 181–83 with bibliography on earlier proposals of a similar date. Zimmermann 1992: 93–94 accepts the 470s for similar reasons and also because of the meter.

[113] Käppel 1992: 189 makes this same point from a different perspective, finding the poem at the boundary of the genre *paian*.

more complicated relationship between performers and audience than does community poetry.

There is one victory ode, however, that does make prominent use of female figures for a special reason, one related to the effects sought by the poems considered so far. In this ode, *Olympian* 6, Pindar uses the figure of a mother in order to position the chorus in relationship to victor and community. He resorts to this method because the shared community of chorus, audience, and victor must be created by the poem itself. *Olympian* 6 was written for Hagesias of Syracuse after his victory with the mule-cart, perhaps in 468. Through his mother, Hagesias was related to the Iamidai, a family of seers who claimed descent from Iamos and who had the right to practice divination at Olympia. His mother's kin, also presumably Iamidai, lived at Stymphalos in Arcadia (77–78). Rather than return to Syracuse for the victory celebration, Hagesias visited his mother's family at Stymphalos, where the ode was performed (99). When Pindar undertook to compose this ode, he faced a special problem: the people of Stymphalos were not Hagesias' own community. Indeed, the end of the ode indicates that Hagesias is about to return to Syracuse. And while Hagesias may well have visited before, he seems to have been an associate of Hieron's at Syracuse (judging from the end of the ode), so he was probably not often in Arcadia. Pindar had to compose a poem in which a community welcomed one who was not really their own. We do not know who the performers or the audience for the ode were.[114] I assume that both were drawn from the community of Stymphalos, including relatives of Hagesias.

The opening section of the ode speaks primarily to the audience, introducing Hagesias and vouching for him. In the imagery of the poem, the chorus-members begin by building the entrance as if to a marvelous building (1–4).[115] They say they will bear witness, swearing a great oath (20–21).[116] They therefore begin as mediators (as in Hermokles' *paian*) between Hagesias and the audience. The story of Euadne and the birth of Iamos near the middle of the poem is a pivot; it establishes a community around the mother within which the chorus can include Hagesias with itself and with the audience at large. After the birth story the chorus is speaking primarily for the audience in praising Hagesias; thus the poem

[114] See the Introduction for my view of the first person in Pindar's epinician odes as the chorus *in performance*.

[115] For a study of the richness of the poem's imagery and the multiplicity of its referents, see Goldhill 1991: 146–66.

[116] An oath is sworn by speaking it aloud. An oath is the kind of performative in which the words perform an action (to say "I swear" under felicitous conditions is to do so), so the voice here is of necessity the chorus's. An oath of Pindar's, spoken by the chorus, would be meaningless.

signals its assumption that the audience no longer perceives Hagesias as an outsider. In this poem, then, the model, the new stage, comes first and consists of making Hagesias an honored member of the community, and the reflection, the celebration of communal ties, comes second. This is the opposite of the sequence in the Alkman and Tyrtaios poems and, less distinctively, of most of the poems we have looked at.

To illustrate the switch in mode of addressing the audience, we can observe the motif of jealousy of the victor. It comes up twice: once before the central myth and once (74–76) after. The first passage is (4–9):

εἰ δ᾽ εἴ-
η μὲν Ὀλυμπιονίκας,
5   βωμῷ τε μαντείῳ ταμίας Διὸς ἐν Πίσᾳ,
συνοικιστὴρ τε τᾶν κλεινᾶν Συρακοσ-
σᾶν, τίνα κεν φύγοι ὕμνον
κεῖνος ἀνήρ, ἐπικύρσαις
ἀφθόνων ἀστῶν ἐν ἱμερταῖς ἀοιδαῖς;

ἴστω γὰρ ἐν τούτῳ πεδί-
λῳ δαιμόνιον πόδ᾽ ἔχων
Σωστράτου υἱός.

If one should be an Olympic victor and steward of the prophetic altar of Zeus at Pisa (= Olympia) and cofounder of famous Syracuse, what song would that man escape, meeting with unjealous fellow-townsmen in seductive melodies? Let the son of Sostratos (= Hagesias) know that he has his god-assisted foot in this sandal.

The praise owing to Hagesias is cast as a question, allowing the audience to supply the answer and so assent mentally to his glorification. The question is immediately qualified by a participial phrase ("meeting with unjealous townsmen in seductive melodies") that could be taken either as conditional ("if he meets . . . ") or as causal ("since he meets . . . "). Anyone who resists welcoming Hagesias will hear the conditional and his or her own response labeled jealousy. Since the chorus is singing a "seductive melody," the speakers both imply that they are unjealous fellow-townsmen and invite the audience to identify with them. The actual charm of the performance, if it moved the audience to pleasure, was part of the persuasive logic set up in these lines.

The third-person imperative that follows, opening the antistrophe, is still addressed to the audience and further invites them to assent. The phrase τούτῳ πεδίλῳ (8, "this sandal") functions as a metaphor for either of the conditions of the previous sentence. It could mean that Hagesias *is* in the situation of being Olympic victor and steward; then the sentence means, "Let Hagesias know that he meets the criteria for praise." Or it could mean, "Let Hagesias know that he meets with unjealous townsmen." Each construction implies the other: if Hagesias is praised, then the townsmen are unjealous, and the reverse. Here is the modeling function of the poem, skillfully persuading the audience to move to the new stage of offering Hagesias their admiration. But the chorus has not yet acted as representative of the audience in linking praise of Hagesias with the identity of the community so that his praise becomes their praise, his honor a projection of their character.

After the story of Euadne and her son Iamos, the chorus speaks for the audience. The narrative has given the audience a (renewed?) imaginative investment in the Iamidai and has established the idea of a community of "Arcadians." As the myth comes to an end, the chorus praises the whole Iamid *genos* (extended family), then brings up the theme of jealousy again: "blame from others who are jealous" (74) hangs over Olympic victors who are also handsome. The jealous are no longer "townsmen" but "others," that is, those who are not among the current company. In the last epode Hagesias, who is to return to Syracuse, is said to go "from home to home" (99) and the chorus prays that the god furnish an illustrious destiny for "these friends and those" (102). Stymphalos has become home.

The linking of Hagesias and the audience into a single community is the function of the myth that comes between these two passages. Its outline is as follows: Iamos' mother Euadne is born from the union of Pitana, eponymous nymph of the town Pitana, and Poseidon. Pitana orders that the baby be carried to the house of Aipytos, a mythical king of Arcadia.[117] There Euadne, when grown, is embraced by Apollo and conceives Iamos, founder of the Iamid clan. She gives birth and leaves the baby in the thicket, where he is fed by snakes; she calls him "Iamos" after the violets in which he lies. When grown, Iamos calls on his father Apollo, who leads him to Olympia and gives him the ability to prophesy. The chorus tells this myth without first-person intervention, unlike the performers of Isyllos' *paian*. Adoption of female character is subtler and more indirect here than in Isyllos' poem.

In this myth the mother is a paradigm figure. The first consideration, of course, is the fact that Hagesias was related to the Iamid seers at Olympia and to his Stymphalian relatives through his mother. By projecting the theme of an Iamid mother back to the original, the mother of Iamos, the poem ensures that the community at Stymphalos can celebrate a mythic ancestry that it shares with Hagesias. For the birth story Pindar probably

[117] The tomb of Aipytos at the foot of Mt. Kyllene is mentioned in *Iliad* 2.603–4. Pausanias mentions Aipytos as acceding to the kingship of Arcadia in 8.4.7 and his tomb in 8.16.2–3.

had no more than the genealogical data, which he expanded by means of conventional motifs and vivid description.[118] What the expansion notably accomplishes is to characterize Arcadia as a natural world haunted by divinity.[119] Euadne gives birth: "Iamos came from her womb into the light instantly in response to delightful labor pains" (43–44). She abandons the baby in a landscape lush with color. This land is sheltering and nurturant; the baby is safe in his hiding spot, fed by snakes with the "blameless poison of bees" (45–47).[120] When Iamos is grown, he wades into the Alpheus at night under the sky to call on his father. All takes place in a world without human settlement. Euadne herself blends into Arcadia (while her mother Pitana implies connections with neighboring Lakedaimon, for Pitana was a Spartan town).[121] The only other character to receive attention, King Aipytos, rushes away to Delphi before the birth and cannot find the baby on his return.

The story establishes Arcadia as the origin of Iamos and therefore of Hagesias, the place from which both journeyed to Olympia. Insofar as the chorus and audience identify themselves as Arcadian and feel attachment to the land, they can adopt the maternal position of Euadne in relation to Hagesias. Then in the triad and a half after the myth ends, identifications with a mother are both advanced and retracted in a delicate positioning of Iamidai, chorus, and audience. First Hagesias is drawn into the ambit of the myth (77–81):

εἰ δ᾽ ἐτύμως ὑπὸ Κυλλά-

    νας ὄρος, Ἁγησία, μάτρωες ἄνδρες

ναιετάοντες ἐδώρη-

σαν θεῶν κάρυκα λιταῖς θυσίαις

πολλὰ δὴ πολλαῖσιν Ἑρμᾶν εὐσεβέως,

ὃς ἀγῶνας ἔχει μοῖράν τ᾽ ἀέθλων,

[118] Wilamowitz-Moellendorff 1886: 176–77 thinks of a poem on the birth of Iamos located at Olympia, which Pindar expanded. Goldhill 1991: 152–53 points out the mythic patterns of the hero's birth which Pindar uses. Rubin 1980–81 suggests that birth is for Pindar an image of his creativity.

[119] One could compare the Attic orators' habit of calling Athenian men "autochthonous" in the yearly military funeral orations by analogy with Erechtheus. On autochthony and its relationship to gender, see Loraux 1986: 145–50.

[120] Stern 1970 finds ambivalence in both landscape and language, resolved by the immortality bestowed by Pindar's poetry. I agree that the poem subsumes the landscape, but to Arcadians the evocation of Arcadia would have a different meaning from that produced by reading the text.

[121] Wilamowitz-Moellendorff 1886: 179–83 points out the Peloponnesian politics involved in claiming kinship with Sparta when Sparta had just (?) subjected Arcadia at the battle of Dipaia. The Spartan connection would have pleased the Dorian Syracusans as well, whom Pindar also has in mind.

80   Ἀρκαδίαν τ' εὐάνορα τιμᾷ·

      κεῖνος, ὦ παῖ Σωστράτου,

      σὺν βαρυγδούπῳ πατρὶ κραίνει σέθεν εὐτυχίαν.

If truly the men on (your) mother's side, Hagesias, living below Mt. Kyllene, often begifted the herald of the gods piously with many sacrifices of supplication, Hermes, who holds the games and has contests as his portion and honors Arcadia of good men, he, O child of Sostratos, with his deep-thundering father, brings about your good fortune.

The μάτρωες ἄνδρες (men on the mother's side) are the kin of Hagesias' real mother, but the phrase resonates with the myth. Reinforcing the resonance is the reference to Mt. Kyllene, for Hermes was born in a cave on that mountain.[122] Again, a baby hidden in a protective landscape is suggested, and again the Arcadians are linked with maternity. The word μάτρωες absorbs the floating maternal imagery, but the addition of ἄνδρες simultaneously masculinizes the idea, so that maternal imagery only enriches their male identity.[123] Hermes himself honors his birthplace, "Arcadia of good men."

Up to this point the chorus has not adopted the imagery generated by the myth to characterize itself. The performers have established a relationship between Hagesias and his relatives, drawn Hagesias into Arcadia, and asserted that Arcadian Hermes is the favoring deity responsible for his victory. Now it is their turn to locate themselves and the audience in the community they have constructed. After a declaration that they are impelled by inspiration, they speak of themselves (84–90):

      ματρομάτωρ ἐμὰ Στυμ-

        φαλίς, εὐανθὴς Μετώπα,

85   πλάξιππον ἃ Θήβαν ἔτι-

        κτεν, τᾶς ἐρατεινὸν ὕδωρ

      πίομαι, ἀνδράσιν αἰχματαῖσι πλέκων

      ποικίλον ὕμνον. ὄτρυνον νῦν ἑταίρους,

      Αἰνέα, πρῶτον μὲν Ἥραν

        Παρθενίαν κελαδῆσαι,

      γνῶναί τ' ἔπειτ', ἀρχαῖον ὄνειδος ἀλαθέσιν

90   λόγοις εἰ φεύγομεν, Βοιωτίαν ὖν.

My mother's mother is Stymphalian, flowery Metope, who bore horse-spurring Theba, (Metope) whose delightful water I drink as I weave a variegated song for

---

[122] *Homeric Hymn to Hermes* 227–30. The story was taken up in Panhellenized poetry but was a local myth also; cf. Pausanias 8.16.1 and 8.17.1.

[123] Note that Pindar never mentions Hagesias' real mother.

spear-bearing men.[124] Now rouse (your) companions, Aineas, first to celebrate Hera Parthenia, then to judge whether in true words we flee the old censure, Boeotian sow.

The fresh stimulus of inspiration leads the chorus-members to an emphatic personal declaration, their first since the end of the first triad. They announce their own maternal genealogy, which links them also to the Arcadian natural world; the water they drink may be both nurture and inspiration. The listeners too drink the water of Stymphalian Metope, so they are included in the chorus's first person. However, since the chorus drinks from the maternal source, it does not adopt the figure of mother as its own identity. Instead it places itself in parallel with Hagesias/Iamos, the offspring of an Arcadian mother. By doubling ("mother's mother"), the chorus allows room for a human mother like Hagesias' and a mythic one like Iamos' or alternatively repeats the double story of Iamos' conception. The analogy between Pitana and Metope is strengthened by yet one more birth; Metope bore Thebe, one of the many daughters of Metope and the River Asopos in mythology.[125] However, the abundance of mothers requires a balancing masculine association, provided in the participial phrase: the chorus drinks as it weaves a song for spear-bearing men. These latter could be either the audience or Hagesias' retinue.

Throughout these lines, approaches to adopting the maternal identity of Arcadia play in counterpoint with references to men and masculine activities (games, war). A double imaginative relationship develops: the Arcadians are the maternal, protective community from which Hagesias departed to find glory but to which he returns; and the Arcadians are, like Hagesias, sprung from Arcadia the mother but involved in competition and war.[126] In the interplay of the two possibilities, a community emerges

[124] Lines 84–87 are arranged so that grammatically the relative pronoun in the clause "whose water I drink" could be referred either to Metope or to Thebe. The scholiasts, even though they assume that the first person is Pindar, refer the phrase "whose water I drink" to Metope (I 186 Dr.). Thebe was not a spring nymph (as her epithet "horse-spurring" shows); the spring at Thebes was Dirke. At Stymphalos the lines would naturally seem to refer to their own spring, and the chorus would be perceived as proclaiming its identity, just as the chorus in *paian* 2 does. Modern scholars (e.g., Mullen 1982: 35), less sensitive to categories of nymphs, generally attribute the water to Thebe and take the speaker to be Pindar drinking the water of inspiration.

[125] Bacchylides 9.40–65 and Jebb 1967: 205–6; Diodoros 4.72; Pausanias 5.22.5. The number varies; up to twenty are mentioned. Thebe is regularly named as one of the daughters of Asopos, but there was a river Asopos in Boeotia also. Korinna (654 col. iii 12–21; cf. 48–51 *PMG*) makes the Boeotian Asopos the father of many daughters. Pausanias remarks (2.5.6) that the Thebans claim that Thebe was the daughter of Boeotian Asopos, not the Arcadian one. The version used here honors the Arcadians by linking Thebe with their Asopos (and provides an implicit reference to Pindar and justification for importing his poem).

[126] The theme of return is significant in this section of the poem. Iamos "returns" as Hagesias. Hermes returns from Olympia if he is present to receive offerings. Hera returns

to which Hagesias, the chorus, and the audience can subscribe. The Stymphalians are ambiguously mothers and brothers to Hagesias. The ambiguity creates simultaneously unity of family and fellowship among men.

The references to Hagesias' μάτρωες ἄνδρες (mother's male kin) and the chorus's ματρομάτωρ (mother's mother) at the end of antistrophe and epode (though not in metrically equivalent places) form a pair, thematically and aurally linking Hagesias and the chorus. The following lines (quoted above) contain another pair, Hera Parthenia and a sow, explicitly coupled by the text. The chorus asks Aineas to rouse the companions, "first to celebrate Hera Parthenia (Hera the Maiden), then to judge whether in true words we flee the old censure, Boeotian sow." The second request seems most peculiar. It is usually taken as Pindar (who was Boeotian) speaking in his own person, but to attribute it to Pindar does not explain its presence; why would Pindar raise the possibility that someone might call him a sow?[127] Why would he ask the Arcadians of all people, a group whose great families did not patronize him, about his reputation? Nothing else like it appears in any other ode. The remark must be understood in the first instance in the context of performance. I will examine each request separately in turn, then the two as a contrasting pair.

Hera Parthenia is apparently the goddess of a local cult about which Pausanias gives some information; his notice makes it possible to understand the reference in light of the themes I have been tracing. According to Pausanias (8.22.2):

> They say the ancient Stymphelos is where Temenos son of Pelasgos lived, and that Temenos brought up Hera, and founded three sanctuaries of that goddess and gave her three titles: he called her the Child when she was still a young virgin, and Perfect when she married Zeus, and while she was quarrelling with Zeus and came back to Stymphelos, Temenos called her the Widow.[128]

Like Iamos/Hagesias, Hermes, and the chorus (and audience), Hera found protection and nurture in Arcadia. She too departed—for Olympus, not Olympia. And like Iamos/Hagesias and Hermes, she returned and was welcomed back with new honor. In this case, however, the gender terms are reversed: the baby who grows up and departs is female, the protector

---

from Olympus in the myth. These returns must be connected with the phrase "home to home" at the end of the ode. Goldhill 1991: 150–58 and 164–65 points out the prominence of journey imagery. Garner 1992 links the elements of journey, female-dominated genealogy, and Iamos' "initiation" to mystery religions.

[127] Slater 1969a: 90 lists this passage as one of only five in the epinician odes in which Pindar separates himself from the chorus by addressing it. His question then becomes an odd indirect boast.

[128] Translation from Levi 1971: II 421. In Pausanias' account Hera's first title is *pais*, not *parthenos*, but the two words could be used interchangeably for young women, and it is generally assumed that Pausanias and Pindar refer to the same cult.

male.[129] Hera's story, if recalled by the audience, allows Pindar to cap his submerged image of masculine nurturance with an allusion to an explicit case. The corollary implication, that Hagesias is a bride, provides a formula for his imagined original and his upcoming departure that does not signal rejection of the community. All of this was present to the minds of the audience only by free association to the *aition* of Hera's cult, but the motif of the male "mother" in her cult, if it was current in Pindar's day, must certainly have been evoked by this ode.[130]

One of the odd things about the second request, "to judge whether in true words we flee the old censure, Boeotian sow," is the implication that someone has called the speakers by that epithet.[131] As the sentence is constructed, "Boeotian sow" comes at the end, separated from the phrase "old censure" (which stands first in the clause) by four words. Whatever the audience was expecting to hear as the content of the censure, it cannot have been "Boeotian sow"! This insult has been substituted for whatever might have stood there; it must have provoked a laugh, so inappropriate is it to Arcadians. But it was also meaningful. First, at the level of humor it disavows association with Pindar. If a sense of community is to be created, it undermines the enterprise to have a foreigner fabricate it. The chorus here proclaims in effect that it has not given up its communal function of reflecting local identity in performing this foreigner's composition but has sung an Arcadian song. The joke comes precisely at the moment when Aineas is praised because he is responsible for the choral production. He is an "upright messenger, a message-stick of the well-tressed Muses, a sweet mixing bowl of resounding songs" (90–91) because he has mediated well between the Stymphalians, the poet, and Hagesias and has "mixed" a performance that all can welcome. The chorus's first-person plural ("we flee," 90) includes Aineas with them in approving his community-mindedness. At this level the contrast with Hera Parthenia lies in the fact that she receives local cult and so anchors Stymphalian identity. It seems no accident that this jocular ethnic put-down should be used in an ode for an audience whose home was not a cosmopolitan center and regular scene of Panhellenic performance.

---

[129] Cf. the *Hymn of the Kouretes,* discussed above, pp. 148–49.

[130] See Too 1991 for the question whether the celebration of Hera is another song or is fulfilled by very mention of Hera. He argues that *Olympian* 6 as a whole is the song for Hera.

[131] Schol. *ad loc.* (I 188 *Dr.*) quote a similar reference from one of Pindar's dithyrambs (fr. 83; *SM* print it with fr. 75) and the word Συοβοιωτοί from the comic poet Kratinos; cf. Plutarch *Moralia* 995e. It refers to stupidity in these passages. They also (I 187 *Dr.*) call Βοιωτία ὖς a saying referring to ignorance and rusticity. The sentence continues: τούς τε βουλομένους εἰς ἀπαιδευσίαν ἐπισκώπτειν τινὰς, τοῦτο λέγειν· Βοιωτία ὖς (and those wishing to mock others for lack of education say this: Boeotian sow). The implication is that the phrase was not used only of Boeotians (any more than similar slurs are in English; "Dutch uncle," for instance, is not addressed only to the Dutch).

The contrast between Hera Parthenia and "Boeotian sow" also links up with themes I have been tracing. But the disjunct is so enormous that no common ground as basis for the contrast is perceptible—except the fact that both Hera and the sow are female. Some aspect of the female is being rejected in order to protect the image of a nurturant-and-masculine community. It looks as though the ethnic contrast serves as displacement or disguise for a contrast in male modes of becoming female; Arcadian men as "mothers/nurses" of a god (and prophet and Olympic victor) are nothing like the ignorant and stupid "female" men of the slur. For chorus and audience, the birth-giving and household-defining role of women is partially and implicitly shifted to men, while identification with a female figure who embodies the negative traits attributed to women is rejected. In addition, the phrase "Boeotian sow" refers to lack of culture, and since the chorus has demonstrated its musical education it escapes from the insult and simultaneously from the gender label. The approach toward and retreat from identification with the female that I mentioned earlier reaches its culmination here.

Behind this contrast, again, is another, concerned with the female characters of the myth. *Sow* is a slang term for a woman as sexual.[132] Hera Parthenia is set in opposition to an image of unregulated female sexuality. We remember that the myth contained two instances of *parthenoi* giving birth. They are aligned with Hera, both because of the echo (παρθενίαν in 31; Παρθενίαν in 88) and because all three were taken by gods. From this point of view, the contrast dissociates their offspring, Iamos in particular, from the insult of illegitimacy. In sum, the female as associated with Arcadian land and divinity, as a figure for the identity of a nurturant community, is linked additively to male identity via the figure of mother, while the female as undifferentiated fecund body is rejected in the figure of the sow.

In this ode images of the female are manipulated to produce an identity for the chorus. Pitana, Euadne, Hagesias' mother, Maia (mother of Hermes), Stymphalian Metope, the mothers of the chorus, Hera, and the sow all serve to locate the men involved. The chorus's own self-presentation at the end puts the female to the most extended uses: Metope is grandmother and water; they are collectively aligned with the man who raised Hera; and they differentiate themselves from the female-as-sow. In a summarizing image at the end of the ode, Stymphalos is called "mother of Arcadia of

---

[132] *Sow* refers to the female genitals. The most frequent term is χοῖρος, but ὗς is also used, e.g., Aristophanes *Ach.* 741 and *Lys.* 683. So Henderson 1991: 131–32, who shows that ὗς and δέλφαξ refer to mature women. Responding to the attack by the chorus of old men, the old women in *Lysistrata* say: λύσω τὴν ἐμαυτῆς ὗν ἐγὼ δή (683, "I will let loose my sow, I will"). *Sow* stands for anger, but as Henderson points out, the metaphor contains a sexual threat.

good flocks" (100). The unifying image of the mother, now Stymphalos itself, joins Hagesias to chorus and audience in a final embrace.[133]

Olympian 6 is not straightforward communal poetry, for Syracuse looms in the background. But Pindar borrowed the form of communal poetry and gave the chorus a means to stage itself as well as praise the victor. Exigencies of writing for a less sophisticated audience than usual and of creating a sense of community have caused him here to work more deeply into integrative modes of communal self-representation than usual in his epinician poetry.

---

[133] Syracuse is brought in by similar imagery. Mention of Ortygia (92) brings Arethusa to mind, the spring nymph pursued by the Arcadian river Alpheus, and Demeter and her daughter are worshiped there (94–95) along with Zeus of Aetna (96).

CHAPTER FOUR

Bardic Poetry

I

WITH THIS CHAPTER we turn to performance of a different kind. Dactylic hexameter poetry, which I will call bardic poetry, was sung or recited solo by specialists.[1] Bardic poetry includes heroic epic, songs to and about the gods, wisdom literature, and genealogy. It had a long prehistory as "oral poetry," for bards preserved traditional material and passed it on, not in fixed form but through recomposition-in-performance.[2] How and when such poetry began to be recorded in writing and to what extent performers in the archaic period recited fixed, memorized poems rather than recomposing are matters of little evidence and much debate.[3] Nor are memorizing and recomposing exclusive alternatives; most bards throughout the archaic and classical period probably used both techniques, although there was a slow (I imagine) shift toward repeating fixed texts as these became canonized via writing.[4] A multiform body of shared but evolving narratives, always splitting into new versions and being rejoined in new ways, must have been perceived as bards' own accounts of events whose outlines were known, although personae developed into which bards might insert themselves.[5]

[1] A performer is sometimes called "singer" (ἀοιδός), sometimes "rhapsode" in the ancient sources; the latter did not accompany himself on a lyre (phorminx). The same poetry could be delivered either way. See West 1981; Ford 1988: 303. I use the term *bard* to cover both types of performer. For later performers (after the sixth century), *rhapsode* is the appropriate term.

[2] For the technique of recomposition-in-performance (which used to be termed *improvisation*), see Lord 1965.

[3] These are separate questions. On the date when the *Iliad* (the longest and seemingly earliest poem) was fixed, presumably by writing, cf. Janko 1982: 228–31 and the table on 200; Nagy 1992b discusses various views and gives bibliography.

[4] By "canonized" I mean more than recorded in writing: the written form comes to be regarded as definitive. In this case the public cherishes the poem-in-itself and wants bards, like actors, to realize it. Bakker 1993a: 15–18 speaks of writing as canonizing a performance for repetition.

[5] Cf. Lord 1965: 26–29 on Yugoslav performers; Bakker 1993a. "Traditional" poetry is far from unchanging, even when its practitioners say that it is, and Greek bards did not claim to reproduce a tradition but to sing new songs. Cf. Murray 1981: 97 apropos of Phemios' claim to be self-taught: "The general point of Phemius' claim is that he does not simply repeat songs he has learnt from other bards, but composes his songs himself."

At some point, in some places, bards had their task redefined as one of repeating particular poems, now thought to be the work of particular "authors"; Homer's poetry is actually the only known case.[6] That situation does not concern me. In this chapter I study the stage at which a bard presented a poem as his own utterance. In other words, I assume a situation before the poem in question was canonized or prescribed, although it may already have been recorded somewhere. Audience belief that the words are the bard's own is essential to my discussion, for the audience's knowledge that a poem exists in a paradigm version alters the bard's source of authority in ways that we cannot follow here. Much bardic poetry probably continued to be performed throughout the classical period without achieving a single authoritative form.[7]

With this new kind of poetry, we must begin again by establishing the conditions of performance and asking what sort of psychological efficacy performance aspires to. There were other kinds of solo performance similar to bardic poetry, and evidence about them will add to the picture. The principal alternative to bardic narrative was kitharodic song, a narrative in somewhat more complex metrical pattern sung to a kithara (a concert lyre).[8] Long narrative poems might be composed in elegiac meter also.[9] Since very little of either of these latter types survives, and we know nothing definite about the performance of the fragments we have, I will not say much about them in the body of the chapter, but they competed with epic.

The evidence tells us two things that largely conditioned bardic (and other solo) performance in the seventh through fifth centuries: it was often performed by itinerant bards, and it was competitive and/or in the service of political entities. The *Odyssey* depicts a local bard performing at banquets and at public festivals sponsored by the noble family and refers to a resident bard.[10] There may have been such, but all our other information

---

[6] See the Introduction, pp. 15–16.

[7] Ford 1992: 67–79 points out that the "field" of material for song is described as very large. The bard must select his path through it.

[8] On kitharody see West 1981, esp. 125; Koller 1956. For phorminx and kithara see West 1992a: 48–70. Stesichoros was possibly a kitharode, as West 1971 argues, or he may have composed for chorus (since his poetry is triadic). Burkert 1987b: 51–52 proposes that he had a traveling professional chorus and that this new narrative style, more exciting than epic, was meant to oust the latter from its place of privilege. There is no evidence for professional choruses in this period. Shapiro 1992: 58–60, 65–70 discusses kitharodes and kitharists (instrumentalists), with illustrations.

[9] Bowie 1986: 28–35 discusses these. Mimnermos' *Smyrneis* (9 *W*) and Simonides' Persian War elegies (1–4 *W²* on Artemision, 10–18 *W²* on Plataia) are the only well-attested examples. For Simonides, see below.

[10] The marvelous description of Demodokos in *Odyssey* 8 has been taken as Homer's self-portrait. The resident bard is the one Agamemnon set as guardian of Clytemnestra (*Odyssey* 3.267–72). Nagy 1990b: 21–24 points out that the internal epic picture of performance is obsolete.

172 · Chapter Four

from the archaic age is about bards, singers, and musicians who traveled widely. The testimony is well-known, so I give just a brief discussion.[11] The *Odyssey* itself describes a singer as a traveler (17.382–86). The performer of the *Homeric Hymn to Delian Apollo* speaks of himself as a Chian who journeys "over the earth to well-populated cities" (174–75). Sparta, a center of music and poetry in the seventh century, drew performers. Terpander went there from Lesbos; he won a victory as a kitharode at the Spartan Karneia in its first year.[12] He also won four times at Delphi.[13] Perikleitos, called the last of the Lesbian school of kitharodes, was in Sparta and won at the Karneia.[14] Sakadas from Argos and Thaletas from Gortyn, composers who were also aulete (pipes-player) and kitharode, respectively, we are told, helped establish the Spartan festival of the Gymnopaideia.[15] Also named as their cofounders are Polymnestos of Kolophon and the more obscure Xenodamos of Kythera and Xenokritos of Lokri in Italy. Festivals at Argos and in Arcadia are attributed to the same peripatetic group; these must have had musical contests also. Arion of Lesbos, who worked for a long time at Corinth under the patronage of Periander, toured Sicily.[16] Kynaithos is said to have been a Homerid (a member of a guild of bards) from Chios who introduced the poems of Homer into Syracuse.[17] Hesiod crossed from Aulis to Euboea to participate in a contest at the funeral games of the aristocratic Amphidamas (*WD* 654–59). The Ephesian rhapsode Ion encounters Socrates on his arrival at Athens to compete in the Panathenaia after winning a rhapsodic contest at Epidauros (Plato *Ion* 530ab). Olympia, with no musical contests, must even so have attracted bards eager to demonstrate their virtuosity informally.[18]

This list of the movements of performers simultaneously reveals the activity of states, tyrants, noble families, and religious centers in soliciting

[11] Inter alios Thalmann 1984: 117–23 has a good discussion of occasions for performance in general.

[12] Athenaios 14, 635e citing Hellanikos (*FGH* 4 F85); Ps-Plutarch *On Music* 1132c on Terpander's singing his own and Homer's hexameter verse in competitions. Cf. Barker 1984: 208n.18.

[13] Ps-Plutarch *On Music* 1132e. Cf. Pausanias 10.7.2–4 on musical contests at Delphi.

[14] Ps-Plutarch *On Music* 1133d.

[15] Ibid. 1134 bc (perhaps referring to the founding of musical contests and not the festival itself). Cf. Barker 1984: 214n.66 and 1146bc, where Terpander is said to have calmed a civil war and Thaletas to have cured a plague by means of their music. The particular activities attributed to these musicians are no doubt apocryphal, but the general picture is probably right.

[16] Hdt. 1.23–24. Arion was a kitharode, said also to have been the first to compose dithyrambs. These he may have produced as communal Corinthian poetry for Periander.

[17] Schol. Pindar *Nemean* 2.1 (III 29 Dr.).

[18] Dikaiarchos (fr. 87 Wehrli) is referred to by Athenaios (14, 620d) as saying that Kleomenes the rhapsode recited Empedokles' *Purifications* at Olympia. Kleomenes' date is unknown.

poetry. We could add to it Herodotus' account of Kleisthenes of Sikyon, who forbade rhapsodic performances, as well as transferring choruses from Adrastos to Dionysus, all out of resentment at Argos.[19] It seems that narrative poetry had ideological value in the jockeying for prestige among growing political centers.[20] As the list also betrays, patrons often cast their solicitations in the form of a contest, which was a means not only to attract performers but also to elicit ever more flattering narratives.[21] It follows that bards were always under pressure to outdo one another. Hesiod comments, speaking of the good *eris* (strife), "potter is angry with potter and carpenter with carpenter; beggar is resentful of beggar and bard of bard" (*WD* 25–26). In pairing bards with beggars, his aphorism suggests that members of both groups struggle to top one another's stories.

Richard Martin illuminates the agonistic quality of bardic poetry from another direction, studying the self-presentation of the heroes of the *Iliad*. He shows that their speech-making is bound up with the creation and maintenance of authority yet seeks to win admiration and assent. In his conclusion he applies Homer's depiction of performance to Homer's own activity:

> [T]his is poetry meant to persuade, enacted in public, created by authority, in a context where authority is always up for grabs and to be won by the speaker with the best style. Most important, in my view, is the further implication of this view: that Homeric muthos is inherently antagonistic and that the poet (like Diomedes in his contest with Glaukos) invents incident to overpower opposing versions. The poet of the *Iliad,* as an enactor of a muthos, must by this implication be a poet against others, out to obliterate their performances by speaking in more detail, about more topics—in short, in a more monumental fashion than any other epic performer.[22]

Martin does not envision the bard of the *Iliad* in an actual contest, and indeed that is difficult to imagine. But the *Iliad* may be taken as the end result of bards' competition to produce successful *mythoi* in contests.[23]

Bards, then, do not speak for a community and do not speak to it from

[19] Hdt. 5.67.1. "Argive" occurs often in the Homeric poems as the name for the inhabitants of the eastern Peloponnesus and the collected army at Troy.

[20] Nagy 1990b: 67 speaks of the city as oriented toward both the local and the Panhellenic. Great families also drew on epic heroes for ancestors. On the Peisistratidai see Hdt. 5.65.3–4. On Neoptolemos at Aigina and Delphi, see Ch. 3, pp. 144–47.

[21] See Herington 1985, "Appendices" I–III on contests. Martin 1989: 229 comments that Thamyris' boast that he could outperform the Muses at *Iliad* 2.594–600 is the best evidence that epic was composed under agonistic conditions. Svenbro 1976: 78–82 discusses the economic situation of rhapsodes who made a living by patronage and prize winning.

[22] Martin 1989: 238. See also the Introduction to this volume.

[23] Edwards 1990 and Griffith 1990 also show how the stimulus of competition drives innovation in epic (and other) poetry.

within. Instead, their songs are brought to an audience from without. These conditions, competitive song-making by outsiders with an external perspective, point to a different kind of psychological efficacy: the bard strives to win a livelihood in return for offering the audience a persuasive vision of the cosmos or history or morality, with its ideological implications, a larger conceptual system within which to orient the familiar. Hesiod wins the prize in the *Contest of Homer and Hesiod* (207–10 Allen) because he sings of farming and peace instead of war. Herakleitos—a rival speaker about the cosmos if not a bardic performer—asserts rancorously (42B *DK*) that Homer and Archilochos should be thrown out of the contests and beaten.

Consequently a bard's self-presentation must differ from that of a performer of community poetry. He does not seek to present an exemplary status in social terms; he does not show himself off as marriageable or valiant or politically qualified. He represents himself only as a speaker, but a speaker with special knowledge of a comprehensive "truth," about which he must persuade the audience.[24] The bard's dilemma is that every audience is local (or defined by its relationship to a locality, e.g., Delphi), while he brings an external perspective and must create his own authority to assure its validity.[25] One could say that the bard's access to the place of performance is predicated on his external speaker's role of bringing to an audience an account of the past or the world that will hold for all other people as well, while the audience exerts pressure through its command of rewards to make that "universal" description advantageous to itself.

Before taking up the kind of self-presentation required by these circumstances, then, let us consider briefly various strategies a bard could use to compete in performance. First, the bard must choose how to shape the content of his song.[26] There is tension between an itinerant bard's desire to tell narratives in the same way everywhere, as he has practiced and polished them, and a particular audience's desire to hear something relevant to itself. He must therefore persuade the audience that he speaks "truth"

[24] Nagy 1979: 3 §6n. points out that authority is coded as truth in bardic poetry. Nagy 1990b: 56–61 also connects Panhellenization with the claim to "truth" (*alētheia*). He thus disputes Svenbro 1976: 46–73, who connects "truth" in Hesiod with Hesiod's independence from a system of noble patronage and turn to writing. Other major discussions of poetic "truth" are Detienne 1967, Pucci 1977: 8–44, Puelma 1989. Thalmann 1984: 126–29 collects references to the poet's knowledge in early texts.

[25] Nagy 1990a: 42–47 makes this point. Cf. Loraux 1986: 77–98 on Athenian funeral speeches, which are uneasily positioned between address to other cities and to the Athenians themselves. On 92–97 she analyzes the incompatibility of Panhellenic rhetoric with eulogistic address to the community. The funeral speech never successfully combined the two, although certain orators tried.

[26] Brillante 1993: 15–16 shows that bards represented themselves as exercising choice in their subject matter.

either by adapting his story to local interests (an approach toward community poetry) and winning assent that way or by offering a "Panhellenic" story that includes no concession to the audience but signals its validity through its rhetoric.[27]

Some bards did tell stories adapted to particular audiences. The *Korinthiaka,* an epic attributed to Eumelos of which only a few fragments survive, has a remarkable geographic scheme according to which Medea was of Corinthian descent (3 Bernabé):

> ἀλλ' ὅτε δ' Αἰήτης καὶ Ἀλωεὺς ἐξεγένοντο
> Ἡελίου τε καὶ Ἀντιόπης, τότε δ' ἄνδιχα χώρην
> δάσσατο παισὶν ἑοῖς Ὑπερίονος ἀγλαὸς υἱός.
> ἦν μὲν ἔχ' Ἀσωπός, ταύτην πόρε δίωι Ἀλωεῖ·
> 5 ἦν δ' Ἐφύρη κτεάτισσ', Αἰήτηι δῶκεν ἅπασαν.
> Αἰήτης δ' ἄρ' ἑκὼν Βούνωι παρέδωκε φυλάσσειν,
> εἰσόκεν αὐτὸς ἵκοιτ' ἢ ἐξ αὐτοῖό τις ἄλλος,
> ἢ πάις ἢ υἱωνός· ὃ δ' ἵκετο Κολχίδα γαῖαν.

But when Aietes and Aloeus were born of Sun and Antiope, then the bright son of Hyperion distributed the country in separate parcels to his children. The land which (the river) Asopos bounds he furnished to godlike Aloeus; that which Ephyra claimed he gave in its entirety to Aietes. But Aietes voluntarily turned it over to Bounos to guard until he himself should come or some other from him, a son or a grandson; and he arrived at the land of Kolchis.

According to Pausanias' summary the Corinthians later called Medea from Iolkos when local members of the ruling house failed, and through her Jason became king.[28] The poem claims Medea for Corinth and polishes her reputation. Similarly Pierre Guillon has detected political partisanship in the *Shield of Heracles* and the *Homeric Hymn to Pythian Apollo;* the *Shield* appears to support Thebes and the *Hymn* the Amphiktyonic League in the struggle for influence in Boeotia and the surrounding territory.[29] The other poems of the Trojan Cycle appealed more to regional audiences than did the Homeric epics.[30]

[27] Svenbro 1976: 16–35 has an excellent account of bards' need to please their patrons; itinerant bards had equally to please audiences.

[28] Paus. 2.3.10 = 5 Bernabé. Also quoted under Bernabé 5 is a scholion to Euripides *Medea* 9, which states that according to Eumelos (and Simonides) Medea held the rule at Corinth.

[29] Guillon 1963, esp. 55–74 and 85–98. Even if the details of his reconstructions of the historical situation are speculative, his case for the pro- and anti-Theban bias in the respective poems is good. Janko 1986: 43–48 concurs.

[30] Nagy 1990b: 70–75. Smith 1981 shows that there is no evidence for Aineidai near Troy who would have patronized stories about Aineas, as has been suggested. West 1985b: 4–5 mentions several epics each centered on one area.

Later evidence also suggests that adaptations were common. In the Pseudo-Platonic dialogue *Hippias Major* (285d), the orator Hippias says that when in Sparta he gives speeches on subjects that the Spartans like to hear, particularly genealogies and foundations of cities.[31] The author of the *Contest of Homer and Hesiod* pictures Homer as traveling from city to city and reciting a piece relevant to the locale in each case.[32] In Thebes he recites the *Thebais* and the *Epigonoi* (255–59 Allen), in Argos the Argive section of the "Catalogue of Ships" from the *Iliad* (287–301 Allen), in Delos the *Homeric Hymn to Apollo* (315–18 Allen).[33] These accounts are not actual evidence for what earlier bards did, but they reveal a presumption that audiences liked to hear about their own communities.[34]

The alternative, narratives that do not privilege any particular locale, can be described as Panhellenic. The term implies that they appeal to Greek speakers at large and could be performed anywhere. Gregory Nagy has investigated in detail the process of Panhellenization (detachment from local cult and belief) that some traditional tales underwent and the issues of authority that Panhellenized poems raise.[35] This chapter owes much to his work. I differ from him in emphasis, however, in that I focus on the *contest* of voices and think of it as producing two-way movement, toward localized poetry as well as away. I assume that in any given performance Panhellenic stories could always be challenged by versions oriented to the particular audience, as the story of Jason and the Argonauts has been reshaped for Corinth in the *Korinthiaka*.[36] In order to compete success-

[31] I imagine these to be genealogies relevant to the Spartans and their neighbors. The other subject that they appreciate is moral harangue, cast as a conversation between Neoptolemos and Nestor (286ab). In this we can see the afterlife of the moral and ideological aspect of bardic poetry.

[32] The extant *Contest* belongs to the imperial period, but its prototype goes back to Alkidamas in the fourth century BCE; see Schadewaldt 1942: 93–95n.6; West 1967. Richardson 1981: 1–3 thinks that the idea of the contest may have developed as early as the sixth century; similarly Janko 1982: 259–60n.80.

[33] For the fragments of the *Thebais* and the *Epigonoi,* see Bernabé 1987. Only the first lines are given in the *Contest*.

[34] Another kind of appeal is based on class. Homeric epic supports an aristocratic ideology. Aloni 1985; Morris 1986: 123–26; Janko 1992: 37–38 suggest that this fact influenced transmission of the epic. Similarly, genealogical poetry bolstered the claim of aristocrats: so West 1985b: 8–9 apropos of the *Catalogue of Women*.

[35] Nagy 1979, esp. 59–150, traces patterns of ritual antagonism and cultic symbiosis between hero and god that epic partly generalizes, partly suppresses; Nagy 1990a: 36–47 gives a clear summary. Epic was not at any stage *only* a local phenomenon since it had an Indo-European background. The two-way process I posit could explain why local material was taken up in epic.

[36] Although Eumelos was Corinthian, the *Korinthiaka* is not an example of a pre-Panhellenized stage of heroic epic. On it cf. Huxley 1969: 61–68; for development of the story, Will 1955: 85–129, 237–40.

fully, a bard reciting a Panhellenic poem had to provide superior pleasures or else compensatory validation for its lack of parochial appeal.

To create pleasure, bards could compete in actualization, the techniques for making the story vivid. A carrying voice, range of inflections (cf. *Ion* 535c), and sense of timing must have been essential. Modes of narrative were developed that made the telling as vivid as possible, for ideally bards must have sought to sound like eyewitnesses, or rather, make the audience feel like eyewitnesses.[37] Subtle linguistic, rhythmic, and thematic techniques by which Homeric epic engaged its audience are now being studied in very interesting ways.[38] Fullness in narrative is another aspect of competitive presentation, as Martin observes. Some degree of novelty would be welcome. The *Iliad* and *Odyssey,* thoroughly Panhellenic poems, validate their narrators through the power and immediacy of the narration itself.[39] Yet not all bards were virtuosos and not all subjects lent themselves well to visualization or sheer drama in the telling.

Alternatively, a bard could thematize his own authority as a form of compensatory validation: he could exalt a Panhellenic point of view in opposition to the local one as the product of his superior knowledge. Whereas a bard who adapts a tale to a community's agenda or who concentrates on techniques of dramatic narration could allow his authority as speaker to be implicit in his performance, the bard in this third case must make a more studied self-presentation, one powerful enough to persuade the audience that his perspective overrides theirs. Yet a bard could not merely assert that he knew the truth.[40] He would have to produce his self-presentation and his narrative together as mutually supporting, and he would have to make his claim powerful enough to displace the local viewpoint by attaching the claim to a proposition in which (some part of) the audience had an investment. This is where gender comes in. In this chapter I examine poems in which bards used self-presentation as gendered to signal their possession of truth and negotiate the tension between local and Panhellenic viewpoints.

I will begin with a poem in which the tension is visible, the *Homeric Hymn to Delian Apollo*. The *Hymn to Delian Apollo* is the first part of the composite *Homeric Hymn to Apollo* that has come down in the collection of *Homeric Hymns*. This analysis assumes a separatist answer to the question about whether the *Hymn to Apollo* is one poem or a combination of

[37] Puelma 1989: 68–71; cf. Ford 1992: 52–55 on vividness producing pleasure.

[38] Cf., e.g., Frontisi-Ducroux 1986; De Jong 1987: 60–99; Wyatt 1987–88; Bakker 1990 and 1993b.

[39] Ford 1992: 93–101 shows how the *Iliad* and *Odyssey* evade the issue of competition.

[40] Performers' claims may be met by denials. Cf. the proverb, attributed to Solon (29 *W*): "Bards tell many lies," referring to bards in competition; see Svenbro 1976: 59. Xenophanes denounced Homer and Hesiod for attributing all human failings to the gods (B11 *DK*).

two originally separate ones. Its unity has been argued several times recently, by William Thalmann, Andrew Miller, and Jenny Strauss Clay, but always on thematic and literary critical grounds, which show only that if two poems were combined they produced a viable poem.[41] The three recent studies that consider its diction, narrative techniques, and language, those by Richard Janko, Karl Förstel, and Filippo Càssola, all conclude that the *Hymn to Apollo* is a composite of two hymns from different dates.[42] The performer also establishes a different relationship with the audience in each poem, as we shall see, so on those grounds too the two poems should be considered to have different origins. I will return to the composite hymn later.

The *Hymn to Delian Apollo* belongs to the genre of prooimia, invocations to a god sung as introductions to epic narrative; but like the other long hymns in the collection, it has been expanded into an independent piece. The *Hymn to Delian Apollo,* however, differs from the others in that it refers to its own setting. We learn from the internal reference that in the version that became fixed it was performed at a festival of Apollo on Delos.[43]

The anomalous reference to its own setting is one symptom of the character of this poem: it is a mimesis of communal poetry and correspondingly anti-Panhellenic. The performer has solved the bard's dilemma mentioned above by creating or adapting a poem to espouse a local perspective. The poem's stance is established at the beginning with Apollo's appearance on Olympus: he enters with bow drawn, and all the other gods except Zeus and Leto leap up in fright (2–13). This is portrayed as Apollo's regular mode of entrance to the house of Zeus and has provoked puzzled

---

[41] Aloni 1989: 19–29 points out that unitarians privilege the analysis of structure and narratology, while analysts rely on differences of diction. Thalmann 1984: 64–73 argues that the compositional techniques used include paratactic units connected by repetition; this means that poems could easily be joined (as he acknowledges on 73). Miller 1986: 117 is specifically interested in the composite poem. Clay 1989: 19 makes the strongest argument for *original* unity: "Taken in isolation, neither the Delian nor the Pythian half delineates the full complexity of Apollo," for only at the end of the hymn has the god come into full possession of bow, lyre, and oracular power, the specialties he claims in the Delian section. Further, questions raised in the first half are not answered until the end of the poem. Clay's acute study shows that the hymn as we now have it offers a synthetic view of Apollo and his place in the cosmos, but to show the god in his complexity may have been the aim of a performer who was familiar with the two portrayals of the god; the original Delian poem had different goals.

[42] Janko 1982: 99–100, 106–15; Förstel 1979: 272–81; Càssola 1975: 97–100. Van Groningen 1958: 314–16 (and Ch. 13 generally) thinks that the Delian part was originally separate. Baltes 1981 shows that the style of the first catalogue (30–45) is different from the later two (216–86, 409–29) but argues against the idea of different composers.

[43] On the festival see Nilsson 1957: 144–49; Ch. 3 above. For this and the other *Homeric Hymns* quoted in this chapter I use the text of *AHS*.

or caustic comments from a number of scholars.[44] In fact the scene establishes not only that Apollo's power is greater than that of the others aside from Zeus but, further, that he is not at home on Olympus. His mother Leto of course has nothing to fear from him. Her seat by the side of Zeus, which she has usurped from Hera in this poem, indicates her high rank. Apollo and Leto are powerful, then, by Olympian standards, but Apollo at least is hostile to Olympian company.

The same oppositional attitude carries over to the treatment of terrestrial geography. A long list of places beginning in line 30 reveals itself to be places that rejected Leto when she was seeking a site for the birth of Apollo (45–48); these places all serve as a foil for Delos. Another, generic list of the places that Apollo haunts—islands, groves, peaks—comes after the birth story (140–45), but Apollo delights most in Delos (146). The song claims the god for the island, which means refusing to yield him to Olympus. The festivity on Delos, when to the eyes of a stranger the crowd would resemble the immortals, stands in contrast to the disturbed scene on Olympus, almost as though the performer had transferred the joyous company associated with Olympus to Delos along with Apollo.

Between the opening and the end of the poem, the performer tells of the birth of Apollo, the cult *aition* for the Delian sanctuary of Apollo, Artemis, and Leto. What is perhaps more surprising than has been noted is the fullness with which the birth itself is narrated. Between line 45, where it becomes clear that Leto's story is underway, and the birth in 119, the characters in the narrative (including the island Delos) are entirely female. Delos confesses to Leto the reason that the other lands have rejected her: Apollo, it is rumored, will be a violent god (67–68).[45] Delos too fears; he will have great power among immortals and mortals and might reject her as too insignificant for him. Delos therefore asks Leto to swear to her son's future respect for the island. Leto can speak for Apollo, and Delos accepts her oath. Apollo's ferocity is the other side of the poem's orientation toward the local and female: Delos does gain the fierce god's loyalty, but the bard is at pains to show that Apollo is not rendered feeble by the feminine milieu.

Several goddesses attend the birth. Hera tries to keep Eileithyia, god-

[44] Förstel 1979: 166–75 points out that Apollo is treated as the most powerful of the gods along with Leto and Zeus, but thinks the presentation overworks "pathos." Kirk 1981: 167 refers to Apollo as a figure of burlesque. Clay 1989: 20–29 stresses the potential violence indicated by the scene and remarks (29) that "the progress from terror to delight constitutes the eternal response to the manifestation of Apollo's divinity." But only Leto is said to feel delight (13). The tenses are difficult, but the scene begins and ends in the present tense. See Clay 1989: 23–28 for bibliography.

[45] Clay 1989: 35–38 points out the strangeness of such a characterization. She sees in it an allusion to the succession theme, the possibility that Apollo will replace Zeus as king of the gods.

dess of childbirth, on Olympus. The reason given for Hera's hostility is not jealousy of Zeus' affair with another woman but jealousy of Leto's giving birth (100–101); Zeus is kept out of the picture. Iris entices Eileithyia away to Delos, and as she arrives the birth proceeds. Seldom in Greek literature is actual birth-giving described, as it is here (115–19):

115   εὖτ' ἐπὶ Δήλου ἔβαινε μογοστόκος Εἰλείθυια,
        τὴν τότε δὴ τόκος εἷλε, μενοίνησεν δὲ τεκέσθαι.
        ἀμφὶ δὲ φοίνικι βάλε πήχεε, γοῦνα δ' ἔρεισε
        λειμῶνι μαλακῷ, μείδησε δὲ γαῖ' ὑπένερθεν·
        ἐκ δ' ἔθορε πρὸ φόως δέ, θεαὶ δ' ὀλόλυξαν ἅπασαι.

When Eileithyia of difficult births stepped on Delos, then the moment of birth seized her (Leto) and she strove urgently to deliver. She threw her arms around the palm tree and braced her knees on the soft meadow, and the earth smiled under her. Out he leaped into the light, and all the goddesses cried *ololygē*.

After the birth the goddesses wash the baby. Leto does not suckle him; Themis feeds him ambrosia, smoothly effecting his transition on the spot from the realm of women, dependence, human food, and mortality to participation in the realm of the gods. Apollo bursts out of his swaddling clothes, leaps up, and proclaims his spheres of activity.[46] All is local.

Even Pindar does not neglect Zeus in his brief evocation of the birth in the fragmentary *paian* 12.8–14: " . . . to the Kynthian hill, where they say that cloud-wrapped, lightning-flashing Zeus sitting on the peaks above mounted guard with forethought when the daughter of Koios with gentle thoughts was being released from her delightful labor pains." Similar to *paian* 12 in bringing the father on the scene is Isyllos' *paian,* discussed in Chapter 3. The absence of Zeus is remarkable in the *Homeric Hymn*'s version of the story, a compensation, perhaps, for the external perspective inherent in bardic production.

As remarked, this poem is a mimesis of a communal poem. The performer does not represent the audience, but he does reflect back to it its own situation. By choosing to expand the birth story to his whole narrative, he achieves complete focus on the site of the festival and connection with the themes of the cult complex. The narrative is pictured as taking place on or near the spot where the audience is probably standing.[47]

---

[46] Apollo lists three things (131–32): kithara, bow, and prophecy. All three are connected with the god in the Pythian part, but they are his standard attributes; cf. the *Homeric Hymn to Hermes* 515, 535–38. There may have been an oracle on Delos, but the evidence is late; see *AHS ad* 81.

[47] Förstel 1979: 119. *Contest* 316–17 (Allen) pictures Homer standing beside the horn altar to recite this poem (or the combined poem).

Mount Kynthos, against which Leto leans, is not far from the sanctuary, and the palm tree that she grasps is said to have been beside her (later) temple.[48] Eileithyia received honors on the island.[49] The apostrophe to Leto (14–18), which is abrupt in the text, would seem natural if the bard turned toward her precinct as he spoke it. Beyond these effects, the narrative makes its listeners all imaginatively present at the birth. It makes them, as it were, women of the household, for assisting at birth was their task. We have seen a female figure used as an integrative image in community poetry. Here the performer seems to have capitalized on the importance of Leto in cult to draw his audience into intimate relationship with her and Apollo.[50] The performer, in sum, has appealed to his audience on Delos by privileging Delos against Olympus and the rest of the Greek world, while bringing the audience together as participants in the event that makes Delos special.

The bard himself, by singing this song, seems to be a participant in the collective he has created. His apostrophes and addresses to Apollo, reminiscent of choral lyric, link the god with the island (19–29, 146) and greet him at the moment after birth (120), as he tastes ambrosia (127–29), and at the beginning of the final section on the festival itself (140). Second and third person of the god alternate and connect the audience with the god.[51] The author of the *Contest of Homer and Hesiod,* who pictures Homer receiving various rewards for his performances, has the Ionians honor him by making him a *politēn koinon* (319–20 Allen, "common citizen"). It is quite different from his other compensations, which are gifts.[52] For the author of this piece, at least, the performer seemed to have made himself a member of the same community with his audience.

The poem was claimed at some point by the festival, for it was recorded on whitened boards and displayed in the sanctuary.[53] The medium, wooden boards (rather than stone), suggests that it was written and set up

[48] Odysseus compares Nausikaa, a girl ready for marriage, with the Delian palm tree in *Odyssey* 6.162–69, another indication of the thematic complex of the cult.

[49] Pausanias 1.18.5; Bruneau 1970: 212–19.

[50] Sale 1961: 83 suggests that in the traditional hymn attributed to Olen the birth was not located on Delos; rather the gods came to Delos from Lycia. If so then our hymn is part of Delos' refashioning of myth and ritual.

[51] Norden 1956: 157–72 discusses the form of archaic cult hymns: praise of the deity can be in the second person, addressed to the deity, or in the third person; some hymns (like this one) alternate. On apostrophe and other features typical of lyric poetry in the *Hymn to Apollo*, see Clay 1989: 30–31 with bibliography. Compare Isyllos' *paian,* discussed in Ch. 3.

[52] In addition, the Argives erect a statue and offer sacrifices in return for the generous space they receive in the "Catalogue of Ships" (*Iliad* 2.559–68).

[53] *Contest* 320–21 Allen. It is a question whether the combined *Hymn* or the Delian part only was displayed. Förstel 1979: 71 argues against van Groningen 1958: 315 that there is no way to be sure which it was.

early, although the information is late.[54] Perhaps the Delians made it a prescribed text for performance. The "blind bard" (172, see below) became Homer, whether or not the bard(s) who initially recited the poem meant to refer to him.[55] Such a sequence of events illustrates the drawback of this strategy of self-presentation for a bard. Apart from the fact that the poem might not travel well, it leaves him no way to call attention to his own stature, for, however successful, the poem does not raise him above his listeners by allowing him to present a larger conception of the world than the audience's. The more perfect a mimesis of a local poem he created, the more it would seem to belong to the community and the less to him.

In a coda, therefore, the bard adjusts his relationship with his audience. To compensate for his service to Delos, he puts praise of himself into the mouths of the chorus of Delian *parthenoi* (the Deliades) and portrays himself as an actor on a larger stage than Delos. He thereby creates the paradox that the narrative part of the poem imitates communal poetry, while the coda, in the I-you style of communal poetry, provides Panhellenic authorization for the performer. We must examine the coda in detail (146–76):

> ἀλλὰ σὺ Δήλῳ Φοῖβε μάλιστ' ἐπιτέρπεαι ἦτορ,
> ἔνθα τοι ἑλκεχίτωνες Ἰάονες ἠγερέθονται
> αὐτοῖς σὺν παίδεσσι καὶ αἰδοίῃς ἀλόχοισιν.
> οἱ δέ σε πυγμαχίῃ τε καὶ ὀρχηθμῷ καὶ ἀοιδῇ
> 150 μνησάμενοι τέρπουσιν ὅταν στήσωνται ἀγῶνα.
> φαίη κ' ἀθανάτους καὶ ἀγήρως ἔμμεναι αἰεὶ
> ὃς τότ' ἐπαντιάσει' ὅτ' Ἰάονες ἀθρόοι εἶεν·
> πάντων γάρ κεν ἴδοιτο χάριν, τέρψαιτο δὲ θυμὸν
> ἄνδρας τ' εἰσορόων καλλιζώνους τε γυναῖκας
> 155 νῆάς τ' ὠκείας ἠδ' αὐτῶν κτήματα πολλά.
> πρὸς δὲ τόδε μέγα θαῦμα, ὅου κλέος οὔποτ' ὀλεῖται,
> κοῦραι Δηλιάδες Ἑκατηβελέταο θεράπναι·
> αἵ τ' ἐπεὶ ἂρ πρῶτον μὲν Ἀπόλλων' ὑμνήσωσιν,
> αὖτις δ' αὖ Λητώ τε καὶ Ἄρτεμιν ἰοχέαιραν,
> 160 μνησάμεναι ἀνδρῶν τε παλαιῶν ἠδὲ γυναικῶν

---

[54] Förstel 1979: 79–80. Càssola 1975: 99 takes up van Groningen's remark (1958: 315) that the location, the temple of Artemis, is an odd detail and suggests an early date. Càssola points out that the temple of Artemis was built before the temple to Apollo. But cf. Förstel 321n.113: dedications to Apollo were housed there in later periods, so we cannot be sure that the *Hymn* was recorded at a time when Apollo had no temple.

[55] Förstel 1979: 142–43 views it as the bard's self-description. Burkert 1979: 56–58 thinks the description designates Homer but was disbelieved, so the poem was attributed to a forger identified with Kynaithos (on whom see below).

ὕμνον ἀείδουσιν, θέλγουσι δὲ φῦλ' ἀνθρώπων.
πάντων δ' ἀνθρώπων φωνὰς καὶ κρεμβαλιαστὺν
μιμεῖσθ' ἴσασιν· φαίη δέ κεν αὐτὸς ἕκαστος
φθέγγεσθ'· οὕτω σφιν καλὴ συνάρηρεν ἀοιδή.
165 ἀλλ' ἄγεθ' ἱλήκοι μὲν Ἀπόλλων Ἀρτέμιδι ξύν,
χαίρετε δ' ὑμεῖς πᾶσαι· ἐμεῖο δὲ καὶ μετόπισθε
μνήσασθ', ὁππότε κέν τις ἐπιχθονίων ἀνθρώπων
ἐνθάδ' ἀνείρηται ξεῖνος ταλαπείριος ἐλθών·
ὦ κοῦραι, τίς δ' ὔμμιν ἀνὴρ ἥδιστος ἀοιδῶν
170 ἐνθάδε πωλεῖται, καὶ τέῳ τέρπεσθε μάλιστα;
ὑμεῖς δ' εὖ μάλα πᾶσαι ὑποκρίνασθ' ἀμφ' ἡμέων·
τυφλὸς ἀνήρ, οἰκεῖ δὲ Χίῳ ἔνι παιπαλοέσσῃ,
τοῦ πᾶσαι μετόπισθεν ἀριστεύουσιν ἀοιδαί.
ἡμεῖς δ' ὑμέτερον κλέος οἴσομεν ὅσσον ἐπ' αἶαν
175 ἀνθρώπων στρεφόμεσθα πόλεις εὖ ναιεταώσας·
οἱ δ' ἐπὶ δὴ πείσονται, ἐπεὶ καὶ ἐτήτυμόν ἐστιν.

But, Phoibos, your heart rejoices most in Delos where the trailing-robed Ionians gather for you with their children and modest wives.[56] They delight you as they remember you with boxing and dance and song, whenever they hold their meet. And one who encountered the Ionians when they were gathered would say they were immortal and unaging forever. For he would see the grace of all and delight his heart observing the men and the beautifully attired women and the swift ships and their many possessions. In addition, this is a great wonder, whose fame will never perish: the Delian maidens, servants of the Far-Shooter. After they hymn Apollo first and thereupon Leto and Artemis the arrow-pourer, they sing in recollection of the men and women of old and enchant the tribes of humans. They know how to imitate the voice and rhythm of all humans. Each man would say that he himself was speaking, so beautifully is the song adapted by them. But come, may Apollo be favoring together with Artemis, and farewell, all of you; and remember me in the future whenever some one of humans who live on earth, a much-suffering stranger, should ask on coming here: "O Maidens, what man who comes here on his rounds is sweetest of bards to your ears, in whom do you especially take pleasure?" You then answer, all of you, be sure, concerning us, "a blind man, and he lives in rocky Chios; all his songs stand out as best in later times." In turn we will carry your fame as far as we roam over the earth to well-populated cities of humans; and they will be persuaded, for it is indeed true.

[56] Or if we adopt the reading from Thucydides 3.104.4, "When your heart rejoices most in Delos, then the Ionians gather."

The performer turns to the here and now to praise his audience. Rather than stage himself as the superior figure, he portrays the audience as god-like. But he speaks as an outsider to the scene (152). His praise then turns especially to the Deliades, an established chorus of young women.[57] Just as he has been reflecting the cult story and the local scene, so he praises them for reflecting their audience: they know how to imitate the voice and rhythm of all, so that whoever comes finds himself represented.[58] The Deliades too can create a sense of community by their powers of reflection. But when the bard finally uses the second person to address the Deliades, it is to say farewell (166). At this moment of direct communication and separation, he changes his relationship to the island and its people: he requests that they treat the narrative about their deity as his poem and that they keep him in the community by repeating his words whenever another stranger asks who pleases the most. Since his poem, being oriented toward the local, will enter its discourse, he can append a representation of himself in this setting as well.

And suddenly the bard refers to his own travels: "In turn we will carry your fame . . ." (174). The effect is arresting. It breaks the set of reflections that had played among performer, Deliades, and audience and rivets attention on the performer as an individual. He is more than this poem; he knows other places and other poems. He makes us want to say, "Wait, tell us about your travels!" That is, the community will close in on this scene but he will escape from it to move through the world.

In return for preserving his memory, the bard promises to carry praise of the Deliades abroad. It is as though he wants to continue the set of reflections by splitting it into two sets: if they mirror back his words about himself to others, he will speak their praises elsewhere. But this last gesture of complementarity reveals the decisive difference between communal and bardic performers. On Delos, just as he has mirrored their local story in exemplary fashion, so the Deliades will mirror his words, including his projection of his own fame. Elsewhere he will speak of the Deliades, but he will not repeat their words; instead he will make praise of them the basis for *his* self-representation as knowledgeable. These other audiences, he says, will accept his authority, "and they will be persuaded, for it is indeed true." "True" is the penultimate word in his address to the Deliades; its appearance sums up his change of status, for it is the claim of a Panhellenic performer about his poems.[59] By detaching himself from the scene, he converts the authority derived from telling the community story to his own.

[57] On the Deliades see Ch. 2, p. 110.
[58] Bergren 1982: 93 makes this point.
[59] Miller 1986: 57–65 has a good discussion of the poetics of this passage.

Together with the bard's transformation to Panhellenic performer comes his gendered self-presentation. The bard attributes authority to himself on the basis of his mobility and resultant personal knowledge.[60] In the structure of the coda, he contrasts his travel with the fixity of the Deliades and, in a larger perspective, with that of Leto. Both belong on Delos. Leto traveled, but only until she found a receptive place, and the act of giving birth fixed her connection with the particular spot. Apollo, although also attached to Delos, wanders over islands and among humans at the end. Male mobility and female immobility are an underlying contrast in the text, calling to mind Jean-Pierre Vernant's study of the pair Hestia/Hermes, who represent the opposition of female rootedness (the hearth) and male ability to cross boundaries.[61] To portray himself as mobile implicitly genders the performer. We must see the self-authorization at work in the coda not only as calling attention to the performer's personal authority but also as releasing him from the local world of women, created by telling the birth story, and identifying his larger perspective as a male one.

Here is the kernel of one bardic technique of gendered self-authorization: the performer's distancing himself from a female figure identified with a geographical location. We saw in Chapter 3 that male performers within the community might take on female identity in addition to their own in order to embody a unified, noncompetitive reflection of the community-as-household. The bardic technique is the complementary opposite. The female still represents the community, but the bard is outside it. Thus, without making a direct (and provocative) assertion that his authority is based on masculinity, the bard represents the supracommunal position he claims as a male identity. Because of the switch in stance from communal to noncommunal in the *Hymn to Delian Apollo,* the contrast is clear.

Other poems use a technique similar to the one that ends the *Hymn to Delian Apollo,* coding their performers' authority as distance from the female on either a horizontal or a vertical axis. The fragmentary *Homeric Hymn to Dionysus* is a good example of the latter. The date and context are unknown, but the poem is generally accepted as archaic.[62] The performer begins with a priamel (1–9):

[60] On travel and knowledge as traditionally linked from the *Odyssey* through Pindar to Herodotus, see Nagy 1990b: 231–36. Ford 1992: 41–48 isolates the imagery of song as a path and thinks of shamans, who travel, as well as seers.

[61] Vernant 1983. For gendering of travel cf. also the *Odyssey*'s contrast of women fixed on islands with Odysseus' movement and Herodotus' account of women snatched (or seduced) from their homes by men who move about the Mediterranean (1.1–4).

[62] *AHS* 97–98. The extant manuscript of the *Hymns* was copied from an original that was missing sections (*AHS* xvii–xx), so only the final twelve lines of the *Hymn* are preserved. Diodoros 3.66.3 quotes the first nine lines of a poem that is agreed to be the opening of the

οἱ μὲν γὰρ Δρακάνῳ σ', οἱ δ' Ἰκάρῳ ἠνεμοέσσῃ
φάσ', οἱ δ' ἐν Νάξῳ, δῖον γένος εἰραφιῶτα,
οἱ δέ σ' ἐπ' Ἀλφειῷ ποταμῷ βαθυδινήεντι
κυσαμένην Σεμέλην τεκέειν Διὶ τερπικεραύνῳ,
5   ἄλλοι δ' ἐν Θήβῃσιν ἄναξ σε λέγουσι γενέσθαι
ψευδόμενοι· σὲ δ' ἔτικτε πατὴρ ἀνδρῶν τε θεῶν τε
πολλὸν ἀπ' ἀνθρώπων κρύπτων λευκώλενον Ἥρην.
ἔστι δέ τις Νύση ὕπατον ὄρος ἀνθέον ὕλῃ
τηλοῦ Φοινίκης σχεδὸν Αἰγύπτοιο ῥοάων

For some say of you that it was in Drakanon, some, in windy Ikaros, some, in
Naxos, divine offspring sewn in the thigh (*eiraphiota*), and some say that it was
by the deep-whirling Alpheus River that Semele, pregnant, bore you to Zeus
who delights in thunder, and others say, lord, that you were born in Thebes—
liars. Rather, the father of men and gods bore you, far from men, hiding from
white-armed Hera. There is a place Nysa, the top of a mountain, flowery with
trees, far beyond Phoenicia, near the streams of Egypt . . .

The expectation aroused is that the cap of the priamel will contain a clause
beginning, "but I say . . ." and naming the birthplace to be favored here.
Instead, the bard summarily dismisses all the claims he has mentioned (6).
He then replaces *Semele,* the constant of the priamel, with Zeus. The
words for "father" and "gave birth" are juxtaposed. Replacement of all
local stories by one story that is universally valid is equated with replacement of the female by the male. The mother's story becomes a geographical marker in a panoramic survey of Greek lands, an Olympian father's
point of view.[63]

The other surprising feature of the priamel-cap is the replacement of the
first-person, the expected "but I say . . . ," by the dismissive participle,
ψευδόμενοι (lying, liars). The word *liars* is placed emphatically at the
beginning of the line. The bard thus elevates himself from contender to
judge of truth. His position as judge and Zeus' assumption of Semele's role
are linked and analogous. The local speakers all refer to their particular
Semele, while by merely listing the multiplicity of places claiming Semele
this performer discredits their stories and subsumes their perspective into
his own larger one. Thus the bard dramatizes his own authority by modeling it on male preempting of the power of the female.

The performer's presence and voice have an effect on the meaning con-

---

same poem. The epithet *eiraphiota* occurring in both parts (lines 2, 17, 20) supports the
connection. Càssola 1975: 14–17 has discussion and bibliography.

[63] Nagy 1990a: 43 sees this *Hymn* as rejecting local stories in favor of a single Panhellenic
story.

veyed by these lines. The poet begins by addressing his "true" version to Dionysus directly, an unusual opening; and rather than switch to the third person after the invocation in order to begin the narrative, the poet continues to address the god. Invocation shifts to a mimesis of conversation, and the audience is left out because the unbroken apostrophe, unlike the intermittent apostrophes of the *Hymn to Delian Apollo,* does not form a link between god and listeners. Its effect is to make the god present for the audience, as an actor on the stage can create a second figure in the mind of the audience, but also to distance the performer.

The middle of the poem with the narrative is lost. At the end of the poem the bard again aligns his voice with Zeus', though now in obedience to his command. The narrative comes to an end with a direct speech by Zeus commanding honors for Dionysus. The next line begins with the bard's address to Dionysus, stating the honor in which bards hold him (17–21):

> ἵληθ' εἰραφιῶτα γυναιμανές· οἱ δέ σ' ἀοιδοὶ
> ᾄδομεν ἀρχόμενοι λήγοντές τ', οὐδέ πῃ ἔστι
> σεῖ' ἐπιληθομένῳ ἱερῆς μεμνῆσθαι ἀοιδῆς.
> 20   καὶ σὺ μὲν οὕτω χαῖρε Διώνυσ' εἰραφιῶτα,
> σὺν μητρὶ Σεμέλῃ ἥν περ καλέουσι Θυώνην.

Be propitious, *eiraphiota,* you who drive women mad; we bards sing you as we begin and as we end, nor is it at all possible for one forgetting you to remember holy song. So farewell in joy to you, too, Dionysus *eiraphiota,* with your mother Semele whom they call Thyone.

The bard's voice supervenes on Zeus', addressing a Dionysus who "drives women mad." There are also links with the opening lines. The same obscure vocative epithet, *eiraphiota,* returns again in lines 17 and 20, that is, in each of the last two sentences. Its etymology was lost already in antiquity, but later, at least, it was believed to mean "sewn in the thigh," thus to refer to the very story that this *Hymn* promotes, the story of Dionysus' birth from Zeus' thigh.[64] Càssola suggests the meaning "he who is connected with the bull," that is, "he who reveals himself in the form of a bull."[65] With either meaning, the old and obscure adjective signals both the gender code of the performance and the bard's superior knowledge. It must be remarked that Semele returns at the end as "mother." The bard never meant seriously to deny her, but only to register his own position.

As is clear from the lines right after the lacuna (10–12), the bard ends by

---

[64] See *AHS* ad loc. They give various suggested etymologies.

[65] Càssola 1975: 463–64, based on an Indian cognate meaning "bull" or (generally) "masculine." The etymology is not original with him; see *AHS* ad loc.

recounting Zeus' establishment of a trieteric, that is, a biennial, festival in honor of his son Dionysus. Trieteric festivals to Dionysus were common, and the poet offers a generic *aition*. The poem could have been performed at any number of celebrations and appear to give the overall framework within which the festival was located, Zeus' organization of the cosmos. Thus the bard would appear to sing something relevant but derived from a grander perspective than that of the festival itself. Or the bard could have performed it outside the context of such a festival. It is a poem that can travel.

The persuasive power of this ploy can be deduced by imagining its effect on an audience. Any male auditor—or another bard—would be put in the position of identifying with women against Zeus if he attempted to maintain a parochial perspective against the bard of the *Hymn to Dionysus*. We can label this technique of authorizing an appeal to patriarchy. It is the male as father and universal ruler, summed up by Zeus, that the bard sets up as paradigm for his own authority. The importance of male *birth-giving* is that by its very impossibility in human terms it symbolizes the effectiveness of divine male control and therefore the comprehensiveness of Zeus' point of view. Bards' use of patriarchy as a form of authorization must be connected with the pattern that Ann Bergren has pointed out, which associates truth (and deception) with female figures, from whom male figures wrest it.[66] Bergren links women's possession of truth with their knowing who the father of the baby is. The bards' truth-telling is therefore not correlated just with an elevated or synoptic viewpoint but also with overriding and neutralizing women's secret knowledge. Its appeal to the men in the audience lies in constructing an antidote to their culturally induced suspicion.

The theme of the bard's mobility, by contrast, emphasizes his experiential knowledge and his own ability to synthesize multiplicity and geographic difference. We thus have two modes of gendering by contrast with the female, one that depicts the bard as mobile and one that elevates him to an Olympian perspective.[67] On either the vertical or the horizontal axis, therefore, the bard thematizes his authority by equating a panoramic view with masculine superiority as the basis for his own knowledge of the truth.

The *Hymn to Dionysus* is a good introduction to the *Hymn to Pythian Apollo,* the second half of the *Homeric Hymn to Apollo*. Here the bard employs the same strategy: gender conflict and the triumph of patriarchal

---

[66] Bergren 1983. Cf. also Gresseth 1970.

[67] Richardson 1990: 119–23 (and cf. 137–39 and 192–96) shows that the bird's-eye view of events on earth, which the narrator of the *Iliad* often adopts, is naturalized by being aligned with the perspective of the gods. The bard's "male" Olympian perspective is similarly naturalized.

authority are again foregrounded and arranged in such a way as to align the performer's voice with male divine might. The opening of the poem was presumably lost when it was attached to the Delian hymn, so we cannot tell how the bard initially presented himself.[68] As it stands the poem begins with Apollo's march first to Pytho (Delphi), then to Olympus, where he sets the Muses singing and other goddesses and gods dancing (182–206).[69] Festivity on Delos is replaced by festivity on Olympus, the first sign of this poem's Panhellenic allegiance.[70]

The bard must then choose a topic for his praise of Apollo.[71] The priamel rejecting other (local) stories in favor of the founding of the oracle at Delphi and the beginning of the main narrative are one long address to Apollo with a steady sequence of second-person pronouns and verbs (207–53, resumed in 277–82). Virtuosic this may be in dramatizing the presence of the god as interlocutor for the bard and vivifying the narrative, but by making the audience bystanders, it reflects the bard's implied attitude toward them.[72] When he does switch to the third person, the energy level may have fallen, but nothing suggests a shift in his relationship to the listeners. The effect is very different from the weaving together of god and audience through apostrophe in the *Hymn to Delian Apollo*.

In the first episode of the main narrative, told entirely in the second person, Apollo journeys from Olympus across Euboea to Boeotia, seeking a place to put a temple (216–43). He chooses the site of the spring Telphousa. Directed by the spring-nymph Telphousa to Delphi instead, he lays out his temple and has it built. He then kills a monstrous female snake, the *drakaina*, who inhabits the area. At this point a long excursus on a previous episode in the life of the *drakaina* is inserted (305–55). The *drakaina* once played foster-mother to Typhon, the frightful snake to

---

[68] Förstel 1979: 283–84 reviews Wilamowitz-Moellendorff's suggestion that either two poems were joined or a continuation of the Delian hymn was composed; he thinks the first more likely without ruling out the second. West 1975: 162 prefers the first because of the awkwardness of the join; Càssola 1975: 100–101 prefers the second. Aloni 1989: 74–75 argues most extensively for the view that two prior poems were put together; the second he thinks was recomposed. The question whether one poem imitates the other (on which see Förstel and West with bibliography) is irrelevant to my inquiry.

[69] I take lines 177–81 as a bridge between the poems.

[70] Miller 1986: 68–69 compares the two feasts, Delian and Olympian, with bibliography. These clearly show the orientation of the two poems.

[71] He rejects a series of more or less obscure love stories (208–13). Clay 1989: 57 considers these to be local stories that the bard passes over in favor of a Panhellenic one. Nagy 1990b: 72n.99 remarks, "It goes without saying that love affairs lead to conceptions of heroes, a basic theme of genealogical poetic traditions that promote the localized interests of the status quo."

[72] Richardson 1990: 170–74 treats apostrophe in the *Iliad* as creating intimacy with the characters apostrophized. Bergren 1982: 94–95 points out the remarkableness of this passage and the bard's strategy of turning apostrophe into a demonstration of his ability to re-present the absent god.

which Hera had given birth. The poem recounts Hera's anger at Zeus over his giving birth to Athena and her calling on the powers of Tartaros to impregnate her, her sitting apart for a year and giving birth to Typhon. At the end of the excursus, Typhon disappears from the story and the narrator repeats that Apollo killed the *drakaina*.[73] It would have been known to the audience that Zeus killed Typhon when the latter challenged his rule.[74]

The excursus with the story of Typhon is so abruptly and awkwardly introduced that it was long thought to be an interpolation, especially since it seems to have no function in the poem.[75] It does, however, introduce gender conflict and open the poem up to depiction of Zeus' power, specifically the power to give birth.[76] Whereas in the *Homeric Hymn to Dionysus* stories of Dionysus' birth from a female were rejected as lies in favor of birth from the male, here the child of the female is contrasted—as both monstrous and vulnerable—with the offspring of the male, Athena.

Lest any miss the point, the performer gives Hera a speech underlining the relationship between birth-giving and authority in which she castigates Zeus for his usurpation of her prerogative (311–15, 322–27):

> κέκλυτέ μευ πάντες τε θεοὶ πᾶσαί τε θέαιναι,
> ὡς ἔμ' ἀτιμάζειν ἄρχει νεφεληγερέτα Ζεὺς
> πρῶτος, ἐπεί μ' ἄλοχον ποιήσατο κέδν' εἰδυῖαν·
> καὶ νῦν νόσφιν ἐμεῖο τέκε γλαυκῶπιν Ἀθήνην,
> 315   ἣ πᾶσιν μακάρεσσι μεταπρέπει ἀθανάτοισιν·
>
> . . . .
>
> σχέτλιε ποικιλομῆτα τί νῦν μητίσεαι ἄλλο;
> πῶς ἔτλης οἶος τεκέειν γλαυκώπιδ' Ἀθήνην;
> οὐκ ἂν ἐγὼ τεκόμην; καὶ σὴ κεκλημένη ἔμπης
> 325   ἦα ῥ' ἐν ἀθανάτοισιν οἳ οὐρανὸν εὐρὺν ἔχουσι.
> (325a)   φράζεο νῦν μή τοί τι κακὸν μητίσομ' ὀπίσσω·
> καὶ νῦν μέν τοι ἐγὼ τεχνήσομαι ὥς κε γένηται
> παῖς ἐμὸς ὅς κε θεοῖσι μεταπρέποι ἀθανάτοισιν

Listen to me, all you gods and all you goddesses, to how cloud-gathering Zeus begins to dishonor me, the first to do so, since he made me his devoted wife. And now he has given birth to grey-eyed Athena apart from me, she who is

---

[73] Van Groningen 1958: 54–55 calls it the most extreme case in archaic poetry of absence of a connecting link, but differing only in degree from other examples.

[74] Hesiod, *Theogony* 820–68, where Gaia is mother and the snake is Typhoeus.

[75] Förstel 1979: 260–63 has discussion and bibliography.

[76] Aloni 1989: 86–87 suggests that it is inserted to honor Hera of Samos, but it is hardly an impressive portrait of Hera's power. Förstel 1979: 227–33 sees the hymn as contrasting a period before the founding of the oracle when there was strife on Olympus and a new order in which Apollo extends help to witless humans.

preeminent among all the blessed immortals. . . . Clever wretch, what else will you devise? How did you dare give birth to grey-eyed Athena by yourself? Would I not have borne her? I was called yours, certainly, among the immortals who hold wide heaven. Now beware lest I devise for you some evil in return; and in fact I will invent a way for a child of mine to come forth who will perhaps be preeminent among the immortal gods.

Because Hera and the *drakaina* are related "mothers," Apollo is aligned with Zeus as opponent. Apollo also kills the *drakaina* just as Zeus kills Typhon. In other words the *drakaina* represents, for Apollo, both Hera and Typhon.[77] The excursus therefore guides interpretation of Apollo's fight with the snake as gender conflict. Myth provides no birth-giving episode for Apollo to parallel Zeus' act, but this solution cleverly provides him with an equivalent way to outdo a female.[78] That defeat of a female is the main point of the story is clear not only from Hera's defiant speech but from the unorthodox gender of the snake: most other versions make it male.[79]

The account of Apollo's combat also throws away the chance for excitement by having Apollo dispatch the *drakaina* with a single arrow in a line and a half (357–58).[80] She writhes in agony for several lines while Apollo gloats over her, predicting that she will rot and give the name Pytho (I rot) to the area. Apollo's journey of purification to Tempe is omitted; such a theme would likewise temper the victory. Neglect of the last item illustrates the performer's lack of interest in local specificity, for the journey to Tempe and back was the basis for a major Delphian festival, the Septerion.[81]

[77] She perhaps also replaces Gaia and Themis, who are later said to have held the oracle before Apollo, e.g., Aeschylus *Eumenides* 1–8. Förstel 1979: 234–37 and Clay 1989: 61–63 connect the poem's silence about their priority with its theme of establishing order in the cosmos. Sourvinou-Inwood 1987 argues that the story of earlier owners postdates the *Hymn*.

[78] According to Fontenrose 1959: 16–17, the version in which Apollo as a baby in Leto's arms kills the snake appears in an early-fifth-century vase painting and in Euripides *Iphigeneia in Tauris* 1239–51. If this version is as old as the *Hymn*, then the *Hymn*'s ignoring Leto is another aspect of the gender code.

[79] *AHS ad* 300. Fontenrose 1959: 13–22 distinguishes five versions of the myth of Apollo killing the snake; the version in this *Hymn* "stands somewhat apart from the other four versions, in which his opponent is the male Python and which are closely related one to another" (21). The snake is sometimes described as female in Hellenistic and later sources (14–15).

[80] The *Pythikos nomos* (Pythian tune) for pipes is said to have imitated Apollo's fight with the snake. See Barker 1984: 51–52 for descriptions (Pollux, *Onomastikon* 4.84; Strabo 9.3.10). The middle section, according to Pollux, "includes sounds like those of the *salpinx* [trumpet] and gnashings like those of the serpent as it grinds its teeth after being pierced with arrows." (Barker trans.) The version in which he used one hundred arrows appeared in Simonides (573 *PMG*).

[81] On this festival, also called Stepterion, and its relationship to the fight with the snake, see Nilsson 1957: 150–57 and Fontenrose 1959: 453–56. Simon 1953: 26–34 believes, against doubts that have been raised, that the Septerion originated early.

The *drakaina*'s rotting reduces her to humus, localized material. She marks the spot on the map by giving a name to it, while Apollo ranges freely between earth and Olympus and over the earth itself. His character as god therefore is not defined by a relationship to a particular place; rather he participates in centralized patriarchal power. Apollo's processional march from Delos to Pytho then to Olympus at the beginning of the poem (182–87), followed by his travels in search of a place to set his temple, distinguish him from the *drakaina,* and in the second part of the poem he again ranges abroad, attaching himself to a ship sailing from Crete (391–439). The two themes of mobility and elevation that I identified as indirect ways for a bard to claim male authority are both applied to Apollo.

But so long as these themes are only part of the narrative, they would not directly reflect on the performer's staged identity. The bard, however, has arranged the narrative so as to identify his voice with Apollo's. At the end of the first episode, the one described above, Apollo gloats over the *drakaina*. His speech is directly reported, so the performer's voice is Apollo's and Apollo's triumph is also the performer's. Apollo's vaunt is then the performer's punning (362–74):

ὁ δ' ἐπηύξατο Φοῖβος Ἀπόλλων·
ἐνταυθοῖ νῦν πύθευ ἐπὶ χθονὶ βωτιανείρῃ,
οὐδὲ σύ γε ζωοῖσι κακὸν δήλημα βροτοῖσιν
365 ἔσσεαι, οἳ γαίης πολυφόρβου καρπὸν ἔδοντες
ἐνθάδ' ἀγινήσουσι τεληέσσας ἑκατόμβας,
οὐδέ τί τοι θάνατόν γε δυσηλεγέ' οὔτε Τυφωεὺς
ἀρκέσει οὔτε Χίμαιρα δυσώνυμος, ἀλλὰ σέ γ' αὐτοῦ
πύσει γαῖα μέλαινα καὶ ἠλέκτωρ Ὑπερίων.
370 ὣς φάτ' ἐπευχόμενος, τὴν δὲ σκότος ὄσσε κάλυψε.
τὴν δ' αὐτοῦ κατέπυσ' ἱερὸν μένος Ἠελίοιο·
ἐξ οὗ νῦν Πυθὼ κικλήσκεται, οἱ δὲ ἄνακτα
Πύθειον καλέουσιν ἐπώνυμον οὕνεκα κεῖθι
αὐτοῦ πῦσε πέλωρ μένος ὀξέος Ἠελίοιο.

And Phoibos Apollo boasted, "Now rot here on the man-nourishing earth, nor will you be an evil bane of living people, those who eat the fruit of the much-nourishing earth, who will bring perfect hecatombs here, and neither Typhoeus nor the Chimaera of evil name will ward off grievous death from you at all, but the black earth and bright sun will rot you on this spot." Thus he spoke in boast, but darkness covered her eyes. The pure strength of the sun rotted her there. From that time til now it is called Pytho, and they give its lord the epithet "Pythian" because there on that spot the strength of the sharp sun rotted the monster.

Both the pun on Pytho, as humor, and the following explanation, that
Apollo's words did give a name to the place, break through the narrative
and focus attention on the bard. In lines 363–69 the bard speaks as Apollo
speaking to the snake, but he also directs his words *qua* pun straight to the
audience (for the words are not a pun for the snake). Then in lines 372–74,
speaking as the bard, he tells the audience directly that Apollo's words are
in fact the source of the name Pytho. The bard's identification with
Apollo, followed by his breaking out of narrative containment, means
that Apollo's status as triumphant over the female is extended to the bard
as well. He becomes "male" in his derogation of the female.

As if to confirm that triumph over the female is the key to Apollo's (and
the bard's) status, the bard follows the lines on the *drakaina*'s rotting with
Apollo's punishment of the spring Telphousa. Since she had directed him
to the spot where the *drakaina* lay in wait, he returns and in a brief speech
(379–81) tells her that his fame, not hers, will distinguish the place. He
pushes a cliff into her stream and sets up an altar to himself there. Again the
bard breaks into the narrative briefly to corroborate Apollo's success (385–
87): all venerate Apollo on that spot with the epithet "Telphousian."

The performer takes on Apollo's voice again at the end of the poem. The
second major episode of the poem is Apollo's kidnapping of some Cretan
sailors to become his priests, for once the temple is built and the snake
killed Apollo needs temple servants. He espies a Cretan ship sailing along
and lands on its deck in the form of a dolphin. The ship, despite its crew's
efforts, heads up the west coast of Greece and into the Gulf of Corinth,
coming to land at Krisa, port of Delphi. Apollo leaps in the form of a star
from ship to temple, then reappears as a young man to the Cretans. In
direct discourse he explains their fate to them: they will remain at Delphi
and serve the temple, eating from the sacrifices brought by worshipers.

In this final speech explaining how they will live, the performer speaking as Apollo addresses the detainees as νήπιοι ἄνθρωποι δυστλήμονες
(532, "witless, wretched humans"). At the end he warns them never to
commit hybris or they will be ruled over by foreigners. His threat ends the
poem, except for the usual two-line break-off formula. There is no closure
to the story, so the speech again escapes from the narrative frame and
becomes the bard's as well as Apollo's (540–44; there is a line missing prior
to 540):

540   ἠέ τι τηύσιον ἔπος ἔσσεται ἠέ τι ἔργον,
        ὕβρις θ', ἣ θέμις ἐστὶ καταθνητῶν ἀνθρώπων,
        ἄλλοι ἔπειθ' ὑμῖν σημάντορες ἄνδρες ἔσονται,
        τῶν ὑπ' ἀναγκαίῃ δεδμήσεσθ' ἤματα πάντα.
        εἴρηταί τοι πάντα, σὺ δὲ φρεσὶ σῇσι φύλαξαι.

[But if you err . . .] or there is an uncalled-for word or deed and arrogance, which is typical of humans subject to death, then other men will be commanders over you, under whose control you will be constrained forever. All has been told to you, and you keep it in mind.

Apollo's derogatory language is now neither amusing nor directed at an enemy in whose defeat the audience can share. By virtue of its form of address, "witless, wretched humans . . . ," it takes in the actual audience as well as the internal one, the Cretans. And since, as everyone knew, the Pythia spoke Apollo's oracles, the listeners would finish the story for themselves by concluding that Apollo carried out his threat and replaced the Cretans with a woman.

The effect of the ending on the audience would depend on where the poem was performed. If it was presented at Delphi, it would appear downright hostile, for the Delphians at large, as attendants on the oracle, would be implicated with the Cretans. The unframed speech would bring Apollo's attitude into the present and insinuate that the Delphians had not yet won Apollo's affection. These lines may reflect the results of the first Sacred War, when the Amphiktyones, a league of Boeotian cities, took over control of the oracle, as Pierre Guillon suggests.[82] If so, they indicate that the Delphians are to blame for their present political subservience, while Apollo himself, in whose voice the bard speaks, supports the Amphiktyones. Apollo's warning will have been carried out on a larger scale than the Cretans' loss of privilege: Delphi as a whole has forfeited its autonomy because it did not listen to Apollo. By demonstrating that as privileged interpreters of the god's will the Delphians fail, the bard aligns himself with a foreign power against Delphi and participates in its authority as he validates it. The contrast with Pindar's *paian* 6 for the Delphians, discussed in the last chapter, is instructive, for in that poem Apollo protects and responds to the Delphians, who in turn intercede for the protection of the rest of Greece.

Leading to the same conclusion is the treatment of the place Delphi. The site of Delphi is an accident, suggested by the nymph Telphousa; Apollo himself had wanted to build beside her spring. Very few features of the site of Delphi are mentioned in the poem. The spring Kastalia is ignored. The Krisan plain comes in because the Delphians are not to cultivate it. Much of the poem concerns Apollo's travels, the journey to find a site for the oracle and the commandeering of the Cretan ship, both of them given

[82] Guillon 1963: 95–96. He has found other indications in the geographic catalogue of Apollo's wanderings before founding his temple that the poem favors the Amphiktyones. Discussion and bibliography also in Förstel 1979: 200–202, who argues for a date before the first Sacred War. Robertson 1978 thinks that the Sacred War is a fiction; Lehmann 1980 answers. The war itself is not germane to my argument, and Robertson (48–50) sees a reference to the Amphiktyones in the poem.

extensive geographical explication.[83] Delos, we remember, is set over against other places in that Apollo delights in it most of all. But the *Hymn to Pythian Apollo* makes no appeal to local pride at all.

The poem could be sung outside the environs of Delphi as well, for its local political allegiances are not paramount. An audience elsewhere could imagine the final speech to be addressed to the Delphians and interpret it to mean that Delphi has no special authority in the Greek world. The poem, one could say, wrests the god away from Delphi. Or they could take it as an address to themselves containing an urgent moral message of universal application. Its wider relevance is underlined by the fact that the adjective δυστλήμονες (wretched) in the final speech recalls the song that the Muses sing when Apollo arrives on Olympus at the beginning of the poem (189–93):

Μοῦσαι μέν θ' ἅμα πᾶσαι ἀμειβόμεναι ὀπὶ καλῇ
190 ὑμνεῦσίν ῥα θεῶν δῶρ' ἄμβροτα ἠδ' ἀνθρώπων
τληιμοσύνας, ὅσ' ἔχοντες ὑπ' ἀθανάτοισι θεοῖσι
ζώουσ' ἀφραδέες καὶ ἀμήχανοι, οὐδὲ δύνανται
εὑρέμεναι θανάτοιό τ' ἄκος καὶ γήραος ἄλκαρ·

The Muses all singing together in responsion with beautiful voice hymn the immortal gifts of the gods and the sufferings of humans, burdened with all of which by the immortal gods, (humans) live mindless and helpless lives and cannot find a cure for death and defense against old age.

Apollo then is a moral preceptor for all, apart from cult, and a harsh judge. His oracle provides a negative paradigm of behavior in the persons of his own attendants, as well as offering guidance to anyone who seeks it. The bard then makes the universal moral injunction an expression of his own authority.

The *Homeric Hymn to Delian Apollo* became Panhellenic by being drawn into this system. It and the *Hymn to Pythian Apollo* were joined at some point. It could have been done by the bard Kynaithos, since a scholiast on Pindar attributes the *Hymn to Apollo* to him (saying he passed it off as Homer's).[84] The scholiast also says that Kynaithos introduced Homer's poetry to the Syracusans, so perhaps he created the composite for performance at Syracuse.[85] Or the composite hymn could have been created for a

---

[83] For only 146 lines is the narrative specifically located at Delphi. The two trips take 121 lines of narrative, or 134 if the punishment of Telphousa is included. The excursus on Typhon is 51 lines long.

[84] Schol. Pindar *Nemean* 2.1 (III 29 Dr.).

[85] Wade-Gery 1958: 17–36 makes this suggestion; West 1975: 165–68 attributes the Delian hymn (which he argues is modeled on the Pythian hymn) to Kynaithos and the composite to a redactor.

"Delian-Pythian" festival held by Polykrates, the tyrant of Samos.[86] However it came into being, the composite has the effect of reinterpreting the Delian hymn. The birth-story is no longer complete in itself. Apollo's birth is now just the first stage in his biography; the narrative goes on to bring him into his own as an independent force in the world while shifting his significant attachment from his mother to his father. Delos and Leto are transcended by Apollo's move to Delphi: whereas it was Leto who swore that Apollo would always honor Delos, Apollo founds his own temple at Delphi. But the composite is not attached to Delphi either, as we saw. The composite is Panhellenic in that it acknowledges no particular allegiance.[87] One effect, paradoxically, may have been to give Delos's claim to be Apollo's birthplace greater currency than it would otherwise have had. Other stories were told, locating his birth elsewhere, including possibly Delphi, but the version set on Delos prevailed.[88]

A minor version of the same strategy appears in *Homeric Hymn* 19 to Pan, a later, perhaps fifth-century hymn.[89] This brief hymn describes Pan disporting himself among the nymphs. In the evening he pipes and prances, while the nymphs sing and dance. Their song tells the story of Pan's birth: Hermes was shepherding for a mortal in Arcadia, where he had a sanctuary under the name Kyllenian, out of desire for the daughter of Dryops. Then (35–39):

35 ἐκ δ' ἐτέλεσσε γάμον θαλερόν, τέκε δ' ἐν μεγάροισιν
Ἑρμείῃ φίλον υἱὸν ἄφαρ τερατωπὸν ἰδέσθαι,
αἰγιπόδην δικέρωτα πολύκροτον ἡδυγέλωτα·
φεῦγε δ' ἀναΐξασα, λίπεν δ' ἄρα παῖδα τιθήνη·
δεῖσε γὰρ ὡς ἴδεν ὄψιν ἀμείλιχον ἠϋγένειον.

He consummated a lusty union, and she bore a dear son to Hermes in her chamber forthwith, a wonder to look at, goat-footed, two-horned, much-

[86] Burkert 1979: 59–62. Aloni 1989 takes up his suggestion and argues it in the context of Polykrates' and Peisistratos' propagandistic religious policy. The evidence for the festival is tenuous.

[87] Clay 1989: 17–94 gives an excellent account of the composite. In it the theme of Apollo's violence in the Delian half is shifted from its geographical significance to a historical significance in the establishment of an orderly cosmos.

[88] Ps-Plutarch *On Music* 1132a, credits Herakleides (Pontikos) with the statement that "Philammon of Delphi related in songs the wanderings of Leto and the birth of Artemis and Apollo and was the first to establish choruses at the temple of Delphi." Philammon is mythical; see Barker 1984: 207. His songs about Leto and her children may therefore have been local choral songs that located the births in the vicinity of Delphi.

[89] This date is suggested by *AHS* ad loc. Pan was not a Panhellenic god until the fifth century, and this poem that depicts his Panhellenization is presumably a reaction to that very process of spreading popularity. Càssola 1975: 361–65 thinks it could have originated earlier in Arcadia.

stomping, sweet-laughing. She leaped up and fled, the breast-giver abandoned her child, for she took fright as she saw his unyielding, full-bearded face.

Hermes scooped up the baby and carried him to Olympus, where he was welcomed and named (44–47):

πὰρ δὲ Ζηνὶ καθῖζε καὶ ἄλλοις ἀθανάτοισιν,
45 δεῖξε δὲ κοῦρον ἑόν· πάντες δ' ἄρα θυμὸν ἔτερφθεν
ἀθάνατοι, περίαλλα δ' ὁ Βάκχειος Διόνυσος·
Πᾶνα δέ μιν καλέεσκον ὅτι φρένα πᾶσιν ἔτερψε.

(Hermes) sat down beside Zeus and the other immortals and showed them his son; all the immortals were delighted at heart indeed, but especially Dionysus the Bacchic one. They called him Pan because he delighted the heart of all (*pasin*).

The movement from female and local to male and Olympian is archetypically simple. Welcome by his father and by *the* father, Zeus, Panhellenizes the new god. The only earthly place named in the poem is Arcadia, site of the birth, for Pan's haunts in the first part of the poem are unlocalized. Arcadia is named "mother of sheep" (30), confirming the link between geography and gender.

The performer aligns himself with the male, Olympian side through an echo. In the first two lines of the poem he introduces his subject by describing him before he names him (1–2):

ἀμφί μοι Ἑρμείαο φίλον γόνον ἔννεπε Μοῦσα,
αἰγιπόδην δικέρωτα φιλόκροτον

Sing for me, Muse, about the dear offspring of Hermes, goat-footed, two-horned, stomp-loving . . .

The first two adjectives of line 2 and a variant on the third are repeated in line 37 (quoted above) at his birth. The arrangement means that Pan is celebrated precisely for his unique appearance, the very appearance that causes his mother to leap up and flee. The bard, like the Olympians, is delighted by the creature that a mother could not love. In this poem no politics are at stake; the bard does not construct his pro-Olympian stance in opposition to an earthly cult center (though he steals Pan away from Arcadia).[90] Rather, bard and god appear as free spirits dedicated to music and dance. The effect stages the bard as a mobile professional (who has

[90] Minton 1970: 359–60, following Friedländer 1914, develops the idea of formal hymn-types, of which he distinguishes two, the descriptive and the theogonic; typical of the theogonic type is Friedländer's "Progress to Olympus." Yet birth followed by travel to Olympus occurs only in the *Hymns* to Pan and Hermes and the *Theogony* (on which see below). Minton (361n.9) adds *Hymn* 6, in which Aphrodite is taken to the other immortals,

stolen the nymphs' song and broadcast it), rather than a political or moral guide.[91] If the poem was used to introduce another, the proper function of a prooimion, it would set the tone for pure musical pleasure.

Hermes in the *Homeric Hymn to Hermes* more elaborately and playfully moves between his mother, babyhood, and residence in a cave on Mt. Kyllene in Arcadia, on the one hand, and his father Zeus, possession of honors, and Olympus on the other. This is a difficult poem, with elliptical references to ritual and belief. Its connection of gender with geography is articulated in Hermes' response to his mother's prophecy that he will be in trouble with Apollo for stealing his cattle (167–72):

> οὐδὲ θεοῖσι
> νῶϊ μετ' ἀθανάτοισιν ἀδώρητοι καὶ ἄλιστοι
> αὐτοῦ τῇδε μένοντες ἀνεξόμεθ', ὡς σὺ κελεύεις.
> 170 βέλτερον ἤματα πάντα μετ' ἀθανάτοις ὀαρίζειν
> πλούσιον ἀφνειὸν πολυλήϊον ἢ κατὰ δῶμα
> ἄντρῳ ἐν ἠερόεντι θαασσέμεν·

. . . and we two will not submit to staying here, ungifted and unbeseeched among the immortal gods, as you order. It is better to gossip among the immortals for all our days, rich, wealthy, possessing abundant cropland, than to sit at home in a windy cave.

The "windy cave" of Mt. Kyllene is Maia's home (and a site where Hermes was worshiped, as we saw in Chapter 3), while Hermes gains his niche on Olympus by exchanges with Apollo, half-brother through his father Zeus, and by Zeus' granting of honor.

However, Hermes only wins new possessions and a portion of honor because he created the lyre (24–51) and later the panpipe (512), charmed Apollo with his singing, and made him nervous with his cleverness.[92] In portraying Hermes as the original musician, the performer aligns himself with the god whose inventiveness he celebrates, but a simple movement from local and maternal to Olympus and paternal does not adequately describe the poem. Here again musical and not political authorizing is effected by self-reflexive illustration of the power of music.

As I indicated at the beginning of the chapter, self-presentation as a patriarchal figure is not the only style in which a bard can essay a relation-

---

but Olympus is not mentioned and the emphasis is all on her appearance. The pattern is not a given but is generated by the alignment of patriarchy with Panhellenism.

[91] The nymphs sing of "the blessed gods and high Olympus" (27). The poem from 28 on is a repetition of their song as they dance with Pan, so on returning to earthly haunts Pan brings his Olympian identity with him.

[92] As Bergren 1982: 98–99 says apropos of the cattle tracks going backward, Hermes puts signs into circulation, so neither local nor Olympian identity could sum him up.

ship with his audience. *Homeric Hymn* 6 starts the bard out on other footing altogether, seeking to evoke pleasure. It tells of Aphrodite's coming ashore at Paphos from the sea-foam. The Hours meet her and dress her in beautiful clothes and jewelry. They take her to the other immortals, whom she delights and each of whom prays (!) to have her to wife, "marveling at the appearance of violet-crowned Aphrodite." The singer then asks Aphrodite for victory in "this contest" (19–20). As in Bacchylides' song for the Keans on Delos, discussed in Chapter 3, there is a certain borrowing of female sensuality, a seductive tone: the song should charm the judges as Aphrodite does the (male) Olympians. What contest the poem was meant for and what poem it might have introduced are unknown.

Most of the other *Homeric Hymns* are short (less than twenty lines), meant simply as introductions to longer pieces (as were *Hymns* 6 and 19). They stage the performer as having a special affinity for one god or another or one set of gods. More flexible than an appeal to the Muses, which they may have either replaced or supplemented, these openings too must have helped establish an identity for the performer.

II

What then of the Muses? They represent another system of authorizing more familiar than the appeal to patriarchy or mobility that I have been outlining. According to it bards receive authorization from female figures. The major hexameter poems, those attributed to Homer and Hesiod, open with a request to a Muse or the Muses to speak (the *Theogony* at the end of the proem); similar invocations are found in some of the *Homeric Hymns,* for instance 4, 5, 9, 17, 19, 20. The Muses' function of granting song must go back well into the prehistoric period. As Margalit Finkelberg points out, the Muses allow performers to portray themselves as singing true songs without acknowledging tradition.[93] Under conditions of bardic rivalry on the interstate stage, however, the more assertive, agonistic stance replaced or supplemented the invocation to the Muses if the bard was seeking a form of compensatory validation. In fact, since the Muses are female truth-givers, one aspect of the appeal to patriarchy that I have been outlining must be its tacit competition with the very tradition of invoking the Muses and disparagement of performers who do call on them.

As invokers of the Muses, the Homeric and Hesiodic poems should not be lumped together. The *Iliad* and *Odyssey* make little use of the Muses. In the *Iliad* one can see what was probably the traditional conception of the

[93] Finkelberg 1990. Svenbro 1976: 31–35 explains the Muses as a projection of the audience's pressure on the composing bard, who had to adjust his poem to reflect the audience's convictions. This view sorts well with my argument.

relationship between Muses and bard. Periodic invocations of the Muse call attention to a heightened moment of the bard's recall or narration.[94] In the opening line the request is minimal: "Sing, goddess, . . ." But the passage enacts the relationship the performer imagines: in line 8 he asks a question, "Which of the gods set them to fighting in strife?" addressed to the Muse. The answer comes in the next line, so he presents himself as hearing and repeating the Muse's response, which of course the audience cannot hear. In the famous passage in *Iliad* 2.484–93, the performer is more explicit. The Muses, he says, as goddesses are "on the spot and know all, while we hear rumor merely and know nothing." Of himself he declares (488–93):

> I could not recount or name the throng, not if I had ten tongues and ten mouths,
> an unbreaking voice and a heart of bronze within, if the Olympian Muses,
> daughters of aegis-bearing Zeus, did not remind me of how many came to Ilion.
> In turn, I will tell the leaders of the ships and all the ships.

While calling attention to his own physical stamina, he also presents himself as hearing from eyewitness Muses during performance and repeating the account.[95] The Muses' knowledge is unmediated by any intervening intelligence. The real authority of this poem, however, as remarked earlier, is its dramatic power and monumentality as *mythos*.[96] The poem itself, as it were, validates the performer's assertion of physical strength and access to complete information by its length and inclusiveness.

The opening of the *Odyssey* makes use of the same conception, for after a sketch of the whole story the bard says (10), "beginning at whatever point you like, tell us too of these things, goddess, daughter of Zeus." The next line specifies the point at which the story takes up.[97] Elsewhere in the *Odyssey* the Muse appears to teach poems ahead of time, although her witnessing is implied. Odysseus says to Demodokos (8.488–91):[98]

[94] De Jong 1987: 46–53. Brillante 1993: 10–11 remarks that a bard who claimed autonomy would deprive his song of interest because it would be a merely personal message. I would say that he would require another authorizing strategy.

[95] Jensen 1980: 75 points out that this invocation emphasizes the bard's performance: "What is felt overwhelming here is not the aesthetic beauty of his song, nor even the complicated task of mastering the huge material, but the sheer physical demands that such a long enumeration would make on the organs of speech." De Jong 1987: 46–47, 52 analyzes the relationship of the bard to the Muses as similar to the double motivation of Homeric heroes.

[96] For the alignment of the bard with Achilles in the *Iliad,* see Martin 1989: 220–30. For other internal methods by which the performer's own voice takes on authority, see, e.g., Scully 1986 and Morrison 1991.

[97] See Pedrick 1992 on this opening.

[98] Brillante 1993: 25–26 argues that teaching and informing on the spot are not separate conceptions of the Muses' aid; he also gives bibliography on the Muses.

ἤ σέ γε Μοῦσ' ἐδίδαξε, Διὸς πάϊς, ἤ σέ γ' Ἀπόλλων.
λίην γὰρ κατὰ κόσμον Ἀχαιῶν οἶτον ἀείδεις,
490 ὅσσ' ἔρξαν τ' ἔπαθόν τε καὶ ὅσσ' ἐμόγησαν Ἀχαιοί,
ὥς τέ που ἤ αὐτὸς παρεὼν ἤ ἄλλου ἀκούσας.

Either the Muse taught you, the child of Zeus, or Apollo. For quite in order you
sing the fate of the Achaeans, all that they did and suffered and the labors they
went through, as if somehow either you were there yourself or you heard it
from another.

But the *Odyssey* never represents the Muse as present after the opening. As
Herwig Maehler points out, observing that the Muse plays little part,
curiosity drives both hero and internal listeners in the *Odyssey;* the latter
accept as "truth" what fulfills their desire for descriptions of the larger
world.[99] Beyond that, the text itself is playful about the truth–status of
speaking and the possibility of getting at a reality behind speech. The very
sophistication of the *Odyssey* makes the virtue of calling on the Muses
questionable.[100] Instead, experiential knowledge is valorized. The bard
aligns his voice with Odysseus' as he moves from one immobilized female
to another, identifying traveling bard with traveling hero and allowing the
implicit gender code to mark both.[101]

The two Hesiodic poems, on the other hand, take a different tack and
expand the address to the Muse, altering the Muse's relationship to truth
and to the performer in the process. In the end they produce an appeal to
patriarchy as surely as do the poems previously discussed. The *Theogony* is
no intensely dramatic or playful narrative of adventures but the promulga-
tion of a view of the cosmos that purports to found proper human conduct.[102] The bard's story, the triumph of Zeus and Zeus' imposition of
order on the world, is the ultimate Panhellenic synthesis of the religious
system and requires a weighty compensatory validation.[103] In the narra-

[99] Maehler 1963: 30–34.

[100] See, e.g., Redfield 1975: 36–37 on differences in treatment of narrative time in relation
to time of performance between the two epics.

[101] Kahane 1992 argues that the word *anēr* (man) always refers to Odysseus in the *Odyssey*.
For gender assumptions at work between speakers and audience both within the *Odyssey* and
between the performer and his actual audience, see [Arthur] Katz 1991; Doherty 1992 and
1995.

[102] Detienne 1967: 51–80 envisions the early poet's "efficacious word," which creates
cosmic order (61); however, for Hesiod its effectiveness is already problematic, for it can
deceive (79). To this magical-religious speech Detienne (81–103) opposes another type of
speech: dialogue-speech. In the warrior band speech, like booty, is "in the middle" and
becomes the *isēgoria* (equal right of speech) of the archaic city. These two types could be
associated with bardic and communal poetry.

[103] Maehler 1963: 43 takes Hesiod's intensity to mean that he had no given public for his

tive Zeus' patriarchal rule is established, but the god gains control of the world toward the end of the poem. "Hesiod," the persona identified as the speaker, solves the problem of grounding his authority at the beginning of the poem by turning the Muses into a link between Zeus and himself.[104] The female figures, in other words, are reconceived to serve the performer's patriarchal stance.

The poem opens with a description of the Muses "who hold the great and holy mountain of Helicon" (2) dancing around a spring and altar of Zeus. They appear to be nymphs, who typically dance around springs (although they are immediately set into a world defined by Zeus). When they begin to sing, their subject is the gods, headed by Zeus. Their voices can be heard at night as they go invisibly. These are the nymph-like goddesses who "once taught Hesiod beautiful song, as he was herding sheep below holy Helicon" (22–23). They spoke to "me" first, the bard says, shifting into the first person. The lines the Muses say to him are famous and much-discussed (26–28):[105]

> ποιμένες ἄγραυλοι, κάκ' ἐλέγχεα, γαστέρες οἶον,
> ἴδμεν ψεύδεα πολλὰ λέγειν ἐτύμοισιν ὁμοῖα,
> ἴδμεν δ' εὖτ' ἐθέλωμεν ἀληθέα γηρύσασθαι.

Field-dwelling shepherds, disgraces, mere bellies, we know how to speak many lies like true things and we know, whenever we wish, how to proclaim true things.

Did Hesiod not notice that there is no guarantee that the Muses told *him* the truth?[106] Or is it oversubtle to ask what the significance of their distinction is for Hesiod? Precisely because they are spoken by female figures, who have a dangerous propensity to deceive, these lines *do* unsettle the status of truth and lies.[107] In other words, the bard deliberately raises the question for the audience whether he is dependent on unreliable female

---

work. Puelma 1989: 74–79 emphasizes the different conception of "truth" required by didactic, "engaged" poetry.

[104] For previous scholarship on the *Theogony* proem, see Lenz 1980: 123–26; West 1966 *ad loc.* Lenz's excellent discussion of the structure of the proem views it as establishing the nature of truth, but he ignores the issue of patriarchy, which organizes truth. For the persona of Hesiod, see Nagy 1990a: 48–51, who connects it with cult. Lamberton 1988 warns against assuming either a personal Hesiod or early honor at Askra.

[105] Some scholars, e.g., Maehler 1963: 40–41, see in this account a genuine visionary experience. West 1966 *ad loc.* documents a convention in Greek and other literatures by which seeing a vision is the basis for a demand to be heard. The convention is the basis for the persona.

[106] This is the starting point of Pucci's 1977 study.

[107] In the *Theogony* itself Gaia and Pandora illustrate the theme of female deceit. On Metis in the *Theogony*, see Detienne and Vernant 1978: 57–130.

speech. In doing so, of course, he activates the idea that stable truth is "masculine," but at the same time he makes any mere reliance on the Muses problematic. The proem as a whole constitutes his construction of male authority out of that ambiguous encounter. We can trace the train of thought.

The Muses appear at the beginning to be nymphs. Nymphs are dangerous. An encounter in the mountains with such figures had every chance of being perilous, and indeed their words are not auspicious.[108] But the Muses breathe into "Hesiod" and give him a laurel staff so that he will be able to sing of future and past, and they order him to sing of the gods and first and last of themselves. Certainly the experience *appears* to have changed the bard's life: no longer a shepherd, he stands before his audience holding a staff, the visual sign of his encounter with the Muses, and speaking of the gods, beginning with the Muses. The performer presents himself as having a special power of song because he has gone through an initiatory experience in confrontation with vivid daimonic figures, an experience far more intense than that of bards (like the performer of the *Iliad* and "Hesiod" himself before his encounter) who only hear the Muses.[109]

But the Muses still appear to be unassimilated figures dancing in the mountains. They have given him the power of song, but did they inspire him with the truth?[110] The bard quotes the Muses' lines directly and speaks in their voice. For the audience the bard has co-opted the Muses' words, so that their boast is now his: "I can tell the truth. . . ." A substitute question therefore poses itself to the audience: what is our guarantee that this nympholeptic bard is telling *us* the truth?[111] The audience must perceive its own vulnerability as well as the bard's, for what access to truth does it have except through bards? By raising the question, the bard forces the audience to pay attention to his definition of the Muses in the following lines, in which he establishes his access to "truth."

Hesiod's answer is to integrate the Muses into the order of Zeus. Ac-

---

[108] Latte 1968: 65–68 understands the encounter as one with nymphs. Lenz 1980: 148 remarks that the passage shows that the goddesses of Helicon were personal divinities for Hesiod, whom he reveals to be Muses.

[109] This point is made forcefully by Lenz 1980: 152–53: all other poetry is questionable—not false but undecidable.

[110] Connor 1988: 158–59 points out, citing Plato's *Phaedrus* 238cd, that the one seized by the nymphs may feel increased power of speech; on 160–62 he gives instances of nympholepts (those possessed by the nymphs) who were said to be prophetic.

[111] As Nagy 1992a: 121–24 points out, the verbs have different weights: the Muses would λέγειν (speak) lies, but γηρύσασθαι (sing, cry) the truth. ἀληθέα γηρύσασθαι marks a speech act, "an utterance with special authority and authorising power." The latter phrase also signals Panhellenic status (124–25), so the Muses contrast local accounts (lies) with a universally valid one. If the audience identified the Muses and performer as speaking in a special, inherently authoritative way, they would have a preliminary indication of his trustworthiness.

cordingly, he begins again, after dismissing the wild landscape (35), and the daimonic recedes. Instead the Muses are described as singing on Olympus for "father Zeus" (36–37). Their song begins (45) with the offspring of Earth and Heaven, followed by a song about Zeus, "father of gods and men (sic)," best of the gods and greatest in power, then by an account of humans and giants.[112] At the beginning and end of the passage on their singing, Hesiod says that they delight the mind of Zeus (37, 51). Like a communal chorus the Muses reflect back the community, but here the community is Zeus and the history of the cosmos is required to express his identity. Pleasing him means that their song is identical with reality, for any difference would be a deviation from the order he has instituted.[113]

To fix the Muses more genetically within Zeus' dispensation, the bard next tells of their birth. Zeus begat them and they were born to Mnemosyne (Memory) a short distance away from the peak of Olympus— near enough to belong but just peripheral to the center of power.[114] Then (68–76):

> αἳ τότ' ἴσαν πρὸς Ὄλυμπον, ἀγαλλόμεναι ὀπὶ καλῇ,
> ἀμβροσίῃ μολπῇ· περὶ δ' ἴαχε γαῖα μέλαινα
> 70 ὑμνεύσαις, ἐρατὸς δὲ ποδῶν ὕπο δοῦπος ὀρώρει
> νισομένων πατέρ' εἰς ὅν· ὁ δ' οὐρανῷ ἐμβασιλεύει,
> αὐτὸς ἔχων βροντὴν ἠδ' αἰθαλόεντα κεραυνόν,
> κάρτει νικήσας πατέρα Κρόνον· εὖ δὲ ἕκαστα
> ἀθανάτοις διέταξε νόμους καὶ ἐπέφραδε τιμάς.
> 75 ταῦτ' ἄρα Μοῦσαι ἄειδον Ὀλύμπια δώματ' ἔχουσαι,
> ἐννέα θυγατέρες μεγάλου Διὸς ἐκγεγαυῖαι.

---

[112] According to Lenz 1980: 160–62, the Muses' song encompasses more than Hesiod's does; it tells of everything, whereas Hesiod can only speak of the overall order. Contrast Clay 1988: 332–33.

[113] I use "identical with reality" in a different sense from Pucci 1977: 12–14. Pucci argues that Hesiod raises the problem of language as nonidentical with "things as they are," then avoids it by affirming that the Muses sing a song identical with truth. My point is that Hesiod created a closed system with a central signifier, Zeus.

[114] The Muses were not always the offspring of Zeus in early poetry. The *Iliad* refers to the Muses as daughters of Zeus (2.491, 598). But Eumelos is reported to have made Apollo the father of three Muses (17 Bernabé; cf. 16 Bernabé, where Zeus and Mnemosyne are the parents). Alkman, it is said, calls them the children of Ouranos and Ge (67 *PMGF*; cf. 5 fr. 2.28–29 *PMGF*), although a line is quoted in which he invokes a Muse as daughter of Zeus (28 *PMGF*). Mimnermos reconciles accounts, according to Pausanias (9.29.4), by distinguishing between older and younger Muses, the former offspring of Ouranos, the latter of Zeus, while a separate commentator says that he made them daughters of Ge (evidence collected in 13 *W*). See also Harriott 1969: 10–11.

They then went to Olympus, rejoicing in their beautiful voice, with immortal song; the black earth resounded to their singing, and a lovely beat arose beneath their feet as they went to their father. He rules the heaven, personally possessing thunder and glittering lightning, having defeated his father Kronos by force; he arranged observances for the immortals in every matter and appointed honors. These things the Muses were singing, who dwell in Olympian homes, the nine daughters begotten by great Zeus.

The theme of birth and travel to Olympus is the Panhellenizing motif that we have seen before, but here it is more complex. The Muses are Zeus' daughters, but they travel *to* his house, not from it in marriage as daughters normally would. By returning to father and center, they show that Zeus' rule is a closed system; like Athena at the end of the poem, they remain defined by the father.[115] Equally important, the Muses sing as they go of the power of Zeus and his assignment of ordinances and honors to the gods. Marylin Arthur [Katz] has drawn attention to the importance of the homology between the Muses' song and the father-daughter bond.[116] One can put it even more strongly: the addition of Zeus' fatherhood to the picture of the Muses singing means that Zeus begets the language used to describe the system. This circularity is therefore more profound than in the previous image, for it makes him the origin of the discourse whose identity with his dispensation pleases him. The further circulation of the same discourse on earth equally returns to Zeus, as this poem will.

In their like-minded (60) articulation of order, the Muses are the opposite of Zeus' last enemy, Typhoeus, who threatens confusion of tongues (829–33):

> φωναὶ δ' ἐν πάσῃσιν ἔσαν δεινῆς κεφαλῇσι,
> 830   παντοίην ὄπ' ἱεῖσαι[117] ἀθέσφατον· ἄλλοτε μὲν γὰρ
> φθέγγονθ' ὥς τε θεοῖσι συνιέμεν, ἄλλοτε δ' αὖτε
> ταύρου ἐριβρύχεω μένος ἀσχέτου ὄσσαν ἀγαύρου,
> ἄλλοτε δ' αὖτε λέοντος ἀναιδέα θυμὸν ἔχοντος.

Voices were in all the dreadful heads emitting all sorts of noises indescribably, for sometimes they spoke as if to the gods so they could understand, then again

[115] The Muses were not always virgins. In various accounts they appear as mothers of legendary singers. Three children could possibly be restored to Kalliope in Pindar fr. 128c.5 *SM*. Plato refers to Orpheus as "offspring of the Muses" (*Rep.* 364e). Other references are later. Harriott 1969: Ch. 1 discusses early artistic and literary depictions.

[116] Arthur [Katz] 1983: 108–9. The Muses' song represents the power of language, whose fictionality transcends human corporeality. Her analysis begins from the logic of the text rather than of the performer's self-representation, but my discussion owes much to it.

[117] On the psilosis see West 1966: 91n.1.

(they uttered) the (sound) of a bellowing bull, untameable in might and proud in voice, then again of a lion with shameless heart.

The Muses' allegiance to Zeus and Zeus' defeat of Typhoeus are opposite expressions of Zeus' control of discourse within his order.[118] Zeus' liaison with Mnemosyne is also repeated at the end of the poem (915), so the defeat of Typhoeus is followed by the begetting of Zeus' discourse; the genesis of the poem is also its endpoint. From this standpoint all other speech appears as mere babble.

The performer has now established the Muses within the patriarchal order and defined their song as a reflection of that order. His last step is to assess the relationship between the Muses and human speaking. To kings they give the ability to instantiate Zeus' order in particular judgments that appear to their hearers to be both straight and sweet (80–93); to singers they grant the power to erase care and grief from the minds of listeners with their stories, for delight is also a part of Zeus' dispensation (55).[119] These are speakers who only hear the Muses, or rather, whose tongues the Muses make sweet. Consequently, although they depend on the Muses, they do not have the comprehension to confirm that they speak the truth.[120] "Hesiod" himself is not among the singers, whose songs are described as tales of the glorious deeds of earlier humans and the blessed gods who hold Olympus (100–101), for with his speaker's staff he has affinities with the kings also.[121] He stands between and above the two categories, for he alone reveals the cosmic structure on which the other speakers rely and is therefore able to validate their speech as well.

Looking back from this vantage point to the opening lines, we can see that the change in the description of the Muses at line 36 is a result of their revelation. In turning from local Heliconian to Olympian Muses, "Hesiod" dramatizes the Panhellenization not of the Muses but of the bard himself.[122] Although he initially experiences them as invisible figures whose intentions are unfathomable, after the encounter he can describe the Muses even far off on Olympus. He shows the audience that one conse-

[118] Zeus, of course, also has mastery of deceit, which he sends to earth in the person of Pandora (589): cf. Bergren 1983: 74–75. But in the *Theogony*, unlike *WD* (77–80), Pandora's speech is not mentioned.

[119] Maehler 1963: 44–45 stresses the parallel between the two. Gagarin 1992: 63–71 argues that both rely on persuasive language.

[120] Arthur [Katz] 1983: 110–12 shows that Hesiod sets the speech of kings and bards, reproduction through the mouth, as a male world of pure *logos* into contrast with the world of corporeal necessity; the latter is identified with the *gastēr* (stomach/womb) and displaced downward onto women. Even so, *logos* relies blindly on the Muses.

[121] Detienne 1967: 90 connects the staff with sovereignty. So also Koller 1956: 165–69. Clay 1988: 332–33 views Hesiod's song as surpassing that of the Muses because the staff unites the authority of Zeus and Apollo as well.

[122] Nagy 1990a: 57–58 speaks of the transformation from local to Panhellenic Muses.

quence of their gift of song is his ability to comprehend them, with the result that they move from being the inspirers of his song to being its content. He has transcended dependence on them for knowledge.[123] He implies too that their visibility is an effect of the transparency of their song: the account identical with reality lays open the cosmos as emanating from Zeus. It is clear that he has a different order of knowledge from those who rely on the Iliadic Muses, who have seen everything for themselves. Only by raising for the audience the question of the Muses' reliability could "Hesiod" demonstrate that through their gift *he* is now the one who can "see."

Then, having established his position, the bard ends the proem by calling on the Muses in a string of five imperatives to sing the *Theogony*. The *Theogony* itself gives an account of the gradual shift of power in the cosmos from female to male.[124] Gender organizes the whole poem and provides the legitimation of Zeus' rule.[125] The source of authority, patriarchy, is therefore the same for "Hesiod" and Zeus and provides both with a unitary, synoptic vista.

Finally, we come to the *Works and Days,* an example of "wisdom literature." Not being narrative, the *Works and Days* cannot include the same technique for authorizing its performer. The speaker of wisdom literature does need a persona, however, a role that legitimates his possession of wisdom, especially if he aspires to a more complex production than a collection of gnomes. The speaker of the *Works and Days* opens the ten-line proem by asking the Muses, who create fame in song, to come and speak, singing about their father Zeus (1–2). The next six lines describe Zeus: he makes human men spoken of or not, renowned or not, and raises them or casts down. The last two lines are a direct address to Zeus (9–10):

κλῦθι ἰδὼν ἀιών τε, δίκῃ δ' ἴθυνε θέμιστας
τύνη· ἐγὼ δέ κε Πέρσῃ ἐτήτυμα μυθησαίμην.

Listen, looking and hearing, and set judgments straight with justice, you; and I would be glad to pronounce unerring things to Perses.

This performer repeats in small compass the movement from Muses to Zeus found in the proem of the *Theogony;* he asks them to sing about Zeus' power and caps his indication of the source of power by transferring his

[123] Thalmann 1984, esp. 139, gives only part of the Hesiodic claim when he says of the initiation scene: "In this way Hesiod implicitly claims validity for the *Theogony* as the medium for transmitting a knowledge of the world that would be the gods' sole privilege if it were not for the Muses' intervention."

[124] Arthur [Katz] 1982 shows that the *Theogony* equates justice with the patriarchal family.

[125] Thalmann 1984: 41 points out that Hesiod integrates the cosmogony with its endpoint by repeated proleptic references to Zeus.

own address to Zeus. Finally, by juxtaposing the pronouns "you" and "I" he equates his knowledge of truth with Zeus' dispensation.

It is soon clear that the performer is borrowing the persona of "Hesiod" found in the *Theogony* proem (though not necessarily unique to it), while disputing and correcting "Hesiod's" statements. This performer demands that the system of justice be applied to human relations. It is not enough to describe the cosmos; we must know its consequences for ourselves. The poem proper therefore opens with a disputatious statement revising the *Theogony*'s description of the birth of Strife (11–26). The first narrative section is the story of Pandora (60–105), also found in the *Theogony*.[126] Both are reconsidered in light of their effects on daily life. The parable of the hawk and the dove sarcastically revises the *Theogony*'s description of "Hesiod's" elevation in knowledge beyond kings (202–12). The bard of this poem is in competition with performers of poems like the *Theogony* for the role of "Hesiod."

It looks as though the persona of the Panhellenized celebrant of Zeus' order was an established one, created out of an encounter with the Muses plus a vision of the cosmos controlled by Zeus.[127] An authorizing strategy seems to have evolved into a role, since it could be evoked by mere allusion. Late in the *Works and Days,* in the passage on sailing, the performer makes his usurpation of the persona of the *Theogony* explicit when he announces that he dedicated his tripod, his prize in a song contest, on Helicon at the spot where the Muses set him on the path of song (658–59). By this time the persona has been thoroughly recast as a speaker about human matters, farming and hoarding up goods.[128] The role brings its gender hierarchy with it, but the performer does not make consistent use of it, for the elevation it implies does not sort with his I-you style, his orientation toward the present and dialogue with a human audience.[129]

The *Theogony* and the *Odyssey,* both self-conscious about the problem of the narrator's source of knowledge, could be said to take opposite tacks

---

[126] The performer calls attention to Pandora's voice (61 and 79) as a speaker of "lies and wheedling words" (78).

[127] Nagy 1990a: 47 derives the name Hesiod from roots meaning "emit" and "voice."

[128] Martin 1992 identifies a traditional persona for the wisdom-speaker, that of the *metanastēs,* or "immigrant." The speaker comes from a geographical margin, bringing an external perspective and a free-speaking style to the center. Phoinix's speech to Achilles in *Iliad* 9.434–605 provides the best example, and his speech parallels the content of such poetry. Martin finds evidence of the *metanastēs* figure in *WD* 633–40 in which the speaker says his father immigrated to Askra. This persona, it seems to me, is crossed with "Hesiod."

[129] Hamilton 1989: 72 contrasts the maiden of 519–23 with Pandora and points out that in the second part of the poem, in which good *eris* rather than bad prevails, women are not denigrated. The bard does not totally neglect the elevated stance; cf. *WD* 661, where he says, "I will express the mind of aegis-bearing Zeus."

in transforming Iliadic Muses. The *Odyssey* evokes them in a minimal, distanced way, primarily to validate bards depicted in the narrative, while the *Theogony* elaborates them as captive members of Zeus' regime. The idea of Muses who see all and formulate it to pass on to bards is antithetical to both poems: to the *Theogony* because they would constitute a competing source of knowledge for Zeus, to the *Odyssey* because they would provide a spectator's view of Odysseus and undo his control of the narrative. The *Works and Days* makes use of them only as a link to the persona created in the *Theogony*. Outside the *Iliad* the Muses do not compete seriously with patriarchy as a way of defining a bard's source of knowledge.

In the sixth and fifth centuries, as poetry became a vehicle for less traditional descriptions of the world and of history, more individualistic ways of positioning the singer developed. Some were quite dramatic in the way they used but also transformed the techniques of hexameter poetry. The recently published opening section of Simonides' elegy commemorating the battle of Plataia (11 *W*²), for instance, reveals his strategy for differentiating the performer from Homer: the performer asserts that the Muses gave Homer "the whole truth," but for himself he requests only that the Muse be ἐπίκουρος (foreign military auxiliary). He ends the description of the fall of Troy by saying (13–22):

> τοὶ δὲ πόλι]ν πέρσαντες ἀοίδιμον [οἴκαδ' ἵ]κοντο
>   ]ωων ἀγέμαχοι Δαναοί[,
> 15 οἷσιν ἐπ' ἀθά]νατον κέχυται κλέος ἀν[δρὸς] ἕκητι
>   ὃς παρ' ἰοπ]λοκάμων δέξατο Πιερίδ[ων
>   πᾶσαν ἀλη]θείην, καὶ ἐπώνυμον ὁπ[λοτέρ]οισιν
>   ποίησ' ἡμ]ιθέων ὠκύμορον γενεή[ν.
>   ἀλλὰ σὺ μὲ]ν νῦν χαῖρε, θεᾶς ἐρικυ[δέος υἱέ
> 20 κούρης εἰν]αλίου Νηρέος· αὐτὰρ ἐγώ[
>   κικλήισκω] σ' ἐπίκουρον ἐμοί, π[ολυώνυμ]ε Μοῦσα,
>   εἴ πέρ γ' ἀν]θρώπων εὐχομένω[ν μέλεαι·[130]

And after sacking the much-sung-of [city], the battle-leading Greeks [   ] came [home] (Greeks) [over whom immortal] fame is poured by the agency of the [man] (Homer) who received from the violet-haired Muses the [whole?] truth and [made] the short-lived race of demigods known to younger men. [But] farewell now, O [son] of the glorious goddess, [daughter] of briny Nereus. I however [call?] you to be my auxiliary, [many-named] Muse, if indeed [you care for ?] humans when they pray.

---

[130] For a description of the text, which is heavily restored, see Parsons 1992. He suggests (6) that the poem may have been performed at Plataia to commemorate the victory.

On the field of contemporary battle, the Muses are not the authorities, for eyewitnesses exist, a fact that the performer capitalizes on to distance himself from Homer's derivative knowledge and suggest the immediacy of his own. He combines his demotion of the Muse with an unorthodox invocation to Achilles, creating thereby a military persona for himself in keeping with the subject of his recitation.[131] Although a pro-Spartan tilt appears in it, for the opening of the narrative focuses on Sparta (25–34), the poem must have been intended to provide a version of the battle of Plataia that would be accepted as valid all over the Greek world. Concomitantly, Simonides must create a speaking position for this nontraditional situation that signals a new kind of authority.[132]

Some pre-Socratic philosophers opened their poetic accounts of the world with self-presentations meant to verify their unique access to knowledge. Empedokles has the most spectacular one. In the opening of his *Katharmoi* (1 Inwood = 112 *DK*), he describes himself (1–8):

> ὦ φίλοι, οἳ μέγα ἄστυ κάτα ξανθοῦ Ἀκράγαντος
> ναίετ' ἀν' ἄκρα πόλεος, ἀγαθῶν μελεδήμονες ἔργων,[133]
> 4 χαίρετ'· ἐγὼ δ' ὑμῖν θεὸς ἄμβροτος, οὐκέτι θνητός
> πωλεῦμαι μετὰ πᾶσι τετιμένος, ὥσπερ ἔοικα,
> ταινίαις τε περίστεπτος στέφεσίν τε θαλείοις.
> πᾶσι δ' ἅμ' εὖτ' ἂν ἵκωμαι ἐς ἄστεα τηλεθάοντα,
> ἀνδράσιν ἠδὲ γυναιξί, σεβίζομαι·

O friends, who dwell in the great city of the yellow Akragas River, up on the heights of the city-center, caring for good deeds, greetings! I tell you, as an immortal god—no longer mortal—I come on my rounds, held in honor among all, just as I appear, crowned with ribbons and fresh garlands. Whenever I come to flourishing cities, I am revered by all together, men and women.

He claims both elevation and mobility, but rather than create an analogy with Zeus, he appears to join Zeus—a stance not unrelated to his philosophical system.[134] In fact, the attention-getting opening illustrates one

---

[131] Stehle 1996 studies the performer's self-presentation in this poem.

[132] Stesichoros also adopted an anti-Homeric stance in at least one poem, the *Palinode* (192 *PMGF*, where the testimonia are collected). He declares that Helen never went to Troy, thus canceling her mobility, and portrayed himself as recovered from the blindness that Helen inflicted when he said that she had gone. Since Homer was conventionally thought to have been blind, the performer's sightedness stood for his superior knowledge. Cf. Bergren 1983: 80–82 and 93n.44 on the connections.

[133] I have left out line 3, which was inserted from a separate source but is bracketed by Inwood, whom see *ad loc*.

[134] In what follows I take the opening as an address to the audience, but I wonder whether it was not rather addressed to the gods.

aspect of Empedokles' physical theory.[135] But, to protect him until he can reveal the grounds for his claim, it also creates distance between the performer's persona and the audience. If the poem was performed at Akragas, then the audience could construe his words to mean that others welcome him as a god, taking ὑμῖν (to you) as a dative of interest (I tell you) with πωλεῦμαι (I come on my rounds), while if he performed elsewhere the address to the citizens of the city Akragas would produce a fictional setting that would invite the audience to treat the persona as fictionalized as well. The technique is somewhat like that of Archilochos 98–99 W, discussed in Chapter 1.[136]

I have not taken up the other two long *Homeric Hymns*, the *Hymn to Aphrodite* and the *Hymn to Demeter*, in this chapter because both pose problems for the kind of analysis undertaken here.[137] The *Hymn to Aphrodite* does not use either an appeal to a local audience or the technique of compensatory validation that I have been examining. It includes a birth story in which the mother, Aphrodite, regrets her pregnancy but the father, Anchises, does not gain control of the child (though he will eventually), no cult is founded, and the whole episode takes place in Trojan territory. It is almost a parody of the birth story as cult *aition* or anchor of local identity.[138] Like the story of Aphrodite and Ares sung by Demodokos in the *Odyssey* (8.266–366), the poem has moved far away from the pole of efficacy toward the pole of entertainment and relies on forms of actualization, teasing and titillating its audience.[139] It could be performed anywhere but is too open to multiple interpretations to compete in ideological influence with more didactic poems. I have discussed gender relations in the poem and its appeal to audiences elsewhere.[140]

The *Homeric Hymn to Demeter* is a different issue. It is tied to a particular site, Eleusis, but its relationship to the mystery cult of Demeter and Persephone at Eleusis has not been fully clarified: the story appears to be both localized and Panhellenized.[141] Kevin Clinton, who has long argued

---

[135] Inwood 1992: 52–55.

[136] Xenophanes 8 W and Parmenides 1 DK both use mobility as an authorizing device. On Parmenides see Lesher 1994.

[137] See Clay 1989: 152–201 on the *Hymn to Aphrodite* and 202–65 on the *Hymn to Demeter*. I have passed over the Hesiodic *Catalogue of Women* as well because it is too fragmentary to reveal the speaker's stance it encoded, nor do we know anything about where it was performed. See West 1985b: 29–30 for description, 125–37 for a date ca. 580–520 when the whole heritage was being codified during the last stage of living epic.

[138] Cf. n. 30 above.

[139] See the Introduction for positioning of poems between efficacy and entertainment.

[140] Stehle 1990: 98–99. See Clay 1989: 267–70 on the consolidation of Zeus' rule in response to female challenge in both poems. She sees all the major *Homeric Hymns* as continuing the ideological work of the *Theogony* by assigning honors to the other gods within Zeus' order.

[141] Pausanias (10.38.11) comments about the *Naupaktika*, a lost epic, that it was composed

against a close connection between it and the Eleusinian mysteries, has recently suggested that the poem reflects the Thesmophoria (a Demeter festival celebrated by women) at Eleusis at a period before the mysteries had become prominent, although he also thinks of it as Panhellenized.[142] Helene Foley defends the connection with the Eleusinian mysteries and explains the deviations from local Eleusinian myth in the poem as concessions to nonlocal audiences in the process of Panhellenization.[143] Before studying the self-presentation of the bard, it will be necessary to investigate the relationship between the poem and the mysteries further and also to ask what effect the popularity of the mysteries had on the constitution of audiences.[144]

As remarked at the beginning of the chapter, not all bards thematized male identity as a strategy for claiming authority. Nor can one deduce that a poem was designed for a local audience simply because of the absence of an explicit authorizing strategy. But bards' Panhellenic stance could be supported by patriarchy because the latter provides the model for personal authority that organizes people and lands under a single all-embracing viewpoint. By signaling their own patriarchal authority, bards gained the symbolic stature to explicate the cosmos to an audience—and the same cosmos to all audiences. For male members of audiences, the exaggerated disparity in power of the two sexes and the symbolic male reproductive independence, represented as cosmic verities, must have replaced reflection of local interest as the source of satisfaction and ideological validation in these poems.

---

es gynaikas. Huxley 1969: 69 tentatively suggests that he might mean "for women" as well as "about women" and that it might have been for a festival of Ariadne at Naupaktos. On 68–73 he describes the epic, which included the story of Jason and had northwest Greek connections. To earn Pausanias' description the story must have emphasized women's roles, but we do not know enough about it to know whether it offered any kind of parallel to the *Hymn to Demeter*. Pausanias (9.31.5) uses the same description for the *Catalogue of Women*.

[142] Clinton 1992: 28–37. The defeat of Zeus in this poem is remarkable, although softened by the final solution. It must be accounted for in a study of the dynamics of performance.

[143] Foley 1994: 172–75, responding to Clinton's view that the poem was not connected with the Eleusinian Mysteries; 175–78, agreeing that it was Panhellenic in its intended audience.

[144] The *Homeric Hymn to Hermes* may be a better analogy than the *Hymn to Pythian Apollo* since it is strained between its Panhellenic perspective and the now-mysterious references to local cult (e.g., 121–36) that did not drop out because they are essential to the narrative.

CHAPTER FIVE

The Symposium

I

WE NOW MOVE to another well-attested location for performance, the symposium, or (eating and) drinking party. Here too men were the only performers, or better, the only performers whose discourse counted, for women (usually slave women) might be present as entertainers. Once again we must examine the setting and the function of performance before taking up the question of the gendering of the performer. Symposium groups were heterogeneous in their character and aims, so generalization is even more perilous than in talking about communal and bardic performance, but I will identify some shared characteristics. As always, my attention is on performers, so I assume situations in which the poetry was perceived as the utterance of the performer who sang or recited it. A performer might sing songs that he had learned from another, but so long as he adopted the words as his own and was understood to be doing so, the poetry provided him with a persona, however idealized or artificial it might be.[1] I will therefore refer to the poetry by its traditional authors without meaning to suggest that a poem had a unique singer or occasion or even that the poetry actually stems from these distinct composers with well-defined oeuvres.

The physical setting for symposia is well documented by archaeological remains of dining rooms, both in private houses and in public settings such as sanctuaries. There was a standard layout. The room was small; typically, along each of three walls were ranged two or three couches, on each of which two men might recline. One couch fewer occupied the fourth wall to allow room for a door. Seven- and eleven-couch arrangements are the commonest, meaning that fourteen or twenty-two men could share in a symposium.[2] Other numbers of couches are found (or suggested by the

---

[1] On the first person see Dover 1987, who demolishes the idea that archaic lyric is biography; Rösler 1985; Bowie 1986: 16–17. Slings 1990a: 1–14 gives a historical sketch of views and argues that the "I" is that of the performer (12), while the statements made by "I" may range between the fictional and the biographical. The former occur when the performer takes on the persona of someone he or she is not; the latter are those predicated of the singer in propria persona but can be true or false. Carey 1986: 66–67 remarks that there is no firm evidence that Archilochos ever took on a sustained fictional persona as opposed to a role; likewise Bowie 1986: 18. I think this is right.

[2] Bergquist 1990: 37.

dimensions of some rooms), but the standard range gives us the order of magnitude of a symposium group. Each couch had a low table in front of it. The krater (bowl for mixing wine) stood in the center, and wine-pourers, usually boys or young men, refilled the cups of the symposiasts.[3]

The symposium seems to have been the primary setting in which non-kin men met together socially.[4] It was the place for conviviality among *philoi* (friends), but also for meetings of *hetaireiai* (political groups or clubs), civic organizations, and officers' groups. It is distinguished by its small space and selective membership from public feasts, although these too sometimes had provision for breaking up into smaller groups.[5] Many sanctuaries that hosted public religious festivals had a series of dining rooms among the cult buildings.[6] Who used them is unknown; perhaps a group that wished to celebrate the festival together (apart from their families?) could reserve one for a fee.[7]

Among groups that met in symposia, we can distinguish dinner parties, institutionalized gatherings, and the unformalized self-defining interest group.[8] Examples of the first type are the parties described by Plato, Xenophon, and others. Those present are friends and perhaps see each other often this way, but they do not have an agenda beyond enjoyment of their friendship. Tyrants' circles must have masqueraded as this type. Examples of the second type are connected with the government or have an established civic identity. According to Plutarch (*Lykourgos* 12.3), for instance, the Spartan *syssitia,* or "messes," were divided into groups of about fifteen, each of which was supplied by its members independently. State guests were entertained at the *prytaneion* (town hall) at Athens.[9] Sappho praises her brother, who was a wine-pourer at the *prytaneion* of Mytilene

[3] On the atmosphere of the symposium, including celebration of boys' beauty, see Gentili 1988: 89–104. He discusses Anakreon in particular.

[4] The two most thorough investigations of the symposium as the locus of poetic performance are Reitzenstein 1970 and the essays in Vetta 1983c.

[5] Schmitt-Pantel 1990: 20–23 divides "rituals of commensality" into the banquet (connected with sacrifice and citizens as a group), *xenia* (hospitality), and the symposium, forms that coexist and coalesce. On 25 she asserts the continuity of public feast and symposium but ignores the problem of factions within the city.

[6] Bookidis 1990: 90 says that the sanctuary of Demeter and Persephone at Corinth had at least thirty dining rooms in the late fifth or early fourth c. Most sanctuaries had far fewer; cf. Bergquist 1990.

[7] Cooper and Morris 1990: 77–78 make it appear plausible that the elite, accustomed to reclining, were the ones accommodated in such rooms.

[8] There are various ways of categorizing types of symposia. Bergquist 1990: 37 speaks of private, civic, and ritual symposia. Murray 1990b: 5 identifies four "ideal types": religious festival, military common meal, public meal granted as an honor by the *polis,* and symposium for pleasure. Neither of these lists highlights the interest group or faction.

[9] Cooper and Morris 1990: 78 distinguish between the more democratic *prytanikon* (officials' quarters) where the *prytaneis* (officials) for the month dined seated and the *prytaneion* (town hall) where athletes and state guests reclined.

(203 *V*). Pausanias mentions (2.31.8) a building near the sanctuary of Apollo at Troizen called the "Booth of Orestes," where the descendants of those who purified Orestes dine on certain days. This must have been an aristocratic institution, for it implies a claim to heroic ancestry.[10] Pausanias seems to have been entertained at the *prytaneion* of Elis, for he gives a circumstantial account (5.15.11–12), while forbearing to transcribe the prayers and hymns the Elians used.

Somewhat different from either of these (while grading into them) is the type of symposium group for which some of the extant lyric and elegiac poetry seems to have been composed.[11] This third sort of group is neither ad hoc nor institutionalized but has a contentious agenda to promote, social or political. Its members cooperate in furthering one another's interests because they perceive those interests to be compatible. Alkaios' poetry gives evidence of addressing an organized group; he mentions his *hetairoi* (comrades) with whom he drinks and broods over politics.[12] Archilochos addresses others occupied by soldiering.[13] Unlike the other two groups, this type has a narrower or different set of values from those acceptable in the community as a whole.[14] The discourse that defines the group will

[10] Dining and drinking institutions seem to have been very common. Athenaios mentions a number of organizations and festivals: see for instance 4, 148f–149f for examples from Phigalea and Naukratis; Cooper and Morris 1990: 73–75, with bibliography.

[11] That short elegy had its home in the symposium is cogently argued by Bowie 1986: 13–21. Rösler 1980 argues that elliptical lyric like Alkaios' presupposes a closed group (33–45, esp. 37, where he sets out criteria for positing the *hetaireia* as the audience); Aloni 1981: 24–30 proposes a correlation between a poem's degree of linguistic affinity with epic and the broadness of its audience. About the setting for iambic poetry there is less consensus. West 1974: 32–37 suggests public festivals because a religious background can be traced in names and themes connected with it. I assume a closed setting, not necessarily the standard symposium, for the preserved iambic, which has shed ritual associations. As for Archilochos, Glaukos is the addressee in both elegiac 15 *W* and iambic 48.7 *W*. The name Periklees may also occur in both elegy and trimeter: see 13 and 16 *W* and 28.4 *W* (where -*lees* is found). Glaukos and Periklees were addressed in tetrameters also (131 and 124 respectively), a meter sometimes used for invective by Archilochos. The remark by Kritias (see below) that Archilochos practiced invective against his friends suggests that the same addressees were to be found in poems of both types. Cf. also Fowler 1987: 89 for different meters put to similar uses. Semonides uses iambic meter for both invective and gnomic poetry in the style of Theognis. Hipponax 115 *W* is an invective against a former *hetairos*, which suggests a setting in the symposium. Dover 1987: 97–105 argues against taking elegy and iambic as different genres in Archilochos' time.

[12] 129.16 *V* in a reference to oath-taking. Cf. Rösler 1980: 191–204 on this fragment. Podlecki 1984a: 62–82 discusses the interpretations of Lesbian politics offered by scholiasts. Alkaios was from Lesbos.

[13] E.g., 4, 5, 105, 114 *W*. Burnett 1983: Ch. 2; Aloni 1981: 31–48. Archilochos is associated with the islands Paros and Thasos.

[14] Murray 1990b: 7 remarks, "The *symposion* became in many respects a place apart from the normal rules of society, with its own strict code of honour . . . and its own willingness to establish conventions fundamentally opposed to those within the *polis* as a whole."

then be discourse marking its distinction from the community.[15] Archilochos expresses anticommunal sentiment (14 *W*):

Αἰσιμίδη, δήμου μὲν ἐπίρρησιν μελεδαίνων
οὐδεὶς ἂν μάλα πόλλ' ἱμερόεντα πάθοι.

Aisimedes, no one who worried about the censure of the people would enjoy very many delights.

Theognis describes the banquet as the setting in which his poetry will be sung in the future and makes disgusted political observations about the community.[16] Thucydides comments on the existence of disruptive aristocratic political groups called *hetaireiai* (clubs) at Athens.[17] In a study of Theognis in historical context, Thomas Figueira contrasts the symposium with the communal form of comedy:

> Thus, two ideologies existed in sixth-century Megara. For simplicity, let us call one democratic (or populist) and the other oligarchic, although these terms must not be given their Athenian valence. The social setting for the two ideologies varied as much as their content and generic medium. Elegy and oligarchic ideology appropriated the context of the symposium, while democratic ideology was expressed in a comic performance with its attendant religious activity.[18]

The Greek term *hetaireia* will serve here as an overall name for the symposium group as interest group, although in discussing the poetry I will use it only in connection with Alkaios.[19]

What characterizes all symposium groups, but the *hetaireia* most signifi-

---

[15] See Fisher 1989: 36–38 on the differences between Athenian symposia and the Spartan *syssitia*. For the tone of Spartan common meals, see Alkman 17 *PMGF* and Nannini 1988: 31–33 on its political and poetic symbolism.

[16] Banquet: 239–40. The Theognid corpus is a collection of brief songs under the name Theognis. Most of Book I contains political and social observation; on its teaching as symposium precept, see Edmunds 1988: 85–91. Cf. Donlan 1985: 237–39 for Theognis' recognition of the impossibility of replicating the bonds of friendship in relations with citizens at large.

[17] Thucydides 3.82.6. Connor 1971: 25–29 proposes that the *hetaireia* was the primary organization of political groups at Athens until the late fifth century. Calhoun 1913: 24–39 covers textual evidence for the characteristics of these "clubs."

[18] Figueira 1985: 139. The whole discussion of ideologies and of the attitudes implied in each genre toward distribution and consumption of food (128–43) is relevant to the conception of communal and symposiastic groups.

[19] Among poets Alkaios was demonstrably associated with a formal *hetaireia* (cf. n.12). How large it was is unknown; but rather than one set of men meeting in a symposium, one should probably imagine interconnecting groups who shared songs. Archilochos and his friends seem to have distinguished themselves by military orientation from others. The Theognid corpus embraces a variety of political stances.

cantly, is that they are held together by their own discourse.[20] A dinner party is a success if everyone leaves feeling warmed by the interchange of songs and talk. Institutional dining should promote mutual good will among those who are active in the city's government or have dealings with it; the symposium at the end of the *Lysistrata* turns the truce between Athenians and Spartans into fellowship (1225–1321). But the very existence of the *hetaireia* depends on its members' continuing to prize their *philia* (friendship) with one another above competing allegiances, for no external structure maintains it.[21] Each member must be persuaded that the goals of the group are his also. Each must therefore articulate his loyalty and his worthiness to be part of the group so that mutual trust is constantly reaffirmed. The interchange that gives each individual his turn as the focus of attention and weaves individuals together into a collective sustains the group (which is not to say that their actions outside the walls of the symposium are irrelevant). Singing and formalized modes of discourse, therefore, are common to all types of symposium, but especially useful to the *hetaireia*.[22] This kind of group is the strongest model one can use in considering the dynamics of performance in the symposium, for there the psychological efficacy of performance is most important, but what is true of it is generally true of symposium poetry.

A group defined by exchange of speech must be open to all within it and closed to those outside, traits that characterize the symposium. A symposium, whether party, institution, or meeting of the *hetaireia,* is by nature a closed occasion. A Spartan could join one of the *syssitia* only if all the

---

[20] Jarcho 1990: 37 stresses this: "[W]e can draw the conclusion that despite all the differences in the social surroundings of Archilochos, Sappho, and Theognis, their poetic 'I' arises from personal experience and is at the same time felt as a special communicative code that makes a social group truly homogeneous." (My translation.) Most 1982: 90 describes the symposium group as directing eros to those within the group and invective to those without.

[21] Donlan 1985, esp. 225–26: faithfulness is the key attribute of a friend, but in Theognis' eyes even it is dubious.

[22] The best description of the ideal symposium comes from an anonymous early Hellenistic elegy (*Adespota elegiaca* 27 *W*). It ignores song but pictures harmony rising from exchange of banter and moralizing speech (3–8):

> χρὴ δ', ὅταν εἰς τοιοῦτο συνέλθωμεν φίλοι ἄνδρες
> πρᾶγμα, γελᾶν παίζειν χρησαμένους ἀρετῆι,
> 5   ἥδεσθαί τε συνόντας, ἐς ἀλλήλους τε φ[λ]υαρεῖν
>   καὶ σκώπτειν τοιαῦθ' οἷα γέλωτα φέρειν.
> ἡ δὲ σπουδὴ ἐπέσθω, ἀκούωμέν [τε λ]εγόντων
>   ἐν μέρει· ἥδ' ἀρετὴ συμποσίου πέλεται.

It is proper, whenever we come together as friends for such a purpose, to laugh and joke while observing virtue, to enjoy being together, to banter with one another and mock in such a way as to rouse a laugh. Let seriousness follow, and let us listen to those who speak in turn; that is the virtue of a symposium.

current members agreed to admit him.[23] Alkibiades at the door of
Agathon's dining-room asks whether he can come in or should go away.[24]
Uninvited guests did come, but only as hangers-on of an invited guest;
Archilochos makes fun of one such.[25] Moreover, exchanges within the
symposium must often have been kept from wider circulation. Plutarch
again, speaking of the Spartan *syssitia,* says that boys were permitted to
come but that the eldest member of the *syssition* stood at the door as everyone entered, reminding them that no word should leave the room
(*Lykourgos* 12.8). That poetic discourse in the symposium was itself
"closed," coded so as to mean less to those outside the group, may explain
the allusiveness of some symposium poetry.[26] Through metaphor the
group creates a series of references to which it alone has the key, for having
secrets helps to define a group.[27]

The very organization of the room creates intimate interchange. All face
inward toward each other. Private conversations are difficult since everyone is within easy hearing distance.[28] Performance, whether sung or spoken, went by convention around the circle. In a famous passage Athenaios
describes the sequence of singing at a symposium (15, 694ab):

> There are three kinds of *skolia* (symposium songs), as Artemon of Kassandreia
> says in the second book of his work *On the Use of Books,* comprising all the songs
> sung in social gatherings. Of these the first kind was that which it was custom-
> ary for all to sing in chorus; the second was sung by all, to be sure, but in a
> regular succession, one taking it up after another; and the third kind, which
> came last of all in order, was that no longer sung by all the company, but by
> those only who enjoyed the reputation of being specially skilled at it, and in
> whatever part of the room they happened to be; hence because this method
> implied a kind of disorder . . . it was called the crooked song (*skolion*).[29]

Following this passage he gives twenty-five short songs, the "Attic
skolia," which must belong to the second category, songs sung by each in

[23] Plutarch, *Lykourgos* 12.9–11.
[24] Plato, *Symp.* 212e. Agathon instructs a slave to see who is at the door and send the
person away unless it is an intimate friend (212d).
[25] Archilochos 124b *W.*
[26] Nagy 1985: 24 speaks of the *ainos,* which "entails one code with at least two messages—
the true one for the intended audience and the false or garbled ones for all others." Cf. Nagy
1979: 237–42, esp. 241.
[27] Gentili 1988: 197–215; Nannini 1988: 8.
[28] Bergquist 1990: 39 describes sympotic space as having "the essential characteristic of a
visual and auditory coherence which includes all participants in a *symposion* and stresses
exchange of speech as part of sympotic atmosphere."
[29] Translation from Gulick 1927–41. Cf. Schol. Plato *Gorgias,* 451e, 133–34 Greene, for
similar information.

turn.[30] Likewise, in Plato's *Symposium* the speeches in praise of Love go around the room. Later, when the question what to do next comes up, Eryximachos suggests that each man in turn give a task to the one to the right of him (214c), and Socrates eventually interprets that to mean that each man should praise the one to the right of him (222e). Praises going around the room are the ideal symposium discourse.

Kritias 6 *W* (= 6 *DK*) contrasts Spartan and Lydian symposia. The Lydians started the habit (used by the Greeks) of drinking pledges to one another (5–7):

ἄγγεα Λυδὴ χεὶρ ηὖρ' Ἀσιατογενής,
καὶ προπόσεις ὀρέγειν ἐπιδέξια, καὶ προκαλεῖσθαι
ἐξονομακλήδην ὧι προπιεῖν ἐθέλει.

The Asian-born Lydian art discovered large cups and offering of toasts (going around) to the right and calling by name the one to whose health one wants to drink.

Mutual interchange of affection, we may imagine, knits the group together in spirit. Yet pledging leads to too much drinking, according to Kritias, whereas the Spartans drink only enough to lead their minds to cheer and (16):

εἴς τε φιλοφροσύνην γλῶσσαν μέτριόν τε γέλωτα.

. . .the tongue to cheerfulness and moderate laughter.

Overbalancing is one of the dangers that hang over a symposium; even the flow of good feeling can create excess.[31]

An evening's revelry could be in someone's honor: Pindar and Bacchylides wrote encomia to be performed at banquets; Plato's *Symposium* has Agathon's victory in the tragedy contest at the Lenaia as its occasion. But even so the one feted must share attention with others, as Agathon does. A fragment of a poem of Bacchylides for such an occasion gives a picture of the effects of wine and illustrates the reintegration into the group of the one who had been singled out (fr. 20B 1–16 *SM*):

---

[30] The *skolia* are 884–909 *PMG*, the last not an Attic *skolion*. Reitzenstein 1970: 3–44 studies the *skolia*, pointing out their allusions to known poetry and fable and their political implications. For an exhaustive study of the *skolia*, see Lambin 1986. Harvey 1955: 162–63 explains the contraction in the meaning of the term *skolion* from all symposium poetry to short generic pieces: as the skill and interest in after-dinner singing faded, the term came to be limited to the simple songs sung in turn.

[31] On moderation in Spartan drinking, see Fisher 1989. Warning songs about drinking too much include Anakreon 356b *PMG*, Xenophanes 1 *W*.

ὦ βάρβιτε, μηκέτι πάσσαλον φυλάσ[σων
ἑπτάτονον λ[ι]γυρὰν κάππαυε γᾶρυν·
δεῦρ’ ἐς ἐμὰς χέρας· ὁρμαίνω τι πέμπ[ειν
χρύσεον Μουσᾶν Ἀλεξάνδρωι πτερόγ

5   καὶ συμποσ[ίαι]σιν ἄγαλμ’ [ἐν] εἰκάδεσ[σιν,
εὖτε νέων ἁ[παλὸν] γλυκεῖ’ ἀνάγκα
σευομενᾶν κυλίκων θάλπησι θυμόν,
Κύπριδός τ’ ἐλπὶς ⟨δι⟩αιθύσσηι φρένας,

ἀμμειγνυμένα Διονυσίοισι δώροις·
10   ἀνδράσι δ’ ὑψοτάτω πέμπει μερίμνας·
αὐτίκα μὲν πολίων κράδεμνα λύει,
πᾶσι δ’ ἀνθρώποις μοναρχήσειν δοκεῖ·

χρυσῶι δ’ ἐλέφαντί τε μαρμαίρουσιν οἶκοι,
πυροφόροι δὲ κατ’ αἰγλάεντα πόντον
15   νᾶες ἄγουσιν ἀπ’ Αἰγύπτου μέγιστον
πλοῦτον· ὣς πίνοντος ὁρμαίνει κέαρ.

O lyre, no longer guard the peg or refrain from a seven-toned, clear voice.
Come to my hands. I am eager to send a golden wing of the Muses to Alexander,
an ornament for monthly symposia whenever sweet necessity warms the [ten-
der] hearts of youths, as the cups go swiftly around, and hope of Aphrodite
flutters minds as it mixes with the gifts of Dionysus. It sends men's ambitions
aloft; straightway one breaches the towers of cities and thinks that he will be sole
ruler over all humans; his house glitters with gold and ivory, grain-bearing ships
over the bright sea bring the greatest wealth from Egypt. Thus does the heart of
a drinker leap up.

Alexander son of Amyntas was king of Macedon.[32] The poem for Alexander is the "ornament" of the symposium, and the following lines address him. Yet the poem suggests that all the symposiasts will feel equal to
Alexander while drinking and pledging one another: "One thinks that he
will be sole ruler." An illusion, of course, but the poem excuses in advance
any breaches of the special respect due to him and offers him in exchange a
form of immortality: he will always be present when men pledge one
another.[33] By line 25 the subject is again general (ὁ τυχών). The poem
itself negotiates a special convivial relationship in which Alexander is at

[32] Pindar wrote an encomium for him also, 120–21 SM.
[33] Cf. Theognis 245–50: Kyrnos will be immortalized not "on horseback" but through
singing in the symposium. Nannini 1988: 70–80 sees in the line a rejection of epic and a
replacement of funeral monument by song. Cf. also Ibykos 151.47–48 SLG (= 282 Campbell 1991) for the singer immortalizing the addressee in song.

once singled out and made part of the company. Good fellowship is very fragile, as these poems indirectly testify.

Responsiveness among participants was also created through riddles and capping songs.[34] A number of riddles come down to us under the names of Kleoboulos and of Kleoboulina (1–3 *W*), sometimes said to be his daughter.[35] They are kennings, recherché ways of describing common objects. One of Kleoboulina's more charming kennings runs, "A dead donkey struck me with a horn-bearing shank on the ears." The object is a Phrygian flute.[36] The riddle sounds aggressive, as though a hostile act had been perpetrated, but when one learns its meaning, it turns out to refer to an instrument related to the one used in the symposium. Riddles are also found in Theognis. One unsolvable riddle (861–64) involves a female speaker who may be a free-lance courtesan.[37] Part of the joke may be the feminine "voice," first revealed in the last syllable of the second verse.[38]

Capping could be done by following someone's short song with another that used the same construction but changed the conceit, like two of the *skolia* in Athenaios: "Oh that I were an ivory lyre" and "Oh that I were pure gold."[39] Capping songs are found in the Theognid corpus, e.g., 332a–b and 333–34, and variations on known poems would be easy to produce. Another kind of capping is illustrated by the funny scene in Aristophanes' *Wasps* (1222–39), discussed in the Introduction, in which Bdelykleon tries to instruct his father, Philokleon, in how to behave at a symposium.[40] Bdelykleon several times begins a well-known *skolion*, to which Philokleon should supply a second line. Philokleon improvises outrageously when it is his turn, so it is impossible to tell whether the point was to sing the proper second line or to improvise, perhaps with a graceful compliment to the previous singer (since Philokleon's caps are insults). Either way, capping is a joking challenge that results in a collective production. Much of this kind of singing can be done off the cuff. M. L. West

[34] Athenaios 10, 448f quotes a passage from a comedy of Antiphanes that speaks of men proposing riddles to one another while drinking. For other games and entertainment at the symposium, see Lissarrague 1987: ch. 4.

[35] See Diogenes Laertios 1.89–93 for the "life" of Kleoboulos; West 1974: 17n.26 on Kleoboulina.

[36] 3 *W*, from Plutarch's *Symposium of the Seven Wise Men* 150e. The epithet "horn-bearing" refers to the curved piece at the lower end of a Phrygian flute, actually constructed from a horn. There is also a pun in the verb, which means "strike" but is used for playing an instrument.

[37] Van Groningen 1966 *ad loc.* He is not satisfied with the explanation (331) but rejects the proposed alternatives.

[38] A female speaker also occurs in Theognis 257–60 (a mare). West 1974: 17n.26 thinks that women performed in the symposium.

[39] 900–901 *PMG*. It is conjecture that these variants were used as caps, but a parallel is found in some of Theocritus' *Idylls*.

[40] Reitzenstein 1970: 24–29 and Vetta 1983a discuss this scene.

suggests that elegy was a favorite meter for symposium poetry because it was easy to sing and to use in improvisations.[41]

All of these forms, the singing in turn, praising, propounding, and answering riddles, the new turn on the known song, are designed to keep the discourse collective, while at the same time highlighting each person's contribution. The participants must constantly respond to each other, but the full literary forms (riddle and answer, song and cap, variant heard against the known song) require the work of more than one contributor. One could say that ideally the whole symposium should create one inter-textual web.

The participants were not expected to be self-effacing or spend all their energy in praises of others. In Aristophanes' mock party, a man was expected to do some boasting, but of an unaggressive nature. Thus Bdelykleon asks his father what most manly exploit done in youth, a hunting expedition or a torch race, he would recount while drinking with foreigners (1197–1204). There are boasts in Theognis, but boasts attuned to the speaker's relationship to the group, such as that he has never betrayed a friend (529–30), that his character is trustworthy gold (447–52), that he wishes to aid friends and hurt enemies (869–72). In all of these examples, the boasting furthers the symposium goal of good fellowship.[42] According to Plutarch (*Lykourgos* 12.6) the Spartans enjoyed "jeering" in fun as their symposium talk; they were hardy folk, but there was a tradition of badinage, especially among the young.[43]

The formalized communication at the symposium was designed to ward off the very real danger that conviviality would collapse and the group break up. The *hetaireia* of course was threatened by external pressures. Politicians changed their allegiances. Hipponax (or Archilochos) and Alkaios both rail against erstwhile friends who have betrayed oaths.[44] In Alkaios' case he is speaking about Pittakos, who went on to become a lawgiver for Mytilene and relieve the city of factional fighting. What Archilochos and Alkaios imply is that their groups tried to bind themselves by oath more securely even than fellowship in the symposium could do.[45]

---

[41] West 1974: 17–18. See 14–18 for a description of sympotic elegy, including insult poems and capping games.

[42] Aristotle *Art of Rhetoric* 1418b advises a speaker to put boasting and opposition into the mouth of another, citing Archilochos 19 and 122 *W* as examples.

[43] On jesting in Spartan education, see David 1989: 3–4; Reitzenstein 1970: 26–27n.2 for other references. Hermes in the *Homeric Hymn to Hermes* 55–56 tries out improvisations on his newly invented lyre just as "young men at feasts make mocking innuendos."

[44] Hipponax 115 *W*; Alkaios 129 *V*.

[45] Calhoun 1913: 34–39 discusses the oaths, initiations, and secrecy by which club members bound themselves together. Trumpf 1973 sees an old connection between oath taking and drinking: participants sealed their oath by drinking from a common cup.

Even so, language could not hold them together.[46] Theognis bemoans the choice of all too many men for riches or power over the friendship of the good. Herodotus' story (1.59.3–1.63.2) of the shifting alliances among Megakles, Lykourgos, and Peisistratos in sixth-century Athens illustrates the political milieu in which the symposium group tried to retain members' loyalties.

But danger threatened from within also, from perceived insults and sudden quarrels. Again Theognis is a good witness; he gives advice on running a symposium which grades into a diatribe against drunkenness and ends with the precept that everyone should address the company at large (491–96, also attributed to Euenos):

> ἀνίκητος δέ τοι οὗτος,
>
> ὃς πολλὰς πίνων μή τι μάταιον ἐρεῖ.
>
> ὑμεῖς δ' εὖ μυθεῖσθε παρὰ κρητῆρι μένοντες,
>
> ἀλλήλων ἔριδας δὴν ἀπερυκόμενοι,
>
> 495 εἰς τὸ μέσον φωνεῦντες, ὁμῶς ἑνὶ καὶ συνάπασιν·
>
> χοὕτως συμπόσιον γίνεται οὐκ ἄχαρι.

But that man, notice, is unconquered who in drinking many (cups) says nothing thoughtless. You, too, speak well as you linger around the mixing-bowl, long staving off quarrels from one another, addressing the company at large, one and all at the same time; thus the symposium is not without joy.

Theognis worries about quarrels, for which he uses the sharp word ἔρις, but sees danger if the participants even carry on separate conversations, for collectivity will be lost.[47] The illusions fostered by wine according to Bacchylides' poem to Alexander (quoted above) could easily be punctured. In another poem Theognis demands that his friend recognize his temperament and bear with him even when he is being difficult (97–100). Alkaios laments strife among the members of his audience (70 V). Bdelykleon predicts, after his father's first insulting cap, that he will perish from the shouting if he does that; Philokleon answers with another insulting ditty.[48] Demosthenes mentions two instances in which one man killed another at a party because he thought he had been insulted.[49]

---

[46] Murray 1990a: 153 and 157–58 points out that Andokides (1.67) explained the profanation of the Eleusinian mysteries in 415 BCE as a *pistis*, an illegal act that a group engaged in to seal their trust, since any of them could denounce the others.

[47] Slater 1990 discusses ancient advice on symposium behavior; bad behavior includes quarrels, arrogance, and force. For *eris* in a civic context, see Solon 4.38 *W*.

[48] Philokleon sings an excerpt from a song of Alkaios (141 V) denouncing the tyrant Pittakos (?) in order to characterize Kleon.

[49] 21 *Meidias* 71–73. The second instance appears at first (72) to be a public meal (*koinēi*),

Because it depended on consensus, a *hetaireia* was always fragile, a structure of muted competition and shaky alliance. Each participant presented himself to a group that needed to feel his loyalty and had to be convinced that he was worth their loyalty.[50] To achieve psychological efficacy performance should, ideally, further the harmony of the group but give favorable impression of the speaker.[51] The problem for the performer was to pose himself as a compelling presence while not seeming to elevate himself above the others. Before turning to the ways in which performers presented gendered identities in their songs, I want to show how three poems achieve this effect.

A common strategy used by quite different poems is to posit an "other" against which the symposium group can measure its pleasure and companionableness.[52] For instance, the *skolia* honoring Harmodios and Aristogeiton were popular at Athens. They create a unifying discourse by giving the performer an opportunity to adopt a conventional stance. Athenaios preserves four variations, one of which runs (893 *PMG*):

> ἐν μύρτου κλαδὶ τὸ ξίφος φορήσω
> ὥσπερ Ἁρμόδιος καὶ Ἀριστογείτων
> ὅτε τὸν τύραννον κτανέτην
> ἰσονόμους τ᾽ Ἀθήνας ἐποιησάτην.

I will carry my sword in a branch of myrtle, just as Harmodios and Aristogeiton did when they slew the tyrant and made Athens a place of equality under the law.[53]

---

but is clearly a closed dinner (73); see MacDowell 1990 *ad loc.* In 72 Demosthenes describes hybris as an attitude; the real insult lies not in being struck a blow but in the air with which the attacker does it.

[50] Of course symposium poetry was also meant to entertain, and songs that were amusing or catchy would be effective without any of the special qualities that I discuss below.

[51] Speech itself was potentially suspect, as Theognis points out (979–82):

> μή μοι ἀνὴρ εἴη γλώσσηι φίλος, ἀλλὰ καὶ ἔργωι·
> 980   χερσίν τε σπεύδοι χρήμασί τ᾽, ἀμφότερα·
> μηδὲ παρὰ κρητῆρι λόγοισιν ἐμὴν φρένα θέλγοι,
> ἀλλ᾽ ἔρδων φαίνοιτ᾽ εἴ τι δύναιτ᾽ ἀγαθόν.

May a man not be friendly to me (just) in word, but in deed also; may he be ready with his hands and his money both; and may he not bewitch my mind with words beside the wine bowl but show by his actions whether he is capable of anything good.

[52] Contrast the visual technique of mirroring the symposium back to itself that Lissarrague 1987, esp. Ch. 7, studies.

[53] Lambin 1986: 262–65 thinks the poem has an obscene second meaning: the sword is a phallus and "myrtle" refers to female genitals.

The person who proclaims his partisanship thus is making a boast that every other Athenian would also be prepared to make. The "I" is not disjunctive; the singer is rather announcing his adherence to prevailing ideology. The term ἰσόνομος (equal under the law) is a political catchword that sets itself in opposition to the tyrant, the "other" against whom the singer arms. The tyrant is the perfect opposite of the symposium group because he is isolated, authoritarian, and hated. By choosing a figure that all present (conventionally, at least) would agree to fight, these songs can superimpose an appearance of political unity on those whose political views might in fact vary.[54] It is with a "Harmodios and Aristogeiton" song that Bdelykleon begins his abortive education of his father.[55]

Hipponax (or Archilochos) makes life among foreigners a vivid and horrifying alternative to participation in the symposium group. In this poem one who broke his oath is imaginatively cast out. The quoted excerpts give the flavor (Hipponax 115 *W*, 4–9, 14–16):

[   ]

   κύμ[ατι] πλα[ζόμ]ενος·

5   κἂν Σαλμυδ[ησσ]ῶι γυμνὸν εὐφρονε[

   Θρήϊκες ἀκρό[κ]ομοι

   λάβοιεν—ἔνθα πόλλ' ἀναπλήσαι κακὰ

   δούλιον ἄρτον ἔδων—

   ῥίγει πεπηγότ' αὐτόν· . . .

14   ταῦτ' ἐθέλοιμ' ἂν ἰδεῖν,

   ὅς μ' ἠδίκησε, λ[ὰ]ξ δ' ἐπ' ὁρκίοις ἔβη,

   τὸ πρὶν ἑταῖρος [ἐ]ών.

[   ] driven adrift in the wave; and may the high-haired Thracians with kindly intent (?) capture him naked [   ] at Salmydessos—where may he have full measure of evils as he eats slave's bread—stiff with frost. . . . Thus I would wish to see him who did me injustice and trampled on oaths, though he was previously a comrade (*hetairos*).

He who betrays his allegiance deserves to suffer the opposite of all the symposium is. Isolation is a prominent leitmotif of the poem: he should be

---

[54] Reitzenstein 1970: 27 cites an Athenian law against singing the Harmodios song "for the worse," which shows that it had political symbolism.

[55] See Reitzenstein 1970: 22–23 on the variants. He views the collection of Attic *skolia* as reflecting aristocratic circles after the Persian Wars (14–15). Vetta 1983a finds a more differentiated politics implied in the choice of *skolia* here. Insofar as the *skolia* became identified with a particular group (e.g., aristocratic, anti-Spartan), they would be unifying over a much smaller range of political positions than I have described.

cold and naked, lying like a dog on the beach (11–13). The poem fantasizes a situation that would equalize this man's circumstances to his character. The violent imagery also unites singer and audience in aggression directed outward. The sense of being united is given tremendous charge by this emotional flinging of the betrayer out into the cold.

The symposium group can be buttressed by suggesting that it is the defense against the pains and problems that exist for members elsewhere. Mimnermos, a seventh-century poet from Smyrna, is a subtle practitioner of this art. In 1 *W* he contrasts youthful love with the desolation of old age:

> τίς δὲ βίος, τί δὲ τερπνὸν ἄτερ χρυσῆς Ἀφροδίτης;
>   τεθναίην, ὅτε μοι μηκέτι ταῦτα μέλοι,
> κρυπταδίη φιλότης καὶ μείλιχα δῶρα καὶ εὐνή,
>   οἷ' ἥβης ἄνθεα γίνεται ἁρπαλέα·
> 5 ἀνδράσιν ἠδὲ γυναιξίν· ἐπεὶ δ' ὀδυνηρὸν ἐπέλθῃ
>   γῆρας, ὅ τ' αἰσχρὸν ὁμῶς καὶ κακὸν ἄνδρα τιθεῖ,
> αἰεί μιν φρένας ἀμφὶ κακαὶ τείρουσι μέριμναι,
>   οὐδ' αὐγὰς προσορῶν τέρπεται ἠελίου,
> ἀλλ' ἐχθρὸς μὲν παισίν, ἀτίμαστος δὲ γυναιξίν·
> 10 οὕτως ἀργαλέον γῆρας ἔθηκε θεός.

What life is there, what delight is there, without golden Aphrodite? May I die when these things no longer move me, secret love-making, honeyed gifts, and bed, such as make up the rapt peak of youth for men and women. But when painful old age comes on, which makes a man both ugly and worthless, evil cares continually wear away at his mind, nor does he feel joy seeing the light of the sun, but he is hateful to boys and an object of scorn to women. Thus grievous did the god make old age.

On the page the poem seems sad, but the optatives make the singer's loss of interest in love remote. At the same time, by his voice the singer gives warmth and life to the song, belying the possibility his text raises. In the second half of the poem, old age is described in terms that set it in opposition to the symposium group.[56] An old man is "hateful to boys and an object of scorn to women," but the symposiasts sit surrounded by friends, attended by boys pouring wine, perhaps accompanied by *hetairai* (courtesans).[57] The old man is the "other" that participation in the symposium keeps at bay. The song draws the group together, by its reminder of the fate of being unwanted, but makes each man feel affirmed in his youth and

---

[56] Cf. Theognis 973–78, where the singer contrasts death with the pleasures of the symposium and determines to enjoy the latter while possible. Likewise 983–88 urges enjoyment on the grounds that youth is brief.

[57] Vase-paintings show women at symposia. See Keuls 1985: Ch. 6.

desirability by his presence at the party. The melancholy is contradicted but remains as an undertone that mutes aggressiveness by suggesting that loss of fellowship leads to the futility of feeble old age.

The popularity of nautical images for the symposium may stem from the feeling that on a sea voyage everyone's fate is connected, whether they sink or stay afloat. If the group comprises the rowers, then everyone must row in time or the oars will tangle. Or the group finds common harbor from separate trials at sea. William Slater has traced a metaphor complex of Dionysus coming over the sea to bring illusionary wealth.[58] In addition, the drinkers may be afloat in wine that flows as freely as the waves. Archilochos, Alkaios, and Pindar all used ships and sailing as images of the symposium.[59]

Tyrant, slavery among the Thracians, old age, the threat of the sea all in different ways affirm the group by contrast. They have in common the proposition that the alternative to the symposium is isolation and desolation. Thus each song induces its audience to identify pleasure and security with their present company. At the same time each poem stages its performer as the one feeling the emotion to be induced in the others. The others catch up the singer's mood, helped by the music and the tonalities the singer gives to the words. So each singer adopts a persona whose feelings are sharply drawn and in conveying it to others can feel his own presence in the group validated.

II

With this sense of the psychological efficacy of symposium poetry, it is time to turn to the issue of gender representation. Gender imagery is a powerful source of emotion, yet use of it goes to the heart of the tension created by the symposium. The aggressive, individualistic posture admired in men and identified with masculinity meant that self-representation as "male" among equals could be provocative. To boast of being a man might convey the subtext "more man than you." A man who bragged of sexual conquests portrayed himself apart from his fellows, as well as inviting comparisons. Yet masculinity was very much at issue; some *hetaireiai* were committed to common military action, and in all groups an ineffectual man could shame the others by association. Inevitably, symposium performers found a strategy for representing themselves as men by portraying themselves in relation to women. They neither adopted female identity nor positioned themselves as vanquishers of female forces, unlike the male performers already observed. Their

---

[58] Slater 1976. For nautical images on vases, see Lissarrague 1987: Ch. 6.
[59] Archilochos 4 *W*; Alkaios 73 *V*; Pindar fr. 124 *SM* (a sympotic song).

method in this setting is one that I shall call disconnection from women.[60] Through it they give their masculine identity a particular character without constructing it against other men.

A very simple way to emphasize shared masculinity is to use women as the symposium's "other," like the tyrant, Thracians, or old age. Archilochos does this in one poem (13 *W*):

κήδεα μὲν στονόεντα Περίκλεες οὔτέ τις ἀστῶν
μεμφόμενος θαλίης τέρψεται οὐδὲ πόλις·
τοίους γὰρ κατὰ κῦμα πολυφλοίσβοιο θαλάσσης
ἔκλυσεν, οἰδαλέους δ' ἀμφ' ὀδύνῃς ἔχομεν
5   πνεύμονας. ἀλλὰ θεοὶ γὰρ ἀνηκέστοισι κακοῖσιν
ὦ φίλ' ἐπὶ κρατερὴν τλημοσύνην ἔθεσαν
φάρμακον. ἄλλοτε ἄλλος ἔχει τόδε· νῦν μὲν ἐς ἡμέας
ἐτράπεθ', αἱματόεν δ' ἕλκος ἀναστένομεν,
ἐξαῦτις δ' ἑτέρους ἐπαμείψεται. ἀλλὰ τάχιστα
10   τλῆτε, γυναικεῖον πένθος ἀπωσάμενοι.

Periklees, no one of the citizens or the city either will blame our groans and laments while delighting in festivity.[61] For a wave of the much-sounding sea has washed away such men, and we have lungs swollen in grief. But still, friend, the gods have made strong endurance the drug for incurable ills. Different men suffer this at different times; now it has turned our way and we groan at the bloody wound, but again it will shift to others. So bear up, this minute, pushing womanly grief away.

In the first lines the performer says that citizen and city will not blame the addressee for grieving. Periklees is the addressee, but he need not have been present; the real audience is the group, as indicated by the second-person plural at the end. A fictional or absent addressee allows the performer to take on the role of advisor or rebuker.[62] Then first-person

---

[60] For an illuminating modern parallel, see Stewart 1989. He describes Gypsy men's "celebrations," in which men gather to drink and sing in response to an event like a departure. Their competitive egalitarianism gives way to an attitude of respect for each; songs create a sense of unity; and the men contrast their wives negatively with their "brothers." The songs are more efficacious than entertaining; Stewart remarks (81) that they may seem "repetitive, even dull" to an outsider. His final analysis (95–98) is similar to the dynamic of the symposium as I describe it; cf. esp. 96: "As brothers, without wives, the Rom [i.e., Gypsy] men represent their reproduction through drinking and then singing 'true speech.'"

[61] The distich is ambiguous: either no one will blame while feasting or no one will feast (and thereby blame). Kamerbeek 1961: 2–3 argues for attaching the negative only to "blame."

[62] Rösler 1980: 181–85 discusses second-person polemic and shows that a poem could include address to a hostile absent person. Other special effects could be achieved by address to an absent figure also.

plurals associate the speaker in the addressee's grief, while proposing endurance. In the last line the performer switches suddenly to the second-person plural imperative τλῆτε (endure), followed immediately by γυναικεῖον πένθος (womanly grief). His own shedding of grief is enacted by shifting it onto women, with the suggestion that though the city does not blame grief, he will.[63] The gendering of grief genders the speaker, who shakes it off and gives his hearers an incentive to follow him in a return to "taking pleasure in cheer."

Here too belong sneering references to enemies' lack of manhood.[64] Anakreon is quoted as referring to a bridal-chamber where (7 W):

κεῖνος οὐκ ἔγημεν ἀλλ' ἐγήματο.

That man didn't screw but was screwed.

And a biting little portrait of an enemy as having become a kept woman, so to speak, also comes from Anakreon. A dirty ragpicker and scoff-law has changed his lifestyle (388.10–12 PMG):[65]

10   νῦν δ' ἐπιβαίνει σατινέων χρύσεα φορέων καθέρματα

     †παῖς Κύκης† καὶ σκιαδίσκην ἐλεφαντίνην φορεῖ

     γυναιξὶν αὔτως ⟨ ⟩.

. . . now he rides in (ladies') carriages wearing golden earrings, the child of Kuka (?), and carries an ivory parasol like women.

His success depends on giving up masculinity. The insult perhaps has a double point, for some symposiasts luxuriated in delicate finery. Athenian vases sometimes show men with full beards in what appears to be women's dress, usually in a procession or *kōmos* (revel). These are not fully understood, though they have been strikingly explained as images of controlled exploration of the realm of the other.[66] Gender identity was a live issue for symposiasts; therefore, in some places and times it could be played with, modified by a Dionysiac release.

Some songs in which gender codes are used to position the speaker are more complex. A singer often presented himself as an idealized masculine figure by portraying his separation from women, using women to represent status, kin-networks and community, or sexual partners. Being cut off from these, the singer is both independent and attached to his male companions. The singer can thus depict the group also as a "masculine"

---

[63] Cf. 11 W, where Archilochos rejects crying in favor of festivity as a reaction to grief.

[64] Cf. the Introduction and Stehle 1994 on Timokreon 727 PMG as a poem of sexual insult.

[65] On this poem see Brown 1983: 5–15, esp. 14–15 on the implication that Artemon is now a pathic.

[66] Frontisi-Ducroux and Lissarrague 1990, with illustrations.

alternative to family or community or a "masculine" substitute for emotional satisfaction from women. Women are not necessarily painted in negative terms; they may be described as attractive but unavailable. It is no accident that the strongest forms of this stance are found in Archilochos and Alkaios, for whom the circle of friends was the focus of active life.[67]

In one of his exile poems, Alkaios uses a tableau of women to create a self-portrait that also reflects on the symposium group (130B 1–20 *V*):[68]

> ἀγνοις . . σβιότοις . . ις ὁ τάλαις ἔγω
> ζώω μοῖραν ἔχων ἀγροϊωτίκαν
> ἰμέρρων ἀγόρας ἄκουσαι
> καρυ[ζο]μένας ὦ Ἀγεσιλαῖδα
>
> 5 καὶ β[ό]λλας· τὰ πάτηρ καὶ πάτερος πάτηρ
> κα⟨γ⟩γ[ε]γήρασ' ἔχοντες πεδὰ τωνδέων
> τὼν [ἀ]λλαλοκάκων πολίταν
> ἔγ[ω ἀ]πὺ τούτων ἀπελήλαμαι
>
> φεύγων ἐσχατίαισ', ὡς δ' Ὀνυμακλέης
> 10 ὠθάναιος ἐοίκησα λυκαιχμίαις
> φεύγων τὸν πόλεμον·[69] στάσιν γὰρ
> πρὸς κρ . [   ] . οὐκ †ἄμεινον† ὀννέλην·
>
> [   ] μακάρων ἐς τέμ[ε]νος θέων
> ἐοι[   ] με[λ]αίνας ἐπίβαις χθόνος
> 15 χλι . [   ]ν συνόδοισί μ' αὔταις
> οἴκημι κ[ά]κων ἔκτος ἔχων πόδας,
>
> ὄππαι Λ[εσβί]αδες κριννόμεναι φύαν
> πώλεντ' ἐλκεσίπεπλοι, περὶ δὲ βρέμει
> ἄχω θεσπεσία γυναίκων
> 20 ἴρα[ς ὀ]λολύγας ἐνιαυσίας

. . . wretched I, I live having a place in the fields, longing to hear the assembly announced, Agesilaides, and the council. What my father and father's father have held into old age among these citizens who do each other wrong, from that I am driven, a fugitive at the margins, and like Onomaclees the Athenian I have made a lair, a wolf-man, fleeing the war; for it is not more noble (?) to get rid of

---

[67] For Alkaios, see Fränkel 1975: 188–99; Burnett 1983: 107–205. Rösler 1980 is the most thorough study. On Archilochos, see Burnett 1983: 15–97; Fränkel 1975: 132–51; Aloni 1981; Miralles and Pòrtulas 1983 (which is speculative).

[68] Voigt divides 130 *LP* into two poems (A and B) at line 16.

[69] Lines 10 and 11 incorporate the reading of a new papyrus fragment (*pap. Oxy.* 3711); see Haslam 1986: 117, 123–24.

faction against [   ];[70] [   ] to the sanctuary of the blessed gods
[   ] stepping on the black earth [   ] at gatherings themselves,[71] I live keeping my feet out of troubles where the Lesbian *parthenoi* with trailing robes parade up and down, being judged for their beauty, and the awesome sound of the
yearly sacred cry of the *gynaikes* fills the air. . . .[72]

Driven from his ancestral possessions, living like a wolf-man (?), the
singer bemoans his fate.[73] Unfortunately his explanatory summary on
war and faction is lacunose, but he seems to connect his situation with
staying alive in order to continue political strife (11–12). When he expands
on the description of his surroundings in the second half of the poem, it
seems that he has taken refuge in a sanctuary where Lesbian women
gather. This could be the sanctuary of Zeus, Hera, and Dionysus, common to all the Lesbians, although nothing specific indicates it.[74] The last
stanza (21–24) is too fragmentary to read but contained a question about
the gods' plans, and perhaps a first-person plural verb as the last word of
the poem.

If the song was performed in the symposium, the singer was of course
not actually lurking in the sanctuary.[75] The singer adopts a setting appropriate to first-person lament in order to give immediacy to the idea of
exile.[76] The *hetaireia* is not referred to, for the first half of the poem contrasts exile with political activity in the city. However, the isolated life of
the fugitive makes an effective "other" that should draw the group together. The technique is like Mimnermos' in that the projection of an
alternative makes the present company seem more precious. However,
whereas the singer of Mimnermos 1 *W* could cancel the despondency by

[70] I follow Page 1955 *ad loc.*, who suggests οὐ κάλλιον for the corrupt οὐκ ἄμεινον. If his
suggestion is kept with the new reading, the difference between "war" and "faction" must be
significant. Lloyd-Jones and Lefkowitz 1990: 54 contrast conventional warfare and guerrilla
tactics.

[71] I omit the μ' in this phrase since it is unconstruable. See Page 1955 *ad loc.*

[72] The text does not specify *parthenoi*. I assume that *parthenoi* would be the ones judged on
beauty and that they balance the *gynaikes* who follow.

[73] The word translated "wolf-man" is not otherwise attested except in Hesychios (with
that meaning), and its case and meaning are open to doubt. The nominative "wolf-
spearman" is tentatively proposed by Haslam 1986: 123–24. Lloyd-Jones and Lefkowitz
1990: 53–54 suggest a dative plural meaning "wolf-battles," i.e., guerrilla warfare. See Porro
1992: 23n.1 for further bibliography, although I have not adopted her suggestion.

[74] Alkaios describes it in 129.1–9 *V*, where he also refers to it as "this sanctuary" and prays
for an end to exile, implying that he is sheltering there.

[75] He may have been in exile. A scholion on 114 *V* refers to Alkaios' "first exile," indicating that there was more than one (Page 1955: 179). Cf. the previous note: both 129 and 130B
may have been composed in exile, but the specific situations portrayed are probably fictional.

[76] Rösler 1980: 273–75 treats the poem as a poetic letter. His operating assumption that the
poems reflect their setting with immediacy forces him to accept the distance between speaker
and audience in the poem as real.

his warmth, the singer of this song should use a disconsolate tone. His self-presentation would then contrast jarringly with his actual physical presence to his audience, an effect that would increase his psychological remoteness from the listeners and make the idea of isolation palpable.

Further, the singer's first hint of the source of his troubles comes in lines 6–7: "these citizens who harm one another." Page remarks that this is "the only clear example in the Lesbians of the pronoun ὅδε [this, these] used to denote persons not present in the speaker's company."[77] I wonder, though, whether under the cover of his fictional setting the performer could not gesture toward his audience. If the singer is conjuring up a picture of isolation in exile, he may be reminding his audience of the potential consequences of strife among themselves, for then each would be truly alone (if a group is in exile together) or more vulnerable to being exiled (if the group is not in fact in exile). He also implies that he is the only one left to persist in holding out for his vision of social order, and without support he is being hunted down. The poem is less logical than evocative, since the "citizens" are right there to point at and women come to the sanctuary, while the performer nevertheless portrays himself as living in animal solitude. The isolation portrayed is really psychological, and the singer's first-person projection of the alternative to unity is more effective than any harangue.

The last two stanzas of the poem describe the sanctuary and the activities of the women in whose vicinity the speaker locates himself. The women's ritual of judging beauty and their religious cries, substituting for the call to assembly and the deliberations of the council, increase his portrayal of alienation.[78] Anne Burnett proposes that the poem is a satiric self-portrait in which the speaker progressively undermines his manliness in order to express his shame. The ultimate stage of self-denigration is the speaker's hiding in the company of women, the opposite of a soldier. "[Exile] has taken his function and his class and his pride from him, and he has lost not just the city of the herald's cry, not just the honours that his forefathers knew, but his ferocity and his masculine identity."[79]

His self-portrait is not flattering. Yet the women receive a full stanza of vivid description, too much to account for simply as calling attention to the singer's shame. The Homeric and religious language that delineates them is too impressive. The two are starkly juxtaposed: a wolflike man living "at the margin" beyond civilized life shares the picture with a collective of women celebrating the traditional round of religious observances (perhaps in the "common" sanctuary shared by all Lesbians). Women to-

[77] Page 1955: 204.
[78] Rösler 1980: 283–84 makes this point, adducing the segregation of the sexes that seems to have been pronounced on Lesbos.
[79] Burnett 1983: 180. I do not see him as hiding *among* the women.

gether in ritual, song, and dance were an image of the ideally harmonious community, as we have seen in previous chapters, so here two extremes meet. What would the group of listeners make of it?

How the listener would construe the scene would depend on his feelings about the singer. In an audience of friends suffering from disagreement the singer would draw the listeners to himself by the poignancy of his self-portrayal. At the same time, the picture of the women contained in it reflects the ideal of the symposium in a mirror image: they form a group that is possessed of inner accord. If the women's harmony can be transferred to the singer's group, the group will be more fit to continue the struggle. Even as he creates himself as the lone wolf, emphasizing his character by contrast with the women, he also presents the women as an alluring image of collective purpose that has escaped the *hetaireia,* or has at least been lost to him with exile.

An audience less committed to the singer and his program might detect other resonances. A "wolf" skulking in the same sanctuary with the women makes them seem frighteningly vulnerable. It is not that the speaker gives notice of any intention to attack them but that they lack protection against aggression. If the women represent the community in its ordinary, ritual, and (re)productive life, then the meeting of these two extremes says something about the deleterious effects of the current political situation for both sides: the fighters (in whose number the speaker is) find themselves fugitive, barred from civic participation, and the community is left without protectors. The parts that make up a functioning community are severed and come to share the same space as totally unrelated, noncommunicating entities. In this sense the poem is addressed to the whole city and combines threat, accusation, defense, and plea. How it might have been conveyed to unsympathetic groups we can only guess.

More often symposium poetry treats marriage and wives as that from which the singer is disconnected. The ordinary relationships that bind men to the community are thus contrasted with the singer's undivided loyalty to the *hetaireia.* This theme has many manifestations, from the complaints of Theognis to the invective of Archilochos. In a simple example, Theognis (183–92) contrasts men who value money with men who appreciate good birth. Among the former a good (i.e., well-born) man is willing to marry a bad daughter of a bad father if she has a good dowry, and a woman is willing to be wife to a rich bad man: "wealth confuses birth" (190). The latter, men who value good birth, are by implication the performer's fellow symposiasts, for he addresses Kyrnos (191) as part of a sympotic educational program (cf. 31–38).[80] Preferring money and pre-

[80] On Kyrnos as representative of both the community and the group of friends, see Nagy 1985: 53–56. Theognis' poetry strives at times to stand in for community poetry in prescribing juridical norms.

ferring birth are aligned with marriage and symposium respectively. The effect is not logical, for men who value birth should presumably marry also, but the silence in the poetry about proper marriages leaves the impression that only in the symposium is an alternative to bad marrying behavior found.[81]

Alkaios also sets marriage and the symposium group into opposition. As in Theognis, marriage is an example of opportunistic politics. By marrying into the Penthilidai, one of the noble families of Mytilene, Pittakos gave him an opening; Alkaios takes the opportunity and makes the act of rejecting the *hetaireia* for a marriage, like oath-breaking, a paradigm of faithlessness.[82] The best-preserved poem in which the contrast is found is both fragmentary and complex, for it also speaks of strife among the members of Alkaios' own audience. This poem, like 130B *V,* reveals in the place of the opposite an inverted mirror of what the symposium should be (70 *V*):

[   ]

π[ ]τωι τάδ᾽ εἴπην ὀδ . υ[

ἀθύρει πεδέχων συμποσίω[

βάρμος, φιλώνων πεδ᾽ ἀλεμ[άτων

5   εὐωχήμενος αὔτοισιν ἐπα[

κῆνος δὲ παώθεις Ἀτρεΐδα[ν

δαπτέτω πόλιν ὡς καὶ πεδὰ Μυρσί[λ]ῳ[

θᾶς κ᾽ ἄμμε βόλλητ᾽ Ἄρευς ἐπιτ . ύχε[

τρόπην· ἐκ δὲ χόλω τῶδε λαθοίμεθ[

10   χαλάσσομεν δὲ τὰς θυμοβόρω λύας

ἐμφύλω τε μάχας, τάν τις Ὀλυμπίων

ἔνωρσε, δᾶμον μὲν εἰς ἀυάταν ἄγων

Φιττάκω⟨ι⟩ δὲ δίδοις κῦδος ἐπήρ[ατ]ον.

. . . to say these things [   ] the lyre gambols, sharing in the symposium [   ], feasting [   ] with vain impostors (?) [   ] to (?) themselves; and let him, married into the Atreidai [   ], devour the city as (he did) also with Myrsilos, until Ares wishes to turn us to weapons (?); might we forget this anger; and let us

---

[81] One couplet does affirm marriage (1225–26):

οὐδὲν Κύρν᾽ ἀγαθῆς γλυκερώτερόν ἐστι γυναικός·
μάρτυς ἐγώ, σὺ δ᾽ ἐμοὶ γίνου ἀληθοσύνης.

Nothing, Kyrnos, is sweeter than a good wife; I am a witness, but become yourself (a witness) of its truth to me.

[82] Alkaios seems also to have attacked Pittakos' mother (and her marriage?) in 72 *V:* see Page 1955: 171–74.

relax heart-eating faction and internecine strife, which some one of the Olympians roused, leading the citizenry into disaster and giving delightful glory to Pittakos.

The first preserved stanza describes a symposium. Its relationship to the following stanzas is not clear, but it may be the wedding feast for Pittakos.[83] Certainly the festivity is marked as despicable by the φιλώνων (impostors/braggarts?) who join it.[84] But reprehensible though the company is, this feast sounds surprisingly delightful: the lyre plays as it shares the wine and food. The insult word φιλώνων is actually enclosed by "lyre" and "feasting"; it must have been heard as a pun on φίλων (friends). So, the listener who compares this gathering with his own fractured group finds that imposters act like friends enjoying fellowship, while those who should be friends quarrel.[85]

Line 6 suggests the outcome of the bonhomie in the phrase παώθεις Ἀτρείδαν (married into the Atreidai). The Penthilidai did claim descent from Orestes, according to the scholia, but it is hardly a good omen to characterize the union as an Atreid marriage.[86] No family in Greek mythology was so notorious for intertwining the promise and violation of marriage with the grasp for power. Think of Thyestes' wife, the sacrifice of Iphigeneia, the Trojan War, Clytemnestra and Aigisthos, Orestes' and Neoptolemos' quarrel over Hermione. Since φιλώνων and *Atreidai* resonate, both replacing expected words denoting positive relationships, marriage and symposium are additively infected by violent connivers.

The third-person imperative δαπτέτω (let him devour) at the beginning of line 7 continues the image of the feast, but what is served up is the city. However, the moment of truth about the menu, the peak of denunciation, is also a hinge on which the direction of the poem shifts. Whether sarcastic or dismissive, the imperative signals the performer's refusal to spend more time gaping at his enemies' good cheer as he turns instead to "us" (8). Now that he has roused envy of others' pleasure and focused resentment on Pittakos, he has hope that his own group will drop internal anger and strife.[87] His verbs are no longer imperative; he is now speaking as a mem-

[83] In that case the δέ is continuative: so Rösler 1980: 164n.131.

[84] The meaning of φιλώνων (genitive plural) is unknown. Voigt *ad loc.* lists suggestions: φίλων equivalent to φέλων defined as ἀλαζών (deceiver or braggart) by the ninth century CE grammarian Theognostos; a compound meaning "lover of goods"; "crony."

[85] Burnett 1983: 173–76 treats the poem as an attack on Alkaios' *hetaireia*, with scorn for them and mock-praise for Pittakos, designed to make them truly angry. Rösler 1980: 165 sees the first part of the poem simply as polemic and stresses the negative image of the symposium, ignoring the lyre.

[86] For the Penthilidai see Page 1955: 149–50. For the connection with Orestes, see Rösler 1980: 162–63; he takes the use of *Atreidai* as mocking exaggeration of the nobility of the family.

[87] I take λύα as internal strife in the larger group to which Alkaios belongs; so Burnett

ber of the group, and the verb forms he uses imply rising hope of cohesion in the *hetaireia*. The first, the subjunctive of the indefinite future, puts the initiative into the hands of Ares: "until Ares wishes. . . . " The second is the first-person optative λαθοίμεθα (might we forget) expressing a wish that is now up to "us." The third, χαλάσσομεν (let us relax), is a first-person plural hortatory subjunctive, a more direct call to change than the previous verb.[88] The singer gains energy and optimism as he exhorts his companions to relax their internecine fighting.

The last line returns to Pittakos, reminding the audience of the earlier description. It now seems that Pittakos' cheer and success are the consequence of "our" loss of cheer; by transferring pleasures back to itself, Alkaios' group can find the means to unite in opposition to Pittakos. To abet the reversal, the lyre that is so prominently pictured as playing for that group is actually playing for this one. Thus the festal gathering that begins the fragment functions both as the opposite of the symposium group, a cynical marriage involving abandonment of old loyalties to men, and as an image enticing Alkaios' group to recover festivity for itself.[89]

Mythic marriages and rapes also appear in Alkaios' poetry. Arrogant stealing of a woman is an analogue for political hybris in one poem and probably in another. In 298 *V* Alkaios describes Aias' rape of Kassandra in the temple of Athena and the destruction that Athena wreaked on the Greek fleet (?) in return.[90] As the beginning of the fragment shows, Alkaios uses the episode to illustrate the benefit of killing someone whose behavior brings destruction on many.[91] Similarly, in 42 *V* Alkaios compares Helen and Thetis as brides, emphasizing Thetis' virginity (8, 10).[92] From the latter union came Achilles, who destroyed Paris' city on account of Helen. Against a simple view that the poem contrasts good and bad

---

1983: 174n.44, who refers it to strife among the various anti-Pittakos factions. Rösler 1980: 166–70 takes it to mean civil strife and understands the last stanza to refer to the future, after Alkaios' faction has triumphed: the poem combines abuse of Pittakos and hope for peace, the contradictory tone of a group in exile.

[88] The shift from optative to subjunctive is considered clumsy, and λαθώμεθα has been suggested; see Voigt *ad loc.*

[89] Alkaios appears to reject marriage for himself in 5 *V*, but the text is not well enough preserved to reveal the circumstances. On other possible references to Pittakos' marriage in Alkaios' poetry, 5 *V* and elsewhere, see Burnett 1983: 171–73.

[90] On the text of this poem, see Führer 1977: 27–28; Lloyd-Jones 1990a; Bremer et al. 1987: 98–108 (95–127 for their whole discussion of the fragment). Earlier bibliography in Burnett 1983: 198n.48.

[91] Burnett 1983: 198 draws a parallel with Pittakos.

[92] Rösler 1980: 227–29, taking up earlier suggestions, argues that the addressee was Aphrodite rather than Helen. With this poem compare 283 *V* on Helen; as Burnett 1983: 186–89 shows, Helen is there balanced by the destruction of Troy.

wives is the fact that Thetis did not stay with Peleus.[93] The real contrast was perhaps primarily between the men, for, as Wolfgang Rösler points out, Peleus refused the wife of Akastos.[94] A man who stole another's wife compared with one who resisted an offer—the political application of such a contrast is easy to imagine, especially in light of Pittakos' marriage. Relations with women, then, provided an image of the threat to the symposium group posed by competing loyalties.[95]

In iambic (invective) poetry the singer is more openly disdainful of ties to women. Semonides' poem on wives (7 W) is an unsubtle example. This long diatribe is rather a compendium of topoi than a crafted poem; it lists types of wives, each one fashioned from an animal (or earth or sea), with their characteristics.[96] The overriding complaint is that wives are impossible to control. Either they know too much or they are so dense that nothing gets through to them; they eat too much or refuse to work; they embarrass the husband before the neighbors. The listeners are united as men by having to deal with these stubborn opposites. Two passages will illustrate the kind of frustrations that the poem articulates (12–20, 71–82):

> τὴν δ' ἐκ κυνός, λιτοργόν, αὐτομήτορα,
> ἣ πάντ' ἀκοῦσαι, πάντα δ' εἰδέναι θέλει,
> πάντηι δὲ παπταίνουσα καὶ πλανωμένη
> 15 λέληκεν, ἢν καὶ μηδέν' ἀνθρώπων ὁρᾶι.
> παύσειε δ' ἄν μιν οὔτ' ἀπειλήσας ἀνήρ,
> οὐδ' εἰ χολωθεὶς ἐξαράξειεν λίθωι
> ὀδόντας, οὐδ' ἂν μειλίχως μυθεόμενος,
> οὐδ' εἰ παρὰ ξείνοισιν ἡμένη τύχηι,
> 20 ἀλλ' ἐμπέδως ἄπρηκτον αὐονὴν ἔχει. . . .
> 71 τὴν δ' ἐκ πιθήκου· τοῦτο δὴ διακριδὸν
> Ζεὺς ἀνδράσιν μέγιστον ὤπασεν κακόν.
> αἴσχιστα μὲν πρόσωπα· τοιαύτη γυνὴ

[93] Page 1955: 280–81 takes it to be a contrast in wives but remarks that "such moralizing is almost unique in the Lesbians" (280) and thinks of a reaction to Stesichoros. Rösler 1980: 222–23 remarks that we can ignore the later history of Peleus and Thetis, but why should we? Burnett 1983: 190–98, bringing the myth to bear, sees the two marriages as complementary events in a divine scheme that ends in the destruction of Troy.

[94] Hesiod frs. 208–9 MW; Rösler 1980: 230.

[95] Rösler 1980: 235–38 finds Alkaios' attitude toward women negative. His conclusion, that Alkaios' hostility was connected with his concentration on the symposium group, is close to mine, but he takes it as biographical fact rather than symposium theme.

[96] The poem breaks off after 118 lines. On this poem see Lloyd-Jones 1975, who defends it as being funny (24–25) but does not analyze the assumptions out of which the humor arises.

εἰσιν δι' ἄστεος πᾶσιν ἀνθρώποις γέλως·
75   ἐπ' αὐχένα βραχεῖα· κινεῖται μόγις·
ἄπυγος, αὐτόκωλος. ἆ τάλας ἀνὴρ
ὅστις κακὸν τοιοῦτον ἀγκαλίζεται.
δήνεα δὲ πάντα καὶ τρόπους ἐπίσταται
ὥσπερ πίθηκος· οὐδέ οἱ γέλως μέλει·
80   οὐδ' ἄν τιν' εὖ ἔρξειεν, ἀλλὰ τοῦτ' ὁρᾶι
καὶ τοῦτο πᾶσαν ἡμέρην βουλεύεται,
ὅκως τι κῶς μέγιστον ἔρξειεν κακόν.

And that one is from a dog, a mischief-maker, a veritable mutt, who wants to hear everything and know everything, and peering around and wandering every which way, she barks, even if she doesn't see a single soul. Her husband could not shut her up with threats, not even if in anger he bashed her teeth out with a stone, not even speaking sweetly, not even if she happens to be sitting with guests from elsewhere, but he has constantly an incurable dessication. . . . And another is from a monkey; this one for sure Zeus gave as distinctly the greatest evil to men. Her face is repulsive; such a woman walking through the town is an invitation to all humans to laugh; she is short of neck and can scarcely move, buttockless, in toto a hambone. Ah wretched man who embraces such an evil. She knows all tricks and ways around just like a monkey, and laughter doesn't bother her.[97] She wouldn't do anyone a good deed, but notes and plans this all day: how she might do the greatest evil.

In this poem, in striking contrast to bardic poetry, men have no real power over women. The poem stages the performer as needing his audience, for his litany of complaints acknowledges the difficulty of living in a community in which one's status is always vulnerable, dependent on another, and maliciously assessed by everyone else. The so-called humor distances speaker and listeners from their spouses and displaces shortcomings onto the women, while the symposium is treated by the performer as an alternative location in which a man can present himself as independent of his household. A man's friends replace the neighbors as the ones who understand his real worth.

The last in the list of types of wives is the one created from a bee. She alone earns no blame, for the house flourishes under her and she bears enviable children. Yet, lest some listeners preen themselves on their good luck, the last section of the poem declares *all* women bad, and "if they

---

[97] On the difficulties of translation, see Lloyd-Jones 1975 *ad loc*. On αὐτομήτορα (mother to herself) I do not follow his suggestion ("her own mother's child") because the insult should be stronger. It may refer to having no known parentage (a meaning that would preserve the parallelism with αὐτοπάτωρ, "self-engendered").

seem to benefit one who has (a wife), to him especially she becomes an evil" (97–98). The last section reinterprets the earlier passage on the bee-woman as the view of a deluded husband.[98] This sentiment is expressed at greater length just before the poem breaks off in a passage whose psychology is illuminating (108–14):

> ἥτις δέ τοι μάλιστα σωφρονεῖν δοκεῖ,
> αὕτη μέγιστα τυγχάνει λωβωμένη·
> 110   κεχηνότος γὰρ ἀνδρός, οἱ δὲ γείτονες
> χαίρουσ' ὁρῶντες καὶ τόν, ὡς ἁμαρτάνει.
> τὴν ἣν δ' ἕκαστος αἰνέσει μεμνημένος
> γυναῖκα, τὴν δὲ τούτερου μωμήσεται·
> ἴσην δ' ἔχοντες μοῖραν οὐ γινώσκομεν.

She who most seems chaste is the very one who turns out to commit mortal insult. For as the man stands gaping (*gesture meaning* "there she goes")—and the neighbors happily observe how he too errs. Each man will attentively praise his own wife and decry another man's; and we do not recognize that we all have the same fate.

The man who thinks his wife good is only the more deceived, and because of his ignorance he is secretly an object of greater amusement to the neighbors than if he had a recalcitrant wife with whom he fought. Each listener is threatened with the possibility that he is the fool: note the vividness of "as the man stands gaping," accompanied no doubt by a gesture of head or hand.[99] The effect of this reasoning is to cut each man off from his wife and his neighbors by fostering suspicion that they are all laughing behind his back. It can hardly be countered since the actions of one's wife and the neighbors' reactions will always be partly out of one's sight. It therefore reduces all members of the symposium to the same unhappy marital condition. The sudden first-person plural in line 114 says so decisively: "and we do not recognize that we all have the same fate." The speaker includes himself in this position. The poem both suppresses competition within the symposium group on the basis of family connections and leaves no alternative to the symposium group as the ones with whom one can give and receive trust.[100]

[98] Cf. Loraux 1993: 102–6 on the bee-woman's effect of confusing the categories of praise and blame.

[99] I owe to Alan Boegehold the realization that a sentence that breaks off may be completed by a gesture. On the breaking off of the thought (aposiopesis), see Lloyd-Jones 1975 *ad loc.*

[100] Latte 1953: 37–38 compares this poem to Archilochos' use of animal fables and both to mocking-festivals; this poem, he suggests, is an answer to women's mockery of men (for which see Ch. 2). But the latter are collective, whereas iambic requires a single performer.

For Alkaios, too, although in a more cavalier vein (and not iambic), the symposium is a refuge from women. In a reworking of lines 582–88 of Hesiod's *Works and Days,* he advises (347 *V*):

τέγγε πλεύμονας οἴνωι, τὸ γὰρ ἄστρον περιτέλλεται,

ἀ δ' ὥρα χαλέπα, πάντα δὲ δίψαισ' ὑπὰ καύματος,

ἄχει δ' ἐκ πετάλων ἄδεα τέττιξ . . .

ἄνθει δὲ σκόλυμος, νῦν δὲ γύναικες μιαρώταται

5   λέπτοι δ' ἄνδρες, ἐπεὶ ⟨ ⟩ κεφάλαν καὶ γόνα Σείριος

ἄσδει

Wet your lungs with wine, for the dogstar is on high, the season is harsh and everything thirsts in the heat, the cicada sounds sweetly from among the leaves . . . the thistle flowers, and now women are most pestilential and men are fragile, since Sirius desiccates the head and knees.[101]

The symposium is refuge equally from the heat and from women, for the adjective attached to them connotes pollution and rotting. In Hesiod women are "most wanton" (μαχλόταται), so Alkaios suggests by his echo that women's desire will infect men. As in Semonides men need the haven of the symposium instead.[102]

Another variation on the theme of disconnection from women is Archilochos' collection of diatribes against Lykambes. Very little is left in Archilochos' own words on his enmity with Lykambes, but we have several reports of it and can see the outline.[103] According to it Lykambes had engaged his daughter Neoboule to Archilochos but then broke off the engagement. Archilochos responded so effectively with his invective, insinuating that Neoboule and her sister were no longer virgin, that both women hanged themselves.[104] I take it not as biography but as a fictional situation that allowed Archilochos much scope for staging himself through invective on the subject of loyalty and relations with the community.[105] The singer could always improvise further elaborations on the

---

[101] I owe "pestilential" to Page 1955: 305 but unlike him do not think that the word should be robbed of its strength. On 303 he combines these lines with others that are quoted separately. *WD* 585–88 is quoted in Ch. 2, p. 83.

[102] In 117b *V* Alkaios seems to warn against prostitutes (26–35). On it see Burnett 1983: 148–49.

[103] See Burnett 1983: 19–23 and cf. n.105 below.

[104] Based on an epigram of Dioskourides (*Palatine Anthology* 7.351, given *ad* 30 *W*), Gentili 1988: 185–91 thinks that Archilochos told of encounters with the sisters in a sanctuary of Hera, which would be an insult to the goddess as well.

[105] West 1974: 25–28 sees it as fictional, a part of stock Dionysiac scurrility perhaps derived from old "iambic" religious ritual. Carey 1986 defends the historicity of the event, pointing out that the only characters are Lykambes and two daughters, the only story the loss

theme, and through its fictions he could criticize and evaluate. Women here too play the role of representatives of the community in its character as kin-networks.

From just the outline some aspects of Archilochos' self-staging are clear. Lykambes' name contains the root of "wolf"; he is an isolated figure, the opposite of the symposium group.[106] In not keeping his promise Lykambes violates the trust on which the symposium group relied. On the other hand, in having nubile daughters he offers men the chance to make a marriage alliance and become integrated into the status hierarchy of the community. Lykambes represents both ends of the spectrum, lone wolf and community pillar, against which the symposium group defined itself. The story allows Archilochos to present himself as one who has no marriage alliance to interfere with his allegiance to the symposium group but who, unlike Lykambes, holds oaths inviolable. The illogicality that if Lykambes had held to his oath Archilochos would have had a marriage is irrelevant, for the episode serves the needs of self-portrayal rather than narrative.

In one epode Archilochos charged Lykambes with violating his oath and breaking off the marriage and told the fable of the fox and the eagle, presumably as a prediction to Lykambes that he would suffer retribution.[107] The lines 172 *W may* represent the opening:

πάτερ Λυκάμβα, ποῖον ἐφράσω τόδε;

τίς σὰς παρήειρε φρένας

ἧις τὸ πρὶν ἠρήρησθα; νῦν δὲ δὴ πολὺς

ἀστοῖσι φαίνεαι γέλως.

Father Lykambes, what is this you said? Who stole your wits that you were equipped with before? Now on the other hand you really seem to be a great joke to the townspeople.

A fragment said by Origen to have been addressed to Lykambes (173 *W*) is also assigned to this epode:

---

of the marriage—but this is precisely what Archilochos needs to present his solo masculine identity. As Carey says (67n.31), if it happened, it would be a public affront to Archilochos. I think it fiction, given the apt names, but possibly Archilochos' names are code for real people. Gentili 1988: 294–95n.50 has other bibliography.

[106] On the image of the wolf as a devious slanderer and its use in iambic, see Miralles and Pòrtulas 1983: 53–60.

[107] West collects the fragments that appear to belong to this epode as numbers 172–81 of his edition; West 1974: 132–34 offers a reconstruction of the epode. Epodic verse shares with iambic an affinity for invective, and the name Lykambes also appears in small iambic trimeter fragments, e.g., 38, 71.

ὅρκον δ' ἐνοσφίσθης μέγαν
ἅλας τε καὶ τράπεζαν.

You forsook a great oath, salt and table.

The bond between Lykambes and Archilochos was affirmed by their eating together, precisely the tie enacted in the symposium. Archilochos' invective can thereby take the breaking of symposium trust as its theme. Both fragments are second-person address, so the speaker must have conjured up a confrontation that allowed him to direct the full force of his invective at his victim and demonstrate to his drinking companions how he speaks to those who betray a promise.[108]

The fable of the eagle and the fox itself connects eating and oaths, though in reverse fashion. As told by Aesop, the two animals made a pact and agreed to live near each other to strengthen their friendship.[109] Then the eagle ate the fox's young. The fox prayed for vengeance, which came when the eagle stole a piece of smoldering sacrificial meat and set his nest afire. His young fell out of the blazing nest and were eaten by the fox. Eating in this case is the equivalent of breaking the oath: Archilochos rang a series of changes on the themes of oaths, eating, and marriage that we cannot follow.[110] What can be seen is that Archilochos has so arranged it that his portrayal of himself as cut off from marriage and its community ties also allows him to inveigh against violation of friendship, portray those outside his circle of friends as treacherous, and demonstrate the power of his invective to destroy those who scorn him.[111] His group of friends is given the opportunity to deduce his staunch loyalty from his reaction to Lykambes. Archilochos, or any speaker, makes himself the incarnation of what we could call a man's man.

The Cologne Epode (196a W^2), a long fragment of a poem found on papyrus and attributed to Archilochos, is connected with the Lykambes story because it mentions Neoboule.[112] The fragment is the latter part of a narrative of a sexual encounter.[113] When the preserved section opens, the

---

[108] The speech may have been embedded in a narrative; the Cologne Epode (see below) contains reported direct speech. Even so, the speech offers the performer the opportunity for dramatic declamation.

[109] The text is given in West 1989 p. 10 *ad* Archilochos 172.

[110] Cf. the same set of themes, eating (the city), marriage, and breaking of oaths, in Alkaios' poems about Pittakos (70 *V*, discussed above, and 129 *V*).

[111] Cf. 197 *W* from a different epode: "Father Zeus, I was not given a wedding feast."

[112] First published by Merkelbach and West 1974.

[113] This poem has generated much discussion about how to take the first person: is Archilochos narrating a real event or a fiction; is he acting a role that replaces his actual identity? Rösler 1985: 131–38 rightly rejects the abstract poetic persona of new criticism as inadequate for oral presentation but does not come to a definite answer. Slings 1990a: 23–26 argues against West (above, n. 105) that the "I" is biographical and the story probably false; he thinks

girl is responding to the speaker's proposal, apparently a proposal of a tryst on the spot. She is putting him off; her suggestion is that if he is aroused and his will drives him on, he should consider another girl, whom she calls a *parthenos*. The speaker responds by saying that there are "many delights of the goddess for young men beside the divine thing" (13–15), one of which will do, while they can deliberate on "these things" (what she has said?) later. "I will obey as you order me" (19). After a metaphorical description of what he would like to do, he dismisses the other girl, to whom he gives the name Neoboule, with scorn. He then lays his interlocutor down in the flowers, runs his hands over her body, and releases his "strength" without penetrating her. There is no other poem quite like this, in its almost pastoral, naturalistic, first-person account. How does it fit with the Lykambes theme and a symposium setting?[114] The girl may be Neoboule's sister, Lykambes' other daughter, but she is vague in her description of Neoboule's relationship to her. At all events the speaker distinguishes the two girls (32–38):

]μὴ τοῦτ' εφ . ιταν[
ὅ]πως ἐγὼ γυναῖκα τ[ο]ιαύτην ἔχων
γεί]τοσι χάρμ' ἔσομαι·
35   πολλὸν σὲ βούλο[μαι
σὺ] μὲν γὰρ οὔτ' ἄπιστος οὔτε διπλόη,
ἢ δ]ὲ μάλ' ὀξυτέρη,
πολλοὺς δὲ ποιεῖτα[ι φίλους·

May that not [happen?   ], that I have such a wife and become a laughing-stock to the neighbors. I much prefer you, for [you] are neither faithless nor two-faced, while [she] is much more quickly aroused and makes many men [her friends].

Neoboule, like the wives that Semonides portrays, would make him a butt of laughter, for she is no longer virgin (cf. line 27) but sexually active.[115]

---

that only if Lykambes and his daughters are real people whom the poet wishes to hurt can we find unity in the poem. My view is close to that of Aloni 1981: 133–36, who thinks that the speaker has a fictional persona related to his real one and has modified traditional material. I would not call it a "fictional persona" and do not follow him in supposing the poem to present a paradigm for young men.

[114] Here again I agree with Aloni 1981: 135, who deduces a restricted audience from the style, with its ambiguous metaphors that allow the singer to convey more to his audience than the narrator within the poem to the girl. Although he rejects West's explanation, Slings 1990a: 24–25 oddly keeps the idea that the poem was performed in an open public setting. As he points out, it would not seem humorous to all in the audience (and he also finds the ending too ambiguous for a fiction), whence he must suppose that Archilochos means to insult.

[115] In two Hellenistic epigrams Lykambes' daughters defend themselves (*Palatine Anthol-*

Archilochos seconds Semonides' sour suspicion that the neighbors will be eager to detect a cuckold, but by not marrying he depicts himself as having escaped the entanglement that Semonides says all men share. To an audience familiar with the scenario of the Lykambes poems, Archilochos' abuse of Neoboule also fits his overall theme of the treachery found in the community: she "makes many men friends," that is, does not keep her loyalties exclusive and may abandon one tie for another that seems more attractive, just like her father and just as her name, "New-Plan," predicts.

Even to an audience to whom Lykambes and company were unknown, the contrast between an honest and inexperienced young woman and one who suited herself sexually would be of great interest. The poem catches the audience in a bind between their voyeuristic preference for a fresh virgin beloved and their shocked resentment at someone who threatens to "ruin" daughters. The real suspense would be over what Archilochos actually intended.[116] He calls the girl faithful—she has the quality of a symposium companion—but Archilochos appears to be abusing his admiration for loyalty by employing it as seductive talk. Does he really mouth the words "you are not faithless" just to flatter the girl and get what he wants? Is he promising marriage? Either way, he seems to be about to lose his symposium persona. If his vague words about deliberating later are a smokescreen and his admiration a come-on, then his protestations of fidelity to friends may be hollow too; but if he means to marry her, the vaunted dissociation from the community will come to an end (barring, of course, a second refusal from Lykambes).

The last twelve lines of the Cologne Epode are his description of making love to the girl (42–53):

τοσ]αῦτ' ἐφώνεον· παρθένον δ' ἐν ἄνθε[σιν
   τηλ]εθάεσσι λαβών
   ἔκλινα· μαλθακῆι δ[έ μιν
45 χλαί]νηι καλύψας, αὐχέν' ἀγκάληις ἔχω[ν,
   ]ματι παυ[σ]α μένην
   τὼς ὥστε νεβρ[

---

ogy 7.351 and 352, printed ad 30 W). One can gather that Archilochos elsewhere described meeting them in a temple of Hera and that he called them wanton; we cannot confidently deduce (as West 1974: 26 suggests) that Archilochos described himself having sex with Neoboule.

[116] Zanetto 1985 thinks that the speaker describes intercrural intercourse from behind when he says, "don't begrudge my [hastening?] under the coping and the gates, for I will steer toward the grassy gardens" (21–23). His metaphorical language would let the audience know what he intended without its being clear to the girl. The joke, according to Zanetto (47), is thus in the audience's complicity. This view depends on the idea that the metaphors were standard slang; I suspect it was not obvious what he had in mind.

μαζ]ῶν τε χερσὶν ἠπίως ἐφηψάμην
      ]ρέφηγε νέον
50   ἥβης ἐπήλυσιν χρόα
      ἅπαν τ]ε σῶμα καλὸν ἀμφαφώμενος
      ]ον ἀφῆκα μένος
      ξανθῆς ἐπιψαύ[ων τριχός.

So much I said, and taking hold of the young woman I lay her down in the blooming flowers. Covering [her] with a soft [cloak], holding her neck in the crook of my arm as she held still [with fear ?] like a fawn [   ], I gently touched her [breasts] with my hands [   ] her skin showed freshly the arrival of youth, and stroking her [whole] lovely body I let go my vitality, just touching her light-brown [hair].

She is the daughter of a member of the community, a "respectable" woman, as the tone of the whole piece makes clear. The description here is less lusty than tender. Both of these aspects make these lines almost shocking. The listeners may have held their breath, wondering whether Archilochos was going to describe the deflowering of a citizen girl, the sort of act for which he could get himself killed—and if so when the tone of triumph would emerge.[117] Archilochos veers off in the very last line, *after* the culmination. Performance of this poem is a tour de force of baiting expectations.[118]

Archilochos retrieves his persona in the most spectacular enactment of disconnection from women that symposium poetry offers. He does not (quite) make a mockery of a faithful personality and he does not make a commitment; and if this young woman was one of Lykambes' daughters in the ongoing fiction, he denies to Lykambes belated justification for Lykambes' breach of faith. The performer in the end eludes all the reactions that he has solicited in the course of performance. It is as an enactment of the performer's masculinity and independence and as a confirmation against all expectations of his keeping his promise that the poem stages a symposium persona.

Archilochos 23 *W* is another poem in which the narrator reports a conversation with a woman, apparently as part of a larger narrative, although here the poem ends with his speech.[119] The narrator's reported speech is again about faithfulness, and again he reassures the interlocutor that he

[117] Even as a fiction this is a risky narrative. Contrast the treatment of *parthenoi* in new comedy, on which see Scafuro, forthcoming.

[118] Bremer et al. 1987: 50–51 think that the speaker is deliberately ambiguous about whether he penetrated the girl or not. Zanetto 1985 argues cogently that he did not and gives a large bibliography.

[119] Cf. West 1974: 118–20 with earlier interpretations.

will take thought for something (bad report?), this time adding a defense of himself (7–16):

τὴν δ' ἐγὼν̣τ̣α̣μειβόμ[ην·

"γύνα[ι], φάτιν μὲν τὴν πρὸς ἀνθρώπω[ν κακὴν

μὴ τετραμήνηις μηδέν· ἀμφὶ δ' εὐφ[ρόνηι,

10   ἐμοὶ μελήσει· [θ]υμὸν ἵλαον τίθεο.

ἐς τοῦτο δή τοι τῆς ἀνολβίης δοκ[έω

ἥκειν; ἀνήρ τοι δειλὸς ἂρ' ἐφαινόμην[,

οὐ]δ' οἷός εἰμ' ἐγὼ [ο]ὗτος οὐδ' οἴων ἄπο.

ἐπ]ίσταμαί τοι τὸν φιλ[έο]γ̣[τα] μὲν φ[ι]λεῖγ[,

15   τὸ]ν̣ δ' ἐχθρὸν ἐχθαίρειν τ̣ε [κα]ὶ κακο[

μύ]ρμηξ.[120] λόγωι γυν τ[ῶιδ' ἀλη]θείη πάρ[α."

I answered her, "Woman, don't worry at all about [bad?] report among humans. I will take care of it when night falls (?); make your heart cheerful. Do I really seem to you to have come to this stage of misfortune? I appeared to you to be a wretched man, but I am not that sort, not this fellow, nor the offspring of such people. I know, I tell you, how to be a friend to the one who is my friend and to hate my enemy and [speak?] evil, an ant (?). There is truth in this account."

The symposium theme of fidelity to friends becomes the performer's boast within the framework of address to a woman. Again the second-person forms direct the remonstrance at the audience as the performer acts out his sense of himself.

The imagery of the captured city with which the speaker concludes and that ends the poem is hard to decipher (17–21):

"πό]λιν δὲ ταύτη[ν   ἐ]πιστρέ[φεα]ι

οὔ]τοι ποτ' ἄνδρες ἐξε[πόρθη]σαν, σὺ δ[ὲ

ν]ῦν εἷλες αἰχμῆι κα[ὶ μέγ' ἐ]ξήρ(ω) κ[λ]έος.

20   κείνης ἄνασσε καὶ τ̣[υρα]νγίην ἔχε·

π[ο]λ̣[λοῖ]σ̣[ί θ]ην ζ]ηλωτὸς ἀ[νθρ]ώπων ἔσεαι."

And this city [which now ?] you are walking over men never [plundered?], but you took it just now with a spear and earned [great] fame. Rule it and hold the [tyranny?]; you will no doubt be enviable (?) to [many?] among humans.

The woman has made a conquest, but of what? Perhaps it is of the speaker himself, and Archilochos' stance of disconnection from women is broken

---

[120] Clay 1986: 14 suggests μά]ρμηξ (falcon) as a reference to Gyges' family crest, and also a boast of powerful character. On the relevance of Gyges, see below.

in this instance, but as an explanation that does not quite seem to account for either logic or imagery.[121] The woman appears to fear a bad (?) reputation, perhaps that the speaker will betray her in some way (hence his protest). But it is not a matter of keeping a liaison secret, for he says at the end that she will be famous and envied by many. Since the woman's conquest will not be secret, there must be some other grounds for the bad reputation, which the speaker implies he will not publish—but which the seemingly reassuring final lines may hint at, wittily, for the listeners who can decipher the imagery of sex-role reversal. Alternatively, Jenny Strauss Clay makes the fascinating suggestion that it portrayed King Kandaules' wife confronting Gyges (whom Kandaules stationed in the bedroom so that Gyges could see her naked) with the choice of killing Kandaules or dying himself.[122] The preserved section is then his response to her ultimatum. Whatever the narrative frame, it serves the purpose of highlighting the speaker's ethics while rejecting a woman's view of him.

Confirmation that Archilochos was adopting an anticommunal stance in his animadversions on his lost marriage can be found in a passage of Aelian quoting from Kritias on Archilochos. Kritias (44 *DK*) clearly takes Archilochos' poetry as biography:

> Kritias accuses Archilochos because he speaks so ill of himself. If he hadn't publicized such a reputation about himself to the Greeks, says (Kritias), we would not have learned either that he was the son of the slave-woman Enipo, or that it was on account of poverty and resourcelessness that he left Paros and went to Thasos, or that when he went he became an enemy of the people there, nor indeed (would we know) that he execrated friends and enemies alike. In addition to these things, (Kritias) says, we would not know that he was an adulterer, if we did not learn it from himself, nor that he was lecherous and violently arrogant and, even more shameful, that he threw away his shield.[123]

What Kritias found remarkable was that Archilochos said such shocking and demeaning things about himself. If we take it that Kritias collected first-person statements from Archilochos' poetry, we can consider these

---

[121] The erotic interpretation was proposed by Adrados 1956: 40 and adopted by West 1974: 119 and Burnett 1983: 71–75. Bremer et al. 1987: 6 do not accept it because αἰχμῆι (with a spear) does not seem to fit the metaphor. They take the words at face value: "The woman is apparently a seventh-century Artemisia. . . ." Burnett suggests that Archilochos is affirming his power as a blame-poet.

[122] Clay 1986, with bibliography on previous interpretations. I am not fully persuaded because the speaker's statement that she has conquered the city does not seem quite to fit either the timing or the event. I would take the city as metaphorical and the last stanza as an elaborate insult to another man, but that is only a guess.

[123] Aelian *Varia Historia* 10.13, quoted at Archilochos 295 *W*. Other references to these self-portrayals in Archilochos' poetry are collected by West *ad loc.*

items as manifestations of the Archilochean persona we have been observing.[124] They all emphasize his disconnection from the community. He was poverty-stricken and therefore had no status. He was an enemy of the Thasians among whom he lived. And his mother was a slave-woman named Enipo, so he had no familial grandeur. Like his being rejected as a son-in-law, these details create the picture of a man with no anchors in kinship and nothing he fears to lose, a man whose self-esteem is based purely on his own physical being.[125]

The last item in particular is relevant to the study of Archilochos' use of gender in self-presentation. Enipo, his "mother's" name, is derived from the verb "to blame," so Archilochos identifies his poetic practice with his genealogy.[126] In this case distance from the community is created not by disconnection from his "mother" (though he may have disowned this creature of his imagination also) but by her disconnection from the family structures that define the community. Born from a woman who was perhaps foreign, perhaps available to more than one man, without right to her own person (for these are the implications of being a slave), Archilochos portrays himself as sprung from nowhere, in Greek social terms. The woman herself, through her name Enipo, rejects the integrative function assigned to mothers in communal poetry, for blaming is the divisive opposite of communal poetry. Archilochos' style of masculinity is constructed as radical otherness from the community, repeatedly figured by lack of connections through women.

The Cologne Epode illustrates Archilochos' disconnection from a sexual partner as well as his avoidance of marriage. One wonders whether a riddle in Theognis could not refer to the same denouement as the one in the Cologne Epode. The lines are Theognis 949–54:

νεβρὸν ὑπὲξ ἐλάφοιο λέων ὣς ἀλκὶ πεποιθὼς
950   ποσσὶ καταμάρψας αἵματος οὐκ ἔπιον·
τειχέων δ' ὑψηλῶν ἐπιβὰς πόλιν οὐκ ἀλάπαξα·

---

[124] See Lefkowitz 1981: 25–31 on the fictions that grew up around Archilochos' vivid persona. A hero shrine was dedicated to him on Paros, and two inscriptions recording aspects of his "biography" and some of his poetry have been found; the texts are in Tarditi 1968: 4–11. The Mnesiepes inscription is discussed by Miralles and Pòrtulas 1983: 63–80. Peek 1985 gives a new fragment of the Sosthenes monument.

[125] Lucian in *The Mistaken Critic* 1 confirms this impression in a description of Archilochos (223 *W*):

Being bad-mouthed by one of this sort, Archilochos said that the man had caught a cicada by the wing, comparing himself with a cicada, a creature of babbling nature and without any needs, but whenever seized by his wing crying more resoundingly.

Again, the picaresque portrait must have been in the first person.

[126] West 1974: 28.

ζευξάμενος δ' ἵππους ἅρματος οὐκ ἐπέβην·
πρήξας δ' οὐκ ἔπρηξα, καὶ οὐκ ἐτέλεσσα τελέσσας,
δρήσας δ' οὐκ ἔδρησ', ἤνυσα δ' οὐκ ἀνύσας.

Like a lion sure in its strength, snatching a fawn from under the doe with my feet, I did not drink of its blood. Mounting the high walls, I did not sack the city. Having yoked the horses, I did not mount the chariot. Acting, I did not act, and I did not finish, though I finished, and doing I did not do, and I accomplished, though I did not accomplish.

The images are all known sexual metaphors.[127] If the point is sexual, then like Archilochos the speaker takes the beloved but does not.[128] He is like a lion, he has his opponent or his desire in his grasp, and yet he does not make the last possessive move—killing or plundering or mounting the chariot for competition or war. This little piece in a sense sums up the stance of a symposium performer. Through the sexual metaphor the performer takes his stand in the moment between capacity and triumph, for he must be potent in order to ensure respect, but success would imply his separation from his fellows.

III

Performers of love poetry depict their disconnection from women in the erotic realm as a different version of this state of arrest so precisely described by Theognis: the performer is aroused but not satisfied, somehow separated from the beloved. He does not boast of happy lovemaking but diffuses the force of his desire in the comfort of drinking companions. (The Cologne Epode skirts very close to the edge of this "rule"; that is part of its daring self-presentation.) Such a self-portrait solves the potential problem of sexual competition among members of the group. Then too, unhappy desire is more interesting than happy desire to those who hear about it because it leaves the auditors a role to play: they can offer traditional wisdom, recount their own experiences, feel needed rather than left out.[129]

[127] This poem is one of the puzzles of the Theognid corpus. Several commentators have proposed that it must be a sexual metaphor, for the first distich reappears in Book II; see van Groningen 1966 *ad loc.*, who gives parallels to the erotic use of the final verbs but rejects an erotic interpretation. He thinks the point might be political. Lewis 1985: 218 interprets the first distich as distinguishing hunting from the erotic hunt, which requires restraint.

[128] Nonpenetrating sex would fit both of the claims in the poem, namely (1–4) that the speaker has not taken the last step and "entered" fawn, city, and chariot, and (5–8) that he has both completed and not completed the action.

[129] Cf. Stewart 1989: 94 on Gypsy singing in celebration. There are limits to the acceptable subjects: "A Rom in love cannot sing about his passion."

In love poetry boys more often than girls are the objects of desire, while the latter may be from noncitizen families. This focus too plays into anti-communal postures, for in the community as a whole marriage and begetting of children are of paramount interest. Love poetry is a nonpolitical way to promote feelings of fellowship and express separation from the normative demands of the community. Unsurprisingly, two of the major producers of sympotic love poetry, Ibykos and Anakreon, were associated with tyrants. Both were clients of Polykrates of Samos, and Anakreon went on to the Athens of Hipparchos.[130] They must have sung at the tyrant's table after dinner, where overtly political poetry would have been out of place.

One of the most striking poems of disconnected desire is by Ibykos (286 *PMGF*):

ἦρι μὲν αἵ τε Κυδώνιαι
μηλίδες ἀρδόμεναι ῥοᾶν
ἐκ ποταμῶν, ἵνα Παρθένων
κῆπος ἀκήρατος, αἵ τ' οἰνανθίδες
5   αὐξόμεναι σκιεροῖσιν ὑφ' ἔρνεσιν
οἰναρέοις θαλέθοισιν· ἐμοὶ δ' ἔρος
οὐδεμίαν κατάκοιτος ὥραν.
†τε† ὑπὸ στεροπᾶς φλέγων
Θρηίκιος Βορέας
10   ἀίσσων παρὰ Κύπριδος ἀζαλέ-
    αις μανίαισιν ἐρεμνὸς ἀθαμβὴς
ἐγκρατέως πεδόθεν †φυλάσσει†
ἡμετέρας φρένας

In the spring the quince trees watered by streams from the rivers, where the uncut garden of the Maidens lies, and the waxing vine-blossoms under the shady vine tendrils unfold. But for me eros sleeps at no season. Instead, like (?) Thracian Boreas blazing with lightning, (eros) whipping with scorching madnesses from Kypris, dark, shameless, powerfully sucks up (?) my mind from its foundation.[131]

As Athenaios (who quotes these lines) says, Ibykos cries and shrieks. No person is indicated as the object of Ibykos' desire, at least in the quoted

---

[130] See Bowra 1961: 241–307 on these two poets. Recent studies are Davies 1986b and Woodbury 1985. There is some question about the history of tyranny on Samos and the identity of these poets' patrons (on which see Woodbury 206–18), but it does not affect my discussion.

[131] Accepting in the translation ἀλλ' ἄθ' in line 8 for †τε† and λαφύσσει for †φυλάσσει†, both in Davies' *app. crit.* Campbell 1991 prints the first.

section. Instead an abstract world of sexuality is divided between a virgin enclosure where peace reigns and the space outside. The two are incommensurable. Though the garden is the scene where fulfillment would be found and the weather outside it tempestuous, the speaker makes no attempt to get into the garden; he rather leaves the impression that his entry would bring violence with it and blast the budding luxuriance. Yet the violence he suffers is absorbed by his vivid language and the musical control of his voice and becomes an expression of his character, driving and uncontainable.

Another poem of Ibykos' also avoids suggesting a specific beloved, although here the effect of love is given in a more humorous vein (287 PMGF):

> Ἔρος αὖτέ με κυανέοισιν ὑπὸ
> βλεφάροις τακέρ' ὄμμασι δερκόμενος
> κηλήμασι παντοδαποῖς ἐς ἄπει-
> ρα δίκτυα Κύπριδος ἐσβάλλει·
> 5 ἦ μὰν τρομέω νιν ἐπερχόμενον,
> ὥστε φερέζυγος ἵππος ἀεθλοφόρος ποτὶ γήραι
> ἀέκων σὺν ὄχεσφι θοοῖς ἐς ἅμιλλαν ἔβα.

Eros again meltingly eyeing me from under dark eyelids tosses me into the endless nets of Aphrodite, using every kind of spell. Indeed I tremble at his coming as a yoke-bearing horse, a prize-winner growing old, unwillingly goes into the contest with his swift chariot.

Again an abstraction: Eros himself is the beloved, and the speaker desires the figure of desire. Yet, as the singer of Theognis 949–54 has not yet mounted the chariot, so the singer here stops at the beginning of the race. Gaining the favor of the beloved is cast in competitive metaphor as winning, and the performer has triumphed in the past, yet this time, the time of the song, the performer resists and doubts success. The experience of desire becomes almost an existential state, the definition of symposiastic masculinity.

Anakreon's love poetry arrives at a similar effect by a very different route. Two poems will illustrate. The first (if complete) is very short, like the skolia (360 PMG):

> ὦ παῖ παρθένιον βλέπων
> δίζημαί σε, σὺ δ' οὐ κλύεις,
> οὐκ εἰδὼς ὅτι τῆς ἐμῆς
> ψυχῆς ἡνιοχεύεις.

Oh boy, virgin-glancing, I seek you but you do not hear, for you do not know that you are the charioteer of my soul.

Like the closed garden of Ibykos 286, the boy is desirable because he is virginal; were the speaker to possess him, he would lose his attractiveness. The paradox of his being the charioteer is that he could never actually exercise his ascendancy. Again, however, distance preserves the status quo. Since the boy does not "hear" the singing voice, he must be absent from the scene (at least psychologically), but the present-tense "I seek" confines the activity within the circle of friends. The poem constitutes the object of *eros* as absent, always elsewhere, and the listeners, who do comprehend the "confession," as a group of intimates.

Anakreon's other poem addresses a girl who is depreciated in the very address: she is called a "Thracian filly" (which may mean that she is a slave). This girl is not depicted as absent but as unwilling (417 *PMG*):

πῶλε Θρηικίη, τί δή με
  λοξὸν ὄμμασι βλέπουσα
νηλέως φεύγεις, δοκεῖς δέ
  μ' οὐδὲν εἰδέναι σοφόν;
ἴσθι τοι, καλῶς μὲν ἄν τοι
  τὸν χαλινὸν ἐμβάλοιμι,
ἡνίας δ' ἔχων στρέφοιμί
  σ' ἀμφὶ τέρματα δρόμου·
5 νῦν δὲ λειμῶνάς τε βόσκεαι
  κοῦφά τε σκιρτῶσα παίζεις,
δεξιὸν γὰρ ἱπποπείρην
  οὐκ ἔχεις ἐπεμβάτην.

Thracian filly, why do you look at me askance with your eyes and flee pitilessly, why think that I know nothing involving skill? Take it from me, I could throw the bridle over you neatly and holding the reins could make you do turns around the posts of the course. As it is, you graze in the meadows and play frisking lightly, for you do not have a deft, experienced rider on your back.

The singer threatens to ride her, but the verbs of the threat are in the optative. Its immediacy is drained away, contingent on some unspecified condition. Poised again between capacity and triumph, the singer asserts his masculine identity without abandoning the group for the private pleasure of rape. The image is left of a frisking girl, unprotected by respectable status but as yet untamed. The staging of the performer is through his address to the girl: he asserts his mastery of her verbally, but the ones who assent to his declaration of power are the members of the audience.

These four poems, superficially so different, all show the speaker off as passionate and forceful and the object of passion as aestheticized. Whether virginal or provocative (the set includes one of each by each poet), the unindividuated object becomes the focus of the whole group's feelings of desire. Thus a shared, verbally constituted figure substitutes for the actual individual desires of the symposiasts and creates an experience of collective masculine sexuality. The psychological effect could operate even if individual drinkers admitted to particular desires, for those desires would appear to be instantiations of the ever-unreachable corporate ideal. The poetry of Ibykos and Anakreon was not for the self-defining group or *hetaireia,* so here the staging of the singer as a lover replaces political themes such as are found even in the erotic poetry of Archilochos.

Pindar adopts the same technique for a delicate poem, an encomium probably meant to be sung at a symposium (123 *SM*).[132] When commenting earlier in the chapter on Bacchylides' poem praising Alexander son of Amyntas, I said that the one momentarily singled out must be reunited with the group as well in order to preserve the collective. Pindar employs a depersonalized, suspended effusion of desire to praise Theoxenos and also reintegrate him with the others, combining it with the theme of disconnection from women encoded in the contrast of marriage and symposium:

> χρῆν μὲν κατὰ καιρὸν ἐρώ-
>   των δρέπεσθαι, θυμέ, σὺν ἁλικίᾳ·
> τὰς δὲ Θεοξένου ἀκτῖνας πρὸς ὄσσων
> μαρμαρυζοίσας δρακεὶς
> 5 ὃς μὴ πόθῳ κυμαίνεται, ἐξ ἀδάμαντος
>
> ἢ σιδάρου κεχάλκευται μέλαιναν καρδίαν
> ψυχρᾷ φλογί, πρὸς δ' Ἀφροδί-
>   τας ἀτιμασθεὶς ἑλικογλεφάρου
> ἢ περὶ χρήμασι μοχθίζει βιαίως
> ἢ γυναικείῳ θράσει
> ψυχρὰν† φορεῖται πᾶσαν ὁδὸν θεραπεύων.
> 10 ἀλλ' ἐγὼ τᾶς ἕκατι κηρὸς ὣς δαχθεὶς ἕλᾳ
>
> ἱρᾶν μελισσᾶν τάκομαι, εὖτ' ἂν ἴδω
> παίδων νεόγυιον ἐς ἥβαν·
> ἐν δ' ἄρα καὶ Τενέδῳ
> Πειθώ τ' ἔναιεν καὶ Χάρις
> 15 υἱὸν Ἀγησίλα.

[132] The form of the poem is triadic, which could imply choral performance but need not. Van Groningen 1960: 15–18 points out that no evidence exists for choral performance of *skolia* (the category in which he includes Pindar's "personal" encomia). He assumes that Pindar sang his *skolia* himself, but they may have been commissioned. It is unknown whether this one triad is the whole poem.

One ought, heart, pluck one's loves in due season, with youth; but he who looks at the sparkling rays of Theoxenos' eyes and does not swell with desire has a dark heart forged of adamant or iron in a cold fire and, dishonored by round-eyed Aphrodite, either labors vehemently for money or is carried down the whole length of a cold road by female assertiveness, a servitor. But I melt like the wax of holy bees in the warmth on (Aphrodite's) account, stung whenever I look at the new-limbed youth of boys. Now truly in Tenedos Persuasion and Grace dwell in the son of Hagesilaos.[133]

This poem is often treated simply as an expression of Pindar's love for Theoxenos, but in fact that is not what it says.[134] The movement of the poem as it positions speaker, addressee, and audience is more complex and must be followed carefully. The speaker begins as though he were about to reveal his own ardor, but when he identifies the subject who looks at the rays of Theoxenos' eyes in line 4, it is general: all who are not impervious. Theoxenos excites infatuation in all those present, or so it is implied, for the next step is to distinguish those who do feel passion for him from those who do not. The latter group is cold, seeks money, and suffers subjection to women, the opposite of the sympotic audience. Anyone who does not want to align himself with those sorry souls will agree to find Theoxenos beautiful. In line 10 the speaker returns to his own reaction, but now it is generalized to all lovely youth. The poem therefore opens by staging the speaker in a confession of desire, as the poems of Ibykos and Anakreon also do, but one that draws attention to Theoxenos. Then it embraces the audience with the speaker in admiring him and turns the admiration into a flattering portrait of the audience as a special class. Finally it casts its light back on the speaker, whose steady state of desire shows that Theoxenos is representative. ἀλλ' ἐγώ (but I) in line 10 contrasts directly with the one suffering under γυναικείῳ θράσει (female assertiveness) and depicts the speaker as an exemplary symposiast. What is left at the end is a circle whose collective identity is imaged as preference for the young men who join them over attachment to women. The poem is a study in avoiding expression of any individual relationships, while putting erotic energy into circulation.

Unlike the poems I have been considering, Theognis' generic love po-etry (the so-called Book II, 1231–1389) does connect eroticism and poli-tics, but only in that speech ostensibly addressed to a beloved is in fact directed at the symposium audience.[135] Many of these poems address an undelineated "boy," while some just have a second-person pronoun and

---

[133] On this poem see van Groningen 1960: 51–83, esp. 60–67 on the meaning of the phrase containing γυναικείῳ θράσει. I follow his interpretation.

[134] Athenaios (13, 601d), quoting these lines, says that Pindar was in love with Theoxenos.

[135] See Lewis 1985 on the love poetry as political precept; Edmunds 1988: 81–84 on the speaker's assimilation of love relationships to political ones and fear of domination.

some are gnomic. Desire here is largely an excuse for the singer to profess his virtues and the respect he deserves. But the lover is not successful. That the generic beloved has wronged the singer gives the latter his justification for self-assertion. Lines 1263–66 will serve as an example:

> ὦ παῖ, ὃς εὖ ἔρδοντι κακὴν ἀπέδωκας ἀμοιβήν,
> οὐδέ τις ἀντ᾽ ἀγαθῶν ἐστι χάρις παρὰ σοί·
> 1265 οὐδέν πώ μ᾽ ὤνησας· ἐγὼ δέ σε πολλάκις ἤδη
> εὖ ἔρδων αἰδοῦς οὐδεμιῆς ἔτυχον.

O boy, you who give an evil return to the one who benefits you, there is no gratitude in you in response to favors either. You have in no way done me service; but though I have often done well by you, I meet with no respect.

The technique is similar to Archilochos' use of erotic situations to proclaim his view of reciprocity, but without any of his audience-baiting wit or scene-setting. And in contrast to Archilochos, Ibykos, and Anakreon, Theognis does not induce imaginings of sexual pleasure in his audience, for he does not offer here (and seldom elsewhere) any sensuous language to color his representation of desire and its frustration. The lover's solicitation is merely a minimal framework that enables the performer to assert his own virtues and values and express the general sense that they do not meet with appreciation in the world at large. This is staging through disconnection at its least vivid.

A very different approach to asserting and sharing masculine sexuality in the symposium was to evoke not a state of arrested desire but sexual activity with a partner whom the speaker shares, verbally, with the others. Anakreon's poem on the Thracian filly provided an image vivid enough to engage the libidinous imagination of the audience. The iambographers' way was to describe the act graphically, as if it were public. This approach has a parallel in the end of the *Lysistrata* (1112–88), in which the Athenians and Spartans divide up the body of *Diallage* (Reconciliation). Action as well as desire is thus transformed from self-assertion to mutual experience. The extant fragments of iambic sexual poems are mostly too tattered to read, but the style is discernable. Archilochos 119 *W* is an example:

> καὶ πεσεῖν δρήστην ἐπ᾽ ἀσκόν, κἀπὶ γαστρὶ γαστέρα
> προσβαλεῖν μηρούς τε μηροῖς

. . . and to fall, a workman, on her wineskin and press stomach on stomach and thighs on thighs . . .

It is conceivable that these lines followed a line quoted elsewhere (118 *W*):[136]

---

[136] See Gerber 1975: 183–84 for various suggestions and problems. Gerber rejects the collocation, which does not fit his reading of 119 (with δρήστην meaning "penis" as subject

εἰ γὰρ ὣς ἐμοὶ γένοιτο χεῖρα Νεοβούλης θιγεῖν.[137]

Would that thus it be mine to touch Neoboule's hand.

The combination would produce a more complex effect, for Neoboule belongs to the Lykambes theme. The unrealized, tender-sounding wish would suddenly turn into evocation of the act, and sex into the shaming of Lykambes. Mention of a permissible body part would lead to exposure of hidden parts. Since Neoboule was portrayed as "ruined" already, at least in the Cologne Epode (discussed earlier), she is available for such graphic treatment. True, if 119 is part of the wish construction of 118, the poem offers suspended desire rather than public exposure, but even sharing a fantasy of Neoboule's body in such unvarnished terms shames her. The Cologne Epode is far more discrete in naming what it pictures. An additional effect of the completely speculative combination is that it explains 118, which by itself seems respectful toward Neoboule, as part of the same set of defaming poems rather than a poem from a different stage in the relations between Archilochos and the family of Lykambes.

Hipponax is even more imaginative (84.10–22 *W*):

```
10   ἐκδύγτες α[
     ἐδάκνομέν τε κἀφ[ιλέομεν
     διὲκ θυρέων βλέ[ποντες
     μὴ ἥμεας λάβ[
     γυμνοὺς ἐρυ[
15   ἔσπευδε δ' ἡ μ[ὲν
     ἐγὼ δ' ἐβίνε[ον          ]τε κα[ὶ
     ἐπ' ἄκρον ἕλκων ὥσπερ ἀλλᾶντα ψήχων,
     κλαίειν κελεύ[ων Βού]παλο[ν
     κ[αί] μ' αὐτίκ' ἐξ[          ]σεν ἐκ δεπ[
20   καὶ δὴ 'πὶ τοῖς ἔργοισιν εἴχομ[εν
     ἐγὼ μὲν ὥσπ[ερ ὁ]ρυσὸν ἰστι[
     σφάζειν ὑπέτ[          ]φαλουτ[
```

. . . undressing . . . we were biting and [kissing] . . . looking out the door . . . lest he (?) catch us . . . naked . . . and she was eager . . . and I was fucking . . . and drawing up toward the top as if skinning a sausage, telling Boupalos to go

---

of the infinitive). Fr. 118 need not be taken as "coarse" if the two are joined, for the point would have been in the change of tone.

[137] This is the transmitted text. West prints χειρί since the verb usually takes a genitive; the line then says, " . . . touch Neoboule with my hand." But the accusative is possible; see Gerber 1975: 183.

hang . . . and on the spot . . . me out . . . and in fact we were in the middle of
the job . . . I like a shriveled mast . . . to slay. . . .

The speaker is interrupted.[138] The sexual act is completed, as it were, in
the telling of the poem, and the pornographic humor allows the audience
to share phallic sexuality. There may be further pleasure as well. A man
named Boupalos functioned as the symposium's "other" in the poetry of
Hipponax.[139] If the woman in the narrative is Arete, the girlfriend of
Boupalos, then the speaker shames Boupalos, both taking his place with
Arete and exposing Arete imaginatively to the view of the whole group.
Sex doubles as a victory over the group's opposite. At the same time the
speaker's collapse deflects his own sexual self-presentation into a bawdy
joke.[140]

Symposium poetry is more various than community or bardic poetry,
for it met a wider range of situations and needs. The brief poems had
momentary effects and responded to passing impressions. But the self-
presentation in the symposium must have been a matter of more immediacy for many men than communal performance. Symposium performance was not scripted ahead of time, and its impromptu character made
it an unpredictable arena for the crossing of personalities. In this volatile
atmosphere the leitmotif of male bonding against an outside world helped
guide the fashioning of song and determine the kind of gendered self-
presentation that participants offered to one another.

IV

In Chapter 1 I discussed one of Solon's poems (1–3 W) as a limit case of
community poetry. It invited the community to regroup around the
speaker and accept his advice on fighting for Salamis as communal opinion. I would like to end this chapter by analyzing another of Solon's
poems, one that comments on his past political activity, pointing out this
time that it does not conform to the characteristics of symposium poetry as
I have described them. This poem (36 W) shares with Solon 1–3 W a
detached speaker but carries separation from the audience even further. It
is in iambic trimeter, a meter that suggests an association with iambogra-
phy.[141] I quote two sections (1–7, 15–27):

[138] See Masson 1962 *ad* fr. 84, who interprets the action this way. On the text cf. also
Degani 1991.

[139] Boupalos did exist; he was a sculptor (referred to in Pausanias 4.30.6 and elsewhere).
Boupalos and Arete recur in Hipponax's poetry, e.g., 12, 14–17, 120 W. Their function may
be similar to that of Lykambes and his daughters in Archilochos' poetry.

[140] See West 1974: 28 for other references to sexual activity in Hipponax and Semonides.

[141] Anhalt 1993: 137–38 comments on the dissonances in the poem that make iambic a
good choice.

ἐγὼ δὲ τῶν μὲν οὕνεκα ξυνήγαγον
δῆμον, τί τούτων πρὶν τυχεῖν ἐπαυσάμην;
συμμαρτυροίη ταῦτ᾽ ἂν ἐν δίκηι Χρόνου
μήτηρ μεγίστη δαιμόνων Ὀλυμπίων
5   ἄριστα, Γῆ μέλαινα, τῆς ἐγώ ποτε
ὅρους ἀνεῖλον πολλαχῆι πεπηγότας,
πρόσθεν δὲ δουλεύουσα, νῦν ἐλευθέρη. . . .
15   ταῦτα μὲν κράτει
ὁμοῦ βίην τε καὶ δίκην ξυναρμόσας
ἔρεξα, καὶ διῆλθον ὡς ὑπεσχόμην·
θεσμοὺς δ᾽ ὁμοίως τῶι κακῶι τε κἀγαθῶι
εὐθεῖαν εἰς ἕκαστον ἁρμόσας δίκην
20   ἔγραψα. κέντρον δ᾽ ἄλλος ὡς ἐγὼ λαβών,
κακοφραδής τε καὶ φιλοκτήμων ἀνήρ,
οὐκ ἂν κατέσχε δῆμον· εἰ γὰρ ἤθελον
ἃ τοῖς ἐναντίοισιν ἥνδανεν τότε,
αὖτις δ᾽ ἃ τοῖσιν οὕτεροι φρασαίατο,
25   πολλῶν ἂν ἀνδρῶν ἥδ᾽ ἐχηρώθη πόλις.
τῶν οὕνεκ᾽ ἀλκὴν πάντοθεν ποιεόμενος
ὡς ἐν κυσὶν πολλῆισιν ἐστράφην λύκος.

I, however, of those things for which I called together the people, which of them
have I dropped before accomplishing? The great mother of the Olympian
powers, black Earth, could best bear witness from me to these things in the
court of Time, (Earth) from whom I some time ago pulled up the boundary
stones set in many places, (Earth) in slavery before, now free.
(I rescued those who were enslaved or dispossessed.)
These things I did by force, joining justice and violence together, and I pro-
ceeded as I promised; laws for the bad and the good alike, attaching straight
justice to each, I wrote. Another taking up the goad as I did, an evil-minded and
gain-loving man, would not have held back the people. For if I had wanted what
pleased one set of opponents at the time or again what the others were contriv-
ing for them, this city would have been bereaved of many men. For these reasons, devising protection on all sides, I circled like a wolf among many dogs.

The poem begins with an emphatic first-person pronoun. Superficially its
assertiveness might be compared with Archilochos', but the kinds of
things they assert are very different. In 1 *W* Archilochos makes a first-
person declaration:

εἰμὶ δ' ἐγὼ θεράπων μὲν Ἐνυαλίοιο ἄνακτος
καὶ Μουσέων ἐρατὸν δῶρον ἐπιστάμενος.

I am both a servant of lord Ares and one who knows the lovely gift of the Muses.

Archilochos proffers precisely the identity that legitimates his presence in the circle of military/political figures for whom he sang. Presumably every member of his audience could make the same boast, for the two capacities Archilochos claims were expected of aristocratic figures.[142] Furthermore, the language is cautious, quite different from his projected personality in dialogue with female figures: Archilochos is a "servant" of Ares, not a master of war, and he "knows the gifts" of the Muses, that is, he can sing or recite but does not claim to compose himself.[143] Archilochos' self-characterization does not distinguish him from his listeners even while highlighting his worthiness to be among them.

Solon's assertion, on the other hand, characterizes him in a unique way, for Solon describes not who he is but what he has done.[144] The poem opens with a question to engage its audience, but the question implies that criticism has been directed at Solon; it is really a challenge to opponents. The poem continues by answering the question, preempting any answer from others. His appeal to the earth as witness in the future overrides the present speech of critics. Concomitantly, Solon refuses to identify his point of view with that of any group in the city: they are all dogs (27). The poem is profoundly anti-symposiastic. The isolation of the *ego* at the beginning is matched by λύκος (wolf), the last word of the poem.[145] The wolf has been met with twice in this chapter as the antithesis of the symposium group.[146] In claiming it, Solon excludes himself from the group.

Solon's treatment of the female figure, Ge (Earth), is consistent with his stance. He does not single out Attica as a privileged land, as for instance Delos was singled out in the *Hymn to Delian Apollo*. His action was di-

[142] Bowie 1986: 14–15 notes this in pointing out that symposium elegy tends to identify the singer with the group rather than setting him apart.

[143] Aloni 1981: 31–48, esp. 41, makes a similar point in analyzing the relations of this couplet with epic.

[144] Vox 1983: 517–19 compares Solon with Archilochos but portrays an Archilochos at odds with the community and mocking at his own expense, while Solon was in rapport with the community and "auto-encomistica, quasi auto-agiografica." While agreeing with the final adjectives, I see the communicative effect of these self-presentations differently.

[145] Anhalt 1993: 126–34 explores the imagery of the wolf in other poetry as an isolated figure of blame and suggests (134) that Solon takes on himself the role of scapegoat that will bring the others into unity.

[146] Loraux 1984, esp. 206–7 emphasizes Solon's repeated image of his own isolation, the wolf here echoing his picture of himself as a boundary-marker placed in the middle between factions, in 37.9–10 *W*.

rected simply at "Earth." He is like a bard in bringing himself into relationship with a great mythic female power; but rather than defeat her and
adopt the position of Zeus, he is her heroic champion.[147] He equates political action with heroic action when he claims that he has made earth "free"
(5–7); so when next he says that he freed enslaved citizens and brought
others home (8–15), he speaks as though he had exercised coercion from
outside the political system.

His final action was to write laws. Like his imposition of a new order by
force, writing isolates Solon, for it sets itself above exchange of speech in
assembly or symposium.[148] Only at the end of the poem does Solon explain and shift his self-representation: he held all parties in check, hence can
identify with none. The final image of the wolf then changes the image
from one of coercion to one of combat.

Where then was the poem performed?[149] It could have been performed
anywhere, in a symposium or to a larger public, for no matter where it was
performed, it has the same effect: it monumentalizes Solon. Just as he
wrote laws, so Solon has "written" himself. Rather than poetry designed
for interaction with an audience, this poem is designed to replace the
speaker by an internally constructed, fixed figure whose activity is past
and whose significance is established. Furthermore, the poem can only be
a "true" assertion if the *ego* is Solon. If Solon recited the poem, he was
isolating himself from his audience by its form, and if anyone else did so,
he would become a kind of marker of "Solon," an absent figure replaced
by his text. The poem forces a reciter to lend his voice to the poem to
revive Solon without the reciter's being able actually to take on the first-
person identity.[150]

The closest parallel to this poem is found among the inscriptions discussed in Chapters 2 and 6. One could compare, for instance, the
Phrasikleia monument (Chapter 6, #6), in which *ego* refers to the statue of
the young woman that replaces the living Phrasikleia. In other inscriptions
to be studied in Chapter 6, even closer parallels will be found, inscriptions

[147] Vox 1984 compares Solon's poetry methodically with epic and finds him to be redefining epic heroism for his self-portrait.

[148] Cf. Ford 1985 on Theognis and Hipparchos claiming ownership of fixed texts and
appropriating their political power. Hipparchos used writing, setting up herms that bore his
name and a gnomic couplet (Ps-Plato *Hipparchos* 228cd). In Aeschylus *Suppliants* 942–49
Pelasgos contrasts persuasion and debate with writing.

[149] Vetta 1983b: xvii–xvix argues for a symposium setting for Solon's poetry, as does
Bowie 1986: 18–21. Tedeschi 1982: 38–40 proposes larger gatherings like a feast in the
phratry.

[150] The process of heroizing lawgivers that Szegedy-Maszak 1978 has identified is invited
by this poem. Svenbro 1993: 135–44 calls attention to the tattooed body of Epimenides,
whose *ego* was inseparable from his writing and who therefore became a *sēma* (sign or grave-
marker).

that borrow the reader's voice to address the reader and that preempt the reader's reaction by referring to the future. Solon makes of himself a *stele,* or monument, on which his own program is summed up, both (like the law-code) as a guide to relations in the state and (like a grave-marker) to give the summarized, fixed statement of his own significance. As we saw in Chapter 2, writing, because it disjoined speaker and audience, permitted a kind of self-representation in absence that could be forthright, unmindful of counterclaims. By composing as if he were writing for readers, Solon has made use of the *style* that writing permitted. One significance of writing, as it entered a system of communication dominated by performance, was in the new possibilities for self-representation it intimated—representation of a self not defined through jostling for position within a group.

CHAPTER SIX

Sappho's Circle

I

THE LAST SETTING for performance to be investigated is the women's circle. Women met together apart from men in larger or smaller groups. All the women of a community might celebrate religious festivals like the Thesmophoria, which honored Demeter. Alkaios 130B *V,* discussed in Chapter 5, gives us a vignette of married women (and probably *parthenoi* too) in a sanctuary on Lesbos occupied in judging beauty and celebrating a religious festival. Other festivals such as the Adonia that were not statesponsored and communitywide (at least at Athens) brought smaller groups together, and so did the committees or boards of women who organized the large festivals.[1] Women, especially *parthenoi,* must have met to rehearse for choral performance, and older women were no doubt often in charge of training them; some see a period of segregation and initiation for *parthenoi* in these choral activities, but, as pointed out in Chapter 2, there is no reason to think that their performances were closed to the community. In addition to these opportunities, women met in small groups also, where they might sing for one another: Athenian vasepainting shows women gathered together and listening as one plays and sings.[2] Such groups would be analogous to male groups meeting at symposia and were probably characteristically aristocratic.

In these all-female settings a woman should be (relatively) free of pressure to express alienation from herself as a speaking or a sexual being. The only poetry that survives from such a setting, with the possible exception of Korinna's poetry, is Sappho's, so it is to her that I now turn with this question. Sappho composed wedding songs and other ritual poetry; it will be argued later that these were choral, and as such they would have been performed to a larger audience, more representative of the community. But she also composed poetry addressed to individual women and concerned with feelings and relationships, "personal" poetry whose closest analogue is symposium poetry and whose audience is agreed to be other women. The nature, however, of the women's group for which she sang

---

[1] See Burkert 1985: 230, 242–46; Kraemer 1992: 22–29 for an overview, 30–35 on the Adonia.

[2] West 1992a: plates 7, 22, and 33; Bérard 1989: figure 124; cf. figures 127–34 for groups of women together.

is difficult to reconstruct and has been the subject of recent controversy.[3] There are two broad possibilities. Did Sappho train *parthenoi* in choral performance and, more than that, guide their awakening sexuality through the transition to adulthood, or even oversee a formal initiation process, as the prevalent reconstruction has it? If she was the mentor of *parthenoi*, how much of her poetry was in fact choral and composed for performance by them (therefore reflecting their self-presentation and not hers)? Or was her audience a circle of friends who were adult women like herself, no doubt married?[4] As in the previous chapters, I must begin by considering the setting and the psychological efficacy of performance therein. I must therefore defend my view of her audience first of all, for singing to a group of friends would not call for the same effects or, consequently, the same self-presentation as performance to students. To ground my approach, I examine the external and internal evidence for her collective audience and then the major scholarly reconstructions. In common with most scholars, I assume that Sappho was an adult when she composed her poetry and that women frequently addressed in her poetry were part of the audience. One's view of Sappho's audience colors one's estimation of her sexuality, as I point out later.

There are two passages in much later authors that purport to describe Sappho's life and circle. The tenth-century encyclopedia called the Suda speaks of Sappho as having three ἑταῖραι and φίλαι (companions and friends), Atthis, Telesippa, and Megara, "with respect to whom she also suffered imputation of shameful love," and three μαθήτριαι (students), Anaktoria (emended from "Anagora" in the text) of Miletos, Gongyla of Kolophon, and Euneika of Salamis.[5] Maximus of Tyre in the second century CE gives a list of those whom Sappho loved: Gyrinna, Atthis, and Anaktoria.[6] Gorgo and Andromeda, he says, were ἀντίτεχνοι (rival practitioners). Maximus' list of beloved women includes one named as a "friend" and one called a "student" by the Suda. What grounds the Suda had for distinguishing the two sets of women is unknown, but since the

---

[3] Parker 1993; Lardinois 1994. Parker anticipates many of my own arguments, arrived at independently. I am glad to see that our views are similar.

[4] I assume that Sappho was married, although the information in the Suda (= 253 *V*) that she was married to Kerkylas (κέρκος is a slang term for "penis") of Andros (Isle of Man) looks as though it were derived from jokes in fourth-century Attic comedy, in which Sappho figured as a character. See *pap. Oxy.* 1800 fr. 1 (= 252 *V*) and the Suda for testimony that Sappho had a daughter Kleis, named after her own mother (specific and undisputed information that must derive from her poetry); Hallett 1982 on the nonsexual adjective "beloved" applied to Kleis in 132 *V*.

[5] S.v. Σαπφώ = 253 *V*; Test. 2, Campbell 1982. Campbell 1982 includes text, translation, and testimonia for Sappho; he follows the numbering of Lobel and Page, which is generally the same as that of Voigt. Hereafter citations of "Test." refer to Campbell.

[6] 18.9 = 219 *V*; Test. 20.

"students" are all from other cities, the compiler of the Suda (or rather his source) may have postulated that they were students to explain why Sappho knew them.[7] In addition, two references to Sappho's relations with other women are found in biographical notices recovered on papyrus. One fragment (*pap. Colon.* 5860) describes Sappho as "educating at leisure the best not only of local (female persons) but also of those from Ionia."[8] This statement accords with the information in the much later Suda.[9] Another papyrus containing a capsule biography reports that she was accused by some of being a γυναικε[ράσ]τρια (woman-lover).[10] These four passages are the only testimony bearing on Sappho's audience that purports to be biographical. We may deduce from it that Sappho addressed poems expressing love to "companions" and (if the emendation in the Suda is accepted) to at least one woman from another city.

But what does Sappho mean by "companions"? Internal evidence corroborates that the word is Sappho's own and shows its application. Athenaios quotes a scrap to show that Sappho used the word ἑταίρα to mean "friend" (160 *V*):

τάδε νῦν ἑταίραις
ταῖς ἔμαις †τέρπνα† κάλως ἀείσω

. . . now these delightful things (?) I will sing beautifully to my companions. . . .

If the first person is the singer and the quotation is not from ceremonial poetry, these lines give us our only actual statement about the identity of Sappho's audience. They do not reveal what relationship in age the "companions" have to Sappho, but the other line quoted by Athenaios at the same time helps (142 *V*):

Λάτω καὶ Νιόβα μάλα μὲν φίλαι ἦσαν ἔταιραι

Leto and Niobe were very dear companions.

The line joins two women whose later dispute over their relative childbearing prowess, according to the myth, shows that they were thought of

[7] Parker 1993: 320 puts this idea forward also.

[8] S 261A *SLG;* 214B Campbell 1982. See Gronewald 1974. It must be a deduction, for where outside the poems would information of this sort be preserved? The following statement, that Sappho was in good repute among the citizens, is attributed to Kallias, a Mytilenean of the third/second century BCE, who wrote a commentary on Sappho and Alkaios, according to Strabo 13.2.4, but nothing assures that Kallias is the source of the earlier statement. One would have to posit private records or memoirs or an oral tradition surviving for over four hundred fifty years to reach the time of Kallias, and we do not know that the statement comes from him.

[9] Burnett 1983: 210n.4 remarks that "at leisure" must mean that Sappho took students as a private person. What it may mean is that there was no public evidence of her activity.

[10] *Pap. Oxy.* 1800 fr. 1 = 252 *V;* Test. 1.

as more or less coeval.[11] By analogy, Sappho's "companions" should be of the same age-category, adult women.

Another tantalizing fragment is 24.2–6 *V:*

    [ ]εμνάσεσθ' ἀ[
    κ]αὶ γὰρ ἄμμες ἐν νεό[τατι
    <u>ταῦτ' [ἐ]πόημμεν·</u>

5   πόλλα [μ]ὲν γὰρ καὶ κά[λα
    ]η[   ]μεν, πολι

. . . (you?) will remember [   ] for we also did these things in (our) youth; for many beautiful [   ] we [   ], city (?)

Does the "we" include the audience? Since it follows on what looks like a second-person plural verb, which must be addressed to the audience, and there is no parallelism (e.g., "for we remember") to suggest that "you" and "we" are differentiated, Sappho would appear to be addressing an audience no longer young. The word *city* seems to have stood in line 6, so we have a minimal hint of a civic or political aspect to the memory.

Those who believe that Sappho headed a group of *parthenoi* argue that she applied the term *companion* to them. But there is no reason to think a priori that Sappho would call *parthenoi* ἔταιραι, given the difference in status, for the word (in the masculine) refers either to a notional equal, a "companion," or to a military or intellectual follower, one who differs in ability but not in age category.[12] It should be added that the first papyrus quoted does not identify those Sappho educated as *parthenoi,* and Maximus and the second papyrus use *gynē* (married/adult woman) or a word based on it to name Sappho's kind of love.

All other passages adverting to Sappho's addressees or audience or loves conjure Sappho for some literary purpose of the author's and not with the intention of giving information about her.[13] Hellenistic and Roman

[11] The discussion in Athenaios 13, 571b–572b turns on the two meanings of ἑταίρα, "courtesan" and "friend." The word occurs only one other time in Sappho, in 126 *V,* a line that may be erotic but tells us nothing about relative ages:

    δαύοις(') ἀπάλας ἐτα⟨ί⟩ρας ἐν στήθεσιν

    May you sleep (*or* "sleeping") on the breast of a tender companion.

Howie 1979: 318–19 cites passages of single-sex feasting and pleasure, including some in which male companions of the same age have erotic relationships, e.g., Theognis 1063–64.

[12] And (in the feminine) to a courtesan, but that meaning is ruled out by Athenaios. According to *LSJ* s.v. the meaning "pupil" or "disciple" appears in a philosophical context in the late fifth century. Calame 1977: I 75–77 takes the word in a choral context as "subordinate," parallel to the meaning "follower" in Homer in a military context; members of a chorus of *parthenoi* are ἔταιραι to the chorus-leader to whom they are attached.

[13] See Hallett 1979 on the development of attitudes toward Sappho; Snyder 1989. Dover

writers picture her as a lover. The Hellenistic poet Nossis, a woman, evokes Sappho as a predecessor and writes poems implying erotic response to women.[14] The Roman poets Horace and Ovid describe Sappho as loving *puellae* (girls).[15] *Puella* is not the equivalent of *parthenos* (for which the Latin is *virgo*), and in love poetry it means "girlfriend."[16] These writers give no indication that they thought of Sappho as consorting with *parthenoi*.

Later yet, Philostratos, a second or third century CE novelist, describes a Damophyla of Pamphylia as an associate of Sappho's who is said to have collected *parthenoi* as ὁμιλητρίας (associates/students) in the fashion of Sappho and to have composed poems, both erotic works and hymns.[17] This is the only passage even to suggest that *parthenoi* formed Sappho's circle, and not coincidentally the author is thinking primarily of cult poetry: he says that Damophyla composed "the hymns in Aeolian and Pamphylian modes that they sing to Artemis of Perge" and that these are derived from Sappho. If there were in fact such hymns, sung by *parthenoi*, in the second or third century CE, one can imagine that they were attributed to a probably mythical early poet Damophyla, whom it was tempting to link with Sappho. Philostratos creates the link by making *parthenoi* (who sang the hymns) "students" as well, who would go on to compose their own hymns. An important feature of this passage is its demonstration that by this time interest in Sappho had shifted to include her more ceremonious compositions.

Now Sappho's wedding poetry gains attention, and with the new focus comes reference to *parthenoi*—but as figures in and performers of her poetry and not as Sappho's audience! Four passages mention *parthenoi* as the subject or performers of Sappho's poetry. Himerios, a rhetorician of the fourth century CE, says that Sappho "loved [beauty] together with the lyre and on account of this . . . made *parthenoi* and the Graces the occasion of her songs"; he is presumably referring to her wedding poetry, which he

---

1978: 173–75 gives a skeptical summary of the reliability of biographical evidence and evolving treatment of Sappho as a figure in the literary work of other authors.

[14] The subject of *Anth. Pal.* 6.354 is called a *gynē*, and none is named a *parthenos*. See Skinner 1989 and 1991b for Nossis' interest in women and claim to be a successor to Sappho. In some epigrams (e.g., 6.353) women (presumably young) are like or close to their mothers.

[15] Horace *Odes* 2.13.24–25 = Test. 18; Ovid *Heroides* 15.15–20 = Test. 19; *Tristia* 2.365 = Test. 49.

[16] Horace *Odes* 4.9.12 = Test. 51 calls Sappho herself a *puella*. Lardinois 1994: 64n.30 argues that in Ovid *Tristia* 2.365 *puella* means "unmarried girl." The line is: Lesbia quid docuit Sappho, nisi amare, puellas? (What did Lesbian Sappho teach girls except to love?) However, Ovid is not saying that she instructed virgins in sexual techniques; cf. the parallel with Anakreon, who "advised" mixing wine and love.

[17] *Life of Apollonios* 1.30 = 223 V; Test. 21.

recalls frequently.[18] In another speech Himerios gives a baroque description of Sappho performing the "rites of Aphrodite": Sappho enters the bridal chamber, spreads the bed, [gathers?] the *parthenoi* into the bride's room, brings Aphrodite on the chariot of the Graces, and so on; he attributes to her the motions described in her poetry.[19] Philostratos says, "Sappho loves the rose and always crowns it with an encomium, likening the beautiful *parthenoi* to it."[20] In the twelfth century Sappho is still said to compare a bride to a rose, so this effusion is probably a reference to wedding poetry.[21] A different Philostratos depicts a chorus of *parthenoi* singing a hymn around an altar redolent of Sappho to a statue of modest Aphrodite.[22] Sappho's name helps to set a demurely erotic atmosphere. The same interest in female desire as part of ideal married love that David Konstan documents in the Greek novels may be operating in this conventional and encomiastic literature.[23]

Finally, an undatable epigram from the *Palatine Anthology* (9.189) depicts Sappho as singing for a chorus of dancers in a shrine of Hera. And in a reversion to Sappho's love poetry, Themistios in the fourth century CE says that Sappho and Anakreon praised their παιδικά (beloveds).[24] The term, drawn from male older-younger relationships, is too general to tell us anything. In sum, the literary testimony tells us only what part of Sappho's oeuvre was engaging the imaginations of the time. But none of it except Philostratos' provision of a literary filiation for Damophyla gives any expression to the notion that Sappho ever sang to an assembled audience of *parthenoi*. For that matter, there is nothing to show that any of these later people had ever read Sappho's poetry, since conjuring with her name had become a commonplace of rhetorical technique.[25]

In the fragments of Sappho, all of the occurrences of *parthenos* and words from the same stem, in cases where a context allows us to judge, come in poems associated with weddings (27, 30, 44, 56 probably [see below], 107 probably, 112, 114 *V*) or in poems with a mythical topic (44A *V*).[26] Four instances (17.14, 93, 103Cb, 153 *V*) are impossible to judge because of lack of context. In the first of these, 17, an allusion to the Atreidai stopping on

---

[18] Quotation from *Orations* 28.2 = 221 *V*; Test. 50. There are problems with the text. For his use of Sappho's wedding poetry, see 104b, 108, 194, 218 *V*. He also makes two very general references to Sappho's poetry, 208 and 220 *V*.

[19] *Orations* 9.4 = 194 *V*; 194 Campbell 1982.

[20] *Letters* 51 = 216 *V*.

[21] 194A *V*; 117A Campbell 1982.

[22] *Imagines* 2.1.1–2.

[23] Konstan 1994: 33–35.

[24] *Orations* 13, 170d-171a = Test. 52.

[25] Cf. Demetrios *On Style* 132 = Test. 45; Menander Rhetor *On Display Oratory* 402.17–18 Russell and Wilson = Test. 46.

[26] Parker 1993: 323 makes the same point.

Lesbos to pray to Hera, Zeus, and Dionysus seems to introduce a prayer of the speaker's, in the second line of which π]αρθ[εν is restored (14). Reinhold Merkelbach suggests that the poem was a *propemptikon* (farewell song) for a *parthenos* who was one of Sappho's friends.[27] To call it a *propemptikon* is speculative in itself, but the qualifier "for one of Sappho's friends" has no basis. Moreover, ἄγνα (holy) stands in the line above, which may mean that the *parthenos* was more than human.[28] The text becomes so fragmentary at the point where the prayer begins that nothing definite can be said about it, but whether the *parthenos* was human or divine the poem appears to be ceremonial poetry, in which case it tells us nothing about Sappho's own audience.

The same distribution is found with equivalent words. The word κόρα (girl) appears in a wedding context (108 *V*), a ritual or mythic context as a vocative used by Aphrodite to those lamenting the death of Adonis (140 *V*), and as a description of the Charites (53 *V*). The word πάις (child) is used in a wedding context in 27, 104a (probably), 113 *V;* of Sappho's daughter Kleis in 132; of someone in the past in 49; with mythic reference in 1, 16, 103; to mean "child of" in 155; in an indeterminable context in 58, 64, 164, 95 (not certainly this word), 102 (folksong?), 122 (wedding?).[29] The word νέανις (young woman) is a very doubtful restoration in 94.23 *V*.

One fragment tantalizes us with the possibility that Sappho's relationship to an addressee might be recovered. Atthis (who is probably addressed in 96 *V*) is the addressee of a single preserved line (49.1 *V*):

> ἠράμαν μὲν ἔγω σέθεν, Ἄτθι, πάλαι ποτά

I desired you, Atthis, once long ago.

On the basis of a sentence in Terentianus Maurus (2nd–3rd c. CE), a second line has been connected with this one (49.2 *V*):

> σμίκρα μοι πάις ἔμμεν' ἐφαίνεο κἄχαρις

You seemed to me to be a small child without charm.

Terentianus' testimony is as follows:

> cordi quando fuisse sibi canit Atthida parvam, florea virginitas sua cum foret.

> (Sappho) sings that small Atthis was dear to her heart once when blooming virginity was hers (Sappho's).[30]

---

[27] Merkelbach 1957: 23–24. Cf. Page 1955: 58–62 on this poem. I do not assume that it was "personal"; see below.

[28] Gentili 1988: 216–22, building on earlier studies, shows that at this date ἀγνός does not mean merely "ritually pure" but "inspiring fear or veneration."

[29] Note the context, ripeness for marriage, in which 122 *V* is quoted.

[30] *On Letters, Syllables, etc.* 2154–55, quoted at 49 *V*. Lardinois 1994: 68 argues that the

Note that it is only the word *small* that Terentianus and the second Greek line have in common. Both of the Greek lines are quoted by several people but never together.[31] If we take Terentianus and the two Greek lines together, we construct the statement that Sappho, when ready for marriage, loved Atthis, who was not yet nubile.[32] Atthis cannot have been much younger than Sappho, since Greek women tended to marry young. We could either stretch the difference in age as far as possible, not give much weight to the adverb "long ago," and suppose that the dramatic date of the poem is the point at which Atthis in turn has become ready to marry. On that reading we see Sappho addressing a *parthenos*. Or we could stress the "long ago" and suppose that Atthis and Sappho are both adult at the date of the poem.[33] The poem in that case looks back to the period of entering puberty. If the two lines do not belong together, then no indication of relative ages can be drawn from the first line.

Women who have departed are referred to several times in Sappho's poetry, e.g., 16, 94, 96 *V*. They may have left because they were getting married (which would mean that they were *parthenoi* while with Sappho), but nothing in the poems indicates as much. In 96.6–7 the singer says of the departed woman, "now she is conspicuous among Lydian married women." Does that mean "now she is among the married women" or "now she is among Lydian women (and not among us married women)"? There were certainly other reasons why women moved around. Sappho herself is reported to have been in exile in Sicily.[34]

Christopher Brown argues that, by analogy with its use in the Hesiodic *Catalogue of Women*, ἀμάρυχμα (sparkle) in the description of Anaktoria in

---

reflexive pronoun *sua* (hers) could refer to Atthis rather than (as usual) the subject of the sentence, Sappho. But *parva* (small) implies that Atthis is not yet at the stage of "blooming virginity." Plutarch, quoting the second line, says that Sappho addresses it to one who is not yet at the age for marriage (*Dialogue on Love* 751d, quoted *ad* 49 *V*).

[31] See Voigt *ad loc*. Maximus of Tyre quotes it with no name attached even though a name would strengthen the parallel he is drawing with Socrates and Alkibiades. Note the lack of connective in l. 2 also.

[32] Recent editors (Voigt, Lobel and Page) connect the two Greek lines but do not make them consecutive. Campbell 1982 (*ad loc*.) acknowledges that, if related, the lines should be joined: "The version of Terentianus Maurus suggests that the lines are consecutive, *however unlikely that may seem*" (my italics). Bowra 1961: 193–94 disregards Terentianus because Sappho would not say she loved someone who had no charm: "It seems more likely that in this poem Sappho told how Atthis, who at first did not appeal to her, later won her love" (194). However, without Terentianus nothing indicates that the two lines come from the same poem.

[33] The name Atthis occurs four times in our meager fragments (8, 49, 96.16, 130 *V*), and in a papyrus commentary (90d.15), which suggests that she was a frequent figure in Sappho's poetry. She is the only figure (apart perhaps from Anaktoria) whom the Suda, Maximus, and Ovid all mention. This preponderance by itself tells against her having been a *parthenos* who would have left Sappho's circle.

[34] *Parian Marble* Epoch 36 = 251 *V*; Test. 5.

16.18 *V* shows that she is of marriageable age.[35] But this mode of reasoning ignores the issue of gendered discourse and assumes that Sappho used the word in the same way as a male poetic tradition that focused on female figures only at the moment of readiness for marriage (and of childbirth). Sappho revises themes from mainstream poetry and celebrates married women's beauty (96, Helen in 16 *V*), so she cannot be counted on to restrict the language of praise to nubile *parthenoi*.

Internal and external evidence strongly aligns *parthenoi* with performance of wedding poetry and of other ritual poetry (140, perhaps 17 *V*). The rare and uncertain evidence for the status of Sappho's own audience points to "companions" who belong to the same age-category. Outside wedding and ritual poetry no addressee in Sappho's poetry is demonstrably a *parthenos*.[36] While many passages are indeterminate, nothing contravenes this alignment—unless Philostratos' Damophyla be thrown up against it.

Yet scholars have generally imagined Sappho as the head of an initiation group, school, cult association, or more informal group consisting of *parthenoi* who were preparing for marriage. The most extended arguments for this view, and in particular for the version that puts Sappho in charge of an initiatory group, have been made by Reinhold Merkelbach and Claude Calame.[37] In a summary of earlier German views, Merkelbach lists four reasons for thinking that Sappho's audience consisted of a "Bund" of *parthenoi* preparing for marriage: 1) there were other such groups elsewhere in Greece (e.g., Sparta); 2) Sappho is, as the fragments show, continually surrounded by a whole crowd of young girls who come and go, leaving (it seems) in order to get married; 3) there were other such circles of girls on Lesbos, for Gorgo and Andromeda appear to have been Sappho's closest rivals; 4) "lesbian" love is more understandable against this background, for love is one of the things learned in the "*Bund*" of girls as well as that of

---

[35] Brown 1989.

[36] Lardinois 1994 argues two things, that Sappho's poetry was largely choral and that she sang to and about *parthenoi*. The argument is confused: if Sappho's poetry was choral, then *she* was not addressing anybody; the chorus was. He suggests apropos of 58 *V* that Sappho sang to the *parthenoi* while they danced (67). This arrangement is supported by a speculative conjecture in the fragmentary text and an unpersuasive parallel with Alkman 26 *PMGF*. Moreover, the transmitted explanation of the Alkman lines is not correct (see *PMGF* ad loc.), and we do not know how his poem was performed. Lardinois 69–70 lists eight fragments showing that young women were Sappho's subject outside wedding poetry, six of which are scraps without context. 17 *V*, discussed above, may be public choral poetry. In 58 *V* the speaker describes herself as old and the addressee is singular, so παῖδες (children) in 11 must be a passing reference. 56 *V* (a sentence fragment) may be from a wedding poem; 93 has two legible words; 49.2, 122, and 153 are quotations of a few words each; and 140 appears to be choral ritual poetry. He also forgets that the named women are never referred to as *parthenoi*.

[37] Merkelbach 1957; Calame 1977: I 427–32 and passim.

boys.[38] Of these the first, the paradigm of Sparta, is the real underpinning of the reconstruction.

The second, Sappho's association with *parthenoi,* already assumes a parallel with Sparta. It is essential to understand this in evaluating the idea that Sappho's own audience was an initiation group. As I have shown, it is not possible to demonstrate from Sappho's poetry that the *parthenoi* she mentions in wedding and ritual poetry have any connection with the addressees or audience for her "personal" poetry; except for the married woman in 96.6–7, the age and marital status of Sappho's addressees or of the subjects in her nonritual poetry is never indicated. But at Sparta erotic language was sung by *parthenoi* about a woman. If one assumes on that basis that *parthenoi* and homoerotic language always and everywhere go together, then it is easy to suppose that the addressees of Sappho's love poetry *must* be *parthenoi.* The bald assumption, however, is not justified, and the analogy between Sparta and Lesbos must be demonstrated independently of Sappho's poetry before it is used to interpret her poetry.

Merkelbach's third argument also depends on the parallel with Sparta, for Sappho never says that Gorgo and Andromeda were leaders of any kind of group; they are individuals to whom she was at least sometimes hostile. To posit that they headed groups is already to assume the existence of a particular social organization. The fourth argument is no argument but betrays the attraction of a Spartan parallel: it makes female homosexuality less disturbing by confining it to a preliminary stage before heterosexuality, for most participants, and to women who associated only with these liminal early adolescents.[39] What makes homosexual love "understandable" for the modern interpreter, however, may be quite different from ancient constructions of it. Male homosexual love was of course not confined to initiatory contexts. Merkelbach is careful to underline the fact that his argument is not proof but a hypothesis for which he claims explanatory power.

Some scholars have tried to establish a parallel between Sparta and Lesbos independent of Sappho's poetry by focusing on choral activity in the two places. At Sparta and on Lesbos (and probably everywhere else), *parthenoi* performed choral poetry. Now, as the Chapters 1 to 3 have shown, choral poetry was an embedded part of numerous rituals; the performers, the kind of self-presentation they made, the librettos they sang, and their movements were determined by the function of their perfor-

---

[38] Merkelbach 1957: 4–5, taking up the view of Schadewaldt 1950: 11–15.

[39] Cf. Calame 1977: II 12, who explains that initiatory homosexuality does not have anything in common with "fixed homosexuality," and I 430 where Sappho's homosexuality is said to be "fixed" in the clinical sense but to function nevertheless in its institutional and pedagogical roles. DeJean 1989 addresses this attitude.

mance in the overall event. In other words, choral performance was not an institution unto itself but a medium in which many combinations of self-presentation and cultural credo could be communicated. Yet the route these commentators take in defending an analogy between Sparta and Lesbos and between Alkman's and Sappho's poetry is to treat choral performance by *parthenoi* as an independent institution, always initiatory and always similar in its language and processes. If this were true, then any evidence for choral performance by *parthenoi* would also be evidence for a system of female initiation. The relations among performers indicated in any one instance could be attributed to all other cases. Since the very idea of initiation is that the initiates are removed from their social milieu for a period, the hypothesis that choral groups are initiatory retroactively justifies treating choral groups in isolation from their context in the community.

Given this approach, the fact that Sappho wrote wedding poetry for *parthenoi* to perform is sufficient reason to ascribe a whole system of initiation to Lesbos and make Sappho one of its overseers. Then the parallel with Sparta is drawn. This approach avoids the difficulty inherent in trying to create a parallel directly between Alkman's and Sappho's poetry, but it is no more justified and suffers its own internal contradiction. Once the two communities are equated, the student of initiation must immediately qualify the equation: on Lesbos "initiation" was private and voluntary, unlike the public, state-sponsored system of performances at Sparta.[40] But the hypothesis that choral performance by *parthenoi* is ipso facto a manifestation of a system of initiation practices depends on its being everywhere the same. If the organization of choral performance was different on Lesbos, how do we know that it was connected with a process of initiation? Indeed, the Spartan system existed in the context of a very cohesive society that bears small resemblance to anything we know about faction-ridden Lesbos at the beginning of the sixth century.[41]

Claude Calame takes this approach.[42] He offers an argument for interpreting choral performance as initiatory by beginning from the existence of private Hellenistic organizations of "dancers." Some Hellenistic groups use terms drawn from choral performance to name functionaries and contributions; this link between choral activity and corporate structure Calame interprets as derived from archaic initiatory practices.[43] Calame then

---

[40] Merkelbach 1957: 1–3 and 4n.1.

[41] Parker 1993: 325–31 also argues against analogy with Sparta.

[42] Calame 1977: I 367–71. Lardinois 1994: 73–74n.62 embraces Calame's view without acknowledging that it includes casting Sappho as a teacher, an idea that he admits (57, 76) we should give up.

[43] Calame 1977: I 363–66. Choral performance continued in the Hellenistic period (cf. Ch. 1) and private societies were most likely simply borrowing from contemporary public practice and terminology.

looks for evidence of organizational structures in archaic poetry. He supports the institutional view of Sappho's relations with her audience by adducing, first, Sappho's use of the verb ἀδικεῖν (do an injustice) to describe a resistant beloved in 1.20 *V*, on the grounds that it suggests a legal infraction.[44] But of course legal language (if it was that on Lesbos in 600 BCE) can be used metaphorically, just as military terms can. Second, he interprets the phrase μοισοπόλων οἰκία (house of the servants of the Muses) in a fragment quoted by Maximus of Tyre (150 *V*) as pointing to Sappho's running an institution:

οὐ γὰρ θέμις ἐν μοισοπόλων ⟨δόμωι⟩

θρῆνον ἔμμεν' ⟨   ⟩ οὔ κ' ἄμμι πρέποι τάδε

> For it is not right for lament to take place in the house of the servants of the Muses [   ] this would not befit us.[45]

The "house of the servants of the Muses," considered in isolation as a phrase, could conceivably refer to a "school." But before asserting that as its meaning, we must take into account possible contexts for the fragment. Maximus claims that Sappho said this to her daughter, who was mourning because she (Sappho) was dying. If that was the projected situation in the poem, the most likely subject was Sappho's belief in her poetic immortality. The term "servants of the Muses" then constitutes the reason not to mourn, namely that Sappho will live on through her poetry. In 65 *V* someone (Aphrodite?) appears to address Sappho and promise her "glory everywhere," even when she is in Hades. The "servants of the Muses" stand in contrast to the woman who has no share of the "roses from Picria," who will wander invisible even in the house of Hades (55 *V*). Sappho is proud of her fame as a poet and never elsewhere mentions an official role for herself, so the poem is far more likely to have contrasted Sappho's personal mortality with her poetic immortality than to have insisted on institutional rules *in extremis*. The plural *servants* may point to a group of poets or performers, but demonstrating the existence of an institution requires showing that the statement *must* be a bylaw or that "servant of the Muses" must be an office, and there is no particular reason to think that they are.[46]

Having argued for Sappho's circle as an initiatory institution, Calame then draws the analogy with Spartan choral groups, already interpreted as

---

[44] Calame 1977: I 367–69 for this and the following argument.

[45] The word δόμωι replaces οἰκίαι, which meter rules out.

[46] Lanata 1966: 67 finds a Hellenistic instance of the word as cult title at Thebes, but that has no bearing on Sappho. The word means *poet* at Euripides *Alcestis* 445 and elsewhere. For the plural, which may refer to those with whom she shared poetry-making, cf. 147 *V*: "I say that some other will remember us." Here certainly poetic fame and not office is meant. See Bowra 1961: 206–7 on Sappho's expectation of poetic fame.

initiatory. He casts Sappho in the roles of both Alkman and Hagesichora, as both poet/chorus trainer and chorus leader.[47] Asserting that homosexual relations played an educational role in both places, he equates Sappho's expression of desire for the *parthenoi* (as he thinks) with the Spartan chorus's admiration for Hagesichora.[48] Sappho, he says, expressed love for one *parthenos* in a group and the others participated vicariously through the poetry to her beloved that Sappho performed for all of them.[49] Thus we arrive back at a forced equivalence between Alkman's and Sappho's poetry.

To explain female homoerotic discourse as always and everywhere initiatory may make it "understandable" by placing it within a system of institutionalization, but containment is bought at the price of ignoring all other aspects of the cultural context and making Sappho into a sort of Peter Pan.[50] It forecloses any investigation of what such discourse communicates, including the question how women might use such a discourse among themselves differently from men writing for women's public presentation of themselves.[51]

To get around the problem that the poetry expressing sexual response to women is sung by different performers on Lesbos and at Sparta, Calame tentatively, and following him André Lardinois, propose that Sappho's love poetry was meant for choral performance.[52] One cannot distinguish solo and choral lyric poetry by its formal properties (indeed it will require demonstration that Sappho's wedding poetry was choral), but Sappho's love poetry has none of the marks of community poetry such as were identified and discussed in Chapters 1 to 3. Each of the three partially preserved *partheneia* examined in Chapter 2 was part of a ceremony to

[47] Calame 1977: I 396; for Alkman and Hagesichora see Ch. 2. Calame assigns the function of chorus-leader to Sappho on the basis of *Anth. Pal.* 9.189 (= Test. 59) in which she sings while a chorus dances. This is imaginative literature from a different epoch. Alkman trained the chorus for performance according to a papyrus commentary (Test. 5.30–34 C = TA2.30–34 *PMGF*), whose author may be extrapolating from Alkman's function as poet, but nothing indicates that either he or Sappho performed with the choristers.

[48] Calame 1977: I 438 acknowledges the reversal of the Spartan case but does not discuss it.

[49] Calame 1977: I 428–29. He adduces as an analogy a Cretan system reported by Ephoros (*FGH* 70 F149.21 from Strabo 10.4.21) in which an older youth carries off a younger one to be his beloved for two months spent in the woods hunting. The younger man's friends came along. But since the friends joined them after the older youth had made his choice, the dynamic would be quite different.

[50] It is a feature of such accounts that they must make Sappho simultaneously a teacher of *parthenoi* and equivalent to a *parthenos,* one among the group who pair off in couples. This psychologically impossible picture is essential to maintaining the parallel with Sparta. Even Burnett 1983: 227 accepts it.

[51] Cf. Parker 1993: 326.

[52] Calame 1977: I 127n.171 and 369 with n.18 denies that a choral/monodic distinction is relevant to Sappho's poetry; cf. n.47 above. Lardinois 1994: 61–62 agrees; cf. n.36 above.

which it referred, and two of them, Alkman 1 *PMGF* (= 3 *C*) and Pindar *partheneion* II (= 94b *SM*), had other public functions in retelling of local heroic myth or praise of a prominent family. The third (Alkman 3 *PMGF* = 26 *C*) is too fragmentary to reveal its full frame of reference but alludes to its public context of performance. Sappho's love poetry does not speak to or for a community; it confines its subject to the emotions of the speaker and as such has no communal celebratory dimension. On the other hand, 17 *V,* not a love poem, includes a prayer to Hera and a brief narrative of a myth adapted to the local cult.[53] Since it contains elements typical of community poetry, interpreting it as choral poetry would be reasonable.

Although the fact does not tell us anything directly about performers or audience, it is significant that Sappho's work was divided into categories in antiquity. Philostratos says that Damophyla, like Sappho, composed both erotic poems and hymns.[54] A somewhat different division is found in an epigram by Dioskourides (*Palatine Anthology* 7.407):

> Sweetest prop of passions for the young in love, Sappho, surely Pieria or well-ivied Helicon honors you along with the Muses, you who breathe inspiration equal to theirs, Muse in Aeolian Eressos. Or else Hymen, god of the wedding song, stands over bridal chambers with you holding a flaming torch. Or else, mourning the young offspring of Kinyras together with grieving Aphrodite, you see the holy grove of the blessed. In every place, exalted lady, rejoice equally with the gods, for we still have your songs, immortal daughters.

The three places where Dioskourides imagines Sappho to be correspond with three types of poetry: love poetry, wedding poetry, and songs for the Adonia. The last could be seen as a subset of ceremonial poetry (including hymns). From Sappho's songs for the Adonia, a quotation of two lines (140 *V*) survives, a line addressed to Aphrodite and her rejoinder addressed to κόραι (girls). The plural addressees in Aphrodite's response imply that it was a choral poem. The ancients thus subdivided Sappho's poetry by function, and the function would have determined whether performance was solo or choral.[55]

[53] Cf. Alkaios 130B (discussed in Ch. 5) in which women celebrate in a sanctuary of Hera. *Anth. Pal.* 9.189 is set in a sanctuary of Hera; perhaps the author knew a hymn to Hera of Sappho's, 17 *V* or another.

[54] On Sappho's hymns see also Menander Rhetor *On Display Oratory* 333.8–10 Russell and Wilson = 222 *V;* Test. 47. Fränkel 1975: 171–72, among others, distinguishes Sappho's choral songs for festive occasions from her personal (monodic) poetry.

[55] The Alexandrian edition of Sappho's poetry included wedding poetry in the same book with love poetry (e.g., 30 in book 1, 43 [and 44?] *V* in book 2) because it was organized by meter. There was a separate book of epithalamia (wedding poems), evidenced by 103¹⁷ *V* (in the *app. crit.*), where the heading Ἐπιθα]λάμια stands. Presumably these were poems whose meter did not dictate that they should be included in one of the earlier books; see Page 1955: 123–26. Cf. Lasserre 1989: 18–35 for a different view.

Bruno Gentili, who also accepts the theory of initiatory groups, interprets a remark in a fragmentary commentary on papyrus as referring to sexual initiatory practices. In 213 *V* the commentator explains a line in Sappho as meaning "Pleistodike along with Gongyla will be named the 'yoke-mate' (σύνδυγος) of Gorgo." The word *yoke-mate* can be used to mean "wife," so Gentili suggests a ritual marriage (à trois!).[56] But since "wife" is an extension of the metaphorical meaning "fellow-worker" or "companion" and takes on its specificity from its context, it should not be substituted for "companion" where the context does not warrant it.[57]

English-speaking scholars are less willing to accept the idea that Sappho oversaw initiations. Denys Page argues vehemently against the idea of a school or cult association, pointing out that Sappho's fragments offer no direct evidence of either, and Holt Parker comes to the same conclusion.[58] Page would reject Merkelbach's contention that poetic performance in the archaic period was always called forth by a formal occasion. About the term *student* in the Suda, he comments that it need mean no more than that "Sappho taught her friends the tricks of her poetic trade."[59] (One might wonder how the Suda would have information like that.) Anne Burnett accepts the social configuration derived from the initiation theory but pictures a more informal association of *parthenoi*, educational but not ritually initiatory.[60] I discuss her approach at greater length below.

The evidence of Sappho's poetry, plus *pap. Colon.* 5860, points to three things that Sappho did: 1) performance for "companions," 2) composing of wedding and other ritual poems probably for performance by *parthenoi*, and 3) possible activity as a teacher. The initiation theory tries to combine these into a single synthetic picture. Without the theory one can see these as separate activities. If we posit a circle of adult friends for whom Sappho performed and who performed in turn, then we have a parallel to the symposium group. A number of Sappho's poems would fit best in such a setting—her comments on her two brothers, the sarcastic remarks about other women, the fragments that seem to have political innuendo. There would have been other such groups also, so Gorgo and Andromeda may have belonged to rival circles. Sappho's poetry suggests that the

---

[56] Gentili 1988: 76. Calame 1977: I 370–71 takes it to mean "companion" in accordance with one of its common meanings.

[57] See *LSJ* s.v. συζυγέω etc. In Euripides *Heracles* 673–75, the chorus says that the mingling of Charites and Muses is the ἁδίσταν συζυγίαν (sweetest yoking). Clearly "marriage" is not meant here.

[58] Page 1955: 111–12, 126–40; Parker 1993. Bowra 1961: 176–240 passim and Kirkwood 1974: 101–2 also stress the private nature of Sappho's poetry—private in the sense of being shared among friends or sung to the addressee.

[59] Page 1955: 111n.2. His study predates publication of the papyrus fragment *pap. Colon.* 5860, quoted above.

[60] Burnett 1983: 209–313 discusses Sappho.

women's group was more personal than symposium groups. We do not hear about children or siblings in symposium poetry (except for Alkaios' mention of his brother [350 *V*], who was probably himself welcome in the symposium).

Sappho also composed poetry for weddings and ceremonies, in which *parthenoi* played a role. If they formed a chorus that sang and danced, they would need to be trained. Sappho might have acted as producer, choreographing and rehearsing the chorus. Chorus-trainer is one of the roles that Calame assigns to Sappho, and insofar as she was a poet of choral pieces the role naturally fell to her, just as Alkman, the dramatic poets at Athens, and perhaps Pindar trained their choruses.[61] If Simonetta Nannini is right in interpreting some of Alkman's fragments as sympotic, then Alkman would provide a parallel for Sappho in both singing solo poetry to an audience of peers and preparing choral poetry for choruses to perform.[62] Likewise Anakreon, for Kritias (1 *DK*) calls him a composer of poems for women's song, as well as of symposium poetry, one who will not be forgotten as long as there are symposia and female choruses dance all night long. Sappho by analogy addressed her personal poetry to her peers, not to a group of *parthenoi*. The latter are not her audience, but performers of her choral poetry. If the wedding poems were commissioned, she would not necessarily know the dancers before she began training them.

In that performing in a chorus was itself considered educational, Sappho could be said to be "educating" *parthenoi*.[63] But the Suda names three "students." All three come from elsewhere. Why were they singled out by Sappho? What is the correlation among the three items of foreign residence, being "students," and prominence in Sappho's poetry? As I suggested above, they may have been labeled students simply because they were foreign. One could also speculate that these women were students in a different sense from the chorus-members. They were possibly adult women who came to Sappho to learn choral production: music, composition, choreography, and training of the chorus. Rituals were being developed in the sixth century and cults elaborated, while aristocratic productions like weddings must have been dazzling displays. Someone was needed to produce the songs and celebrations that cities decreed and families planned. Pindar reportedly went to Athens to study with Lasos of Hermione, and Lesbos was well known as a musical center. Other women composed for community performance: in addition to Korinna, Telesilla and Praxilla wrote hymns in the fifth century.[64] It might surprise us to

[61] Calame 1977: I 394.

[62] Nannini 1988: 19–56. For an example of Pindar's sympotic poetry, see Ch. 5. These parallels imply that Sappho was a professional poet.

[63] Plato clearly thought so; see Ch. 1.

[64] See Rayor 1991: 117–20 for the exiguous fragments, Snyder 1989: 54–62 for discussion.

think that women were traveling to study professional work at the end of the seventh century, but it is less surprising than the idea that men might send their unmarried daughters abroad for their education, and of course the women may have been on Lesbos for other reasons. But while I am enamored of the idea, I do not know where such information would have been preserved.

Without the initiation theory we cannot confine Sappho's life and love to an institution and a passing phase of young women's lives. She may have desired some among the *parthenoi* whom she trained; she may have been attracted to married women, younger, older, or coeval. Sappho's poetry does not reveal conformity with the male model of older lover and younger beloved.[65] If we are not committed to institutionalizing Sappho's emotional life, we can leave open the question about the identity of those who attracted her.

I have posited two different audiences for Sappho, her circle of friends and the celebrants at wedding ceremonies and religious events. If Sappho wrote for different audiences, then the psychological efficacy and the gender implications of each kind of performance must be examined separately. I look at the wedding poetry first, then poetry that there is reason to situate in a circle similar to a symposium group. After these investigations I take up the major erotic fragments. I conclude that they were not composed for either setting and that their function is different from that of any poetry investigated so far in this study.

II

Sappho's wedding poetry survives largely in papyrus scraps and brief quotations made by later authors.[66] We are not informed about the setting or style of performance. The best evidence that it was choral and performed by *parthenoi* can be gained from Sappho's description of the wedding of Hector and Andromache, perhaps written for a wedding (44.24–34 *V*):

αὖλος δ' ἀδυ[μ]έλης [   ]τ' ὀνεμίγνυ[το
25   καὶ ψ[ό]φο[ς κ]ροτάλ[ων   ]ως δ' ἄρα πάρ[θενοι
ἄειδον μέλος ἄγν[ον, ἴκα]νε δ' ἐς αἴθ[ερα
ἄχω θεσπεσίᾳ γελ[
πάνται δ' ἦς κὰτ ὄδο[ις
κράτηρες φίαλαί τ' ὀ[   ]υεδε[   ]εακ[

[65] Cf. Stigers [Stehle] 1981. In Aristophanes' *Lysistrata* married women express appreciation of one another's attractions.

[66] Contiades-Tsitsoni 1990 discusses the genre of epithalamium; see 68–109 on Sappho. Lasserre 1989 tries to reconstruct songs from scattered references. Cf. Bowra 1961: 214–23

30   μύρρα καὶ κασία λίβανός τ᾿ ὀνεμείχνυτο
      γύναικες δ᾿ ἐλέλυσδον ὄσαι προγενέστερα[ι
      πάντες δ᾿ ἄνδρες ἐπήρατον ἴαχον ὄρθιον
      πάον᾿ ὀνκαλέοντες Ἐκάβολον εὐλύραν
      ὔμνην δ᾿ Ἔκτορα κ᾿ Ἀνδρομάχαν θεο⟨ε⟩ικέλο[ις.

The sweet-singing pipe and [   ] were mingled and the clack of castanets
[   ] *parthenoi* sang a holy song and the wondrous sound [rose] into the ether
[   ] and everywhere in the streets there was [   ] mixing bowls and libation
saucers [   ] myrrh and cassia and frankincense mingled, while all the older
women gave a ritual shout and all the men called out a delightful high-pitched
paian, invoking the lyre-playing far-shooter (= Apollo), and hymned Hector
and Andromache, (a couple) like the gods.

The scene of celebration must be drawn at least partly from actual weddings. It shows us that *parthenoi* sang as part of the festivity that spilled
through the streets.[67]

Fragment 30 *V* confirms that *parthenoi* participated in other moments of
the marriage proceedings as well (2–9):

      πάρθενοι δ[
      παννυχίσδοι[σ]αι [
      σὰν ἀείδοισ[ι]ν φ[ιλότατα καὶ νύμ-
5   φας ἰοκόλπω.

      ἀλλ᾿ ἐγέρθεις ἤϊθ[ε
      στεῖχε σοὶς ὐμάλικ[ας
      ἤπερ ὄσσον ἀ λιγύφω[νος
      ὔπνον [ἴ]δωμεν.

Parthenoi [   ] celebrating through the night [   ] sing your [love and your]
violet-girt [bride's]. But rising, go [join?] young bachelors (?), your age-mates
[so that ?] we see [less?] sleep than the clear-voiced [nightingale (gets) ?].

Parthenoi sang at the ceremony. It is possible that they sang this song,
despite the third person in line 4.[68] The third person then describes the
scene from the groom's point of view. In the next stanza with its probable
imperative and more assertive tone, a first person plural appears, so either
"we" who are singing are the *parthenoi* just mentioned or this couple has

_____

on the stages of a wedding and the character of Sappho's songs; Page 1955: 119–23. Both
remark on their folk quality.

[67] For wedding processions see also *Iliad* 18.491–95; Ps-Hesiod *Shield* 272–74.

[68] The present tense ἀείδοισ[ι]ν, accepted by Voigt, makes it somewhat more natural to
take it this way than the optative printed by Page 1955: 125 and by Campbell 1982.

two serenading choruses.[69] The song may be a "morning song" meant to greet the couple after their wedding night.[70]

Another fragment sung at daybreak is 43 *V*, a tatter in which only a few words can be read. The last two lines (8–9) have

>] ἀλλ' ἄγιτ', ὦ φίλαι,
>
>], ἄγχι γὰρ ἀμέρα.

But come, o (female) friends [   ], for day is near.

A chorus may well have sung this, for the vocative reveals the presence of plural female figures: what would they be doing there if not singing?[71] If so, the lines are an address by chorus-members to each other. Two fragments (107 and 114 *V*) must be sung by one or more female performers, for they lament the loss of virginity. Did the bride herself sing them, or did a chorus of *parthenoi*, speaking for the bride? The lines could be choral or solo, but in the latter fragment "virginity" answers the girl who regrets its going, an arrangement that suggests at least two voices. Perhaps a chorus of *parthenoi* sang in responsion of a bride's reluctance to change her status. In 27 *V parthenoi* are mentioned as participants at a wedding also, although the fragment is obscure. The evidence, such as it is, supports the view that Sappho's wedding poetry was choral poetry performed by *parthenoi*. In addition, there are a number of other brief quotations assuredly or probably from wedding poems, judging by their content, collected as 104–17 *V*, to which 103B and probably 56, 141, and 161 should be added. The performer of these cannot be determined from the fragments themselves. *Parthenoi* probably sang them because a number praise the bride, and women are more likely to praise other women in public than are men.

Given the state of the evidence, we have no way to discuss the gendered self-presentation of the speaker, interesting as it would be to know how *parthenoi* presented themselves when marriage was the subject. The speaker implied by these fragments does assume an authoritative voice in order to praise. The speaker makes pronouncements, for instance, as judge of the worth of bride or groom in 113, 105, 56, 106 *V*. I quote 113:

[69] Lasserre 1989: 37 denies that the poem is choral on the grounds that its meter is Sapphic strophes and supposes that Sappho herself sang it. There is no evidence to show that Sapphics must be monodic. On the other hand he reconstructs (41–61) a non-strophic choral *hymenaios* out of a mélange of dactylic and pherecratean lines of different lengths, without asking how it would be possible to move pleasingly to such a song.

[70] Or else it might have been sung the morning of the wedding, as Lobel 1951: 123 suggests, which would allow a slightly different reconstruction. See Voigt *ad loc.*

[71] Lasserre 1989: 39 claims, again on the grounds of meter, that this poem was monodic. The meter is not strophic, but choral poems could be stichic: see Ch. 2n.93.

οὐ γὰρ

ἀτέρα νῦν πάις, ὦ γάμβρε, τεαύτα

For there is not now another such girl, o groom.

These are cases of conventional *makarismos* (praise). There are imperatives in fragments 30 and 43 (quoted above), but they direct the addressee to do what the ceremonial proceedings call for anyway. The imperative of 111 ("Raise high the roofbeams, carpenters") is joking praise. In other words, the speaker's assertions and directives are simply a manifestation of what the occasion demands; they thus rely on authority borrowed from the community or the group of celebrants.

At best we can remark on the gender conventions expressed in the praise of bride and groom. They seem familiar. The speaker credits the groom with agency, the bride with beauty (112 *V*):

ὄλβιε γάμβρε, σοὶ μὲν δὴ γάμος ὡς ἄραο

ἐκτετέλεστ᾽, ἔχηις δὲ πάρθενον, ἂν ἄραο.

σοὶ χάριεν μὲν εἶδος, ὄππατα ⟨δ᾽   ⟩

μέλλιχ᾽, ἔρος δ᾽ ἐπ᾽ ἱμέρτωι κέχυται προσώπωι

5   ⟨   ⟩ τετίμακ᾽ ἔξοχά σ᾽ Ἀφροδίτα

Happy groom, the marriage is accomplished as you prayed, and you have the *parthenos* for whom you prayed. (To the bride) Your figure is delightful, (your) eyes [are?] soft, and desirability is poured over your lovely face [   ] Aphrodite has honored you outstandingly.

These lines are actually a synthesis of two overlapping quotations. One source implies that lines 3–5 were addressed to the bride.[72] Together they define a standard attitude toward male and female: the groom is congratulated on having gained what he wanted and the bride for being desirable. Fragment 113, quoted above, was probably also meant to laud the groom's choice. The groom is large, heroic, preeminent, worthy (111, 106, 116 *V*).[73] The bride is beautiful and chaste (105a, 107, 108, 112, 113, 114 *V*). The psychological efficacy of wedding poetry is to promote the success of the marriage, so the principals must be praised according to indisputable standards.

[72] Cf. Voigt *ad loc*. The sentence is in asyndeton, which may suggest a change of referent, formally prepared by mention of the *parthenos* at the end of the previous sentence.

[73] Cf. Demetrios *On Style* 167 = 110 *V* test., who criticizes this bantering poetry as prosaic. 110 *V* concerns the size of the doorkeeper's feet, in which Killeen 1973 sees a double entendre (*contra* Renehan 1983: 20–23). Such joking is more in keeping with the wedding spirit than the flat(-footed?) humor that others, such as Page 1955: 120, find in it. For a parallel to both the joking and the address to the groom, see Theocritus 18.9–21, inspired by Sappho.

Only two of the fragments do not conform in their praise to these themes. In 115 *V* the speaker deliberates over what analogy to use for the groom and chooses the phrase "slender shoot" to describe him.[74] The image almost implies a maternal attitude. In 56 *V* the speaker praises a *parthenos* for her wisdom (or skill):

οὐδ' ἴαν δοκίμωμι προσίδοισαν φάος ἀλίω

ἔσσεσθαι σοφίαν πάρθενον εἰς οὐδένα πω χρόνον

τεαύταν

I do not think that there will be in all of time a single young woman seeing the light of day who (has) such wisdom/skill.

Nothing marks this as an excerpt from a wedding poem except the analogy with 113 *V*, quoted above, and the formality of expression.[75] If it is, then the chorus is giving recognition to a young woman's accomplishment in a public context. The word σοφία and its kin were used by Pindar and others to describe poetic skill, so the chorus may mean that she has musical talent.[76] Whatever its precise application, it is a startling noun to find attached to a *parthenos* and illuminates by its difference the small range of attributes that convention ascribed to *parthenoi*. With these exceptions, the identifiable wedding poetry is joking or laudatory in predictable ways. Its speaker correspondingly has no distinctive character—or so it appears from the scraps of lines vouchsafed by excerptors.

We can turn now to Sappho's circle of friends. Insofar as it was a parallel institution to Alkaios' *hetaireia*—and remember that Alkaios was Lesbian also—poetry composed for it should promote a sense of mutual friendship. As suggested above, such a circle makes a logical setting for Sappho's poems about her family and acquaintances and poems that seem to make political statements. A good example of a poem plausibly sung to friends who are also allies is 5 *V*, a prayer to Aphrodite (?) and the Sea Nymphs for the speaker's brother to recover from difficulties.[77] Best preserved are the first three stanzas (1–12):

[74] Cf. Alkman 3.68 *PMGF*, where a similar image is used to describe Astymeloisa; *Iliad* 18.56–57.

[75] In her *app. crit.* Voigt refers to Kaibel as proposing the same view, and her own citation of Theocritus 18.24ff. and Catullus 61.86ff. implies that she considers it plausible.

[76] Alkman 59b *PMGF* praises a *parthenos* for her poetry or her singing:

The light-haired Megalostrata, blessed among *parthenoi*, demonstrated this gift of the sweet Muses.

Athenaios, who quotes the lines (13, 601a), says that Alkman had fallen in love beyond measure with Megalostrata. The lines may come from a *partheneion*, and the expressions of praise may be those of the *parthenoi*.

[77] This poem may or may not be connected with the story that Herodotus 2.135 (254a *V*)

Κύπρι καὶ] Νηρήϊδες, ἀβλάβη[ν μοι
τὸν κασί]γνητον δ[ό]τε τυίδ' ἴκεσθα[ι
κὤσσα ϝ]οι θύμω⟨ι⟩ κε θέλη γένεσθαι
    πάντα τε]λέσθην,

5   ὄσσα δὲ πρ]όσθ' ἄμβροτε πάντα λῦσα[ι
    καὶ φίλοισ]ι ϝοῖσι χάραν γένεσθαι
      ἔ]χθροισι, γένοιτο δ' ἄμμι
        μ]ῆδ' εἷς·

    τὰν κασιγ]νήταν δὲ θέλοι πόησθαι
10]τίμας, [ὂν]ίαν δὲ λύγραν
    ]οτοισι π[ά]ροιθ' ἀχεύων
    ]να

Cyprian goddess and] Sea Nymphs, grant that [my?] brother arrive here unharmed and that [all] he heartily wishes to have happen be done and that all the things that he earlier did in error he undo, that he become a joy to his [friends] and [a grief?] to his enemies, and may no one be [ ] to us; may he wish to make his sister [the recipient] of honor, but (of?) bitter distresses [ ] previously grieving

If Sappho sang the poem to an audience of "companions," the audience would be included in "us" (7) because Sappho was speaking as one among them. Very discreetly she criticizes her brother; the poem opens with a prayer that he gain his wishes in safety before asking that he change his ways. The word *citizens* in the broken fourth stanza (not quoted), where "accusation of the citizens" is a possible reading, shows that she is concerned about political appearances.[78] Sappho, it seems, dissociates herself from her brother's conduct and aligns herself with her audience, although she also stresses the family connection. We may suppose that the audience included women who felt that they too were implicated, by virtue of their families' political alliances, in the brother's embarrassing behavior. Sappho demonstrates solidarity with her circle in a self-presentation that reveals its similarity to symposium dynamics. If this scenario is correct, then women's groups formed a system of political communication separate from, but interacting with, men's symposium groups.

Fragment 98ab *V* similarly seems to combine personal and political concerns. Sappho describes ways of decorating the hair popular in her

tells about Sappho's brother: he bought the courtesan Rhodopis at great expense and gave her freedom. Fragment 15 *V* seems to speak to this episode, although the woman is called Doricha. That Doricha was Rhodopis may be later embroidery (cf. Strabo 17.1.33 = 254b *V*).
[78] Line 14. Lobel proposed ἐπαγ[ορί]αι ("accusation" [dative], LP *ad loc.*). See Voigt's apparatus; she doubts that the word can be attributed to Sappho.

mother's time and tells the addressee Kleis, her daughter, that she cannot acquire a headband for her. The reason apparently has to do with the political situation. Sardis, "the Mytilenean," the Kleanaktidai (a prominent family), "exile," and "city" are mentioned in b, but the sense cannot be recovered.[79] The usual explanation of the fragment is that it serves to instruct Kleis and other *parthenoi* in the art of dressing the hair, but it sounds more like political comment clothed in a subject considered appropriate to women.[80] The main fragment is the following (98a.1–12 *V*):

]θος· ἀ γάρ μ' ἐγέννα[τ

σ]φᾶς ἐπ' ἀλικίας μέγ[αν

κ]όσμον αἴ τις ἔχη φόβα⟨ι⟩ς[

πορφύρωι κατελιξαμέ[να

5   ἔμμεναι μᾶλα τοῦτο [

ἀλλ' ἀ ξανθοτέρα⟨ι⟩ς ἔχη[[81]

τα⟨ὶ⟩ς κόμα⟨ι⟩ς δάϊδος προφ[

σ]τεφάνοισιν ἐπαρτία[ις

ἀνθέων ἐριθαλέων· [

10   μ]ιτράναν δ' ἀρτίως κλ[

ποικίλαν ἀπὺ Σαρδίω[ν

]αονίας πόλ{ε}ις [

For she who bore me [said that] in her youth a great adornment this was indeed if one had one's hair wound around with a purple [ribbon]. But she who had hair tawnier than a torch [should wear it?] decked with crowns of blooming flowers; [   ] recently a decorated turban from Sardis [   ] cities.

Getting a turban for her daughter is impossible (98b.1–3). The turban may have been the real subject, and Sappho may have been decrying conspicuous consumption in presenting young women in public. The poem is then a comment on the social atmosphere as it impinged on women with nubile daughters. But the reference to the Kleanaktidai and exile (98b.7–8) makes it sound as though Sappho had a more specific situation in mind, so the unavailability of the turban may be symbolic for the situation she is

---

[79] This poem, if it is one poem, consists of two fragments (a and b) plus three misplaced lines that were copied at the bottom of the page and probably belong between a and b. See Page 1955: 98–99; Voigt *ad loc.* Lines 7–9 in b may say, "the city has these [   ] (as?) memorials of the flight of the Kleanaktidai"; see Page 102–3.

[80] Kirkwood 1974: 100–101 points out that a few of Sappho's fragments have political implications, but since she was not known for political poetry he doubts that it was a significant part of her work.

[81] Accepting the interpretation of ἀλλα favored by Page 1955; see his note *ad loc.*

deploring. In either case Sappho appears even more indirect than in 5 *V* (although without the beginning of the poem we cannot be sure of this). She induces nostalgia, and assent, by dwelling on her mother's recollection for three stanzas (quoted above) before introducing politics. As in 5 *V*, she emphasizes family relations. It looks as though political criticism was circumscribed in form (prayer, reminiscence) and content (focus on family and areas of women's interest) even among women. Probably it was as much to defuse tensions among themselves as to preserve decorum in what was after all a public venue, but if these two fragments are indicative, women avoided straightforward appraisal of male political activity in a repeatable medium like song. The dynamics are more muted than those of the symposium, although Alkaios too uses imagery and indirection in political criticism.[82]

Sappho's hostility to other women such as Gorgo and Andromeda may therefore be political hostility.[83] They may have belonged to circles representing other alignments of allegiance, and just like the men, women shifted in their friendships among different groups. Gongyla seems to be close to both Sappho and Gorgo at one time or another (95 and 22 (?) vs. 213 *V*). In 130 *V* Sappho describes Atthis as "flying" to Andromeda. This fragment, however, takes us back to the controversy with which I began, for these lines are quoted together with a complaint about Eros:

> Ἔρος δηὖτέ μ' ὁ λυσιμέλης δόνει,
>
> γλυκύπικρον ἀμάχανον ὄρπετον. . . .
>
> Ἄτθι, σοὶ δ' ἔμεθεν μὲν ἀπήχθετο
>
> φροντίσδην, ἐπὶ δ' Ἀνδρομέδαν πότη⟨ι⟩

Eros again the limb-loosener shakes me, the sweet-bitter irresistible reptile. . . . But, Atthis, you found it odious to give thought to me, and you fly to Andromeda.

Most commentators assume that it is Atthis herself whom Sappho desires. Assuming further that Atthis is a *parthenos,* they suppose that she has transferred herself to a rival educational institution. This reading, however, is self-destructive: it makes the transition from the first two lines to the latter two so abrupt that recent editors separate them (as given above) even though the lines are quoted as one passage.[84] Then too, from the perspec-

---

[82] For instance, his "ship of state" poems, on which see Gentili 1988: 197–215.

[83] On Andromeda cf. 57 *V* with Athenaios' comment (1, 21bc, quoted *ad loc.*) that Sappho is mocking Andromeda.

[84] Blass 1874: 150–51 explains why Hephaistion would have quoted two lines, then skipped down to quote two more: he was looking for examples of all the permutations of the Aeolic base. But the explanation is needed only if one thinks that the lines do not belong together.

tive of the social order, the fragment is surprising: it implies that a *parthenos* could remove herself at will from one "school" to another.

On the other hand, if the burden of the passage is that Sappho has fallen in love but Atthis is not willing to comfort or abet her, then the juxtaposition of lines 1–2 with 3–4 is very effective and we can keep the transmitted form: Sappho accuses Atthis of abandoning her at a moment when Sappho most needs her company. On this view, Atthis is a friend who has shifted her social or political allegiance, perhaps while maintaining ties with Sappho's group as well.

Eros among women was an area of women's interest, one of the subjects on which women did speak among themselves. It is possible, therefore, that this poem is another example of indirection in political comment: Sappho may portray herself as shaken by love so that she can decry Atthis' betrayal as the defection of a confidante, rather than speaking of it in openly political terms. If Sappho sang the poem to the circle with Atthis present, it would be a preemptive warning; or if she sang it in Atthis' absence, she would be accusing her of infidelity by using personal terms.[85]

In another fragment Sappho combines address to a woman who appears to be abandoning Sappho's group with liquid description of song (71 *V*):

>]μισσε Μίκα
>]ελα[ἀλ]λά σ' ἔγωὐκ ἐάσω
>]ν φιλότ[ατ'] ἤλεο Πενθιλήαν[
>]δα κα[κό]τροπ', ἄμμα[
> 5   ] μέλ[ος] τι γλύκερον [
>]α μελλιχόφων[ος
>]δει, λίγυραι δ' ἄη[
>] δροσ[ό]εσσα[

] Mika [   ] but I will not let you [   ] you chose the friendship of the Penthilean women [   ] (you) seeker-after-evil, our [   ] some sweet song [   ] gentle-voiced [sings?], and clear-sounding [nightingales?] dewy

In order to explain Mika (assuming that she is the addressee) as a *parthenos* who wants to leave Sappho, as some would do, one must posit that the women of the Penthilean family had a "school" or circle of initiates. But

---

[85] Sappho's few references to intimacy won are quoted out of context, so we cannot tell what they signify, for example, 48 *V*:

ἦλθες, †καὶ† ἐπόησας, ἔγω δέ σ' ἐμαιόμαν,
ὂν δ' ἔψυξας ἔμαν φρένα καιομέναν πόθωι

You came and (?) acted; I was longing for you, and you cooled my heart burning with desire.

the name Penthilos belonged to a very prominent aristocratic family at Mytilene.[86] I cannot help but think that they would have preferred to cultivate ties with women of greater standing and influence than *parthenoi*. Mika is more plausibly an adult friend of Sappho's who has engaged a new friendship with them, to Sappho's dismay. What Sappho seems to hold out to her audience in contrast to the attractions of friendship with the Penthilean clan is song. The last four lines, whose grammatical relationship to the preceding lines is lost, are a series of sensuous words describing song and singers. Like eros, song is a nonpolitical reason for attachment to Sappho's group, so perhaps yet another veil. But however much she skirts criticism of women's politics, Sappho speaks freely to the women themselves, accusing Atthis and castigating Mika.

Song characterizes Sappho's group. One would expect other members of Sappho's circle to perform as well as Sappho herself. Atthis was a singer (96.5, if Atthis is the addressee as line 16 implies). In fragment 21 *V* the singer, who seems to describe herself as old, asks another to "take [the lyre] and sing for us of the violet-girt one." Note the plural "us" referring to the audience, though one person is directly addressed. The same papyrus that contains the poem to Mika has scraps of a poem (70 *V*) in which the words *I go, harmony, chorus,* and *clear-sounding* appeared, the latter three in successive lines. Members of the circle may have been involved in public choral performance as well as singing to each other for pleasure.[87] Poem 2 *V* belongs in this setting, for it refers to festivity (15), while its diffused sensuousness would be appropriate to a group among whom Sappho used the language of sexual longing and mutual aesthetic delight to describe the bonds that held them together.[88]

Singing and eros for women were among women's interests and the subjects of their songs. These are the topics that Sappho combined to create a self-presentation both passionate and judgmental. The political aspects of Sappho's poetic speech are unrecoverable, but her self-presentation goes beyond the stance of discreet commentator to one of intense subjectivity. She superbly reverses the position that women were

[86] Cf. Alkaios 469 *V*. Pittakos married into this family, which was inimical to Alkaios and his group. See Ch. 5, pp. 234–35.

[87] *Incert. auct.* 35 *V* (= Alkaios 261b col. i *LP*) connects Abanthis with dancing. If the fragment was Sappho's, we may have another reference to choral performance. It was attributed to Alkaios by *LP* because the name of the tyrant Myrsilos occurs in the margin of another poem on the same papyrus (*Incert. auct.* 34² *V* in the *app. crit.*), and the editors did not think of Sappho as referring to political matters.

[88] West 1970a: 317n.25 points out that Athenaios quotes the end of 2 *V* (as we have it) with the addition of "for my companions (ἑταίροις) and yours," which could be a paraphrase of Sappho's ending. Lanata 1966: 68–70 takes the poem as a description of the cult ambience of Sappho's circle. Burnett 1983: 259–76 sees in it a description of physical love and its transformation into praise of Aphrodite; Heikkilä 1992 extends her analysis.

forced to take in open public performance as analyzed in Chapter 2. As a compelling speaker in song and subject/definer of her sexuality through active desire, Sappho displays among women a character to counteract the hegemonic model. Correlatively, confession of admiration and desire for others' beauty and delight in others' song must have been for her modes of maintaining friendship with the members of her circle. Attention to women's problems within families and even issues of style in grooming were other binding themes, but Sappho, we may guess, was remarkable for the sensual responsiveness by which she attached others to herself. Women expressed less anticommunal collectivity than did symposium groups—witness the emphasis on family in 5 and 98 V—but a seductive atmosphere apart from family life must have fused women's individual ties into a common intimacy.[89]

III

Love among women was an area of women's interest, so one would expect that Sappho's love poetry was performed to her circle.[90] But Sappho's love poetry does not support the analogy with the symposium poets; the major poems and fragments are antithetical to the creation of collective bonhomie. It is not just that they intimately address one person but that they implicitly reject the circle. Given their disinterest in striving for the psychological efficacy of renewing the group, I think that these poems had another function. To demonstrate my reason for thinking that the circle was not their primary setting, I begin by examining 31 V, then I propose a setting for it that makes more sense of its communicative strategy.

Here is the poem, one over which there has been much dispute:[91]

> φαίνεταί μοι κῆνος ἴσος θέοισιν
> ἔμμεν' ὤνηρ, ὄττις ἐνάντιός τοι
> ἰσδάνει καὶ πλάσιον ἆδυ φωνεί-
> σας ὑπακούει
>
> 5 καὶ γελαίσας ἰμέροεν, τό μ' ἦ μὰν
> καρδίαν ἐν στήθεσιν ἐπτόαισεν·

---

[89] 23 V mentions *eros*, seems to compare the addressee to Helen rather than Hermione, and contains the verb "to celebrate an all-night festival." Possibly it is wedding poetry, but in its combination of eroticism and celebration, it seems an ideal sketch of the atmosphere of Sappho's circle.

[90] See Saake 1972: 13–36 for a history of scholarship to circa 1963 and 1971 for bibliography on problems connected with the major fragments. Gerber 1976: 105–15 and 1987: 132–44 gives annotated bibliographies.

[91] For bibliography on the question whether this was a wedding poem and how to take the man in the first line, see Saake 1971: 19–22; Burnett 1983: 232–34 notes. For a history of scholarship on the poem, see Bonelli 1977: 463–85.

ὠς γὰρ ⟨ἔς⟩ σ᾽ ἴδω βρόχε᾽ ὤς με φώνη-
___ σ᾽ οὐδὲν ἔτ᾽ εἴκει,[92]

ἀλλὰ †καμ† μὲν γλῶσσα †ἔαγε†, λέπτον
10 δ᾽ αὔτικα χρῶι πῦρ ὑπαδεδρόμακεν,
ὀππάτεσσι δ᾽ οὐδὲν ὄρημμ᾽, ἐπιβρό-
___ μεισι δ᾽ ἄκουαι,

†ἔκαδε† μ᾽ ἴδρως κακχέεται, τρόμος δὲ
παῖσαν ἄγρει, χλωροτέρα δὲ ποίας
15 ἔμμι, τεθνάκην δ᾽ ὀλίγω ᾽πιδεύης
___ φαίνομ᾽ ἔμ᾽ αὔτ[αι.

ἀλλὰ πὰν τόλματον, ἐπεὶ †καὶ πένητα†

He appears to me to be equal to the gods, that man who sits facing you and listens to you sweetly speaking right near him and laughing enchantingly—a thing that truly makes the heart in my breast cower. For as I look at you fleetingly I can no longer utter a thing, but my tongue is shattered (?), instantly light fire runs through my flesh, I see nothing with my eyes but my ears re-sound, sweat flows down me and a shiver seizes me whole, I am a fresher green than grass, and I seem to myself to lack little of death. But all is bearable, since even a poor man (?) . . .

The song puts the speaker into a fictional situation: she is looking at a man and woman conversing. She also addresses the woman in this scene ("you" in lines 2 and 7), who by the logic of the setting cannot hear her. The singer must be speaking to herself.[93] The audience must overhear her since her imaginary situation means that she is not speaking to it. The singer shifts her attention to her own state in the second stanza, and there-after she is speaking about herself to herself. After describing the symp-toms of emotional distress that afflict her each time she looks at the woman, Sappho reasserts emotional control at line 17, at the moment of

___

[92] For a recent discussion of the text of these two lines, see Lidov 1993. I do not accept his emendation because I do not think that Sappho describes a single occasion but something that will always happen. Cf. Latacz 1985: 85–86 on the indicative. As to βρόχε᾽, which Lidov says does not mean "briefly" at this time, it is already metaphorical in *Iliad* 10.226, which he cites (514), so it could easily be applied to time.

[93] Cf. Johnson 1982: 1–23 on meditative verse compared with address to an audience; I do not think that this is meditative verse (see below). Latacz 1985: 80–81 points out the fiction-ality of the address but denies that it is inner monologue; he pictures Sappho performing in the presence of the young woman and projecting a scene that will soon take place (86–87). McEvilley 1978 thinks that Sappho is recreating for her circle of *parthenoi* the feelings she had while offering praise to a bride. Rösler 1990b: 282–83 points out that the verb *appear* in 1 and 16 marks the intervening section as fantasy, and Burnett 1983: 230 takes it as inner mono-logue. For the latter three scholars the poem is essentially meditative. For the views of Rösler and Burnett on the conditions of performance, see below.

near fainting. Her recovery is reflected in the few remaining words of that line: "all is bearable."[94] The tight inward focus of "I seem to myself" in line 16, followed by her recall of some mitigating idea, further denies the audience its obvious role as sympathetic substitute for the woman who affects Sappho. Far from striving to affirm her membership in a circle of friends, the singer of 31 *V* does not allow room for the listeners' presence in her fiction or insinuate that the group has any function in relation to her.[95]

I have characterized this poem as "overheard," but the image is not adequate to describe the communicative situation that the poem establishes. The singer's visible and audible control as she sings, the beauty of the highly organized words, mean that the listeners must suppose a radical disjunction between outer poise and inner turmoil. More than that, the singer describes herself immediately as unable to speak.[96] What then are we hearing as we hear the poem performed? In the fourth stanza the singer adds that she is *looking* distressed—sweating, trembling, and pale. The singer in the here and now is not the same as the speaker constituted by the text of the poem.[97] A split between the physically present performer (the singer) and the poem's first-person self-representation (the speaker) has opened up.[98]

The separation of singer and speaker combined with the fictional situation described and the soliloquizing creates a fictional character within the poem whose inner emotional state is laid open to secret observers—a remarkable configuration for archaic lyric. To see the difference from symposium poetry, we can recall several of the poems discussed in Chapter 5. Symposium poets address absent figures: Archilochos, for instance, accosting Lykambes in 172 *W*. But his speech is meant to be public, as public as possible, for Archilochos is engaged in shaming Lykambes. The address therefore renders Lykambes imaginatively present so that the symposium group can share in denigration of him. Anakreon addresses a boy who, he

[94] The following words, "even a poor man," may be corrupt.

[95] Rösler 1990b: 277–78 thinks the poem could not have been performed in the presence of the girl about whom it speaks because Sappho's self-consolation at the end has nothing to do with her. Burnett 1983: 241–43 (who believes that the poem is about approaching a new love, not about departure) thinks that the consolation consists of gaining the confidence to seek out the woman the speaker desires. Neither scholar allows a role for the audience.

[96] O'Higgins 1990: 158–59 describes the threat that non-speaking poses to oral poetry; it means the end of poetic creation. Cf. 164: silence assails Sappho repeatedly, and the act of creating poetry resists it.

[97] Rösler 1990b: 282 also notes this: "Sappho" becomes part of the imaginary picture within the poem; the "Sappho" who glances is a different person from the one who sings.

[98] It is standard new-critical procedure to distinguish the biographical subject (the poet) from first-person speaker in a poem. Kirkwood 1974: 112, for instance, distinguishes Sappho the woman from Sappho the speaker in the poems. Note that I am distinguishing the speaker in the poem from the *performer*.

says, cannot hear him (360 *PMG*). However, he does not establish a fictional situation for himself, so the remark is not overheard; rather, the boy's failure to "hear" marks the boy as absent or uncomprehending. Anakreon's poem therefore functions both as an admission of love and as a comment to the audience about the paradox of desirable innocence. Ibykos, by contrast, exploits the disjunct between singer's control and inner chaos to express his very being as love-torn, but his poems have no addressee or fictional setting. They are presented as confessions to the actual audience.

The symposium poets also create fictions in their poetry. Alkaios' poem from exile (130B *V*)—the closest parallel—posits a fictional situation for the speaker but does not inhibit identification of speaker and singer. He therefore threatens his audience by portraying his assumed isolation, while Sappho's poem takes it as a given. Alkaios' poem has an addressee, Agesilaidas, whose identity is unknown. He is a sympathetic figure, for the singer complains to him. He is probably a member of the group or someone who could be imagined as a participant, in which case the address to him represents communication to the group. Conceivably Agesilaidas' identity was such that speaking to him precluded speaking to the *hetaireia*. Barring the latter possibility, utterance is still communication from actual singer to actual audience, even though it must be thought of as traversing a distance. Hipponax too offers a partial parallel with Sappho, though with utterly different effect, but despite the lively fictional accounts of lowlife doings, usually told in the past tense, his short and broken fragments do not appear to split singer and speaker. The poems that are narratives are directed to their actual audience and the prayers are a humorous form of self-staging as rogue.[99]

The various aspects, therefore, of Sappho's technique are found in symposium poetry. But no extant symposium poem uses all of Sappho's devices together: the fictional situation, the unreachable addressee, the inward focus, the coherent exposition of psychosomatic devastation; nor does any symposium poem push them so far. In its creation of fantasy scene and inner monologue, Sappho's poem actually denies the situation of performance by detaching the speaker from the actual setting, singer, and collected audience. This is certainly not a poem for a group like a symposium group, one that used performance to reinforce a sense of collectivity. How then can we understand the poem as performance?

To one who would study it as performed communication, the poem presents two choices. One can pursue the idea that the poem was performed to a group of a different sort, a group within which it was appropriate for the singer to make a point of her distance and detachment from

[99] E.g., 79 and 92 *W* (narratives), 34 *W* (prayer). See the translations in West 1993: 116–23 for the flavor.

the audience in her self-presentation. Or else one can look for an altogether different performance context for it. The first is Anne Burnett's approach. Burnett notes Sappho's detachment (which she finds in the content and tone of the poetry, not in performance dynamics). She also accepts an informal version of the initiation theory and sees the audience as a circle of *parthenoi* preparing for marriage.[100] She therefore takes Sappho's aloofness as a didactic stance. Thus in this poem Sappho uses herself as a model to demonstrate a method of recovering self-possession: the poem begins with a statement that "smilingly" compliments the addressee (to sit near you is the highest happiness) and articulates an extreme sense of the difference between the speaker's position and the man's; but it ends by redefining the difference in mundane terms (poor versus rich) that might easily change—a hopeful idea that revives the speaker.[101] Love, says the poem, is both immortalizing and ephemeral. Overall Burnett finds Sappho's lesson in the need to transmute desire into appreciation of beauty.[102] In sum, Sappho's strategy is to demonstrate her ultimate detachment from any erotic involvement and to bring detachment within the circle as an ideal, promoting an aesthetic sensuality in response to the ineluctable problem of women's being separated by their families' command.

But would 31 *V* be heard that way? If Sappho in person sang the poem to a group of *parthenoi* who knew her, they would inevitably take it as an expression of her attitude toward them. If they thought that she had a specific person in mind, the rest would feel emotionally left out, for the contrast between Sappho's intense reaction to one and her disregard for all the others present would be evident. If they thought that she had no one in mind, her description of her symptoms would seem mocking. It seems to me that as a didactic piece the poem would fail because an impersonal attitude projected within a small group will be read as rejection of friendship with other members of the group.

Let us make the other choice and think further about a performance context for the poem. The only way 31 can be heard without appearing to ignore or spoof the emotions of its audience is for each auditor to take it as meant for herself alone. As a result, the poem gains immediacy as each listener loses consciousness of any rival auditor.[103] But members of a

[100] Burnett 1983: 209n.2: "It is the assumption of the present study that the group met in daily intimacy and informality, and that most of Sappho's songs were first performed before this assembly of pupils who were also friends and temporary wards."

[101] Burnett 1983: 241–42, accepting the final two words as part of the poem. West 1970a: 312–13 proposes by analogy with Theognis 657–64 that Sappho said, "All is bearable, since god suddenly makes even the poor man rich."

[102] Burnett 1983: 277–312, esp. 309–12. Burnett's approach reveals that the very effort to locate the poems in a group context exposes their lack of engagement with the audience.

[103] West 1970a: 310, commenting on the lack of names in several of Sappho's poems, suggests that like Theognis' songs, Sappho's could be resung. On 315 he describes her songs as freed from their context.

group with established relationships, affections, and jealousies could not banish each other from mind. The poem would achieve its greatest emotional impact, therefore, if a woman sang it to herself. Instead of hoping that Sappho envisioned her, she would envision Sappho. The separation of speaker and singer effected by the poem means that a woman who sang the poem could simultaneously hear it as another's voice. The fictional setting invites her to imagine herself in that situation, feeling "Sappho's" eyes on her and hearing "Sappho's" thoughts. She could easily picture "Sappho," since the latter gives such full description of herself. To be its focus makes the poem thrilling to any auditor.

From the singer/addressee's point of view, the poem has two powerful effects. First, the poem creates an illusion of communication with "Sappho." Within the framework of the fictional setting, "Sappho's" speech is telepathic, for the addressee becomes cognizant of it as she speaks to the man. Nor does "Sappho" withdraw: since the poem does not begin as a soliloquy for the addressee (as it does for other listeners), she would take lines 8 and following as the continuation of "Sappho's" address to her.[104] The result is two-way interchange: since "Sappho" describes herself, the addressee knows what "Sappho" feels and sees "Sappho" along with "Sappho" seeing her and seeing herself. From the recipient's point of view, each woman is seeing herself and the other; she also hears "Sappho"—and can imagine "Sappho" hearing her thoughts. The poem actually invites her participation in a secret conversation.

Dependent on the first effect is the second: the addressee would have to imagine herself as desirable to others, for she would find both "Sappho" and the man beside her in thrall to her, and the reactions of both would guide the representation of herself that she projects into the picture.[105] And how unconventionally Sappho goes about signaling her attractiveness! To feel the full impact of the scene of the addressee's speaking to the man, we must compare it to one of Greek culture's most prevalent narratives of female beauty, the rape. The loveliness of a young woman in myth is routinely represented by her ability to attract a god or hero, who seizes the opportunity for an act of intercourse and then is off. Examples are mentioned in Chapter 2. In Sappho's poem, by contrast, the man seems "like a god" but sits immobilized. Instead of acting, he listens to "you" talking and laughing. Since she is thus the one who defines the situation rather than the object of his wilful desire, she finds herself represented as a speaking subject in the mirror of the poem. Even if the addressee does not construe the man as important, his behavior reflects on the image of herself that she is invited to create.

[104] Contrast O'Higgins 1990: 164, who reads the effect psychologically: the act of making a poem replaces passion.

[105] Hallett 1979 argues that Sappho's poetry has the function of awakening young women's sexuality.

With respect to "Sappho," the revisionist image granted the addressee is even stronger: "Sappho" both listens and sees her but does not objectify her, since "Sappho's" perception leads to an overwhelming sense of her very being. The addressee accordingly perceives herself not as a body caught in "Sappho's" gaze, but as a presence for others.[106] Her subjectivity and desirability are inseparable in the phrases "sweetly speaking" and "laughing enchantingly." Thus the poem provides its addressee with an ideal image of herself in terms that resist the culture's objectification of women, just as Sappho reversed the dominant construction of the female in her own self-presentation.

We can see that when we explore its effects from the position of a unique recipient the poem comes most to life as communication and appears to have the greatest psychological efficacy; that is, it has the power to influence the auditor positively in ways that one can imagine Sappho wanted. It creates more impression of interchange, paradoxically, than if Sappho were to sing it to a group as an illustration of her feelings. The earlier analysis of the disjunct between speaker and singer has already shown that the poem is not a libretto for self-presentation: the fictional speaker cannot be realized by the singer but must rely on the auditor's imagination. Let us take these two aspects of the poem together: they suggest that the poem was created as *text*, as Sappho's projection of herself into a form that would be independent of her presence. I propose, therefore, that Sappho composed this poem as a gift for a woman from whom she expected to be cut off for some reason. Poems 16, 94, and 96 *V* show that separation was a painful reality for women. The poem then has as its function to keep a sense of contact alive over time and distance. In blurring subject–object distinctions as she does, Sappho tries not only to foster the fantasy of continued intimacy but to reproduce the sense of mutual affirmation that women must have gotten from Sappho or in her circle. We can add that the telepathic communication implied within 31 mirrors its actual mode of communication, writing, which is silent and able to traverse distance. The repeatability of the scene (the man sits in the continuative present and Sappho collapses every time she looks) reflects the reiterability of the written statement. If I am right, then Sappho was one of the first major poets to exploit the textual possibilities of writing, with its ability to project an implied speaker independent of the physical mode of transmission. I return to this issue at the end of the chapter.

How, then, should we think about gendered speech in this poem? Since it is not a poem designed for a singer's self-presentation to a circle of friends, we should look at the en-gendering of the singer/addressee who creates an image of herself for herself as she performs it. I have already

---

[106] See Stehle 1990: 107–8; Greene 1994: 42–43. Sara Lindheim reminds me of the importance of stressing this.

pointed out that she can perceive the force of her presence by its effect on the other figures in the poem. Yet more subtly, the poem forces the recipient to define her own desire by construing the scene. The extant lines never name "Sappho's" emotion, only its symptoms, so the singer/ addressee can decide what "Sappho" feels, depending on what she wants from "Sappho." The man might or might not be important, depending on her inflection of the scene. He might function for an addressee simply to indicate a setting in which "Sappho" cannot approach, or she might find the idea of proximity to a man or the implication of marriage exciting. Nor must the man be a future husband; a listener could think of him as an alternative to her present husband, for imagination is free. The poem provides a field in which the recipient can arrange a variety of relationships centered on herself, while she must act as subject in positioning the other figures emotionally.

In singing the poem, the addressee speaks of herself through the mouth of another whom she creates in imagination. Within the poem she sees and hears herself through the others' eyes and ears. She therefore conceives herself as a split subject, finding herself in another's consciousness of her; but because she creates the other whose voice she uses to represent herself, hers is a self-conscious split subjectivity. Her performance therefore counteracts women's gendered public self-presentation as unaware objects for others. The significance of Sappho's poem must be seen in light of the stance assigned to women speakers as we uncovered it in Chapter 2: in public performance women dramatized their dissociation from their bodies and voices. None of the poems examined there comes from Lesbos, but, as the wedding poetry shows, the same assumptions about male and female seem to have been prevalent on Lesbos. When juxtaposed with Alkman's *partheneia*, 31 *V* seems subversive: it elicits the singer/recipient's awareness of herself as desiring and desirable in addition to fabricating a female speaker who speaks of her own desire.[107]

If 31 *V* had no specific performance context because it was written for a woman to sing to herself, we have no hope of identifying the age of the recipient or her actual relationship to Sappho. Sappho may have given 31 to a *parthenos* whom she had trained for performance but would not expect to see again. She may have composed it for a companion from her circle. The separation would not necessarily result from one woman's departure from Lesbos, for the shifts of political alignment alone probably barred women from seeing one another at times. Sappho may in fact have been a lover of the one she begifted, but her poems do not reveal actual relation-

---

[107] In this 31 *V* is like 16 *V*. In Stehle 1990: 109–12 I analyze 16, a description of Helen acting on her desire in going to Troy, as a validation of women's subjectivity in a cultural world defined by men. Poem 16 has a different rhetorical structure; it has no addressee but makes a general proposition, so performance in the circle would suit it.

ships. They use the expression or intimation of desire to bridge the distance and keep contact with her emotionally alive. It is a striking fact that Sappho's declarations and descriptions of love and desire are always mediated by distance, the inaccessibility of one even to the other's speech by normal channels.[108] Desire in Sappho's poetry, then, is a form of and metaphor for contact despite separation.

In 1 *V* Sappho achieves similar effects by another route. Sappho begins by calling on Aphrodite not to tame her with pains but to come as she has come before in her sparrow-drawn chariot. I quote the latter part of the poem (13–28):

> αἶψα δ' ἐξίκοντο· σὺ δ', ὦ μάκαιρα,
> μειδιαίσαισ' ἀθανάτωι προσώπωι
> 15 ἤρε' ὄττι δηὖτε πέπονθα κὤττι
>   δηὖτε κάλημμι
>
> κὤττι μοι μάλιστα θέλω γένεσθαι
> μαινόλαι θύμωι· τίνα δηὖτε πείθω
>]σάγην ἐς σὰν φιλότατα;[109] τίς σ', ὦ
> 20   Ψαπφ', ἀδίκησι;
>
> καὶ γὰρ αἰ φεύγει, ταχέως διώξει,
> αἰ δὲ δῶρα μὴ δέκετ', ἀλλὰ δώσει,
> αἰ δὲ μὴ φίλει, ταχέως φιλήσει
> 25   κωὐκ ἐθέλοισα.
>
> 25 ἔλθε μοι καὶ νῦν, χαλέπαν δὲ λῦσον
> ἐκ μερίμναν, ὄσσα δέ μοι τέλεσσαι
> θῦμος ἰμέρρει, τέλεσον, σὺ δ' αὔτα
>   σύμμαχος ἔσσο.

. . . swiftly they arrived; and you, blessed one, with a smile on your immortal face, asked what again I suffer and why again I call and what I most wish in my mad heart to have happen; whom again should I persuade to [   ] into your affection (*or* lead you back into her affection)? Who does you injustice, Sappho? For even if she flees, soon she will chase, and if she does not accept presents, she will nevertheless give them, and if she does not love, soon she will love, even if unwilling. Come to me now also, free me from harsh cares, bring to fulfillment all that my heart yearns to accomplish, and you yourself be my ally.

[108] Carson 1986: 17 and passim refers to this effect as "triangulation."

[109] A papyrus fragment appears to give ψ as the second letter in this line. One could therefore restore ἄψ σ' ἄγην ἐς ϝὰν φιλότατα (to lead you back into her friendship), which Campbell 1982 prints. There are details that do not seem to accord with this reading, so it remains tentative. See Page 1955 *ad loc.;* Voigt *ad loc.*

In the poem the address to Aphrodite becomes a recalled conversation, which switches from indirect into direct discourse, blurring the time difference. The past appears to be now, the divinity there in "Sappho's" presence. A collective audience would be reduced to the status of ignored observers as the narration of a past event turns into a dramatic projection in the present. This poem, like 31 *V,* does not present its singer to the audience as one among them or constitute its auditors as a group.

The dramatic situation is further displaced from the actual context of performance by the treatment of the first person. The whole poem is an address to Aphrodite, but within that address the singer narrates to Aphrodite a previous epiphany of the goddess's. This narration begins in mediated form: "you" remains Aphrodite from the opening address through the first part of the narration, while "I" is the singer. Then in mid-stanza (line 18) the construction switches to direct discourse and "I" becomes Aphrodite.[110] Two successive first-person verbs (θέλω and πείθω) have different referents. Just after the moment when the singer's voice becomes Aphrodite's, "Aphrodite" addresses "Sappho" by name. The effect of this transfer is to detach the character "Sappho" from the singer and make her a figure in the imagination of the listener.

The poem withholds even knowledge from a collective audience: the woman who causes "Sappho's" pain is not named, and the listeners would be left in the dark. Nor do I think that her identity would be known to the audience from real life, given that the poem would seem gloating if the woman had (re)turned to Sappho and risky if she had not: if the woman did not soon reconcile with Sappho, Sappho's influence with Aphrodite would appear to have faded. And the poem makes a rather remarkable claim: Aphrodite once told Sappho that she would coerce *whomever* Sappho wanted (back?) (18–24). How many current intimates, ex-lovers, or rivals for others' affection would want to hear that?

Like 31, the poem is textual; it presents a fictional "Sappho" to be created in imagination by a singer/recipient who identifies herself as the "she" of whom "Sappho" speaks. She would overhear "Sappho's" determination to gain (or recover) intimacy (φιλότας) with her.[111] She would hear herself described by Aphrodite as bound to become an active pursuer, an agent of her own desire. The second of the two effects treated above, portrayal of the other woman as at once desiring and desirable, seems to operate in this poem too. On the other hand, this poem sounds very different in tone and attitude from 31. Aphrodite's speech has an aggressive edge, which "Sappho" seconds with her military metaphor in the last line.

---

[110] See Führer 1967: 3–4 for other examples of the switch from indirect to direct discourse in lyric; none is a switch between first and second person. Cf. also his p. 60.

[111] Wilamowitz-Moellendorff 1913: 48 has a biographical version of this point: the poem might have made the girl aware that she was the one meant and inspired love in her in turn.

Aphrodite's repeated "again" makes it clear that she has been summoned before. These features are reminiscent of 130 and 71 V, discussed above as poems about women who appear to be transferring their loyalty to new friendships. The beauty of the other woman is not mentioned, and the problem is not unbridgeable distance but the other woman's refusal to close the distance. I would therefore hazard a guess that 1 V offers a singer who identifies with "she" the motivation to come (or return) to Sappho's circle. She hears that Aphrodite is likely to compel her despite her own resistance, just as Aphrodite has brought others (back). Aphrodite moreover thinks that she is committing "injustice" by staying away. If the singer/recipient is torn between the impulse to come and advice from others not to come, this poem will give her both precedent and justification for yielding to impulse. Sappho's unparalleled use of legal and military language, as well as her unique request that Aphrodite take practical steps to bring a woman (back), indicate that Sappho seeks a different effect from that of 31 V. Like the poems discussed in the last section, this may be a political poem veiled in the language of personal need. The term φιλότας can mean either "love" or "friendship," so would be well-suited to link Sappho's fictional self-presentation as desiring to her actual meaning of seeking political intimacy within a circle.[112]

The textuality that we discovered, put to use in 31 V to counteract the effects of separation, is deployed here to undo separation. If Sappho sent the poem to the woman she meant, the woman could always renew and justify her attachment to Sappho through the imagery of erotic compulsion. She might notice the veiled threat as well, contained simply in the lack of a specifying pronoun in lines 23–24: Aphrodite does not say whether the other woman will pursue "you" (i.e., "Sappho") or will pursue some other (and learn what it is to be disdained).[113] Sappho clearly seeks reciprocity of attachment, so if the woman was inclined to return to Sappho she could supply "you" without making anything of its absence.[114] But if she resisted the idea of joining Sappho, she might hear Aphrodite's promise as a threat to make her pursue others.

Some will object that I have demoted 1 V from a love poem to a political poem. I do not think that any of the love poems are a candid cry of emotion or even a taming of ardor by controlled expression. They are rather the vehicle for expenditure of emotion: Sappho lent her body and desire to others in order to sustain them with the energy of her response to them.

---

[112] Page 1955 ad loc. discusses the meanings of the word in Sappho.

[113] Page 1955: 14–15 remarks that διώκω means "pursue someone who flees." This is not always true, but Sappho's use of the verb may carry overtones. For Giacomelli [Carson] 1980 the justice of Aphrodite consists of making the one who spurns someone's love fall hopelessly in love with another.

[114] As Greene 1994: 50–55 argues.

We, who cannot pretend to know her personally and are not engaged by her political life, must approach her power by creating a biography of loves, but the desire we feel to know her desire attests to her power to draw women to her, even absent an expectation of becoming lovers. Poem 1 *V* may be both a love poem and a political protreptic, but at the least its vocabulary gives it an additional field of reference missing in the other love poems.

For her project in 1 *V,* Sappho uses a bold technique: she portrays herself in conversation with a god. Interchange with divinity is another method by which Sappho creates a fictional textual character separate from the singer, for such privilege belongs to mythical and heroic figures.[115] Like a hero the speaker calls on her favoring deity; the full stanza it takes Aphrodite to arrive is a measure of the distance the speaker's voice can reach. Like a hero she can endure the undisguised presence of a god. The listener who creates a fictional Sappho can either take the epiphany as "real" and imagine Sappho in quasi-mythical terms or can take it as imagined by the fictional Sappho, who becomes a figure of intense inward emotions.[116]

This method has a further dimension that the portrayal of psychosomatic chaos in 31 *V* lacks: it lends authority to the speaker. She is like a bard as well as a hero, for she can also "see" Aphrodite leave Olympus and can make her visible to the audience. On the other hand, Sappho uses bardic authorizing techniques in counterpoint to bards' practice: Aphrodite validates her speaking, not Zeus; she chooses as her "ally" in this poem the god whom Athena mocked in the *Iliad* as a useless adjuvant in war (21.423–33).[117] Sappho's authority is antipatriarchal, and she gains thereby an alternative source of "truth."

In other fragments as well, the speaker portrays herself in conversation with a god. In fragment 95 *V* Sappho appears to report a conversation with a god; her interlocutor this time may be Hermes.[118] She repeats a speech she made to him in which she expressed longing to die and see "the lotusy, dewy banks of Acheron" (8–13). Images of loss of consciousness and renewal interact in the description.[119] Of the addressee or the dramatic context for the reported speech, almost nothing is preserved: the name

---

[115] See Marry 1979 for Sappho's implicit equation of herself with a Homeric warrior in 1 *V*.

[116] Earlier commentators (e.g., Page 1955: 18) considered whether Sappho had actually experienced the epiphany of Aphrodite. If the poem is taken as a straightforward self-presentation, then the question is a legitimate one.

[117] See Skinner 1991a on Sappho's calling on Aphrodite (rather than the Muses) for poetic inspiration. Greene 1994: 53 discusses Sappho's reconfiguration of military language in this poem.

[118] Ἔρ]‖μας is a possible restoration of the end of line 6 (Voigt *ad loc.*)

[119] Boedeker 1979 makes this point; she also reviews earlier literature on the fragment, in which a biographical approach predominates.

Gongyla and the word *sign* are almost the only other words of significance that can be read. We cannot tell, then, how Sappho used the figure she created as speaker in this poem, but perhaps she again revealed intense longing for another woman.

Other small fragments hint at Sappho's habit of fictionalizing herself by revealing her interaction with divinities. In 96.21–23, which may open a new poem, the speaker says, "It is not easy for us (?) to equal the goddesses in lovely shape . . ." In the following two stanzas, something is said about Aphrodite, who "poured nectar from golden [pitchers?]" (26–28). The speaker's idea about whether mortal women resemble the gods gains weight from her personal vision of Aphrodite. A line is quoted by Maximus of Tyre with the explanation that Aphrodite is speaking to Sappho (159 *V*):

> σύ τε κἄμος θεράπων Ἔρος

You and my attendant Eros

The goddess addresses Sappho, as she does in 1 *V*, with the added distinction that Sappho is paired with the daimonic Eros; we can see how this poem might have detached the speaker from the singer and created a mythicized figure of "Sappho." Another quotation (134 *V*) seems to say, "I narrated a dream to (?) Aphrodite," and yet another, garbled passage is reported as spoken to Aphrodite (101 *V*). Sappho must have used the technique frequently.

Poem 96 *V* is somewhat different from 31 and 1. Though the opening is lost, it appears to have been addressed to Atthis, to judge from the name in the genitive in line 16. The extant part, beginning with scraps of what may well be the first stanza, evokes a woman who is now in Lydia; she may have been named as well:

>] σαρδ[
>
> πόλ]λακι τυίδε [   ]ων ἔχοισα
>
> ὤσπ[   ]ώομεν, [
>
> σε †θεασικελαν ἀρι-
>
> 5   γνωτα†, σᾶι δὲ μάλιστ' ἔχαιρε μόλπαι·
>
> νῦν δὲ Λύδαισιν ἐμπρέπεται γυναί-
>
> κεσσιν ὤς ποτ' ἀελίω
>
> δύντος ἀ βροδοδάκτυλος ⟨σελάννα⟩
>
> πάντα περ⟨ρ⟩έχοισ' ἄστρα· φάος δ' ἐπί-
>
> 10   σχει θάλασσαν ἐπ' ἀλμύραν
>
> ἴσως καὶ πολυανθέμοις ἀρούραις·

ἀ δ' ⟨ἐ⟩έρσα κάλα κέχυται, τεθά-
λαισι δὲ βρόδα κἄπαλ' ἄν-
θρυσκα καὶ μελίλωτος ἀνθεμώδης·

15   πόλλα δὲ ζαφοίταισ' ἀγάνας ἐπι-
μνάσθεισ' Ἀτθιδος ἰμέρωι
λέπταν ποι φρένα κ[ ]ρ[ ] βόρηται·

κῆθι δ' ἔλθην ἀμμ[   ]ισα τόδ' οὐ
νωντα[ ]υστονυμ[   ] πόλυς
20   γαρύει [ ]αλογ[   ]τ̣ο μέσσον·

. . . Sardis (?) [   ] often turning her [mind] in this direction [   ], [she
honored ?] you like a manifest goddess (?),[120] and she delighted most in your
song and dance, but now she stands out among the Lydian women as sometimes, when the sun has set, the rosy-rayed moon outshines all the stars; its light
reaches equally over the briny sea and the flower-filled fields; and the beautiful
dew settles and the roses and tender chervil and fragrant clover are in bloom.
Often pacing up and down, remembering gentle Atthis with longing, she is
consumed [   ] in her delicate heart (?).[121] But for us to go there [   ] this
(is) not [possible ?] much [   ] sounds [   ] middle.

The poem does not detach its speaker from the singer. Instead its speaker
pronounces with an air of oracular authority about the thoughts and feelings of the woman in Lydia, offering no explicit self-presentation at all. It
too concentrates on one addressee and allows the audience no way to
participate, so I take this poem also as one intended for the addressee to
perform for herself. The addressee is not described as distant from the
speaker, but through the poem she can recall a woman who is gone. We
could say that "Sappho" portrays the woman in Lydia as playing the same
role toward Atthis that "Sappho" herself fills for the addressee in 31 and 1,
with the same two effects. On one hand, the woman in Lydia attests to
Atthis' desirability and subjectivity in that she used to compare Atthis to a
goddess and loved her singing. On the other, her longing allows Atthis to
think of the intimacy as continuing across the distance that separates them.
"Sappho" speaks for the absent woman; in her name she offers magnifi-
cent praise of Atthis, for the phrase "manifest goddess" (4–5) recalls a
passage from the *Odyssey* in which Nausicaa is compared to Artemis
(6.107–9).[122] "Sappho" also reveals her to Atthis, pacing and yearning.

[120] Accepting in the translation -σε θέα⟨ι⟩ σ' ἰκέλαν ἀριγνώτα⟨ι⟩ (where -σε is the end
of the verb), which Page 1955 prints. See his note *ad loc.*
[121] This line has not been reconstructed in a satisfactory way. See Burnett 1983: 309–
10n.92 for attempts; Bonanno 1990: 119–21.
[122] Marzullo 1952: 90–92. The text is uncertain; some think that ἀριγνώτα is the name of

Poem 96 therefore confirms the intent of 31 by showing us the same mystic communication, arranged by the speaker now but affecting two others. In what was perhaps the last stanza (18–20), as in 31 *V*, the speaker acknowledges separation—unless line 21 is not the opening of a new poem, in which case the speaker goes on to suggest that Atthis looks like a goddess, compensation proffered for the other woman's absence.

Since it involves three figures, 96 *V* has even more of a polymorphous quality than does 31 *V*. Atthis could sing the poem to herself and feel "Sappho's" urgency, as well as the longing of the woman in Lydia. The woman's beauty like the moon, an image that seems to overflow the simile and drench the poem in its light, would call forth Atthis' own desire for the absent woman—and perhaps for Sappho too as the producer of such sensuous imagery. "Sappho's" sentiment for Atthis is unspecific, if heartfelt: is she comforting or seductive?[123] Perhaps she wishes to draw Atthis to herself. Atthis could construct the scene as she wished. The woman in Lydia could also sing it to herself and hear herself described in terms of beauty and sexual subjectivity together, the latter as the one who praises Atthis. The poem implies by its existence that Atthis longs for her. She could also imagine that "Sappho," who extols her beauty, desires her. The power of "Sappho's" feeling for Atthis, or for the woman in Lydia, or both, gives her recreation of their intimacy its force, as though they both draw from her their energy of desire for one another. The poem thus creates a play of intersubjectivity in which each woman who sings and puts herself into the song is desirer and desired. For each woman it offers, in the course of creating a fiction of continued communication, the possibility of mutual interchange in escape from the subject-object division encoded in hegemonic culture.

Fragment 22 *V* shows us another dimension of Sappho's project. I quote the best-preserved section (9–17) from Campbell:[124]

```
        [              κ]έλομαι σ' ἀ[είδην
10    Γο]γγύλαν ['Άβ]ανθι λάβοισαν ἀ[
        πᾶ]κτιν, ἆς σε δηὖτε πόθος τ[
        ἀμφιπόταται
```

the woman in Lydia. Marzullo gives arguments *contra*. Voigt's preference (*ad loc.*) is to take the word as a name in the vocative; then four women would be implicated: the speaker, the Lydian woman, Arignota, and Atthis.

[123] For Hague 1984 Sappho is comforting; for Schadewaldt 1950: 123 Sappho expresses her own desire for Atthis while disguising it as that of the woman in Lydia; Saake 1972: 81 sees Sappho's attitude as seductive.

[124] 22 Campbell 1982. The restored text, although speculative, gives a better idea of possibilities than Voigt's. See also Di Benedetto 1986: 21–25 on the text.

τὰν κάλαν· ἀ γὰρ κατάγωγις αὖτα[ς σ'
ἐπτόαισ' ἴδοισαν, ἔγω δὲ χαίρω·
15   καὶ γὰρ αὖτα δήπο[τ'] ἐμέμφ[ετ' ἄγνα
     Κ]υπρογέν[ηα,

ὠς ἄραμα[ι
τοῦτο τῶ[πος
β]όλλομα[ι

[   ] I order you [to sing of Gongyla, Abanthis ?] taking [   ] lyre [   ] while desire yet again [   ] flies around you, the lovely one. For her (?) garment overwhelmed [you?] when you (?) saw it, and I rejoice, for even the [holy?] Cyprian herself (= Aphrodite), no less, once rebuked (me) on the grounds that I pray [   ] this word (?) [   ] I want [

The papyrus does not show whether line 9 is the opening of a new poem, but it looks as though it could be, and I will assume that it is. As in 96, there may have been specific names, although the restorations in line 10, Gongyla and Abanthis, are uncertain. Edgar Lobel does not think that "Gongyla" fits the trace of a letter at the edge of the papyrus.[125] The name Abanthis is borrowed from an unattributed fragment of Aeolic lyric.[126] Other completions of the visible letters are possible, and the whole restoration is tentative; it is not implausible, however, so with that caveat I will adopt it.[127]

"Sappho" speaks to one woman about another, recreating a past moment of attraction. The fragment does not reveal whether Gongyla is now absent, but the parallel with 96 *V* suggests that she is. If so, Sappho is again the link between the two women by her observation and memory of what once transpired. Sappho also fictionalizes herself through conversation with Aphrodite as in 1 *V* and more overtly than in 96. Since the poem shows the same features as these two poems, I analyze it too from the recipient's perspective.

From this angle one can see that Sappho devises a new mode of fostering another woman's subjectivity. The speaker asserts Abanthis' desire and desirability, as we have seen in other poems, but does not create the illusion of continued communication between Abanthis and Gongyla. She does not evoke Gongyla in the present for Abanthis or convey her thoughts like a seer. Instead she orders Abanthis to compose and sing for

---

[125] See *LP* ad loc.; Voigt *ad loc.* and *ad* 95.4.

[126] *Incert. auct.* 35 *V;* cf. n.87 above. Di Benedetto 1986: 22 thinks that it is not long enough to fill the lacuna but that a name did stand there. Alternatively, the word could be an imperative.

[127] Cf. λάβοισα and ἄεισον in 21.11–12 *V*.

herself. We should therefore examine the effect on the recipient more closely.

The speaker opens by telling one woman, Abanthis, to sing about another for whom she feels longing. At the same time she (the speaker) attests to Abanthis' beauty, for τὰν κάλαν (the lovely one) should refer to the nearer accusative (σε in 11). But the adjective does not simply stay put: because it stands at the beginning of the line and has the same metrical shape as Γογγύλαν two lines above, it could be heard as applying to Gongyla also and epitomizing what Abanthis should sing about her. What the speaker says about Abanthis, Abanthis should say about Gongyla. Then too the phrase "desire . . . flies around you" must refer to the longing that Abanthis feels, but in its vivid unspecificity it suggests the longing that Abanthis causes as well. Like Erotes fluttering about a bride or beautiful woman in later Greek vase-painting, longing flying around Abanthis hints at a double movement of desire between her and another who also finds her desirable.

The next sentence specified that one woman's dress made the other lose her breath, but because of the ambiguity, or rather two-way nature, of the relationship between the two women, we cannot decide between two possible restorations, αὔτας σ' or αὔταν, at the end of line 13.[128] The first yields the statement "her dress overwhelmed you when you saw it," and the second the reverse, "your dress overwhelmed her when she saw it." The second creates mutual attraction, for Gongyla responds to Abanthis as well. Even if the original line was the first (as given above), the double movement of desire from and to Abanthis would not be canceled, for Abanthis is the "lovely one" and the focus of the poem. The dress itself is an object onto which desire is deflected to generalize it.[129] Abanthis would surely hear confirmation of her desire and desirability in the poem.

"Sappho" shifts attention to herself in line 14, describing her own reaction to the moment just mentioned: she "rejoices" at the sight of one woman overwhelming the other. Her delight must mean that she sees in Abanthis assailed by desire another like herself, and therein lies her reason for commanding Abanthis to sing. Abanthis, who is like "Sappho" in the intensity of her emotions, should become like her also in articulating her acute responsiveness to another and presenting herself as the subject of her sexuality.

On the other hand Aphrodite reproves "Sappho" for wanting [   ]. "Sappho," for her part, seems to refuse to give up the fervor of her own

---

[128] The accusative is restored in Page 1955: 135 although not in his edition of the same year; see also Voigt *ad loc.* Campbell 1982 prints αὔτα[ς σ' from West 1970a: 319. Di Benedetto 1986: 23–24 disputes West, preferring αὔτα[ν.

[129] Cf. the eroticized landscape in 96 *V;* Snyder 1994.

desire despite the criticism. One who not only converses with a god but insists on her own perspective makes herself a subject in the face of powerful authority. Because Abanthis should imitate her, "Sappho" provides a paradigm for the addressee to follow by expressing her self-knowledge in spite of others' disfavor. Abanthis therefore should compose and sing songs herself, whatever those around her make of her passion. Like 1 *V,* this is a poem of resistance: it establishes a counterweight to other pressures in the recipient's immediate life. It is more vital to understanding Sappho's overall endeavor than 1 *V,* however, because it does not seek to produce a specific action but to make the recipient more autonomous in expressing her own emotional states.

Yet two problems must be addressed if I am to include this poem with those a recipient sings to herself. First, because the speaker's communication with Abanthis in the fragment appears to be direct and unhindered, the poem seems to be one that Sappho could sing to Abanthis among other women in the circle of friends. Second, the verb "I order" in line 9 (which I take to be the first line of the poem) seems odd in a poem urging another to speak autonomously about her desire. In fact, the two problems cancel each other out. If Sappho were to sing this poem to Abanthis, she would impose herself, with her "I order you" and her interchange with Aphrodite, as superior in power (even if playfully). The poem would then be contradictory in its effect, for Abanthis' singing would not be an expression of her own desire to speak and therefore not a sign of her desire. The impossibility of the verb "I order" in this poem if Sappho meant to sing it to Abanthis shows that the poem must be treated otherwise. If Abanthis, however, were to sing the poem, she would issue the command to herself, and by projecting it onto a mythicized figure whom she creates in imagination she would gain the authority (in her own eyes) to speak about herself as a sexual subject. Claiming divine or mythic validation was of course a normal form of authorizing one's speech or actions in Greek culture. Thus, the split subjectivity Abanthis creates by uttering another's command to her is the springboard to her own freedom to speak.

Fragment 95 *V,* discussed earlier, could be classed with 22 *V* as offering a model for speaking. As in 22 *V* "Sappho" uses her account of interaction with divinity to emphasize her human difference, for she asks not for immortality or gratification but for death. She appears to speak as soon as Hermes arrives: the word εἶπον (I said) is positioned at the beginning of the stanza (8), highlighting her act of speech. Poem 1 *V* likewise shows Sappho speaking, compelling Aphrodite's response despite the latter's smile. As remarked earlier, "that man" in 31 can stand in for the whole social system in separating "Sappho" and the addressee. Persistence in subjectivity in spite of lack of power in fact describes all of Sappho's love poetry, composed in the face of the dominant culture, but 22 manifestly propels another to take up Sappho's resistance to the cultural definition of women.

One more poem, 94 *V*, combines all these functions and shows Sappho urging the role of speaker on another. It is made difficult by the loss of at least one line from the beginning. The text follows:

. . . .

τεθνάκην δ' ἀδόλως θέλω·

ἄ με ψισδομένα κατελίμπανεν

πόλλα καὶ τόδ' ἔειπέ [μοι·

ὤιμ' ὠς δεῖνα πεπ[όνθ]αμεν,

5   Ψάπφ', ἦ μάν σ' ἀέκοισ' ἀπυλιμπάνω.

τὰν δ' ἔγω τάδ' ἀμειβόμαν·

χαίροισ' ἔρχεο κἄμεθεν

μέμναισ', οἶσθα γὰρ ὠς ⟨σ⟩ε πεδήπομεν·

αἰ δὲ μή, ἀλλά σ' ἔγω θέλω

10   ὄμναισαι [   ]ε̣αι

ο̣σ̣[   ] καὶ κάλ' ἐπάσχομεν·

πό[λλοις γὰρ στεφάν]οις ἴων

καὶ βρ[όδων   ]κίων τ' ὔμοι

κα[   ] πὰρ ἔμοι π⟨ε⟩ρεθήκα⟨ο⟩

15   καὶ πόλλαις ὐπαθύμιδας

πλέκταις ἀμφ' ἀπάλαι δέραι

ἀνθέων ἐ̣[   ] πεποημέναις.

καὶ π[   ] μύρωι

βρενθείωι [ ]ρυ[ ]ν

20   ἐξαλ⟨ε⟩ίψαο κα[ὶ βασ]ι̣ληίωι

καὶ στρώμν[αν ἐ]πὶ μολθάκαν

ἀπάλαν παρ[   ]ργων

ἐξίης πόθο[ν   ]νίδων

κωὔτε τις [οὔ]τε̣ τι

25   ἶρον οὐδ' ὐ[

ἔπλετ' ὄππ[οθεν ἄμ]μες ἀπέσκομεν,

οὐκ ἄλσος [

I truly want to die. She left me weeping much and said this [to me]: "oh! how terribly we are suffering; Sappho, in truth I leave you unwillingly." I answered her thus: "Go in joy and remember me, for you know how we sought you out. Or if you don't, then I want to remind you [   ] and we 'suffered' lovely things. For many wreaths of violets and roses and [crocuses?] together and [   ] you put around yourself, beside me, and many plaited garlands made of flowers [you put?] around your tender neck and [   ] with much (?) fragrant myrrh [   ] you anointed yourself and with royal (perfume), and on a soft bed, tender [   ] you satisfied longing for [   ], and no [   ] and no shrine [   ] was there from which we stayed away, no grove [

One must decide to whom to attribute the first extant line, the speaker of the poem or the woman who is departing. Anne Burnett argues for the view that it was spoken by the leave-taker. Her "Sappho" expresses no sentiment, which allows her to take the poem as a straightforwardly didactic one.[130] Burnett assumes that the girl addressed is one whom Sappho loved. Sappho's lesson for her, repeated for the others, is that she must accept the fact that the circle will continue without her and that Sappho will have other loves; in the dreamlike sensuousness of perfume and flowers she is to give up the specificity of her experience.[131] On the other hand, no parallel offers itself among the fragments for a quoted speech begun, interrupted, and taken up again, as we must assume if the other woman speaks the line.[132]

Emmet Robbins makes a persuasive case for giving the line to "Sappho."[133] In that case, as often noticed, "Sappho" confesses that she cannot take her own advice to remember the past without pain.[134] This is a more ironic but conceptually almost as simple a poem: pain leads to rehearsal of now-lost pleasures, which must lead to fresh access of pain (or to some consoling thought).[135] The didactic version of the poem actually gives the later stanzas more point, but the confessional one more typically superimposes present and past and is rhetorically the more likely.

In either version the audience is irrelevant to the speaker. Either "Sappho" could calmly lose all of her auditors or else no one can distract her from the loss of one. Or if Sappho were to sing "I truly want to die" one

[130] Burnett 1983: 293–95. Her reason is that the rhetorical intensifier *truly* is indicative of an attempt to persuade, appropriate to the other speaker. Greene 1994: 47 concurs. Howie 1979: 302–5 discusses various proposed interpretations of the first line.

[131] Burnett 1983: 296–300.

[132] McEvilley 1971: 4–5n.7 prefers to assign it to "Sappho" on the grounds that Sappho's poems typically begin in the present and move to the past. As Burnett 1983: 293 points out, however, we do not know that this is the first stanza of the poem.

[133] Robbins 1990: 114–18, who bases his argument on a subtle rhetorical analysis.

[134] The disparity between the first line, if it is attributed to "Sappho," and the tone of the reported speech is noted, e.g., by Schadewaldt 1950: 116–18; Saake 1971: 189–204.

[135] Some see in the poem the implication that the addressee has now forgotten Sappho. Caduff 1972 defends this reading, earlier proposed by Wilamowitz-Moellendorff, but rejected by most commentators since.

day and appear cheerful the next, her protestations of emotion would seem overblown. Unless it is grandstanding, the statement is too extreme to serve as a singer's self-presentation among a group of those with whom she has close ties.

Let us instead read the poem as I have been doing, as a text that another woman could sing to herself, taking the first extant line as "Sappho's."[136] The singer/recipient would hear "Sappho's" confession that she misses the leave-taker and discover that "Sappho" now reviews the (perhaps fictional) final conversation with emotions different from those she conveyed then. She could interpret "Sappho's" intense but unspecific expression of emotion as she wished—as erotic desire or more diffuse sense of emotional loss. There follows, embedded in the first-level narrative, a reported conversation that takes over as the envisioned scene, just as in 1 V. The recipient speaks first in the interchange, so in singing the song she repeats her (alleged) words, addressing "Sappho" by name. Thus the direct discourse returns the recipient in fantasy to communication with "Sappho." "Sappho's" response, sung by the recipient, allows her to hear Sappho again and carries the scene presented to her mind still farther back, to the time when she was a member of a group around Sappho. Thus she can soothe her sense of loss and fulfil "Sappho's" admonition to remember.

At the same time, in "Sappho's" embedded speech she would find mirrored her own enjoyment of herself, her ways of enhancing her sensuousness. Two of the verbs are middle voice ("you put around yourself" in 14 and "you anointed yourself" in 20), focusing attention back on the addressee's own body.[137] Sappho's desire for her is a possible subtext within the embedded recollection, for "beside me" in line 14 gives license to it. And even as she sees herself through "Sappho's" eyes, the woman also finds reminders of her interaction with a whole group. This second theme appears with the verb πεδήπομεν (8, "we sought out"), which does not mean "we cherished," as it is often translated.[138] Some take it as Sappho's reminder of her own love for the addressee, but they must overtranslate and deny any weight to the plural.[139] In line 23 also, the noun expressing

[136] Burnett 1983: 292 points out that the poem could be sung later by any of the girls in order to reinforce their memories of delight after they in turn had left.

[137] McEvilley 1971: 9–11 reads the poem in psychological terms as the creation of an imaginary world, a world empty of anyone but the speaker and the beloved. Howie 1979: 310–29 analyzes it as consolation. Though his approach is very different, his conclusions complement mine.

[138] The verb does not normally refer to an emotional state. LSJ s.v. creates a special category just for this instance, but it gets special treatment only because the poem is taken to be a love poem.

[139] Burnett 1983: 296 notes the plural: "The lover who begins by saying 'Remember me'

the persons or things for whom the addressee satisfied desire is plural.[140] The poem recalls for the singer a broader set of affirmative relationships within the imaginatively restored communication with "Sappho."

Still, "Sappho" appears to undermine her own advice by her confession, "I simply wish to die." Is this inconsistency more than ironic? Logically, "Sappho" contrasts her despair now with the advice she gave then to enjoy the memory. But as the poem moves, the memory replaces despair. Or, as Ellen Greene puts it, narrative gives way to reciprocal apostrophes, which give way to "a detemporalized mode of discourse."[141] Thus the recipient can indulge both in the pleasure of believing that Sappho misses her and in positive recollection of her participation in a group. In portraying herself as devastated, Sappho lends her erotic energy to the catalogue of mutual pleasures that follows, vivifying it and enabling the addressee to revive her memories without the torment of feeling forgotten by those she leaves behind.

Furthermore, "Sappho's" confession is contained in a poem that must be performed with discipline and harmony, so the move that she recommends, to forge self-defining speech from painful experience, she herself has already made. From this perspective "Sappho's" admission of current pain is essential to her point. As the recipient sang the song, she too would replace weeping with poetry that is at the same time remembering—she would remember Sappho, other times, and the poem itself. Sappho's song sets itself in implicit contrast with weeping and shows the recipient the difference. The poem also seduces the recipient into extending the poem's mode of speaking about the past. "Sappho's" list of pleasures is not individualized to specific events, yet it would induce memories of particular days. The addressee's remembering would leap beyond these generic activities and impel her to continue the recitation, to extend her speech about the past and thus become the speaker that "Sappho" urges her to be. In light of 22 *V* we can interpret this poem as an inspiration to the recipient to transcend the split subjectivity created by singing Sappho's songs and compose her own.

If this is a poem for an addressee to sing to herself, it sets up the same interplay between two figures who are separated but still in communication as we found in the other poems. We can now return to the problem of

---

in an instant offers to revive the girl's knowledge of how the whole group had gathered adoringly about her."

[140] The supplement νε]ανίδων (young women) in line 23 has been suggested but cannot be taken as probable. Page 1955 *ad loc.* says that, whatever the first visible letter was, it was not α. Burnett 1983: 298n.56 takes the genitive that stood there as subjective, "the desire that girls feel" (accepting the supplement), thus avoiding the idea that the recipient was involved with someone other than Sappho.

[141] Greene 1994: 48.

the opening. Most scholars think (or hope) that there is only one missing line. But Sappho does not usually begin so abruptly as this poem appears to, so perhaps a full stanza plus a line is gone.[142] The first stanza could have framed the poem as a report to a god; then it would be imagined by its singer/recipient as a confession she overhears, like 1 and perhaps 95 *V*. "Sappho's" self-presentation as despairing (a fictionalizing technique like that of 31) would be contained within another framework that displaced the song from the context of performance, making the fictionality of the speaker even clearer.

The poem, like the others, represents resistance to emotional passivity. It also confirms my reading of the other poems in that it shows "Sappho" creating a discourse for the addressee to adopt that will maintain (or create) both a living sense of intimacy with Sappho and an erotic subjectivity. That is to say, it shows us the genesis of poems like 1, 31, 96 *V* in which the recipient is invited to imagine her own emotional state in response to the speaker's longing. Like 22 *V* it also commands the addressee to shape her own speech in song. Poem 94, therefore, is the most revealing of the extant poems about the role Sappho envisioned for her poetry. It provides the addressee with a model speaker as well as a friend or lover for whom she continues to be a presence and who bears witness to her desire/desirability.

Poems for performance in a women's group, poems that commented on political life and celebrated common activities but that used the language of eros to characterize Sappho, are distinguishable from poems that detach themselves from performer and context. The latter appear within the category of love poetry that Dioskourides identified and can be characterized as poems that require a speaker constructed in the imagination and gain psychological efficacy when sung by one who identifies herself as the subject or addressee. These poems vary in the circumstances and relationships they imply, but they have a common theme in soliciting women's sense of subjectivity. Desirable, according to "Sappho," the recipient is also portrayed as desiring and invited to articulate her desire, even when making a song of it may be her only possible form of expression.

Sappho's poetry for others to perform relies on the kind of self-representation possible in writing. The heightened, mythicized speaker, whose emotion is at an absolute pitch and who consorts with the gods, is a figure created in a text. No singer performing as herself could claim to be the person who speaks from these poems of Sappho's. It is through this fictional character that Sappho can dramatize her unyielding energy of desire and convey it to other women as what they should recollect about

[142] In 31 and 95 *V* she describes the scene before speaking of her own state. Poem 31 begins with her speech, and so in this poem also she could open with an address to the divinity.

her and take as a model for themselves. Yet Sappho wrote for those who knew her, and she must have wanted them to dress the textual speaker in their mental picture of her physical self. "Sappho" is not only a fiction but the woman raised to full power. That she speaks with such immediacy, surviving the fragmentation of Sappho's poetry, is an effect of oral style fleshed out (to speak in paradox) by the representation of the speaker included in the text to stand in for Sappho when others perform her poems.

IV

Sappho's mode of communication in the poems just analyzed is unique among the kinds of poetry we have examined. It is poetry detached from performance, that is, poetry as written text. I do not mean simply that Sappho wrote her poems down but that she exploited the possibilities of textual utterance.[143] Solon's poetry also approached the textual in a different way, as we saw in Chapter 5. What Sappho discovered in writing was not only a way to produce an assertion of the self that is independent of the speaker (as Solon did) but a way to preserve communication in the face of separation. The speaker in her poetry may focus on herself or on the other, but either way a relationship of desire that is affirmative for the other is created.

In Chapter 2 I pointed out that women could represent themselves in writing, where they were not bodily present. Authoritative speaking was taken up by the inscribed object, so the woman's own voice was not represented, but in this displaced form women put their names and actions before the public. I see similarities between Sappho's poetry and the rhetoric of inscriptions.[144] Sappho, I think, may have drawn from inscriptional practice a way of lending herself authority outside the context of the women's circle; at the same time writing offered her the idea of creating a fictional "I" not recuperable by a singer and using it to simulate communication. Common to Sappho's poetry and inscriptions is address to a singular "you" by a voice that is not the performer's, a voice that brings together, often by evocation of the past, two figures who are not present to each other. I end the chapter by exploring the similarity. Most of the

---

[143] Rösler 1990b: 285–86 argues that although Sappho's poetry has its "Sitz" in her circle, it is "written" in that its refinement exceeds its hearers' comprehension; this is different from my meaning but compatible with it. Svenbro 1993: 145–59 very interestingly reads 31 V as an allegory in which Sappho expresses jealousy of "you," the poem, which will "speak" to him, the reader. (But what did Sappho mean by making the reader male?) In both his view and mine, Sappho distances herself from "you," while commending "you." So long, however, as the poem is taken as communication rather than meditation, it will address other women.

[144] Svenbro 1993: 148–52 compares Sappho's "I" to that of inscriptions but sees her poetry as transcription from performance.

inscriptions I adduce are later than Sappho's poetry, but they show that from the beginning inscriptions exploited the potential of writing to create effects different from those of performance.

Inscriptions portray themselves as speaking by referring to themselves in the first person.[145] In a culture of speakers in which utterances are assessed by reference to their origin, this construction is not surprising.[146] Paradoxically, the effect is to create a textual "I," that is, an "I" detached from a speaker and constructed from the text itself. In inscriptions the "I" may simply repeat the identity of the object it is on, but it may also define the object, at which point the text begins to become autonomous. A series of examples shows the range of relationships between textual "I" and object:

1. *CEG* 354, ca. 600–550? From Perachora.

δραχμὰ ἐγό, hέρα λευϙ[όλενε,   ]λαι.

I (am) a bundle of spits, white-[armed] Hera, [   ]

2. *CEG* 144, ca. 650–600? From Corcyra.

[   ]τίμου ματρὸς ἐγὸ hέστακ᾽ ἐπὶ τύμοι
Πολυνόϝας· [   ]πετο ματϙ[   ].

[A marker?], I stand on the tomb of the mother of [   ]timos, Polynowa. [   ] mother.

3. *CEG* 137, ca. 600? From Methana.

Εὐμάρες με πατὲρ Ἀνδροκλέος ἐντάδε σᾶμα
ποιϝέσανς καταέθεκε φίλο μνᾶμα hυιέος ἔμεν.

Eumares set me up here, the father of Androkles, making a marker to be a memorial of his dear son.

4. *CEG* 334, ca. 550–525? From the Ptoion at Thebes.

καλϝὸν ἄγαλμα ϝάνακτι ϝ[εκαβόλοι Ἀπόλονι]
[   ]ορίδας ποίϝεσέ μ᾽ Ἐχέστροτος· αὐτὰρ ἔπεμφσαν
[   ]ον Πτοιἔϝι,
τὸς τύ, ϝάναχς, φεφύλαχσο, δίδοι δ᾽ ἀρ⟨ε⟩τάν [τε καὶ ὄλβον].

Echestrotos son of [   ] made me, a lovely delight for the lord [far-shooting Apollo]; and [and   ] sent [me as a gift ?] to Ptoian (Apollo); you, lord, keep them safe and give excellence [and wealth ?].

---

[145] This is a common construction in early inscriptions: Häusle 1979: 44; Friedländer 1948: 10.

[146] It has been studied several times, usually as an example of the naïveté or animism of the

5. *CEG* 47, ca. 525–500? From Attica.

ἐνθάδ' ἀνὲρ ὄμοσε[ν κα]τὰ ḥόρκια παιδὸς ἐρα[σ]θὶς
νείκεα συνμείσχι[ν] πόλεμόν θ'ἄμα δακρυόεντα.
Γναθίο, τõ σφυχὲ ὄλετ' ἐ[ν δαΐ], ḥιερός εἰμι
τõ ḥεροιάδο.
    [Γνά]θιϙ, αἰεὶ σπευδε[

Here a man swore oaths, out of desire for a boy, to mingle in quarrels and tearful war. Of Gnathios (H)eroiades, whose life was lost in [battle?], I am (the) consecrated (marker). Gnathios, always be eager (?) [

6. *CEG* 24, ca. 540? From Attica.

σῆμα Φρασικλείας. κόρε κεκλέσομαι αἰεί,
    ἀντὶ γάμο παρὰ θεõν τοῦτο λαχõσ' ὄνομα.
'Αριστίον Πάρι[ος μ' ἐπ]ο[ίε]σε.

The tomb of Phrasikleia. I shall be called a maiden forever, having been allotted this name by the gods in place of marriage. Aristion of Paros made [me].

In the first example the "I" identifies itself as the object; writing repeats visual identity. The first person is assumed in order to address Hera. In the second example the object defines itself through its activity (standing on the tomb).[147] The third explains itself in terms of its history, recalling its maker. The fourth inscription demonstrates a larger step in the direction of autonomy. It is engraved on a plain black-painted tile, yet the "I" asserts its beauty. Writing allows the dedicator to replace an inherently valuable object by an assertion of value.[148] The inscription in this case is the real "delight," for it defines the relationship between humans and god as the tile in its ordinariness does not.

The fifth inscription supplies a narrative not about the grave marker as material object but about Gnathios, the person whose decease it marks. It also characterizes itself as consecrated, as though the tomb approximated a hero shrine. In the mutilated last line, it addresses him. This marker uses

early Greeks. Burzachechi 1962 argues that the objects were felt to be alive. Raubitschek 1967: 11–12 rejects Burzachechi's view and suggests that the inscription was thought of as part of the monument. Häusle 1979: 60–61 finds a developing rationalism in the shifts in first-person referent.

[147] Grave inscriptions exhibit more variety of discourse and rhetorical form than do dedicatory inscriptions. Many have the form, "This is the marker (or memorial) of X." Svenbro 1993: 31–37 argues that before about 550 the rubric "this marker" is to be understood as first person.

[148] Friedländer and Hoffleit 1948: 41 say of it: "The contrast between the plain object and the grand style of the dedicatory verses is . . . remarkable. . . . These workmen raised themselves above the level of the banausos [artisan] with the help of Homeric poetry."

three different techniques (narrative, heroization, address) to recreate Gnathios' presence, all of them constructed by the writing itself, for the gravestone as material object is even less the focus of attention than in the case of the tile.

Finally, the last example: the Phrasikleia inscription is famous because the statue associated with it has also survived. The statue represents a young woman holding a flower. Here the living person is replaced by an image that "speaks" through writing.[149] Another person, by looking at the statue and reading the inscription, can reanimate Phrasikleia, as it were, by speaking her words for her. All of these inscriptions, in fact, when read aloud, borrow the reader's voice. The self-definition attached to the first person means that the "I" does not become the performer's. This writing marks its textuality precisely by blocking the performer's assumption of the role of speaker.

When inscriptions contain a second person, they can be used to represent communication across the distance represented by absence. The bundle of spits in #1 addresses Hera. Gnathios' tomb addresses him. A god or the deceased are frequent addressees. Two examples of a different type follow:

7. *CEG* 152, ca 700–650? From Amorgos.

Δηϊδάμαν, Πυγμᾶς ὁ πατὲρ τόνδ' οἶϙ[ον ?ἔτευϙσεν].

Daidaman, Pygmas (your) father [constructed?] this house.

8. *CEG* 19 ca. 550–530? From Attica.

[   ]ς αἰχμετο̄, Χσενόκλεες, ἀνδρὸς [ἐπισ]τὰς
σε̄μα τὸ σὸν προσιδὸν γνό[σετ]ϙι ἐν[ορέαν?].

[Each person ?], Xenoklees, standing near and looking at your tomb will recognize the [courage?] of a spear-wielding man.

These are different from the previous inscriptions in that they do not contain a first person. The written statement, when read, becomes the reader's address to the deceased and the grave-marker becomes an object about which the reader communicates with him. What is actually communication to a reader is constructed as communication by him or her to another. The reader of the first inscription addresses the dead on behalf of the father. Writing is here even less attached to its material referent than in the previous cases. For example, inscription #8 must have been attached to an image of Xenoklees, but instead of animating the statue (as the Phrasikleia inscription does) the reader acknowledges the "readability" of the repre-

---

[149] Svenbro 1993: 8–25 studies the relationship of writing and speaking constructed by the monument.

sentation. Here writing preempts the reader's interpretation of the visual image by asserting that all viewers in the future will interpret the image in the same way. Projection beyond the present reduces any one reader to making an assertion about future readers; it renders the individual reader contingent and the representation eternal.

More exploitative of textuality yet are inscriptions that borrow the reader's voice to address the reader.

9. *CEG* 34, ca. 530? From Attica.

['Α]ντιλόχο ποτὶ σῆμ' ἀγαθδ καὶ σόφϱονος ἀνδϱὸς
[δάκϱυ κ]άταϱ[χ]ϱον, ἐπεὶ καὶ σὲ μένει θάνατος.
(on right side) Ἀϱιστίον μ' ἐπόεσεν.

In front of the marker of Antilochos, a good and prudent man, make a preliminary offering of [tears?], since death awaits you also. Aristion made me.

10. *CEG* 28, ca. 540–530? From Attica.

ἄνθϱοπε hὸστείχε[ι]ς καθ'οδὸν φϱασὶν ἄλα μενοινδν,
στῆθι καὶ οἴκτιϱον σῆμα Θϱάσονος ἰδόν.

O you person who comes along the road eager for other things in your mind, stand and take pity, seeing the marker of Thrason.

These inscriptions draw the reader into an imaginative interchange in which the reader must perform both parts, the recorded utterance and his or her response. In both cases the addressee is singular and is represented as mortal or unaware. Both inscriptions use the characterization rhetorically to elicit emotion from the reader: confronting the reader with his or her own condition persuades him or her to give a moment of sorrow to the deceased.

The treatment of the "speaker" in these inscriptions can be compared with that of Sappho's poems. In 1 and 31 *V* the performer is detached from the speaker, as she or he is in the case of the first and the third set of inscriptions (#1–6, 9–10). In 1 and 94 *V* the use of Sappho's name blocks another performer's adoption of the first person, as self-identification does in the inscriptions. The performer lends a voice to a textual "I" that remains separate from the him or her. Furthermore, like the third set of inscriptions, poems 31 and perhaps 96 *V* focus their attention on a singular addressee who is unidentified (or belatedly identified). At any given reading the addressee is exclusive, so the performer who lends the text a voice can feel that the text is addressed specifically to herself or himself. The inscriptions request emotion rather than describing it, but in both cases the addressee's reaction is solicited as a way to simulate communication. In 96 and inscriptions #4, 7, 9, and 10, the textual speaker brings the addressee into relationship with the absent figure. These comparisons bring out the textuality of Sappho's construction of a speaker.

It is not only in the rhetoric of address and self-presentation that Sappho's poetry and inscriptions can be compared. Both create fictional speakers who use the language of epic and religion with an assumed authority. Because they have a disembodied speaker, inscriptions can make idealizing assertions about their subjects of a kind not possible in performance, where social pressure controls self-presentation. For instance:

11. *CEG* 344, ca. 600–550? From Phokis.

τάσδε γ' Ἀθαναίαι δϙαϝεὸς †Φαϝ εάϙιστος† ἔθεϰε
hέϙαι τε, hος ϰαὶ ϰἔνος ἔχοι ϰλέϝ ος ἄπθιτον αἰϝεί.

Phawearistos (?) dedicated these vessels (?) to Athena and Hera so that he also might have undying fame forever.

12. *CEG* 31, ca. 540–520? From Attica.

[ἔν] γὰϙ hαπάσες
νõν τε ϰαὶ ἀνϙ[ϙέ]αν ἔχσοχος hελιϰίας.
[οὐϰ ἀνε]πιστέμον τόδ' ἐπόε hιπόστ[ϙατ]οσᾶμα.

[   ], for [he was] outstanding in intelligence and courage of all his generation. Hippostratos made this marker [not un]skillfully.

The epic language of the first dedication is striking. Phawearistos, an iron-age man, reproduces by means of writing the privilege of heroes. He chooses as recipients the two goddesses of the *Iliad* who care for great warriors and expects to receive in return the epic reward for glorious fighting prowess, ϰλέος ἄφθιτον (undying fame). Phawearistos' fame is confirmed in the very reading of the inscription, for his name and deed are revived thereby. The absence of the dedicator parallels the death of the hero. The second inscription locates its subject among his contemporaries but claims preeminence for him. The second figure (who did not achieve undying fame, for his name is gone) relies on the unanswerable quality of writing to assure his preeminence. No confrontation with other opinions can change what the inscription says. It thus opposes itself in its isolation to the living jostle of competing claims. The two epitaphs of the second set (#7–8) also, because they are not imperatives but assertions of fact, present themselves as absolute. The speaker becomes a surrogate for the monument's act of bearing witness. Sappho's poems likewise draw on epic themes and rework them, as she does for instance in calling on Aphrodite.[150] Spoken by and about humans in verbal interchange, these descrip-

---

[150] See Stanley 1976 on Sappho's combining of epic with Lesbian vernacular to create an intertwined pattern of violent emotions and reflectiveness; Winkler 1981 and Rissman 1983, who study Sappho's ironic revisions of Homer in a number of poems.

tions would appear conventional or grandiose, but in written form they create the figures whom they describe.

Yet for all the indisputable authority assumed by writing, the detachment from speakers (and hence the absoluteness) of its assertions, the inscriptions gain their full impact by participating in another signifying system, that either of grave monuments or of dedications to a god. The placement, visual impressiveness, sculptural iconography of a grave monument signal the importance of the family and the status of the deceased. The system of gravemarkers in turn refers to funerals, with their memorializing performance of praise for the deceased. Grave inscriptions therefore both recall performance and transform it into another medium.[151] Any one inscription must be read in light of the whole system.

Sappho's poetry too can be seen as a system, the whole serving to construct a speaker whose character then informs any one of the poems. The most striking aspect of Sappho's self-creation as extraordinary is her treatment of the gods, with whom she frequently depicts herself as conversing. The erotic power that she claims by this strategy can be extended to all the love poems—something that readers of her collected poetry do easily. I say more about this in the conclusion. Sappho's statements about the beauty and desirability of others gain their definitive quality from the authority of this aggrandized figure defined by writing.

What, then, can be said about Sappho's self-presentation as gendered? When Sappho sang her poetry, the "Sappho" she created was embodied in herself and demonstrably female. Yet the text does very little to articulate the gender of its speaker.[152] Sappho does not refer to herself (or her addressees) as women, so only when she uses adjectives or participles is her gender even specified. Her depiction of herself in converse with the gods allows her to sidestep any question about the status of her speaking. Human men are absent from the poems discussed in part III of this chapter (except for "that man" in 31 *V*). Since women are the only inhabitants of the world of these poems, they become the norm.[153]

Indirectly, of course, Sappho's poetry does acknowledge the cultural construction of gender, precisely by her silence (a way of refusing to concede) and by her various reworkings of bardic stance and subjects (cf. above).[154] And her portrayal of human obstinacy in confrontation with

[151] Cf. Day 1989.

[152] DeJean 1989: 17–22 comments on Sappho's elusiveness, calling her (21): "a poet who proclaims the death of the subject, the prophet of today's widely prevalent critical desire for a subject that celebrates (in terms both literary and sexual) a mode beyond difference, beyond categories such as male/female, masculine/feminine."

[153] Svenbro 1984: 71–72 describes Sappho as a "transgressive" poet for making the domain of Aphrodite both exclusively feminine and symmetrical (that is, equal) with the world of war. She substitutes another set of values for that of the public world of war and marriage.

[154] Cf. Winkler 1981 for an excellent study of Sappho's double-entendres and ironic juxtaposition of male and female consciousness.

the gods I have read as a reflection of her resistance to the impositions on women's emotions found in the world at large. Her project, as I have interpreted it, of providing a means for other women to feel continuing contact with her when they had departed and to take on the role of speakers to themselves about their own desire/desirability shows that, on Lesbos as well as elsewhere, only among women could women perform as self-defining subjects.

Conclusion

LOOKING BACK over the range of performance covered, we can see its part in the contest of voices that characterized Greek culture at all levels. It is too bad that we do not know how some of the most interesting voices were presented, those of the pre-Socratic philosophers. Some philosophers entered the lists against established views through poetry that must have been performed in public, in some milieu that challenged the audience to hear the difference between their systems and, say, Hesiod.

As an institution for aristocratic self-presentation, choral performance was more significant in the early period. Alkman, Sappho, perhaps Stesichoros, created texts for aristocrats' public demonstration of the gods' favor—their bodily attractiveness, wealth, *paideia* (culture)—and of their embodiment of ideal community identity. But the system was not static. Throughout this period it expanded. At Athens choral performance was democratized in the dithyrambic contests. In the Dorian world especially, it was adapted by wealthy families to celebrate athletic and other victories as a way to declare the meaningfulness of victory within their home communities. Pindar composed a choral ode (*Nemean* 11) so that Aristagoras of Tenedos could celebrate his election to councilman in style. Even in radically democratic Athens, this sort of advertisement could be found: the ostentatious Alkibiades commissioned a victory ode from Euripides.[1] Even as it escalated, however, choral performance yielded its political importance, certainly at Athens and probably elsewhere, to more individualistic and flexible kinds of self-representation in oratory and debate. At Sparta choral performance remained important for the young, and Plutarch notes the attention that the fourth-century king Agesilaos gave to it.[2] At Epidauros around 300 BCE Isyllos' ceremony was anachronistic and Dorianizing, a deliberate attempt to use an old form to promote an obsolete conception of government.

For a community's collective self-representation, choral performance continued to be a viable form, as Hermokles' ithyphallic song for Demetrios and inscriptional records show.[3] The singer-dancers in the many

---

[1] Plutarch *Alkibiades* 11.

[2] Plutarch *Agesilaos* 21.7.

[3] See Käppel 1992: 386–91, *paianes* 43–46, for inscriptions preserving poems and notices of poems; and cf. 327–28, test. 95 (*SIG*³ 450, dated to 230–220 BCE), an inscription by the Delphians that honors Kleochares for his composition of a processional song, *paian,* and hymn for a boys' chorus to sing at the Theoxenia and instructs the chorus master to teach the songs each year and present them at the Theoxenia.

320 · Conclusion

choral productions from the later fifth century into and through the Hellenistic period were no doubt generally not the most eminent or ambitious
of citizens, but they cannot have been slouches. Our lens is not powerful
enough to bring into focus the local civic kudos that performance must
have continued to generate. Regional gatherings that had developed as
occasions for cities to represent themselves to each other in choral performance, as at Delphi and on Delos, continued to elicit performance. In the
Hellenistic period professional choral groups are attested, who might be
called on to represent a city.[4] At the village level the yearly round of
celebrations went right on, and festivals sometimes underwent a revival as
exhibitions of ethnicity or became displays for tourists, like the Spartan
Hyakinthia.

Singing in the symposium went through a similar arc, inspiring complex poetry in the seventh through early fifth centuries but losing its grip
on symposium decorum by the later fifth century.[5] As the practice of
singing in choral performance declined, it must have had an impact on
men's ability to perform the more sophisticated symposium poetry and
song.

The change in the performance of epic followed a somewhat different
trajectory. Its performers were not seeking political influence so much as
prizes and prestige, but the material they sang had political implications,
and if one can generalize from the case of Athens and of Sikyon (where
rhapsodic performance was banned by Kleisthenes), states acted to assert
control over what might be presented to their citizens. Thus the demand
for performing fixed texts changed bards' habits, and with less call for
them to put on extemporaneous performance they would have begun to
lose the art.

The seventh through early fifth centuries are thus the period in which
the system of performance outlined in this book was at its peak, but its
long afterlife and its usefulness in the eyes of the old Plato of the *Laws*
testify to its potency in linking performers, words, and audience in a
delight-inducing affirmation of shared ideology.

I want as a final rumination on the system of self-presentation in performance to point out in turn two questions that this book raises, larger
questions about gender ideology and about writing. In performance, as I
have shown, performers displayed visually constructed gender identities,
inevitably, and also spoke about themselves to guide the audience's interpretation of their bodies as the locus of social and political meanings. Male
performers enriched their identity as male—too much a norm for nuanced

[4] E.g., "Delphic Paean II" (*CA* pp. 149–59; Käppel 1992: 389–91, *paian* 46), performed in
128 BCE by the "Technicians of Bacchus."
[5] Cf. Aristophanes' *Clouds* 1354–58: the son replies to his father's request for a song after
dinner with the sneer that singing over wine is old-fashioned.

self-representation—by positioning themselves in relation to the category "female." It has never (so far as I know) been observed that the pronouncements on male and female so common in early Greek poetry are a product of the system of performance. What are the implications for our understanding of gender ideology in early Greece?

Certainly we cannot take these statements simply as assertions of settled views. No particular utterance from epic or symposium poetry, for instance, is a summary of what "the Greeks" or indeed any particular Greek man thought about gender relations, for conceptions were shaped to serve the rhetorical purposes of individuals under particular conditions; they changed with the location and goals of the speaker. And, as we saw, undergirding representations of the female is a figuration of the community as female. Statements, therefore, are not (just) about women but about a political entity. John Winkler observes apropos of ancient Greek culture that androcentrism is an "utterly conventional arrangement, . . . both an unquestioned truth and a universal fib." He draws the consequence, "Instead of snipping opinions from their context . . . and treating them as objective dogma, we should learn to see the various kinds of spin and misdirection that qualify the meaning of such pronouncements in their full social context, the unspoken stage directions that are understood but not voiced by the social actor."[6] In the stagy performance culture of ancient Greece, the conditions of performance determine some of the spin and misdirection.

Yet we cannot draw the conclusion that all these statements about the female are irrelevant to actual relations between men and women. Women in performance could not adopt the same images for their self-presentations. Rather than identify the community with themselves, they speak of, or, to put it more strongly, they *enact* their lack of subjectivity, the availability of their bodies to men, and the yielding up of their children. The sign *woman* as it functioned in public discourse is not one that women could claim. We must imagine that bluff characterized women's performance as well as men's, but only by ironizing their self-presentations could women signal their awareness of the implications of their speech (and thus claim subjectivity). And irony must have been a limited strategy in public performance. Women were thoroughly constrained by the same system that used *female* as a political idea.

Nor did the contradictions created in ideological representations of women by the exigencies of performance, with its political tropes and inconsistencies, undermine the patriarchal conceptual structure. Instead, patriarchy meant men's right to define *female,* which is to say that the category *female* does not exist in mainstream Greek discourse. Thus David

---

[6] Winkler 1990a: 5.

Halperin's observation, speaking of Diotima in Plato's *Symposium,* is borne out by this study: there are no women but only feminine "difference" appropriated by men.[7] Socrates, speaking in praise of love, says that he was taught about the subject by the priestess Diotima, and he repeats what she said to him as his contribution to the evening's discussion of the nature of love (201d ff.). In Plato's text, as Halperin shows, representation of woman serves male identity and "lends men a fullness and totality that enables them to dispense (supposedly) with otherness altogether."[8] What Halperin says of the *Symposium* is most pertinent to performance culture (which the *Symposium* mimics), for in performance the appropriation is physical as well as intellectual. *Woman* is an empty sign to be positioned and filled *ad lib.* It can be attributed to male bodies, deflected into the landscape (as in *Olympian* 6), equated with decay in order to contrast it with male bodies. Young women's scripted denial of subjectivity in public speech is in part a way to preserve the "emptiness" of the sign. The operation of men's appropriation is evident if we imagine a reader of Plato's *Symposium* for whom performance culture was the norm "speaking" the dialogue aloud in his head. He would *hear* Socrates speaking Diotima's words.[9] Diotima's remonstrances would emerge as examples of Socratic irony. Socrates would appear to be the one bringing beautiful thoughts to birth. Men's speech in performance is only about men.

Yet Sappho's poetry, one "voice" from outside the system of male public discourse about men, has survived. Marilyn Skinner points out that Sappho must have been composing in a long tradition of women speaking among themselves; this separate women's tradition provided a way for Sappho to escape from male definition of gender relations.[10] I believe that Skinner is absolutely right to envision a tradition behind Sappho's poetry, which means that we must not think of Sappho as an isolated genius but as a representative of a now-lost system of women's discourse about women. But why did Sappho's poetry, uniquely, survive to become canonized? Normally, it would seem, poetry created by women outside the area of community performance was not recorded; there are, for instance, no texts of laments, although by analogy with modern Greece one might guess that some laments were remembered and repeated, by men as well as women.[11] Skinner suggests that Sappho articulated desire so compellingly

---

[7] Halperin 1990b: 145–47. His cogent summary could stand as my conclusion about performance culture.

[8] Halperin 1990b: 151.

[9] In fact, it is not Socrates but the narrator speaking; Plato marks the unavailability of Socrates' voice even as he recreates it.

[10] Skinner 1993.

[11] Seremetakis 105–6 and passim. Pausanias 4.16.6 records a very brief song extemporized and sung by women honoring Aristomenes of Messenia.

that men found her poetry emotionally accessible as a "delightfully idyllic and romantic" escape from the constraints of masculinity.[12] Though important, I do not think that Sappho's offering an alternative subject position for men is a sufficient explanation by itself for her appeal. The obvious place for men to sing Sappho's poetry would be in the symposium, but I doubt that it would have found the kind of widespread and continuous performance that would lead to its being collected and preserved through symposium culture.[13] Her poetry is not functional for the symposium; it does not affirm a group, let alone meet the needs of self-representation by symposiasts.

However, as I argued in Chapter 6, some of Sappho's poetry does more than offer a subject position. When a poem separates the speaker from the singer, it creates a fictional, textual "Sappho," a speaker who reveals her inward emotions in secret communication and who must be created in the listener's imagination. This poetry, I suggested, was composed for women to carry away from their association with Sappho or to have as a substitute for her presence. It was meant to travel beyond the intimacy of the women's group. Women hearing and singing it would be maintaining a sense of communication among women, recreating the discourse through which they could speak their subjectivity and creating a flow of erotic feeling between women.

A male listener encountering one of these poems would not necessarily be responsive to the creation of female subjectivity, but he could feel that he had heard "Sappho" speak. If he wished to know more, he would become engaged with her *texts*. I do not mean that he would not listen to and sing her poems but that he would value a song as an autonomous object and not primarily as a vehicle for self-representation.[14] Sappho did create an alternative subject position that men might adopt, as Skinner says, but, more important, she made herself a source of fascination rather than just a producer of resingable songs. And once the name Sappho had become famous, men could sing her songs as hers without presenting themselves as "female." I thus propose that Sappho's poetry survived because it was designed to escape the tyranny of the performance culture and remain her "voice," that is, to circulate as text from the beginning. If she literally gave her poems to other women, copies of her poetry would have existed as prized possessions. When collected (whether by herself or by those for whom the fictional "Sappho" was meaningful), her poetry

[12] Skinner 1993: 137.

[13] I do not mean that symposium poetry was orally preserved but that its circulation both orally and in writing was driven by demand; only those poems that men wanted to sing over and over would get collected.

[14] See Ricoeur 1976: 25–44 on the difference in character between spoken and written communication; the latter has "semantic autonomy."

would seem more compelling yet, as recurring names and situations seemed to fill out a portrait.

This brings me to the second question, the use of writing. Skinner contrasts oral culture, which has room for women's traditions, with writing, in which masculine cultural hegemony was solidified.[15] There was in Sappho's time no accumulation of learning in written form, the authority of which controlled the forms of discourse. But precisely because authority inhered in public speaking, writing offered a medium to the voiceless and an opportunity for a different mode of self-presentation from public speech. For women it was a vehicle for making a public record of their names, so seldom acknowledged in men's speeches. Sappho used it to recreate women's traditions of speaking among themselves in an imaginative, permanently accessible form.

Writing allowed other authors to escape from the tyranny of performance as well. Solon created a monumental self, Pindar exploited the difference between performance and writing to make the written version of his epinicians appear to be his own utterance, and Plato recreated a speaking "Socrates" through writing. Those of the first generation of readers who knew Socrates could supply his voice mentally while finding him depicted in the text. The effect is the same as the one I think Sappho created for her friends. Pindar and Plato may have learned it from her.

Transcription of performance is another matter. Recording performance texts in writing flattens them out; the unspoken stage directions inherent in the speaking situation are lost. The statements in them no longer seem positional, as John Winkler warns us they are, but like considered summaries of long-term beliefs. In the case of gender, an overwrought patriarchy and misogyny appear rather than manipulation of the definition of "female," for the topic seems to be women. Yet it is the written text that liberates us to trace other voices behind the speaker's own. In the text of the *Symposium,* when read, not only Diotima but Socrates is constructed, and we can take them as equivalent fictions. Skinner opposes Halperin's view and sees "a dash of actual female subjectivity" in the Diotima of Plato's *Symposium* on the grounds that the idea of sexual reciprocity comes from Sappho.[16] It is in the text that we can trace Sappho's influence, because Socrates' voice does not turn Diotima (or Sappho) into a facet of his own self-representation.

This study, then, suggests that writing could not equal the power of

---

[15] Skinner 1993: 131–33; she is responding to Luce Irigaray's criticism of representational language as inherently "masculine." Of course, if that is so, then women speaking among themselves will no more afford an alternative discourse than Aristotle does. But why yield language to the men; why not say that grammar was invented by women, seeking like Scheherazade to defer the impact of the signifier on their bodies?

[16] Skinner 1993: 137.

speech to represent the speaker, to persuade, to enact significant gestures like prayer, oath, prophecy, or praise, but that to those whose public face was determined by others it provided an alternative mode for self-expression. Implicit in such a view is a radically different idea about the way in which writing entered Greek culture from the usual assumption of a slowly spreading comprehension of its possibilities.[17] In sum the power of performance must be taken into account in the study of both gender ideology and writing.

[17] For the idea that writing spread slowly, see Thomas 1992; Robb 1994. Latacz 1990 is closer to the view suggested here.

Chronology of Primary Sources

Chronological list of the principal authors and anonymous works quoted and discussed in the book. Dates are taken from *Der kleine Pauly*, ed. K. Ziegler and W. Sontheimer, 5 vols., Munich, 1975. Many of the dates are estimates. I have simplified some, since my aim is only to provide a general guide for the non-classicist. Dates are BCE unless otherwise specified.

Homer: 8th c.

Hesiod: 7th c.

Homeric Hymns: various dates, mostly 7th-5th c.

Eumelos: 7th c.

Kallinos: 7th c.

Archilochos: ca. 680–640.

Mimnermos: 7th c.

Tyrtaios: mid-7th c.

Alkman: ca. 650–600.

Semonides: second half of 7th c.

Solon: ca. 640–560.

Sappho: before 630–after 595.

Alkaios: ca. 630–570.

Stesichoros: late 7th-early 6th c.

Theognis: 6th c.; poetry collected under his name ranges from 7th to 5th c.

Ibykos: 6th c.

Anakreon: second half of 6th c.

Hipponax: second half of 6th c.

Simonides: ca. 557/56–468/67.

Aeschylus: 525/24–456/55.

Pindar: 522 (or 518)–after 446.

Bacchylides: ca. 517–after 452.

Timokreon: first half of 5th c.

Korinna: 5th c. (or Hellenistic).

Sophocles: 497–406/05.

Euripides: 485/84 (or 480)–406.

Herodotus: ca. 484–after 431.

Empedokles: ca. 483–ca. 423.

Thucydides: before 455–ca. 400.

Kritias: second half of 5th c.

Aristophanes: ca. 450–after 388.

Xenophon: ca. 428–after 355.

Plato: 428/27–349/48.

Demosthenes: 384/83–322.

Philodamos of Skarpheia: second half of 4th c.

Hermokles: late 4th c.

Isyllos: second half of 4th c.

Theocritus: first half of 3rd c.

Callimachus: 3rd c.

Dioskourides: second half of 3rd c.

Polybios: ca. 200–ca. 118.

Strabo: 64/63 BCE–after 23 CE.

Plutarch: after 45–after 120 CE.

Pausanias: ca. 113–after 180 CE.

Contest of Homer and Hesiod: after 138 CE. Taken from late 4th c. work.

Athenaios: active ca. 200 CE.

Proklos: 412–485 CE.

Transliterated (and Some Anglicized) Terms Used

agora — marketplace, center of public city life.
aischrologia — mocking, obscene jesting.
aition, pl. *aitia* — origin story.
antistrophe — second stanza of a triad (which see).
Charites — Graces.
chorēgos, pl. *chorēgoi* — chorus leader *or* sponsor of a chorus.
chorus — a group of performers who sing and (usually) dance or process
   also.
daphnēphorikon, pl. *daphnēphorika* — song for a festival of Apollo.
daphnēphoros — laurel-bearer in procession honoring Apollo.
deme — village, local community in the territory of a polis.
dēmos — people, collective citizenry.
dithyramb — danced song for a god, usually Dionysus.
drakaina — monstrous female snake.
ephebe — young man entering adulthood and military service.
epode — third stanza in a triad (which see).
encomium, pl. encomia — song of praise, sometimes sung at a symposium.
epinician — victory (adj.), victory song for victory in athletic games.
epithalamium — wedding song.
gnome — brief expression of conventional wisdom, maxim.
gynē, pl. *gynaikes* — married woman, adult woman.
hecatomb — large animal sacrifice.
hetaireia, pl. *hetaireiai* — political club.
hymenaios — wedding song.
hyporchēma, pl. *hyporchēmata* — dance song.
iambos — mocking, sometimes obscene poetry, often in an iambic meter.
ithyphallic — with upright phallus.
kithara — concert lyre.
kitharode — performer who sings solo and plays the kithara.
kōmos — reveling procession or dance.
mimesis — imitation, reenactment.
monody — song for solo performance.
mythos, pl. *mythoi* — authoritative speech.
ololygē — ritual shout by women.
paian, pl. *paianes* — cult song, usually for Apollo.
pannychis — all-night celebration at a festival.
partheneion, pl. *partheneia* — song for a chorus of *parthenoi* to sing.
parthenos, pl. *parthenoi* — young unmarried woman.

philos, pl. *philoi* — friend, political ally.

polis — city, city-state.

prooimion — preliminary song introducing epic narrative.

prytaneion — town hall.

pyrrhichē — dance in armor.

rhapsode — performer who recites epic poetry.

skolion, pl. *skolia* — short song sung in the symposium.

stichic — composed in a meter that repeats by the line.

strophe — first stanza of a triad (which see).

symposium — small gathering of men who eat then drink and sing together.

syssitia — Spartan messes.

triad — a three-part metrical arrangement of a choral song: the first two stanzas (strophe, antistrophe) are alike metrically, and the third (epode) differs. A choral ode may have several triads.

Bibliography

EDITIONS

Allen, T. W. 1912. *Homeri Opera*. Vol. 5: *Hymni, Cyclus, Fragmenta, Margites, Batrachomyomachia, Vitae*. Oxford.

Allen, T. W., W. R. Halliday, and E. E. Sikes. 1980 [1936]. *The Homeric Hymns*. 2d ed. Amsterdam.

Austin, C. 1968. *Nova Fragmenta Euripidea in Papyris Reperta*. Berlin.

Barrett, W. S. 1964. *Euripides, Hippolytos*. Oxford.

Bernabé, A. 1987. *Poetarum Epicorum Graecorum. Testimonia et Fragmenta*. Vol. 1. Leipzig.

Bremer, J. M., A. M. van Erp Taalman Kip, and S. R. Slings. 1987. *Some Recently Found Greek Poems*. Leiden.

Calame, C. 1983. *Alcman*. Rome.

Campbell, D. A. 1982. *Greek Lyric*. Vol. 1: *Sappho and Alcaeus*. Cambridge, MA.

————. 1988. *Greek Lyric*. Vol. 2: *Anacreon, Anacreontea, Choral Lyric from Olympus to Alcman*. Cambridge, MA.

————. 1991. *Greek Lyric*. Vol. 3: *Stesichorus, Ibycus, Simonides, and Others*. Cambridge, MA.

————. 1992. *Greek Lyric*. Vol. 4: *Bacchylides, Corinna, and Others*. Cambridge, MA.

Càssola, F. 1975. *Inni Omerici*. Milan.

Davies, M. 1991. *Poetarum Melicorum Graecorum Fragmenta*. Vol. 1. Oxford.

Degani, E. 1991. *Hipponactis Testimonia et Fragmenta*. 2d ed. Stuttgart.

Denniston, J. D. 1939. *Euripides, Electra*. Oxford.

Diels, H., and W. Kranz. 1954. *Die Fragmente der Vorsokratiker*. 7th ed. 3 vols. Berlin.

Dittenberger, W. 1915. *Sylloge Inscriptionum Graecarum*. Vol. 1. 3rd ed. Leipzig.

Dover, K. J. 1968. *Aristophanes, Clouds*. Oxford.

Drachmann, A. B. 1966–69 [1903–27]. *Scholia Vetera in Pindari Carmina*. 3 vols. Leipzig.

England, E. B. 1976 [1921]. *The Laws of Plato*. 2 vols. New York.

Farnell, L. R. 1961 [1932]. *Critical Commentary to the Works of Pindar*. Amsterdam.

Fraenkel, E. 1950. *Aeschylus, Agamemnon*. 3 vols. Oxford.

Gentili, B. 1958. *Anacreon*. Rome.

Gentili, B., and C. Prato. 1979–85. *Poetarum Elegiacorum Testimonia et Fragmenta*. 2 vols. Leipzig.

Greene, W. C. 1938. *Scholia Platonica*. Haverford.

Hansen, P. 1983. *Carmina Epigraphica Graeca Saeculorum VIII-V a.Chr.n.* Berlin.

Haslam, M. 1986. "3711. *Lesbiaca* (Commentary on Alcaeus)." In *The Oxyrhynchus Papyri* 53. Ed. M. Haslam. London. 112–25.

Henderson, J. 1987. *Aristophanes, Lysistrata*. Oxford.

Inscriptiones Graecae. 1913-. Berlin.

Inwood, B. 1992. *The Poem of Empedocles*. Toronto.

Jacoby, F. 1954–69. *Die Fragmente der griechischen Historiker*. Leiden.

Jebb, R. C. 1967 [1905]. *Bacchylides, The Poems and Fragments*. Hildesheim.

Kaibel, G. 1887–90. *Athenaei Naucratitae Dipnosophistarum Libri XV*. 3 vols. Leipzig.

Lobel, E., and D. Page. 1955. *Poetarum Lesbiorum Fragmenta*. Oxford.

MacDowell, D. M. 1971. *Aristophanes, Wasps*. Oxford.

———. 1990. *Demosthenes, Against Meidias (Oration 21)*. Oxford.

Masson, O. 1962. *Les Fragments du poète Hipponax*. Paris.

Meiggs, R., and D. Lewis. 1988. *A Selection of Greek Historical Inscriptions to the End of the Fifth Century B.C.* Rev. ed. Oxford.

Merkelbach, R., and M. L. West. 1967. *Fragmenta Hesiodea*. Oxford.

———. 1974. "Ein Archilochos-Papyrus." *ZPE* 14: 97–113.

Mineur, W. H. 1984. *Callimachus, Hymn to Delos*. Leiden.

Page, D. L. 1951. *Alcman, The Partheneion*. Oxford.

———. 1953. *Corinna*. London.

———. 1955. *Sappho and Alcaeus*. Oxford.

———. 1962a. *Poetae Melici Graeci*. Oxford.

———. 1962b [1942]. *Select Papyri III: Literary Papyri: Poetry*. Cambridge, MA.

———. 1974. *Supplementum Lyricis Graecis*. Oxford.

Parsons, P. J. 1992. "3965. Simonides, *Elegies*." In *The Oxyrhynchus Papyri* 59. Ed. E. W. Handley, H. G. Ioannidou, P. J. Parsons, and J.E.G. Whitehorne. London. 4–50.

Pfeiffer, R. 1949–53. *Callimachus*. 2 vols. Oxford.

Powell, J. U. 1970 [1925]. *Collectanea Alexandrina*. Oxford.

Prato, C. 1968. *Tyrtaeus*. Rome.

Rabe, H. 1906. *Scholia in Lucianum*. Leipzig.

Radt, S. L. 1958. *Pindars Zweiter und Sechster Paian*. Amsterdam.

———. 1977. *Tragicorum Graecorum Fragmenta*. Vol. 4: *Sophocles*. Göttingen.

Roche-Pereira, M. H. 1989. *Pausaniae Graeciae Descriptio*. 2d ed. 3 vols. Leipzig.

Russell, D. A., and N. G. Wilson. 1981. *Menander Rhetor*. Oxford.

Schroeder, O. 1900. *Pindari Carmina*. Leipzig.

Smyth, H. W. 1900. *Greek Melic Poets*. London.

Snell, B., and H. Maehler. 1970. *Bacchylides*. Leipzig.

———. 1987–89. *Pindarus*. 2 vols. Leipzig.

Sokolowski, F. 1962. *Lois sacrées des cités grecques. Supplément*. Paris.

Supplementum Epigraphicum Graecum. Ed. J.J.E. Hondius et al. Leiden 1923–.

Tarditi, G. 1968. *Archilochus*. Rome.

Van der Weiden, M.J.H. 1991. *The Dithyrambs of Pindar*. Amsterdam.

Van Groningen, B. A. 1966. *Theognis, le premier livre*. Amsterdam.

Vetta, M. 1980. *Theognis, Elegiarum Liber Secundus*. Rome.

Voigt, E.-M. 1971. *Sappho et Alcaeus*. Amsterdam.

Wehrli, F. 1944–49. *Die Schule des Aristoteles*. 10 vols. Basel.

West, M. L. 1966. *Hesiod, Theogony*. Oxford.

———. 1978. *Hesiod, Works and Days*. Oxford.

———. 1989. *Iambi et Elegi Graeci I*. 2nd ed. Oxford.

———. 1992b. *Iambi et Elegi Graeci II*. 2nd ed. Oxford.

Woodhead, A. G., ed. 1958. *Supplementum Epigraphicum Graecum* 15. Leiden.
Wright, M. R. 1981. *Empedocles, The Extant Fragments*. New Haven.
Ziegler, K. 1959–73. *Plutarchi Vitae Parallelae*. Vols. I.1, I.2, III.2. Leipzig.

TRANSLATIONS OF POETRY DISCUSSED AND OF SOME MAJOR SOURCES OF EVIDENCE
FOR PERFORMANCE

Note: See also the editions of Campbell, Inwood, Jebb, McDowell 1990, Page
1955 listed above.

Barker, A. 1984. *Greek Musical Writings*. Vol 1: *The Musician and His Art*.
  Cambridge.
Burstein, S. 1985. *The Hellenistic Age from the Battle of Ipsos to the Death of Kleopatra
  VII*. Cambridge.
Fagles, R. 1990. *Homer. The Iliad*. Harmondsworth.
Friedländer, P., and H. B. Hoffleit. 1948. *Epigrammata: Greek Inscriptions in Verse*.
  Berkeley.
Grene, D. 1987. *The History of Herodotus*. Chicago.
Gulick, C. B. 1927–41. *Athenaeus, The Deipnosophists*. 7 vols. Cambridge, MA.
Lattimore, R. 1947. *The Odes of Pindar*. Chicago.
———. 1965. *The Odyssey of Homer*. New York.
Levi, P. 1971. *Pausanias, Guide to Greece*. 2 vols. Harmondsworth.
Rayor, D. 1991. *Sappho's Lyre: Archaic Lyric and Women Poets of Ancient Greece*.
  Berkeley.
Sandys, J. 1937. *The Odes of Pindar, Including the Principal Fragments*. Cambridge,
  MA.
Saunders, T. J. 1970. *Plato, The Laws*. Harmondsworth.
Sargent, T. 1973. *The Homeric Hymns: A Verse Translation*. New York.
Wender, D. 1973. *Hesiod and Theognis*. Harmondsworth.
West, M. L. 1988. *Hesiod, Theogony and Works and Days*. Oxford.
———. 1993. *Greek Lyric Poetry: The Poems and Fragments of the Greek Iambic,
  Elegiac, and Melic Poets (Excluding Pindar and Bacchylides) Down to 450 BC, Trans-
  lated with Introduction and Notes*. Oxford.

STUDIES, COMMENTARIES, DICTIONARIES

Adrados, F. R. 1956. "Sobre algunos papiros de Arquiloco (P. Oxyrh. 2310–
  2313)." *La Parola del Passato* 11: 38–48.
Alexiou, M. 1974. *The Ritual Lament in Greek Tradition*. Cambridge.
Aloni, A. 1981. *Le Muse di Archiloco: Ricerche sullo Stile Archilocheo*. Copenhagen.
———. 1983. "Eteria e Tiaso: I Gruppi Aristocratici di Lesbo tra Economia e
  Ideologia." *Dialoghi di Archeologia* ser. 3, 1: 21–35.
———. 1985. "L'Intelligenza di Ipparco (II): La Presenza degli Eroi Attici in
  Omero e nelle Tradizioni Arcaiche." In *Graeco-Latina Mediolanensia. Quaderni di
  Acme* 5: 11–27.
———. 1989. *L'Aedo e i Tiranni: Ricerche sull' Inno Omerico a Apollo*. Rome.
Anderson, W. D. 1966. *Ethos and Education in Greek Music: The Evidence of Poetry
  and Philosophy*. Cambridge, MA.

Andrewes, A. 1938. "Eunomia." *CQ* 32: 89–102.

Anhalt, E. K. 1993. *Solon the Singer: Politics and Poetics*. Lanham.

Arthur, M. [Katz]. 1982. "Cultural Strategies in Hesiod's *Theogony*: Law, Family, Society." *Arethusa* 15: 63–82.

———. 1983. "The Dream of a World without Women: Poetics and the Circles of Order in the *Theogony* Prooemium." *Arethusa* 16: 97–116.

Athanassakis, A. N., ed. 1992. *Ramus* 21: *Essays on Hesiod*.

Bakker, E. J. 1990. "Homeric Discourse and Enjambement: A Cognitive Approach." *TAPA* 120: 1–21.

———. 1993a. "Activation and Preservation: The Interdependence of Text and Performance in an Oral Tradition." *Oral Tradition* 8: 5–20.

———. 1993b. "Discourse and Performance: Involvement, Visualization and 'Presence' in Homeric Poetry." *Classical Antiquity* 12: 1–29.

Baltes, M. 1981. "Die Kataloge im Homerischen Apollonhymnus." *Philologus* 125: 25–43.

Barrett, W. S. 1954. "Bacchylides, Asine, and Apollo Pythaieus." *Hermes* 82: 421–44.

———. 1961. Review of *The Oxyrhynchus Papyri* 24, ed. E. Lobel, C. H. Roberts, E. G. Turner, and J.W.B. Barns. *Gnomon* 33: 682–92.

Bauman, R. 1978. *Verbal Art as Performance*. Rowley, MA.

Bauman, R., and J. Sherzer, eds. 1989. *Explorations in the Ethnography of Speaking*. 2d ed. Cambridge.

Belfiore, E. 1986. "Wine and *Catharsis* of the Emotions in Plato's *Laws*." *CQ* n.s. 36: 421–37.

Bérard, C. 1989. "The Order of Women." In *A City of Images: Iconography and Society in Ancient Greece*. Tr. D. Lyons. Princeton.

Bergquist, B. 1990. "Sympotic Space: A Functional Aspect of Greek Dining-Rooms." In Murray 1990c: 37–65.

Bergren, A.L.T. 1982. "Sacred Apostrophe: Re-presentation and Imitation in the Homeric Hymns." *Arethusa* 15: 83–108.

———. 1983. "Language and the Female in Early Greek Thought." *Arethusa* 16: 69–95.

Blass, F. 1874. "Zu den griechischen Lyrikern." *Rheinisches Museum* 29: 149–58.

Bloch, M., ed. 1975. *Political Language and Oratory in Traditional Society*. London.

Boedeker, D. D. 1979. "Sappho and Acheron." In Bowersock et al. 1979: 40–52.

Bonanno, M. G. 1990. *L'Allusione Necessaria: Ricerche Intertestuali sulla Poesia Greca e Latina*. Rome.

Bonelli, G. 1977. "Saffo, 2 Diehl = 31 Lobel-Page." *L'Antiquité Classique* 46: 453–94.

Bookidis, N. 1990. "Ritual Dining in the Sanctuary of Demeter and Kore at Corinth: Some Questions." In Murray 1990c: 86–94.

Borthwick, E. K. 1970. "P. Oxy. 2738: Athena and the Pyrrhic Dance." *Hermes* 98: 318–31.

Bowersock, G. W., W. Burkert, and M.C.J. Putnam, eds. 1979. *Arktouros: Hellenic Studies Presented to Bernard M. W. Knox*. Berlin.

Bowie, E. L. 1986. "Early Greek Elegy, Symposium and Public Festival," *JHS* 106: 13–35.

———. 1990. "*Miles Ludens*? The Problem of Martial Exhortation in Early Greek Elegy." In Murray 1990c: 221–29.

Bowra, C. M. 1961. *Greek Lyric Poetry from Alcman to Simonides*. 2d ed. Oxford.

Brelich, A. 1969. *Paides e Parthenoi*. Vol 1. Rome.

Bremer, J. M. 1981. "Greek Hymns." In *Faith, Hope and Worship: Aspects of Religious Mentality in the Ancient World*. Ed. H. S. Versnel. Leiden. 193–215.

———. 1990. "Pindar's Paradoxical ἐγώ and a Recent Controversy about the Performance of His Epinicia." In Slings 1990b: 41–58.

Bremmer, J., ed. 1987. *Interpretations of Greek Mythology*. London.

Brillante, C. 1993. "Il Cantore e la Musa nell' Epica Greca Arcaica." *Rudiae: Ricerche sul Mondo Classico* 4: 7–37.

Brown, C. G. 1982. "Dionysus and the Women of Elis: *PMG* 871." *GRBS* 23: 305–14.

———. 1983. "From Rags to Riches: Anacreon's Artemon." *Phoenix* 37: 1–15.

———. 1989. "Anactoria and the Χαρίτων ἀμαρύγματα." *QUCC* n.s. 32: 7–15.

Bruit, L. 1990. "The Meal at the Hyakinthia: Ritual Consumption and Offering." In Murray 1990c: 162–74.

Brumfield, A. C. 1981. *The Attic Festivals of Demeter and Their Relation to the Agricultural Year*. New York.

Bruneau, P. 1970. *Recherches sur les cultes de Délos à l'époque hellénistique et à l'époque impériale*. Paris.

Bruschi, L. 1994. "Alcmane, Fr. 26.64–72 C. = 3 D." *ZPE* 101: 38–48.

Bundy, E. L. 1962. *Studia Pindarica I* and *II*. Berkeley.

Burkert, W. 1979. "Kynaithos, Polycrates, and the Homeric Hymn to Apollo." In Bowersock et al. 1979: 53–62.

———. 1985. *Greek Religion*. Tr. J. Raffan. Cambridge, MA.

———. 1987a. *Ancient Mystery Cults*. Cambridge, MA.

———. 1987b. "The Making of Homer in the Sixth Century B.C.: Rhapsodes versus Stesichoros." In *Papers on the Amasis Painter and His World*. Malibu. 43–62.

Burnett, A. P. 1964. "The Race with the Pleiades." *CP* 59: 30–34.

———. 1983. *Three Archaic Poets: Archilochus, Alcaeus, Sappho*. Cambridge, MA.

———. 1985. *The Art of Bacchylides*. Cambridge, MA.

———. 1988. "Jocasta in the West: The Lille Stesichorus." *Classical Antiquity* 7: 107–54.

Burzachechi, M. 1962. "Oggetti parlanti nelle epigrafi greche." *Epigraphica* 24: 3–54.

Butler, J. 1990. "Performative Acts and Gender Constitution: An Essay in Phenomenology and Feminist Theory." In *Performing Feminisms: Feminist Critical Theory and Theatre*. Ed. S.-E. Case. Baltimore. 270–82.

Caduff, G. 1972. "Zu Sappho Fragment 94 LP. (= 96 D.)." *Serta Philologica Aenipontana II*. Ed. R. Muth. Innsbruck. 9–12.

Calame, C. 1977. *Les Choeurs de jeunes filles en Grèce archaïque*. 2 vols. Rome.

———. 1986. "Spartan Genealogies: The Mythological Representation of a Spatial Organisation." Tr. A. Habib. In Bremmer 1987: 153–86.

———. 1990. "Narrating the Foundation of a City: The Symbolic Birth of Cyrene." In *Approaches to Greek Myth*. Ed. L. Edmunds. Baltimore. 275–341.

Calame, C. 1995. *The Craft of Poetic Speech in Ancient Greece*. Tr. J. Orion. Ithaca.

Calhoun, G. M. 1913. *Athenian Clubs in Politics and Litigation*. Austin.

Campbell, J. K. 1964. *Honour, Family and Patronage: A Study of Institutions and Moral Values in a Greek Mountain Community*. Oxford.

Carey, C. 1986. "Archilochus and Lycambes." *CQ* n.s. 36: 60–67.

———. 1991. "The Victory Ode in Performance: The Case for the Chorus." *CP* 86: 192–200.

Carson, A. 1986. *Eros the Bittersweet: An Essay*. Princeton.

———. 1990. "Putting Her in Her Place: Woman, Dirt, and Desire." In Halperin et al. 1990: 135–70.

Caudatella, Q. 1972. "Sugli Scoli A, B al *Partenio* I di Alcmane." In his *Intorno ai Lirici Greci*. Rome. 21–41.

Clay, J. S. 1986. "Archilochus and Gyges: An Interpretation of Fr. 23 West." *QUCC* n.s. 24: 7–17.

———. 1988. "What the Muses Sang: *Theogony* 1–115." *GRBS* 29: 323–33.

———. 1989. *The Politics of Olympus: Form and Meaning in the Major Homeric Hymns*. Princeton.

Clinton, K. 1992. *Myth and Cult: The Iconography of the Eleusinian Mysteries*. Stockholm.

Coldstream, J. N. 1968. "A Figured Geometric Oinochoe from Italy." *BICS* 15: 86–96.

Cole, S. G. 1993. "Procession and Celebration at the Dionysia." In *Theater and Society in the Classical World*. Ed. R. Scodel. Ann Arbor. 25–38.

Connor, W. R. 1971. *The New Politicians of Fifth-Century Athens*. Princeton.

———. 1987. "Tribes, Festivals and Processions: Civic Ceremonial and Political Manipulation in Archaic Greece." *JHS* 107: 40–50.

———. 1988. "Seized by the Nymphs: Nympholepsy and Symbolic Expression in Classical Greece." *Classical Antiquity* 7: 155–89.

Contiades-Tsitsoni, E. 1990. *Hymenaios und Epithalamion: Das Hochzeitslied in der frühgriechischen Lyrik*. Stuttgart.

Cooper, F., and S. Morris. 1990. "Dining in Round Buildings." In Murray 1990c: 66–85.

Cowan, J. K. 1990. *Dance and the Body Politic in Northern Greece*. Princeton.

Crowther, N. B. 1985. "Male 'Beauty' Contests in Greece: The Euandria and Euexia." *L'Antiquité Classique* 54: 285–91.

D'Alessio, G. B. 1992. "Immigrati a Teo e ad Abdera (SEG XXXI 985; Pind. fr. 52B Sn.-M)." *ZPE* 92: 73–80.

———. 1994. Review of L. Käppel, *Paian*. *Classical Review* 44: 62–65.

D'Alessio, G., and F. Ferrari. 1988. "Pindaro, *Peana* 6, 175–83: Una Ricostruzione." *Studi Classici e Orientali* 38: 159–80.

Danielewicz, J. 1990. "*Deixis* in Greek Choral Lyric." *QUCC* n.s. 34: 7–17.

David, E. 1989. "Laughter in Spartan Society." In Powell 1989: 1–25.

Davies, J. K. 1971. *Athenian Propertied Families, 600–300 B.C.* Oxford.

Davies, M. 1986a. "Alcman and the Lover as Suppliant." *ZPE* 64: 13–14.

———. 1986b. "Symbolism and Imagery in the Poetry of Ibycus." *Hermes* 114: 399–405.

———. 1988a. "Corinna's Date Revisited." *Studi Italiani di Filologia Classica* 81: 186–94.

———. 1988b. "Monody, Choral Lyric, and the Tyranny of the Hand-Book." *CQ* n.s. 38: 52–64.

Davison, J. A. 1968. *From Archilochus to Pindar: Papers on Greek Literature of the Archaic Period*. New York.

Day, J. W. 1989. "Rituals in Stone: Early Greek Grave Epigrams and Monuments." *JHS* 109: 16–28.

De Jong, I.J.F. 1987. *Narrators and Focalizers: The Presentation of the Story in the Iliad*. Amsterdam.

DeJean, J. 1989. *Fictions of Sappho 1546–1937*. Chicago.

Denniston, J. D. 1954. *The Greek Particles*. 2nd ed. Oxford.

Detienne, M. 1967. *Les Maîtres de vérité*. Paris.

Detienne, M., and J.-P. Vernant. 1978. *Cunning Intelligence in Greek Culture and Society*. Tr. J. Lloyd. Hassocks, Sussex.

Deubner, L. 1962 [1932]. *Attische Feste*. Hildesheim.

Di Benedetto, V. 1986. "Integrazioni al *P. Oxy.* 1231 di Saffo (frr. 27 e 22 V.)." *QUCC* n.s. 24: 19–25.

Diels, H. 1896. "Alkmans Partheneion." *Hermes* 31: 339–74.

Doherty, L. E. 1992. "Gender and Internal Audiences in the *Odyssey*." *AJP* 113: 161–77.

———. 1995. *Siren Songs: Gender, Audiences, and Narrators in the Odyssey*. Ann Arbor.

Donlan, W. 1985. "Pistos Philos Hetairos." In Figueira and Nagy 1985: 223–44.

Dougherty, C. 1994. "Pindar's Second Paean: Civic Identity on Parade." *CP* 89: 205–18.

Dover, K. J. 1978. *Greek Homosexuality*. Cambridge, MA.

———. 1987. "The Poetry of Archilochos." In *Greek and the Greeks: Collected Papers I*. Oxford. 97–121.

duBois, P. 1988. *Sowing the Body: Psychoanalysis and Ancient Representations of Women*. Chicago.

Easterling, P. E., and B.M.W. Knox, eds. 1985. *Cambridge History of Classical Literature*. Vol 1: *Greek Literature*. Cambridge.

Edmunds, L. 1988. "Foucault and Theognis." *Classical and Modern Literature* 8: 79–91.

Edwards, M. W. 1990. "Neoanalysis and Beyond." *Classical Antiquity* 9: 311–25.

Ehrenberg, V. 1968. *From Solon to Socrates*. London.

Eisenberger, H. 1991. "Zu Alkmans Partheneion Fr. 3 Calame." *Philologus* 135: 274–89.

Fairbanks, A. 1900. *A Study of the Greek Paean*. Ithaca.

Farnell, L. R. 1977 [1896–1909]. *The Cults of The Greek States*. 5 vols. New Rochelle.

Ferrari, F. 1991. "Tre Papiri Pindarici: In Margine ai Frr. 52n(a), 94a, 94b, 169a MAEHLER." *Rivista di Filologia e di Istruzione Classica* 119: 385–407.

Figueira, T. J. 1985. "The Theognidea and Megarian Society." In Figueira and Nagy 1985: 112–58.

Figueira, T. J., and G. Nagy, eds. 1985. *Theognis of Megara: Poetry and the Polis*. Baltimore.

Fingerle, A. 1939. *Typik der homerischen Reden*. Diss. Munich.

Finkelberg, M. 1990. "A Creative Oral Poet and the Muse." *AJP* 111: 293–303.

Finnegan, R. H. 1977. *Oral Poetry: Its Nature, Significance, and Social Context*. Cambridge.

Fisher, N.R.E. 1989. "Drink, *Hybris* and the Promotion of Harmony in Sparta." In Powell 1989: 26–50.

Fluck, H. 1931. *Skurrile Riten in griechischen Kulten*. Endingen.

Flückiger-Guggenheim, D. 1984. *Göttliche Gäste: Die Einkehr von Göttern und Heroen in der griechische Mythologie*. Bern.

Fogelmark, S. 1972. *Studies in Pindar with Particular Reference to Paean VI and Nemean VII*. Lund.

Foley, H. P., ed. 1981. *Reflections of Women in Antiquity*. New York.

———. 1993. "The Politics of Tragic Lamentation." In *Tragedy, Comedy, and the Polis*. Ed. A. H. Sommerstein, S. Halliwell, J. Henderson, and B. Zimmermann. Bari. 101–43.

———, ed. 1994. *The Homeric Hymn to Demeter: Translation, Commentary, and Interpretive Essays*. Princeton.

Foley, J. M. 1992. "Word-Power, Performance, and Tradition." *Journal of American Folklore* 105: 275–301.

Fontenrose, J. 1959. *Python: A Study of Delphic Myth and Its Origins*. Berkeley.

Ford, A. L. 1985. "The Seal of Theognis: The Politics of Authorship in Archaic Greece." In Figueira and Nagy 1985: 82–95.

———. 1988. "The Classical Definition of ΡΑΨΩΙΔΙΑ." *CP* 83: 300–307.

———. 1992. *Homer: The Poetry of the Past*. Ithaca.

Förstel, K. 1979. *Untersuchungen zum Homerischen Apollonhymnos*. Bochum.

Fowler, R. L. 1987. *The Nature of Early Greek Lyric: Three Preliminary Studies*. Toronto.

Fränkel, H. 1975. *Early Greek Poetry and Philosophy*. Tr. M. Hadas and J. Willis (from 2d German ed., 1962). Oxford.

Friedländer, P. 1914. "Das Prooimium der Theogonie." *Hermes* 49: 1–16.

Frisch, H. 1942. *The Constitution of the Athenians: A Philological-Historical Analysis of Pseudo-Xenofon's Treatise De Re Publica Atheniensium*. Copenhagen.

Frontisi-Ducroux, F. 1986. *La Cithare d'Achille: Essai sur la poétique de l'Iliade*. Rome.

Frontisi-Ducroux, F., and F. Lissarrague. 1990. "From Ambiguity to Ambivalence: A Dionysiac Excursion through the 'Anakreontic' Vases." In Halperin et al. 1990: 211–56.

Führer, R. 1967. *Formproblem-Untersuchungen zu den Reden in der frühgriechischen Lyrik*. Munich.

———. 1977. Review of *Supplementum Lyricis Graecis*, ed. D. Page. *Göttingische Gelehrte Anzeigen* 229: 1–44.

Fuqua, C. 1981. "Tyrtaeus and the Cult of Heroes." *GRBS* 22: 215–26.

Gagarin, M. 1992. "The Poetry of Justice: Hesiod and the Origins of Greek Law." In Athanassakis 1992: 61–78.

Gallavotti, C. 1972. "Le Pernici di Alcmane." *QUCC* 14: 31–36.

Garner, R. 1992. "Mules, Mysteries, and Song in Pindar's *Olympia* 6." *Classical Antiquity* 11: 45–67.

Garvie, A. F. 1965. "A Note on the Deity of Alcman's *Partheneion*." *CQ* n.s. 15: 185–87.

Gentili, B. 1988. *Poetry and Its Public in Ancient Greece from Homer to the Fifth Century.* Tr. A. T. Cole. Baltimore.

———. 1990. "L «io»' nella Poesia Lirica Greca." In *Lirica Greca e Latina: Atti del Convegno di Studi Polacco-Italiano, Pozna'n 2–5 maggio 1990.* Rome: 9–24.

Gentili, B., and G. Paioni, eds. 1985. *Oralità: Cultura, Letteratura, Discorso: Atti del Convegno Internazionale (Urbino 21–25 luglio 1980).* Rome.

Gerber, D. E. 1975. "Archilochus Fr. 119 W." *Phoenix* 29: 181–84.

———. 1976. "Studies in Greek Lyric Poetry: 1967–1975." *CW* 70.2: *Special Survey Issue.*

———. 1982. "Bacchylides 17,124–29." *ZPE* 49: 3–5.

———, ed. 1984. *Studies in Honour of Leonard Woodbury.* Chico.

———. 1987. "Studies in Greek Lyric Poetry: 1975–1985, Part I." *CW* 81.2.

———. 1988. "Studies in Greek Lyric Poetry: 1975–1985, Part II." *CW* 81.6.

Giacomelli [Carson], A. 1980. "The Justice of Aphrodite in Sappho Fr. 1." *TAPA* 110: 135–42.

Gleason, M. W. 1990. "The Semiotics of Gender: Physiognomy and Self-Fashioning in the Second Century c.e." In Halperin et al. 1990: 389–415.

Goff, B. E. 1990. *The Noose of Words: Readings of Desire, Violence, and Language in Euripides' Hippolytos.* Cambridge.

Golder, H., and S. Scully, eds. 1995. *The Chorus in Greek Tragedy and Culture, One.* Arion ser. 3, 3.1.

Goldhill, S. 1990. "The Great Dionysia and Civic Ideology." In Winkler and Zeitlin 1990: 97–129.

———. 1991. *The Poet's Voice: Essays on Poetics and Greek Literature.* Cambridge.

Gouldner, A. W. 1965. *Enter Plato: Classical Greece and the Origins of Social Theory.* New York.

Graf, F. 1985. *Nordionische Kulte: Religionsgeschichtliche und epigraphische Untersuchungen zu den Kulte von Chios, Erythrai, Klazomenai und Phokaia.* Rome.

Greene, E. 1994. "Apostrophe and Women's Erotics in the Poetry of Sappho." *TAPA* 124: 41–56.

Gresseth, G. K. 1970. "The Homeric Sirens." *TAPA* 101: 203–18.

Griffith, M. 1990. "Contest and Contradiction in Early Greek Poetry." In *Cabinet of the Muses: Essays on Classical and Comparative Literature in Honor of Thomas G. Rosenmeyer.* Ed. M. Griffith and D. J. Mastronarde. Atlanta. 185–207.

Griffiths, A. 1972. "Alcman's Partheneion: The Morning After the Night Before." *QUCC* 14: 7–30.

Gronewald, M. 1974. "Fragmente aus einem Sapphokommentar: Pap. Colon. inv. 5860." *ZPE* 14: 114–18.

Guillon, P. 1963. *Etudes Béotiennes: Le Bouclier d'Héraclés et l'histoire de la Grèce centrale dans la période de la première guerre sacrée.* Aix-en-Provence.

Hague, R. 1984. "Sappho's Consolation for Atthis, fr. 96 LP." *AJP* 105: 29–36.

Hallett, J. P. 1979. "Sappho and Her Social Context: Sense and Sensuality." *Signs* 4: 447–64.

Hallett, J. P. 1982. "Beloved Cleïs." *QUCC* n.s. 10: 21–31.

Halperin, D. 1990a. "The Democratic Body: Prostitution and Citizenship in Classical Athens." In his *One Hundred Years of Homosexuality and Other Essays on Greek Love*. New York. 88–112.

———. 1990b. "Why Is Diotima a Woman?" In his *One Hundred Years of Homosexuality and Other Essays on Greek Love*. New York. 113–51.

Halperin, D. M., J. J. Winkler, and F. Zeitlin, eds. 1990. *Before Sexuality: The Construction of Erotic Experience in the Ancient Greek World*. Princeton.

Hamilton, R. 1974. *Epinikion: General Form in the Odes of Pindar*. The Hague.

———. 1989. *The Architecture of Hesiodic Poetry*. Baltimore.

Hampe, R. 1941. "Zu Pindars Paian für Abdera." *Hermes* 76: 136–42.

Harriott, R. 1969. *Poetry and Criticism Before Plato*. London.

Harris, W. V. 1989. *Ancient Literacy*. Cambridge, MA.

Harvey, A. E. 1955. "The Classification of Greek Lyric Poetry." *CQ* n.s. 5: 157–75.

Häusle, H. 1979. "ΖΩΟΠΟΙΕΙΝ-ῨΦΙΣΤΑΝΑΙ: Eine Studie der frühgriechischen inschriftlichen Ich-Rede der Gegenstände." *Serta Philologica Aenipontana III*. Ed. R. Muth and G. Pfohl. Innsbruck. 23–139.

Havelock, E. A. 1963. *Preface to Plato*. New York.

———. 1982. *The Literate Revolution in Greece and Its Cultural Consequences*. Princeton.

Heath, M., and M. Lefkowitz. 1991. "Epinician Performance." *CP* 86: 173–91.

Heikkilä, K. 1992. "Sappho Fragment 2 L.-P.: Some Homeric Readings." *Arktos* 26: 39–53.

Henderson, J. 1991a. *The Maculate Muse: Obscene Language in Attic Comedy*. 2d ed. New York.

———. 1991b. "Women and the Athenian Dramatic Festivals." *TAPA* 121: 133–47.

Henrichs, A. 1978. "Greek Maenadism from Olympias to Messalina." *HSCP* 82: 121–60.

Herington, J. 1985. *Poetry into Drama: Early Tragedy and the Greek Poetic Tradition*. Berkeley.

Herrmann, H.-V. 1972. *Olympia: Heiligtum und Wettkampfstätte*. Munich.

Herzfeld, M. 1985. *The Poetics of Manhood: Contest and Identity in a Cretan Mountain Village*. Princeton.

Hoekstra, A. 1962. "The Absence of the Aeginetans." *Mnemosyne* ser. 4, 15: 1–14.

Holst-Warhaft, G. 1992. *Dangerous Voices: Women's Laments and Greek Literature*. London.

Homolle, T. 1890. "Comptes et inventaires des temples Déliens en l'année 279." *Bulletin de correspondance hellénique* 14: 389–511.

Hooker, J. T. 1979. "The Unity of Alcman's Partheneion." *Rheinisches Museum* 122: 211–21.

Howie, J. G. 1979. "Sappho *Fr.* 94 (LP): Farewell, Consolation and Help in a New Life." *Papers of the Liverpool Latin Seminar* 2: 299–342.

Hubbard, T. K. 1985. *The Pindaric Mind: A Study of Logical Structure in Early Greek Poetry*. Leiden.

———. 1987. "Pindar and the Aeginetan Chorus: *Nemean* 3.9–13." *Phoenix* 41: 1–9.

Huxley, G. L. 1965. "Xenomedes of Keos." *GRBS* 6: 235–45.

———. 1969. *Greek Epic Poetry from Eumelos to Panyassis.* London.

———. 1984. "Teos in Pindar." *Studies Presented to Sterling Dow on his Eightieth Birthday.* Ed. K. J. Rigsby. Durham. 149–52.

Hymes, D. 1962. "The Ethnography of Speaking." In *Anthropology and Human Behavior.* Ed. T. Gladwin and W. C. Sturtevant. Washington, D.C. 13–53.

Ieranò, G. 1987. "Osservazioni sul Teseo di Bacchilide (*Dyth.* 18)." *Acme* 40: 87–103.

Jaeger, W. 1966. "Tyrtaeus on True Arete." In *Five Essays.* Tr. A. M. Fiske. Montreal. 101–42.

Janko, R. 1982. *Homer, Hesiod and the Hymns: Diachronic Development in Epic Diction.* Cambridge.

———. 1986. "The Shield of Heracles and the Legend of Cycnus." *CQ* 36: 38–59.

———. 1992. *The Iliad: A Commentary.* Vol 4: *Books 13–16.* Cambridge.

Jarcho, V. N. 1990. "Das poetische 'Ich' als gesellschaftlich-kommunikatives Symbol in der frühgriechischen Lyrik." In Slings 1990b: 31–39.

Jeanmaire, H. 1939. *Couroi et Courètes: Essai sur l'éducation spartiate et sur les rites d'adolescence dans l'antiquité hellénique.* Lille.

Jensen, M. S. 1980. *The Homeric Question and the Oral-Formulaic Theory.* Copenhagen.

Johnson, W. R. 1982. *The Idea of Lyric: Lyric Modes in Ancient and Modern Poetry.* Berkeley.

Jones, N. F. 1987. *Public Organization in Ancient Greece: A Documentary Study. American Philosophical Association Memoirs* 176. Philadelphia.

Kadletz, E. 1980. "The Race and Procession of the Athenian *Oscophoroi.*" *GRBS* 21: 363–71.

Kahane, A. 1992. "The First Word of the *Odyssey.*" *TAPA* 122: 115–31.

Kamerbeek, J. C. 1961. "Archilochea." *Mnemosyne* ser. 4, 14: 1–15.

Käppel, L. 1992. *Paian: Studien zur Geschichte einer Gattung.* Berlin

Katz, M. A. *Penelope's Renown: Meaning and Indeterminacy in the Odyssey.* Princeton.

Keuls, E. C. 1985. *The Reign of the Phallos: Sexual Politics in Ancient Athens.* New York.

Killeen, J. F. 1973. "Sappho Fr. 111." *CQ* n.s. 23: 198.

King, H. 1993. "Bound to Bleed: Artemis and Greek Women." In *Images of Women in Antiquity.* 2d ed. Ed. A. Cameron and A. Kuhrt. Detroit. 109–27.

Kirk, G. S. 1981. "Orality and Structure in the Homeric «Hymn to Apollo»." In *I Poemi Epici Rapsodici non Omerici e la Tradizione Orale: Atti del Convegno di Venezia, 28–30 settembre 1977.* Ed. C. Brillante, M. Cantilena, C. O. Pavese. Padua. 163–82.

Kirkwood, G. M. 1974. *Early Greek Monody: The History of a Poetic Type.* Ithaca.

———. 1982. *Selections from Pindar.* Chico, CA.

Knox, B. 1985. "Books and Readers in the Greek World 1, from the Beginnings to Alexandria." In Easterling and Knox 1985: 1–16.

Koller, H. 1956. "Das Kitharodische Prooimion: Eine formgeschichtliche Unter-suchung." *Philologus* 100: 159–206.

Konstan, D. 1994. *Sexual Symmetry: Love in the Ancient Novel and Related Genres.* Princeton.

Konstan, D., and M. Nussbaum, eds. 1990. *differences* 2.1: *Sexuality in Greek & Roman Society.*

Kraemer, R. S. 1992. *Her Share of the Blessings: Women's Religions among Pagans, Jews, and Christians in the Greco-Roman World.* Oxford.

Kranz, W. 1961. "Sphragis: Ichform und Namensiegel als Eingangs- und Schluss-motiv antiker Dichtung." *Rheinisches Museum* 104: 3–46.

Krummen, E. 1990. *Pyrsos Hymnon: Festliche Gegenwart und mythisch-rituelle Tradi-tion als Voraussetzung einer Pindarinterpretation (Isthmie 4, Pythie 5, Olympie 1 und 3).* Berlin.

Kullmann, W., and M. Reichel, eds. 1990. *Der Übergang von der Mündlichkeit zur Literatur bei den Griechen.* Tübingen.

Kurke, L. 1991. *The Traffic in Praise: Pindar and the Poetics of Social Economy.* Ithaca.

Kyle, D. G. 1992. "The Panathenaic Games: Sacred and Civic Athletics." In Neils 1992: 77–101.

Lamberton, R. 1988. "Plutarch, Hesiod, and the Mouseia of Thespiai." *Illinois Classical Studies* 13: 491–504.

Lambin, G. 1986. *Les Chansons de banquet dans la Grèce antique.* Thèse de doctorat, Univ. de Lille.

Lanata, G. 1966. "Sul linguaggio amoroso di Saffo." *QUCC* 2: 63–79.

Lardinois, A. 1994. "Subject and Circumstance in Sappho's Poetry." *TAPA* 124: 57–84.

Lasserre, F. 1989. *Sappho: Une autre lecture.* Padua.

Latacz, J. 1985. "Realität und Imagination. Eine neue Lyrik-Theorie und Sapphos φαίνεταί μοι κῆνος-Lied." *Museum Helveticum* 42: 67–94.

———. 1990. "Die Funktion des Symposions für die entstehende griechische Lit-eratur." In Kullmann and Reichel 1990: 227–64.

Latte, K. 1953. Review of H. Fränkel, *Dichtung und Philosophie des frühen Griechen-tums. Göttingische Gelehrte Anzeigen* 207: 30–42.

———. 1968. "Hesiods Dichterweihe." *Kleine Schriften.* Munich. 60–75.

Leclerc, M.-C. 1993. *La Parole chez Hésiode: À la recherche de l'harmonie perdue.* Paris.

Lefkowitz, M. R. 1981. *The Lives of the Greek Poets.* Baltimore.

———. 1991. "The First Person in Pindar." In her *First-Person Fictions: Pindar's Poetic 'I.'* Oxford. 1–71.

Lehmann, G. A. 1980. "Der 'Erste Heilige Krieg' – Eine Fiktion?" *Historia* 29: 242–46.

Lehnus, L. 1979. *L'Inno a Pan di Pindaro.* Milan.

———. 1984. "Pindaro: Il Dafneforico per Agasicle (Fr. 94b Sn.-M.)." *BICS* 31: 61–92.

Lenz, A. 1980. *Das Proöm des frühen griechischen Epos.* Bonn.

Lesher, J. H. 1994. "The Significance of κατὰ πάντ' ἄ⟨σ⟩τη in Parmenides Fr. 1.3." *Ancient Philosophy* 14: 1–20.

Lewis, J. M. 1985. "Eros and the Polis in Theognis Book II." In Figueira and Nagy 1985: 197–222.

Ley, G. 1993. "Monody, Choral Song, and Athenian Festival Performance." *Maia* 45: 105–24.

Liddell, H. G., R. Scott, and H. S. Jones. 1968. *A Greek-English Lexicon*. 9th ed. Oxford.

Lidov, J. 1993. "The Second Stanza of Sappho 31: Another Look." *AJP* 114: 503–35.

Lissarrague, F. 1987. *The Aesthetics of the Greek Banquet: Images of Wine and Ritual*. Tr. A. Szegedy-Maszak. Princeton.

Lloyd-Jones, H. 1975. *Females of the Species: Semonides on Women*. London.

———. 1990a. "The Cologne Fragment of Alcaeus [= Page, SLG S 262]." In Lloyd-Jones 1990b: 38–52.

———. 1990b. *Greek Epic, Lyric, and Tragedy: The Academic Papers of Sir Hugh Lloyd-Jones*. Oxford.

Lloyd-Jones, H., and M. Lefkowitz. 1990. "Λυκαιχμίαις." In Lloyd-Jones 1990b: 53–54.

Lobel, E., ed. 1951. *The Oxyrhynchus Papyri* 21. London.

Longo, O. 1981. *Techniche della comunicazione nella Grecia antica*. Naples.

Loraux, N. 1984. "Solon au milieu de la lice." In *Aux origines de l'Hellénisme*. Paris. 119–214.

———. 1986. *The Invention of Athens: The Funeral Oration in the Classical City*. Tr. A. Sheridan. Cambridge, MA.

———. 1988. "Solon et la voix de l'écrit." In *Les Savoirs de l'écriture en Grèce ancienne*. Ed. M. Detienne. Lille. 95–129.

———. 1990. *Les Mères en deuil*. Paris.

———. 1993. *The Children of Athena: Athenian Ideas about Citizenship and the Division between the Sexes*. Tr. C. Levine. Princeton.

———. 1995. *The Experiences of Tiresias: The Feminine and the Greek Man*. Tr. P. Wissing. Princeton.

Lord, A. B. 1965 [1960]. *The Singer of Tales*. New York.

Maclean, M. 1987. "Oppositional Practices in Women's Traditional Narrative." *New Literary History* 19: 37–50.

MacMullen, R. 1980. "Women in Public in the Roman Empire." *Historia* 29: 208–18.

Maehler, H. 1963. *Die Auffassung des Dichterberufs im frühen Griechentum bis zur Zeit Pindars*. Göttingen.

Marcovich, M. 1988. *Studies in Graeco-Roman Religions and Gnosticism*. Leiden.

Marry, J. D. 1979. "Sappho and the Heroic Ideal: ἔρωτος ἀρετή." *Arethusa* 12: 71–92.

Martin, R. 1989. *The Language of Heroes: Speech and Performance in the Iliad*. Ithaca.

———. 1992. "Hesiod's Metanastic Poetics." In Athanassakis 1992: 11–33.

Marzullo, B. 1952. "Arignota l'Amica di Saffo." *Maia* 5: 85–92.

McEvilley, T. 1971. "Sappho, Fragment Ninety-Four." *Phoenix* 25: 1–11.

———. 1978. "Sappho, Fragment Thirty One: The Face Behind the Mask." *Phoenix* 32: 1–18.

Meier, C. 1989. "Zur Funktion der Feste in Athen im 5. Jahrhundert vor Christus." *Das Fest*. Ed. W. Haug and R. Warning. Munich. 569–91.

Merkelbach, R. 1957. "Sappho und ihr Kreis." *Philologus* 101: 1–29.

———. 1973. "Der Theseus des Bakchylides (Gedicht für ein attisches Ephebenfest)." *ZPE* 12: 56–62.

Miller, A. M. 1986. *From Delos to Delphi: A Literary Study of the Homeric Hymn to Apollo*. Leiden.

Minchin, E. 1990–91. "Speaker and Listener, Text and Context: Some Notes on the Encounter of Nestor and Patroklos in *Iliad* 11." *CW* 84: 273–85.

Minton, W. W. 1970. "The Proem-Hymn of Hesiod's Theogony." *TAPA* 101: 357–77.

Miralles, C., and J. Pòrtulas. 1983. *Archilochus and the Iambic Poetry*. Rome.

Molyneux, J. H. 1992. *Simonides: A Historical Study*. Wauconda.

Morgan, K. A. 1993. "Pindar the Professional and the Rhetoric of the ΚΩΜΟΣ." *CP* 88: 1–15.

Morris, I. 1986. "The Use and Abuse of Homer." *Classical Antiquity* 5: 81–138.

Morrison, J. V. 1991. "The Function and Context of Homeric Prayers: A Narrative Perspective." *Hermes* 119: 145–57.

Morrow, G. R. 1960. *Plato's Cretan City: A Historical Interpretation of the Laws*. Princeton.

Most, G. W. 1982. "Greek Lyric Poets." In *Ancient Writers*. Vol 1. Ed. T. J. Luce. New York. 75–98.

———. 1985. *Measures of Praise*. Göttingen.

Muellner, L. C. 1976. *The Meaning of Homeric εὔχομαι through Its Formulas*. Innsbruck.

Mullen, W. 1982. *Choreia: Pindar and Dance*. Princeton.

Murray, O. 1990a. "The Affair of the Mysteries: Democracy and the Drinking Group." In Murray 1990c: 149–61.

———. 1990b. "Sympotic History." In Murray 1990c: 3–13.

———, ed. 1990c. *Sympotica: A Symposium on the* Symposion. Oxford.

Murray, P. 1981. "Poetic Inspiration in Early Greece." *JHS* 101: 87–100.

Nagy, G. 1979. *The Best of the Achaeans: Concepts of the Hero in Archaic Greek Poetry*. Baltimore.

———. 1985. "Theognis and Megara: A Poet's Vision of His City." In Figueira and Nagy 1985: 22–81.

———. 1990a. "Hesiod and the Poetics of Pan-Hellenism." In his *Greek Mythology and Poetics*. Ithaca. 36–82.

———. 1990b. *Pindar's Homer: The Lyric Possession of an Epic Past*. Baltimore.

———. 1992a. "Authorisation and Authorship in the Hesiodic Theogony." In Athanassakis 1992: 119–30.

———. 1992b. "Homeric Questions." *TAPA* 122: 17–60.

Nannini, S. 1988. *Simboli e Metafore nella Poesia Simposiale Greca*. Rome.

Neils, J., ed. 1992. *Goddess and Polis: The Panathenaic Festival in Ancient Athens*. Princeton.

Nilsson, M. P. 1957 [1906]. *Griechische Feste von Religiöser Bedeutung*. Stuttgart.

———. 1972 [1950]. *Cults, Myths, Oracles and Politics*. New York.

Norden, E. 1956 [1913]. *Agnostos Theos*. Stuttgart.

Notopoulos, J. A. 1966. "Archilochus, The Aoidos." *TAPA* 97: 311–15.

Ober, J. 1989. *Mass and Elite in Democratic Athens: Rhetoric, Ideology, and the Power of the People.* Princeton.

O'Higgins, D. 1990. "Sappho's Splintered Tongue: Silence in Sappho 31 and Catullus 51." *AJP* 111: 156–67.

O'Sullivan, J. N. 1981. "Asius and the Samians' Hairstyle." *GRBS* 22: 329–33.

Page, D. L. 1959. Review of *The Oxyrhynchus Papyri* 24, ed. E. Lobel, C. H. Roberts, E. G. Turner, and J.W.B. Barns. *Classical Review* 9: 15–23.

Parker, H. 1993. "Sappho Schoolmistress." *TAPA* 123: 309–51.

Patterson, C. 1986. "Hai Attikai: The Other Athenians." In *Rescuing Creusa: New Methodological Approaches to Women in Antiquity.* Ed. M. Skinner. *Helios* n.s. 13.2: 49–67.

Pavese, C. O. 1992. *Il Grande Partenio di Alcmane.* Amsterdam.

Pedrick, V. 1992. "The Muse Corrects: The Opening of the *Odyssey.*" *Yale Classical Studies* 29: 39–62.

Peek, W. 1985. "Ein neues Bruchstück vom Archilochos-Monument des Sosthenes." *ZPE* 59: 13–22.

Petropoulos, J.C.B. 1994. *Heat and Lust: Hesiod's Midsummer Festival Scene Revisited.* Lanham.

Pickard-Cambridge, A. W. 1962. *Dithyramb, Tragedy and Comedy.* 2d ed. rev. by T.B.L. Webster. Oxford.

———. 1968. *The Dramatic Festivals of Athens.* 2d ed. rev. by J. Gould and D. M. Lewis. Oxford.

Pitt-Rivers, J. A. 1977. *The Fate of Sechem; Or, the Politics of Sex.* Cambridge.

Podlecki, A. J. 1980. "Festivals and Flattery: The Early Greek Tyrants as Patrons of Poetry." *Athenaeum* 58: 371–95.

———. 1984a. *The Early Greek Poets and Their Times.* Vancouver.

———. 1984b. "Poetry and Society in Archaic Sparta." In *Actes du VIIe Congrès de la Fédération Internationale des Associations d'Etudes Classiques* 1. Ed. J. Harmatta. Budapest. 175–82.

Pomeroy, S. B. 1977. "Technikai Kai Mousikai." *American Journal of Ancient History* 2: 51–68.

Porro, A. 1992. "A Proposito di Alc. fr. 130 B Voigt." *QUCC* n.s. 41: 23–27.

Poursat, J.-C. 1968. "Les Représentations de danse armée dans la céramique attique." *Bulletin de correspondance hellénique* 92: 550–615.

Powell, A., ed. 1989. *Classical Sparta: Techniques Behind Her Success.* London.

Prins, Y. 1991. "The Power of the Speech Act: Aeschylus' Furies and Their Binding Song." *Arethusa* 24: 177–95.

Pritchett, W. K. 1979. *The Greek State at War.* Part III: *Religion.* Berkeley.

Prudhommeau, G. 1965. *La Danse Grecque antique.* 2 vols. Paris.

Pucci, P. 1977. *Hesiod and the Language of Poetry.* Baltimore.

Puelma, M. 1977. "Die Selbstbeschreibung des Chores in Alkmans grossem Partheneion-Fragment." *Museum Helveticum* 34: 1–55.

———. 1989. "Der Dichter und die Wahrheit in der griechischen Poetik von Homer bis Aristoteles." *Museum Helveticum* 46: 65–100.

Race, W. H. 1992. "How Greek Poems Begin." *Yale Classical Studies* 29: 13–38.

Raubitschek, A. E. 1967. "Das Denkmal-Epigramm." In *L'Epigramme grecque. Entretiens Hardt* 14: 1–36.

Rayor, D. J. 1987. "Competition and Eroticism in Alcman's Partheneion [1 PMG]." *American Philological Association Annual Meeting 1987 Abstracts.* Decatur. 80.

———. 1993. "Korinna: Gender and the Narrative Tradition." *Arethusa* 26: 219–31.

Redfield, J. 1975. *Nature and Culture in the Iliad: The Tragedy of Hector.* Chicago.

———. 1990a. "Drama and Community: Aristophanes and Some of His Rivals." In Winkler and Zeitlin 1990: 314–35.

———. 1990b. "From Sex to Politics: The Rites of Artemis Triklaria and Dionysos Aisymnētēs at Patras." In Halperin et al. 1990: 115–34.

Rehm, R. 1992. *Greek Tragic Theatre.* London.

Reitzenstein, R. 1970 [1893]. *Epigramm und Skolion.* Hildesheim.

Renehan, R. 1983. "The Early Greek Poets: Some Interpretations." *HSCP* 87: 1–29.

Richardson, N. J. 1981. "The Contest of Homer and Hesiod and Alcidamas' *Mouseion.*" *CQ* n.s. 31: 1–10.

Richardson, S. 1990. *The Homeric Narrator.* Nashville.

Richter, G.M.A. 1968. *Korai: Archaic Greek Maidens.* London.

Ricoeur, P. 1976. *Interpretation Theory: Discourse and the Surplus of Meaning.* Fort Worth.

Rissman, L. 1983. *Love as War: Homeric Allusion in the Poetry of Sappho.* Königstein/Ts.

Robb, K. 1994. *Literacy and Paideia in Ancient Greece.* New York.

Robbins, E. 1984. "Intimations of Immortality: Pindar, *Ol.* 3.34–35." In Gerber 1984: 219–28.

———. 1990. "Who's Dying in Sappho Fr. 94?" *Phoenix* 44: 111–21.

———. 1994. "Alcman's *Partheneion*: Legend and Choral Ceremony." *CQ* n.s. 44: 7–16.

Robertson, N. 1978. "The Myth of the First Sacred War." *CQ* n.s. 28: 38–73.

———. 1987. "Government and Society at Miletus, 525–442 B.C." *Phoenix* 41: 356–98.

Rosenmeyer, T. G. 1966. "Alcman's *Partheneion I* Reconsidered." *GRBS* 7: 321–59.

Rösler, W. 1980. *Dichter und Gruppe.* Munich.

———. 1983. "Über Deixis und einige Aspekte mündlichen und schriftlichen Stils in antiker Lyrik." *Würzburger Jahrbücher für die Altertumswissenschaft* n.s. 9: 7–28.

———. 1985. "Persona reale o persona poetica? L'interpretazione dell' 'io' nella lirica greca arcaica." *QUCC* n.s. 19: 131–44.

———. 1990a. "*Mnemosyne* in the *Symposion.*" In Murray 1990c: 230–37.

———. 1990b. "Realitätsbezug und Imagination in Sapphos Gedicht ΦΑΙΝΕΤΑΙ ΜΟΙ ΚΗΝΟΣ." In Kullmann and Reichel 1990: 271–87.

Rubin, N. F. 1980–81. "Pindar's Creation of Epinician Symbols: *Olympians* 7 and 6." *CW* 74: 67–87.

Rutherford, I. C. 1988. "Pindar on the Birth of Apollo." *CQ* n.s. 38: 65–75.

———. 1990. "*Paeans* by Simonides." *HSCP* 93: 169–209.

——. 1992. "Two Heroic *Prosodia*: A Study of Pindar, *Paeans* XIV-V." *ZPE* 92: 59–72.

——. Forthcoming. *Pindar's Paeans: A Reading of the Fragments with a Survey of the Generic Context*. Oxford.

Rutherford, I. C., and J.A.D. Irvine. 1988. "The Race in the Athenian Oschophoria and an Oschophoricon by Pindar." *ZPE* 72: 43–51.

Saake, H. 1971. *Zur Kunst Sapphos: Motiv-Analytische und Kompositions-technische Interpretationen*. Munich.

——. 1972. *Sapphostudien: Forschungsgeschichtliche, biographische und literarästhetische Untersuchungen*. Munich.

Sale, W. 1961. "The Hyperborean Maidens on Delos." *Harvard Theological Review* 54: 75–89.

Scafuro, A. C. 1990. "Discourses of Sexual Violation in Mythic Accounts and Dramatic Versions of 'The Girl's Tragedy.'" In Konstan and Nussbaum 1990: 126–59.

——. Forthcoming. *The Forensic Stage: Settling Disputes in Graeco-Roman New Comedy*. Cambridge.

Schachter, A. 1981. *Cults of Boiotia*. Vol. 1: *Acheloos to Hera*. *BICS Supplement* 38. London.

Schadewaldt, W. 1942. *Legende von Homer dem Fahrenden Sänger: Ein altgriechisches Volksbuch*. Leipzig.

——. 1950. *Sappho. Welt und Dichtung: Dasein in der Liebe*. Potsdam.

Schechner, R. 1976. "From Ritual to Theatre and Back." In Schechner and Schuman 1976: 196–222.

Schechner, R., and M. Schuman, eds. 1976. *Ritual, Play, and Performance*. New York.

Schmidt, D. A. 1990. "Bacchylides 17 – Paean or Dithyramb?" *Hermes* 118: 18–31.

Schmitt-Pantel, P. 1990. "Sacrificial Meal and *Symposion*: Two Models of Civic Institutions in the Archaic City?" In Murray 1990c: 14–33.

Scodel, R. 1984. "The Irony of Fate in Bacchylides 17." *Hermes* 112: 137–43.

Scully, S. P. 1986. "Studies of Narrative and Speech in the *Iliad*." *Arethusa* 19: 135–53.

Seaford, R. 1977–78. "The 'Hyporchema' of Pratinas." *Maia* 29–30: 81–94.

Segal, C. 1979. "The Myth of Bacchylides 17: Heroic Quest and Heroic Identity." *Eranos* 77: 23–37.

——. 1983. "Sirius and the Pleiades in Alcman's Louvre Partheneion." *Mnemosyne* ser. 4, 36: 260–75.

——. 1985. "Archaic Choral Lyric." In Easterling and Knox 1985: 165–201.

Seremetakis, C. N. 1991. *The Last Word: Women, Death, and Divination in Inner Mani*. Chicago.

Shapiro, H. A. 1992. "Mousikoi Agones: Music and Poetry at the Panathenaia." In Neils 1992: 53–75.

——. 1993. "Hipparchos and the Rhapsodes." In *Cultural Poetics in Archaic Greece: Cult, Performance, Politics*. Ed. C. Dougherty and L. Kurke. Cambridge. 92–107.

Shey, H. J. 1976. "Tyrtaeus and the Art of Propaganda." *Arethusa* 9: 5–28.

Sifakis, G. M. 1971. *Parabasis and Animal Choruses: A Contribution to the History of Attic Comedy*. London.

Simon, E. 1953. *Opfernde Götter*. Berlin.

Skinner, M. B. 1989. "Sapphic Nossis." *Arethusa* 22: 5–18.

———. 1991a. "Aphrodite Garlanded: Erōs and Poetic Creativity in Sappho and Nossis." In *Rose di Pieria*. Ed. F. de Martino. Bari. 77–96.

———. 1991b. "Nossis Thêlyglōssos: The Private Text and the Public Book." In *Women's History and Ancient History*. Ed. S. B. Pomeroy. Chapel Hill. 20–47.

———. 1993. "Woman and Language in Archaic Greece, or, Why Is Sappho a Woman?" In *Feminist Theory and the Classics*. Ed. N. Sorkin Rabinowitz and A. Richlin. New York. 125–44.

Slater, W. J. 1969a. "Futures in Pindar." *CQ* n.s. 19: 86–94.

———. 1969b. *Lexicon to Pindar*. Berlin.

———. 1976. "Symposium at Sea." *HSCP* 80: 161–70.

———. 1984. "*Nemean One*: The Victor's Return in Poetry and Politics." In Gerber 1984: 241–64.

———. 1990. "Sympotic Ethics in the *Odyssey*." In Murray 1990c: 213–20.

Slings, S. R. 1990a. "The I in Personal Archaic Lyric: An Introduction." In Slings 1990b: 1–30.

———, ed. 1990b. *The Poet's I in Archaic Greek Lyric*. Amsterdam.

Smith, P. M. 1981. "Aineiadai as Patrons of *Iliad* XX and the Homeric *Hymn to Aphrodite*." *HSCP* 85: 17–58.

Snodgrass, A. 1980. *Archaic Greece: The Age of Experiment*. London.

Snyder, J. 1989. *The Woman and the Lyre: Women Writers in Classical Greece and Rome*. Carbondale, IL.

———. 1994. "The Configuration of Desire in Sappho Fr. 22 L-P." *Helios* 21: 3–8.

Sourvinou-Inwood, C. 1987. "Myth as History: The Previous Owners of the Delphic Oracle." In Bremmer 1987: 215–41.

Stanley, K. 1976. "The Rôle of Aphrodite in Sappho Fr. 1." *GRBS* 17: 305–21.

Starr, C. G.1986. *Individual and Community: The Rise of the Polis, 800–500 B.C.* New York.

Stehle, E. 1990. "Sappho's Gaze: Fantasies of a Goddess and Young Man." In Konstan and Nussbaum 1990: 88–125.

———. 1994. "Cold Meats: Timokreon on Themistokles." *AJP* 115: 507–24.

———. 1996. "Help Me to Sing, Muse, of Plataea." *Arethusa* 29.

Stehle, E., and A. Day. 1996. "Women Looking at Women: Women's Ritual and Temple Sculpture." In *Sexuality in Ancient Art*. Ed. N. Kampen. Cambridge. 101–16.

Stern, J. 1967. "The Structure of Bacchylides' Ode 17." *Revue belge de philologie et d'histoire* 45: 40–47.

———. 1970. "The Myth of Pindar's *Olympian* 6." *AJP* 91: 332–40.

Stewart, A. 1982. "Dionysus at Delphi: The Pediments of the Sixth Temple of Apollo and Religious Reform in the Age of Alexander." In *Macedonia and Greece in Late Classical and Early Hellenistic Times*. Ed. B. Barr-Sharrar and E. Borza. Washington. 205–27.

Stewart, M. 1989. "'True Speech': Song and the Moral Order of a Hungarian Vlach Gypsy Community." *Man* 24: 79–102.

Stigers, E. [Stehle]. 1979. "Romantic Sensuality, Poetic Sense: A Response to Hallett on Sappho." *Signs* 4: 465–71.

———. 1981. "Sappho's Private World." In Foley 1981: 45–61.

Svenbro, J. 1976. *La Parole et le marbre: Aux origines de la poétique grecque.* Lund.

———. 1984. "La Stratégie de l'amour: Modèle de la guerre et théorie de l'amour dans la poésie de Sappho." *Quaderni di Storia* 19: 57–79.

———. 1993. *Phrasikleia: An Anthropology of Reading in Ancient Greece.* Tr. J. Lloyd. Ithaca.

Szegedy-Maszak, A. 1978. "Legends of the Greek Lawgivers." *GRBS* 19: 199–209.

Taplin, O. 1992. *Homeric Soundings: The Shaping of the Iliad.* Oxford.

Tedeschi, G. 1978. "L'Elegia parenetica-guerriera e il simposio: a proposito del fr. 1 W di Callino." *Rivista di Studi Classici* 26: 203–9.

———. 1982. "Solone e lo spazio della comunicazione elegiaca." *QUCC* n.s. 10: 33–46.

Thalmann, W. G. 1984. *Conventions of Form and Thought in Early Greek Epic Poetry.* Baltimore.

Thomas, R. 1992. *Literacy and Orality in Ancient Greece.* Cambridge.

Too, Y. L. 1991. " Ἥρα Παρθενία and Poetic Self-Reference in Pindar 'Olympian' 6.87–90." *Hermes* 119: 257–64.

Trumpf, J. 1973. "Über das Trinken in der Poesie des Alkaios," *ZPE* 12: 139–60.

Van Groningen, B. A. 1935–36. "The Enigma of Alcman's Partheneion." *Mnemosyne* ser. 3, 3: 241–61.

———. 1958. *La Composition littéraire archaïque grecque: Procédés et réalisations.* Amsterdam.

———. 1960. *Pindare au banquet.* Leiden.

Vernant, J.-P. 1983. "Hestia-Hermes: The Religious Expression of Space and Movement in Ancient Greece." In his *Myth and Thought among the Greeks.* London.

———. 1988. *Myth and Society in Ancient Greece.* Tr. J. Lloyd. New York.

Vetta, M. 1983a. "Un Capitolo di Storia di Poesia Simposiale." In Vetta 1983c: 119–55.

———. 1983b. Introduzione. In Vetta 1983c: xiii-lx.

———, ed. 1983c. *Poesia e Simposio nella Grecia Antica.* Rome.

Vian, F. 1952. *La Guerre des géants: Le Mythe avant l'époque hellénistique.* Paris.

von Arnim, H. 1909. "Pindars Päan für die Abderiten." In *Wiener Eranos zur 50. Versammlung deutscher Philologen und Schulmänner in Graz 1909.* Vienna. 8–19.

Vox, O. 1983. "Le Muse Mute di Solone (e lo Specchio del Suono)." *Belgafor* 38: 515–22.

———. 1984. *Solone Autoritratto.* Padua.

Wade-Gery, H. T. 1943. "The Spartan Rhetra in Plutarch *Lycurgus VI*." *CQ* 37: 62–72; continued in 1944. *CQ* 38: 1–9, 115–26.

———. 1958. *Essays in Greek History.* Oxford.

Webster, T.B.L. 1970. *The Greek Chorus.* London.

Weege, F. 1926. *Der Tanz in der Antike.* Halle.

West, M. L. 1965a. "Alcmanica." *CQ* n.s. 15: 188–202.

West, M. L. 1965b. "The Dictaean Hymn to the Kouros." *JHS* 85: 149–59.

———. 1967. "The Contest of Homer and Hesiod." *CQ* n.s. 17: 433–50.

———. 1970a. "Burning Sappho." *Maia* 22: 307–30.

———. 1970b. "Corinna." *CQ* n.s. 20: 277–87.

———. 1971. "Stesichorus." *CQ* n.s. 21: 302–14.

———. 1974. *Studies in Greek Elegy and Iambus*. Berlin.

———. 1975. "Cynaethus' Hymn to Apollo." *CQ* n.s. 25: 161–70.

———. 1981. "The Singing of Homer and the Modes of Early Greek Music." *JHS* 101: 113–29.

———. 1985a. "Archilochus: New Fragments and Readings." *ZPE* 61: 8–13.

———. 1985b. *The Hesiodic Catalogue of Women: Its Nature, Structure, and Origins*. Oxford.

———. 1990. "Dating Corinna." *CQ* n.s. 40: 553–57.

———. 1992a. *Ancient Greek Music*. Oxford.

Wheeler, E. L. 1982. "*Hoplomachia* and Greek Dances in Arms." *GRBS* 23: 223–33.

Whitehead, D. 1986. *The Demes of Attica, 508/7-ca. 250 B.C.: A Political and Social Study*. Princeton.

Wilamowitz-Moellendorff, U. von. 1886. *Isyllos von Epidauros*. Berlin.

———. 1913. *Sappho und Simonides*. Berlin.

———. 1922. *Pindaros*. Berlin.

Wilhelm, A. 1949. "ΔΙΑΦΟΡΑ." *Symbolae Osloenses* 27: 25–39.

Will, E. 1955. *Korinthiaka: Recherches sur l'histoire et la civilisation de Corinthe des origines aux guerres médiques*. Paris.

Winkler, J. J. 1981. "Gardens of Nymphs: Public and Private in Sappho's Lyrics." In Foley 1981: 63–89.

———. 1990a. *The Constraints of Desire: The Anthropology of Sex and Gender in Ancient Greece*. New York.

———. 1990b. "The Ephebes' Song: *Tragōidia* and *Polis*." In Winkler and Zeitlin 1990: 20–62.

———. 1990c. "Phallos Politikos: Representing the Body Politic in Athens." In Konstan and Nussbaum 1990: 29–45.

Winkler, J. J., and F. Zeitlin, eds. 1990. *Nothing to Do with Dionysos? Athenian Drama in Its Social Context*. Princeton.

Wissowa, G., ed. 1893-. *Paulys Realencyclopädie der classischen Altertumswissenschaft, neue Bearbeitung*. Munich.

Woodbury, L. 1985. "Ibycus and Polycrates." *Phoenix* 39: 193–220.

Wyatt, W. 1987–88. "Homer in Performance: *Iliad* I.348–427." *Classical Journal* 83: 289–97.

Young, D. C. 1968. *Three Odes of Pindar: A Literary Study of Pythian 11, Pythian 3, and Olympian 7*. Leiden.

Zanetto, G. 1985. "Archiloco: La ΤΕΡΨΙΣ e la ΝΕΒΡΟΣ." In *Graeco-Latina Mediolanensia. Quaderni di Acme* 5: 35–47.

Zeitlin, F. 1985. "The Power of Aphrodite: Eros and the Boundaries of the Self in the *Hippolytus*." In *Directions in Euripidean Criticism*. Ed. P. Burian. Durham. 52–111.

———. 1986. "Configurations of Rape in Greek Myth." In *Rape*. Ed. S. Tomaselli and R. Porter. Oxford. 122–51.

———. 1990. "Playing the Other: Theater, Theatricality, and the Feminine in Greek Drama." In Winkler and Zeitlin 1990: 63–96.

Zimmermann, B. 1992. *Dithyrambos: Geschichte einer Gattung*. Göttingen.

Index Locorum

General Index

Note: This index is oriented to performance. Mythological and historical names and place-names generally appear in it only insofar as they are connected with performing. Greek words are transliterated.

contradiction in performance of, 72–73; local differences in roles of, 117–18; mockery by, 111–13, 239n.100

gynaikes, as solo performers. *See* Korinna; Sappho as historical figure; Sappho, love poetry of; women's circle

Hagesias, 160–69

Hagesichora: deauthorized, 78; as marriageable, 32, 36; as ritually most beautiful, 82; stands in for men in relation to chorus, 77–78

Halperin, D., 321–22, 324

hamin, in *Louvre partheneion,* 37–38, 81

Hansen, P., 116

Harmodios song at Athens, 6–7, 224–25

Helen: *Louvre partheneion* for, 81; as model chorus-leader at Sparta, 82n.38; at Sparta, 82n.38, 86; Stesichoros *Palinode* for, 210n.132

Hera: at Argos, 87; and Boeotian sow, 166–68; dedications for, 312, 316; at Elis, 104–5; on Lesbos, 231, 267–68, 275; (Hera) Parthenia at Stymphalos, 166–68; on Samos, 24; at Sparta, 90–91n.64

Heracles, Theban festival for, 56

Heraia (Olympia), 104–5

Herakleitos: blames Archilochos and Homer, 174

Herington, J., 22, 31

Hermes, *Homeric Hymn* for, 198

Hermokles, song at Athens, 42–46, 126

Hesiod, as persona: in bardic contest, 172; in *Contest of Homer and Hesiod,* 174; in *Theogony,* 202–3, 206–7; in *WD,* 208

hetaira, of Sappho, 264–65

hetaireia: in Alkaios' poetry, 231–37; defined by discourse, 216–17, 233; as interest group, 214–16; on Lesbos, 215, 222, 231–36; masculinity in, 227; threats to, 222–24

Himerios, recalls Sappho's wedding poetry, 266–67

Hipparchos, 13, 16n.44, 250, 260n.148

Hippias (sophist) as performer at Sparta, 176

Hippodameia, chorus at Elis for, 104–5

hode in Alkaios (130B.6 *V*), 232

Hoekstra, A., 138

Homer: blamed by Herakleitos, 174; blind

bard as, 182; as competitive bard, 10, 173; in *Contest of Homer and Hesiod,* 176, 181; at Panathenaia, 16, 171–72; poems of, prescribed for recitation, 15–16, 171; in Simonides' Plataia elegy, 209–10

Homeric Hymn to Apollo: as composite, 177–78, 189, 195–96; Delian, 178; Leto in, 181; Pythian part, 191–93, 194–95. *See also* Index Locorum

Homeric Hymns. See Index Locorum

Homeridai, 15–16, 172

homosexuality, female: interpreted as initiatory, 87–88, 270–71, 274–76; in later tradition on Sappho, 263–64, 266; in Sappho's poetry, 285–88, 294–99, 301–2, 304, 308–9; at Sparta, 87–88, 93, 118

Hyakinthia (Sparta): description of, 59; ethnic tradition at, 66; lament at, 59; kings perform at, 23–24

Hybristika: at Argos, 112–13; at Epidauros, 112

hyporchēma, 121n.8, 125

I-you style: in bardic poetry, 182, 208; in community poetry, 20, 33, 35–38, 46–47n.63. *See also* speaking for and to audience

iambic (invective): sex in, 255–57; Solon 36 *W* as, 257; as symposium poetry, 215n.11; wives in, 237–39. *See also* Index Locorum, s.v. "Hipponax"; "Semonides"

Ibykos, poetry for tyrant's circle, 250, 253. *See also* Index Locorum

improvisation: by bards, 170; in symposium, 221–22; by women, 322n.11

initiation of young: on Delos, 110n.128, 155n.104; idea of homoeroticism in, 31, 81–82n.35, 87–88, 93, 270–71, 274–76; lack of evidence for, 31n.23, 87–88; Sappho as overseer of, 270–76, 285–87, 292

inscriptions: rhetoric of, 114–15, 312–17; Sappho's poetry compared to, 311–12, 315–17; Solon 36 *W* compared to, 260–61; women as subjects of, 114–17

invective. *See* iambic

Ion of Ephesos, as rhapsode, 5, 16–17, 172

iostephanoi, in Pindar fr. 76 *SM,* 13

Ismenion: birthing-couch of Melia in, 50,

About the Author

Eva Stehle is Associate Professor of Classics at the
University of Maryland at College Park.